by Cynthia Snyder

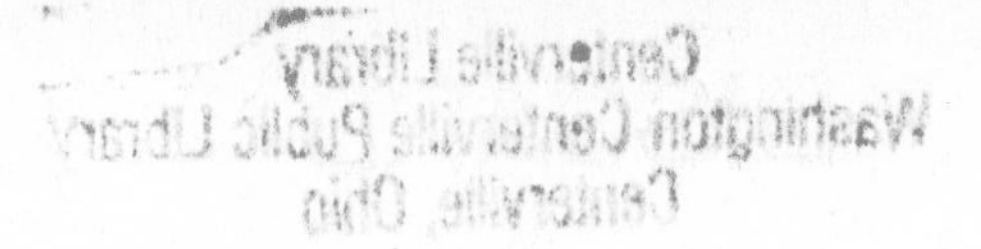

PMP® Certification All-in-One For Dummies®, 2nd Edition

Published by: **John Wiley & Sons, Inc.,** 111 River Street, Hoboken, NJ 07030-5774, www.wiley.com

Published simultaneously in Canada

For general information on our other products and services, please contact our Customer Care Department within the U.S. at 877-762-2974, outside the U.S. at 317-572-3993, or fax 317-572-4002. For technical support, please visit www.wiley.com/techsupport.

Wiley publishes in a variety of electronic formats and by print-on-demand. Some material included with standard print versions of this book may not be included in e-books or in print-on-demand. If this book refers to media such as a CD or DVD that is not included in the version you purchased, you may download this material at http://booksupport.wiley.com. For more information about Wiley products, visit us at www.wiley.com.

Library of Congress Control Number: 2013944334

ISBN 978-1-118-54012-1 (pbk); ISBN 978-1-118-53973-6 (ebk); ISBN 978-1-118-61253-8 (ebk); ISBN 978-1-118-61244-6 (ebk)

Manufactured in the United States of America

10 9 8 7 6 5 4 3 2 1

Contents at a Glance

Table of Contents

Chapter 3: Getting the Word Out to Stakeholders and Contractors . . .493

Book VII: Controlling Scope and Schedule 519

Chapter 1: Monitoring, Controlling, and Managing Change. 521

Chapter 2: Controlling Project Scope 555

Introduction

The PMP is the preeminent certification in project management. Getting your PMP certification will enhance your career opportunities in your current or future positions. In addition, studying for the exam really helps you understand project management principles. I know that I became a better project manager after months of studying this material!

About This Book

PMP Certification All-in-One For Dummies, 2nd Edition is designed to be a hands-on, practical guide to help you pass the PMP exam on your first try. This book is written in a way that will take the information in the standard for project management, the *PMBOK Guide, Fifth Edition,* and help make it easily understandable so you can pass the exam.

This book provides all the information you will need to pass the exam (you just have to apply the time and effort) and practical information to help you in the real world. Except for the first chapter in Book I (which covers the nuts and bolts of taking the exam), each chapter covers various elements to help you pass your PMP exam:

- ✦ As an exam prep guide, you will find all the information you need to pass the exam. And it's presented in an easy-to-understand way in terms of inputs, tools, techniques, and outputs. This is how it's presented in the *PMBOK Guide* as well as on the PMP exam. Pay particular attention to the For the Exam icons, which point out specific information you should keep in mind for the exam.
- ✦ As a reference to help you on your job, you can rely on my years of experience as an active project manager, a professional trainer, and an author to help you see how you can apply this information on a daily basis.
- ✦ **Quick Assessment:** Chapters start with a pretest to help you quickly identify what you already know or need to study in the chapter. These are simple fill-in-the-blank or true/false questions.
- ✦ **Icons:** Icons draw your attention to information that will help you on the exam or in the real world. For more information on the icons, check out the later section, "Icons Used in This Book."
- ✦ **Key terms:** So much of the PMP exam depends on your understanding the terms in the *PMBOK Guide* and the specific definitions associated with them. Throughout the book, I use definitions straight from the

PMBOK Guide Glossary, and each chapter lists all these terms at the end of the chapter. You should quiz yourself and make sure you understand every term listed in the "Key Terms" section.

- **Chapter summary:** At the end of chapters, I summarize the key points discussed. If you're unclear about something after reading these summaries, go back through the chapter for review.
- **Prep Test:** Each chapter concludes with practice questions. These are presented as multiple-choice questions, just like the PMP exam. And, yes, I give you the answers there to explain the correct answer and tell you where to find that information.
- **The Online Prep Exam:** The companion website contains a practice exam designed to mimic the real exam. This computerized test version will tell you how many you got right and how many you got wrong.
- **Web addresses** appear in monofont. If you're reading a digital version of this book on a device connected to the Internet, note that you can click the web address to visit that website, like this: `www.dummies.com`.

Foolish Assumptions

I make a few assumptions about you as a reader and have written this book with these assumptions in mind:

- **You're interested in attaining your PMP Certification.** After all, the focus of this book is to help you do just that!
- **You have a copy of the *PMBOK Guide* in its fifth edition, as of this writing.** Much of the information on the PMP exam is based on the fifth edition of the *PMBOK Guide.* Although this book will help you understand and apply that information, you really should buy that book and study it!
- **You will put the time in to pass the exam.** This is not an easy exam. If your plan is to cram for two weeks and then sit for the exam, you will likely be disappointed in the result. Many people take classes, use books like this one, and study for four to six months prior to sitting for the exam. You should probably go over the *PMBOK Guide* at least once, read through this book two or more times, do the labs, use the practice questions, and find other ways to prepare (flash cards, study groups, online communities, and so on).

How This Book Is Organized

Like all *All-in-One For Dummies* books, chapters are organized into minibooks. The chapters in each minibook are related by a specific theme or topic. For example, Book VI presents all the processes in the Executing Process Group.

This section tells you what you can find in each minibook.

Book I: PMP Foundation

In Chapter 1 of this first minibook, I discuss how the PMP exam is developed and scored as well as the application process and some test-taking tips. The next three chapters cover fundamental concepts you will need to master to do well on the exam.

Book II: Starting Off Right

Book II covers how projects are selected and processes you need to initiate a project. I talk about the chartering process and identifying project stakeholders.

Book III: Planning Integration, Scope, and Schedule

The first chapter in Book III discusses the elements in a project management plan. In the second chapter, I discuss the importance of planning the project scope by collecting requirements, defining the scope, and decomposing scope by using a work breakdown structure. The next chapter goes through the six processes necessary to develop a viable project schedule.

Book IV: Planning Cost, Quality, Human Resources, and Communication

Book IV covers four important aspects of planning your project. For cost, I look at developing estimates and establishing the project budget. For quality, I discuss some basic statistics and how to establish the quality requirements and standards for the project. A discussion of human resources develops a human resource management plan with a responsibility assignment matrix and a staffing management plan. The communications management plan rounds out this minibook.

Book V: Planning for Risks, Procurement, and Stakeholder Management

I cover five risk assessment processes in the first chapter in Book V. In the next chapter, I discuss the various types of contracts you can use, procurement documents, and a procurement management plan. The last chapter describes how to develop a plan that will optimize stakeholder engagement.

Book VI: Managing Your Project

Book VI covers what you do when you're managing the project. A lot of the information focuses on the interpersonal skills you apply when managing and developing your team and when you're managing stakeholder expectations. I also discuss distributing project information and conducting project procurements.

Book VII: Controlling Scope and Schedule

Book VII discusses how you monitor the progress of your project and control change. You will also see information on how to validate and control scope. The minibook wraps up by discussing how to control the schedule.

Book VIII: Controlling Cost, Quality, and More

This minibook starts out by discussing how to control cost, including a special section that discusses earned value management. Controlling quality applies many technical techniques, which I explain and illustrate with examples that demonstrate the concepts. I spend some time discussing the similarities and differences in controlling communications and controlling stakeholder engagement in Chapter 3. Monitoring and controlling risks entails risk reassessment and looking at project and product risk. The section on contracts discusses how to monitor contractor performance and manage the claims, payments, and disputes aspects of contracting.

Book IX: Closing Your Project and the Code of Ethics and Professional Conduct

Book IX covers the two closing processes: Close Project or Phase and Closing Procurements. It also covers the information in the PMI Code of Ethics and Professional Conduct. The Code of Ethics and Professional Conduct is not tested per se, but the standards in the Code are integrated into the test questions.

Appendixes

The appendixes provide useful quizzes and tools to help you study for the exam.

Appendix A. Turn to this appendix for more on how to access and take the online Prep Exam that accompanies this book.

Appendix B. Find 100 test questions, topically weighted by subject area percentage just like the actual PMP exam. Take this practice test after you've been through the material in this book at least once. You should be able to get at least 70 of the 100 questions right on this mini-test before you sit for the exam.

Appendix C. This appendix contains labs, where you find exercises for matching definitions with terms, conduct calculations, and answer fill-in-the-blank questions to ingrain the key information into your brain.

Appendix D. This appendix has a matrix that maps which chapters in this book cover the exam objectives.

Appendix E. The glossary lists all of the *PMBOK Guide* definitions you'll need to know for the exam.

Icons Used in This Book

I use a number of icons in this book to draw your attention to pieces of useful information.

This icon gives you a heads-up on information you should absolutely know for the PMP exam.

This icon presents meanings of terms as they are defined in the *PMBOK Guide* Glossary.

This icon gives you information on how to apply information in real life, or how to make your job easier.

This icon points out something you should avoid or not do at all.

This icon flags information that I already presented, or helps you remember things that will help you on your job.

Beyond the Book

I have written some extra content that you won't find in this book. Go online to find the following:

- The Cheat Sheet for this book is at

  `www.dummies.com/cheatsheet/pmpcertificationaio`

  Here, you'll find handy collections of info you'll need to master, from scheduling relationships and estimating techniques to strategies for conflict resolution and quality control tools.

- Online articles covering additional topics can be found at

  `www.dummies.com/extras/pmpcertificationaio`

  You'll find links to the articles on the parts pages at the beginning of each minibook, and, if relevant, at helpful points in the chapters, too. You'll find articles on

  - Initiating knowledge and skills
  - The role of the project management plan
  - Planning knowledge and skills
  - The importance of project stakeholder management
  - Quick tips for working with your team
  - Executing knowledge and skills
  - Monitoring and controlling knowledge and skills
  - Earned value basics: It's not about the numbers
  - Closing knowledge and skills

- Updates to this book, if any, are at

  `www.dummies.com/extras/pmpcertificationaio`

  Updates will be posted to the Downloads tab on the book's product page.

- You'll find the online prep exam on the Downloads tab at

  `www.dummies.com/extras/pmpcertificationaio`

  The exam has more than 200 questions that will prepare you for taking the official exam. With each question, you find out whether you answered the question correctly by clicking the Explanation button. If you answered incorrectly, you are told the correct answer with a brief explanation of why it's correct. Read Appendix A for more on how to access the exam on the Downloads tab.

Where to Go from Here

You can start reading this book at any chapter you like. If I mention something that appeared earlier in the text, I will put a reference to point you to the book and chapter where you can find the information. If you want to focus on a specific process group, you can start at the appropriate minibook. For example, Initiating processes start in Book II, Planning processes in Book III, Executing processes in Book VI, Monitoring and Controlling processes in Book VII, and Closing in Book IX. If you're familiar with the PMP Exam, you can skip Book I, Chapter 1.

There are a lot of websites and blogs that have practice test questions, discussion groups, and tips for passing the exam. There are also a number of apps you can get download onto your smartphone that offer a tip of the day or a bank of questions you can work through any time you have a few minutes. Try entering **PMP Exam Questions** or **PMP Prep Blog** into a search engine, and pages of options will come up. The point is, there are many ways that you can augment your preparation for the exam in addition to this book. So don't be shy — try out some!

Book I

PMP Foundation

getting started with PMP Certification

Visit www.dummies.com for great Dummies content online.

Contents at a Glance

Chapter 1: The PMP Exam

Chapter Objectives

- The PMP exam blueprint
- The exam domains
- The application process
- Taking the exam

So you decided to take the Project Management Professional Certification Exam. That's a big step in moving forward in your profession.

The Project Management Professional (PMP) certification is developed by the Project Management Institute (PMI), which has more than 400,000 members worldwide. Its credentialing program is designed to ensure competence and professionalism in the field of project management. PMI offers several credentials, and the PMP certification is the most well known by far. In fact, the PMP is the most widely recognized project management certification in the world, and there are more than 500,000 certified PMPs around the globe.

Adding this certification to your resume is important in the growing and competitive field of project management. A PMP certification gives employers confidence that existing employees have the level of knowledge to do their jobs well. It also gives employers a yardstick with which to measure new hires. And your project stakeholders can have confidence in your proven knowledge and experience when you have a PMP credential. Bottom line: With a PMP certification, you have more opportunities in your career path.

Before spending the next 700 or so pages helping you prepare, I want to walk you through some information about the exam and the application process.

How the PMP exam is developed

To develop a valid exam, you have to start by identifying the knowledge and skills that a certified professional should be able to demonstrate. This is done by conducting a *role delineation study*, which ensures that the content on the exam is valid and actually tests skills and knowledge that a certified professional should have. Based on the information from the role delineation study, an exam blueprint is developed.

The PMP Exam Blueprint

The exam content is based on an exam blueprint that defines the domains that should be tested as well as the percentage of questions in each domain. The domains and percentages for the current exam are

Domain	Percentage
Initiating the project	13%
Planning the project	24%
Executing the project	30%
Monitoring and controlling the project	25%
Closing the project	8%
Total	**100%**

Knowledge and skills

Each domain has tasks associated with it as well as the knowledge and skills needed to carry out the task successfully. For example, you might see something like this:

Task

Analyze stakeholders to identify expectations and gain support for the project.

Knowledge and skills

- Stakeholder identification techniques

The tasks for each domain have been translated into the exam objectives you see at the beginning of each chapter, starting in Book II. At the end of the final chapter for each domain, a sidebar summarizes the knowledge and skills needed for that domain and provides the location where you can find information related to the knowledge and skills. Here is the minibook and chapter where you find each domain's required knowledge and skills.

Initiating	Book II, Chapter 3
Planning	Book V, Chapter 3
Executing	Book VI, Chapter 3
Monitoring and controlling	Book VIII, Chapter 4
Closing	Book IX, Chapter 1

Cross-cutting skills

In addition to knowledge and skills specific to a domain, you need cross-cutting skills. A *cross-cutting skill* is one that goes across all domains (such as active listening, problem solving tools and skills, and leadership tools and techniques). At the start of the first chapter in a domain, I identify certain cross-cutting skills that you should pay particular attention to in domain. Always keep in mind that cross-cutting skills go across all domains. I just give specific examples in certain domains so you have a concrete example of the cross-cutting skill. Specifically, you can find the cross-cutting skill examples listed in the following minibooks and chapters.

Initiating	Book II, Chapter 1
Planning	Book III, Chapter 1
Executing	Book IV, Chapter 1
Monitoring and controlling	Book VII, Chapter 1
Closing	Book IX, Chapter 1

Code of ethics and professional conduct

The PMI Code of Ethics and Professional Conduct ("the Code") identifies four ethics standards — responsibility, respect, honesty, and fairness — and divides them into *aspirational* standards (those that we, as project managers, should strive to achieve) and *mandatory* standards (those that we must follow). Both standards use statements that describe behavior, such as, "We negotiate in good faith" or "We listen to other's points of view, seeking to understand them."

Pre-test questions

Of the 200 test questions, only 175 are scored. The other 25 questions are "pre-test" questions, which is a bit of a misnomer because they don't come before the other questions but are sprinkled in with them. Those 25 unscored questions are a trial. PMI is looking at the performance of those questions to see whether they can eventually be integrated into the exam as scored questions. That's actually a good quality control process and good news for you because you can be assured that only questions that have been through a rigorous validation process are actually on the exam.

The PMP exam does not test on the Code of Ethics and Professional Conduct explicitly although the standards are integrated into the test questions; therefore, you must be familiar with the Code to do well on the exam. To help you understand how the Code can show up on exam questions, I identify where specific content from the Code could be integrated into test questions throughout the book. Additionally, the final chapter (Book IX, Chapter 2) addresses the Code specifically. By spending time with the Code, you will be familiar with the ethical context of the questions you encounter on the exam.

Exam scoring

The PMP exam has 200 questions, and you are allowed four hours to complete all 200 questions. "Pre-test" questions are not scored. Therefore you will only be scored on 175 questions. In addition to receiving a pass/fail for the exam overall you will attain one of three proficiency levels for each domain:

- **Proficient:** Your performance is above the average for the domain.
- **Moderately proficient:** Your performance is average for the domain
- **Below proficient:** Your performance is below the average for the domain.

The Exam Domains

The five domains on the exam have specific topics that they test. Here is a summary of the topics by domain.

Initiating the project

The initiating domain is worth 13% of the exam score. This domain comprises the initial project definition, identifying stakeholders, and getting project approval. You will see information about

- Evaluating project feasibility
- Defining high-level scope and related success criteria
- Analyzing stakeholders
- Proposing an implementation approach
- Completing a project charter
- Gaining project charter approval

Planning the project

The planning domain is worth 24% of the exam score. Topics in this domain cover all aspects of planning the project from scope, time and cost to risks, change, and holding the kick-off meeting.

- Gathering and documenting requirements
- Documenting assumptions and constraints
- Creating a work breakdown structure (WBS)
- Estimating and budgeting costs
- Developing a project schedule
- Defining project team roles and responsibilities and the organizational structure
- Developing a communication management plan
- Planning project procurements
- Defining how to engage and communicate with stakeholders over the life of the project
- Creating a change management plan
- Identifying risks and risk strategies
- Developing the project management plan
- Obtaining project management plan approval
- Conducting a project kick-off meeting

Executing the project

The executing domain is worth 30% of the exam score. These questions deal with the day-to-day management of the project after the majority of the planning is done.

- Managing internal and external resources and stakeholders to perform project activities
- Creating deliverables on time and in budget
- Following the quality management plan
- Following the change management plan
- Employing risk management techniques
- Providing leadership, motivation, and other skills to maximize team performance

Monitoring and controlling the project

Monitoring and controlling questions make up 25% of the test. The questions are about managing performance and controlling change.

- Measuring project performance
- Applying change management
- Controlling quality for project deliverables
- Conducting risk management
- Managing issues
- Communicating status
- Managing procurements

Closing the project

This domain makes up 8% of the questions. The questions deal with closing a phase, a procurement, or the overall project.

- Closing contracts
- Gaining final acceptance
- Transferring ownership and management
- Conducting a project review
- Documenting lessons learned

- Writing the final project report
- Archiving project records
- Measuring customer satisfaction

Applying for the Exam

The *PMP Credential Handbook* has all the information you need to apply for, pay for, and schedule the exam. It includes information on cancelling and rescheduling, the audit and appeals processes, and the continuing certification requirements. In this section, I touch on a few highlights from the handbook, but I don't cover everything. For that, you need to download and review the handbook. Go to www.pmi.org and click the Certification tab. In the Quick Links box on the right, click Project Management Professional (PMP). Using the Quick Links box again, select PMP Handbook.

To take the exam, you need to meet the following qualifications:

- **A four-year college degree**

  If you don't have a four-year degree, you can take the exam if you have 7,500 hours of project management experience over at least five years.
- **At least three years of experience managing projects**
- **At least 4,500 hours of experience managing projects**
- **35 contact hours of project management education**

PMI audits a percent of the applications submitted for the exam. If your application is selected for audit, PMI may call your employer to validate your hours, or you may have to produce evidence to validate the information on the application. If you cannot validate the information, you cannot take the exam.

The application process

You can fill out your application online at the PMI website (www.pmi.org). Enter **PMP Application** in the Search field to get where you need to go.

Filling out the entire application is time consuming. The easy stuff is the demographics and contact information. Even the education and training sections are relatively quick to fill out. But then you need to document your 4,500 hours of experience. That's right: You have to answer questions about projects you've worked on, and fill in the number of hours until you reach that 4,500-hour milestone. That can take a long time, so be prepared!

Then there is that not-so-small issue of payment. If you're a PMI member, your exam fees are currently $405 US or €340 European. If you're not a PMI member, you pay $555 US or €465 European.

To become a PMI member, just go the PMI website (`www.pmi.org`). Click the Membership tab to get all the information you need to join. The price for a one-year membership is currently $129.

After you start your application process, you have 90 days to submit the application. Then, PMI has five days to review your application for completeness. To make sure your application isn't returned to you, follow these steps:

1. **Write your name exactly as it appears on your government-issued identification that you will present when you take the examination.**

   Read more about the acceptable forms of ID in the upcoming section, "Exam day."

2. **Ensure the application includes your valid e-mail address.**

   This is PMI's primary way of communicating with you throughout the credential process.

3. **Document your attained education and provide all requested information.**

4. **Document 35 contact hours of formal project management education in the experience verification section of the application.**

   You must have completed the course(s) you're using for this eligibility option before you submit your application.

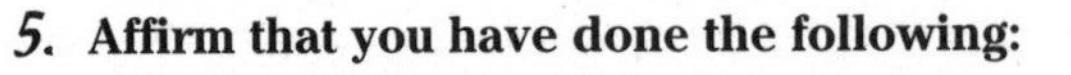

5. **Affirm that you have done the following:**

   - Read and understand the policies and procedures outlined in the credential handbook.
   - Read and accept the terms and responsibilities of the PMI Code of Ethics and Professional Conduct. This is included in the *PMP Credential Handbook*.
   - Read and accept the terms and responsibilities of the PMI Certificate Application/Renewal Agreement.

6. **Affirm that you provided true and accurate information on the entire application, understanding that misrepresentations or incorrect information provided to PMI can result in disciplinary action(s), including suspension or revocation of your examination eligibility or credential.**

Make sure you fill out your application early enough to leave yourself time to go through the application and acceptance process and schedule your exam. I recommend giving yourself at least six weeks prior to when you want to take the exam.

Scheduling your exam

After your application is accepted and you submit payment for the exam, you can schedule your exam. You have one year from the date your application is approved to take your exam.

PMI will send you scheduling instructions and direct you to the Prometric website (`www.prometric.com`) to schedule your exam date. Prometric is a global testing service that administers the PMP exam for PMI. You will need to go to a Prometric testing center to take the exam, but don't worry, there are hundreds of exam centers.

Scheduling your exam is a simple process. On the Prometric website, select the exam you want to take from the For Test Takers drop-down menu, select the country and state, and follow the prompts from there. The scheduling process should take less than five minutes.

Do not misplace the unique PMI identification code you receive when PMI notifies you that your application was approved. This code will be required to register for the examination. In addition, you should print and save all examination scheduling verifications and correspondence received from Prometric for your records.

Because PMI cannot guarantee seating at the testing centers, PMI recommends that you schedule your exam six weeks prior to when you want to take the test and at least three months before your eligibility expires.

If you're scheduling your exam around the time a new exam is coming out, you should give yourself at least four months prior to the exam cut-over date. Many people try to get in before the new exam comes out!

Taking the Exam

Taking the PMP exam can be stressful, to say the least. To help ease the stress a bit, here are five tips to keep in mind for the 24 hours before the exam.

- **Don't cram.** The night before the exam, you should know everything you need to know for the exam. Try to have a nice evening.
- **Get plenty of sleep.** "Have a nice evening" doesn't mean you should go out and stay up late. Your mind will be much clearer if you get a good rest.
- **Leave plenty of time to arrive at the exam site.** You cannot take the exam if you are late. Build in plenty of time for traffic snarls, getting lost, and so forth. Beforehand, perhaps take a practice test drive at the time of day you're scheduled to take the exam, just to see how long it takes.

- **Don't drink too much caffeine.** Or any kind of liquid for that matter.
- **Use the restroom before you start the exam.** After you start the exam, don't count on leaving the room until you finish.

Exam day

When you get to the exam site, you need to show a valid and current form of government-issued identification with your photograph and signature. The name on the ID must exactly match the name on your application. You also have to show them your unique PMI identification number. The following are acceptable forms of government-issued identification:

- Valid driver's license
- Valid military ID
- Valid passport
- Valid national ID card

The following *are not* acceptable forms of identification:

- Social Security cards
- Library cards

There are serious restrictions on what you can bring into the testing areas. You *may not* bring anything into the testing area or to the desk where you take the exam, including

- Purses
- Food and beverages
- Book bags
- Coats or sweaters
- Luggage
- Calculators
- Eyeglass cases
- Watches
- Pagers
- Cellular telephones
- Tape recorders
- Dictionaries
- Any other personal items

Also, you may not bring anyone into the testing area, including

- Children
- Visitors

Calculators are built into the computer-based training (CBT) exam. The testing center administrator provides scrap paper and a pencil to all credential candidates on the day of the exam.

You take the exam on a computer. When you go into the exam testing area, you have the opportunity to take a tutorial and a survey. These are optional. You have 15 minutes to do this.

Use this time to do a memory dump on your scratch paper. Write down equations, tips, the process matrix, and any other memory joggers that will help you during the exam.

During the exam, you have the opportunity to flag questions to come back to them. Make sure to first go through and answer all the questions you're sure about and relatively sure about. For those questions that you're not sure about, flag them to return to later.

Types of questions

The exam has several types of questions:

- **Situational:** The majority of questions are situational. In other words, you need the experience to know what they are talking about. These can be difficult. I include many of these in the test prep questions in this book, and they start something like this:

  Assume you are the PM on a project to upgrade the physical security on a university campus.

  Then you review a situation:

  The Dean of Students wants to make sure that all campus housing can only be accessed by the student, faculty, or staff ID cards. The Security Director states that the only way to provide 100% security is to use a biometric scanner. The Finance Director doesn't care what you do as long as you reduce the current operating costs by 15%.

  Finally, the question:

  What document should you use to record the expectations of each of these stakeholders?

- **Only one possible correct answer:** Some questions appear to have two correct answers; however, the exam allows only one correct answer per question. For those questions, ask yourself, "What is the first thing I would do? What is the best thing to do?" Remember that the *PMBOK Guide* is the source for many exam questions, so think of the PMBOK-ish response.
- **Distracters:** *Distracters* are a technique that test questions writers use to, well, distract you. In other words, they put in extra information that you don't need to answer the question.
- **MSU (made stuff up):** You might see some cool words slung together and think it makes sense. If you haven't heard of it before, it probably doesn't exist: for example, "charter initiation process." There are initiating processes, and one of the outputs of the initiating processes is a charter, but there is no charter initiation process.
- **Calculations:** There are a fair number of calculation questions. About 8 to 10 questions will have earned value (EV) information and equations, and about 8 to 10 questions will have other types of calculations. If you know your equations, these are some of the easiest questions on the test.
- **Identifications:** Expect about 20 to 25 questions where you have to know a specific process name, input, tool, technique, or output.

Some tests are *adaptive.* That is, the more questions you get right, the harder the questions become. If you miss questions, the easier the questions become. However, the PMP is *not adaptive.* The questions are not adjusted based on your answers.

Exam-taking tips

These tips should help you when the going gets tough:

- **Keep moving.** Don't spend a lot of time trying to figure out one question. You could lose the opportunity to answer many others.
- **Skip to the end of a question.** If you get a lengthy question, read the end of the question first. That usually tells you the question you need to answer. The rest of the information is just background.
- **Go with your instincts.** Your first choice is usually correct, so don't second-guess yourself! Change your answer only if you're certain that it should be changed.
- **Think in broad terms.** The exam is global and across all industries. If you apply too much of what you do on a day-to-day basis, you could miss some of the questions. Think about the questions from a global cross-industry perspective.

Getting your results

When you're done with the exam, you submit your test at the computer. This is a scary moment! To make it worse, the computer will ask you whether you are sure. (And, no, the computer isn't hinting that you failed.) Select Yes, and *voilà!* You're informed whether you passed or failed. (I know you will pass!) The exam administrator will hand you a printout of your exam results, indicating your pass/fail status. The printout will also give you an analysis of your results indicating by area whether you are proficient, moderately proficient, or below proficient.

About six to eight weeks after passing the exam, you will receive a congratulations letter, a certificate, and information on how to maintain your certification.

In the unlikely event that you do not pass the exam, you may take the test up to three times during your one-year eligibility period. If you do not pass within three attempts, you need to wait for a year to reapply. There is more information on this in the *PMP Credential Handbook.*

Preparing for the Exam

In addition to the PMP certification, PMI also puts out the *Guide to the Project Management Body of Knowledge*, or the *PMBOK Guide*. While information in the exam blueprint overlaps information in the *PMBOK Guide*, the exam blueprint identifies tasks, knowledge, and skills, and the *PMBOK Guide* identifies the *artifacts,* or the "what" of project management. Let me show you what I mean.

Earlier in this chapter, I demonstrate how the exam blueprint might address information about stakeholders:

Task

Analyze stakeholders to identify expectations and gain support for the project.

Knowledge and skills of

- Stakeholder identification techniques

The *PMBOK Guide* doesn't discuss knowledge and skills the same way that the exam blueprint does. The *PMBOK Guide* identifies the outputs needed to fulfill the task, such as a stakeholder register and a stakeholder management strategy.

Although the *PMBOK Guide* isn't the only source of information for the PMP exam, it is the primary source. The *PMBOK Guide* describes project management practices that, generally, are considered good for most projects. That means there is wide agreement that the outputs from the processes are appropriate and that the tools and techniques used to develop the outputs are the correct tools and techniques. It does not mean, though, that you should use every input, tool, technique, or output on your project. The *PMBOK Guide* is just a guide, not a methodology or a rulebook.

Additionally, the *PMBOK Guide* provides a common vocabulary for project management practitioners. For example, when you want to "decompose" your project into a set of deliverables, you use a "work breakdown structure" (WBS). You don't use a "scope management plan" or a "requirements traceability matrix." By having a common set of terms with an agreed-upon meaning, you can communicate better with your project stakeholders. By becoming familiar with the *PMBOK Guide* and using this book to help you study, you'll be in good shape to pass the exam.

It's time to get started. The next chapter covers some of the foundational principles you have to be familiar with to pass the exam.

Good luck!

Chapter 2: Foundations of Project Management

Chapter Objectives

- **Define key project management terms to provide an understanding of foundational concepts**
- **Compare projects, programs, and portfolios**
- **Introduce the competing demands that project managers have to manage to achieve a successful project**
- **Describe the functions of Project Management Offices (PMOs)**
- **Introduce enterprise environmental factors and their affect on projects**

Before discussing the project management process, you need a foundation of key project management definitions and concepts. In this chapter, I discuss how projects relate to programs, portfolios, and the PMO. I also introduce the important concept of competing demands. Understanding how competing demands require you to balance time, cost, scope, quality, risk, and resources is important before looking at those topics individually in later minibooks.

Competing demands can constrain your project, but they aren't the only things that you have to keep in mind when managing a project. You need to consider your internal and external environment. In this chapter, I also discuss enterprise environmental factors (EEFs) and their effect on your project.

Quick Assessment

1 A project is unique and ______.

2 Balancing scope, schedule, cost, quality, resources, and risk is managing the ______ ______.

3 Deciding how much rigor to apply to each process is ______.

4 (True/False). A portfolio is a group of related projects, subprograms, and program activities managed in a coordinated way to obtain benefits and control not available from managing them individually.

5 Market conditions and regulations are ______ ______ ______ that constrain how you can manage your project.

6 Successive iterations of planning where each iteration gets into more detail is ______ ______.

7 Managing one or more portfolios to meet a strategic objective is ______ ______.

8 (True/False). This following is an example of a technical advance: Your organization initiates a project to improve the efficiency in operations.

9 (True/False). In an administrative PMO, you will find a place that develops policies, procedures, templates, and forms to support project managers.

Answers

1 Temporary. Projects have a distinct beginning and end, as opposed to operations that are ongoing. *Look over the "Definition of a project" section.*

2 Competing constraints. Balancing scope, schedule, cost, quality, resources, and risk is managing competing constraints, which are also known as competing "demands." *For more on this topic, see the "Competing constraints" section.*

3 Tailoring. You will tailor the project management process and tools you use to fit the needs of your project. *Check out the "What makes a successful project manager" section.*

4 False. A *program,* not a portfolio, is a group of related projects, subprograms, and related program activities managed in a coordinated way to obtain benefits and control not available from managing them individually. *See the "Projects, programs, and portfolios" section for more information.*

5 Enterprise environmental factors. Market conditions and regulations are enterprise environmental factors that constrain how you can manage your project. *Look over the "Understanding Environmental Constraints" section.*

6 Progressive elaboration. Progressive elaboration is a technique used to provide more detail when more information is known. *You can find more information on progressive elaboration in the "What makes a successful project manager" section.*

7 Portfolio management. A portfolio of projects is grouped so that organizations can achieve strategic objectives. The projects can be independent or interconnected. *Review the "Projects, programs, and portfolios" section for more information.*

8 False. Improving operations is a business need. Automating them would be a technological advance. *You can find out more in the "Projects and organizational strategy" section.*

9 True. The administrative PMO creates processes and documents to provide a consistent way of applying project management in the organization. *Find more in the "The Project Management Office" section.*

Grasping the Terminology

The *PMBOK Guide* and the PMP exam use terms very specifically. Therefore, you should be familiar with the definitions I call out throughout this book.

Definition of a project

Starting with the term "project," I identify important terms with the Definition icon. You should understand the specific way these terms are defined because they apply to the PMP exam. The majority of the definitions come from the Glossary in the *PMBOK Guide*.

For the exam, you need to distinguish between projects and operations:

- **Project:** A project is temporary and has a beginning and an end. Additionally, a project creates something unique.
- **Operations:** Operations are ongoing and produce identical or similar outputs.

Project. A temporary endeavor undertaken to create a unique product, service, or result.

Frequently, a project is used to launch something that's eventually taken over by operations. A project that launches a new product or a new product line is temporary and unique. After the product goes into production, though, it belongs to operations.

Another aspect about a project is that it creates a unique product, service, or result. Here are some examples of each:

- **Product:** An artifact or a component of an artifact
  - A new computer component
  - A new office park
  - A new factory
- **Service:** A function or a series of steps and actions that supports the business or a stakeholder
  - Process improvement
  - Supply chain management
  - Online support capabilities

✦ **Result:** An outcome, information, or knowledge
  • Market research
  • Clinical trials
  • Annual studies

The *PMBOK Guide* doesn't define *service,* but it does define *product, result,* and *deliverable.*

Product. An artifact that is produced, is quantifiable, and can be either an end item unto itself or a component item. Additional words for products are *material* and *goods.*

Result. An output from performing project management processes and activities. Results include outcomes (integrated systems, revised process, restructured organization, tests, trained personnel, and so on) and documents (policies, plans, studies, procedures, specifications, reports, and so on).

Deliverable. Any unique and verifiable product, result, or capability to perform a service that is required to be produced to complete a process, phase, or project.

Projects, programs, and portfolios

I want to talk about some close relatives of projects: programs and portfolios.

A *program* is a group of projects. It might have an aspect of ongoing operations as part of the program.

Program. A group of related projects, subprograms, and program activities managed in a coordinated way to obtain benefits and control not available from managing them individually.

Program Management. The application of knowledge, skills, tools, and techniques to a program to meet the program requirements and obtain benefits and control not available by managing projects individually.

Programs aren't just giant projects. Rather, they are a collection of projects that supports a common goal. Here are some examples:

✦ Building a ship or an aircraft

✦ Producing a large event, such as the Olympics

✦ Developing a new product line with multiple products and distribution channels

Program management includes managing the integration of multiple projects, the integration of projects with ongoing operations, governance throughout the program, and realizing the benefits the program was initiated to deliver.

Portfolios are more strategic than projects. They are a group of projects or programs that are grouped together to meet strategic business objectives.

Portfolio. Projects, programs, subportfolios, and operations managed as a group to achieve strategic objectives.

Portfolio Management. The centralized management of one or more portfolios to achieve strategic objectives.

An organization may have a portfolio of development projects and a portfolio of maintenance projects. Another way to group portfolios is by product line or geography.

Project management

Some additional definitions you need to be aware of are *project management* and, of course, *project manager.*

Project Management. The application of knowledge, skills, tools, and techniques to project activities to meet the project requirements.

Project Manager (PM). The person assigned by the performing organization to lead the team that is responsible for achieving the project objectives.

Shortly, I talk about some fundamentals of what makes a successful project manager.

The three main aspects of project management are

- ✦ Identifying requirements
- ✦ Managing stakeholder expectations
- ✦ Managing the competing constraints (or demands)

I cover requirements and stakeholders extensively in later chapters. For now, I want to discuss the concept of competing constraints.

Competing constraints

For years, project management was taught around the concept of balancing scope, schedule, and cost. Then project managers started asking, “Well, scope is fine, but what about quality? What about risk?" While you are at it, you might as well ask about resources and stakeholder satisfaction, too.

In essence, you're balancing competing constraints or demands. In reality, your project will have its own unique constraints. Consider safety as a constraint upon a construction site, or regulatory constraints for a new drug. Therefore, part of your job as a project manager is to first identify the competing constraints and then manage your project to balance them appropriately. The *PMBOK Guide* explicitly lists the following six constraints, as shown in Figure 2-1:

- ✦ Scope
- ✦ Quality
- ✦ Schedule
- ✦ Budget
- ✦ Resources
- ✦ Risk

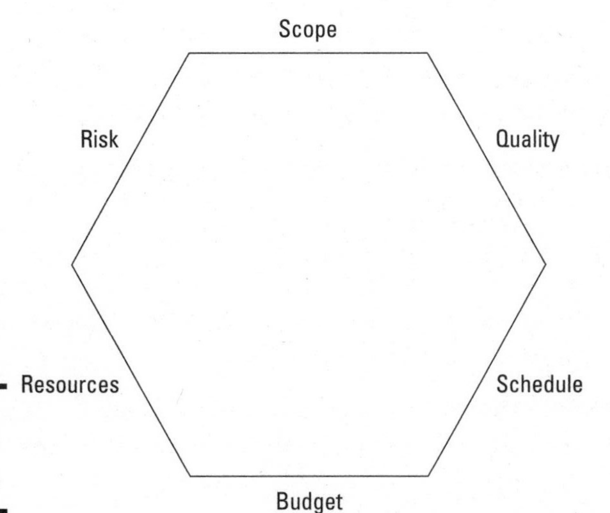

Figure 2-1: Competing constraints.

When any constraint changes, it affects one or more additional constraints. For example, a team losing a key resource will probably affect quality, schedule, and risk. If budget is reduced, that should affect scope and/or quality; if it doesn't, then the risk increases. A shortened schedule usually affects scope, quality, budget, and/or risk.

What makes a successful project manager

It isn't enough to know what's in the *PMBOK Guide*, or pass the PMP exam, to be a successful project manager. You also need subject matter knowledge, the appropriate personality, and good performance. Beyond that, you need to master progressive elaboration and the fine art of tailoring.

- **Knowledge:** Think about it: Without the requisite subject matter knowledge, how would you know whether an estimate a team member gives you is reasonable or out in left field? You have to know something about the type of project you're managing. How else can you expect people to respect you and your expertise?
- **Personality:** Another key aspect in project success comprises your personal traits. Your attitude, personality, and leadership ability are key aspects in your success. It might not seem fair that personality plays a role, but really, this job is not for everyone. Someone who is withdrawn or hypercritical won't do well in this job.
- **Performance:** You can know everything about project management and your industry and technical area, and you can be well liked and respected, but if you can't deliver or perform, you won't be successful.

Don't be surprised if you run into a question that indicates that the project manager has to be knowledgeable about the technical and professional aspects of the project.

Progressive elaboration and tailoring

One of the key techniques that project managers use to ensure success is *progressive elaboration*. There is no way you can know everything about a project when it's first handed over to you. The planning process helps you learn more about the scope and requirements of the project. This in turn helps you develop more detailed and refined cost and time estimates as well as build more accurate schedules and budgets.

Progressive Elaboration. The iterative process of increasing the level of detail in a project management plan as greater amounts of information and more accurate estimates become available.

All areas of your project are progressively elaborated from assumptions to risks and requirements to resources.

Another critical aspect in being successful is what I call "tailoring." You have to figure out how formally you will apply the various project management processes. You might do a very robust and thorough job of gathering and documenting requirements. However, you might not spend as much time in the procurement processes if you have a long-standing strategic relationship with a vendor who is familiar with your organization. Your ability to tailor the degree of rigor you bring to the project is one way you can make your job easier.

Although there are no exam objectives that tie directly to the information in this chapter, you still need to know all the concepts. The concepts and definitions in this chapter are integrated into exam questions. For example, a question may present a scenario that requires a risk response. Information in the question may indicate the priorities between the competing demands that you need to understand to answer the question correctly. Therefore, even though you aren't expected to name the competing demands, you need to understand the concept to be successful on the exam. The same applies to the definitions of project, programs, portfolios, progressive elaboration, and so forth.

Projects and organizational strategy

I mention earlier that projects are initiated to meet strategic objectives. The *PMBOK Guide* lists these strategic reasons for initiating a project:

- **Market demand:** This includes new products and updating existing products.
- **Business need:** This can include projects to make operations more efficient and thereby increase net profits.
- **Social need:** Projects that improve the quality of life, such as improving literacy, drinking water, or reducing disease.
- **Environmental consideration:** This includes projects such as environmental remediation, improving air or water quality, or projects that reduce waste and environmental impact.
- **Customer request:** A customer request can occur via a bid process, or an existing customer can approach you and ask you to perform work.
- **Technological advance:** Anything that helps automate operations or helps your company do things better, faster, or less expensively.
- **Legal requirements:** When a new law or regulation is passed, you need to understand the implications and make sure your organization can comply.

The word "objective" is frequently misunderstood.

Objective. Something toward which work is to be directed, a strategic position to be attained, or a purpose to be achieved; a result to be obtained, a product to be produced, or a service to be performed.

Did you notice that the definition has three of the key words from the definition of project? It talks about a product, service, or result. We undertake projects to achieve objectives. Objectives are enumerated in the project charter, which I talk about in Book II. When you initiate a project, you usually have scope and quality objectives: in other words, what you want to accomplish. And, generally, there are some expectations for schedule and budget objectives as well. These objectives guide the project manager in making decisions and trade-offs throughout the project.

The Project Management Office

A Project Management Office (PMO) is common these days. PMOs can have all different functions, depending upon the needs of the organization.

Project Management Office (PMO). An organizational structure that standardizes the project-related governance processes and facilitates the sharing of resources, methodologies, tools, and techniques.

The responsibilities of a PMO can range from providing project management support functions to actually being responsible for the direct management of a project.

Here are the three basic types of PMOs:

- **Supportive:** A supportive PMO develops policies, procedures, templates, forms, and reports for project management in the organization. The supportive PMO also serves as a project repository for project management resources. It has a low degree of control.
- **Controlling:** A controlling PMO also provides develops policies, procedures, templates, forms, and reports for project management in the organization; however, they require compliance with the project management methodology, the usage of the forms, policies, templates, and so forth. This type of PMO has a moderate level of control.
- **Directive:** Some large projects have a PMO set up to manage a specific project. The degree of control is high.

Of course, PMOs can provide multiple functions, or a little bit of each, but those in the preceding list are the general descriptions of the most common services that PMOs provide. You may also see a PMO that is a home for project managers. In this type of PMO, all project managers (PMs) report to the director or head of the PMO. The head of the PMO assigns PMs to projects, monitors progress, and serves as the functional manager for project management. This PMO also serves as a communication hub and allocates resources across multiple projects.

Understanding Environmental Constraints

All projects are constrained by the environment in which they are performed. If you think about it, your company culture has a lot to do with how you manage your project. If you've managed projects in only one company, you might not see this as clearly as if you had worked with several different companies. Think about where you work. Do you have lots of policies, procedures, forms, rules, and so forth that guide how you manage projects? Or do you work somewhere that has very little formal structure, and you use your personal influence and ingenuity to get things done? Do PMs have a lot of position power or very little?

A company's culture includes

- vision, values, and beliefs
- and procedures
- y relationships, leadership, and hierarchy
- ic, code of conduct, and work hours
- rance
- nd motivation systems

e environmental factors

vironmental Factors. Conditions, not under the immediate team, that influence, constrain, or direct the project, program,

culture, as described earlier, is an example of an enterprise factor (EEF). EEFs can be the result of any or all the enter- in the project; and in addition to company culture, include

- , codes, and regulations
- The organizations infrastructure, such as IT systems, supply chains, and organizational structure
- Marketplace conditions, including the availability of material and technical skills
- Stakeholder risk tolerances and the ability to work with uncertainty
- Extreme geography and weather

Generally, EEFs are considered to be a constraint. They might be almost transparent, but you need to keep them in mind while you plan and execute your project. You will see EEFs as an input to many of the project management processes throughout this book.

TIP

FOR THE EXAM

When you see EEFs as an input to a process, take some time to think about the various things in both the internal and external environment that could influence how you perform the process. This will get your brain used to thinking about how EEFs affect projects rather than being a bunch of words strung together.

The following responsibility standard from the Code of Ethics and Professional Conduct relates to EEFs:

> We inform ourselves and uphold the policies, rules, regulations and laws that govern our work, professional and volunteer activities.

Project governance

The organization's governance structure can also be considered a constraining factor. Project governance follows the organization's governance structure, but it is focused on the project life cycle. Governance is a framework for conducting the project and includes

- Guidelines for aligning organizational and project governance
- Project life cycle and phase reviews
- Decision-making processes
- Issue resolution procedures
- Change management procedures
- Project organizational chart and the relationship among the team, the organization, and external stakeholders

Key Terms

These terms are foundational to understanding the rest of the information in this book. Make sure you understand them well enough to be able to explain them to a novice project manager.

- Project
- Product
- Result
- Deliverable
- Project manager
- Project management

- Progressive elaboration
- Program
- Program management
- Portfolio
- Portfolio management
- Objective
- Project Management Office (PMO)
- Enterprise environmental factor (EEF)

Chapter Summary

The main points in this chapter are defining projects, project management, competing demands, PMOs, and enterprise environmental factors (EEFs). You will see these concepts repeated throughout this study guide, so make sure you are comfortable with them.

- A project is a temporary endeavor undertaken to create a unique product, service, or result. Projects produce deliverables to project requirements.
- Project management is the application of knowledge, skills, tools, and techniques to project activities to meet the project requirements.
- To manage projects successfully, you need to identify and balance the competing constraints. You will also need to practice progressive elaboration and tailor the various project management processes to meet the needs of your specific project.
- Programs manage a group of projects, subprograms, and program activities in a coordinated way to obtain benefits and control not available from managing them individually.
- Portfolios are projects, programs, subportfolios, and operations managed as a group to achieve strategic objectives.
- Projects are initiated to meet the organization's strategic objectives. An objective is a position to be attained or a purpose to be achieved.
- A Project Management Office (PMO) can have various structures and provide various roles to support project management in the organization.
- An organization's culture, infrastructure, organizational structure, IT systems can constrain (or enhance) the way a project is managed. These are enterprise environmental factors (EEFs). Other EEFs include regulations, market conditions, and available skill sets.

Prep Test

1 Performing routine maintenance for a company campus is an example of

A ❍ Project management
B ❍ Operational management
C ❍ Functional management
D ❍ Program management

2 Which of the following is not one of the PMI-identified competing constraints?

A ❍ Market conditions
B ❍ Quality
C ❍ Schedule
D ❍ Resources

3 Your project sponsor wants to know why the schedule you gave her has milestones listed with only the first 90 days worth of work defined in detail. You explain to her that you can provide a more detailed schedule as the project progresses, when you can have a greater understanding of what is involved. You tell her that this concept — common in project management — is

A ❍ Planning
B ❍ Life cycle planning
C ❍ Progressive elaboration
D ❍ Progressive estimating

4 You are tasked with completely updating your organization's communication infrastructure. You decide to break this into several components: one each for telephones, IT, and radio communication. Each will have its own manager. This is an example of

A ❍ A project
B ❍ A portfolio
C ❍ A program
D ❍ Operations

5 The centralized management of one or more portfolios — including identifying, prioritizing, authorizing, managing, and controlling projects, programs, and other related work to achieve strategic business objectives — is

A ❍ Program management
B ❍ Portfolio management
C ❍ Strategic management
D ❍ Forecasting

6 **Your company won a contract to update the security system for the local courthouse. This project is an example of**

- **A** ❍ A market demand
- **B** ❍ A business need
- **C** ❍ A customer request
- **D** ❍ A legal requirement

7 **Your company works with a number of chemical compounds. Your project is to update the handling and disposal of all chemicals to ensure that everyone is handling them correctly. You are doing this because of**

- **A** ❍ A market demand
- **B** ❍ A business need
- **C** ❍ A customer request
- **D** ❍ A legal requirement

8 **A PMO that develops policies and procedures and ensures compliance with the project management processes is what kind of PMO?**

- **A** ❍ Administrative
- **B** ❍ Supportive
- **C** ❍ Project specific
- **D** ❍ Bureaucratic

9 **You work for a commercial roofing contractor. You are asked to do a job in Barrow, Alaska. Which EEF do you need to pay closest attention to?**

- **A** ❍ Company culture
- **B** ❍ Infrastructure
- **C** ❍ Weather
- **D** ❍ Availability of resources

10 **The custom homebuilder you work for has a contract to build a 10,000–square foot home. The customer wants marble from Florence, Italy. To work with the tile, you need extremely skilled craftsmen with special tools. This EEF is an example of**

- **A** ❍ Company culture
- **B** ❍ Infrastructure
- **C** ❍ Weather
- **D** ❍ Availability of resources

Answers

1. **B.** Operational management. Routine maintenance is an example of operations. *Review "Definition of a project."*
2. **A.** Market conditions. Market conditions might be an enterprise environmental factor, but they're not one of the competing constraints. *Look over "Competing constraints."*
3. **C.** Progressive elaboration. Progressive elaboration is continuing to provide more detail as more is known about the project. *Check out "Progressive elaboration and tailoring."*
4. **C.** A program. This is a program. Each component is a project. *Look at "Projects, programs, and portfolios."*
5. **B.** Portfolio management. This is the definition of portfolio management. *See "Projects, programs, and portfolios."*
6. **C.** A customer request. The fact that you won this from a bid on a contract defines it as a customer request. *Go to "Projects and organizational strategy."*
7. **D.** A legal requirement. Ensuring the correct handling and disposal of chemicals is a regulatory requirement. *Look over "Projects and organizational strategy."*
8. **A.** Administrative. Setting policies and procedures and ensuring compliance is the role of an administrative PMO. *Check out "The Project Management Office."*
9. **C.** Weather. In Alaska, weather is always an EEF! *Review "Understanding Environmental Constraints."*
10. **D.** Availability of resources. The material and the labor to work with it are constraints associated with the availability of resources. *Go back to "Understanding Environmental Constraints."*

Chapter 3: Project Life Cycles, Organizational Structures, and Organizational Process Assets

Chapter Objectives

- **Project life cycles provide a framework to manage projects by breaking them into phases. Each phase has a specific intent and deliverable(s).**
- **The organizational structure affects how you manage your projects. Organizations can be set up functionally, in a matrix, or project-oriented (also known as "projectized").**
- **Organizational process assets include policies, templates, information from previous projects, and similar tools to support project managers in managing projects.**

In the preceding chapter, I look at some foundational concepts and definitions used in project management. I want to discuss a few more key concepts before getting into the project management processes.

To begin, I want to discuss a project life cycle and look at the various types of life cycles. Next, I discuss organizational structures and how they affect how you manage your project. The organizational structure is one of those enterprise environmental factors (EEFs), as discussed in the preceding chapter. In this chapter, I look at how the range of structures from functional to projectized influences how you can manage your project.

I finish this chapter by looking at organizational process assets that can aid you in managing your project. Sometimes those pesky policies and procedures can seem like a pain in the neck to follow, but think about how chaotic it would be if everyone managed projects based on their own system and if everyone used different processes. Established processes, templates, and historical information are organizational process assets that can help you manage your project.

Quick Assessment

1. The series of phases that a project passes through from its initiation to its closure is a(n) ______ ______ ______.

2. (True/False). You might have several instances of a project life cycle inside the product life cycle.

3. A collection of logically related project activities that culminates in the completion of one or more deliverables is a ______ ______.

4. In the beginning of the project, the ability of stakeholders to influence the project is ______, and the cost of changes is the ______.

5. The organizational structure where the PM has the most power is a(n) ______ structure.

6. Elements that influence the project's success, such as policies and processes, are called ______ ______ ______.

Answers

1. Project life cycle. The series of phases that a project passes through from its initiation to its closure. *Read more about this in the "The Project Life Cycle" section.*

2. True. You might have several instances of a project life cycle inside the product life cycle. Often, the initial development of a product is a project. There might be projects along the way to improve product. Sometimes retiring a product is a project as well. *This is discussed in the "Product versus project life cycle" section.*

3. Project phase. Project life cycles are made up of project phases, each of which has a specific set of activities or results associated with it. *For more information, see the "Project phases" section.*

4. Highest, lowest. The ability of stakeholders to influence the project is highest in the beginning of the project, and the cost of changes is the lowest. *Look over information in the "Project phases" section.*

5. Projectized. The organizational structure where the PM has the most power is a projectized structure. *See the "Projectized organization" section.*

6. Organizational process assets. Elements that influence the project's success, such as policies and processes, are called "organizational process assets." *You can read more about this in the "Leveraging Your Organization's Assets" section.*

The Project Life Cycle

All projects have certain things in common: They begin, there is some amount of organizing and planning, plans are turned into actions, and then they close. That is an example of a very simple project life cycle. A project life cycle is a framework for managing a project. The life cycle depends on the nature of the work. You wouldn't manage a technology project the same way you would manage a process improvement project. However, managing similar projects in a similar way is useful. And using a life cycle can provide the framework to help you do that.

Project Life Cycle. A series of phases that a project passes through from its initiation to its closure.

The three types of life cycles are predictive, iterative and incremental, and adaptive. Each type of life cycle uses phases to better manage the work.

Project phases

You can make a project life cycle more specific to your type of projects by thinking about the specific type of work and the particular deliverables you have during the project. In other words, what are the various phases your project goes through?

Project Phase. A collection of logically related project activities that culminates in the completion of one or more deliverables.

Project phases are mainly completed sequentially, but they can overlap in some project situations. A project phase is a component of a project life cycle. A project phase is not a project management process group.

For example, an information technology project might have the following phases:

- Concept definition
- Requirements gathering
- Planning
- Development
- Test
- Deploy

Those phases are appropriate for IT projects. However, for a process improvement project, you would have different phases in the project life cycle — perhaps something like the following:

- ✦ Establish goals and objectives
- ✦ As-is process mapping
- ✦ Planning
- ✦ To-be process development
- ✦ Process deployment

Product development, construction, pharmaceutical development, and other industries have their own life cycles. Many industries have similar life cycles, but the needs of the organization and the project should ultimately determine the number of phases and the deliverables associated with each phase.

As I discuss earlier in this minibook, part of your governance role as the project manager is determining how to tailor an existing life cycle to fit your project — or, if your organization doesn't have a set life cycle, figuring out the appropriate phases and their relationships.

Predictive life cycles

A predictive life cycle is used for projects where there is a clear understanding of the project scope. The scope, schedule, resources, and cost are determined as soon as possible in the project, and plans are developed to meet the project objectives. Figure 3-1 shows a predictive life cycle with a sequential relationship between phases. A sequential relationship means that one phase ends before the next phase begins. This is known as a "waterfall" life cycle in some industries.

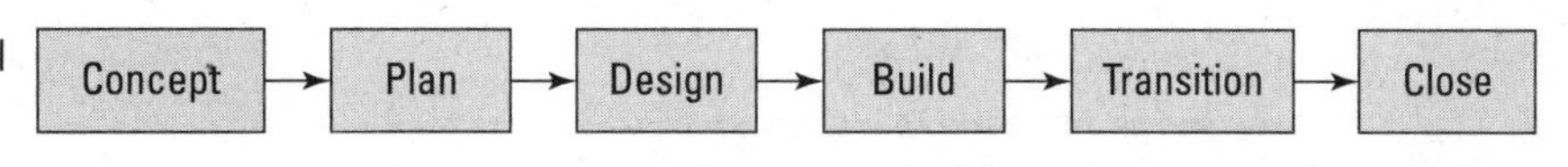

Figure 3-1: A sequential project life cycle.

An alternative to a sequential relationship is an overlapping relationship where you overlap phases, such as design and construction. For example, you might be able to start some of the rough construction before all the detailed design is complete. In Figure 3-2, the project life cycle shows phases of plan, design, and build that are overlapping. Sometimes this is called *fast tracking*.

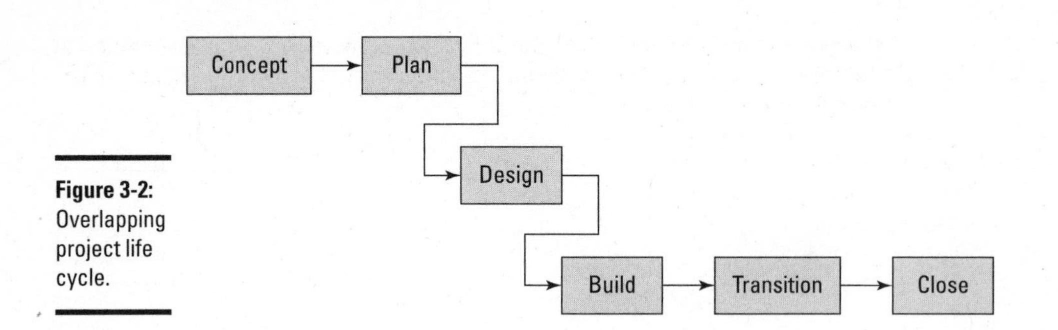

Figure 3-2: Overlapping project life cycle.

You may be familiar with the term "fast tracking" as it is used when referring to schedule compression. Overlapping project phases compresses the overall project duration. I talk more about fast tracking in Book III, Chapter 2.

Another way of showing an overlapping project life cycle (see Figure 3-3) is to have multiple deliverables developed independently and then transition them at the same time. Sometimes an additional phase — integration — is in this type of life cycle.

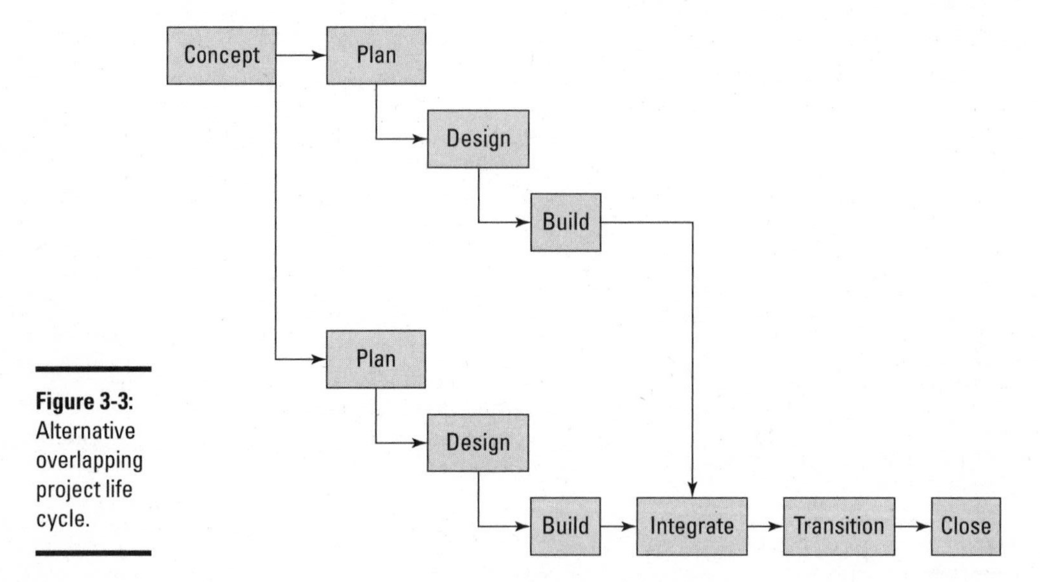

Figure 3-3: Alternative overlapping project life cycle.

Iterative and incremental life cycles

In contrast to predictive life cycles, some projects have an iterative life cycle. For example, design-build-feedback would go through several iterations before finalizing the end product. In an iterative life cycle, each iteration refines and improves the deliverable. An incremental life cycle adds functionality to the product in each phase. Figure 3-4 shows an iterative or incremental life cycle.

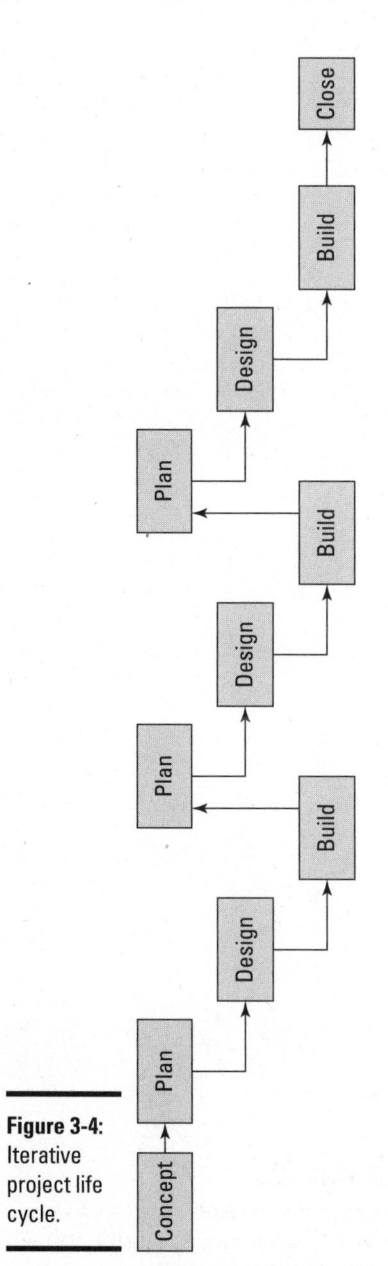

Figure 3-4: Iterative project life cycle.

In many iterative life cycles, high-level visioning and planning is conducted at the beginning of the project. Detailed planning at the phase level is completed one iteration or increment at a time.

Iterative and incremental life cycles are useful when scope is not well defined or is subject to change. This type of life cycle can also be used when a deliverable with partial functionality is a viable option. Future iterations are used to add functionality. Many times, the iterations or increments are designed to incorporate stakeholder feedback in order to improve the product or service.

Adaptive life cycles

Adaptive life cycles are iterative and incremental, but the phases are rapid compared with a non-adaptive life cycle. Adaptive life cycles are also known as *agile methods.* At the end of each iteration (sometimes known as a *sprint*), the customer reviews a functional deliverable. At the review, the customer provides feedback, and the team updates the project backlog of features and functions to prioritize the next sprint based on customer feedback.

One of the benefits of the adaptive life cycle is that making changes earlier in the life cycle is much easier. Project stakeholders have much more influence on the direction of the project and approach to the project in the early phases of the life cycle. An adaptive life cycle that gains stakeholder feedback early and often can reduce the number of changes that come late in the project. Figure 3-5 shows how changes to the project are much more costly to implement later in the project.

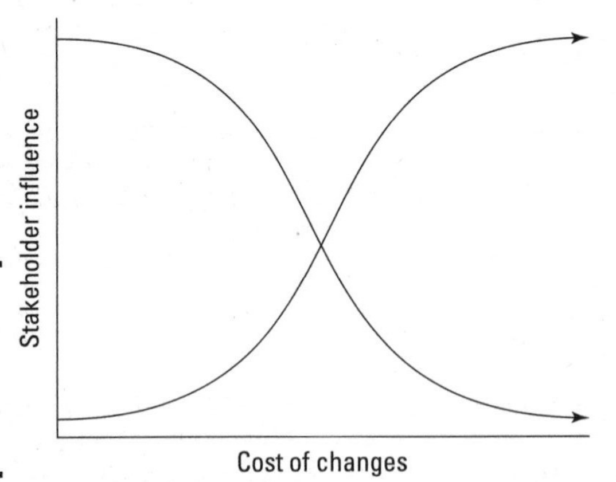

Figure 3-5: Stakeholder influence in the project life cycle.

Phase reviews

It is a common practice at the end of a phase to have a *phase gate review,* during which you should compare your planned accomplishments against the actual deliverables. This is also a good time to refine your plans for the next phase and conduct a "lessons learned" session that will ultimately feed into the overall lessons learned document at the end of the project. You can find more information about lessons learned in Book IX, Chapter 1.

Some organizations use the phase "gate review" to determine whether a project should continue. If the results are not as intended, the need for the project has changed, or the risk is too great, management may decide to cancel the project. Therefore, some organizations call phase gate reviews "kill points." In reality, it's better for a project to be killed early rather than continue expending resources on something not viable or no longer needed.

Product versus project life cycle

Sometimes confusion occurs about the difference between a product life cycle and a project life cycle. A *product life cycle* is the life of a product from conception through retirement. It is common for the development of a new product to be considered a project. However, at some point, the development project ends, and the product continues.

Product Life Cycle. The series of phases that represent the evolution of a product, from concept through delivery, growth, and maturity to retirement.

Generally, a project life cycle is contained within one or more product life cycles. Throughout the product life, the organization may use projects to update and modify the product. Therefore, you can say that product life cycles can include multiple project life cycles.

The PMP exam deals with *project* life cycles, not *product* life cycles. You might see one or two questions that have to do with the relationship between the two, so make sure you to read the question carefully so you understand which life cycle is being discussed.

Organization Structures

I describe enterprise environmental factors (EEFs) earlier in Chapter 2 of this minibook; in particular, I describe the company culture. I want to expand on that a bit from the perspective of a company's hierarchy and organizational structure. The three basic types of organizational structure are functional, matrix, and projectized. The three types of matrix organizations I will talk about as part of this discussion are weak, balanced, and strong.

Functional organization

A *functional organization* is the traditional hierarchical organization. It is organized by function, with a strong chain of command. A functional manager has almost total control over resources. In this situation, the project manager is usually part-time, has very little authority, and does not control the budget. Team members do project work when they can fit it into their daily activities.

Functional Organization. A hierarchical organization where each employee has one clear superior, and staff are grouped by areas of specialization and managed by a person with expertise in that area.

Matrix organization

A matrix organization is a project-friendly structure (more so than the functional organization). As I mention earlier, the three types of matrix organizations I talk about here are weak, balanced, and strong.

Matrix Organization. Any organizational structure in which the project manager shares responsibility with the functional managers for assigning priorities and for directing the work of persons assigned to the project.

- **Weak:** A weak matrix closely resembles a functional organization, but there is a little more understanding that projects require cross-functional communication and that project management is a discipline that can help a project's success.

  In a weak matrix, you might hear the project manager called a *project expediter* or a *project coordinator.*

  - A *project expediter* is similar to an administrative assistant and coordinates communications but has no decision-making or enforcement authority.
  - A *project coordinator* is similar to an expediter but has a bit more authority. The increased authority can be because of reporting to a higher-level manager than the expediter.

- **Balanced:** In a balanced matrix, you will see a full-time project manager position. This person has more authority to make decisions, can have some budgetary accountability, and might even have administrative support. Team members have more time to dedicate to projects, and there is usually a beginning or even full-fledged project management methodology.
- **Strong:** A strong matrix organization has dedicated project managers with a high level of authority, full-time administrative support, and team members who are fully dedicated to the project. They usually control the budget.

Projectized organization

A projectized organization is the opposite of a functional organization. In this type of organization, work is organized around projects. The functions are primarily in support of project work. The project manager has full authority for the work and the budget. Project staff report directly to the project manager as opposed to a functional manager.

Projectized Organization. Any organizational structure in which the project manager has full authority to assign priorities, apply resources, and direct the work of persons assigned to the project.

Comparing organization types

There are pros and cons to each type of organization. Some large organizations take a mixed approach. Perhaps some sections of the enterprise are projectized, some are matrix, and some are functional. Such a blend is a composite organization. Table 3-1 outlines some of the benefits and pitfalls common to different organizational structures.

Table 3-1 Comparison of Organizational Structures

	Description	*Advantages*	*Disadvantages*
Functional	The functional department performs the project. A member of the department is the project manager.	Broad specialist base available Shared knowledge of latest technology Flexible resource scheduling	No one responsible for the total project Little PM authority Complex coordination
Matrix	An interdisciplinary team performs the project. The PM is responsible for all management functions. Project team members report to their functional departments.	Good project control Early identification of problems Better interdepartmental coordination Timely responses to changes	Conflicts between departments Information and work flowing in multiple directions Reporting duplication Team members with two bosses

(continued)

Table 3-1 (continued)

	Description	*Advantages*	*Disadvantages*
Projectized	An ad hoc group, project department, or project office group performs the project. The organization is separate from the functional departments. The PM has full authority and responsibility.	Single focal point for the project Team members reporting to one manager Strong interdisciplinary communication Rapid reaction to changes High project commitment project	Low career security Duplication of resources Team members out of touch with specialty High corporate cost

Figure 3-6 summarizes the PM's authority level and the time commitment from team members relative to the type of organization.

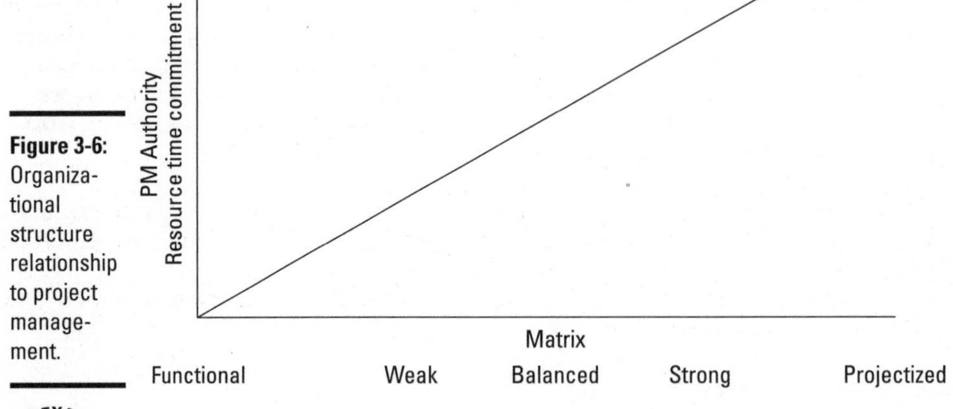

Figure 3-6: Organizational structure relationship to project management.

A *tight* organization is one in which all the team members work in the same location.

Although you may not see questions on the exam that ask about a project life cycle or organizational structure specifically, this information might be integrated into a question, and you will have to understand it to answer the question correctly. For example, you might see a question like

> *You are working in a weak matrix organization with your team members located in different locations. You are developing a communications management plan and want to make sure you identify all the stakeholders that need information about the project status. What type of information should you send to your team members' managers?*

By understanding the nature of a weak matrix (more power to the functional manager), you know that the functional managers will need to know how long their employees will be working on project activities. If you were in a strong matrix, it is more likely that team members would be assigned full-time, or would report to you directly.

Leveraging Your Organization's Assets

As an organization moves along the continuum from functional to projectized, more information and more assets are available that project managers can use to help them perform their duties. A purely functional organization has little or no common terminology, scheduling software, understanding of the competing constraints, or information from past projects. On the other hand, a purely projectized organization has a robust project management methodology complete with governance, policies, procedures, templates, risk databases, estimating guidelines, and so on. These items are organizational process assets (OPAs).

Organizational Process Assets. Plans, processes, policies, procedures, and knowledge bases that are specific to and used by the performing organization.

The two major groups of process assets are processes and procedures, and the corporate knowledge base:

- **Processes and procedures**
  - Policies, procedures, processes, forms, and templates
  - Standard guidelines, work instructions, and performance thresholds
  - Guidelines for proposal evaluation criteria, estimating, communication, audits, and project evaluations

✦ **Corporate knowledge base**

- Historical information from prior projects, past project files, and lessons learned
- Risk databases, estimating databases, and configuration management knowledge bases
- Prior change logs, assumption logs, issue logs, decision logs, and defect logs

You can see how having access to this type of information would make your life a lot easier. You could spend more time problem-solving and managing stakeholder expectations rather than reinventing the proverbial wheel.

When you see OPAs as an input to a process, take some time to think about the various assets in the organization that could influence how you perform the process. This will get your brain used to thinking about how OPAs influence projects.

If you have a few spare moments to study, go through the glossary. The glossary in this book is consistent with the glossary in the *PMBOK Guide*. Understanding the way terms are defined will give you an edge during the exam.

Key Terms

The following terms represent important concepts that you need to remember to do well on the exam. Make sure you can explain each of them.

✦ Project life cycle

✦ Project phase

✦ Product life cycle

✦ Functional organization

✦ Matrix organization

✦ Weak matrix

✦ Balanced matrix

✦ Strong matrix

✦ Projectized organization

✦ Composite organization

✦ Tight matrix

✦ Organizational process assets

Chapter Summary

This chapter covers more fundamental concepts in project management. Although there are no direct exam objectives tied to this information, there are questions on the exam that reference the information. Make sure you are comfortable with these concepts before moving on.

- Projects are managed by using a project life cycle. The project life cycle is composed of phases. Each phase has a specific purpose and ends with defined deliverables. The name and number of the phases depend on the nature of the project. A project life cycle is different from a product life cycle.
- How organizations are structured affects how you can manage your project. In a functional organization, the PM is part-time, has part-time team members, and has very little authority. As the organization moves along a continuum to a matrix and then a projectized organization, the PM's authority, dedication of team members, administrative support, and control over the budget all increase.
- Organizational process assets help you manage your project. Some assets are policies, procedures, and processes; others are historical information and databases of information.

Prep Test

1. **You're setting up your project and need to manage it so that you complete one phase and get customer sign-off before beginning the next phase. What type of project life cycle should you use?**

   A ❍ Overlapping
   B ❍ Sequential
   C ❍ Fast tracking
   D ❍ Iterative

2. **You want to start creating some high-level designs before all your requirements are collected and approved. You would also like to do some testing before all the work is complete. What type of life cycle should you use?**

   A ❍ Overlapping
   B ❍ Sequential
   C ❍ Waterfall
   D ❍ Iterative

3. **Which type of organizational structure is the traditional style where employees report up through their specialty area?**

   A ❍ Functional
   B ❍ Tight matrix
   C ❍ Balanced matrix
   D ❍ Projectized

4. **You report up through your organization's PMO. You don't have unlimited authority for your project, but you do control the budget, and most of your team members are dedicated to the project full-time. What type of organizational structure are you in?**

   A ❍ Weak matrix
   B ❍ Composite
   C ❍ Projectized
   D ❍ Strong matrix

5 **Which of the following is characteristic of a matrix organization?**

A ❍ An interdisciplinary team performs the project.
B ❍ The organization is separate from functional departments.
C ❍ The PM has full authority and responsibility.
D ❍ The functional department performs the project.

6 **Which of the following is an advantage of working in a projectized organization?**

A ❍ Interdepartmental coordination
B ❍ Shared knowledge of the latest technology
C ❍ Better reporting
D ❍ Team members reporting to one manager

7 **Which of the following is a disadvantage of working in a functional organization?**

A ❍ Duplication of reporting
B ❍ No one responsible for the total project
C ❍ High corporate cost
D ❍ Low career security

8 **The organizational structure that combines functional, matrix, and projectized structures, depending on the area, is**

A ❍ A balanced matrix
B ❍ A tight matrix
C ❍ Composite
D ❍ Combined

9 **Which of the following is not an organizational process asset?**

A ❍ Risk database
B ❍ Information from past projects
C ❍ Change control policies
D ❍ Risk tolerance

10 **You are assigned a project to upgrade the organization's operating system. You expect this to take six months. A similar upgrade was performed two years ago. Which organizational process asset should you look at first to help you plan?**

A ❍ Configuration management database
B ❍ Project close out procedures
C ❍ Assumption logs, issues logs, and decision logs from the prior project
D ❍ Proposal evaluation criteria

Scenario 1

Your project is to produce the half-time show for a major football game. The customer wants a light show, a marching band, a well-known pop star, and an acrobat troop. You decide that the best way to do this is to start with the main concept for the show and then get customer sign-off. During the next phase, you fill in more details, get customer feedback, incorporate it, and get sign-off. You do several rounds of this until you receive approval for the whole show. What type of project life cycle is this?

A ❍ Overlapping
B ❍ Sequential
C ❍ Fast tracking
D ❍ Iterative

Answers

Multiple Choice

1 **B.** Sequential. A sequential project life cycle requires you to complete one phase before initiating the next phase. *See "Project phases."*

2 **A.** Overlapping. An overlapping project life cycle allows you to begin one phase before the previous phase is complete. *Look over "Project phases."*

3 **A.** Functional. In a functional organizational structure, employees report up through their functional specialties. This is the traditional structure. *Check out "Functional organization."*

4 **D.** Strong matrix. A strong matrix gives you a lot of control, but not total control. *Review "Matrix organization."*

5 **A.** An interdisciplinary team performs the project. In matrix organizations, team members from different departments work on the project. *Go over "Comparing organization types."*

6 **D.** Team members reporting to one manager. In a projectized organization, team members report to the project manager. *Read about this in "Comparing organization types."*

7 **B.** No one responsible for the total project. In a functional organization, no one takes accountability for cross-functional success of the project. *Review "Comparing organization types."*

8 **C.** Composite. A composite organization has some divisions that are functional, some that are matrix, and some that are projectized. *Look at "Projectized organization."*

9 **D.** Risk tolerance. Risk tolerance is an enterprise environmental factor (EEF). *Check out "Leveraging Your Organization's Assets."*

10 **C.** Assumption logs, issues logs, and decision logs from the prior project. The logs from the previous project will be most helpful in the beginning of the project. You might need the other information later in the project. *Go to "Leveraging Your Organization's Assets."*

Scenario 1

D. Iterative. An iterative project life cycle allows you to evolve the concept, adding detail as you get customer input. *Look over "Project phases."*

Chapter 4: It's All about the Process

Chapter Objectives

- **Project management processes**
- **Learning the process groups**
- **Getting acquainted with the knowledge areas**
- **Mapping the processes**

In this chapter, I cover the framework for the rest of this book. This chapter corresponds to the information in Annex A1 of the *PMBOK Guide,* which identifies the processes needed to manage a project and the inputs and outputs associated with each process.

Although the information in the Annex isn't very exciting, it is important because it establishes the framework for the *PMBOK Guide* and provides the architecture of the processes used in managing a project, by introducing the five process groups and the ten knowledge areas that the project management processes belong to.

I give you a lot of information in this chapter. Don't expect to absorb it all in one sitting. Come back to this chapter every so often. By the time you're ready to take the exam, the information here should make sense. In fact, you should be able to re-create it for yourself. After you can do that, you are ready for the exam!

Quick Assessment

1 The five process groups are ______, Planning, ______, Monitoring and Controlling, and ______.

2 (True/False). The process groups are the same as a project life cycle.

3 A charter is an output from which process group?

4 (True/False). Project Contract Management is the knowledge area used to manage goods and purchases for the project.

5 ______ ______ are those processes performed to establish the total scope of the effort, refine the objectives, and define the course of action required to attain the objectives the project was undertaken to achieve.

6 Is the requirements traceability matrix part of the project management plan, or is it a project document?

7 Problem solving to determine appropriate corrective and preventive action takes place in which process group?

8 How many processes are in the Closing process group?

9 There are ______ process groups, _____ knowledge areas, and ______ processes.

Answers

1 Initiating, Executing, Closing. These five process groups contain all the processes used to manage a project. *Read more about this in "Understanding Project Management Process Groups."*

2 False. Process groups are a collection of processes used to manage a project. The project life cycle is a series of phases used to develop the product service or result. *I discuss this in "Understanding Project Management Process Groups."*

3 Initiating. A charter formally authorizes a project and is an output from the Initiating process group. *Find more information in "Initiating processes."*

4 False. Project Procurement Management is the knowledge area used to manage the procurement of goods and services. *Find the definition in the section on "Project Procurement Management."*

5 Planning processes. Per the glossary definition, "Planning processes are those processes performed to establish the total scope of the effort, refine the objectives, and define the course of action required to attain the objectives the project was undertaken to achieve." *See "Planning processes" for more information.*

6 Project document. The requirements traceability matrix is a project document that helps manage the project, but it is not a part of the project management plan. *This is discussed in "Planning processes."*

7 Monitoring and Controlling process group. Problem solving to determine appropriate corrective and preventive action takes place in the Monitoring and Controlling process group as part of the Monitor and Control Project Work process. *Look over the information in "Monitoring and Controlling processes."*

8 Two. The two processes in the Closing process group are Close Procurements and Close Project or Phase. *Refer to "Closing processes" for more information.*

9 5, 10, 47. There are 5 process groups, 10 knowledge areas, and 47 processes. *See the section, "Mapping the 47 Processes."*

Managing Your Project Is a Process

A *process* is a set of interrelated of actions and activities performed to create a pre-specified product, service, or result. You manage projects via a series of processes, which have *inputs* that are needed to initiate the process. Then you apply tools and or techniques to transform the inputs into outputs. A simple example is making a cup of coffee. The inputs are the beans, water, a grinder, a pot, a heating mechanism, a filter, and a cup. The techniques you use are grinding the beans and boiling the water. The output is a cup of coffee. Here are the *PMBOK Guide* definitions for these terms.

Input. Any item, whether internal or external to the project, that is required by a process before that process proceeds. May be an output from a predecessor process.

Tool. Something tangible, such as a template or software program, used in performing an activity to produce a product or result.

Technique. A defined systematic procedure employed by a human resource to perform an activity to produce a product or result or deliver a service, and that may employ one or more tools.

Output. A product, result, or service generated by a process. May be an input to a successor process.

Inputs can be outputs from previous processes, and outputs can become inputs to subsequent processes.

PMI defines 47 project-related processes used to manage projects. Each process is part of one of five process groups:

- Initiating processes
- Planning processes
- Executing processes
- Monitoring and Controlling processes
- Closing processes

In addition, each process belongs to one of the ten knowledge areas:

- Project Integration Management
- Project Scope Management
- Project Time Management
- Project Cost Management

- Project Quality Management
- Project Human Resource Management
- Project Communications Management
- Project Risk Management
- Project Procurement Management
- Project Stakeholder Management

I talk about the process groups next and then the knowledge areas later in the chapter.

You also need to apply product-related processes to your project, but those are dependent upon the nature of the product and thus are not covered by the *PMBOK Guide*. An example of a product-related project might be integration testing prior to deploying a new system, or editing before printing a technical manual. Those processes are dependent upon the nature of the work and are governed by your organization's policies.

Understanding Project Management Process Groups

The project management process groups (hereafter referred to as *process groups*) of Initiating, Planning, Executing, Monitoring and Controlling, and Closing interact with each other in each project phase and throughout the project as a whole.

Project management process group. A logical grouping of project management inputs, tools and techniques, and outputs. The project management process groups include Initiating processes, Planning processes, Executing processes, Monitoring and Controlling processes, and Closing processes. Project management process groups are not project phases.

Notice that the domains tested on the PMP are the same as the process groups identified in the *PMBOK Guide*. This means that the exam is based around your skills and knowledge in the various process groups, even though most of the information presented in the *PMBOK Guide* is presented by knowledge area.

Many people make the mistake of thinking that the process groups are a project life cycle. They are not. Rather, they are a way of categorizing the various processes by the nature of the work involved in the process. I describe the project life cycle in Chapter 3 of this minibook if you want to read up on the purpose and definition.

- You apply each process group in each phase of the project life cycle although to varying degrees. Figure 4-1 shows how the process groups interact.

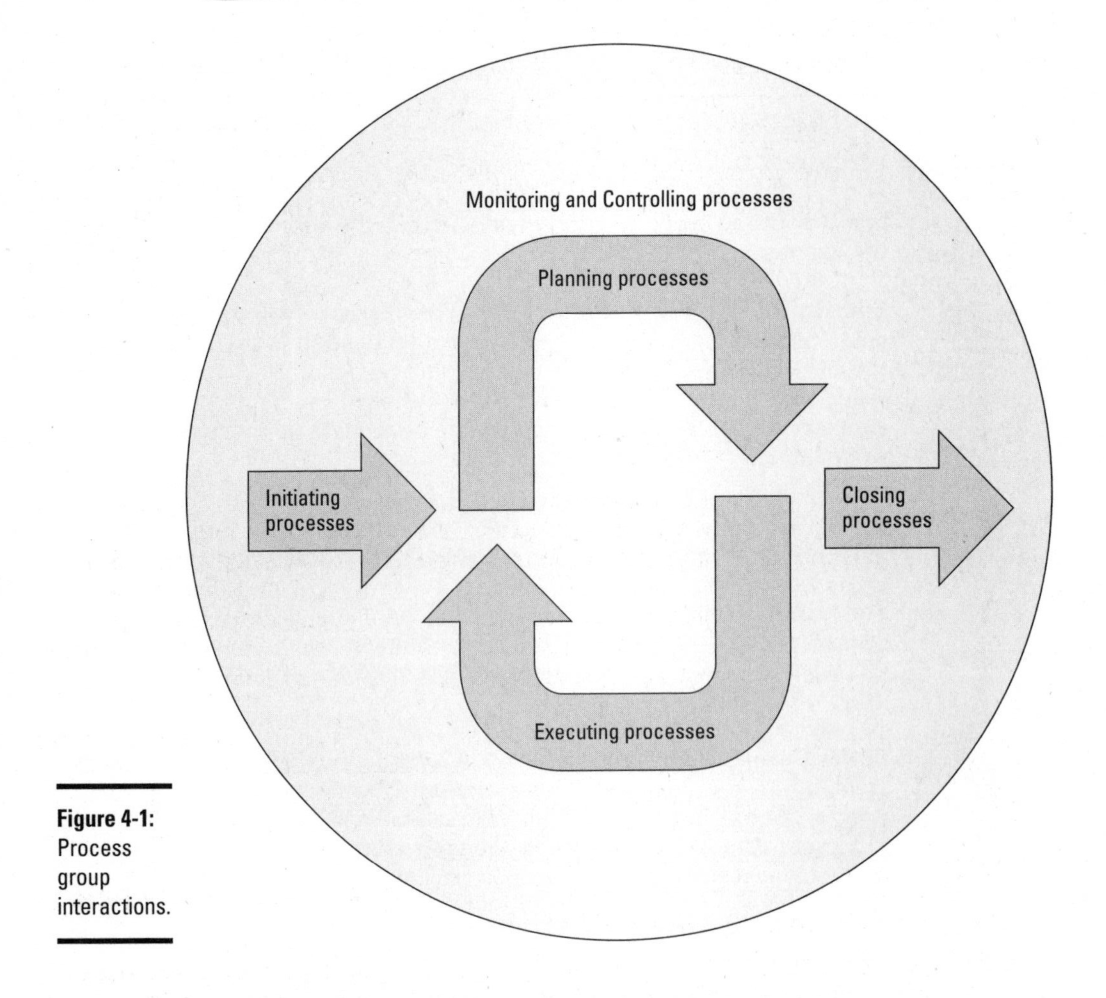

Figure 4-1: Process group interactions.

You can see that when you enter a phase of a project, you go through the Initiating processes. After that is complete, you begin the Planning processes, which lead to Executing processes. However, along the way, you will likely have to replan or progressively elaborate your plans. (I discuss progressive elaboration in Chapter 2 of this minibook.) Therefore, you are planning and executing throughout the majority of the project. Throughout all the processes groups, you conduct activities from the Monitoring and Controlling processes to make sure that the results from the Executing processes are on track with the plans from the Planning processes. When the project objectives have been met, you close out the phase or the project. Figure 4-2 shows how the process looks with a project with three phases.

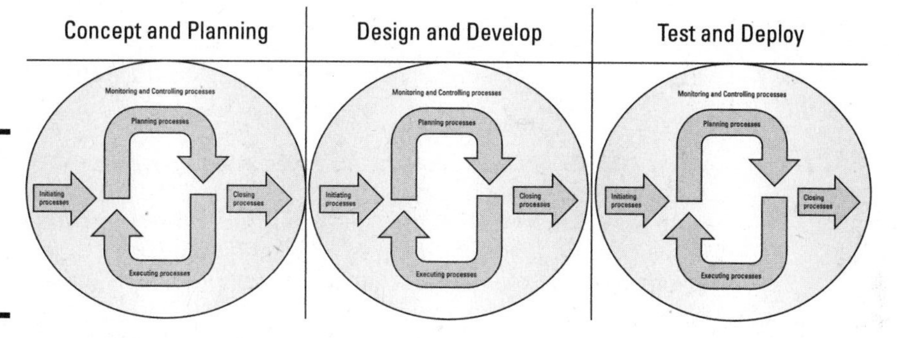

Figure 4-2: Project life cycle and process groups.

Before the Project Begins

I want to talk about some of the activities that happen before the project begins, and then I'll get into the initiating processes. In Chapter 2 of this minibook, I talk about the reasons why projects are initiated: a customer request, regulatory reasons, a technological advance, and so on. In that same chapter, I also discuss programs, portfolios, and Project Management Office (PMOs). Typically, one of these entities has the authority to initiate a project based on the preceding needs.

The decision to initiate a project isn't made in a vacuum. Several steps occur before a project is initiated. Here is a brief generic summary of some of the activities that take place:

1. Someone defines a need or proposes a concept.
2. Some high-level project definition is done, and alternatives to meet the need are developed and discussed.
3. A business case is put together, which can include market opportunity, financial investment, payback period, net present value, and other financial metrics.
4. The business case is presented to the person or group with the authority to initiate projects.

You might see a couple of questions on the exam that ask where projects come from, or about the work done prior to project initiation. Remember that some work is done prior to authorizing a project. Book II covers some of the information used to justify investing in a project.

Initiating processes

Initiating processes happen at the beginning of a project and are revisited at the start of each project phase.

Initiating Processes. Those processes performed to define a new project or a new phase of an existing project by obtaining authorization to start the project or phase.

To help you absorb the information about each process in the process groups, Table 4-1 shows the process name, the activities you perform as part of that process, and the resulting outputs from the process. The activities aren't a complete list, but they are complete enough to give you the idea of what happens in each process. Of course, the complete list of activities would depend upon the specific project. The outputs aren't the full list of outputs, but they are the major outputs from each process. I won't always list outputs, such as organizational process asset updates or change requests and so on. However, the information listed is a solid summary of the information for each process.

Table 4-1 Initiating Processes, Activities, and Outputs

Process	*Activities*	*Output*
Develop Project Charter	Assign a project manager (PM). Identify objectives. Identify stakeholder needs and expectations. Turn stakeholder needs and expectations into high-level requirements. Define high-level project scope. Review information from similar previous projects. Identify order of magnitude budget. Identify summary milestones. Define success criteria. Use organizational policies, procedures, and templates to develop the project charter. Present the charter for approval and formal authorization.	Project charter
Identify Stakeholders	Identify stakeholders. Determine how to manage stakeholders. Communicate how the project is aligned with the organizations' strategic goals.	Stakeholder register

Use the information in all the process group tables to quiz yourself. Try to look at the process and identify the activities and outputs.

Planning processes

Planning processes occur throughout the project. The bulk of your time planning will occur right after the project charter is approved. At some point, you will have done sufficient planning to finalize the project management plan and the baselines contained within it. At that point, you begin managing your performance according to those baselines. However, planning doesn't end after you baseline. You will need to replan based on changes, risk events, and performance. For large projects, you should be engaged in *rolling wave planning,* where you have details for work in the near future and higher-level information for work later in the future. A good time to develop detailed plans for the upcoming phase is when you're closing out one phase and initiating another.

Rolling wave planning. An iterative planning technique in which the work to be accomplished in the near term is planned in detail, while the work in the future is planned at a higher level.

Planning Processes. Those processes performed to establish the total scope of the effort, define and refine the objectives, and develop the course of action required to attain those objectives.

In Table 4-2, outputs in regular type are part of the project management plan. Outputs that are italicized are project documents. Project documents are not part of the project management plan, but they help you manage the project. A list of project management plan elements and project documents is in Book III, Chapter 1.

Table 4-2 Planning Processes, Activities, and Outputs

Process	*Activities*	*Outputs*
Develop Project Management Plan	Determine how to manage scope, schedule, and cost for the project and document the information in a management plan. Determine how to manage change for the project and document the information in the change management plan. Determine the appropriate level of configuration management and document it in a configuration management plan. Document the project life cycle. Determine how performance will be measured and reviewed. Determine which processes are needed for the project and the degree of rigor. Review information from past projects. Identify and follow organizational policies, procedures, processes, and templates used for planning. Identify EEFs* that will influence your project. Identify organizational interfaces and other projects you need to integrate with. Determine the methods used to monitor and control the project. Negotiate and prioritize project constraints. Baseline the plan. Get formal approval and sign-off on the project management plan. Hold a team kick-off meeting.	Project management plan

Process	*Activities*	*Outputs*
Plan Scope Management	Document the approach to develop a scope statement and WBS.** Describe how the WBS will be maintained and approved. Describe how formal acceptance of deliverables will take place. Determine how scope changes will be integrated with the project change control system. Describe how requirements activities will be planned, conducted and documented. Document how configuration management for requirements will be carried out. Define requirements prioritization. Identify the metrics and acceptance criteria for requirements. Determine the requirements traceability structure.	Scope management plan Requirements management plan
Collect Requirements	Employ brainstorming, role playing, negotiating, facilitating, interviewing, and consensus-building skills to identify and agree on project requirements. Document and prioritize project and product requirements.	Requirements documentation Requirements traceability matrix
Define Scope	Document what is in and out of scope. Describe project deliverables and their acceptance criteria. Document assumptions. Document constraints.	Project scope statement
Create WBS	Decompose work into deliverables. Describe each work package.	WBS dictionary Scope baseline
Plan Schedule Management	Document how the schedule will be developed and managed throughout the project.	Schedule management plan

(continued)

Table 4-2 *(continued)*

Process	*Activities*	*Outputs*
Define Activities	Identify activities needed to create deliverables.	Activity list Activity attributes Milestone list
Sequence Activities	Put activities in order.	Network diagram
Estimate Activity Resources	Determine resource requirements.	Resource requirements Resource breakdown structure
Estimate Activity Durations	Estimate project duration.	Duration estimates
Develop Schedule	Develop preliminary schedule.	Project schedule Schedule baseline
Plan Cost Management	Document how cost estimates will be developed. Describe how contingency funds will be determined and managed. Describe how the project budget will be developed. Identify the control mechanisms that will be used to monitor and control the project budget.	Cost management plan
Estimate Costs	Estimate project costs.	Cost estimates
Determine Budget	Develop project budget.	Cost performance baseline Project funding requirements
Plan Quality Management	Document project quality standards and requirements.	Quality management plan Quality metrics Quality checklists Process improvement plan
Plan Human Resource Management	Document project roles and responsibilities. Develop project organization chart. Determine how to manage project staff.	Human resource plan

Process	*Activities*	*Outputs*
Plan Communications Management	Document who needs what information, in what format, and how often.	Communications management plan
Plan Risk Management	Document approach to risk management.	Risk management plan
Identify Risks	Interview stakeholders for threats and opportunities. Document project threats and opportunities.	Risk register
Perform Qualitative Risk Analysis	Assess probability and impact of risks.	Risk register updates
Perform Quantitative Risk Analysis	Apply simulation, expected monetary value, decision trees, and other quantitative analysis techniques to risk events.	Risk register updates
Plan Risk Responses	Brainstorm risk responses and develop strategies to effectively manage threats.	Risk register updates
Plan Procurement Management	Document approach to procurements. Select contract types. Develop procurement documents, including an SOW.***	Procurement management plan Make-or-buy decisions SOWs Procurement documents Source selection criteria
Plan Stakeholder Management	Identify and documents methods to effectively engage stakeholders in the project. Determine how to manage stakeholder expectations.	Stakeholder management plan

**EEF: enterprise environmental factor*
***WBS: work breakdown structure*
****SOW: statement of work*

You can see that a lot of work goes on in the planning processes!

Table 4-2 doesn't show the loops and iterative nature of planning. However, considering that you're at the point of taking the PMP exam, you've been managing projects long enough to know that you go through many iterations of planning before you reach a point where the key stakeholders can reach an agreement. For example, you might go around several times in the scope, schedule, cost, and risk processes to find an agreeable approach.

All plans are preliminary until you do a thorough risk analysis and incorporate the risk management activities, risk responses, and contingency reserves into your scope, schedule, and cost documents. Only then can you baseline. You can find more about the risk management processes in Book V, Chapter 1.

Planning goes on throughout the project. You can and will revisit any or all of these processes and activities at various points in the project.

Executing processes

The Executing processes are where the majority of the project budget is expended and the majority of time is spent. This is where the project team creates the deliverables and meets the requirements and objectives of the project. See Table 4-3.

Executing Processes. Those processes performed to complete the work defined in the project management plan to satisfy the project objectives.

Table 4-3 Executing Processes, Activities, and Outputs

Processes	*Activities*	*Outputs*
Direct and Manage Project Work	Coordinate people and other resources to execute project activities. Problem-solve issues and risks, and analyze the best approach to them. Implement changes, corrective and preventive actions, and defect repairs. Implement risk responses as required.	Deliverables Work performance data
Perform Quality Assurance	Audit utilization and effectiveness of the quality plan.	Change requests

Processes	*Activities*	*Outputs*
Acquire Project Team	Negotiate and influence to ensure the appropriate type and number of resources are assigned to the team.	Staff assignments
Develop Project Team	Motivate, team build, and mentor to improve individual and overall team performance.	Team performance assessments EEF updates
Manage Project Team	Manage and lead team throughout the project. Resolve conflicts and solve problems.	EEF updates Organizational process asset updates Change requests Project management plan updates
Manage Communications	Develop communications. Collect and distribute information.	Project communications
Conduct Procurements	Negotiate contract elements, terms, and conditions.	Selected sellers Contracts/agreements
Manage Stakeholder Engagement	Document, negotiate, and resolve issues and conflicts. Facilitate meetings and present information to ensure a common understanding among stakeholders. Communicate to manage stakeholder expectations.	Issue logs Change requests Project management plan updates Project document updates

Monitoring and Controlling processes

Monitoring and Controlling processes measure the performance of the project, take action based on the performance analysis, and maintain the integrity of the baseline by ensuring that only approved changes are integrated into the project management plan.

Monitoring and Controlling Processes. Those processes required to track, review, and regulate the progress and performance of the project, identify any areas in which changes to the plan are required, and initiate the corresponding changes.

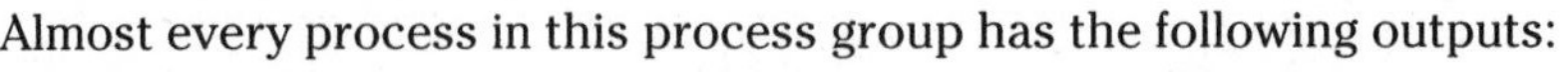

Almost every process in this process group has the following outputs:

- ✦ Change requests
- ✦ Project management plan updates
- ✦ Project document updates
- ✦ Organizational process asset updates

Table 4-4 lists the four consistent outputs only once, but you should know that they are common outputs from the Monitoring and Controlling processes.

Table 4-4 Monitoring and Controlling Processes, Activities, and Outputs

Processes	*Activities*	*Outputs*
Monitor and Control Project Work	Measure and analyze project performance to identify any variances from plan. Problem-solve to determine appropriate corrective and preventive action. Perform a root cause analysis of variances. Manage time and cost reserve allocation.	Organizational process asset updates Project management plan update Project document updates
Perform Integrated Change Control	Evaluate change request impacts. Negotiate competing constraints with stakeholders for requested changes. Maintain baseline integrity by ensuring only accepted changes are integrated into the project. Communicate status of project changes to all impacted stakeholders.	Approved change requests
Validate Scope	Inspect deliverables for acceptance.	Accepted deliverables
Control Scope	Measure performance against the baselines.	Work performance information
Control Schedule	Perform EV* analysis.	
Control Cost	Calculate estimates to complete.	Forecasts

Processes	*Activities*	*Outputs*
Control Quality	Inspect and review all deliverables for compliance with specifications. Apply control charts, histograms, cause-and-effect charts, and other quality control tools to deliverables. Identify areas to improve project and product performance.	Quality control measurements Verified deliverables
Control Communications	Determine the effectiveness and efficiency of the communications management plan and update it as necessary.	Work performance information
Control Risks	Continually monitor status of existing risks. Identify new risks to the project. Negotiate risk response strategies with stakeholders. Problem-solve to identify appropriate risk responses. Evaluate effectiveness of risk management processes and risk responses.	Risk register updates
Control Procurements	Inspect vendor work and work sites.	Procurement documentation
Control Stakeholder Engagement	Determine the effectiveness and efficiency of the stakeholder management plan and update it as necessary.	Work performance information

**EV: earned value*

Monitoring and Controlling processes are applied throughout the project. They are conducted for each phase and for the project as a whole.

Closing processes

Even though there are only two processes in the Closing process group, several activities occur. See Table 4-5.

Closing Processes. Those processes performed to finalize all activities across all project management process groups to formally close the project or phase.

Table 4-5 Closing Processes, Activities, and Outputs

Processes	*Activities*	*Outputs*
Close Project or Phase	Review project management plan to ensure all aspects of the project are complete. Follow all organizational policies regarding phase exit criteria or project closure. Evaluate and document team member performance and update information on new skills as appropriate. Interview stakeholders and document lessons learned. Objectively evaluate project performance and write a project closeout report. Present final project results. Collect, compile, and organize all project records for archives. Interview and survey stakeholders to analyze and rate customer satisfaction. Acknowledge team members with rewards and/or celebrations. Release and return all project resources.	Final product transition Organizational process assets updates
Close Procurements	Review contracts to ensure all contractual obligations have been met. Negotiate and manage conflict to resolve any open issues or claims associated with procurements. Manage and coordinate relationships with internal procurement resources and vendors. Obtain sign-off from legal and the vendors to close contracts. Organize all procurement documentation for archives. Conduct a procurement audit to improve the procurement process in the future.	Closed procurements Organizational process assets updates

Figure A1-2 in the Annex of the *PMBOK Guide* has a high-level view of how the various process groups interact with one another. You should study this and make sure you understand it and can explain the interactions.

The Ten Knowledge Areas

Another way of looking at the project management processes is by grouping them in knowledge areas. There are ten knowledge areas.

Project Management Knowledge Area. An identified area of project management defined by its knowledge requirements and described in terms of its component processes, practices, inputs, outputs, tools, and techniques.

In the following pages, I give you the *PMBOK Guide* definition of the knowledge area, and then list the processes contained in that area. The glossary definitions for each process and significantly more detail about each process are included in upcoming chapters.

Project Integration Management

This knowledge area is the centerpiece of project management: Here's where you combine and coordinate the work of all the processes so they flow smoothly.

Project Integration Management. Project Integration Management includes the processes and activities needed to identify, define, combine, unify, and coordinate the various processes and project management activities within the Project Management Process Groups.

- Develop Project Charter
- Develop Project Management Plan
- Direct and Manage Project Work
- Monitor and Control Project Work
- Perform Integrated Change Control
- Close Project or Phase

Project Scope Management

Scope management is the backbone from which all the rest of the knowledge areas build. Scope processes are concerned with requirements, defining project and product scope, creating the work breakdown structure (WBS), getting acceptance of the scope, and managing changes to the scope.

Project Scope Management. Project Scope Management includes the processes required to ensure that the project includes all the work required — and only the work required — to complete the project successfully.

- Plan Scope Management
- Collect Requirements

- ✦ Define Scope
- ✦ Create WBS
- ✦ Validate Scope
- ✦ Control Scope

Project Time Management

Project Time Management processes create and control the schedule. The processes needed to create a reliable schedule can be done at one time, especially for smaller projects, but they are presented here as discrete processes because the skills and techniques used are distinct for each process.

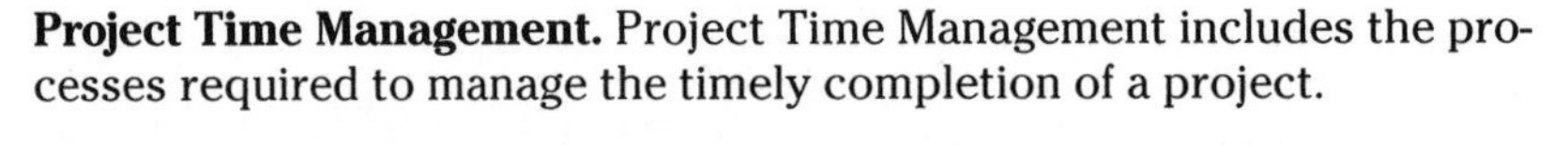

Project Time Management. Project Time Management includes the processes required to manage the timely completion of a project.

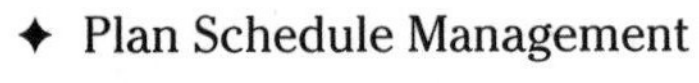

- ✦ Plan Schedule Management
- ✦ Define Activities
- ✦ Sequence Activities
- ✦ Estimate Activity Resources
- ✦ Estimate Activity Durations
- ✦ Develop Schedule
- ✦ Control Schedule

Project Cost Management

The cost estimates and project budget are some of the most closely scrutinized elements in the project management plan. Estimating costs can be one of the more challenging activities you undertake. This knowledge area looks at estimating and budgeting costs. It also looks at controlling them and introduces earned value (EV) management.

Project Cost Management. Project Cost Management includes the processes involved in planning, estimating, budgeting, financing, funding, managing, and controlling costs so that the project can be completed within the approved budget.

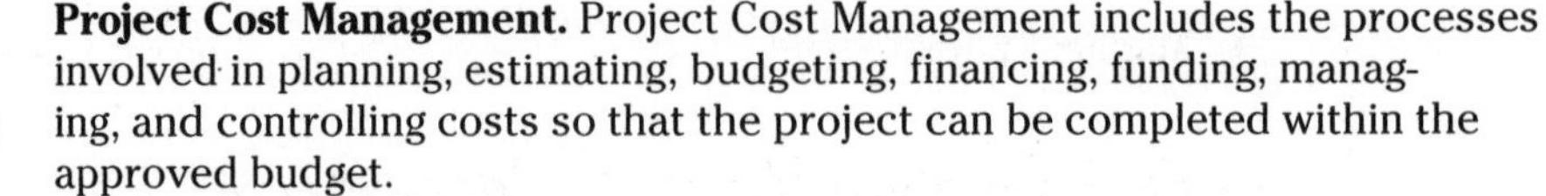

- ✦ Plan Cost Management
- ✦ Estimate Costs

- Determine Budget
- Control Costs

Project Quality Management

If project scope is about what the project and product are supposed to deliver, project quality is about how good it has to be. These processes look at project and product quality from the perspective of planning, maintaining, and controlling.

Project Quality Management. Project Quality Management includes the processes and activities of the performing organization that determine quality policies, objectives, and responsibilities so that the project will satisfy the needs for which it was undertaken.

- Plan Quality Management
- Perform Quality Assurance
- Control Quality

Project Human Resource Management

Much of the *PMBOK Guide* is about the techniques and outputs associated with managing a project. For this knowledge area, I talk about the most important component of performing the work: the people. This knowledge area focuses on the tools you use as well as many of the interpersonal skills needed to effectively manage the project team.

Project Human Resource Management. Project Human Resource Management includes the processes that organize and manage the project team.

- Plan Human Resource Management
- Acquire Project Team
- Develop Project Team
- Manage Project Team

Project Communications Management

Project Communications Management is where you make sure the right people get the needed information in the most effective and efficient way and at the appropriate time.

Project Communications Management. Project Communications Management includes the processes required to ensure timely and appropriate planning, collection, creation, distribution, storage, retrieval, management, control, monitoring, and ultimate disposition of project information.

- ✦ Plan Communications Management
- ✦ Manage Communications
- ✦ Control Communications

Project Risk Management

You can have the best plans in the world, but if you don't incorporate risk management into your project planning, your plans can all go down the tube in an instant. This knowledge area defines the processes needed to keep project risk to an acceptable level.

Project Risk Management. Project Risk Management includes the processes concerned with conducting risk management planning, identification, analysis, responses, and monitoring and control on a project.

- ✦ Plan Risk Management
- ✦ Identify Risks
- ✦ Perform Qualitative Risk Management
- ✦ Perform Quantitative Risk Management
- ✦ Plan Risk Responses
- ✦ Control Risks

Project Procurement Management

In many projects, your organization won't have the skills or capacity to perform all the activities or create all the deliverables necessary. Therefore, procurement management is an important part of managing your projects. The larger the project, the more likely you are to need to procure project scope.

Project Procurement Management. Project Procurement Management includes the processes to purchase or acquire the products, services, or results needed from outside the project team to perform the work.

- ✦ Plan Procurement Management
- ✦ Conduct Procurements

- Control Procurements
- Close Procurements

Project Stakeholder Management

You can meet every milestone, have a fully functioning product, and come in on budget, but if your stakeholders are not happy, you can't really call your project a success. The larger your projects are, the more important it is to manage your stakeholders.

Project Stakeholder Management. Project Stakeholder Management includes the processes required to identify all people or organizations impacted by the project, analyzing stakeholder expectations and impact on the project, and developing appropriate management strategies for effectively engaging stakeholders in project decisions and execution.

- Identify Stakeholders
- Plan Stakeholder Management
- Manage Stakeholder Engagement
- Control Stakeholder Engagement

Interestingly enough, the *PMBOK Guide* presents the project management processes by their knowledge areas. However, the PMP exam evaluates exam performance based on process groups. Because the exam is based on process groups, I present the information by process group and then by knowledge areas in the process groups.

Mapping the 47 Processes

Because each process is part of a process group and part of a knowledge area, it's useful to see how those intersect. Table 4-6 shows how each process maps to a knowledge area and a process group.

One of the best study tips I can give you is to create a table like the one shown in Table 4-6 and fill it in with the processes. Being able to identify the process, the process group, and the knowledge area will help you recollect the information you will need as you take the exam. In fact, I suggest to my students that when they get into the exam, they take a moment and re-create that chart on a piece of paper to reference during the exam.

Table 4-6 Project Management Process Groups and Knowledge Areas

	Initiating	*Planning*	*Executing*	*Monitoring and Controlling*	*Closing*
Integration	Develop Project Charter	Develop Project Management Plan	Direct and Manage Project Work	Monitor and Control Project Work Perform Integrated Change Control	Close Project or Phase
Scope		Plan Scope Management Collect Requirements Define Scope Create WBS		Validate Scope Control Scope	
Time		Plan Schedule Management Define Activities Sequence Activities Estimate Activity Resources Estimate Activity Durations Develop Schedule		Control Schedule	
Cost		Plan Cost Management Estimate Costs Determine Budget		Control Costs	
Quality		Plan Quality Management	Perform Quality Assurance	Control Quality	

	Initiating	*Planning*	*Executing*	*Monitoring and Controlling*	*Closing*
Human Resources		Plan Human Resource Management	Acquire Project Team Develop Project Team Manage Project Team		
Communi-cation		Plan Communications Management	Manage Communications	Control Communications	
Risk		Plan Risk Management Identify Risks Perform Qualitative Analysis Perform Quantitative Analysis Plan Risk Responses		Control Risks	
Procure-ment		Plan Procurement Management	Conduct Procurements	Control Procurements	Close Procurements
Stake-holder	Identify Stakeholder	Plan Stakeholder Management	Manage Stakeholder Engagement	Control Stakeholder Engagement	

Key Terms

There are many terms in this chapter. You don't have to know the definitions verbatim, but you should be able to describe the main points associated with each term.

- Input
- Tool
- Technique
- Output
- Project management process group
- Initiating processes
- Rolling wave planning
- Planning processes
- Executing processes
- Monitoring and Controlling processes
- Closing processes
- Project management knowledge area
- Project Integration Management
- Project Scope Management
- Project Time Management
- Project Cost Management
- Project Quality Management
- Project Human Resource Management
- Project Communications Management
- Project Risk Management
- Project Procurement Management
- Project Stakeholder Management

Chapter Summary

In this chapter, I explain how projects are managed via processes. Processes are categorized by process group and knowledge area. Here are the high points:

✦ Projects are managed via a series of processes. Processes receive inputs and then apply tools and/or techniques to develop outputs.

✦ Processes can be grouped into five process groups: Initiating, Planning, Executing, Monitoring and Controlling, and Closing. The process groups are applied in each phase of the project. They are not a life cycle. Each process group has distinct activities leading to specific outputs.

✦ Processes can also be categorized by ten different knowledge areas. Each knowledge area highlights a specific aspect of the project:

  - Integration
  - Scope
  - Time
  - Cost
  - Quality
  - Human Resources
  - Communications
  - Risk
  - Procurement
  - Stakeholders

Prep Test

1. **Which of the following is not a process group?**

   A ❍ Closing
   B ❍ Integrating
   C ❍ Executing
   D ❍ Planning

2. **The initiating processes have two outputs. Which of the following are the outputs?**

   A ❍ Project charter
   B ❍ Stakeholder register
   C ❍ Stakeholder management plan
   D ❍ Business case

3. **An iterative planning technique in which work to be accomplished in the near-term is planned in detail, and work in the future is planned at a higher level, is called**

   A ❍ Detailed planning
   B ❍ Phase gate planning
   C ❍ Life cycle planning
   D ❍ Rolling wave planning

4. **In which process group should you document the project life cycle?**

   A ❍ Initiating
   B ❍ Planning
   C ❍ Integration
   D ❍ Develop Project Management Plan

5. **During which process group is the majority of the project budget expended?**

   A ❍ Executing
   B ❍ Planning
   C ❍ Integrating
   D ❍ Monitoring and Controlling

6 **You just got the majority of your project team on board and are getting ready to do some team building with them. Which process group are these activities a part of?**

A ❍ Initiating
B ❍ Planning
C ❍ Executing
D ❍ Monitoring and Controlling

7 **Accepted Deliverables is an output from which process in the Monitoring and Controlling Process group?**

A ❍ Control Quality
B ❍ Perform Quality Assurance
C ❍ Validate Scope
D ❍ Control Scope

8 **Conducting Procurements is part of which process group?**

A ❍ Initiating
B ❍ Planning
C ❍ Executing
D ❍ Monitoring and Controlling

9 **Collecting requirements is part of which knowledge area?**

A ❍ Integration
B ❍ Quality
C ❍ Communication
D ❍ Scope

10 **In which process group do you identify stakeholders?**

A ❍ Scope
B ❍ Stakeholders
C ❍ Initiating
D ❍ Planning

Answers

1. **B.** Integrating. Integrating is not a process group. Project Integration Management is a knowledge area. *Look over "Understanding Project Management Process Groups."*

2. **A and B.** Project charter and stakeholder register. The business case is an input to the Develop Project Charter process, which is an Initiating process. The stakeholder management plan is an output of Plan Stakeholder Management. *Go to "Initiating processes."*

3. **D.** Rolling wave planning. Rolling wave planning allows you to plan near-term work in detail and keep the work in the far future at a high level. *See the definition in the "Planning processes" section.*

4. **B.** Planning. You document the project life cycle as part of the developing the project management plan. *Review "Planning processes."*

5. **A.** Executing. The majority of the time and funds are expended in the Executing process group. *Look at "Executing processes."*

6. **C.** Executing. Acquiring the project team and developing the project team are part of the Executing process group. *Review "Executing processes."*

7. **C.** Validate Scope. Accepted deliverables are an output from the Validate Scope process. *Review "Monitoring and Controlling processes."*

8. **C.** Executing. Conducting Procurements is part of the Executing processes. *See "Executing processes."*

9. **D.** Scope. Collecting requirements is part of the Project Scope Management knowledge area. *Review "Project Scope Management."*

10. **C.** Initiating. Stakeholders are identified in the Initiating Process Group. *Check out "Initiating processes."*

Book II

Starting Off Right

Power/Support Grid

POWER	Resistor	Neutral	Advocate
High			Morgan Cuthbert HR department Legal department Facilities department
Medium			Project manager Project team Parents Project vendors
Low	City	Existing vendors Suppliers	Cynergy2 employees Children Caregivers Administrators

SUPPORT

Check out the article on initiating knowledge and skills at `www.dummies.com/extras/pmpcertificationaio`.

Contents at a Glance

Chapter 1: OMG! It's a Project!

Exam Objective

- **Meet with the sponsor, customer, and other subject matter experts and review available information to evaluate the feasibility of new products or services, keeping in mind given assumptions and constraints.**

It seems that everything is a project these days, whether you are reorganizing the company, launching a new product, or even having a holiday party.

Where do all these projects come from? In this chapter, I discuss the internal and external factors — such as business needs and market demands — that initiate the need for a project.

Next, I talk about the methods that organizations use to select the right projects, given that there are usually more projects than there are resources to do them. Some variables that organizations look at include strategic alignment, funding, and project risk.

I wrap up the chapter by describing some of the metrics — such as return on investment (ROI), net present value (NPV), and payback period — that are commonly used to evaluate the financial impact of investing in projects.

Quick Assessment

1. The seven reasons for initiating a project are ______ ______, ______ ______, ______ ______, ______ ______, ______ ______, ______ ______, and ______ ______.

2. A business process improvement project is an example of starting a project because of a/an ______ ______.

3. Retrofitting your electrical system to bring it up to code is an example of initiating a project based on a/an ______ ______.

4. If your organization decides to upgrade to the latest new operating system, this is an example of a project that was initiated based on a/an ______ ______.

5. Organizations can do projects for financial benefits or for nonfinancial benefits. A holiday toy drive is an example of which kind of project?

6. ______ ______ is the amount of time it takes you to recover your initial investment in a project.

7. The three items you need to know before you can compute the present value of investing in a project are ______ ______, ______ ______, and ______ ______ ______ ______.

8. (True/False). Present Value calculates the future value of current cash flows.

Answers

1 Market demand, organizational need, customer request, technological advance, legal requirement, ecological impacts, and social need. The *PMBOK Guide* lists these seven things as reasons for initiating a project. *See "Internal Needs or External Influences."*

2 Organizational need. A business process improvement project is responding to a need the organization has to improve its operations and become more efficient. *Go over "Internal Needs or External Influences."*

3 Legal requirement. Meeting building codes is a legal requirement. *Look over "Internal Needs or External Influences."*

4 Technological advance. A new operating system is an advancement in technology. You might think this is an organizational need, and they really aren't mutually exclusive, but the fact that the project is based on the new technology makes this a better answer. *See "Internal Needs or External Influences."*

5 Nonfinancial benefit. The toy drive does not contribute to the organization's bottom line, but it does provide value to the organization's reputation, employee morale, and the community. *Look over "Criteria for project selection."*

6 Payback period. The amount of time it takes you to recover your initial investment in a project is the payback period. *Take a look at "Payback period."*

7 Future value, interest rate, and number of time periods. These are the three items you need to know before you can compute the present value of investing in a project. *Check out "Present Value."*

8 False. Present Value calculates the current value of future cash flows. *Look at "Present Value."*

Knowledge and Skills for the Initiating Processes

The Initiating process group is the first set of processes you perform when you start a project or start a new phase in a project. To be successful, you will need to bring the following skills to the processes in this group:

- Active listening
- Facilitation
- Oral and written communication techniques, channels, and applications
- Stakeholder impact analysis

As you go through the chapters in this minibook, keep these in mind and see where you would apply them to make your project a success.

Internal Needs or External Influences

Some projects are initiated because of internal needs, and others are initiated because of external influences. The *PMBOK Guide* lists seven reasons why projects can be initiated:

- **Organizational need:** Internal projects that help an organization operate better.
- **Market demand:** Projects that respond to external influences in the market. These projects can be initiated in response to a change in the market, new markets, or developing markets.
- **Customer request:** Projects generally initiated based on external influences, such as responding to a customer request or winning a competitive bid. There are times when an internal customer in an organization requests a project, such as a division asking the IT department for a new functionality in company software.
- **Technological advance:** Projects that can be the result of internal needs or external influences. They are initiated to take advantage of better or faster results because of new technology or technology upgrades.
- **Legal requirement:** External influence projects that are mandatory in nature. They respond to regulatory, legal, or compliance issues.
- **Ecological impacts:** Projects that reactively clean up ecological problems, or proactively implement ecologically sound practices.
- **Social need:** Projects that improve the quality of life. They can be reactive to a particular situation, or proactively planned, such as developing a new medical device.

Organizational need

Organizational need is the umbrella term for internal needs. Examples of organizational needs include

- The company has grown, and the payroll system is no longer sufficient to meet the needs of the company.
- The organization wants to reduce the amount of time it takes to bring new employees on board from eight weeks to four weeks.
- To improve production time and reduce defects, the production line is being reorganized. The reorganization includes staff, production equipment, processes, quality control, and supply chain management.

You can see that these types of projects can be quite complex, depending upon the organization. They can include business process improvement projects, relocations, reorganizations, or any kind of project designed to improve the efficiency and effectiveness of the organization.

The next sections cover the external influences that initiate projects.

Market demand

A *market demand* can include projects that are designed to create new markets, respond to changes in the marketplace, or gain market share. These projects support the reason why the organization is in business. They address the product, service, or result that the organization provides. Here are some examples:

- Because of the high cost of gasoline, a car manufacturer initiates a project to develop a car that runs on biofuel.
- A new type of mobile phone comes out, and your organization decides to create a line of products that can be downloaded onto the phone.
- A competitor has released a new product that's eroding your market share, and your company needs to develop a competing product ASAP!

Customer request

Customer requests can be the result of bidding on a contract. In this case, the statement of work (SOW) in the contract becomes the driving force in initiating the project. You see more information about a statement of work in Book V, Chapter 2.

DEFINITION

Statement of Work. A narrative description of products, services, or results to be delivered by the project.

A customer request can also come from an existing customer asking you to change, increase, or improve something about an existing product or service you're providing. Here are some situations where a customer request would initiate a project:

- ✦ Your engineering firm is designing a new world headquarters for a client. The client is so pleased that they ask your firm to design the new service center they'll be opening after headquarters is complete.
- ✦ The state has issued a Request for Proposal (RFP) to resurface 150 miles of road. Your company responds to the RFP and wins the bid.

Request for Proposal. A type of procurement document used to request proposals from prospective sellers of products or services.

Find more information about RFPs in Book V, Chapter 2.

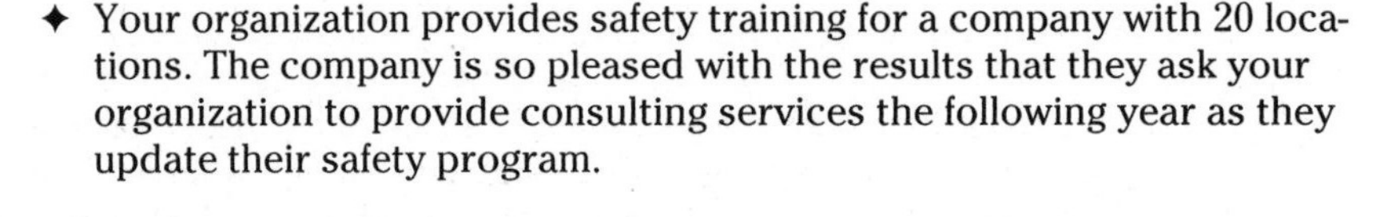

- ✦ Your organization provides safety training for a company with 20 locations. The company is so pleased with the results that they ask your organization to provide consulting services the following year as they update their safety program.

Technological advance

These types of projects can affect internal operations or market place opportunities. Because of the rate of technological advances as well as the need to keep up with the market's adaptation of technological advances, these types of projects have increased dramatically. They can be smaller projects lasting a couple of months or huge programs that take years to complete. Examples of technological advances that can lead to the initiation of a project are

- ✦ A new version of your organization's inventory control system has been released, and you initiate a project to upgrade to the new version.
- ✦ A technological advance in microprocessors has made it possible to store much more data in a smaller space. Your firm initiates a project to redesign an entire line of products to take advantage of the smaller size and lighter weight now possible.
- ✦ Your organization does sensitive work for the government. Because of heightened security concerns and the development of cost-effective retinal-imaging systems, your organization is upgrading the security protocols for entrances, exits, and computer access to sensitive data.

Legal requirement

Legal requirements can include new laws, regulations, code compliance, safety requirements, or any other type of situation where a government agency imposes a new requirement. For example

- The emissions standards for a specific chemical that your organization uses have gotten more restrictive. Your organization initiates a project to upgrade or replace several pieces of equipment and be recertified by the enforcing agency.
- Because there have been several instances of organizations in your field misappropriating funds and not following good accounting practices, the government has passed new reporting, accountability, and transparency regulations for reporting. Your reporting system doesn't support the new requirements, so a project is initiated to implement the new reporting regulations.
- Your company builds high-end custom homes. Last month, a number of homes in the area were damaged by mud and debris run-off from a particularly wet rainy season. The local city council enacted a law that requires all retaining walls to support heavier weight. Your company initiates a project to retrofit all homes in the impacted area.

Ecological impacts

These types of projects are often mandated, and thus in some cases can be considered a combination of ecological impact and legal requirements. For example

- To become more environmentally conscientious, your company institutes a recycling program. The initial start-up of the program is considered a project.
- To reduce wastewater treatment costs, your organization decides to build its own wastewater treatment facility and sell the treated water back to the city for irrigation and other nonpotable uses.
- To be considered an "eco-friendly" firm, your organization undertakes a project to get all its buildings Leadership in Energy and Environmental Design (LEED) certified.

Social need

Many government agencies do projects based on social needs. These projects can also be in response to a disaster. Some organizations undertake social need projects to be good corporate citizens. Examples of social needs that can lead to the initiation of a project are

- ✦ An earthquake causes significant damage to a Third World country. Your organization provides 10 workers for 20 weeks to help rebuild the infrastructure.
- ✦ A county agency initiates a project to collect coats and blankets for the homeless and poor for the coming winter months.
- ✦ A hospital produces a 10K run to raise awareness for heart-healthy eating habits and exercise.

Selecting the Right Projects

As you can see, there are many different avenues that lead to projects. Most times, there are more projects than there are resources to work on them; therefore, organizations need a way to select the projects they will work on now and those they will delay. Organizations have different ways of selecting projects. Some organizations have a very structured process, and others don't seem to have any kind of process whatsoever.

Questions on the exam assume that an organization has a structured project-selection process. This selection process can entail using a project portfolio committee, a Project Management Office (PMO), or some other method to evaluate in which projects to invest.

Project portfolio committee

One method that organizations use to select projects is a project portfolio committee, which

1. Selects new projects
2. Prioritizes projects
3. Measures the progress of existing projects
4. Makes decisions when to cancel projects

The project portfolio committee generally has guidelines for financial and nonfinancial contributions that need to be met in order to launch a project.

The project portfolio committee may be known by other names, both in organization and for the exam. Some examples include *portfolio steering committee, project selection committee,* and *project evaluation committee.*

Project Management Office (PMO)

Another approach to selecting projects is to use the Project Management Office (PMO) — sometimes known as the Project Office (PO) — to select and manage projects. The PMO or PO undergoes a similar process as a project selection committee (see the preceding section) when deciding which projects to launch.

Of course, some projects must be done, such as projects that address changes to legislation or regulations. These projects will still go through the selection process, but they will be automatically approved.

Criteria for project selection

Many variables influence project selection. The importance of these variables is different for each organization; generally, the bullets toward the top of the list that follows tend to be more influential than the bottom of the list.

- **Strategic alignment:** Is the proposed project aligned with the company's strategic plan? Does it help the company meet stated objectives or key performance indicators as documented in an annual operating plan, or similar document? If it doesn't, it should not be selected.
- **Environmental factors:** Do competitive factors necessitate undertaking the project? Will doing the project create a competitive advantage or respond to an opportunity in the market?
- **Expected financial benefit:** Because commercial entities are in business to make a profit, the financial payback is a significant driver in deciding whether to begin a project. In the next section, I present different ways of evaluating the financial benefit of projects.
- **Available funding:** What is the estimated cost of the project? Are sufficient funds available for the year and for the entire project life cycle? Will other projects need to be canceled to afford the proposed project?
- **Availability of resources:** Regardless of how appealing a project may be, if you don't have enough human resources available, the project should not be initiated. If it is, other projects should be canceled or delayed. Starting new projects without concern for the resources availability will eventually lead to one or more projects in the portfolio failing.
- **Riskiness of the project:** High-risk projects are generally less appealing than those with lower risk. If the rest of the project portfolio is conservative, sometimes initiating a higher risk project is acceptable as long as the organization has the resources to recover if the project doesn't pay off. Another consideration is if the reward is substantial, an organization may be willing to take on more risk.

- **Balance in the portfolio of types of projects:** Most organizations that have a formal portfolio of projects balance the type of projects they are undertaking. Some are internal, some are market driven, some are to gain market share, some are product development, and so on. It is wise to balance the types of projects so that no one type of project dominates the portfolio.
- **Project size:** Strive for a balance in the size of projects in the portfolio. Undertaking too many jumbo projects is risky. Most projects should be small to medium in size, with only a few large projects going on at any one time.
- **Expected nonfinancial benefits:** As important as profit is, it isn't the only reason to do a project. Some projects are done for social needs. Public works projects are not done for profit. Therefore, the nonfinancial benefits need to be considered as well.

Selecting the right projects can be complicated. Generally, this process takes place at a level above the project manager's level. However, as a project manager, you should understand the variables associated with selecting projects and balancing a project portfolio. You will find a few questions on the PMP exam that expect you to understand these concepts.

Alphabet Soup: ROI, NPV, FV and Other Project-Selection Metrics

The first part of this chapter discusses where projects come from and how they are selected. In this section, I cover some of the project selection metrics — financial and otherwise — that project portfolio committees use to determine which projects to initiate. These metrics are used to evaluate the feasibility of new products or services. I will also describe some finance and accounting terms you may see on the exam. These don't require any calculations, but you should be familiar with the concepts.

Financial metrics

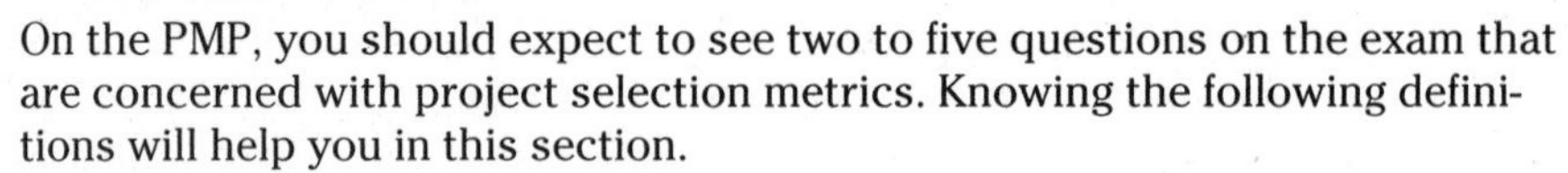

On the PMP, you should expect to see two to five questions on the exam that are concerned with project selection metrics. Knowing the following definitions will help you in this section.

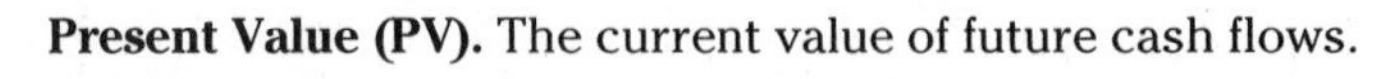

Present Value (PV). The current value of future cash flows.

Net Present Value (NPV). The present value minus the cost over the time periods the costs are invested.

Future Value (FV). The value in the future of funds invested now.

Payback period. How soon you will recapture your investment and begin making a profit

Benefit-cost ratio. Compares the benefit or revenue of a project with the cost or investment of a project.

Present Value

$$PV = FV / (1 + r)^n$$

where

PV = Present Value

FV = Future Value

r = Interest rate

n = Number of time periods

Here is an example of a question you might see on the exam:

Your company provides project management consulting and outsourcing. The selection committee is deciding whether to invest in a Project to update and upgrade your PMO information systems infrastructure with all new software, cloud computing, collaboration sites, and real-time reporting software. The new capabilities will not be available until Year 2. The enhanced infrastructure is projected to increase business by $2,500,000 in Year 2; $5,250,000 in Year 3; and $6,000,000 in Years 4 and 5. After that, you expect to need a new upgrade to keep pace with changes in technology.

The other viable project the selection committee is looking at is developing a new line of business by creating a virtual project management training curriculum. The projected revenue is $1,500,000 in Year 1, and $3.500.000 in Years 2–5.

If the money were invested, the assumed interest rate is 5%.

Given the PV equation, you would end up with the following calculations:

PMO Upgrade	***Future Value***	***Present Value***	***Virtual Training***	***Future Value***	***Present Value***
Year 1	0	0	Year 1	1,500,000	1,428,571
Year 2	2,500,000	2,267,573	Year 2	3,500,000	3,174,603
Year 3	5,250,000	4,535,147	Year 3	3,500,000	3,023,432
Year 4	6,000,000	4,936,214	Year 4	3,500,000	2,879,459
Year 5	6,000,000	4,701,157	Year 5	3,500,000	2,742,342
Total		**16,440,093**			**13,248,406**

Based on solely this information, the investment in the PMO infrastructure has a higher PV and is the better choice.

For PV calculations, the higher PV is the better investment!

Present value is just one way of evaluating the value of a project. Notice that you don't see the investment in this equation. You will see the amount invested if you use a Net Present Value calculation. In addition, when selecting a project, you should look at ancillary benefits, such as the benefits the project infrastructure has to other business units or the opportunity to leverage the virtual training into additional lines of business.

Be careful of the abbreviation PV. It can mean Present Value, as presented here, or Planned Value. Planned Value is an Earned Value Management term that describes the budgeted value for the planned work. You can read a lot more about this in Book VIII, Chapter 1.

Net Present Value

Net Present Value (NPV) takes the PV amount and subtracts the cost over the time periods they are invested. Like the PV, the higher the NPV, the better the project opportunity.

For the exam, you won't have to calculate the NPV, but you should be able to select the best project opportunity given the NPV of multiple projects.

Future Value

Future Value (FV) looks at the value in the future of funds invested now. To calculate the FV of current funds you need to know the interest rate and the number of time periods. The equation is

$$FV = PV \times (1 + r)^n$$

Assume that you can invest $500,000 to upgrade your production facility now and expect an increase in efficiency of 7% for each year for five years.

Another option is to invest in $500,000 in a new product, which should give you a 20% return in Year 1, but then only a 5% return in Years 2 and 3, and then need to be retired.

By calculating the options, you can determine that the FV of the $500,000 of investing in the production facility is $701,276, and the FV of investing in the new product is $661,500. Therefore, the investment in the production facility is a better investment.

Production facility: $FV = \$500{,}000(1.07)^5$

New product: $FV = (\$500{,}000 \times 1.2) \times 1.05^2$

For FV calculations, the higher future value is the better investment!

Payback period

The payback period calculates how soon you will recapture your investment and begin making a profit. This calculation doesn't take into consideration the time value of money the way PV, NPV, and FV do.

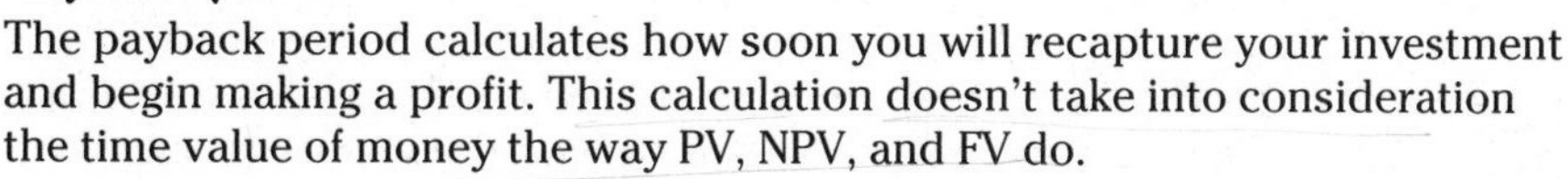

You might see a question like this on the exam:

> *Assume that you're investing $2,300,000 in a project to automate a manual process. Your calculations show that during the first year, you will gain $550,000 in efficiency. Every year after that, you expect to save $710,000 annually. What is the payback period?*

	Year 1	*Year 2*	*Year 3*	*Year 4*
Annual savings	$550,000	$710,000	$710,000	$710,000
Cumulative savings	$550,000	$1,260,000	$1,970,000	$2,680,000

You can see that the payback period occurs in Year 4.

Benefit-cost ratio

Benefit-cost ratio compares the benefit or revenue of a project with the cost or investment of a project. The benefit number is always the first number. Therefore, if you have a project that involves a $2,000,000 investment and will return $2,500,000, you calculate the benefit-cost ratio as

2,500,000 / 2,000,000 = 1.25

You can see that the higher the ratio, the better the project. Any project with a benefit-cost ratio higher than 1.0 means the project will be profitable.

You might see questions on the exam that expect you to calculate a benefit-cost ratio, or you might need to select between various projects with different ratios, or even define what a particular ratio means.

Financial terms

The metrics in the preceding section are the most prevalent metrics used in analyzing the financial contribution a project will make to the organization. This section describes some financial and accounting terms you should also be familiar with although you won't have to use them for calculations.

Sunk cost

Sunk cost is an accounting principle that states that money you have already spent should not be factored into future expenditures. In other words, just because you already spent $5 million on a project, that doesn't justify spending another $2 million. The $5 million is a sunk cost.

Opportunity cost

Opportunity cost is incurred by selecting one project over another. For example, say you have a budget for projects, and you have Project A with an NPV of $2 million and Project B with an NPV of $1.5 million: You should select Project A. However, the opportunity cost of selecting Project A is the $1.5 million NPV of Project B.

Table 1-1 offers a synopsis of the financial metrics you need to know for the exam.

Table 1-1 Financial Metrics Summary

Metric	*Summary*	*Higher or Lower*
Present Value (PV)	Current value of future cash flows	Higher is better.
Net Present Value (NPV)	PV minus costs	Higher is better.
Future Value (FV)	The future value of funds currently invested	Higher is better.
Payback period	How long to recapture investment and make a profit	Lower is better.
Benefit-cost ratio	Revenue divided by cost	Higher is better.

Nonfinancial metrics

In addition to the financial metrics, organizations often include nonfinancial contributions or impacts from investing in projects. Some of the more common ones are

- Customer satisfaction and retention
- Employee satisfaction
- Employee retention
- Process improvement
- Organizational learning

✦ Public opinion

✦ Synergistic effect of doing specific related projects

The financial metrics and nonfinancial considerations are only part of what goes into evaluating the feasibility of a new project. In Chapter 2 of this minibook, I look at how assumptions, constraints, and other variables are reviewed before a project is formally authorized.

Key Terms

The terms from this chapter are all finance related. If you can describe what each of these means, you will be in good shape!

✦ Project portfolio committee

✦ Present value (PV)

✦ Net present value (NPV)

✦ Future value (FV)

✦ Payback period

✦ Benefit-cost ratio

✦ Sunk cost

✦ Opportunity cost

Chapter Summary

The information in this chapter usually occurs before a project is chartered; therefore, you, as a project manager, may not be involved in this pre-project work. However, you need to understand what goes into selecting projects. The PMP reflects the importance of these topics by including questions that cover this information on the exam.

✦ Projects can be initiated based on internal or external factors.

✦ The Project Management Institute (PMI) assumes there is some type of project portfolio committee that selects projects.

✦ Projects are selected based on a set of criteria.

✦ Financial and nonfinancial metrics are used when selecting projects.

Prep Test

1 **Your organization has eight divisions, and they all have their own project management procedures and templates. You have been designated as the project manager and assigned to lead a team in reviewing all existing project management policies and procedures across the organization. Your team will identify gaps, develop policies to fill the gaps, eliminate redundancies, and make recommendations on how to improve the adoption of the new policies and procedures across all divisions. This is an example of initiating a project based on**

A ❍ A technological advance
B ❍ A regulatory requirement
C ❍ Market demand
D ❍ Organizational need

2 **Your company builds medical devices. You want to modify an existing device so it can send back more data to the physician's office. Your project is to conduct a clinical study for the FDA to prove that the modified device is effective and safe. This is an example of**

A ❍ Technological advance
B ❍ Legal requirement
C ❍ Ecological impact
D ❍ Social need

3 **You have just been notified that your company won a bid to conduct an independent verification and validation of requirements for a new campus in the state university system. You will be assessing the construction, IT, quality of life, and administrative processes prior to the campus opening. This is an example of**

A ❍ Customer request
B ❍ Legal requirement
C ❍ Ecological impact
D ❍ A social need

4 **A new project manager approaches you, annoyed that her software upgrade project has been put on hold and all her project resources have been pulled to work on a big new initiative. You explain to her that this decision is actually good because**

A ❍ The new project has a better strategic alignment with the organization.
B ❍ It is better to cancel or put other projects on hold rather than run too many projects without enough resources.
C ❍ The nonfinancial benefits outweigh the financial benefits.
D ❍ Doing too many large projects at one time is risky.

5 **Your organization provides a multitude of electronic components to the aircraft industry. You have heard there are likely to be layoffs in the commercial aircraft companies. You put together a presentation that shows the financial benefits of providing temporary staff to these companies after they downsize. The portfolio steering committee turns down the project because**

A ❍ The information is unreliable.

B ❍ There are too many large projects going on right now to start up a new company.

C ❍ It is not strategically aligned with the organization's business.

D ❍ The temporary staffing industry has a historically low rate of return.

6 **You work for a state agency that sets up literacy programs for economically challenged counties and cities. Which of the following is not a criterion that your agency would use when selecting projects?**

A ❍ Strategic alignment

B ❍ Nonfinancial benefits

C ❍ Riskiness of the project

D ❍ Financial benefits

7 **Which financial measurement identifies how soon you will recapture your investment and start making a profit?**

A ❍ Benefit-cost ratio

B ❍ Payback period

C ❍ Net present value

D ❍ Sunk costs

8 **If the future value, four years from now, of a project investment is $8,500,000, and the interest rate is 6%, what is the present value, rounded to the nearest 100?**

A ❍ $6,732,800

B ❍ $6,351,700

C ❍ $7,136,700

D ❍ $10,731,100

9 **What is the future value of $4,200,000 in three years at an interest rate of 5.5%, rounded to the nearest 100?**

A ❍ $5,203,100

B ❍ $4,931,800

C ❍ $3,576,800

D ❍ $3,773,500

10 **Your organization is weighing which project to invest in. Project Alpha has a benefit-cost ratio of 1:1.1, Project Beta has a benefit-cost ratio of 1:1.33, and Project Charlie has a benefit-cost ratio of 1:1.17. Using a financial analysis, which project is the best investment?**

A ❍ Not enough information to determine the answer

B ❍ Project Alpha

C ❍ Project Beta

D ❍ Project Charlie

Answers

1 **D.** Organizational need. Improving project management processes and capabilities will help the organization. *Look at "Organizational need."*

2 **B.** Legal requirement. Performing a study for the FDA is an example of a legal requirement. *Check out "Legal requirements."*

3 **A.** Customer request. Winning a bid is an example of responding to a customer request. *See "Customer request."*

4 **B.** There are times when it is better to cancel a project or put it on hold to avoid over-allocating resources. *Review "Criteria for project selection."*

5 **C.** It is not strategically aligned with the organization's business. The organization supplies parts. Establishing a temporary staffing organization isn't in alignment with the company's core competency even though it serves the same industry. *Review "Criteria for project selection."*

6 **D.** Financial benefits. A state agency provides services. It's not looking to make a profit; rather, its mission is to provide value to citizens. *See "Criteria for project selection."*

7 **B.** Payback period. The payback period calculates the initial investment and the estimated income over time to determine when you should recapture your investment. *Look over "Payback period."*

8 **A.** \$6,732,800. \$8,500,000 / 1.06^4. *Take a look at "Present Value."*

9 **B.** \$4,931,800. \$4,200,000 × 1.055^3. *Look over "Future Value."*

10 **C.** Project Beta. Project Beta has the best benefit-to-cost ratio. *Review the information from "Benefit-cost ratio."*

Chapter 2: Chartering Your Project

Exam Objectives

- **Given business and compliance requirements, define the high-level scope needed to meet customer expectations.**
- **Use historical data, information on the environment, and expert judgment to identify and document high-level risks, assumptions, and constraints. Use the information to propose an approach to carry out the project.**
- **Analyze stakeholder requirements to document the scope, milestones, and deliverables, and complete a project charter.**
- **Gain commitment for the project and formalize project management authority by obtaining approval for the project charter.**

Before a project is officially authorized, there is work to be done. The first thing you have to do on a project is come to an agreement on the scope of the project with the sponsor and the customer. As part of defining the scope, you also identify boundaries and limitations for the project. This means documenting some of the high-level risks associated with the project as well as any constraints, such as funding limitations, hard due dates, and so forth.

For those areas you can't define, you will have to document some assumptions. For instance, you may have to assume you will have the resources you need inhouse or that funding will be available at specific intervals. Until you have done more work on the scope, you may not know these things for certain, but you document them as assumptions for later validation. Working through the scope, high-level risks, constraints, and assumptions helps you to appropriately set customer expectations and gain acceptance to initiate the project.

A *project charter* is the very first piece of official documentation for a project. Of course, you will probably see previous documents that go into evaluating whether to initiate a project. You will find information about those in Chapter 1 of this minibook. After the decision to initiate a project is approved, the project charter documents the high-level information and becomes the first written communication about the project.

Quick Assessment

1 The four main purposes for a charter are to _____ _____ _____, identify the project manager, authorize the project manager to apply organizational resources, and link the project to the organization's strategic plan.

2 The _____ _____ demonstrates the project's value to the organization.

3 Which input to the charter provides a narrative description of the project?

4 (True/False). Marketplace conditions influence project initiation.

5 A template provided by your PMO can assist you in completing the project charter. This template is an example of a/an _____ _____ _____.

6 The charter should identify the project manager's authority level and limitations with regards to _____, _____ _____, _____ _____, and _____ _____.

7 (True/False). You should document the initial communication strategy in the project charter.

Answers

1 Authorize the project. See the section, *"What a Project Charter Is and Why You Need One."*

2 Business case. The business case provides financial and nonfinancial metrics that show how the proposed project benefits the organization. *Peruse the section "Business case."*

3 Statement of work. The statement of work (SOW) describes the business needs the project will fulfill and provides a narrative description of the product. *Look over "Project statement of work."*

4 True. The marketplace conditions, such as resource availability, lending rates, and competition definitely influence whether a project is initiated and the approach to the project. *Review "Enterprise environmental factors."*

5 Organizational process asset. A charter template is something the organization can provide that can assist you while you're completing the charter, by saving you time and organizing the information you need to initiate a project. *Check out "Organizational process assets."*

6 Staffing, technical decisions, conflict resolution, and budget management. *For more detail, peruse "Develop Project Charter: Outputs."*

7 False. The communication strategy will be in the project management plan, not in the project charter. *Look over "Develop Project Charter: Outputs."*

What a Project Charter Is and Why You Need One

The first process you undertake when you start a project is Develop Project Charter. As you can read in Book I, Chapter 4, each process belongs to a process group and to a knowledge area. This process is in the Initiating process group and in the Project Integration Management knowledge area. If you want a refresher on the knowledge areas or process groups, you can find it in Book I, Chapter 4.

Developing a project charter entails developing a document that formally authorizes a project or a phase and documenting initial requirements that satisfy the stakeholder's needs and expectations. Simply put, a *project charter* is the official document that authorizes a project. A charter is the green light that gives the project manager the authority to expend organizational resources to achieve project objectives.

Project Charter. A document issued by the project initiator or sponsor that formally authorizes the existence of a project and provides the project manager with the authority to apply organizational resources to project activities.

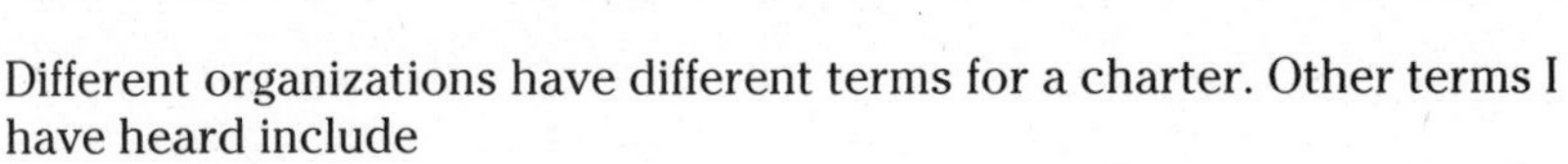

Different organizations have different terms for a charter. Other terms I have heard include

- Project initiation document
- Project description
- Project authorizing document

Regardless of the name that your organization gives the initial project documentation, the project charter document has the following characteristics:

- **Identifies the project sponsor and the project manager**

  Someone other than the project manager initiates projects. This person could be the project sponsor, a customer, the Project Management Office (PMO), a portfolio steering committee, or senior management. The initiator should have authority consistent with the size, complexity, and critical nature of the project.

- **Demonstrates commitment for the project and formalizes project manager authority**

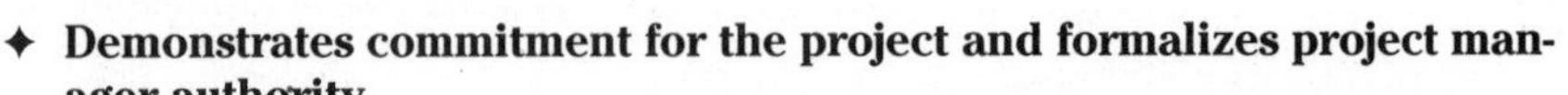

- **Links the project to the strategic plan of the organization and shows how the project aligns with the organization's operations**

  Obviously, organizations should undertake only those projects that tie explicitly to a strategic plan.

Some organizations refer to their chartering documents as a Statement of Work (SOW). A Statement of Work is defined as "a narrative description of products, services, or results to be delivered by the project." PMI does not consider a SOW and a charter to be the same thing!

Develop Project Charter: Inputs

Preparing a useful project charter requires gathering a good bit of information about the project's purpose and its expected benefits to the organization. The *PMBOK Guide* identifies these five inputs for the Develop Project Charter process:

- **Project statement of work (SOW):** This narrative description of a project does the following:
  - Explains the business need that the project will fulfill
  - Clarifies the product of the project
  - Tells how the project aligns with the organization's strategic plan
- **Business case:** This information demonstrates the project's value to the organization. Such value can be judged by these metrics:
  - *Financial:* Increased revenue, expense reduction
  - *Nonfinancial:* Customer loyalty, innovation
- **Agreement:** For a project based on a contractual obligation, the agreement (contract) is an input to the project charter. Its contents include
  - The contract statement of work
  - Contractual requirements, terms, and conditions
- **Enterprise environmental factors (EEFs):** These internal factors (such as organizational structure and human resource capabilities) and external factors (such as competition and regulations) affect whether you do a project and how you approach it. I talk about EEFs in Book I, Chapter 2.
- **Organizational process assets (OPAs):** These comprise the policies, procedures, templates, and prior-project documentation that organizations use to manage projects in a consistent way. I talk about OPAs in Book I, Chapter 3.

Project statement of work

Not all organizations create a formal statement of work (SOW), so don't be surprised if you haven't seen one. For organizations that do have a formal project SOW, it could be created by the person requesting the project, or by a portfolio steering committee, the project sponsor, or the PMO.

When the *PMBOK Guide* refers to a SOW, it isn't necessarily referring to one from a contract. Instead, this use of SOW refers to a narrative description of the project. If the SOW is from a contract, the term *contract* will be used in conjunction with SOW.

The SOW describes the business need and how the project will meet that need. It can also describe how the project is in alignment with the organization's strategic plan.

The following is a fictional SOW for creating an on-site childcare facility at Cynergy, Inc. corporate headquarters:

> *Cynergy, Inc. Childcare Facility Statement of Work*
>
> *Our company values state that we are an organization that values a work-life balance. We believe that our employees are our greatest asset, and we strive to make the work environment a supportive place for our employees.*
>
> *We have a young work force. Forty percent of our employees are under 35, and as such, there are many young families. Commercial childcare facilities have varying quality and can have restrictive hours and policies. To alleviate the stress and issues associated with childcare needs, we have decided to open an on-site childcare facility at our corporate headquarters.*
>
> *The project will identify the childcare wants and needs for all local employees and develop a proposal for meeting those wants and needs. Once an approach is agreed upon, the project manager will create a full set of requirements, project documents, and a project management plan to fulfill the project objectives. Project work includes hiring and managing a contractor to develop plans and construct the facility. Staffing, furnishing, installing playground equipment, and landscaping are included in the project scope.*
>
> *The finished childcare facility will have a capacity for up to 75 children ages 3 months to 5 years. It will include separate rooms for age groups and special activities, such as art, music, nap time, etc. There will be a food area that includes a place to store cold snacks and room-temperature snacks, but no food preparation. The outside play area will have separate sections that are age appropriate.*

You can see where the following elements are documented:

- Narrative description
- Business need

✦ Product description

✦ Alignment with strategic plan

Business case

The business case documents the business reason for undertaking the project as well as the cost-benefit analysis. Much of the financial information used in the cost-benefit analysis comes from the project selection process described in Chapter 1 of this minibook. Many organizations use nonfinancial metrics to justify a project as well, such as customer loyalty, business process improvement, reduced employee turnover, innovation, and so on.

Review the business case periodically throughout the project to ensure that the assumptions on which the business case was built are still valid. If they're not, the portfolio steering committee (or another body that selects projects) may want to revisit the project and determine whether it should continue.

Agreements

Agreements can take the form of contracts, memorandums of understanding (MOU), letter of intent, or other written agreements. When doing work for an external customer a contract is used. If this is the case, you use the SOW contained in the contract to document information in the charter. You would also look at any terms and conditions that provide direction on how the project should be performed, key milestone dates, funding constraints, and any other relevant information in the contract.

Enterprise environmental factors

Think about some of the enterprise environmental factors (EEFs) that might constrain or guide how a project is chartered. What are some of the internal factors? What are some of the external factors?

Internal factors that you definitely want to keep in mind include

✦ Organizational structure of any organizations that are involved in the project

✦ Information systems in an organization and their ability to share information

✦ Human resources: their skills and availability

✦ Portfolio management policies and processes

✦ Project Management Office (PMO) policies and processes

✦ Estimating, risk, and defect-tracking databases

External factors that can influence your project include

- Industry standards that apply to products or services
- Regulatory laws or codes you need to comply with
- Governmental policies, restrictions, and political climates
- Marketplace conditions that influence pricing and availability of materials and services
- Competitor information, such as the number of competitors, opportunities, and threats based on your competition
- Financing availability and rates
- Pending legislation that could impact your products, services, and processes
- Availability of resources, both physical and labor
- Changes in the market, either from competition or economic factors
- Economic influences, such as unemployment and availability of credit

All these EEFs can have an effect on whether you do a project, and how you approach it. Here are a few quick examples:

- You work in a weak matrix organization. Therefore, your ability to negotiate for team members will frequently be overridden by functional managers. Additionally, most of your team members will have their regular work, and work for your project and other projects. This is an example of an internal environmental factor that relates to the organization. For more information on organizational structure, see Book I, Chapter 3.
- Your organization does work for a government agency. The government is getting ready to mandate a particular type of reporting for all projects. This external environmental factor relates to governmental and regulatory topics.
- The interest rate for borrowing money has been rising lately. Assumptions about the cost of money now may be different than it will be in six months when you're estimating needing to draw from a line of credit. This is an example of an external environmental factor that relates to financing and the economy.

Organizational process assets

Organizational process assets (OPAs) are supposed to help you do your project. I know it often seems that they don't really help, but that is PMI's approach to this category of inputs. Some of my favorites for this particular process include

- Organizational policies, procedures, and intranet sites
- Templates for forms, reports, and documentation

✦ Documentation from prior projects

✦ Lessons learned from prior projects

I see many organizations that have plenty of policies and procedures. Some have templates. But, surprisingly, information from prior projects is not centralized, easily accessible, or easily searchable. I see the same thing on lessons learned. Every organization says, "We must do 'lessons learned'!", so people do it. However, I rarely see project manager consulting lessons learned from prior projects before embarking on new projects. Although the *PMBOK Guide* has this lessons learned concept throughout many of the processes, it isn't always implemented well in the real world. You read more about lessons learned in Book IX, Chapter 1.

Develop Project Charter: Tools and Techniques

Putting together the information from the SOW, the business case, and the contract takes a fair amount of organization, analysis, and synthesis, especially for large and complex projects. This analysis needs to be done with a keen eye for the EEFs and OPAs that influence the way you do the project. It takes *expert judgment* to accomplish all this thinking!

You will notice that *expert judgment* is the primary technique for all the Project Integration Management processes. Here's what expert judgment really means, according to the *PMBOK Guide* Glossary:

Expert Judgment. Judgment provided based upon expertise in an application area, knowledge area, discipline, industry as appropriate for the activity being performed. Such expertise may be provided by any group or person with specialized education, knowledge, skill, experience, or training.

Think about the types of expertise you might need for developing a project charter. Who could help you? What kind of knowledge would they need? You should consider resources both internal to the organization and external to the organization.

Some internal resources might include

✦ Sponsor

✦ Potential team members

✦ Prior team members and project managers (PMs)

✦ Other key stakeholders and subject matter experts

✦ The PMO

External resources you might consider include

- ✦ Consultants
- ✦ Industry and professional associations

You can also do research either online or using various publications.

Developing a charter is not done in a vacuum, so you will likely need *facilitation techniques,* such as meeting management, conflict resolution, brain storming, and problem solving to come to agreement on the high-level scope of the project.

Develop Project Charter: Outputs

After all this information gathering and analysis, you can start to document information in an organized fashion, and *voilà!* The charter is created. In some organizations, the charter is created by the sponsor, customer, PMO, or some other entity and then handed to the PM. In other organizations, the PM either assists in the creation or actually creates the charter and then gets approval from the sponsor, PMO, or whoever is appropriate. Regardless, it is a good practice to make sure that the project manager is involved in some manner when developing the charter.

The charter should provide a summary of the project with enough information that the initial project team can read it, absorb it, and then use progressive elaboration to plan the project in detail. Table 2-1 shows the items that the *PMBOK Guide* says are contained in the charter.

The needs of the organization and the project should determine the actual contents.

Table 2-1 Sample Charter Contents

Charter Content Item	*What It Does*
Purpose and justification	The reason why the project is being undertaken. May refer to the business case, the strategic plan, external factors, a contract, or any other document or reason for performing the project.
Objectives	The strategic position the project is being undertaken to deliver, or the result to be achieved. There are usually multiple objectives, such as objectives for scope, schedule, cost, quality, customer satisfaction, and so on.

Charter Content Item	What It Does
Success criteria	Measurable criteria that correspond to each objective to indicate that the objective has been successfully met.
High-level requirements	The high-level business and compliance requirements must meet customer expectations. (These are not detailed requirements but merely initial, high-level requirements.)
Assumptions and constraints	The initial assumptions about scope, resources, funding, approach, and other project variables. Constraints are the initial limitations, such as a fixed due date or budget.
High-level project description	A summary-level description of the project. May include information on high-level project and product deliverables as well as the approach to the project.
High-level risks	The initial risks. These will later be progressively elaborated and entered into a risk register.
Summary milestones	Significant events in the project. May include the completion of deliverables, phases or product acceptance.
Summary budget	The initial range of estimated expenditures for the project.
Stakeholder list	The initial list of stakeholders who can influence or will be influenced by the project, product, service or result.
Approval requirements	Who can approve and sign off on each deliverable and the criteria for acceptance.
PM Authority: Staffing	The authority to hire, fire, discipline, accept, or not accept project staff.
Technical decisions	The authority to make technical decisions about deliverables or the technical approach.
Conflict resolution	The authority to resolve conflict within the team, the organization, and external stakeholders.
Budget management	The authority to commit, manage, and control project funds. Includes variance thresholds.
Sponsor, PM signatures, and other relevant signatures	Demonstrates commitment and approval for the project.

In some organizations, you see high-level assumptions and constraints documented in the charter. In others, you might see an Assumption and Constraint log that would start with the high-level assumptions during project initiation. While the project progresses, you would see more detailed assumptions. Examples of high-level assumptions include

- *We will use internal resources to staff the project.*
- *The market will accept the new product.*
- *Funding will be available.*

Examples of high-level constraints can include regulations, fixed delivery dates, and a budget cap.

I'll show you an example of a project charter for the childcare center. Assume that since receiving the statement of work, you have identified the following additional information:

- The facility must be open from 6:30 a.m. to 6:00 p.m.
- It needs to be completed by December 31 of the current year.
- The budget is $2.5 million.
- The facility will use 20,000 square feet of space not currently occupied at Cynergy, Inc.
- There is a 2,500–square feet outdoor area for play.
- Cynergy, Inc. is located in a temperate climate with daytime lows of 40° in the winter and daytime highs of 90° in the summer.
- There are local strict building and licensing codes for childcare facilities.
- You have a team of six people, not including vendors. These people have already been identified and assigned to your team.
- Team members are available approximately 50 percent of their time, and they are all excited about working on the project.
- Cynergy, Inc. is a matrix organization.

For areas you don't have information about, you would make an assumption and document it. Figure 2-1 shows a sample project charter.

Go to the beginning of this chapter and review the exam objectives. See whether you can explain the content in this chapter and how it meets the exam objectives.

PROJECT CHARTER

Project Title: Childcare Center

Project Sponsor: Morgan Cuthbert **Date Prepared:** May 1

Project Manager: You! **Project Customer:** Cynergy2, Inc. Employees

Project Purpose or Business Justification

Cynergy2, Inc. employees are primarily made up of families with young children. 40 percent of the employees are under 35 and many have toddlers and pre-schoolers. Consistent with our core values of work-life balance, valuing our employees, and having a supportive work environment, Cynergy2, Inc. has decided to open an onsite childcare facility at our corporate headquarters. We believe this will increase employee retention, improve employee satisfaction, reduce work loss time due to childcare issues and promote a healthy and happy work environment.

Project Description

The project will identify the childcare wants and needs for all local employees and develop a proposal for meeting those wants and needs. All project management plans necessary to deliver the project successfully are included in the project scope.
An outside contractor will develop plans and construct the facility.
The facility will be fully staffed, furnished, landscaped and have all playground equipment installed.

Project Objectives	Success Criteria	Person Approving
Scope:		
20,000 square foot facility built out for 75 children age 3 months to 5 years. 2500 square foot outdoor area. Fully furnished and equipped. All staff hired. All landscaping.	The space is ready to accept 75 children beginning January 1. All playground equipment and landscaping is installed. Staff report to work on January 1.	Morgan Cuthbert
Time:		
Complete by 12/31.	All permits are approved and children can enroll by 12/31.	Morgan Cuthbert
Cost:		
Within the approved budget of $2,500,000.	All project work is completed and vendors paid within the allocated budget amount.	Morgan Cuthbert
Quality:		
All permits and licenses obtained.	Permits and licenses on file by 12/31.	City Hall

Project Requirements

Can house up to 75 children.
Care is provided for children 3 months to 5 years old.
Separate space and supplies for art and music.
Food storage area, including refrigerators.
Age appropriate outside play areas.

Page 1 of 3

Figure 2-1: A sample solution.

PROJECT CHARTER

Summary Milestones	Estimated Due Date
Project management plans complete	6/1
Contractor hired	7/1
Blue prints approved	8/1
Interior framed	10/1
Interior finished	12/1
All furniture and fixtures installed	12/15
Outside play area complete	12/1
All play ground equipment installed	12/20
Landscaping complete	12/31
Staffing complete	12/20
Supplies purchased and delivered	12/29

Estimated Budget:

$2,500,000

Risks:

Because the team is only part time, and it is a matrix environment we have limited authority over resources.
Because we have a fixed deadline for enrollment we may have to work overtime to meet it, impacting the budget.
Because the city license and permitting requirements are stringent we may require rework or multiple visits by the permitting agency causing a schedule delay.

Project Manager Authority Level

Staffing Decisions:

The staff has been pre-assigned. Any staffing issues should be escalated to Morgan Cuthbert.

Budget Management and Variance:

The variance threshold is +10% for the approved scope. Any indication that the project will have a greater variance must be escalated to Morgan Cuthbert with a root cause analysis and proposed corrective action.

Technical Decisions:

The general contractor has authority for all construction decisions.
The project manager has the authority to make all project management related decisions.
Playground, Inc. has authority to make all playground and equipment decisions.

Page 2 of 3

PROJECT CHARTER

Conflict Resolution:

The PM will work with the team to resolve any team conflicts.
The PM will work with vendors to resolve any conflicts, however, if there is a contractual implication the legal department must be involved.
Any conflict that cannot be resolved by the PM will be escalated to Morgan Cuthbert.

Escalation Path for Authority Limitations:

Any decisions, issues or situations beyond the PM's authority will be escalated to Morgan Cuthbert.

Approvals:

	Morgan Cuthbert
Project Manager Signature	Sponsor or Originator Signature
	Morgan Cuthbert
Project Manager Name	Sponsor or Originator Name
Date	Date

Page 3 of 3

Key Terms

Congratulations! You just finished the first process! Here are a few key terms associated with initiating a project and developing the project charter.

- Project charter
- Project statement of work (SOW)
- Business case
- Expert judgment
- Objectives
- Success criteria

Chapter Summary

In this chapter, I discuss the components that go into a project charter. Projects don't fall from the sky. They need to align with corporate objectives and have a business case that justifies the investment. Keep the following in mind as you prepare for the exam:

- A *project charter* is the very first piece of documentation for a project. A project charter officially authorizes a project. It links the project to the strategic plan of the organization and shows how the project aligns with the organization's operations.
- The *charter* should provide a summary of the project with enough information that the initial project team can read it, absorb it, and then use progressive elaboration to plan the project in detail.
- The *statement of work* (SOW) provides a narrative description of the project. If you are performing the work under contract, you will use the SOW in the contract.
- The *business case* identifies financial and nonfinancial metrics to demonstrate value to the organization.
- You must keep in mind the enterprise environmental factors (EEFs) and organizational process assets (OPAs) and how they can influence and impact your project!

- ✦ Use expert judgment and needed facilitation techniques with all the inputs to document the high-level scope, risks assumptions, and constraints for the project.
- ✦ Expert judgment is used throughout the Project Integration Knowledge Area. Any group or person with specialized education, knowledge, skill, experience, or training can provide expert judgment.

Prep Test

1 **Which of the following is an enterprise environmental factor (EEF) that would influence charter development?**

A ❍ Charter from a similar project that was done eight months ago
B ❍ Documentation that describes lessons learned from a similar project
C ❍ Charter template
D ❍ Ability to get funding for the project

2 **You are preparing your project charter. You need to find a narrative description of the project. What document will provide you with what you are looking for?**

A ❍ Statement of work (SOW)
B ❍ Business case
C ❍ Scope statement
D ❍ Strategic plan

3 **You are preparing to pitch a project to the portfolio steering committee. You want to demonstrate the value of the project to the organization, not just in financial terms but also in terms of developing customer satisfaction and loyalty. Where would you document this information?**

A ❍ Statement of work (SOW)
B ❍ Business case
C ❍ Project charter
D ❍ Concept of operations

4 **Your company has won a bid to conduct research on the impact of CO_2 in a remote part of the Northwest Territories. You have been assigned to lead the project. Your sponsor, the VP of Research, wants to see a charter for the project on his desk next Tuesday. What document should you pay particular attention to as you develop the charter?**

A ❍ Requirements documentation
B ❍ Business case
C ❍ Contract
D ❍ Stakeholder analysis

5 **Your organization outsources the IT Help Desk to another company. You need to use them on a project you were just assigned. Because they are a vendor, there are certain protocols you have to follow. This is an example of**

A ❍ Assumption
B ❍ Enterprise environmental factor (EEF)
C ❍ Organizational process asset
D ❍ Risk

6 **You are helping a junior project manager on his first project. You walk him through a repository of forms that include business case templates, charter templates, and a myriad of other helpful forms. This repository is an example of**

A ❍ Organizational process asset (OPA)
B ❍ Enterprise environmental factor (EEF)
C ❍ Constraint
D ❍ Statement of work (SOW)

7 **The project justification, summary milestones, and project manager (PM) authority are described in which document?**

A ❍ Statement of work (SOW)
B ❍ Stakeholder analysis
C ❍ Business case
D ❍ The charter

8 **Which of the following persons or entities is not typically authorized to initiate a project?**

A ❍ The project manager
B ❍ The project sponsor
C ❍ The Project Management Office (PMO)
D ❍ The portfolio steering committee

9 **If you are seeking expertise *(expert judgment)* to help develop your project charter, which resource are you most likely to use?**

A ❍ The functional managers
B ❍ The accounting department
C ❍ The PMO
D ❍ The chief operating officer

10 **Which of the following is not included in the project charter?**

A ❍ High-level requirements
B ❍ Contingency funds
C ❍ Objectives
D ❍ Success criteria

Answers

1 **D.** Ability to get funding for the project. The ability to get funding is an external environmental factor (EEF) that influences the project. The other options are organizational process assets (OPAs). *See "Enterprise environmental factors."*

2 **A.** Statement of work (SOW). The statement of work (SOW) provides a narrative description of the work to be done. *Take a look at "Project statement of work."*

3 **B.** Business case. The business case demonstrates the financial metrics as well as nonfinancial metrics to justify undertaking a project. *Review "Business case."*

4 **C.** Contract. Because this project was won in a bidding situation, there will be contractual obligations that are outlined in the contract. These need to be reflected in the project charter. *Look at "Agreements."*

5 **B.** Enterprise environmental factor (EEF). The company's staffing is an external environmental factor (EEF) you need to consider. *See "Enterprise environmental factors."*

6 **A.** Organizational process asset (OPA). Forms and templates are organizational process (OPAs) assets that assist project managers in doing their jobs. *Check out "Organizational process assets."*

7 **D.** The charter. All these items are documented in the charter. The statement of work and the business case may provide relevant information, but the charter pulls it together and documents it in one place. *Spend some time with "Develop Project Charter: Outputs."*

8 **A.** The project manager. The project manager is not usually authorized to initiate a project. They may participate in developing a charter. *See Develop Project Charter: Outputs."*

9 **C.** The PMO. The PMO often has the expertise to help you with high-level information needed for your charter. *Review "Develop Project Charter: Tools and Techniques."*

10 **B.** Contingency funds. Contingency funds are used to protect the project from risk. This information is not available when a charter is developed. *Check out "Develop Project Charter: Outputs."*

Chapter 3: Identifying Project Stakeholders

Exam Objective

- **Analyze stakeholders to identify expectations and gain support for the project.**

This chapter focuses on identifying those people and groups of people who can affect your project — or think they can! They are *stakeholders.* You will see ways to identify them and then analyze their interests, involvement, and potential impact on your project.

Stakeholders may also be affected by your project, sometimes negatively, sometimes positively. Identifying affected stakeholders and understanding their interests and influence will help you manage their engagement level on your project. Ultimately, your goal is to maintain stakeholder satisfaction during the execution of your project.

Keeping track of all your stakeholders can be challenging, so read this chapter to discover such techniques as brainstorming, interviewing, and methods to identify, categorize, and document information about project stakeholders. Then you can develop effective strategies for working with them and getting them to work with you!

Quick Assessment

1 (True/False). Stakeholders are only those people who are positively affected by your project and are working to help it succeed.

2 (True/False). A sponsor is a key stakeholder on a project.

3 Someone who provides resources to help you perform your project is a(n) ______. After you identify stakeholders on your project, you should ______ them.

4 A way to record the level of authority and the degree of involvement of stakeholders is to create a(n) ______ ______ grid.

5 Someone who actively and vocally does not support your project is a(n) ______.

6 Someone who provides resources to help you perform your project is a(n) ______.

7 The ______ ______ is where you record information about your project stakeholders.

8 (True/False). Vendors and suppliers are not considered stakeholders because they are external to the organization.

Answers

1 False. Stakeholders can be affected positively or negatively by your projects, and not all stakeholders want you to succeed. *Read about this in the section, "Who Cares about Your Project?"*

2 True. Sponsors can significantly influence the project, and they are very interested in the outcome. *Review the content in "Common stakeholders."*

3 Supporter, classify. The first step in working with stakeholders is to identify them. After that, you classify them. *Look over "Stakeholder analysis."*

4 Power/Influence grid. A Power/Influence grid maps the level of authority and the amount of participation of each stakeholder. *Check out "Stakeholder analysis."*

5 Resistor. A resistor exerts a negative influence on accomplishing your project. *You can learn more about this in the "Stakeholder analysis" section.*

6 Supporter. Supporters provide resources, such as staff to your project. *Look over "Stakeholder analysis."*

7 Stakeholder register. This contains details about the stakeholders on your project. *Find more in "Identify Stakeholders: Outputs."*

8 False. Vendors and suppliers should definitely be considered stakeholders because they can affect your project and can be affected by your project's outcome. *Peruse the section, "Common stakeholders."*

Who Cares about Your Project?

After you have your charter (which you can read about in the preceding chapter of this minibook), you should start identifying those people who are affected by your project, have expectations or needs associated with your project, or can influence your project. These people (and sometimes things) are *stakeholders.* In the Glossary of the *PMBOK Guide,* PMI expands the definition of a stakeholder a bit. You should know this definition for the exam:

Stakeholder. An individual, group, or organization who may affect, be affected by, or perceive itself to be affected by a decision, activity or outcome of a project.

Identifying stakeholders and understanding their needs and expectations is critical to the success of your project. Think about the implications of not identifying key stakeholders. Most likely, they will have requirements that need to be part of the project. If you don't incorporate their interests from the start, you will most likely need to make changes when you do identify them as stakeholders. And changes that occur late in the project are much more expensive than those that are identified early on. Therefore, thinking through all the people and groups involved in or affected by your project early and often will help you identify the correct approach for each stakeholder.

Identify Stakeholders: Inputs

So how do you go about finding these stakeholders? Start with the project charter. Look at procurement documents, and don't overlook enterprise environmental factors (EEFs), organizational process assets (OPAs), and common stakeholders.

Identify Stakeholders. Identify Stakeholders is the process of identifying the people, groups, or organizations that could impact or be impacted by a decision, activity, or outcome of the project; and analyzing and documenting relevant information regarding their interests, involvement, interdependencies, influence, and potential and impact on project success.

Project charter

A good place to start is the project charter. The purpose, project description, and requirements are a good first place to look to identify people who will be involved with your project, or will have an interest in the outcome. Pay particular attention to the project sponsor, customer, and stakeholders that will be significantly affected by the project.

Procurement documents

If you're outsourcing part of your project or purchasing goods or services, you should look at your procurement documents. For example, if you need to bring in consulting help or perhaps temporary workers, the consultant, temp agency, and the workers are all stakeholders. You have to consider their needs and expectations to be successful. For example, a consultant hired to help plan the childcare center might have expectations that he or she would have office space on-site, a company computer, and access to the network while working for Cynergy2, Inc.

Enterprise environmental factors

Enterprise environmental factors (EEFs) that affect this process include regulations and the company culture. (To refresh your memory about EEFs, read Book I, Chapter 2.) If your project needs any kind of permit, license, or approval by any kind of agency, that agency is a stakeholder. Believe me: That can exert influence, and it's almost always negative! So identify those stakeholders early on and identify a plan to keep them satisfied.

Your company culture will influence how detailed your stakeholder analysis is and also the type of decision making that is prevalent. Some organizations have very collaborative atmosphere that makes certain that all stakeholders have a chance to voice their opinion and influence project direction. Other organizations require cursory communication and a top-down style of information distribution about the project. The culture will influence the time and techniques you will use to identify and analyze your stakeholders.

Organizational process assets

The organization infrastructure can also have an influence if you're considering IT systems and infrastructure components as stakeholders.

Organizational process assets (OPAs) you can use include

- Information from prior projects
- Policies and procedures for identifying stakeholders
- Templates or forms to record information about your stakeholders

For a refresher on OPAs, review Book I, Chapter 3.

Common stakeholders

Think about the projects you have worked on. Who and what are the stakeholders that are present on almost every project? You can probably come up with a list with five to ten common stakeholders, like the following:

- Customer
- Sponsor
- Project manager
- Project management team
- Project team
- End user

You can easily expand this list to include additional stakeholders, such as

- Functional managers (because they provide the team members)
- The Project Management Office (PMO) or a portfolio steering committee
- Program office (if you have one)

Additional stakeholders will be project-dependent, but the preceding list is a decent starting place.

Now look at the example from the Cynergy2, Inc. Childcare Center, as discussed in the preceding chapter. Using the Project Charter shown in Figure 2-1 in the previous chapter, you can identify the following stakeholders:

- **Sponsor:** Morgan Cuthbert
- **Project manager:** You
- **Project team**
- **Project customer:** Cynergy2, Inc. Employees
- **Parents**
- **Children**
- **Human Resources department**
- **Legal department**
- **Facilities department**

- **Project vendors:** Playground, Inc., General Contractor, Carpentry, HVAC, Electrical, Plumbing
- **Suppliers:** Furniture, equipment, supplies
- **Existing vendors:** Maintenance, janitorial, food prep
- **Childcare teachers/caregivers**
- **Childcare administration**
- **City**

As the project continues into the planning phase, you will probably expand the list, filling in the names of the stakeholders instead of their positions in the company. This is an example of progressive elaboration, which I discuss in Book I, Chapter 2.

However, for a first round, this is a good start. The next step is to understand stakeholders' interests and influence.

Identify Stakeholders: Tools and Techniques

Identifying stakeholders is the first step. Here are some techniques you can use to identify stakeholders and analyze the degree of influence that individual stakeholders can have on your project.

Stakeholder analysis

Face it: Not all stakeholders have the same degree of influence on your project. Furthermore, not all stakeholders care that much about your project. Some stakeholders will be affected positively by your project and others negatively. Understanding which stakeholders are influential, which are concerned, and which can help or harm your project are necessary to help you develop strategies to maximize the influence of project supporters while minimizing the influence of resistors.

The three steps to analyze stakeholders are

1. Identify stakeholders.

   This initial step includes identifying and recording stakeholder roles, interests, influence, and expectations. After you identify and record information about the most common stakeholders, you can expand the list by interviewing the identified stakeholders to uncover additional stakeholders.

2. Classify stakeholders.

   Classify stakeholders based on the potential degree of support, influence, and power they have on the project.

3. Assess support.

   Consider how each stakeholder would react in various situations. Then determine the best way to influence them to enhance their support for your project and minimize any negative influence they might exert.

One simple way to consolidate stakeholder information is to create a grid that maps stakeholder positions across two variables. Here's an example: Say you want to figure out who has the most influence and who is the most supportive of your project. You can create a Power/Support grid like the one shown in Figure 3-1. You analyze each stakeholder to determine whether she is an advocate, neutral, or a resistor and whether she has a high, medium, or low amount of power.

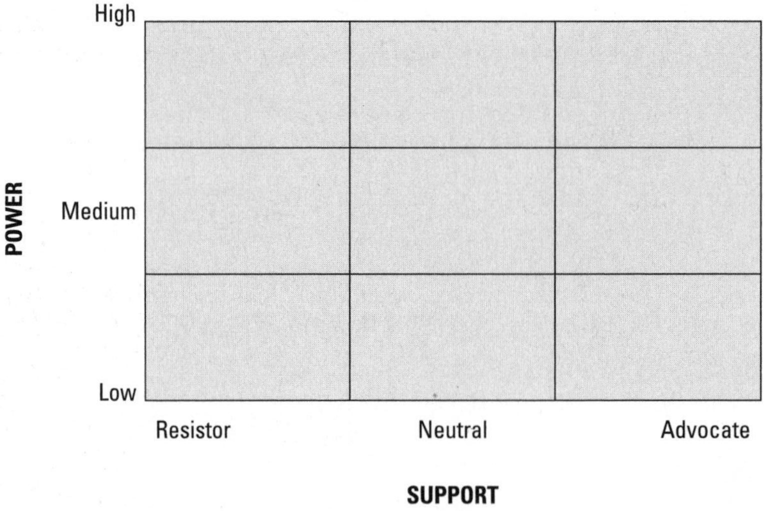

POWER
High
Medium
Low
Resistor
Neutral
Advocate
SUPPORT

Figure 3-1: Use a Power/Support grid to assess stakeholders.

The *PMBOK Guide* shows an example of a Power/Interest grid. The grid in the *PMBOK Guide* is a 2 x 2 grid, and the one in Figure 3-1 is 3 x 3. Point being, you can create any kind of grid, depending on what you think is best for the project, but the overall goal is to develop a strategy for managing stakeholders and for planning your project communications.

✦ **Resistor:** A *resistor* actively and vocally does not support your project. He can cause disruption to your project and take up your time in trying to work with him. You want to find ways to show the resistor the WIIFM *(What's in it for me?)* in supporting your project. You may also try to find ways to minimize his influence on the project. Here's an example: A resistor for the childcare center may be an employee without children who would rather see the space used as a workout area.

✦ **Neutral:** A neutral stakeholder doesn't support or detract from your project. Ideally, you want her to support your project, but she won't do any real harm by being neutral. A neutral stakeholder for the childcare center might be someone without children who doesn't care whether there is a childcare center on-site.

✦ **Advocate:** An advocate is actively and vocally in favor of your project. Try to find ways to encourage him to voice his support and try to maximize his influence. An advocate for the childcare center could be someone with one or more children who will use the center and is thrilled to have quality daycare nearby.

Using the list of stakeholders you identified earlier for the childcare center, you can then plot them on a Power/Support grid as shown in Figure 3-2.

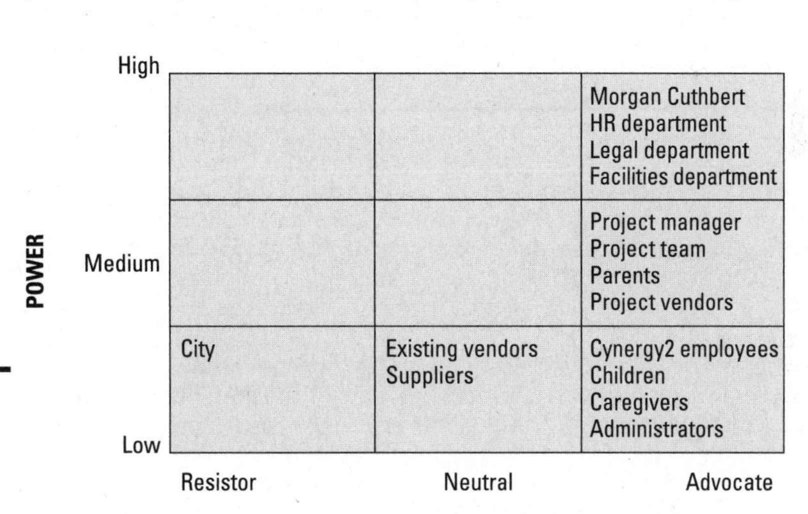

Figure 3-2: Filled-out Power/ Support grid.

The childcare center scenario is an unusual situation because there are few resistors. In most projects, you will usually have at least a few. For example, a resistor could be someone who likes the status quo and doesn't want change. In the case of a childcare center, though, which will improve the quality of work-life balance, not too many people will likely speak out against it.

You might disagree with some of the placement of stakeholders on this grid. In the real world, the project manager and the team would discuss the placement and work together to come to consensus on the placement and the correct strategy.

Another way to categorize stakeholders is to analyze the types of role they have on the project:

- **Driver:** A person who has the authority to determine the direction of the project and make decisions that affect the project. Morgan Cuthbert is a driver for the childcare center.
- **Supporter:** A person who provides assistance or resources used by the project to meet objectives. Department managers who are providing team members to work on the project are supporters.
- **Observer:** A person who does not interact with, or directly influence, the project. The janitorial services vendor is an observer.

This information is entered into the stakeholder register along with the information from the Power/Support grid. I show you an example and describe a stakeholder register in the next section.

You may see different names for the stakeholder grid. For example, interest/influence, interest/support, power/interest, and so forth. The important point is to understand the variables that are being assessed.

Expert judgment

For smaller projects, identifying all the stakeholders isn't difficult. However, the PMP focuses on larger projects. For large projects, you want to pull together people that can help you identify the various stakeholders. For example, you can interview senior management or the key stakeholders you have already identified. You may want to send questionnaires to project managers who have worked on similar projects.

Other groups you can consider include

- Other organizational units
- Subject matter experts in the technical or business area

- Industry groups
- Consultants
- Associations

Meetings

You can gather and compare information about stakeholders in meetings with any of the people mentioned in preceding section on expert judgment. Meetings may consist of a brainstorming session, interviews, focus groups, or virtual meetings to help you identify the pool of stakeholders that you need to analyze.

Identify Stakeholders: Outputs

The stakeholder register, which records relevant information for each stakeholder or group of stakeholders, is a wonderful tool to keep information organized. This will become an input into the communications management plan because communication is the main way you can manage stakeholder engagement. You can read more information on the communications management plan in Book IV, Chapter 4 and about planning stakeholder management in Book V, Chapter 3.

Stakeholder register

You can have whatever fields in the stakeholder register you want. Common fields include

- Name
- Position
- Expectations
- Information from your stakeholder analysis

Figure 3-3 shows an example of a generic stakeholder register.

Another approach is to use the example from the childcare center (see Figure 3-4). In Figure 3-4, I don't list expectations, but I do list information from the stakeholder analysis and the stakeholder function on the project. Again, like all things in the project management world, tailor the use of the forms and techniques to suit your needs!

STAKEHOLDER REGISTER

Project Title: ____________ Date Prepared: ____________

Name	Position	Role	Contact Information	Requirements	Expectations	Influence	Classification

Figure 3-3: Sample stakeholder register.

Figure 3-4: Filled-out stakeholder register.

STAKEHOLDER REGISTER

Project Title: Cynergy2, Inc. Childcare Center **Date Prepared:** ______

Name	Role	Power	Support	Function	Expectations	Influence	Classification
Morgan Cuthbert	Driver	H	H	Sponsor			
You	Driver	M	H	Project manager			
Project Team	Driver	M	H	Project members			
Cynergy2, Inc. employees	Observer	L	H	Provide input			
Parents	Supporter	M	H	End user			
Children	Observer	L	H	End user			
HR department	Supporter	H	H	Staffing			
Legal department	Supporter	H	H	Compliance and contracts			
Facilities department	Supporter	H	H	Vendor selection, management and oversight			
Project vendors	Supporter	M	H	Build out			
Existing vendors	Observer	L	M	Ongoing maintenance			
Suppliers	Observer	L	M	Provide equipment and supplies			
Caregivers	Supporter	L	H	Day-to-day interaction with children and parents			
Administrators	Supporter	L	H	Day-to-day management			
City	Observer	H	L	Permits			

Initiating summary

The chapters in this minibook are all about initiating the project. This process group comprises 13% of the test, or 26 questions. For these questions, you need to have knowledge and skills in the following techniques:

- Cost-benefit analysis — Book II, Chapter 1
- Business case development — Book II, Chapter 2
- Project selection criteria — Book II, Chapter 1
- Risk identification techniques — Book II, Chapter 2
- Elements of a project charter — Book II, Chapter 2
- Stakeholder identification techniques — Book II, Chapter 3

This process and the process to develop the project charter interact. Notice the exam objectives in the prior chapter reference analyzing stakeholder requirements to complete the project charter. Therefore, you should expect to conduct these processes concurrently and iteratively until your charter is signed off and approved and you have identified your project stakeholders to the extent possible during project initiation.

Key Terms

The terms in this chapter provide a means to identify, analyze, and document information about stakeholders.

- Stakeholder
- Resistor
- Neutral
- Advocate
- Driver
- Supporter
- Observer
- Stakeholder register

Chapter Summary

The intent of identifying and analyzing stakeholders is to identify the appropriate approach for each stakeholder to gain support for your project.

- ✦ Identifying stakeholders and understanding their needs and expectations is critical to the success of your project.
- ✦ Information about stakeholders is progressively elaborated throughout your project.
- ✦ Use expert judgment from groups and individuals in the organization to identify a robust list of stakeholders.
- ✦ You can use a grid to map stakeholders against specified variables, such as power, interest, influence, type of role, or support.
- ✦ Record information about your stakeholders in a stakeholder register.

Prep Test

1 **People who have an interest in your project, or who can influence your project, are called**

A ❍ Observers
B ❍ Drivers
C ❍ Customers
D ❍ Stakeholders

2 **Your organization has an enterprise architecture that is tightly controlled. All new IT projects must comply with the enterprise architecture. This is an example of**

A ❍ A stakeholder
B ❍ An enterprise environmental factor (EEF)
C ❍ An organizational process asset (OPA)
D ❍ A constraint

3 **Which of the following is not a stakeholder you are likely to see on most projects?**

A ❍ Sponsor
B ❍ End user
C ❍ Regulatory agency
D ❍ Project team

4 **You are collecting information about people involved with your project. Where should you document that information?**

A ❍ A stakeholder register
B ❍ A stakeholder management strategy
C ❍ A Power/Influence grid
D ❍ A stakeholder management record

5 **You are assessing the amount of help each stakeholder will give you and the ability they have to steer the project. What type of vehicle should you use to record this information?**

A ❍ A stakeholder register
B ❍ A stakeholder management strategy
C ❍ A Power/Support grid
D ❍ A Power/Interest grid

6 **What type of grid would you use to record the amount of involvement and the ability to effect changes on a project?**

A ❍ Interest/Influence
B ❍ Power/Support
C ❍ Power/Observer
D ❍ Support/Interest

7 **There are three steps in analyzing project stakeholders. Which of the following is not one of those steps?**

A ❍ Identify stakeholders.
B ❍ Classify stakeholders.
C ❍ Assess support.
D ❍ Plan engagement strategies.

8 **Which processes provide inputs to the Identify Stakeholders process?**

A ❍ Plan Communications and Develop Project Charter
B ❍ Plan Procurements and Develop Project Charter
C ❍ Develop Project Charter and Conduct Procurements
D ❍ Collect Requirements and Plan Communications

9 **Which stakeholder categories would be appropriate for a project sponsor?**

A ❍ Observer, supporter
B ❍ Driver, resistor
C ❍ Driver, advocate
D ❍ Supporter, neutral

10 **Which document provides input to the Identify Stakeholders process and lists the sponsor, team members, and others participating in the project?**

A ❍ The project scope statement
B ❍ The statement of work
C ❍ A contract
D ❍ A project charter

Answers

1. **D**. Stakeholders. A stakeholder is someone who is actively involved in your project or who is affected by the execution or completion of the project. *Check out the definition in "Who Cares about Your Project?"*

2. **B**. An enterprise environmental factor (EEF). The organization's infrastructure, including the enterprise architecture, is an enterprise environmental factor. *See "Enterprise environmental factors."*

3. **C**. Regulatory agency. Regulatory agencies are not involved in all projects. The others listed are part of almost all other projects. *See "Common stakeholders."*

4. **A**. A stakeholder register. The stakeholder register is the document used to record stakeholders, their interests, and other relevant information. *Review "Stakeholder register."*

5. **C**. A Power/Support grid. The amount of help a stakeholder can give you refers to whether a stakeholder is an advocate or resistor of your project; the ability to steer the project refers to the stakeholder's power. *Look at "Stakeholder analysis."*

6. **A**. Interest/Influence. The amount of involvement refers to the interest in the project and the ability to affect changes refers to the amount of influence on the project. *See "Stakeholder analysis."*

7. **D**. Plan engagement strategies. You will plan stakeholder management and stakeholder engagement strategies in the planning processes. The initiation process of Identify Stakeholders is concerned only with identifying stakeholders and documenting information about them. *Peruse "Stakeholder analysis."*

8. **B**. Plan Procurements and Develop Project Charter. The project charter and procurement documents are inputs to this process. They come from the Develop Project Charter and the Plan Procurements processes. *Check out "Project charter" and "Procurement documents."*

9. **C**. Driver, advocate. The sponsor has the authority to determine the direction of the project, and as a project champion, advocate for the project. *Look at "Stakeholder analysis."*

10. **D**. A project charter. The project charter can identify the sponsor and team members. It is an input to this process. *Check out "Project charter."*

Book III

Planning Integration, Scope, and Schedule

ID	Task Name	Duration
1	Start	0 days
2	Activity A	5 days
3	Activity B	3 days
4	Activity C	4 days
5	Activity D	6 days
6	Activity E	7 days
7	Activity F	6 days
8	Activity G	2 days
9	Activity H	3 days
10	Activity I	4 days
11	Finish	0 days

Take a look at the article on the role of the project management plan at www.dummies.com/extras/pmpcertificationaio.

Contents at a Glance

Chapter 1: Constructing the Project Management Plan

Exam Objectives

- **Define and document how changes will be addressed to track and manage changes throughout the project.**
- **Present the project management plan to attain approval before executing the project.**
- **Hold a kick-off meeting to start the project and communicate key project information.**

I begin this minibook by identifying the cross-cutting skills you will need when planning a project. Skills such as active listening and decision-making are necessary when developing a *project management plan,* which is the master plan for the project. It comprises all the other subsidiary management plans, the project baselines, and additional components that are used to execute, monitor, control, and close the project. Nearly all (22 of the 47 processes are directly related to the Develop Project Management Plan process covered in this chapter. For more on this, turn to Figure 4-5 in the *PMBOK Guide,* which shows how these processes provide inputs to, and receive outputs from, this process.

The project management plan is started after the project charter is approved. However, it is developed iteratively, as the subsidiary plans and the baselines evolve. When the initial detailed planning is complete, the project management plan should be baselined. This controlled document should be changed only via a defined change control process. I discuss the change control process and a change control plan in this chapter.

The elements of the project management plan are dependent upon the needs of the project. The plan may be robust and detailed or high level. The real art of project planning takes place in integrating, combining, and unifying the planning information while making trade-offs between the project constraints and managing stakeholder expectations. Projects are successful to the degree that you can balance and integrate all the project management processes. The project management plan is the vehicle to do that.

A kick-off meeting introduces the team to the project, communicates the relevant project information, and outlines the high-level milestones.

Quick Assessment

1. The ______ ______ system is a collection of formal documented procedures that define how project deliverables and documentation will be controlled, changed, and approved.

2. The project management plan is a controlled document. This means it can be changed only by using a defined ______ control process.

3. The project management plan comprises subsidiary management plans, ______, and various other documents that give direction on executing, monitoring, controlling, and closing the project.

4. The following are not part of the project management plan, but you need them to help manage the project: issue log, milestone list, resource requirements, and risk register. These, and many other elements, are called ______ ______.

5. (True/False). The source selection criteria are part of the project management plan.

6. The cost baseline, which is part of the project management plan, is an output from which process?

7. Which subsidiary plan identifies team member training needs?

8. Two plans that are developed as part of the Develop Project Management Plan process are the ______ management plan and the ______ management plan.

9. (True/False). The change control plan is part of the project management plan.

10. You announce the start of the project and communicate key milestones via a(n) ______-______ ______.

Answers

1. Change control. The change control system should, at the very least, define how to submit a change, describe how the change should be analyzed, and who can approve changes. *For more on this topic, see "Planning for change."*

2. Change. The project management plan is a controlled document. This means that it can be changed only by using a defined change control process. *You can find this discussion in the "The Project Management Plan and the Executing, Controlling and Closing Processes" section.*

3. Baselines. The scope, schedule, and cost baselines are part of the project management plan. *This information is contained in the "Develop Project Management Plan: Inputs" section.*

4. Project documents. The following are not part of the project management plan, but you need them to help manage the project: issue log, milestone list, resource requirements, and risk register. These and many other elements are called "project documents." *To read more about this, see "Project documents."*

5. False. The source selection criteria are part of a project document. *Find a list of the project documents in the "Project documents" section.*

6. Determine Budget. The cost baseline, also known as the performance measurement baseline, is an output from the Determine Budget process. *You will see the documents that each process contributes to the project management plan in the section "Develop Project Management Plan: Inputs."*

7. Human resource plan. The human resource plan includes training, rewards, and recognition, and how team members will be added and released from the team. *Find more on this is in the "Develop Project Management Plan: Inputs" section.*

8. Change, configuration. These plans are developed when developing the project management plan. *Take a look at the "Planning for change" section.*

9. True. The change control plan and (if needed) the configuration management plan are components of the project management plan. *See the "Develop Project Management Plan: Inputs" section and the "Planning for change" section.*

10. Kick-off meeting. The kick-off meeting officially announces the beginning of the project and goes over the key milestones. *This is discussed in the "The project kick-off meeting" section.*

Knowledge and Skills for the Planning Processes

There are more processes in Planning than in any other process group. Many of the cross-cutting skills described in Book I, Chapter 1 are represented strongly in this process group. The following is a list of skills you need to apply to plan your project successfully. Keep these in mind as you go through the chapters in the next three minibooks.

- Active listening
- Brainstorming techniques
- Conflict-resolution techniques
- Cultural sensitivity and diversity
- Data-gathering techniques
- Decision-making techniques
- Facilitation
- Information management tools, techniques, and methods
- Leadership tools and techniques
- Negotiating
- Oral and written communication techniques, channels, and applications
- Problem-solving tools and techniques
- Project management software
- Relationship management
- Stakeholder impact analysis
- Targeting communications to intended audiences (for example, team, stakeholders, customers)

The Project Management Plan

The project management plan is the master document where all subsidiary plans and the project approach are documented. It also contains standard information you will use for the project, such as organizational policies and procedures, templates, the project life cycle, and any project-specific information needed to develop a robust road map for conducting the project.

Project management plan. The document that describes how the project will be executed, monitored, and controlled.

Develop Project Management Plan. The process of defining, preparing and coordinating all subsidiary management plans and then integrating them into a comprehensive management plan.

Develop Project Management Plan: Inputs

The information in the project management plan comes from the planning processes discussed in this minibook and also Books II, IV, and V. Most of the subsidiary management plans come from the other planning processes, the exceptions being the change management plan and the configuration management plan, discussed later in this chapter. Table 1-1 shows the contributions from the outputs from various planning processes.

Table 1-1 Planning Process Outputs

Process	*Contribution*
Plan Scope Management	Scope management plan Requirements management plan
Define Scope	Project scope statement
Create Work Breakdown Structure (WBS)	Scope baseline
Plan Schedule Management	Schedule Management Plan
Develop Schedule	Schedule baseline
Plan Cost Management	Cost Management Plan
Determine Budget	Cost performance baseline
Plan Quality Management	Quality management plan Process improvement plan
Plan Human Resource Management	Human resource plan
Plan Communications Management	Communications management plan
Plan Risk Management	Risk management plan
Plan Procurement Management	Procurement management plan
Plan Stakeholder Management	Stakeholder management plan

Table 1-2 lists the subsidiary management plan content for each knowledge area. (See Book I, Chapter 4 for a list of the knowledge areas.) This is a generic list. You will need to tailor it for your project, but it's sufficient to get an idea of what each type of plan has for the exam.

Table 1-2 Subsidiary Plan Content

Plan	*Content*
Scope management plan	Guidance for how scope will be defined, documented, verified, managed, and controlled Information on how to create the WBS Instructions for gaining formal acceptance and verification of project deliverables Process for controlling changes to the project scope
Requirements management plan	Describes how requirements will be collected, tracked, and reported Describes the configuration management plan for requirements Defines requirements prioritization Defines the product metrics Establishes a requirements traceability structure
Schedule management plan	Describes the scheduling methodology Identifies the scheduling tool Sets the format for developing the project schedule Establishes criteria for controlling the project schedule
Cost management plan	Defines the precision level of estimates Defines the units of measure Establishes cost control thresholds Defines earned value (EV) rules Provides reporting formats
Quality management plan	Identifies quality management roles and responsibilities Defines the quality assurance approach Defines the quality control approach Defines the quality improvement approach
Process improvement plan	Describes the steps to analyze processes Defines process metrics Identifies targets for improvement
Human resource plan	Outlines roles, authority, and responsibility Sets the project organizational structure Describes staff acquisition and release processes Identifies training needs Establishes criteria for rewards and recognition Outlines information on regulations, standards, and policy compliance Describes policies for informing about and enforcing safety procedures
Communications management plan	Describes the type of information that will be distributed, including level of detail, format, content, and so on Identifies the person responsible for communicating information Outlines the timing and frequency of distribution Documents a glossary of terms

Plan	Content
Risk management plan	Describes the risk methodology Outlines roles and responsibilities for risk management Identifies budgeting and timing for risk management activities Describes risk categories Provides definitions of probability and impact Provides a probability and impact (PxI) matrix Describes reporting formats
Procurement management plan	Outlines procurement authority, roles, and responsibilities Documents the standard procurement documents Identifies the contract type Documents selection criteria Defines constraints and assumptions Lists integration requirements
Stakeholder management plan	Identifies the current and desired level of stakeholder engagement for categories of stakeholders Identifies relationships and interdependencies among stakeholders Outlines communication requirements for stakeholders Discusses the impact of a change to stakeholders

You will also have a change management plan and possibly a configuration management plan as part of your project management plan. In addition to the information from the subsidiary management plans listed earlier, industry standards, organizational policies, expert judgment, and project management plans from previous projects will have information that should go into the project management plan as well. For example, depending on your industry, there may be standards for such areas as

- Safety
- Information security
- Validation
- Training
- Transition
- Integration
- Testing

Obviously, this list is not complete, but it should give you an idea of the types of additional information that you can expect to see in a complete project management plan. In addition to the various plans, you should indicate the organizational policies and/or procedures that will be used on your project. For example:

- ✦ Work authorization procedures
- ✦ Guidelines for tailoring the project management plan and project documents
- ✦ Reporting requirements
- ✦ Project life cycle identification and Go/No-go decision criteria
- ✦ Acceptable variance thresholds
- ✦ Performance measurement guidelines
- ✦ Key management reviews
- ✦ Baseline management and control

The enterprise might require specific information or specific ways of tracking information. Consider the following:

- ✦ Systems to track progress and costs
- ✦ Document management and control systems
- ✦ Change control systems
- ✦ Configuration management systems
- ✦ Portfolio management systems

A project management plan is not a schedule. Many times, I hear people refer to their project schedule as a "project plan." On the exam, pay attention to language. The exam might use *project plan* and *project management plan* interchangeably. However, it will not use *project schedule* and *project management plan* interchangeably!

Planning for change

I discuss change control and configuration management in detail in Book VIII. For now, you should understand the definitions of the change control system and the configuration management system as well as the type of information you would find in a change control plan and a configuration management plan.

Change control system. A set of procedures that describes how modifications to the project deliverables and documentation are managed and controlled.

The change control plan outlines at least the following information:

- ✦ How change requests will be submitted
- ✦ The process for evaluating change requests

- Who should sit on the change control board
- Levels of authority for approving changes

Figure 1-1 shows a sample of a simple change management plan.

CHANGE MANAGEMENT PLAN

Project Title: ______________________ Date Prepared: ______________________

Change Management Approach:

Describe the degree of change control, the relationship to configuration management, and how change control will integrate with other aspects of project management.

Definitions of Change:

Schedule change:Define a schedule change versus a schedule revision. Indicate when a schedule variance needs to go through the change control process to be rebaselined.
Budget change:Define a budget change versus a budget update. Indicate when a budget variance needs to go through the change control process to be rebaselined.
Scope change:Define a scope change versus a change in approach. Indicate when a scope variance needs to go through the change control process to be rebaselined.
Project document changes:Define when updates to project management documents or other project documents need to go through the change control process to be rebaselined.

Change Control Board:

Name	Role	Responsibility	Authority
Individual's name.	*Position on the change control board.*	*Responsibilities and activities required of the role.*	*Authority level for approving or rejecting changes.*

Change Control Process:

Change request submittal	*Describe the process used to submit change requests, including who receives requests and any special forms, policies, or procedures that need to be used.*
Change request tracking	*Describe the process for tracking change requests from submittal to final disposition.*
Change request review	*Describe the process used to review change requests, including analysis of impact on project objectives such as schedule, scope, cost, etc.*
Change request disposition	*Describe the possible outcomes, such as accept, defer, reject.*

Attach relevant forms used in the change control process.

Figure 1-1: A change management plan.

Introduction to configuration management

The configuration management plan outlines how you will identify product components and project documents. It describes the processes and approvals needed to change a configuration item's attributes. The process for configuration verification and audit are also outlined along with the roles and responsibilities associated with configuration management.

Configuration management system. A subsystem of the overall project management system. It is a collection of formal documented procedures used to apply technical and administrative direction and surveillance to: identify and document the functional and physical characteristics of a product, result, service, or component; control any changes to such characteristics; record and report each change and its implementation status; and support the audit of the products, results, or components to verify conformance to requirements. It includes the documentation, tracking systems, and defined approval levels necessary for authorizing and controlling changes.

Figure 1-2 shows a sample of a simple configuration management plan.

Develop Project Management Plan: Tools and Techniques

The two broad tools and techniques for this process are expert judgment and facilitation techniques.

Expert judgment

You must make sure your team will have the expert judgment needed to determine how the components and the details should work within the project management plan for your project. Consider the following areas where expert judgment is required:

- Tailoring the components in the project management plan to meet the project needs
- Defining the change control process
- Providing technical details and information for the project management plan
- Providing input for the appropriate life cycle
- Identifying the resources and skill levels needed to perform the work
- Identifying the items and documents that should be under configuration control

CONFIGURATION MANAGEMENT PLAN

Project Title: ______________________ Date Prepared: ______________________

Configuration Management Approach:

Describe the degree of configuration control, the relationship to change control, and how configuration management will integrate with other aspects of project management.

Configuration Identification:

Component	Identification Conventions
Identify the attributes of the product that will be tracked. For example, if the project is to build a new car, define the deliverables that make up the car that will be identified, tracked, and managed. This could include the engine, the transmission, the chassis, and the frame as components that are subject to configuration control. Each of the parts and pieces that make up these deliverables would then be listed and tracked throughout the life of the product.	*Describe how the elements of individual deliverables will be identified. For example, determine naming conventions for all parts of the engine, transmission, chassis, and frame.*

Document Configuration Control:

Configuration-Controlled Documents	Identification Conventions
List all documents that are subject to configuration control.	*Describe how the documents will be named and identified.*
Version-Controlled Documents	**Identification Conventions**
List all the documents that are subject to version control.	*Describe how the documents will named and identified.*

Configuration Change Control:

Describe the process and approvals required to change a configuration item's attributes and to rebaseline them. This includes physical components and documents under configuration control.

Configuration Verification and Audit:

Describe the frequency, timing, and approach to conducting configuration audits to ensure that the physical attributes of the product are consistent with plans, requirements, and configuration documentation.

Page 1 of 2

Figure 1-2: A configuration management plan.

CONFIGURATION MANAGEMENT PLAN

Configuration Management Roles and Responsibilities:

Roles	Responsibilities
List the roles involved in configuration management.	*List the responsibilities and activities associated with the roles.*

Attach any relevant forms used in the configuration control process.

Page 2 of 2

Facilitation techniques

The process of developing the project management plan is lengthy. It starts immediately after the project charter authorizes the charter and continues throughout the planning process. During the iterative development of the project management plan, you will have plenty of need for facilitation techniques. Here are a few examples:

- **Brainstorming:** You might use brainstorming to help define workflows, approaches to accomplish project work, and the processes you will use on your project.
- **Problem solving:** Projects that work with new technology or new processes are often fraught with problems, issues, and challenges. You may find yourself needing to plan work about which you have very little information. You will need to engage in a problem-solving session with your team members to identify solutions to problems and challenges.

- **Conflict resolution:** During the beginning stages of a project, there may be conflict as people get to know one another and establish a hierarchy. This is called *storming,* which I discuss in greater detail in Book VI, Chapter 2.
- **Meeting management:** You can't have a project without meetings! You also can't have a successful project without well-managed and productive meetings. You will need to exercise your meeting facilitation skills to ensure that your agenda is covered, people's questions are answered, and you achieve the results you want from the meeting.

Develop Project Management Plan: Outputs

The project management plan is an input to all the initial planning processes in each knowledge area (such as Plan Scope Management, Plan Schedule Management, and so forth). Updates to the project management plan are an output from many of the planning processes. In other words, it is an iterative process.

Consider that the framework or a template for the project management plan is an input to the initial planning processes in each knowledge area. The template would have a placeholder for each subsidiary management plan, such as the scope management plan, schedule management plan, and so on. After these subsidiary management plans are created, they update the project management plan by being incorporated as part of the plan.

The form in Figure 1-3 shows an example of a simple project management plan framework, which offers places for a description of the life cycle, variance and baseline management, project reviews, and tailoring decisions. The form also has room to address each subsidiary management plan either as a paragraph or as an attachment. Finally, note the area that requires attaching the scope baseline (Book III, Chapter 2), the schedule baseline (Book III, Chapter 3) and the cost baseline (Book IV, Chapter 1).

PROJECT MANAGEMENT PLAN

Project Title: ______________________ **Date Prepared:** ______________________

Project Life Cycle:

Describe the life cycle that will be used to accomplish the project. This may include phases, periods within the phases, and deliverables for each phase.

Variances and Baseline Management:

Schedule Variance Threshold: *Define acceptable schedule variances, variances that indicate a warning, and variances that are unacceptable.*	Schedule Baseline Management: *Describe how the schedule baseline will be managed, including responses to acceptable, warning, and unacceptable variances. Define circumstances that would trigger preventive or corrective action and when the change control process would be enacted.*
Cost Variance Threshold: *Define acceptable cost variances, variances that indicate a warning, and variances that are unacceptable.*	Cost Baseline Management: *Describe how the cost performance baseline will be managed, including responses to acceptable, warning, and unacceptable variances. Define circumstances that would trigger preventive or corrective action and when the change control process would be enacted.*
Scope Variance Threshold: *Define acceptable scope variances, variances that indicate a warning, and variances that are unacceptable.*	Scope Baseline Management: *Describe how the scope baseline will be managed, including responses to acceptable, warning, and unacceptable variances. Define circumstances that would trigger preventive or corrective action or defect repair and when the change control process would be enacted.*
Quality Variance Threshold: *Define acceptable performance variances, variances that indicate a warning, and variances that are unacceptable.*	Performance Requirements Management: *Describe how the performance requirements will be managed, including responses to acceptable, warning, and unacceptable variances. Define circumstances that would trigger preventive or corrective action or defect repair and when the change control process would be enacted.*

Project Reviews:

List any project reviews, for example phase gate reviews, customer product reviews, quality reviews, etc.

Tailoring Decisions:

Indicate any decisions made to combine, omit, or expand project management processes. This may include defining the specific processes used in each life cycle phase and the whether it is a summary or detailed application of specific processes.

Page 1 of 2

Figure 1-3: A project management plan.

PROJECT MANAGEMENT PLAN

Project-Specific Considerations:

This may include specific information about the environment, stakeholders, product integration, or any other aspects of the project that warrant special attention.

Subsidiary Management Plans:

Area	Approach
Either define the approach to each subsidiary plan in narrative form or indicate the plan is an attachment.	
Requirements Management Plan	
Scope Management Plan	
Schedule Management Plan	
Cost Management Plan	
Quality Management Plan	
Process Improvement Plan	
Human Resource Management Plan	
Communications Management Plan	
Risk Management Plan	
Procurement Management Plan	
Change Management Plan	
Configuration Management Plan	

Baselines:
Attach all project baselines.

Page 2 of 2

The Project Management Plan and the Executing, Controlling, and Closing Processes

After you understand where the information that contributes to the project management plan comes from, you need to know where it goes. The project management plan, including specific components included in it, will be inputs to processes in the Executing Process Group, the Monitoring and Controlling Process Group, and the Closing Process Group. The following list shows nonplanning processes that have the project management plan as an input:

- **Executing processes**
  - Direct and Manage Project Work
- **Monitoring and Controlling processes**
  - Monitor and Control Project Work
  - Perform Integrated Change Control
  - Control Scope
  - Control Schedule
  - Control Costs
  - Control Quality
  - Control Communications
  - Control Risks
  - Control Procurements
  - Control Stakeholder Engagement
- **Closing processes**
  - Close Project or Phase
  - Close Procurements

Project documents

You might wonder why not every planning process contributes to the project management plan, or why not every executing and monitoring and control process updates the project management plan. Many documents that you use to manage projects aren't part of the project management plan. For lack of a better term, they are called "project documents." Take a look at the documents in the following list to see how the other planning processes contribute to project documents.

Activity attributes	Activity cost estimates	Activity duration estimates
Activity list	Activity resource requirements	Agreements
Assumption Log	Basis of estimates	Change log
Charter	Change requests	Forecasts
Issue log	Milestone list	Project funding requirements
Proposals	Procurement documents	Project organizational structure

Quality control measurements	Quality checklists	Quality metrics
Responsibility assignment matrix	Requirements traceability matrix	Resource breakdown structure (RBS)
Resource calendars	Resource requirements	Risk register
Roles and responsibilities	Schedule	Schedule data
Sellers list	Source selection criteria	Stakeholder analysis
Stakeholder management strategy	Stakeholder register	Stakeholder requirements
Statement of work (SOW)	Team performance assessments	Work performance information
Work performance measurements	Work performance data	

Project management plan approval

After the plan and all its components are finalized, you need to get it approved and signed off. At the very least, the sponsor and the customer need to approve your approach to the project. The stakeholder register and communication management plan will identify the specific stakeholders that need to sign off on the plan. After the plan is agreed to and signed off, it can be rolled out to the project team.

The project kick-off meeting

Depending on the size of the project and the project team, you might hold a kick-off meeting to introduce the project to the team. For a small project, the project team will probably have been intimately involved with creating the project management plan. The kick-off meeting would have been held after the project charter was developed. However, for a large project with more than 100 team members, the project management plan approval allows the project to move into the development phase, and the kick-off meeting is the appropriate venue to accomplish that.

You will want to have all the key stakeholders at the kick-off meeting. At that meeting you will introduce the project, describe the intended outcomes and discuss the key milestone deliverables and target due dates. If there is other relevant information, such as teaming agreements, external influences, a specific development methodology, and so on, you should discuss that as well.

Key Terms

As you kick off the planning processes, here are some terms you should be familiar with:

- Project management plan
- Change control system
- Configuration management system
- Project documents

Chapter Summary

The project management plan is a foundation for the repository of the information from all planning processes. It provides the initial template to collect the planning information from each knowledge area and puts it into one cohesive project management plan.

- The project management plan defines how the project will be executed, monitored, controlled, and closed. It comprises subsidiary management plans, baselines, and other information necessary to effectively manage the project.
- The project management plan compiles and combines information from many planning processes and develops an integrated plan.
- Information on how to manage and control change and implement configuration management is documented in the plan as well.
- Some project documents that are not part of the project management plan are used to help manage the project.

Prep Test

1 The requirements management plan is an output from which process?

A ○ Plan Scope Management
B ○ Collect Requirements
C ○ Define Scope
D ○ Develop Project Management Plan

2 The requirements management plan, risk management plan, and procurement management plan are referred to as

A ○ Project documents
B ○ Supporting documentation
C ○ Subsidiary management plans
D ○ The project management plan

3 Elements that help you manage the project, but are not part of the project management plan, are called

A ○ Subsidiary management plans
B ○ Supporting documentation
C ○ Backup
D ○ Project documents

4 Which subsidiary management plan defines the precision level of estimates, the units of measure, and reporting formats?

A ○ Quality management plan
B ○ Cost management plan
C ○ Earned value plan
D ○ Configuration management plan

5 Where would you find a description of how to submit change requests and the process for evaluating them?

A ○ The configuration management plan
B ○ The scope management plan
C ○ The change management plan
D ○ The project documents

6 **Which system is used to apply technical and administrative direction and surveillance to identify and document the functional and physical characteristics of a product, result, service, or component?**

A ❍ Change control system
B ❍ Configuration management system
C ❍ Project control system
D ❍ Project management information system

7 **The tools and techniques used in the Develop Project Management Plan are**

A ❍ Expert judgment and facilitation techniques
B ❍ Project management information system and analytical techniques
C ❍ Information-gathering techniques and expert judgment
D ❍ Expert analysis and enterprise environmental factors

8 **Which of the following is not a component of the project management plan?**

A ❍ Change management plan
B ❍ Communications management plan
C ❍ Cost performance baseline
D ❍ Requirements traceability matrix

9 **Depending on the nature of the project, you might have many people approving your project management plan. What is one signature you should be sure to get?**

A ❍ The chair of the change control board
B ❍ The core team
C ❍ The sponsor
D ❍ The PMO Director

10 **For a large project, what is the appropriate time to introduce the project and get team buy-in on the project management plan?**

A ❍ At the kick-off meeting
B ❍ After the baselines are set
C ❍ After the project charter is signed
D ❍ At the end of the project planning phase

Answers

1. **A.** Plan Scope Management. Both the requirements management plan and the scope management plan are outputs from the Plan Scope Management process. *Go over "Develop Project Management Plan: Inputs."*

2. **C.** Subsidiary management plans. Subsidiary management plans are usually outputs from other planning processes, such as the Collect Requirements, Plan Risk Management, and Plan Procurements processes. *Look at "Develop Project Management Plan: Inputs."*

3. **D.** Project documents. Project documents are not part of the project management plan, but they help you manage the project. *Check out "Project documents."*

4. **B.** Cost management plan. The cost management plan defines the level of precision, units of measure, reporting formats, and more. *Review "Develop Project Management Plan: Inputs."*

5. **C.** The change management plan. The change management plan describes how to submit change requests and the process for evaluating them. *Look into "Planning for change."*

6. **B.** Configuration management system. The configuration management system defines how to apply technical and administrative direction and surveillance and much more. *Review "Introduction to configuration management."*

7. **A.** Expert judgment and facilitation techniques. You need people familiar with the product and also your ability to facilitate brainstorming, conflict management, and problem solving. *You'll see reference to this in the section, "Develop Project Management Plan: Tools and Techniques."*

8. **D.** Requirements traceability matrix. The requirements traceability matrix is a project document. *Look at the "Project documents" section.*

9. **C.** The sponsor. You should at least have the project sponsor and the customer sign off on the project management plan. *Check out "Project management plan approval."*

10. **A.** At the kick-off meeting. The kick-off meeting is the right time to introduce the team to the project and the project management plan. *Go over "The project kick-off meeting."*

Chapter 2: Defining Project Scope

Exam Objectives

- **Using the project charter, lessons learned, and requirements gathering techniques (such as interviews, brainstorming, focus groups, and so on), assess the detailed project requirements, assumptions, and constraints to determine project deliverables.**
- **Deconstruct the project into a WBS in order to manage the project scope.**

Everything in the project is a function of the project and product scope. Therefore, getting the scope right and managing it effectively are the best ways to ensure project success. The first step in this process is to plan how you will gather requirements, define project and product scope, organize the scope using a work breakdown structure (WBS), validate the scope with the customer, and control the scope.

Gathering requirements will transition your project from the Initiation process group into the Planning process group. If you need a refresher on process groups, review Book I, Chapter 4. Your ability to fully identify, document, organize, and control requirements and scope is the difference between a successful project and a nightmare!

After you know your requirements, then you can define the scope with a scope statement. When your scope is understood, you develop a WBS to organize the scope into deliverables. This then becomes the foundation for the planning processes in the other knowledge areas, such as time, cost, quality, and so forth.

Quick Assessment

1. (True/False). Project scope refers to all the features and functions you need to deliver to meet project objectives.

2. Completion of the product scope is measured against product ______.

3. (True/False). Requirements are the foundation for developing the work breakdown structure (WBS).

4. Developing requirements begins with analyzing the ______ ______ and the ______ ______.

5. Project deliverables and their acceptance criteria are documented in the ______ ______ ______.

6. The ______ ______ ______ is the foundation for all future planning. It is a deliverable-oriented hierarchical decomposition of the work to be done on the project.

7. The lowest level of the WBS is the ______ ______.

8. The document that provides details about the components in the WBS is the ______ ______.

9. A ______ ______ ______ links requirements to their origin and tracks them throughout the project life cycle.

10. (True/False). The best way to organize a WBS is by phase.

Answers

1 False. Project scope refers to all the work you need to do to create the features and functions. The features and functions are the product scope. *Look at "Project and Product Scope."*

2 Requirements. Product scope completion is measured against requirements. Project scope completion is measured against the project management plan. *Go over "Project and Product Scope."*

3 True. Requirements documentation is an input of the scope statement and the work breakdown structure (WBS). *See "Define Scope: Inputs" and "Create WBS: Inputs."*

4 Project charter, stakeholder register. These two documents are outputs from the Initiating process group and are inputs for collecting requirements. *See "Collect Requirements: Inputs."*

5 Project scope statement. The information from the project charter is progressively elaborated in the project scope statement. Among other information, the deliverables and acceptance criteria are documented in the project scope statement. *See the "Define Scope: Outputs" section.*

6 Work breakdown structure. The work breakdown structure (WBS) organizes the project work. After deliverables are identified in the WBS, the schedule, budget, quality requirements, and procurement decisions can be developed. *Review the information in "Create WBS: Inputs."*

7 Work package. The work package is where you can assign resources. You will see how to decompose work packages into schedule activities in the next chapter. *Go over "Create WBS: Tools and Techniques."*

8 WBS dictionary. The WBS dictionary describes the work that needs to be done in the WBS element, the resources needed, the duration and costs, and other information as appropriate. *See "Create WBS: Outputs" for more information on this topic.*

9 Requirements traceability matrix. The requirements traceability matrix is used to organize and manage requirements throughout the life of the project. *You can find more information on this topic in the "Collect Requirements: Outputs" section.*

10 False. The needs of the project dictate the best way to organize the WBS. *Go over the information in "Create WBS: Outputs."*

Project and Product Scope

All projects start out by defining what is supposed to be accomplished: the *scope*. But did you know about the two types of scope?

Product scope. The features and functions that characterize a product, service, or result.

Project scope. The work performed to deliver a product, service, or result with the specified features and functions.

When reading exam questions, keep in mind that *project scope* and *product scope* look pretty similar. If you read over these two terms quickly, you might misinterpret the question. Take your time on the exam and make sure to read the question right!

Using my threaded example of a childcare center (see the preceding chapters), here's how to identify some of the product and project scope deliverables.

- **Product scope** is easy because it comprises all deliverables for the childcare center. Product scope includes tangible things, such as a playground, a food-prep area, furniture, and so forth.
- **Project scope** is a little trickier, though, because to identify it, you have to think a bit harder. Consider activities, such as preparing procurement documentation for the general contractor, creating the project management plan and project documents, reporting project status for the childcare center, and so forth.

Here are some common types of project scope:

- Documentation
- Testing
- Training
- Planning
- Reporting
- Collecting requirements
- Creating project documents and the project management plan
- Managing risk
- Managing change
- Managing the project team, vendors, and other stakeholders
- All other project management work

Here's another comparison: *Product* scope completion is measured against the product requirements. *Project* scope completion is measured against the project management plan.

Plan Scope Management

Speaking of the project management plan, one of the components in the project management plan is a scope management plan. Because the scope management plan describes how you will plan, manage, and control project and product scope, it is one of the first documents you create. Here is the official definition of the Plan Scope Management process.

Plan Scope Management. The process of creating a scope management plan that documents how the project scope will be defined, validated, and controlled.

Plan Scope Management: Inputs

The primary inputs to consider when developing a scope management plan are the project charter and the project management plan. The project charter contains

- ✦ High-level project description
- ✦ Product characteristics
- ✦ Project statement of work (SOW)

For more information on the project charter, you can check out Book II, Chapter 2.

In the preceding chapter, I discuss how the project management plan is an input to the first planning process in each knowledge area. It provides a framework for planning the project and describes the life cycle for the project. Because the development of the project management plan is iterative, the project management plan is an input to creating the scope management plan — and the scope management plan becomes a component of the project management plan.

The organizational culture, such as whether the organization is very structured or perhaps more agile in its approach to project management will influence scope management planning. Information from past projects as well as policies, procedures, and templates can assist the project manager in developing the scope management plan.

Plan Scope Management: Tools and Techniques

The two techniques used to plan scope management are expert judgment and meetings. Expert judgment can come from team members who understand the scope of the project and how to decompose, validate, and control the scope. Additionally, team members who are experienced with eliciting, documenting, and controlling requirements are helpful in determining how to manage the requirements collection, validation, and control activities on the project.

Meetings should include those stakeholders who will be collecting and managing requirements, validating the scope, and helping control the scope.

Plan Scope Management: Outputs

The scope management plan and the requirements management plan are the two outputs from the Plan Scope Management process.

Scope management plan

The scope management plan describes how the rest of the scope planning processes will be managed. As such, it is an input to the other scope planning processes.

Scope Management Plan. A component of the project or program management plan that describes how the scope will be defined, developed, monitored, controlled, and verified.

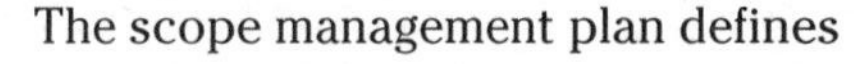

The scope management plan defines

- ✦ Techniques that will be used to define the project scope, such as product analysis or structured workshops
- ✦ How to structure the work breakdown structure (WBS)
- ✦ The elements in the WBS dictionary
- ✦ Methods that will be used to validate deliverables
- ✦ The process for managing and controlling scope change, including membership on the change control board, the change submittal process, and so forth

Requirements management plan

Any project manager can tell you that one of the most common reasons for project failure is the lack of requirements management. This is a key contributor to scope creep. Missing requirements, changes to requirements, and losing control of requirements all lead to failure in meeting project objectives. Therefore, you should establish a plan to manage them.

Requirements management plan. A component of the project or program management plan that describes how requirements will be analyzed, documented, and managed.

Your requirements management plan should describe

- ✦ How you will elaborate your existing requirements (if needed)
- ✦ The method for documenting requirements
- ✦ How you will show traceability
- ✦ Relationships among requirements and methods for verification

Your requirements management plan should also contain a section on configuration management. I discuss configuration management in more detail in Book VII, Chapter 1 (where I discuss change management). For purposes of this process, though, you should establish a system that will do or have the following:

- ✦ Define an identification system, such as a numbering system that allows for parent/child relationships
- ✦ A traceability structure that tracks specified relationships
- ✦ The authority levels to add, delete, or change requirements
- ✦ A system to audit and determine whether the process is being used and is effective

Some projects assign a Requirements Manager to control requirements. This person is in charge of documenting, managing, tracking, controlling, and verifying requirements. In some organizations, a Business Analyst performs this role.

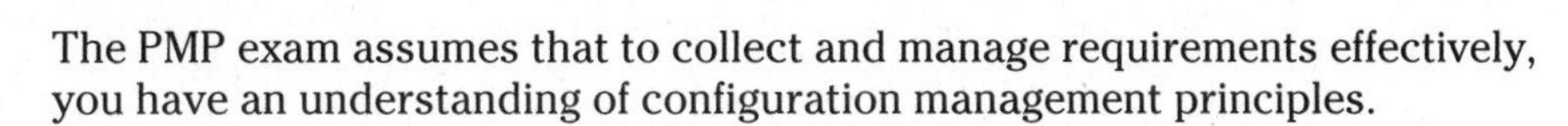

The PMP exam assumes that to collect and manage requirements effectively, you have an understanding of configuration management principles.

Collect Requirements

One of the first questions you should ask when you get a new project is, "What are the requirements?" Another way of asking this is, "What do you need? What do you want? What conditions have to be met for you to be satisfied?"

Requirement. A condition or capability that is required to be present in a product, service or result to satisfy a contract or other formally imposed specification. Requirements include the quantified and documented needs, wants, and expectations of the sponsor, customer, and other stakeholders.

Collect Requirements. The process of determining, documenting, and managing stakeholder needs and requirements to meet the project objectives.

You can group or categorize requirements however it makes sense for your project. Some examples of requirements categories include

✦ **Solution requirements,** such as functional and nonfunctional requirements. Nonfunctional requirements include reliability, supportability, performance, and so forth.

✦ **Stakeholder requirements,** such as communication and reporting requirements.

✦ **Project requirements,** such as business or project management requirements.

✦ **Quality requirements** that define the conductions that need to be met for the end result to be acceptable.

While you collect requirements, you should also determine how to prove that they are met. To help you do that, make sure that all requirements are quantifiable. In other words, stating that you want "the employee hiring process to work better" isn't quantifiable. Comparatively, stating that you want "the process reduced from 16 steps to 7 steps" is quantifiable. Stating that you want "the new process to be 40% faster" is also quantifiable.

Collect Requirements: Inputs

Stakeholders are the sources of requirements, so you need to start with your stakeholder register. As I discuss in the preceding minibook, some people also document high-level requirements or expectations — such as "improve employee productivity by 20%," or "the new system needs to be easy to maintain" — in the stakeholder register. If this is the case for your project, you can progressively elaborate the high-level requirements into detailed requirements in this process. You may document how you are going to manage stakeholder engagement in a stakeholder management plan — for example, you may manage external stakeholders differently than internal stakeholders, or you may collect requirements from technical stakeholders differently than business stakeholders.

You also need to have your project charter. As I also discuss in the preceding minibook, the charter describes the justification for the project and should include high-level requirements.

The scope management plan and requirements management plan developed in the previous process provide guidance in eliciting requirements to develop the product scope.

Using information from your charter, stakeholder register, and various management plans, you can begin gathering and documenting project requirements. During this process, you transition from the high-level business requirements that you documented in the charter to detailed requirements for the product and project.

Collect Requirements: Tools and Techniques

Because all projects are different and because some projects have many stakeholders, there are several ways you can collect requirements. The most obvious one is interviewing people, but you can also use focus groups, workshops, surveys, brainstorming, and other group techniques.

In addition to the inputs listed in the previous section, the exam assumes you have knowledge of requirement-gathering techniques, as discussed in the following sections.

To perform these activities well, you're expected to have skills in negotiating, active listening, brainstorming, and facilitating.

Interviews

Interviews can be informal or formal, done one-on-one or conducted in groups. Many times, an interview is the first step in identifying requirements.

Using my running example of the childcare center, you might meet with the facilities manager, several parents, and the legal department to discover their product and project requirements.

Focus groups

Focus groups are a more formal method of gathering requirements. A group of prequalified or preselected stakeholders is brought together with a facilitator who asks questions about the stakeholder's expectations for the end product. When selecting members for a focus group, make sure to get a diverse group. You don't want the information you collect to be skewed or represent only one viewpoint. Focus groups can have an established set of questions, or they can be more of a dialog with which you generate and capture ideas, feelings, and reactions.

For the childcare center, you could bring together a group of 5 to 10 parents and discuss their needs and expectations for the center.

Facilitated workshops

For larger projects — especially IT, high-tech, or new product development projects — facilitated workshops can be highly productive. Key stakeholders are brought together to identify their requirements and work through any conflicting requirements.

The IT sector often has joint application development (JAD) sessions. In these sessions, system engineers, end users, developers, and business analysts can all work together to identify product features and functions.

Group creativity techniques

"Group creativity techniques" is a catch-all phrase for working with a group of people to generate information. There are a number of group creativity techniques, many of which you will no doubt recognize:

- Brainstorming
- Nominal group technique
- Delphi technique
- Idea/mind mapping
- Affinity diagram
- Multicriteria decision analysis

By the way, these aren't presented in any particular order. No technique is better or more common than another technique.

Brainstorming

When you employ brainstorming to identify requirements, make sure you have representation from all the various stakeholder groups. This helps ensure you have input from everyone impacted by the product and project.

Nominal group technique

The nominal group technique is often used in conjunction with brainstorming. When all the requirements have been generated (or as many as can be generated at the time), the group ranks them. This can be as simple as members listing their top five requirements. The requirements are then prioritized for development, based upon the stakeholder ranking.

Delphi technique

The Delphi technique was designed to bring a group of experts to consensus. The thought process is that a group of experts reaching a conclusion is better than any one expert's conclusion.

Delphi technique

The RAND think tank developed the Delphi technique for forecasting (thus the reference to the Oracle of Delphi, a Greek prophetess in the eighth century BC) the impact of technology on warfare.

Some benefits to using the Delphi technique are that it allows you to get information from a wide group of people that are geographically disbursed, and you can do it easily by using an automated survey tool.

Here are the steps for the Delphi technique:

1. A group of stakeholders or experts are identified, depending on the needs of the project.
2. Each stakeholder is sent a list of high-level requirements and asked to expand that list and send it back to the facilitator.
3. The facilitator compiles a comprehensive list of requirements and sends it back to the stakeholders for prioritization.
4. Each stakeholder prioritizes the requirements and sends it back to the facilitator.
5. Several rounds of this take place until you can reach a reasonable amount of consensus on the requirements and their priority.

One of the important things to know about the Delphi technique is that stakeholders must remain anonymous to each other, at least for the first couple of rounds. This allows free and unbiased participation by participants. Being anonymous also frees stakeholders from being intimidated by people with more knowledge, or a bigger title, or more experience. Sometimes, the facilitator will modify the technique by conducting a round or two anonymously and then gather the group to finalize the list.

If you were using this technique to gather requirements for the childcare center, here are some example questions you could send to the parents:

- What type of outdoor activities would you like at the center?
- What type of indoor activities would you like at the center?
- What topics would you like to see taught?
- What types of food do you think should be available?

After you generate options, you could then ask the parents to rank all the possible requirements.

Idea/mind mapping

A *mind map* is a technique that starts with the idea (or in this case, the project) in the middle, and then stakeholders branch out from the central idea and generate more ideas (or in this case, requirements).

A mind map can give you an overview of the project. This overview allows you to determine whether there is an imbalance in requirements or whether one set of needs was weighted more heavily than others. Figure 2-1 shows a mind map for the childcare center. You can see the overview of the activities planned for the children.

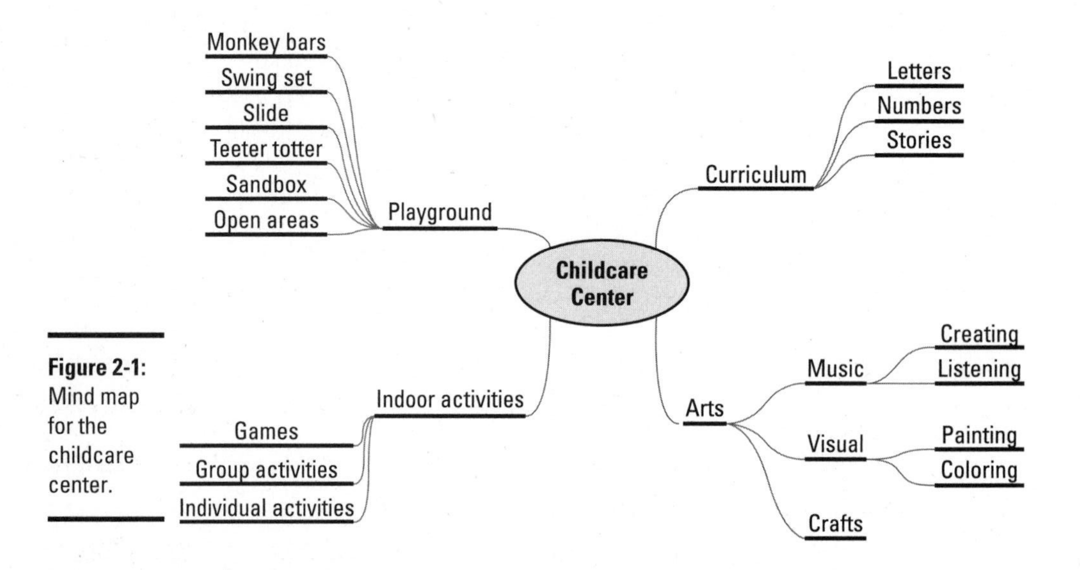

Figure 2-1: Mind map for the childcare center.

Affinity diagram

An *affinity diagram* takes ideas and groups them into categories with similar ideas or requirements. Thus, they are grouped with ideas that they have an "affinity" with. Affinity diagrams can be used alone or in conjunction with brainstorming and the nominal group technique. Figure 2-2 shows a sample affinity diagram with the same information as the mind map, but the display here is in a list versus the visual display in the mind map.

Figure 2-2: Affinity diagram for the childcare center.

Arts	Curriculum	Playground	Indoor Activities

• Music
  ∘ Listening
  ∘ Creating
• Visual
  ∘ Painting
  ∘ Coloring
• Crafts
	• Letters
	• Numbers
	• Stories
		• Open areas
		• Sandbox
		• Monkey bars
		• Swing set
		• Slide
		• Teeter totter
			• Games
			• Group activities
			• Individual activities

Multicriteria decision analysis

When gathering requirements, you often need to balance several criteria to determine the best set or requirements for a product, service, or result. Multicriteria decision analysis identifies the various criteria that you will use to evaluate requirements and then assigns a weighted value to each criteria. Then solutions are rated against the criteria.

For the childcare center, assume that requirements for the cafeteria vendor were

- ✦ Healthy meals
- ✦ Locally sourced ingredients
- ✦ Experience in a preschool environment
- ✦ Price

Three vendors were evaluated against all criteria, which were weighted differently and then ranked on a scale of 1 to 5 (1 being low, and 5 being high). You could set up a table to show how each vendor scored to establish a quantitative method for selecting the best vendor based on the requirements.

Vendor		*Banana Bob's*		*Jodi's Kitchen*		*Tasty Tots*	
Criterion	*Weight*	*Rating*	*Score*	*Rating*	*Score*	*Rating*	*Score*
Healthy	.50	2	1	3	1.5	4	2
Locally sourced	.15	3	.45	5	.75	4	.60
Preschool experience	.25	4	1	3	.75	3	.75
Price	.10	5	.50	4	.40	3	.30
Total	**1.0**		**2.95**		**3.40**		**3.65**

To determine the score, follow these steps:

1. **Identify the criteria you will use to evaluate the requirements.**
2. **Establish a weight for each criterion.**

   The sum of the criteria weights needs to add to 1.0.
3. **Rate each vendor with regards to how well they meet the criteria.**
4. **Multiply the weight times the rating to determine a score for each criterion.**
5. **Sum the scores for each vendor and select the vendor with the highest score.**

Combining group creativity techniques

You aren't limited to using just one group creativity technique. Using the running childcare center example, you can see how a specific technique is well suited for one phase and then easily flows into using another technique.

Start by having a meeting with 20 or so parents. Then, see how your requirement gathering evolves:

1. **Brainstorming:** You lead a session to collect parents' needs, wants, and expectations, all of which are written on sticky notes and put on the wall.
2. **Affinity diagram:** You ask the parents to come up to the wall and start putting the sticky note ideas into groups. You'll probably see some negotiating about how to arrange and group the sticky notes, but eventually, people will settle on something they can live with.
3. **Nominal group technique:** Finally, you prioritize the sticky notes into your list of requirements.

Group decision-making techniques

Some of the preceding techniques can help you make decisions, such as the Delphi technique and the nominal group technique. These decisions are based on the group coming to a unanimous decision, or at least having a majority in consensus. Sometimes, though, the project manager has to establish a structure for making decisions to finalize the requirements. For those times, many decision-making techniques are available. The *PMBOK Guide* identifies four methods of reaching group decisions:

- **Unanimity:** Everyone agrees.
- **Majority:** More than one-half the people agree to a course of action.
- **Plurality:** The largest group of people supports a decision, even if they're not the majority.
- **Dictatorship:** One person makes the decision.

There really isn't one best way to make a decision. It would be nice if every decision had unanimous approval, but that isn't realistic. Therefore, you have to apply the technique that makes the most sense in any given situation. This can sometimes require a trade-off on getting complete group buy-in and, for the sake of time, making a decision and moving on.

Questionnaires and surveys

Questionnaires and surveys are a good way to gather information from large groups of stakeholders. You can automate the process by asking people to answer a set of questions online and then collating the results. This makes completing and submitting the information fast and easy. If you give people multiple-choice questions or ask them to rate information quantitatively, you can easily total and tabulate your results.

For the childcare center example, you could use this technique to prioritize playground equipment choices, hours of operation, food options, and the like.

Observations

Observation is useful when you want to see how end users interact in a scenario or with a product. Observation can also help you understand unconscious or unspoken requirements.

If you were looking at options for designing the floor plan for the example childcare center, you might observe several similar sites and watch the traffic flow for dropping off children, how the children migrate from activity to activity, what the process is for picking up children, and so on. Then you could design the site to best accommodate those processes.

Prototypes

Prototypes are used to create a model or a mock-up of an end product. They might have limited or no functionality, but they give stakeholders an opportunity to visualize the end product and make changes or additions to the requirements early in the process. For the childcare center example, the architect might create a model and discuss the various features and processes that would be used in the center.

Prototyping is often used in new product development, agile software development, and construction.

Benchmarking

Benchmarking involves identifying best practices in an industry or organization and comparing the existing practices against best practices as a means to improve performance. Test scores and customer satisfaction scores are examples of measurements that can be benchmarked.

Context diagrams

Context diagrams show a business system or model and depict how people or other systems interact with it. Oftentimes in context diagrams, people providing inputs or receiving outputs are referred to as *actors*. The benefit of a context diagram is that it shows a visual display of a process and the interactions associated with the process.

Document Analysis

Document analysis consists of analyzing documentation that can help in identifying requirements. Examples of documentation you might analyze to elicit requirements include the following:

- Process flows
- Data flow diagrams
- Interface documentation
- Use cases
- Issue and defect logs
- Policies, procedures, forms, regulations, and information from previous similar projects

Collect Requirements: Outputs

As you collect your requirements, remember to document and organize them so that it's easy to demonstrate when they are complete, as well as how they impact and interact with other requirements. Additionally, you want to think about how to manage and control your requirements.

Requirements documentation

Depending on the type and complexity of your project, your requirements documentation can be relatively simple or very complex. One way to keep requirements organized is to create a requirements register that documents all the requirements for the project. You can do this in a table or a spreadsheet for small projects. For large complex projects, software programs can help you organize, track, and manage requirements. A simple requirements register should at least include the following:

- Stakeholder name or position
- Requirement description
- Category or type of requirement
- Priority
- Acceptance criteria

Writing requirements

Writing good requirements can be challenging. Attributes of good requirements include the following:

- **Clear and unambiguous:** You goal is one — and only one — way to interpret the requirement. Having a quantitative or measurable statement will help here.
- **Concise requirements:** There is only one requirement in each statement.
- **Testable:** You can prove a requirement has been met.
- **Consistent:** Different requirements can't conflict. For example, you can't have a requirement that personal information is encrypted to protect privacy yet another requirement that a person's e-mail address is available.
- **Complete:** All known requirements are documented.
- **Accepted:** Your stakeholders have signed off on the requirements.

Categorizing requirements

As you start to progressively elaborate your requirements, you want to categorize them to maintain visibility and control. Commonly used categories include

- **Product requirements**
  - Technical
  - Performance
  - Size, weight, and appearance
  - Maintainability
  - Environmental and interface
  - Safety and security
  - Operability
- **Project requirements**
  - Business requirements
  - Interface requirements
  - Training and documentation
  - Cost and schedule

Clearly, the nature of the product will determine your requirement categories. The *PMBOK Guide,* Fifth Edition has additional examples that you should be familiar with as well.

It is very important in your job, and for the exam, that your stakeholders agree to the requirements. You may want to get sign-off or some other written form of agreement for the requirements.

Requirements traceability matrix

Because requirements drive scope, and because scope determines the schedule, cost, and everything else about the project, you should be able to tie your requirements to various aspects of the project. A *requirements traceability matrix* can help you do that. For complex projects, you will need software that manages all the requirements and relationships for you. For simpler projects, though, you can create a database or spreadsheet. Here are some examples of what you'll be tracing and tracking:

- How your requirements trace to a deliverable
- How your requirements trace to an objective
- How detailed requirements relate to high-level requirements
- How technical requirements relate to business requirements
- Which verification and validation method will be used for a requirement
- Which stakeholder provided the requirement

Having this information documented and easily accessible will simplify the process of analyzing the impact of changes and help you understand the relationships between requirements.

Define Scope

Defining scope covers defining the project and product scope in more detail. Clearly defined scope enables project success. I'm sure you've been on a project where the scope was not clearly defined, or where it kept changing, or where stakeholders had different opinions about the project scope. Ill-defined scope leads to conflict, rework, and stakeholder dissatisfaction. Therefore, time spent to fully understand project and product scope is time well spent.

Define Scope. The process of developing a detailed description of the project and product.

Define Scope: Inputs

You use the high-level information from the project charter, guidance from the scope management plan, and the more detailed requirements documentation to develop a project scope statement.

Project scope statement. The description of the project scope, major deliverables, assumptions, and constraints.

The project scope statement helps stakeholder understand what is in and out of scope and provides a documented basis for making decisions. For organizations with robust project management processes, you will probably find policies and procedures that give direction to defining the scope. You will probably also find some templates as well.

Define Scope: Tools and Techniques

To move from a high-level understanding of the project, as documented in the project charter and as detailed in the requirements documentation, you need to work with people who understand the product, project, and the technical details. Another way of saying this is that you need expert judgment, and that might come in the form of team members, consultants, customers, or professional organizations.

You might opt to gather these experts and have a facilitated workshop as described in the earlier section, "Collect Requirements: Inputs." A JAD session will often assist in collecting the information needed to develop a robust scope statement.

In practice, gathering requirements and documenting the project scope happen at the same time. It is an iterative cycle that continues until the requirements are complete and information on the project scope is fully defined.

Product analysis

For many projects, the end result is one or more products that can be broken down into component parts or deliverables. By analyzing the end product and determining the component elements, you can get a better understanding of the deliverables and appropriate acceptance criteria.

Depending on the type of project you're working on, you might hear this process referred to as *system engineering, product breakdown, requirements analysis,* or *value engineering.*

Alternatives generation

In project management, there is usually more than one way to go about meeting objectives. You can take into consideration the benefits, costs, risks, and feasibility of various options, be it as simple as deciding whether to outsource work or do work in-house, or assessing whether to use an existing product as a starting place, or reinventing something by starting with a blank slate.

As your team goes through the process of analyzing the product and generating alternatives, project scope becomes clearer, and you can begin to develop the project scope statement.

Define Scope: Outputs

The project scope statement can be as detailed as needed to understand and control the scope. At a minimum, it should include, either directly or by reference to other documents, the following:

- **Product scope description:** A narrative description of the product. It should contain more detail than the project charter.
- **Acceptance criteria:** A description of the conditions or criteria that must be met for the customer to accept the final product or product components.
- **Deliverables:** Include not only the product deliverables but also the project deliverables. This can include training, documentation, reports, research, and the like.
- **Project exclusions:** Clarifying what is *not* in scope. These exclusions should be implicitly stated to minimize misunderstandings and conflicts later in the project.

One of the easiest ways to control your scope is to clearly define what is excluded. Many stakeholders will assume that if something is not excluded, it is included. Those of us who have fought this battle a few times have learned to insert this simple sentence into the exclusions: "Anything not specifically included, is excluded."

- **Project constraints:** A limitation or restriction. Many times, a fixed budget or contractually agreed-upon milestone dates are constraints. Certain regulatory standards are also constraints.

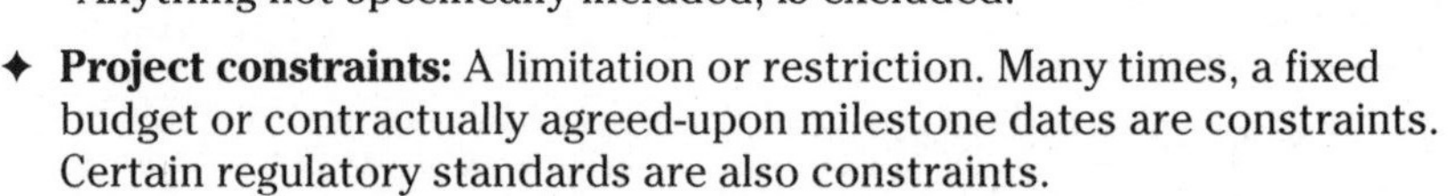

- **Project assumptions:** Aspects of the project that are thought to be true but aren't proven should be documented. For example, you could assume that a cafeteria food service vendor will do any food preparation. This won't be certain until a contract for the extra work is completed, but at this point, you can assume this to be true for planning purposes.

Assumptions. Factors in the planning process that are considered true, real, or certain without proof or demonstration.

Constraint. A limiting factor that affects the execution of a project, program, portfolio, or process.

An example of a schedule constraint is any limitation or restraint in the project schedule that affects when a schedule activity can be scheduled, such as a fixed delivery date or milestone.

Many project managers move their assumptions to an Assumption Log as they are progressively elaborated. You can refer to the log in the scope statement, or keep high-level assumptions in the scope statement and more detailed ones in the Assumption Log.

Figure 2-3 shows a sample project scope statement for my example Childcare facility.

PROJECT SCOPE STATEMENT

Project Title: Childcare Center **Date Prepared:** May 15

Product Scope Description:

Daycare facility. The 20,000 square foot facility will have a place to check children in the morning. 75 cubbies will be available for children's coats and other personal effects. There will be a large open area where several groups of children can participate in group activities with their child care specialist. There will be separate areas for the following needs:

- Children 3 months to 1 year will have a separate area
- There will be a separate area for children who are not feeling well
- There will be a breakout area for music
- There will be a breakout area for art projects
- There will be a library of picture books and pre-school reading materials

Mats will be provided for nap time and quiet time.
All furniture will be child-sized with the highest safety ratings.
The kitchen area will have a refrigerator to store food for snacks and cafeteria prepared lunches. A separate refrigerator will be available for children who bring their own lunch.
Playground. There will be 2 playgrounds, one for children 2 and under and one for children 3 and older. The playgrounds will be located in a courtyard that is not visible or accessible to the street. Playgrounds will be equipped with the safest equipment available. Ground pads will be made of ecologically friendly material. An outdoor water area will be available for warmer months.

Product Acceptance Criteria:

The daycare facility will be accepted when the requirements* have been met, the inspections are complete and the punch list has been completed.
The playground will be accepted when the requirements* have been met, the inspections are complete and the punch list has been completed.

*All requirements are documented in the requirements documentation.

Project Deliverables:

- Daycare operations manual
- Safety and security procedures
- Daycare staff and administration orientation and training
- Project management plan, including
  - Project schedule
  - Project budget
  - Requirements management plan
  - Change management plan
  - Procurement management plan
  - Communications management plan
  - Staffing plan
  - Training plan
- Requirements documentation
- Risk register
- Assumption log
- Issue log
- Change log
- Monthly status reports

Page 1 of 2

Figure 2-3: Childcare center project scope statement.

PROJECT SCOPE STATEMENT

Product Exclusions:

Any children of parents that are not Cynergy2, Inc. employees
Any medical expertise other than basic First Aid
After hours care
After school care
Care for any children older than 5 or younger than 3 months
Pre-school or kindergarten education
Anything not specifically included is excluded

Project Constraints:

Center must be complete by December 31
Center must be staffed by January 1
Budget is fixed at 2.5 million
All children must be current on vaccines
No children with a temperature over 100 or who are actively contagious are permitted on site
All childcare specialists must pass a Department of Justice background check and drug screening

Project Assumptions:

There are sufficient numbers of childcare center architects to allow a competitive bid
There are sufficient numbers of trained childcare specialists to fully staff the center
All funding will be available as needed, within the budget
Team members will be available as promised
There will be sufficient interest to fill the 75 slots
Existing food, janitorial and maintenance vendors will be able to expand their contracts to include childcare center work without substantial increase in rates

Page 2 of 2

Create WBS

The project scope statement provides an overview of the entire project scope. The requirements provide detailed information about the objectives, needs, and expectations. This information is necessary to successfully manage the project, but it doesn't organize the information in a way that allows the team to easily plan, manage, and control the project. That's what a work breakdown structure (WBS) is for. The WBS organizes the project scope. It starts at a high level and progresses downward to decompose the deliverables into finer levels of detail so that the team can identify all the deliverables necessary to meet the project objectives.

Create WBS. The process of subdividing project deliverables and project work into smaller, more manageable components.

Work breakdown structure. A hierarchical decomposition of the total work to be carried out by the project team to accomplish the project objectives and create the required deliverables.

The WBS organizes and defines the total scope of the project. Many practitioners create WBSs that are *deliverable-oriented* — meaning that the WBS is based on the end products, not the *work* necessary to create the end products. The work is represented in the activity list that is part of the schedule. I discuss the schedule in the next chapter.

Create WBS: Inputs

The scope management plan, the scope statement, and the requirements documentation are the key inputs for this process. You might be able to use certain organizational process assets to help create your WBS. In particular, if your organization does similar projects (for example, creating websites, designing networks, product development, or even construction), there might be a template available you can use to begin your WBS. Of course, your particular project will need to modify the template to reflect the unique aspects of your project, but templates and information from prior projects provide a nice starting point.

Create WBS: Tools and Techniques

Decomposition and expert judgment are the only techniques used in developing the WBS. Here is the *PMBOK Guide* definition of decomposition.

Decomposition. A technique used for dividing and subdividing the project scope and project deliverables into smaller, more manageable parts.

The PMP Examination Outline uses the term *deconstruct.* The *PMBOK Guide* uses the term *decompose*. They mean the same thing: taking a chunk of work and breaking it down into smaller chunks of work.

Expert judgment comes into play when project teams decompose the WBS by starting with the highest level, which is the project. The next level down is how you will organize the project. Many technology projects use the project life cycle as the next level down. However, that's certainly not the only way to organize the WBS, and perhaps not even the best way. Other options include major deliverables or geography (given multiple locations). After this level is established, it's just a matter of taking each high-level element and decomposing it into finer levels of detail. This approach — the most common — is a top-down approach.

The converse approach is a bottom-up approach, which starts with the lowest level of deliverables and works up the chart to see where deliverables naturally group themselves.

The lowest level of the WBS is called a *work package,* which is the level where duration and cost can be estimated reliably.

Because the WBS represents all the work in the project, you must make sure you aren't overlooking anything! Sometimes people forget to put in "project management." If you need a WBS to reliably estimate cost and duration, you will significantly underestimate if you leave out the project management deliverables!

I usually put project management as a box in the second level down. And, this is the only branch of the WBS where I might not constrain myself to identifying deliverables only. So much of our job is action-oriented that I might put an entry such as *stakeholder management,* or *communication,* or *change management.* These placeholders identify the type of work I do when I manage a project. Another option is to put the process groups under project management. You will see both these options a bit later in the chapter.

As I mention, the work package is the lowest level of the WBS, but reporting progress at the work package level is probably too detailed. A large project has hundreds of work packages. You can't report cost and schedule status for each one and then expect the sponsor or steering committee to read your report! Instead, you establish *control accounts,* which are where you can reasonably report progress. A control account encompasses the work packages beneath it and can have multiple work packages. Looking at it from the other side, each work package can belong to only one control account. Here are the definitions for work packages and control accounts.

Work package. The work defined at the lowest level of the work breakdown structure for which cost and duration can be estimated and managed.

Control account. A management control point where scope, budget, actual cost, and schedule are integrated and compared to earned value for performance measurement.

You might not be able to define all the deliverables in the WBS at the start of the project. Commonly, the WBS is established at a high level (three levels or so) at the start of the project, and as more information is known, the levels are further decomposed. This is an example of progressive elaboration known as *rolling wave planning.*

Rolling wave planning provides more detail for work happening in the near future, but leaves work further out in the future at a higher level. This doesn't mean you don't have to account for the cost and schedule for future work; you just hold it at a higher level of detail until you know what the lower level of detail looks like.

Figure 2-4 shows part of a WBS for the childcare center. This WBS is arranged by phases at level 2 along with project management. You can see that the earlier work in the project is decomposed to a lower level than the work later in the project (construction, operational readiness), demonstrating rolling wave planning. I would consider Requirements and Plans to be control accounts and the deliverables under them as work packages.

Because the WBS is deliverable-oriented, it comprises nouns, not verbs. Many people have difficulty thinking in terms of deliverables instead of actions. With practice, it gets easier: Just think in terms of nouns.

Deliverable	***Verb***	***Comment***
Playground equipment	Install playground equipment	"Install" implies action. On the WBS, you want only the deliverable.
Curriculum plan	Plan curriculum	Where you place the terms changes the deliverable from a noun to a verb.

To see the converse in action — decomposing work into verbs — see the next chapter.

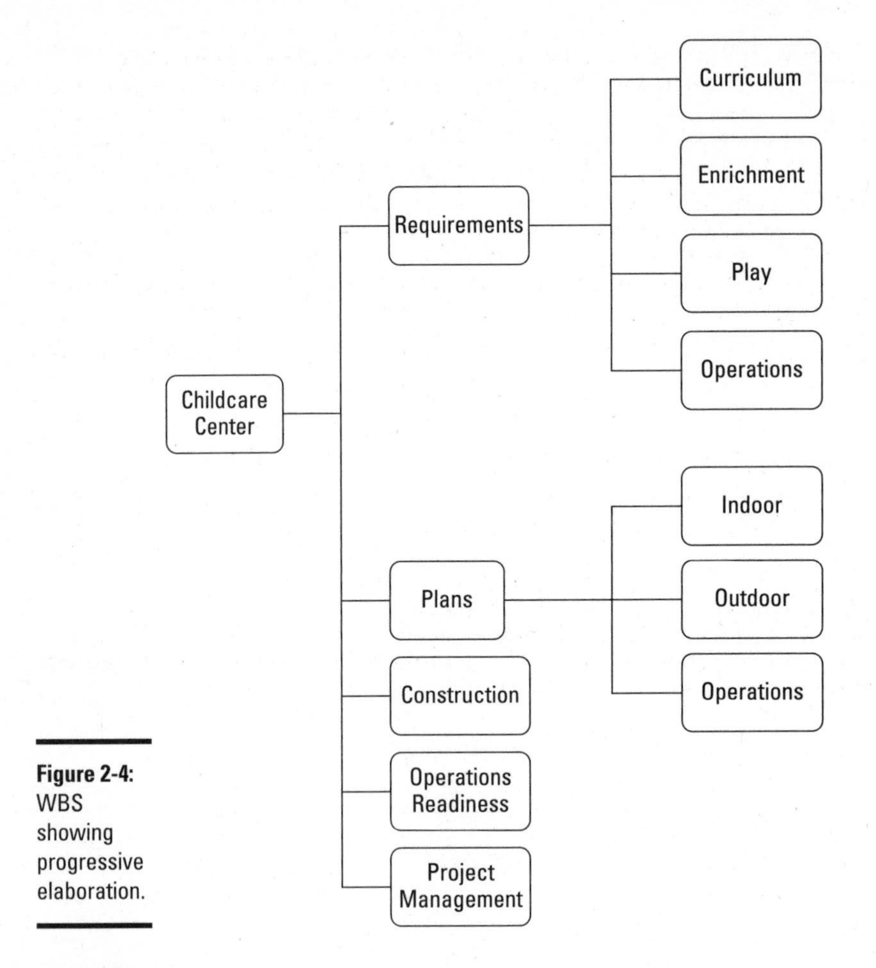

Figure 2-4: WBS showing progressive elaboration.

You can arrange your WBS with the project at the top level and deconstruct it downward, or you can approach the deconstruction shown in Figure 2-4 and deconstruct from left to right.

Not all branches of the WBS can be decomposed to the same level. Some work might stay at three levels because that level is where the deliverables are. Other branches might be decomposed five or six levels.

I've been asked numerous times how low to go on a WBS. The answer is, "That depends." For a very large project, a work package might represent $1 million worth of work. For a small project, it might represent $25,000 worth of work, or even less.

When your WBS becomes fairly robust, you should develop a numeric coding structure to keep track of the levels. For instance, the first level is 1.0. At the second level, you would have 1.1, 1.2, 1.3, and so on. The third level would have 1.1.1, 1.1.2, 1.1.3, and then 1.2.1. 1.2.2, and so on. You can see a numeric coding structure in upcoming Figures 2-5 and 2-6. Many organizations that do large projects already have a coding structure as part of their organizational process assets.

To make it easier to remember, look at these steps:

1. Analyze the scope statement and requirements to understand the project work.
2. Determine how you will structure the WBS (by major deliverable, subproject, phase, and so on).
3. Decompose the work until you have work packages or until you can't realistically decompose it into deliverables.
4. Identify control accounts for reporting purposes.
5. Establish a numeric coding structure.
6. Verify that your WBS is well organized and decomposed to an appropriate level.

Now you're ready for the outputs of this process.

Create WBS: Outputs

Here are a couple of samples of a WBS for the childcare center so you can see different approaches. Figure 2-5 shows a WBS decomposed by major deliverables.

Either approach to the WBS will work. Maybe you would arrange it differently. There is no one correct way to arrange your WBS. The point is to make sure all the work is represented in the deliverables with nothing left out. It should be complete and logical, and help you manage and control your project. So set it up in a way that works for you and your team.

Note, too, that the WBS samples in Figures 2-5 and 2-6 are presented in outline format. Many times, people start with sticky notes and develop a WBS that looks like an organizational chart, as shown in Figure 2-4. You can do that down to about three levels (or about 50 sticky notes) before it gets too unwieldy. Still, this approach is a good way to get a global picture of the project.

Childcare Center
- 1 Indoor
  - 1.1 Blueprints
  - 1.2 Carpentry
    - 1.2.1 Rough
    - 1.2.2 Finish
  - 1.3 Electrical
    - 1.3.1 Rough
    - 1.3.2 Finish
  - 1.4 Plumbing
    - 1.4.1 Rough
    - 1.4.2 Finish
  - 1.5 HVAC
    - 1.5.1 Rough
    - 1.5.2 Finish
  - 1.6 Finishes
    - 1.6.1 Flooring
    - 1.6.2 Paint
    - 1.6.3 Windows
    - 1.6.4 Doors
  - 1.7 Permits
    - 1.7.1 Building
    - 1.7.2 Occupancy
- 2 Outdoor
  - 2.1 Design
  - 2.2 Landscape
    - 2.2.1 Trees
    - 2.2.2 Plants
  - 2.3 Equipment
    - 2.3.1 3 months to 2 years
    - 2.3.2 3+ years
  - 2.4 Surfaces
    - 2.4.1 Pads
    - 2.4.2 Cement
  - 2.5 Permits
- 3 Operations Preparation
  - 3.1 Supplies
  - 3.2 Staffing
    - 3.2.1 Administration
    - 3.2.2 Childcare
  - 3.3 Documentation
- 4 Project Management
  - 4.1 Vendors
    - 4.1 New
    - 4.2 Existing
  - 4.2 Project management plan
  - 4.3 Stakeholder management

Figure 2-5: WBS based on major deliverables.

Figure 2-6 shows a WBS arranged by phases.

```
Childcare Center
        1  Requirements
           1.1   Curriculum
           1.2   Enrichment
           1.3   Play
           1.4   Operations
        2  Plans
           2.1   Indoors
           2.2   Outdoors
           2.3   Operations
        3  Construction
           3.1   Indoors
           3.2   Outdoors
        4  Operations Readiness
           4.1   Staffing
           4.2   Training
           4.3   Documentation
           4.4   Permits
        5  Project management
           5.1   Initiating
           5.2   Planning
           5.3   Executing
           5.4   Monitoring and Control
           5.5   Closing
```

Figure 2-6: WBS based on phases.

WBS dictionary

Your WBS is a key output of this process, but there are others. The *WBS dictionary* is an output that's used on larger projects to provide a detailed explanation for each component of the WBS.

Work breakdown structure dictionary. A document that provides detailed deliverable, activity, and scheduling information about each component in the work breakdown structure.

For each WBS component, the WBS dictionary includes a brief definition of the scope or statement of work, defined deliverable(s), a list of associated activities, and a list of milestones. Other information may include responsible organization, start and end dates, resources required, an estimate of cost, charge number, contract information, quality requirements, and technical references to facilitate performance of the work.

You won't need a WBS dictionary for all projects, but a WBS dictionary is helpful as a communication tool for large projects to make sure that all the details of a work package are fully understood. Figure 2-7 shows a sample blank WBS dictionary form.

WBS DICTIONARY

Project Title: ________ Date Prepared: ________

Work Package Name: WBS ID:

Description of Work:

Milestones: Due Dates:

1.
2.
3.

ID	Activity	Resource	Labor			Material			Total Cost
			Hours	Rate	Total	Units	Cost	Total	

Quality Requirements:

Acceptance Criteria:

Technical Information:

Contract Information:

Figure 2-7: Sample WBS dictionary form.

Scope baseline

The *scope baseline* is composed of three elements: the scope statement, the WBS, and the WBS dictionary. This is the sum total of the project scope, and is part of the project management plan. Any changes to project or product scope will impact one or more of the elements in the scope baseline, and most likely many other project documents as well.

Scope baseline. The approved version of a scope statement, work breakdown structure (WBS), and its associated WBS dictionary, that can be changed only through formal change control procedures and is used as a basis for comparison.

The scope baseline should be tightly controlled after it's agreed upon.

When creating your WBS, WBS dictionary, and scope baseline, you might need to go back and update or modify other project documents.

Key Terms

I introduce you to many new terms in this chapter. You may be familiar with some of these from your job. Sometimes they are in use, but known by different names. For purposes of the exam, make sure you can identify the concept with the term presented here.

- Scope management plan
- Requirements management plan
- Nominal group technique
- Delphi technique
- Affinity diagram
- Multicriteria decision analysis
- Requirements traceability matrix
- Project scope statement
- Assumptions
- Constraint
- Work breakdown structure
- Work package
- Control account
- Work breakdown structure dictionary
- Scope baseline

ter Summary

- Project scope management is concerned with project scope and product scope.
- A scope management plan and requirements management plan provide guidance for the remaining scope planning processes.
- Understanding the project and product scope starts with gathering stakeholder requirements.
- Requirements need to be documented in a clear, unambiguous, and concise way. They need to be testable, consistent, complete, and accepted by stakeholders.
- The project scope statement records the product scope description, product acceptance criteria, project deliverables, and project exclusions.
- The work breakdown structure (WBS) organizes and defines the total scope of the project.
- The WBS dictionary is an extension of the WBS that provides detail about the WBS components.
- The scope statement, WBS, and WBS dictionary make up the scope baseline.

Prep Test

1 **A condition or capability that is required to be present in a product, service, or result to satisfy a contract or other formally imposed document is a**

A ❍ Specification
B ❍ Requirement
C ❍ Stakeholder need
D ❍ Metric

2 **Monday morning, your project sponsor stops by your cubicle and tells you that he needs you to create a new report that correlates each work package on your project to the company's strategic objectives. He needs it by the end of the week. The work to create the report is an example of**

A ❍ Project scope
B ❍ Product scope
C ❍ Requirements traceability
D ❍ Stakeholder expectation

3 **While collecting requirements for the new accounts payable system, you walk around to see how various people use the existing system. You notice a lot of workarounds, shortcuts, and duplication of effort. This technique of collecting requirements is**

A ❍ Observation
B ❍ Focus groups
C ❍ Interviewing
D ❍ Facilitated workshops

4 **If you want to gather information from a large number of people and have it easily quantified, what is the best tool to use?**

A ❍ Prototyping
B ❍ Delphi technique
C ❍ Interviewing
D ❍ Surveys and questionnaires

5 **You expect that you will have four full-time and two part-time programmers on your team from December through March. Therefore, you plan your work to account for these resources. You would document this as a(n) ______ in the ______ ______ ______.**

A ❍ Constraint, project scope statement
B ❍ Assumption, project scope statement
C ❍ Requirement, project requirements documentation
D ❍ Requirement, requirement traceability matrix

6 What information do you need to create a project scope statement?

- **A** ❍ Project charter and requirements documentation
- **B** ❍ Requirements documentation and project management plan
- **C** ❍ Requirements management plan and project charter
- **D** ❍ Project charter and WBS

7 You need to identify and organize all the deliverables for your project. What is the appropriate way to do that?

- **A** ❍ Create a project scope statement.
- **B** ❍ Hold a JAD session.
- **C** ❍ Develop a WBS dictionary.
- **D** ❍ Create a WBS.

8 The level used to report status is

- **A** ❍ Control account
- **B** ❍ Work package
- **C** ❍ Level 3
- **D** ❍ Determined based upon the size of the project

9 Which document records information about WBS elements?

- **A** ❍ The schedule
- **B** ❍ The scope baseline
- **C** ❍ The WBS dictionary
- **D** ❍ The WBS encyclopedia

10 The scope baseline comprises which three elements?

- **A** ❍ WBS, scope statement, WBS dictionary
- **B** ❍ WBS encyclopedia, charter, requirements documentation
- **C** ❍ Scope management plan, WBS, WBS dictionary
- **D** ❍ Scope statement, scope management plan, WBS

Answers

1 **B.** Requirement. This is the definition from the *PMBOK Guide. See the section on "Collect Requirements: Inputs."*

2 **A.** Project scope. Reports are *project* scope, not *product* scope. They are work associated with the project, not the features and functions of the product. *Review "Project and Product Scope."*

3 **A.** Observation. You are observing how people do their jobs. Your observations will help you build requirements for the new system. *Check out the "Observations" section.*

4 **D.** Surveys and questionnaires. Automated surveys can get information from a large number of people and rapidly quantify it. *Check out the "Questionnaires and surveys" section.*

5 **B.** Assumption, project scope statement. You're assuming that you will have those four full-time and two part-time people for planning purposes. However, until you know for sure, it is still an assumption. Assumptions are documented in the project scope statement initially. They might move to their own Assumption Log in time. *See the definition for assumption in "Define Scope: Outputs."*

6 **A.** Project charter and requirements documentation. These are the inputs into the Define Scope process. *Peruse "Define Scope: Inputs."*

7 **D.** Create a WBS. The WBS is used to identify and organize all the project deliverables. *Look over "Create WBS: Inputs."*

8 **A.** Control account. The control account is the level used to report status for scope, schedule, and cost. *Read the definition of control account in "Create WBS: Tools and Techniques."*

9 **C.** The WBS dictionary. The WBS dictionary documents detailed information about WBS elements. *Review the definition in "Create WBS: Outputs."*

10 **A.** WBS, scope statement, WBS dictionary. These three elements make up the scope baseline. *Read more in "Create WBS: Outputs."*

Chapter 3: Creating Your Schedule

Exam Objective

- **Using the scope and resource plan, create a project schedule to manage the timely completion of the project.**

Your project schedule is one of the most important pieces of documentation for your project. It contains all kinds of information, identifying the following:

- Activities needed to get the work done
- Milestone events and dates
- The sequence in which the activities need to occur
- The resources you need to accomplish the work
- The duration and effort estimates
- When activities should start and finish
- Activities that can slip without impacting the due date
- The critical path

Because a project schedule communicates so much information, many people mistakenly refer to it as project *plan.* In fact, the schedule is only one component of the project plan, but it is an important one. The project plan (or project management plan) is covered in Chapter 1 of this minibook.

The PMP exam doesn't have questions that relate to any kind of scheduling tool (software). Instead, the exam focuses on the schedule data needed to develop an effective schedule. Therefore, you must be familiar with the theory and mechanics necessary to build a schedule.

Quick Assessment

1 The process of approximating the number of work periods needed to complete individual activities with estimated resources is ______ ______ ______.

2 A significant point or event in the project is a(n) ______.

3 *I can't complete editing the User Instructions until I finish writing them.* This is an example of a(n) ______ ______ ______ relationship.

4 (True/False). Lag and float are synonymous.

5 Effort is estimated in ______ ______, and duration is generally estimated in ______ ______.

6 If you have an activity with a good deal of uncertainty or risk, the preferred method of developing an estimate is ______ ______.

7 To calculate the late-start and late-finish dates for a schedule, you would complete a(n) ______ ______.

8 The document that establishes how you will develop, manage, and control your schedule is the ______ ______ ______.

9 A graphic representation of the flow of activities through the project is a(n) ______ ______.

10 The difference between the early start of an activity and the late start of an activity is ______ ______.

Answers

1 Estimate Activity Durations. This is the process name and definition per the *PMBOK Guide* Glossary. *You can find this in the "Estimating Activity Durations" section.*

2 Milestone. A milestone marks a significant event or achievement in a project. It can be the start or end of a phase, or the completion of a significant deliverable. *Look over "Define Activities: Inputs" for further information on milestones.*

3 Finish-to-finish. The completion of editing is dependent upon the completion of writing. *See "Sequence Activities: Tools and Techniques."*

4 False. Lag is a directed delay. *Float* is the amount of time that a schedule activity can be delayed from its early start without delaying the project finish date or violating a schedule constraint. *Lag is described in "Sequence Activities: Tools and Techniques," and float is described in "Developing the Schedule."*

5 Labor units, work periods. *Effort* is the amount of labor units it takes to complete an activity. *Duration* is the number of work periods it takes to complete an activity. Effort is usually shown in hours, and duration is usually shown in days or weeks. *This is defined in "Estimating Activity Durations."*

6 Three-point estimating. By identifying optimistic, most likely, and pessimistic estimates, you are more likely to get an accurate expected duration estimate. *For more information on three-point estimating, look over "Estimate Activity Durations: Tools and Techniques."*

7 Backward pass. A *backward pass* identifies the latest date when an activity can start and finish without impacting the finish date or a schedule constraint. *You see more information on the backward pass in "Developing the Schedule."*

8 Schedule Management Plan. Before you start to create your schedule, take time to identify the processes and procedures that you will use to develop and manage your schedule. *Check out the information in "Planning Schedule Management" to see the order of events in scheduling.*

9 Network diagram. The network diagram shows the flow of activities from start to finish. *You find more information on the network diagram in "Sequence Activities: Outputs."*

10 Total float. *Total float* is the difference between a late and an early start. It signifies the amount of time that an activity can slip without impacting the finish date of the project, or any other project constraint. *You read about this in "Developing the Schedule."*

Planning Schedule Management

Developing your project schedule is an iterative process. You will repeat the following scheduling processes numerous times before you end up with an acceptable schedule:

- Identify Activities
- Sequence Activities
- Estimate Activity Resources
- Estimate Activity Durations
- Develop Schedule

In addition to the scheduling processes, you have to incorporate human resource availability, risk, and cost processes as well.

Although the planning involved in creating a viable schedule is significant, the majority of your time will be spent maintaining and controlling it. To assist you with the development, management, and control, you can develop a schedule management plan.

Schedule management plan. The component of the project management plan that establishes criteria and the activities for developing, monitoring, and controlling the project schedule.

Plan Schedule Management: Inputs

The project management plan provides the elements in the scope baseline. The work breakdown structure (WBS) is particularly useful when creating your schedule because it identifies all the deliverables that make up the product scope. As the project management plan is progressively elaborated, it will also contain the budget, information on risks, and the human resource management plan. The charter (described in Book II, Chapter 2) includes the high-level milestones for the project.

Enterprise environmental factors (EEFs) that influence how an organization develops and manages the schedule include the company culture, resource skills, and available software. For example, Alpha Company does not have a mature project management practice, instead relying on resources who work on projects part time and as available. Alpha Company develops schedules in a spreadsheet or in a table. The emphasis is on operational challenges rather than project needs.

Contrast Alpha's approach with Theta Company, which has a robust project management practice. Theta Company employees dedicate some or all of their time to project work. The team members have a familiarity and understanding of scheduling, can create and read a schedule that was developed in scheduling software, and estimate their work and duration much more accurately. Theta Company makes use of organizational process assets, such as information from previous projects, lessons learned, prior estimates and schedules, and information on risk events that materialized.

Plan Schedule Management: Tools and Techniques

The three techniques used to develop the schedule management plan integrate well: expert judgment, analytical techniques, and meetings. Resources with expertise in the discipline, estimating, and scheduling tools meet and discuss the various options for developing a schedule. Topics at the meeting can include

- Whether critical path methodology, critical chain methodology, agile methodology, or some combination of the three is the best approach for the project
- Which deliverables durations should be estimated using an analogous approach, a parametric approach, or three-point estimating; and also what the duration range and confidence levels should be for estimates
- Whether project management software should be used, as well as the level of detail the schedule should show

Plan Schedule Management: Outputs

The schedule management plan is the sole output from this process. The schedule management plan can be high-level with only a few paragraphs. Or the plan can be quite detailed, containing the following:

- Scheduling software
- Scheduling methodology
- Levels of accuracy required at different life cycle phases
- Control thresholds for preventive and corrective action
- Guidelines for establishing and using contingency reserve
- Measurement methods for recording progress
- Estimating methods
- Schedule report formats

Even though most of us call the output of these processes a *schedule,* scheduling gurus refer to it as a *schedule model.* And they're right! The schedule is just a model of what could happen if all the assumptions in the schedule data (such as activities, sequences, durations, and resources) are correct.

From the purist perspective, the project information is entered into a tool (scheduling software). That is combined with a scheduling methodology (such as critical path or critical chain) to develop the schedule model. The output can be in the form of a bar chart or network diagram with dates or any other presentation that meets the need.

Define Activities

After the initial planning for the schedule has been completed, you need to determine all the work that needs to be done.

Define Activities. Identifying and documenting the specific actions to be performed to produce the project deliverables.

The terms *activity* and *task* can be used interchangeably in practice, literature, and the exam.

Define Activities: Inputs

The schedule management plan provides guidance on the level of detail you will use to record the project activities. To define activities, start with the scope baseline: in particular, the WBS. (I discuss both in the preceding chapter.) The *WBS* contains the work packages that you will decompose to determine activities. The *scope statement* — which gives a detailed narrative description of the project — contains assumptions and constraints that need to be considered.

You can use organizational process assets (OPAs), such as information from previous projects or templates, to help you. The organization's information system, including the preferred software for schedule development, is an EEF that guides your approach to recording the activities.

Define Activities: Tools and Techniques

When you create your WBS, you decompose the work to create work packages. (See the preceding chapter for more on work packages.) For creating the schedule, though, you decompose work packages to create schedule activities. For smaller projects, this may occur simultaneously. If you were redoing your backyard, you might identify the deck as a deliverable but then go right into the activities needed, such as set posts, cement posts, build frame, set planks, and build railing. It is such a small project that breaking it into two steps (identifying deliverables and the activities) doesn't make sense. You can do them at the same time. Generally, though, on larger projects, the WBS is agreed to first, and then the decomposition into activities occurs.

Activities are the actions needed to create work packages. In other words, activities are verbs. Your WBS should be noun-centric, but your activity list should be verb-centric. Here is part of the table from the preceding chapter. Look at it from the perspective of defining the activities.

WBS Deliverable	*Schedule Activities*	*Comment*
1.0 Playground equipment	1.1 Determine equipment needs 1.2 Conduct market research 1.3 Order equipment 1.4 Equipment delivered 1.5 Install equipment	The activities are all the actions needed to complete the deliverable. The numbering scheme from the WBS is elaborated with the schedule activities.

Using rolling wave planning is common when identifying all the activities and developing the schedule. I talk about it in the previous chapter when I discuss decomposing scope. For long projects, though, identifying all the activities that will need to take place two years in the future isn't feasible. Therefore, identify only those detailed activities that you need to accomplish in a 90- to 120-day range and keep the information "in the future" at a higher level. With this approach, you can see how the process of planning and developing the schedule occurs throughout a project.

Usually, your team members identify the activities needed to complete the work packages. They have the subject matter expertise necessary to identify all the steps and all the work needed. In some organizations, you will be able to use a schedule from a similar project to get a head start, but you will still need to have your team members review it and modify it to meet the needs for your particular project.

Define Activities: Outputs

The first output for this process is a list of activities. For a shorter project, you should build a comprehensive list. Comparatively, for a longer project, your list should have sufficient detail to build a realistic schedule.

For complex projects, it's appropriate to extend the description of the activities by documenting activity attributes. Activity attributes can include

- Activity identifier or code (usually an extension from the WBS numbering scheme; see the preceding chapter)
- Activity description

- Predecessor and successor activities
- Logical relationships
- Leads and lags
- Imposed dates
- Constraints
- Assumptions
- Required resources and skill levels
- Geographic location of performance
- Type of effort

Note that at this point in time you don't have effort or duration information. That comes later. You can always add that information to your activity attributes as a form of progressive elaboration. A list of activity attributes might be too detailed for your project. Generally, documenting activity attributes is reserved for projects that meet the following criteria:

- Large projects with a lengthy duration
- Complex projects with many interdependencies and stakeholders
- Projects with much uncertainty or risk
- Projects that include technology that's unproven or experimental in nature
- When contractual arrangements are in place that necessitate clear and complete definition

Figure 3-1 shows an example of a form you can use to record activity attributes.

Tailor your project to meet your needs. If you don't need to record activity attributes, don't. If you need only specific information, create a form that suits your needs.

A final output of this process is a milestone list. This records all the milestones and communicates if they are mandatory (as required by a contract) or optional.

Milestone. A significant point or event in the project.

ACTIVITY ATTRIBUTES

Project Title: ____________ Date Prepared: ____________

ID:		Activity:			
Description of Work:					
Predecessors	Relationship	Lead or Lag	Successor	Relationship	Lead or Lag
Number and Type of Resources Required:		Skill Requirements:		Other Required Resources:	
Type of Effort:					
Location of Performance:					
Imposed Dates or Other Constraints:					
Assumptions:					

Figure 3-1: Activity attribute form.

Sequence Activities: Inputs

After identifying all the activities that need to be accomplished, the next step is to put them in order. Sometimes you will order them in conjunction with identifying activities; sometimes you won't.

All activities should have a predecessor (except the first one), and all activities should have a successor (except the last one). For those activities that take place throughout the project, such as risk management or stakeholder management, you can create an activity that starts at the beginning of the project and goes until completion.

Sequence Activities. The process of identifying and documenting relationships among the project activities.

At this point, you aren't establishing how long activities will take: only the sequence in which they will occur. To do this, you use all the outputs you generated in the previous processes:

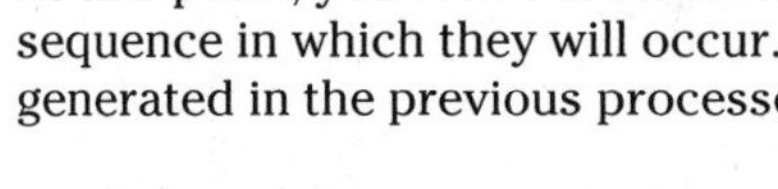

- Schedule management plan
- Activity list
- Activity attribute (if you need these)
- Milestone list

You may also reference the scope statement in case you have any assumptions or constraints that indicate the order of events. Any information from past projects can be useful as well.

Relationships between activities are *logical relationships.* This doesn't mean there are such things as illogical relationships: It simply refers to the way activities are sequenced in relationship to one another. For example, one activity has to end before another can start, or two activities should happen simultaneously.

Logical relationship. A dependency between two activities, or between an activity and a milestone.

The four possible types of relationships are

- Finish-to-start
- Finish-to-finish
- Start-to-start
- Start-to-finish

Read more about these relationship types in the upcoming section, "Precedence diagramming method."

Sequence Activities: Tools and Techniques

Here are three main aspects to sequencing activities:

- Determining the logical relationships
- Determining the type of dependency
- Applying leads and lags

These tasks are often done simultaneously, but they each have their own terminology, as I discuss in the following sections.

Precedence diagramming method

The precedence diagramming method (PDM) is the preferred method of establishing logical relationships. In this method, each activity is represented as a box, connected to other boxes (activities) with an arrow (see upcoming Figure 3-2).

Precedence diagramming method (PDM). A technique used for constructing a schedule model in which activities are represented by nodes and are graphically linked by one or more logical relationships to show the sequence in which the activities are to be performed.

Here are the four types of relationships used in PDM:

- **Finish-to-start (FS):** This is the most common type of relationship. The predecessor activity must finish before the successor can begin. For example:

  I have to finish gathering requirements before I start the design.

- **Finish-to-finish (FF):** The predecessor activity must finish before the successor activity can finish. A sample scenario is

  I have to finish writing the User Instructions before I can finish editing them.

- **Start-to-start (SS):** The predecessor activity must start before the successor activity can start. As an example:

  I need to start writing test questions before I can start writing test answers.

- **Start-to-finish (SF):** This is the least common relationship. You will not see this on the exam, but I include it here to be complete. The successor activity has to start before the predecessor can finish. Consider this scenario:

  A new accounting system has to be up and running before the previous system can be shut down.

Dependency determination

Many times, the relationships in the preceding list are mandatory, but other times they are more discretionary. Some relationships are based on external constraints. The nature of the dependency impacts the flexibility you have in your schedule. Take a look at the different types of dependencies.

- **Mandatory:** These dependencies are required based on the nature of the work involved. For example, you can't test something not yet developed. Note that *mandatory* doesn't refer to a policy or regulation; instead, it's based solely on the physical and logical limitations of the relationship. Using my running example of a childcare center, a mandatory dependency would be the rough electrical work (wiring throughout the space) that has to be done before the finish electrical (hooking up lights, switches, and outlets).
- **Discretionary:** These relationships are determined by a best practice or resource availability. A best practice example is "I recommend gathering all the requirements before designing the solution, but you can do some design without having the requirements complete and finalized." Using my running childcare center example, a resource availability discretionary dependency might be planting trees and plants. If the landscaper has one resource that will do both, he can do either task first. The relationship is discretionary and based on his choice.
- **External:** An external dependency is based on something or someone outside the project. Requiring a permit, waiting on a vendor delivery, needing a deliverable from another project, or meeting a regulatory requirement are all examples of external dependencies. The building occupancy permit for the childcare center example is an external dependency.

You can see that mandatory and external dependencies are constraints on how you schedule a project. Discretionary dependencies have the greatest flexibility in your schedule. However, you can still find ways to adjust mandatory dependencies by applying leads and lags.

Leads and lags

A *lead* is a modification to a relationship that allows you to accelerate the timing between two activities. For example, if I have an FS relationship between gathering requirements and designing the childcare center, I could apply a lead to accelerate designing the center.

Lead. The amount of time whereby a successor activity can be advanced with respect to a predecessor activity.

Here's an example of a lead: In a finish-to-start dependency with a ten-day lead, the successor activity can start ten days before the predecessor activity has finished. A negative lead is equivalent to a positive lag.

See Table 3-1 for a list of the scheduling abbreviations you'll need to know. In the childcare center example, the lead would sound like this:

> *Two weeks before I am done gathering the requirements, I will start designing the center.*

This is represented as

FS – 2w

where

- *FS* is the finish-to-start relationship.
- A lead is shown as a minus sign.
- *2w* signifies two weeks.

Table 3-1 Scheduling Abbreviations

Abbreviation	*What It Means*
FS	Finish-to-start
FF	Finish-to-finish
SS	Start-to-start
SF	Start-to-finish
m	Month
w	Week
d	Day
+	Add time (a lag)
–	Subtract time (a lead)

Here's another example. I have to finish the rough carpentry by April 1, so I need to have the blueprints signed off three weeks before. That results in FF – 3w, which shows a finish-to-finish relationship with a three-week lead.

The other type of modification to a relationship is a *lag,* which indicates a delay in the relationship between two activities. As you can likely guess, a lag is shown as a plus sign.

Lag. The amount of time whereby the successor activity can be advanced with respect to a predecessor activity.

Here is an example of a lag: In a finish-to-start dependency with a ten-day lag, the successor activity cannot start until ten days after the predecessor activity has finished.

Say I want to start an activity 10 days after I start the predecessor activity. Here's how that would look:

SS + 10d

where

- *SS* signifies the start-to-start relationship.
- The plus sign is a lag.
- *10d* is ten days.

Here is another example of a lag. I will start writing offer letters five days after I finish interviewing. I'd write that as FS + 5d. The offer letters are dependent upon the completion of the interviews, with a five-day lag.

Sequence Activities: Outputs

A *network diagram* (also known as a *project schedule network diagram*) is a schematic display of the relationships of all the activities in the project. The network diagram is always drawn from left to right to reflect project work chronology.

Figure 3-2 shows an example of a network diagram.

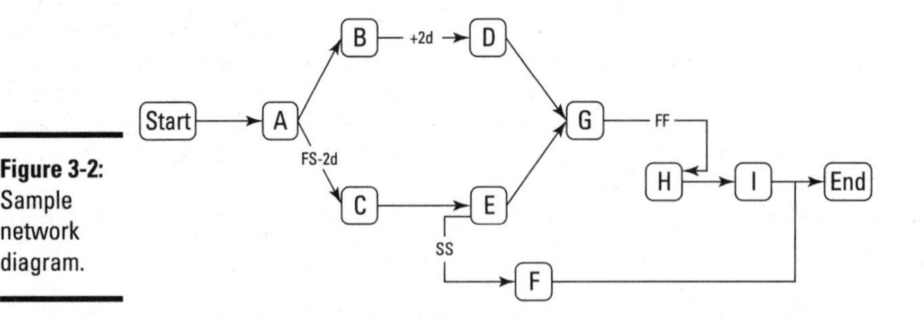

Figure 3-2: Sample network diagram.

Notice the two-day lead between activities A and C and the two-day lag between activities B and D. There is an SS relationship between E and F and an FF relationship between G and H.

Project schedule network diagram. A graphical representation of the logical relationships among the project schedule activities.

"Project schedule network diagram" is the formal name of the schematic display. In practice, it's called a *network diagram.* Use information from this process to elaborate the activity attributes you started when defining activities.

Estimate Activity Resources: Inputs

Completing the scheduled work requires a variety of resources. Some of the common categories include

- People
- Equipment
- Material
- Supplies

Facility space is sometimes considered a resource. After all, if you need a particular site or room for specific activities and that site is in high demand, you probably want to consider it a resource and treat it as such.

Estimate Activity Resources. Estimating the type and quantities of material, human resources, equipment, or supplies required to perform each activity.

Estimate Activity Resources: Inputs

To determine the resources needed for each activity — and, therefore, each work package — start with your schedule management plan, which will inform you of the levels of accuracy you need for resource estimates as well as the units of measure (gallons, yards, hours, and so forth). Next you will consult your activity list and activity attributes. You should also consider using a resource calendar, which can be as simple as looking at team member availability. Of course, a resource calendar can be quite complex. Information you might compile for a resource calendar includes

- Skill levels of human resources (such as Junior, Intermediate, and Expert)
- Geographic location, such as where the work will take place

  This is particularly important if a resource (such as a lab or training room) is in high demand.
- Percent of time the resources are available, such as hours per week
- Corporate calendars that show company holidays or other nonworking times
- Information on multiple shifts or constraints on the number of hours per day a resource can be used

You should consult the activity cost estimates because the cost of resources can be a determining factor in how to resource your project. Risks can also contribute to decisions on resources. For example, if you need ten servers for a project, but they are functioning only as overflow or redundant servers for an inventory system, you can probably select a lower-quality and less-expensive server. However, if you need ten servers for a mission-critical project where lives are at stake and there is a high impact of failure, you should use the highest-quality servers you can buy.

As you can see, the needs of the project and the various resources have a lot to do with the information necessary to determine resource requirements.

Some of the EEFs you should consider are the skill sets available in the organization and also the level of commitment of those resources. Many organizations suffer from equipment bottlenecks or resource constraints on a few key resources. You need to plan for these potential obstacles to build an accurate schedule.

OPAs that you can use include policies for staffing, outsourcing, renting or leasing equipment, and information from previous projects.

Estimate Activity Resources: Tools and Techniques

Your team members will provide the expertise needed to determine the types and amounts of resources you will need. For projects that include new or emerging technology, or where your organization has a lack of experience, you will want to brainstorm alternative approaches. This can include finding new ways of doing something, determining the best mix of resources and skill sets, procuring skills or deliverables versus developing them inhouse, and similar types of alternative analysis.

In some cases, the information on the work package or activities is at too high of a level to be able to estimate the resources accurately. In this case, you will have to decompose it further to get a bottom-up estimate. Some industries, such as construction, have published unit costs for trades, material, equipment, and geography. The published rates are great for an initial estimate. However, you will want to use your knowledge and expertise to refine the estimate for your particular circumstances.

This process is very closely linked to the Estimate Costs process, which you can read about in Book IV, Chapter 1. The cost of resources can drive how you perform the project.

You can use software to slice and dice resource information in a number of different ways. You can create resource utilization histograms or a resource breakdown structure. (See examples of these histograms in upcoming Figures 3-4 and 3-5.)

Estimate Activity Resources: Outputs

Activity Resource Requirements. The types and quantities of resources required for each activity in a work package.

Activity resource requirements include the type, number, and skill level of the needed resources. It's useful to include the assumptions that led to the estimates and the basis of estimates. Table 3-2 shows an example.

Table 3-2 Activity Resource Requirements Example

Resource Need	*Assumptions*
Senior Engineer	Senior Engineers have 10–15 years of experience and have worked on similar projects. They have skills using CAD/CAM software.
Intermediate General Contractor	General Contractors at an intermediate level have 5–10 years of experience and have worked on similar projects. They can interpret architectural drawings as developed by the engineer and provide oversight to lower-level contractors.
Intermediate Carpenters	Carpenters at an intermediate level have 5–10 years of experience and have worked on similar projects. They can construct basic to complex sites with little oversight and rework.
Laborers	Laborers have 6 months to 2 years of experience working on construction sites. They're not licensed. They require instruction and oversight while working. They're skilled in the use of all tools required on-site but are not craftsmen.

In projects with a large number of resources, organizing resources by using a resource breakdown structure can be helpful. A resource breakdown structure is organized like a work breakdown structure, but it uses categories of resources to organize information. Figure 3-3 shows an example of a resource breakdown structure.

Resource breakdown structure. A hierarchical representation of resources by category and type.

RESOURCE BREAKDOWN STRUCTURE

Project Title: ______________________ Date Prepared: ______________________

1. Project
   - 1.1. People
     - 1.1.1. Quantity of Role 1
       - 1.1.1.1. Quantity of Level 1
       - 1.1.1.2. Quantity of Level 2
       - 1.1.1.3. Quantity of Level 3
     - 1.1.2. Quantity of Role 2
   - 1.2. Equipment
     - 1.2.1. Quantity of Type 1
     - 1.2.2. Quantity of Type 2
   - 1.3. Materials
     - 1.3.1. Quantity of Material 1
       - 1.3.1.1. Quantity of Grade 1
       - 1.3.1.2. Quantity of Grade 2
   - 1.4. Supplies
     - 1.4.1. Quantity of Supply 1
     - 1.4.2. Quantity of Supply 2
   - 1.5. Locations
     - 1.5.1. Location 1
     - 1.5.2. Location 2

Figure 3-3: Resource breakdown structure.

Another way to display resource requirements is a resource histogram.

Resource histogram. A bar chart showing the amount of time that a resource is scheduled to work over a series of time periods. Resource availability may be depicted as a line for comparison purposes. Contrasting bars may show actual amounts of resources used as the project progresses.

Here are two examples. Figure 3-4 shows a resource histogram that shows the skill set needed and the months they are needed. Figure 3-5 shows the months and the skills needed by month. Both show the same information but are formatted in different ways. There is no set way to present the information; decide what works best for you.

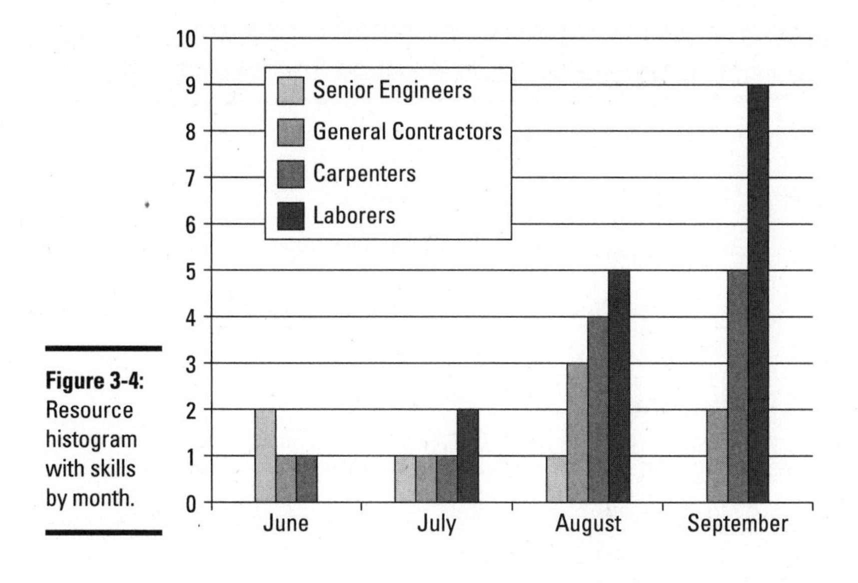

Figure 3-4: Resource histogram with skills by month.

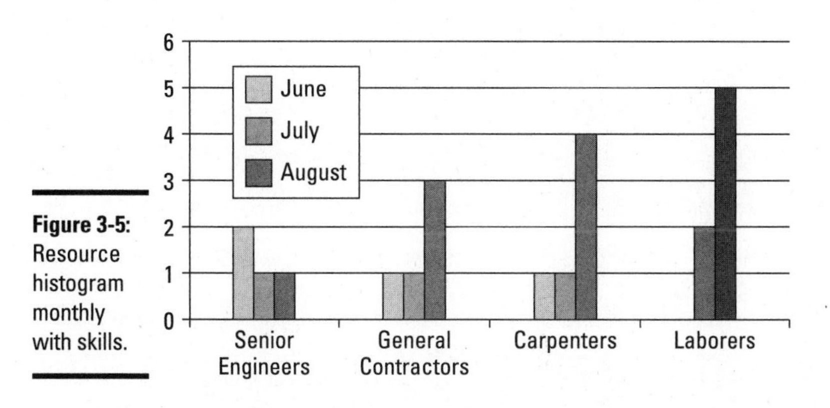

Figure 3-5: Resource histogram monthly with skills.

Information from this process can be used to elaborate the activity attributes you first developed when defining activities and to update resource calendars.

Estimating Activity Durations

Developing accurate estimates — for resources, durations, or costs — is one of the most challenging and contentious parts of managing a project. The customer always wants the deliverables as soon as possible. Team members assume everything will go as planned. Project managers assume resources will be available as promised. All the above contribute to projects running longer than they were originally scheduled to run. The sponsor and the customer usually drive the project manager to unrealistic expectations, things don't go as planned, and resources aren't always available as promised. No wonder projects run late even though team members work overtime trying to get caught up! To get out of this vicious cycle, it helps to understand the nature of estimating:

1. You must fully define project and product scope to have any hope of estimating accurately, whether those estimates are for resources, durations, or costs.

   Oftentimes, we are held to an estimated delivery date when the scope isn't even finalized.

2. Understand the nature of estimating.

   The more you understand about the scope, available resources, the nature of the work, and the environment, the more accurate your estimates will be. Therefore, at the beginning of a project, you are likely to have a range of estimates that can end up being 35–50% more optimistic than in the final duration. This is even truer with projects that are developing new technology or using unproven processes. Often, you can't derive an accurate estimate until you're ready to obtain a baseline and take into account your risks, stakeholder management needs, funding availability, procurement needs, actual resources, and so forth. Then you can get an estimate that is +/–5% to 10% of the final result.

3. Take into account the difference between the effort needed to accomplish the work and the duration, which indicates how many work periods (activity duration) it will take.

   For example, say you have 80 hours of effort and two resources who are working full-time. You can assume that it will take 5 days, or 1 business week, to accomplish the work. If you have only 1 resource working at 50%, it will take 20 days, or 1 business month, to get the work done. Calculations like this get even more complicated if you consider that not all resources work at the same rate. Some people are more productive, and some people require more rework to get things right. In addition, for every 40 hours spent at work per week, folks are productive only about 34 hours.

If you consider all these elements, it's no wonder why projects come in late! Still, that's not reason enough to give estimating less than your best shot. Several estimating techniques are available that can help you develop estimates, depending on the nature of the work. I start by looking at the difference between effort and duration, and then I discuss what you need to develop accurate estimates.

Effort. The number of labor units required to complete a schedule activity or work breakdown structure component, often expressed in hours, days, or weeks.

Duration. The total number of work periods (not including holidays or other nonworking periods) required to complete a schedule activity or work breakdown structure component. Usually expressed as workdays or workweeks. Sometimes incorrectly equated with elapsed time.

Elapsed time refers to calendar time. Thus, a duration of 20 days would be the equivalent of 4 workweeks of elapsed time. Most scheduling software turns duration into elapsed time by assuming that your work calendar doesn't include weekends. You can change this by adjusting the calendar on your scheduling software. Or, you can enter the duration with a suffix that indicated elapsed days. For example, 20ED could mean 20 elapsed days. Check your software to determine exactly how it works.

You need to know only effort and duration. You do not need to consider elapsed time.

Estimate Activity Durations. Estimating the number of work periods needed to complete individual activities with estimated resources.

Estimate Activity Durations: Inputs

To determine effort and duration, you need to incorporate information from the previous time-management processes:

- Schedule management plan
- Activity list
- Activity attributes
- Activity resource requirements
- Resource breakdown structure

The scope statement includes assumptions and constraints that you should take into consideration, such as availability or resources, available skills, contractual information, and so forth.

Your resource calendars will provide availability and resource load information for both internal resources and external resources (for example, if you're using contract labor or rented equipment).

The risk register can provide information on WBS elements that have risks associated with delivery dates, materials, technology, resource availability, and any other type of risk that could impact duration estimates.

Organizations that have a degree of maturity in project management might have EEFs such as estimating databases, productivity metrics, or published estimating data. Some of the OPAs you're likely to use include historic information from past projects and "lessons learned" information.

Estimate Activity Durations: Tools and Techniques

Sometimes, it seems like people pick estimates by snatching them out of the air or by consulting their Magic 8 Ball. There is an art and a science to estimating. The art comes from the expert judgment that team members and estimators bring to the process. Their experience and wisdom from past projects is very valuable in developing estimates, determining the best method to use to develop an estimate, and being able to look at an estimate or the assumptions behind the estimate to assess the validity.

In addition to the artful contribution of experts, team members, and estimators, there are a number of methods that make up the science of estimating.

Analogous estimating

Analogous estimating is the most common method of estimating. The aforementioned experts normally conduct this form of estimating. In its most basic form, analogous estimating compares past projects with the current project, determines the areas of similarity and the areas of difference, and then develops an estimate based on that.

A more robust application determines the duration drivers and analyzes the relationship between past similar projects with the current project. This can include size, complexity, risk, and number of resources, weight, or whatever other aspects of the project influence duration.

To use this method effectively, projects must be similar in fact, not just in appearance. A software upgrade may sound similar, but there are vast differences, so they are not really similar. The difference between moving from Office 2007 to Office 2010 is much different from moving from Office 2007 to Lotus Notes. The conversion time is very different!

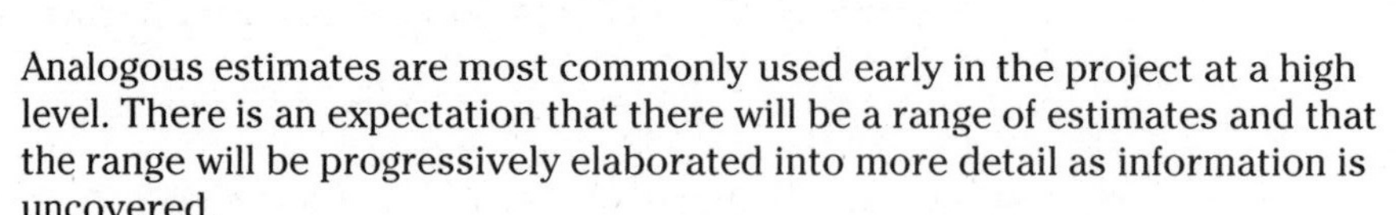

Analogous estimates are most commonly used early in the project at a high level. There is an expectation that there will be a range of estimates and that the range will be progressively elaborated into more detail as information is uncovered.

The benefits of using analogous estimates are that they are relatively quick to develop, and they're not very costly to develop. However, because they're usually done at a high level, they're not the most accurate method.

Say you need to develop training materials for the childcare center staff. The training will take two days. You developed a similar training program a few months ago, but that program was three days long. Therefore, you reduce your estimate by 33%. However, this new training program is relatively complex compared with the earlier one; it includes first aid, food prep, and safety training. Therefore, you increase the duration by 10% for a complexity factor. The first training class required four hands-on demonstrations, but this one needs only three. Given this information, you can access the prior project to find the durations and modify them based on current information. Table 3-3 shows how.

Table 3-3 Training Class Analogous Estimate

Last Class	*Effort*	*This Class*	*Modifier*	*Modified Estimate*
3 days	200 hours	2 days	–33%	133
Easy	Included	Complex	+10%	20
4 demonstrations	40 hours	3 demonstrations	–25%	30
Total	**240 hours**			**183 hours**

Parametric estimating

Parametric estimating uses a mathematical model to determine durations. Not all work can be estimated this way, but when you can, it's fast and easy. You multiply the quantity of work by the number of hours it takes to accomplish it. For example, if a painter can paint 100 square feet per hour and you have 6,000 square feet to paint, you can assume 60 hours of effort. And if you have three people painting (60 / 3), then it should take 20 hours, or the equivalent of 2.5 days.

Three-point estimates

When a lot of uncertainty, risk, or unknowns surround an activity or a work package, you can use *three-point estimating* to give you a range and an expected duration. You collect three estimates based on the following scenarios.

- **Best case:** The best case (optimistic) scenario means that you have all your required resources, nothing goes wrong, everything works the first time, and so on. This is represented as an *o,* for "optimistic." Or you might see it represented as $\mathbf{t}_o$, for "time optimistic."
- **Most likely:** The most likely scenario takes into account the realities of project life, such as someone being called away for an extended period, work interruptions, things not going exactly as planned, and so forth. This is represented as an *m,* for "most likely." You might see it represented as $\mathbf{t}_m$, for "time most likely."

- **Worst case:** The worst case (pessimistic) estimate assumes unskilled resources, or not enough resources, much rework, and delays in work getting accomplished. This is represented as a *p,* or $\mathbf{t}_p$, for "time pessimistic."

The simplest way to develop the expected duration, or $\mathbf{t}_e$ ("time expected"), is to sum the three estimates and divide by three. You might see this referred to as a *triangular distribution.* However, this isn't the most accurate way because it assumes an equal probability that the best case, most likely, and worst case scenarios would occur — and that's not realistic. In reality, the most likely estimate has a greater chance of occurring than either the best case or worst case scenario. Therefore, weight the most likely scenario and take a weighted average. The most common way of calculating a weighted average is

$$\mathbf{t}_e = (\mathbf{t}_o + 4\mathbf{t}_m + \mathbf{t}_p) / 6$$

The PMP exam might refer to this as a Beta distribution or *PERT estimating.* (PERT stands for Program Evaluation and Review Technique.) This was a technique developed in the late 1950s to derive a range of estimates and an expected estimate, given the uncertainty in a project.

Reserve analysis

Reserve analysis is used for work packages, control accounts, or any level of the WBS. It looks at the complexity and riskiness of the duration estimate and determines whether reserve is needed to account for the uncertainty, risk, or complexity. Sometimes, you will see reserve referred to as *contingency reserve* or *buffer.*

You might see reserve as a percentage of time based on the phase of the project or as a set number of hours. It's a good practice to revisit the reserve and see how much you have used compared with how far along you are in the project. When reserve is used, the reason for it should be documented so you can include the information in "lessons learned" and consider it for the next project.

Reserve is not padding. Pad is bad. If you see the word "pad" on the exam, you can be certain that it's in a negative context! Reserve is developed based on analysis and thoughtful deliberation. Padding is throwing extra time in the schedule because you didn't take time to do the work to develop a well thought-out estimate.

For complex estimates, you may need to employ brainstorming, nominal group techniques, or other decision-making techniques to come to consensus on a duration estimate. For a refresher on group decision-making techniques, see Book II, Chapter 2.

Estimate Activity Durations: Outputs

Your duration estimates approximate the number of work periods you need to complete an activity. Often, you will see a range of estimates or the probability of achieving the estimate. For example, you might see something like

> *I think the duration will be 4–6 weeks, but I am going to say 5 weeks for my estimate.*
>
> *There is an 80% likelihood that we will be complete within 5 weeks.*

After developing your estimates, you want to include this information in your activity attributes and also update your Assumption Log with any assumptions you made while estimating. (Read about Assumption Logs in the previous chapter.)

Developing the Schedule

All the work up to now leads to developing a schedule for the project. However, you will most likely need to revisit the preceding processes numerous times before you get a schedule that's acceptable to all your stakeholders. You might need to go back to your network diagram to look for ways to compress the duration by overlapping activities by using leads and lags and modifying the dependency relationships. You can also inquire into getting more resources as a way to shorten the duration. In other words, developing the schedule is an iterative process that you might need to go through several times before you have a schedule that everyone can live with.

Develop Schedule. Analyzing activity sequences, durations, resource requirements, and schedule constraints to create the project schedule model.

Develop Schedule: Inputs

To begin this process, you take outputs from the previous scheduling processes:

- Schedule management plan
- Activity list
- Activity attributes
- Network diagram
- Activity resource requirements
- Resource calendars

- ✦ Activity duration estimates
- ✦ Resource breakdown structure

In addition, check your scope statement for any schedule constraints or project assumptions. Project staff assignments should be consulted for the actual staff assigned to schedule activities. Your risk register will have lots of information associated with risks to resources, duration estimates, staff availability, constraints, and so forth. The EEF you are most likely to use is the organization's scheduling tool (software). OPAs include schedules from previous similar projects and any scheduling methodology, templates, or procedures.

Develop Schedule: Tools and Techniques

Using a scheduling tool (such as Microsoft Project, Primavera, or others) is a necessity for any project with more than 50 activities. Most scheduling tools can show you schedule models as a network diagram, bar chart, or table. The technique of schedule network analysis is composed of applying either the critical path methodology or the critical chain methodology. In both methods, you are likely to use the following techniques:

- ✦ Resource optimization
- ✦ Modeling
- ✦ Schedule compression
- ✦ Leads and lags

I start by discussing critical path and critical chain methodologies and then move into describing the preceding techniques.

Critical path

Critical path — the most common form of teaching scheduling — is also the method that most software employs. The *critical path method* determines the date ranges in which activities can occur by calculating the earliest and the latest dates when activities can start and then the earliest and the latest dates when activities can finish based on the network diagram and the duration. Most critical path analyses are done prior to loading resource availability into the schedule. After resources are loaded, the duration of the project can change. The critical path method has several terms you need to be familiar with.

Critical path method (CPM). A method used to estimate the minimum project duration and determine the amount of scheduling flexibility on the logical network paths within the schedule model.

Early start date (ES). In the critical path method, the earliest possible point in time when the uncompleted portions of a schedule activity can start, based on the schedule network logic, the data date, and any schedule constraints.

Early finish date (EF). In the critical path method, the earliest possible point in time when the uncompleted portions of a schedule activity can finish, based on the schedule network logic, the data date, and any schedule constraints.

Late finish date (LF). In the critical path method, the latest possible point in time when the uncompleted portions of a schedule activity can finish based on the schedule network logic, the project completion date, and any schedule constraints.

Late start date (LS). In the critical path method, the latest possible point in time when the uncompleted portions of a schedule activity can start based on the schedule network logic, the project completion date, and any schedule constraints.

Total float. The amount of time that a schedule activity can be delayed or extended from its early start date without delaying the project finish date or violating a schedule constraint.

Free float. The amount of time a schedule activity can be delayed without delaying the early start date of any successor or violating a schedule constraint.

Forward pass. A critical path method technique for calculating the early start and early finish dates by working forward through the schedule model from the project start date or a given point in time.

Backward pass. A critical path method technique for calculating the late start and late finish dates by working backward through the schedule model from the project end date.

Critical path. The sequence of activities that represents the longest path through a project, which determines the shortest possible duration.

Here are the steps to analyze the schedule, using the critical path method:

1. Draw the network diagram.
2. Box the network diagram.
3. Enter durations into the diagram.
4. Conduct a forward pass.
5. Conduct a backward pass.

6. Calculate float.

7. Identify the critical path.

I talk about each of these in the following sections.

Draw the network diagram

The first step is to create a network diagram that shows the logical relationship among activities. (I discuss the network diagram earlier in this chapter.) I use the network diagram from Figure 3-2 as an example to explain the remaining steps.

Box the network diagram

"Boxing the diagram" means setting up the network diagram with a box for each activity and a place to enter the duration, the early and late start dates, the early and late finish dates, and the float. You can use any structure you want. The following table shows one common way of showing the information for each activity.

Early Start	***Duration***	***Early Finish***
	Activity	
Late Start	***Float***	***Late Finish***

Figure 3-6 shows how the sample diagram would look after it's boxed.

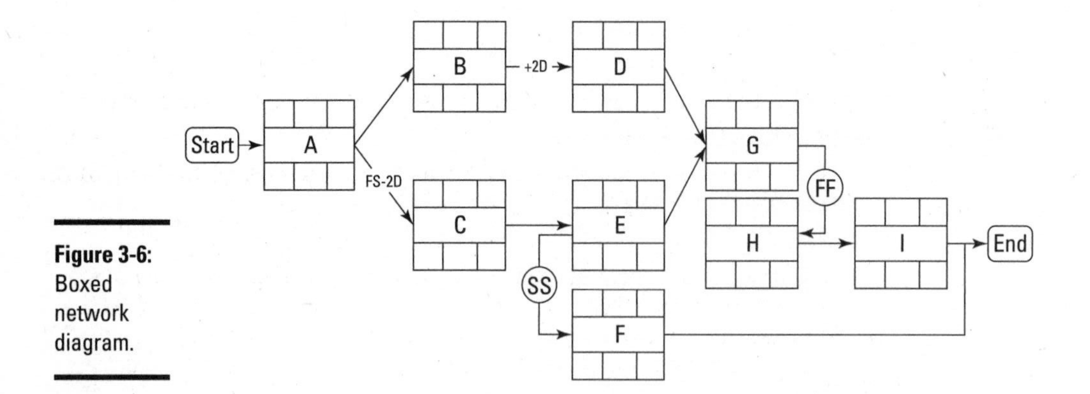

Figure 3-6: Boxed network diagram.

Enter durations

The next step is to enter the durations into the boxed diagram, as shown in Figure 3-7.

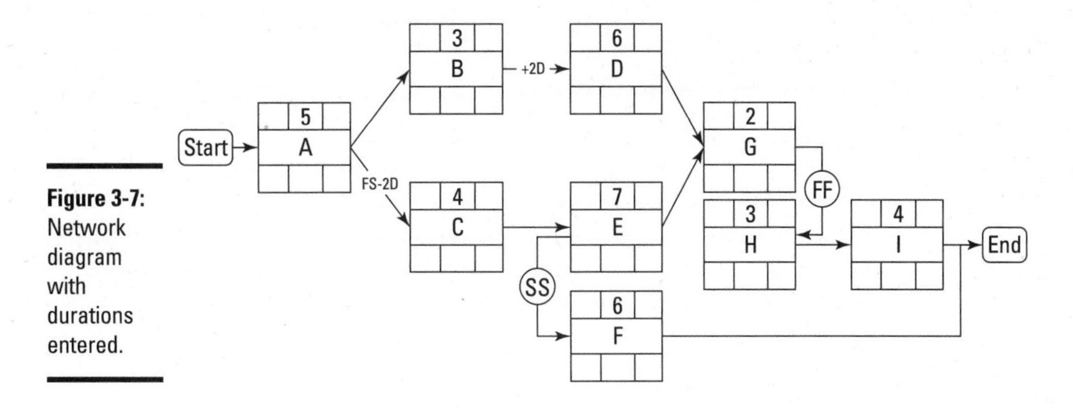

Figure 3-7: Network diagram with durations entered.

Conduct a forward pass

Now you're ready to conduct a forward pass. The forward pass will tell you what the earliest dates are that activities can start and finish, based on the network logic. Here are the steps to conduct a forward pass:

1. **Set the early start for the first activity ("Activity A") or activities to 1.**

   Scheduling software assumes that an activity starts at 8 a.m. and is complete at 5 p.m. on its due date. Therefore, the next activity starts the next morning at 8 a.m.

2. **Add the duration of the activity to the early start and then subtract 1.**

   Now you have your early finish date.

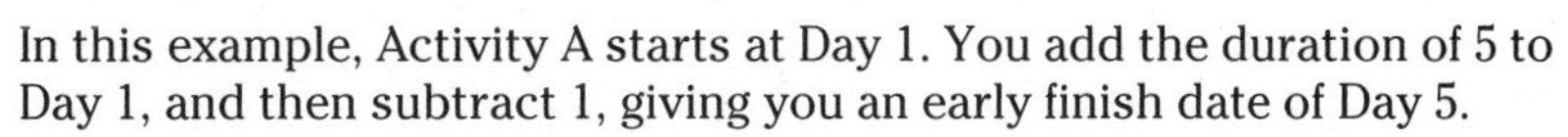

   In this example, Activity A starts at Day 1. You add the duration of 5 to Day 1, and then subtract 1, giving you an early finish date of Day 5.

   Always subtract 1 from the early start plus the duration because you start on Day 1, not Day 0.

3. **Add 1 to the early finish to determine the early start of the immediate successor activities.**

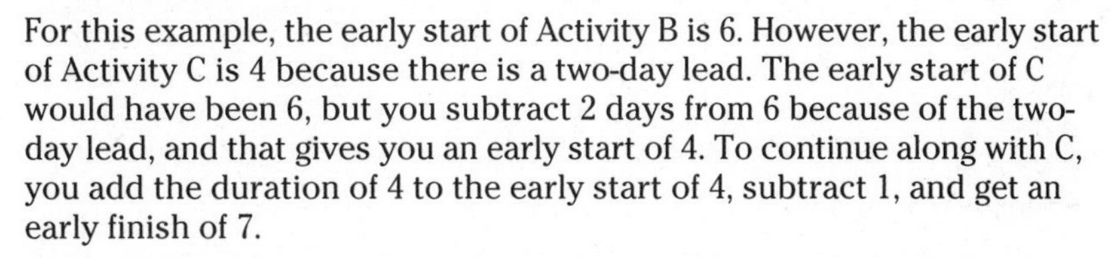

   For this example, the early start of Activity B is 6. However, the early start of Activity C is 4 because there is a two-day lead. The early start of C would have been 6, but you subtract 2 days from 6 because of the two-day lead, and that gives you an early start of 4. To continue along with C, you add the duration of 4 to the early start of 4, subtract 1, and get an early finish of 7.

   Going to Activity B, you add the early start of 6 and the duration of 3, subtract 1, and get an early finish of 8. There is a two-day lag between B and D, so Activity D starts two days after B finishes. This means that D will start on Day 11.

Continue in this fashion until you reach the end of the network. Figure 3-8 shows a network diagram with a forward pass completed.

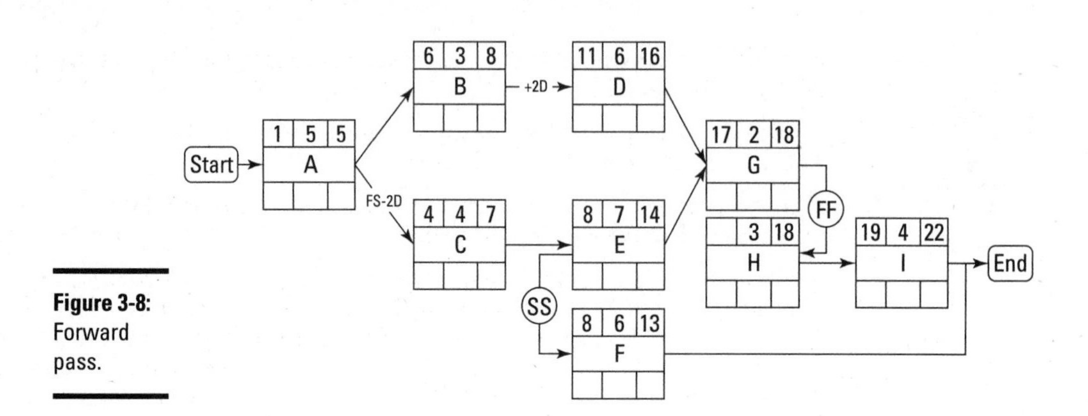

Figure 3-8: Forward pass.

Note these areas of interest in this diagram:

- ✦ Activity F has the same early start as Activity E because there is a start-to-start relationship. Activity F can start after Activity E starts.
- ✦ Activity G and Activity H have a finish-to-finish relationship. This means that Activity H can finish after Activity G finishes.
- ✦ Activity D and Activity E both have to finish before Activity G can start. Activity D has an early finish of 16, and Activity E has an early finish of 14. When there is a path convergence in a forward pass, the highest number always carries forward.

After you finish calculating your forward pass, you will see the earliest finish date. This is the soonest the project can finish, given the information available. For this example, the early finish date is 22 days.

Conduct a backward pass

The next step is to conduct a backward pass, which tells you the latest time activities can start and finish without violating a schedule constraint (such as a mandatory milestone) or without causing the project to be late.

If you have a hard schedule constraint, such as a mandatory review date or a contractually required delivery date, you can enter that as the late finish date. This might cause a situation called *negative float;* I will talk about float shortly.

For a backward pass, follow these steps:

1. **Take the early finish date of the *last* activity in the network and enter that number as the late finish date as well.**

   Therefore, your early finish and late finish for the last activity will be the same. For this example, it's 22 days.

2. **Subtract the duration and add 1 to establish the late start for the last activity in the project.**

   Because you start the project at Day 1, instead of Day 0, you need to add the 1 day back in to get accurate dates.

3. **Using the late start date, subtract 1 to derive the late finish date for any immediately preceding activities.**

   My running example has two final activities: Activity I and Activity F. I use the highest number as the late finish date. Activity I finishes on Day 22, and Activity F finishes on Day 13. Therefore, the late finish for the project is Day 22. For Activity I, you subtract the duration of 4, add 1 and get a late start of 17. Day 17 is the latest date when Activity I can start and not cause the project to be late. For activity H the late start date minus 1 carries backward to become the late finish for Activity H. Figure 3-9 shows how the sample network looks after a backward pass.

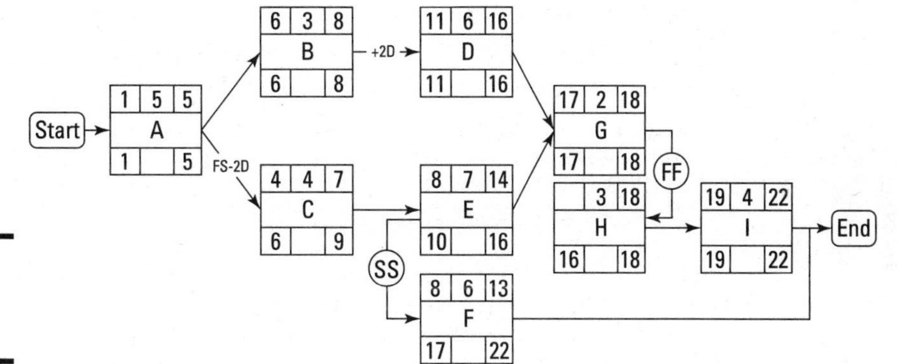

Figure 3-9: Backward pass.

Note these areas:

- ✦ Activity H does not have an early start, but it does have a late start because in this scenario, I'm not so much worried about when Activity H can start. Rather, I'm more concerned about when it finishes. In a real-life scenario, you would have more information about the nature of the activity in the activity attributes. That would give you insight into whether Activity H would need to start on Day 16, or whether it could start anytime.
- ✦ The late start of Activity D is 11, but the late finish of its predecessor (Activity B) is not 10, but 8, because there is a two-day lag. You treat that lag as if it were a mini-activity called "don't do any work here." Therefore, calculate the late start of B as 10, and you subtract 2 to get a late finish of 8 for Activity B.

- The relationship between Activity E and Activity F is start-to-start. It would seem that the late start of Activity F would drive the late start of Activity E. However, in this case, the late start of Activity G drives the late finish of Activity E, which in turn determines the late start. This demonstrates an important rule in the backward pass:

When you have two possible options for a late start or finish, the lowest one is the one you select.

Determine float

After you calculate the early and late start and finish dates, you can determine the float. *Float* is the difference between the late and early dates. For finish-to-start relationships, the difference between early start and late start dates will be the same as the difference between the early finish and late finish dates. However, when you have a start-to-start or a finish-to-finish relationship, you have to determine the difference between each and take the lowest number as the amount of float. Figure 3-10 shows a sample diagram.

If you have a finish-to-start relationship, and the difference between your late and early start is not the same as the difference between your late and early finish, there is an error in your math!

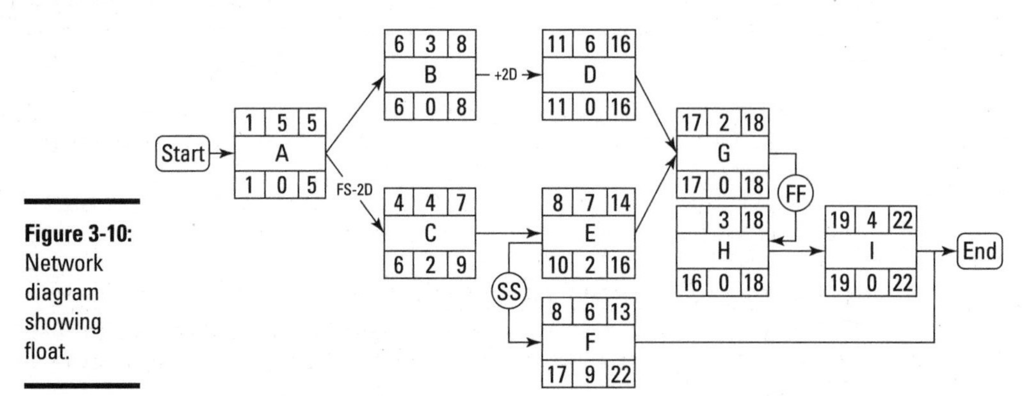

Figure 3-10: Network diagram showing float.

Only Activities C, E, and F have total float. Activity F has the most, with nine days of float: It can finish up to nine days later than its early finish date and not cause the project to be late. As I mention earlier, to calculate the nine days of float, you subtract the early finish from the late finish, or the early start from the late start. Activities C and E both have two days of float. However, that float is shared between them. Any float that Activity C uses isn't available for Activity E. If Activity C starts on Day 5 instead of Day 4, then Activity E will start on Day 9 and have only one day of float.

There is something special about Activities E and F: They have *free float.* They are the last activities on a path. Therefore, if they start late or finish late, within their float, no other activities are affected. Even though Activity C has total float, if it starts late, then both E and F start late. But if Activity F starts late, it doesn't cause any disruption in any other activity, as long as it finishes by Day 22.

If Activity E starts late, then F starts late, but if E finishes late by less than two days, then no other activities are impacted. Therefore, you can see that those activities with free float are the most flexible in the network. You can delay them and reallocate resources to activities that have little or no float to ensure on-time performance, assuming that resources have the right skill sets.

Identify the critical path

Finally, identify the *critical path,* which is the path with the least amount of float. For this example, the critical path is A-B-D-G-H-I. Usually, the critical path is presented as the path with zero float. However, say that you're given a mandated end date, and you calculate your critical path, and you have negative float. That tells you that you cannot meet the end date, given the current information — meaning, you have to find ways to compress the schedule or negotiate a new end date.

Conversely, if you have positive float, you have a little time to spare. In both circumstances, the path with the least amount of float is your critical path.

If you see a question that states you are in a negative float situation, that means you are late.

Another option for calculating the critical path

For the exam, you have to figure out the critical path manually, and the "+1 day/–1 day method" is a bit clunky to emulate when you're doing a manual calculation.

To make it easier, use Day 0 as an early start for the first activity; that way, you don't have to worry about adding or subtracting days based on the start or end of the business day.

Be careful, though, because the early start date and late start date will be different than if you use the +1/–1 method. The early and late finish dates will be the same, and the float will be the same.

Critical chain

The critical chain method comes from the world of manufacturing. In manufacturing, the rate of production is determined by bottlenecks in the process. If you can clear a bottleneck in production, you can get more product through the production line. Therefore, all processes are designed around exploiting that bottleneck — and in projects, the bottlenecks are usually resources. Thus, the critical chain methodology focuses on resolving resource constraints.

To determine the critical chain, you start with the critical path and then load resources. This usually causes a change to the critical path, based on resource constraints. The resource-constrained critical path is the *critical chain.*

To account for the uncertainty associated with the critical chain, you add buffers. Buffer at the end of the project — *project buffer* — is used to protect the delivery date. Along the critical chain are paths that feed into the critical chain. If any path is late, the critical chain is impacted. Therefore, buffers are put into the schedule at these points: *feeder buffers.* For critical chain scheduling, you manage the remaining buffer, as opposed to critical path where you manage the float.

Some of the other details associated with the critical chain methodology include

- All resources doing work on the critical chain are protected. This means that they are not pulled off their work to do other work, go to unrelated meetings, or are otherwise distracted from the work at hand.
- Resources that are in limited supply, or that are the bottlenecks, are exploited. In other words, work is scheduled around their availability to maximize their efficiency.
- All duration estimates are aggressive. Team members are asked to give the duration that they have about a 50/50 chance of attaining.
- Buffer is used to protect those activities that don't meet their estimated end date.
- Activities are scheduled at the late start and finish dates.
- This method can be used to increase the throughput of projects in a portfolio, especially when you have one or only a few resources that are working on many projects. The individual project dates may be sacrificed for the good of the portfolio.

Optimizing your resources

Resource optimization is done after the initial critical path is identified. At that point, you load your resources into the scheduling tool. Often, you will find that one or more resources are over-allocated. For example, you may have a resource scheduled to work full time on more than one activity. Another example is if you have a resource for a limited amount of time (say, 10 hours per week), but you have scheduled them for more than that. Sometimes you can resolve these resource allocation issues by using float to optimize the schedule without extending the due date. Other times, you will find that the schedule is extended, and you have a new critical path based on resource availability.

Resource optimization techniques. A technique used to adjust the start and finish dates of activities that adjust planned resource use to be equal to or less than resource availability.

There are two ways to optimize your resources: level them or smooth them.

Resource leveling adjusts activity start and finish dates so that resources are no longer over-allocated. Leveling frequently extends the due date. For example, if Sarah is scheduled to work on Activity A and Activity B during the week of March 1 through March 5, and both activities require five days of full time commitment, resource leveling would extend the start date of Activity B to begin on March 8 and end on March 12.

Another type of resource leveling is to reduce peaks and valleys in resource utilization. Instead of working 40 hours one week and 10 the next, resource leveling seeks to have a resource work 25 hours each week.

Resource smoothing adjusts activities within their float amounts but does not change the critical path. In other words, some resources may remain over-allocated.

Modeling techniques

So much uncertainty is associated with projects that it's nearly impossible to determine actual durations, future risks, stakeholder issues, actual resource availability, and so on. One way to account for the uncertainty is to think through different scenarios that could impact the project and see what happens to the schedule based on those scenarios.

What-if scenario analysis

For example, what if a critical resource is available only one-half of the time, as opposed to full time? Or, what if a key component is delivered late? Or design issues cause rework? These are common occurrences on projects. Building several schedule scenarios helps you to identify the impact of these scenarios upfront when you can still adjust the schedule to account for them, and update the risk register to take actions to minimize their impact on the schedule.

Simulation

Another modeling technique is simulation. Simulation involves calculating the project schedule with different assumptions about activity durations. One particular type of simulation is a Monte Carlo simulation. I discuss that concept more when talking about analyzing risk in Book V, Chapter 1.

Schedule compression

Compressing a schedule involves looking for ways to shorten the overall project duration without reducing the project scope. The two main types of schedule compression are crashing and fast-tracking.

Crashing

Crashing looks for cost/schedule trade-offs. In other words, you look for ways to shorten the schedule by applying more resources or by spending more. The intent is to get the most schedule compression for the least amount of money. Some common ways of accomplishing this include

- **Bringing in more resources:** Sometimes, more people working, or using additional equipment, can speed up progress.

  Be careful. Sometimes adding resources actually extends the duration because coordination, communication, and conflict actually take more time than they save!
- **Working overtime:** Many times, staff can work longer hours or work weekends. However, this is useful only for a couple of weeks. After that, people burn out and are less productive, so this is but a short-term fix. You also have to take into consideration any union or labor regulations.
- **Paying to expedite deliverables:** This solution can include overnight shipping and paying bonuses to contractors for early delivery.

You could certainly crash some activities for my running childcare center example. For example, you could bring in an extra carpenter, electrician, plumber, HVAC person, or painter and reduce the duration. You could also ask those resources to work more hours (depending on any labor union restrictions). Bringing in more resources might even reduce the time without increasing cost because the extra resources will shorten the duration.

However, overtime is usually billed at time and a half, so that option may cost more.

You can't crash everything. For example, you can't pay to have two inspectors to do one occupancy permit inspection. And you can't pay them to expedite the process.

Crashing usually increases spending, so weigh the benefit of earlier delivery against cost. Bottom line: You're looking for the most time for the least amount of cost!

Fast-tracking

Fast-tracking shortens the schedule by overlapping activities that are normally done in parallel. One way of doing this is changing the network logic by using leads and lags (read about these earlier in this chapter). For example, you can change a finish-to-start relationship to a finish-to-start with a lead. This causes the successor activity to start before the predecessor is complete. You can also change it to a start-to-start or finish-to-finish with a lag. Take a look at a few examples from my running childcare center example:

✦ Suppose you set up your schedule with finish-to-start dependencies among blueprint activities, carpentry, electrical, plumbing, and HVAC. You can probably conduct the electrical, plumbing, and HVAC in parallel instead of sequentially.

✦ You can change a finish-to-start relationship in plumbing to a finish-to-start with a lead. For example, after the bathrooms have all the pipes, the fixtures can be installed. The finish work doesn't have to wait until the kitchen or the outside plumbing is roughed in.

✦ You can install the windows and doors after the rough carpentry is done by modifying the relationship to a finish-to-finish relationship with a lag.

Fast-tracking can increase your risk on the project and might necessitate rework. Make sure you understand the real relationship between activities when you fast-track, or else you will end up with a schedule that doesn't make sense and can't be executed.

Develop Schedule: Outputs

The project schedule is one of the most important project artifacts that project managers create. There can be different versions of the schedule and different ways to display it. In this section, I walk through the different ways of displaying it, and then I describe some of the more common versions of the schedule.

The project schedule can be presented as a table, network diagram, bar chart, or milestone chart:

- **Tables** provide activity detail, such as planned start and end dates, percent complete, resources, actual start and finish dates, and many other column options.
- **Network diagrams** with planned start and finish dates show relationships among activities.
- **Bar charts** show the planned duration of activities.
- **Milestone charts** show the planned dates for major accomplishments.

Many times, you see a combination of a network diagram and a bar chart — often referred to as a *Gantt chart.* In fact, a Gantt chart is a bar chart. But because most of the software refers to a bar chart that shows dependencies as a Gantt chart, that has become the common way of referring to it. Figures 3-11 through 3-14 show various ways to display a schedule.

Activity	Duration	Planned Start	Planned Finish	Predecessor
Activity A	5d	Mon 3/1	Fri 3/5	–
Activity B	3d	Mon 3/8	Wed 3/10	A
Activity C	4d	Thu 3/4	Tue 3/9	A FS-2d
Activity D	6d	Mon 3/15	Mon 3/22	B FS+2d
Activity E	7d	Wed 3/10	Thu 3/18	C
Activity F	6d	Fri 3/19	Fri 3/26	E SS
Activity G	2d	Tue 3/23	Wed 3/24	D, E
Activity H	3d	Mon 3/22	Mon 3/22	G FF
Activity I	4d	Thu 3/25	Tue 3/30	H
Finish	0d	Tue 3/30	Tue 3/30	F, I

Figure 3-11: Schedule table.

Most scheduling tools provide you many different views for the schedule. You can pretty much pick what fields and information you want displayed and the way you want to see it, and *shazam!,* there it is.

Now, take a look at different versions of the schedule. You'll probably manage your project from a detailed schedule with the start and end dates of each activity and the resources assigned to the activity. You might also include the planned start and finish dates along with the actual start and finish dates and the percent complete. This gives you good visibility into the progress being made. However, you don't necessarily want to publish that schedule for the customer, sponsor, or anyone other than the project team. In fact, they probably don't really want to see it, either, because it's way too detailed.

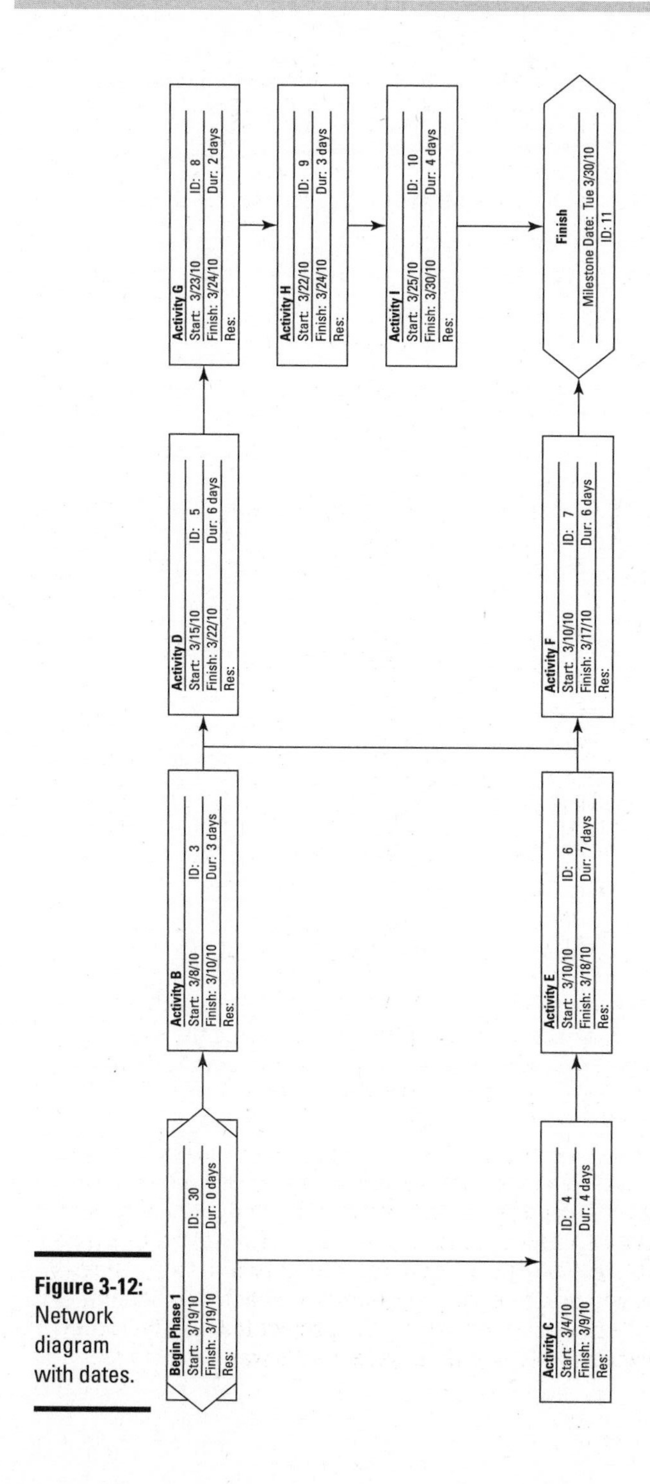

Figure 3-12: Network diagram with dates.

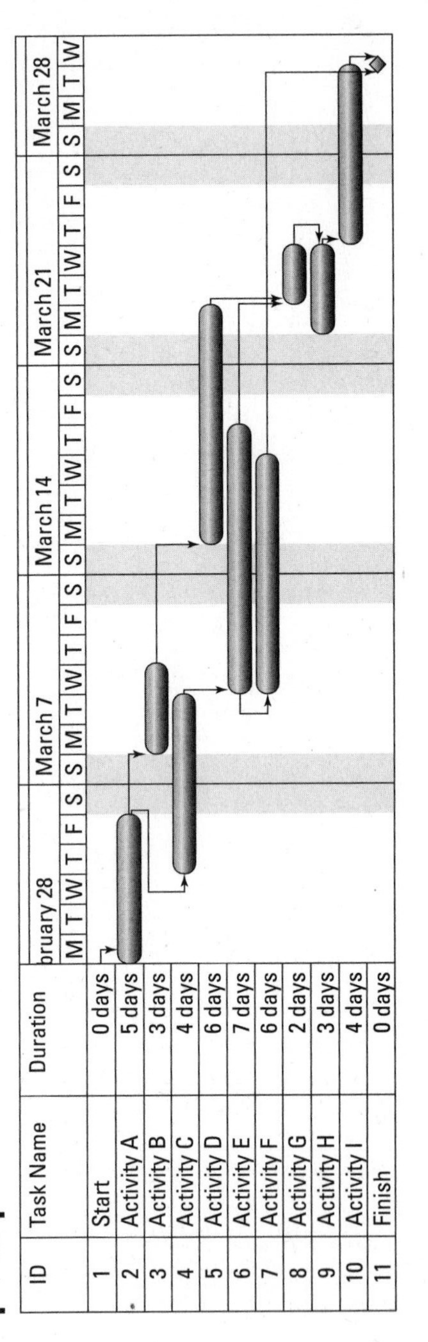

Figure 3-13: Bar chart.

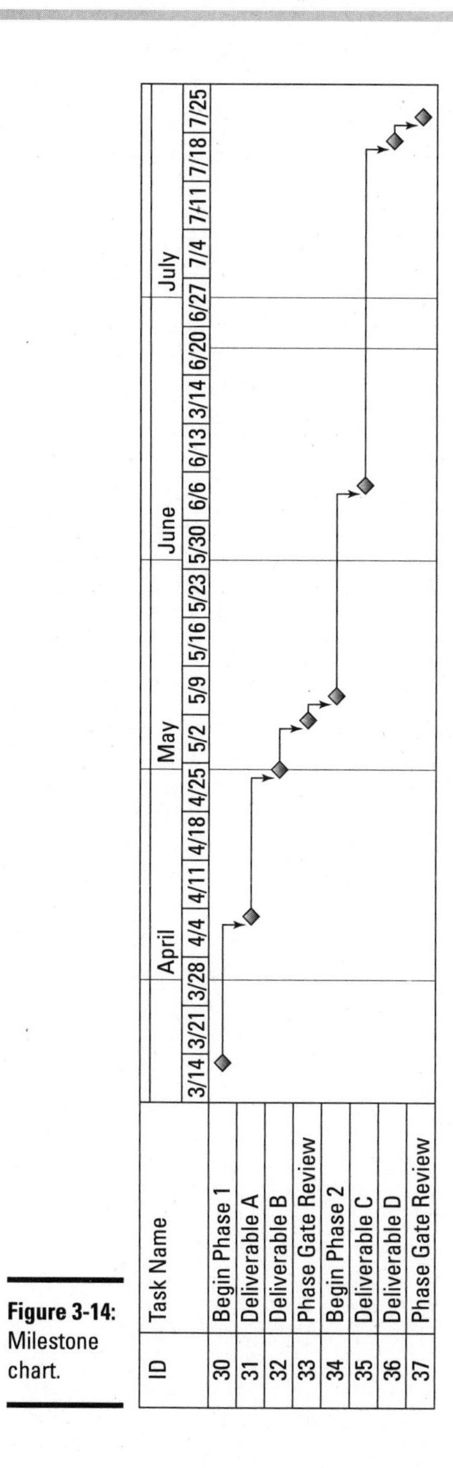

Figure 3-14: Milestone chart.

So, a schedule baseline is a good schedule to show your sponsor. The schedule baseline, which has the agreed-upon start and finish dates for the project, is usually shown at a milestone or summary level. The baseline is part of the project management plan and will be used to evaluate the project status.

Additional schedule options can be based on aggressive dates or best case scenarios, or schedules resulting from what-if scenarios the team generated.

In addition to the schedule, you've developed all kinds of schedule-related data. For example, you have the information to create resource histograms that show the usage of resources over time, assumptions associated with project performance and resource utilization, and the basis of your duration estimates.

Based on all the work done to develop the schedule, you might find yourself updating the project calendar (project working days), elements of the project management plan, or project documents. Your resource requirements, risk register, Assumption Log, and cost estimates are prime targets for updating.

Key Terms

There is a lot of scheduling vocabulary to remember! It is a pretty specialized language.

Study hint: Put each term on an index card with its definition on the back. Memorize the definition with the term.

- Schedule management plan
- Activity attribute
- Milestone
- Logical relationship
- Precedence diagramming method
- Finish-to-start
- Finish-to-finish
- Start-to-start
- Start-to-finish
- Mandatory dependency
- Discretionary dependency

- External dependency
- Lead
- Lag
- Project schedule network diagram
- Resource breakdown structure
- Resource histogram
- Effort
- Duration
- Analogous estimate
- Parametric estimate
- Bottom-up estimate
- Three-point estimate
- Critical path methodology
- Early start date
- Early finish date
- Late start date
- Late finish date
- Total float
- Free float
- Forward pass
- Backward pass
- Critical path
- Critical chain
- Buffer
- Resource optimization
- Resource leveling
- Resource smoothing
- Crashing
- Fast-tracking

Chapter Summary

Here are the main points you need to remember for the scheduling:

- To build a schedule, you start by decomposing work packages into activities.
- Milestones mark a significant event in a project.
- Develop a network diagram to create a visual display of the activity relationships.
- You can have FS, FF, or SS — or, occasionally, SF — relationships.
- You can modify relationships with leads and lags.
- Some dependencies are mandatory, some are discretionary, and still others are external.
- Project resources include people, equipment, material, and supplies.
- Duration estimates can comprise labor units and/or work periods.
- Analogous estimating compares the current project with past similar projects.
- Parametric estimating uses a mathematical relationship to derive duration estimates.
- Bottom-up estimates decompose work to the work package level to determine the duration.
- Three-point estimates are used when there is a large degree of uncertainty associated with the estimate.
- Critical path methodology creates a schedule that shows the range of dates that activities can start and finish without causing the project to be late or without breaking a schedule constraint. It is focused on managing float.
- Critical chain methodology starts with the critical path but considers resource constraints. It works to exploit the most critical resources and focuses on the remaining buffer.
- You can compress a schedule by crashing or fast-tracking.
- The project schedule can be presented in a table, network diagram, bar chart, or milestone chart.

There is no substitute for practice. I encourage you to make a couple of network diagrams, load in some fictional durations, and practice your forward and backward passes. That will give you more confidence on the exam.

Prep Test

Multiple Choice

1 The difference in decomposing the work to develop the WBS and decomposing the WBS to determine the activities is

A ❍ Decomposing work to develop the WBS is a team effort, but the WBS to determine activities is done individually.

B ❍ The WBS is decomposed into deliverables using nouns; activities are decomposed into actions using verbs.

C ❍ The WBS can be developed using progressive elaboration, but activities can use only rolling wave planning.

D ❍ The WBS goes down to three levels, and the activities are decomposed below that.

2 *I can't begin laying the deck planks until the deck framework is done.* This is an example of which kind of dependency?

A ❍ Discretionary

B ❍ Finish-to-finish

C ❍ Mandatory

D ❍ Start-to-start

3 Ellen is responsible for writing Chapters 6, 8, and 10. She can do them in any order. This is an example of

A ❍ A discretionary dependency

B ❍ An assumption

C ❍ An external dependency

D ❍ A resource constraint

4 As soon as Bill begins publicizing the concert, the tickets can go on sale. This is an example of what kind of relationship?

A ❍ Start-to-finish

B ❍ Finish-to-finish

C ❍ Finish-to-start

D ❍ Start-to-start

5 **The phase gate is scheduled for one week after the integration test is complete. This is an example of**

A ❍ Finish-to-finish with a lead
B ❍ Finish-to-start with a lead
C ❍ Finish-to-finish with a lag
D ❍ Finish-to-start with a lag

6 ***We need to finish the walk-through four days before we are done with the quality review.* This is an example of**

A ❍ Finish-to-finish with a lead
B ❍ Finish-to-start with a lead
C ❍ Finish-to-finish with a lag
D ❍ Finish-to-start with a lag

7 **You want to categorize your people, equipment, materials, and supplies by type and skill level so you can get an overview of all the types of resources you need for the project. What is a good way to document this?**

A ❍ A resource traceability matrix
B ❍ A resource calendar
C ❍ A project resource diagram
D ❍ A resource breakdown structure

8 **You've been assigned a project that is in the concept phase. You have a high-level understanding of the requirements, and the WBS is decomposed only to level 2. You have done this type of project before. The sponsor wants an initial timeline: nothing detailed, just milestone dates. What technique should you use to provide the duration estimate?**

A ❍ Analogous estimating
B ❍ Parametric estimating
C ❍ Three-point estimating
D ❍ Monte Carlo simulation

9 **Which type of duration estimating technique is best if you have a quantitative data to work with, such as square footage?**

A ❍ Analogous estimating
B ❍ Parametric estimating
C ❍ Three-point estimating
D ❍ Monte Carlo simulation

10 **You developed three duration estimates based on everything going right, everything going wrong, and what's likely to occur. Your optimistic estimate is 6 weeks; your pessimistic estimate is 16 weeks; and you think it's likely to take 8 weeks. What is your expected duration, using a PERT technique?**

A ❍ 8 weeks

B ❍ 8.7 weeks

C ❍ 9 weeks

D ❍ 10 weeks

11 **If you need to reduce schedule duration and you want to overlap activities, you would**

A ❍ Crash the schedule.

B ❍ Add more resources.

C ❍ Fast-track.

D ❍ Work overtime.

Scenario 1

Use the following network diagram with durations to answer the next two questions.

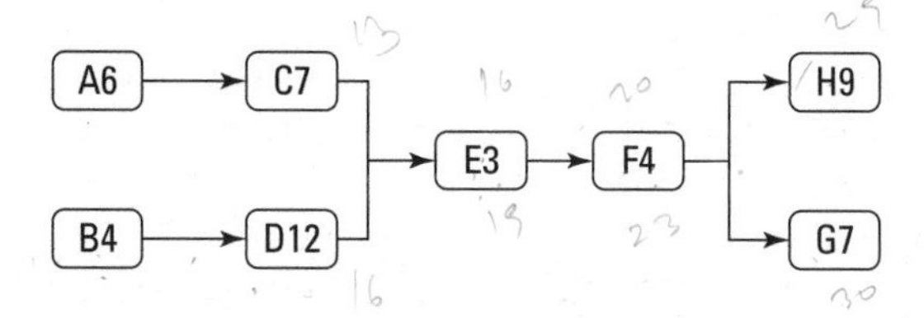

1 **For the figure, what is the critical path?**

A ❍ A-C-E-F-G

B ❍ B-D-E-F-G

C ❍ B-D-E-F-H

D ❍ A-C-E-F-H

2 **For the figure, what duration would the critical path be if the relationship between B and D were SS?**

A ❍ 29 days

B ❍ 28 days

C ❍ 27 days

D ❍ 32 days

Answers

Multiple Choice

1 **B.** The WBS is decomposed into deliverables using nouns; activities are decomposed into actions using verbs. Because the WBS is deliverable-oriented, nouns are used to identify the deliverables. Verbs describe the actions needed to create the deliverables. *See "Define Activities: Tools and Techniques."*

2 **C.** Mandatory. The planks need to rest on the framework. Therefore, the nature of the word dictates that the framework comes before the planks. *Check out "Sequence Activities: Tools and Techniques."*

3 **A.** A discretionary dependency. Because any chapter can come first, it is up to Ellen's discretion to set the order. *Review the information in "Sequence Activities: Tools and Techniques."*

4 **D.** Start-to-start. The start of the ticket sales is dependent upon the start of the publicity. *Review "Sequence Activities: Tools and Techniques."*

5 **D.** Finish-to-start with a lag. The phase gate is dependent upon the end of the integration test, and there is a one-week delay between the two. *See "Leads and lags."*

6 **A.** Finish-to-finish with a lead. The end of the walk-through is based on the end of the quality review, and it needs to happen four days prior to the end of the quality review. *See "Leads and lags."*

7 **D.** A resource breakdown structure. The resource breakdown structure identifies categories of resources and then decomposes them into types, skill levels, or other subcategories as appropriate. *Take a look at "Estimate Activity Resources: Tools and Techniques."*

8 **A.** Analogous estimating. Analogous estimating is used for projects during the early phases when there aren't a lot of details. *Go back over "Analogous estimating."*

9 **B.** Parametric estimating. Parametric estimating is used when you have a quantitative basis for estimating. *Look at the information in "Parametric estimating."*

10 **C.** 9 weeks. $(6 + (4 * 8) + 16) / 6 = 9$ weeks. *See "Three-point estimates."*

11 **C.** Fast-track. Fast-tracking is doing activities in parallel that would normally be done sequentially. *Look at "Schedule compression."*

Scenario 1

1 **C.** B-D-E-F-H. This path is the longest duration through the network. *Review "Identify the critical path."*

2 **A.** 29 days. The critical path with the difference in the network diagram is now A-C-E-F-H and is 29 days. *Look at "Identify the critical path."*

Book IV

Planning Cost, Quality, Human Resources, and Communication

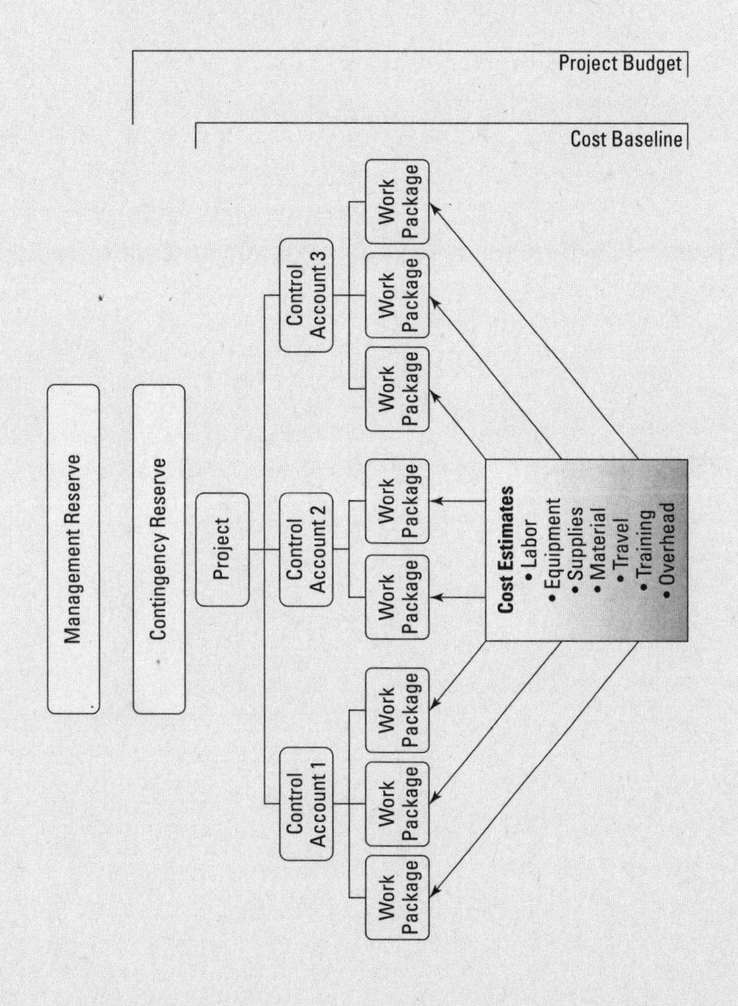

Read the article on planning knowledge and skills at www.dummies.com/extras/pmpcertificationaio.

Contents at a Glance

Chapter 1: Estimating the Price Tag

Exam Objective

- **Using cost-estimating techniques, develop a budget based on the project scope in order to manage project cost.**

Project cost is one of the most sensitive areas of your project. Your sponsor and customer are very concerned with cost estimates, total budget, and the flow of funding. They will want to find ways to minimize costs while maximizing quality and reducing the schedule, yet not giving up scope. Remember, customers generally want more scope, faster and for less cost.

Your job is to resist the pressure to give overly optimistic estimates. You need to make sure that your team has the time to define the scope in enough detail that you can develop accurate cost estimates. In addition, you need to make sure you have sufficient time to plan and estimate your costs, and that you understand the uncertainty associated with the cost estimates and budget. This includes estimating the funding needed to account for uncertainty, undefined scope, project changes, and unplanned in-scope work. None of this is easy, but all of it is important. More than any other objective, in the short term, the success of the project is judged by your ability to deliver on budget as well as in the time allotted.

If you've already read Book III, Chapter 3, many of the techniques used to estimate costs will seem familiar to you: They're the same ones used to estimate effort and duration for the schedule.

Quick Assessment

1. (True/False). At the time of completing the charter, most projects will have cost estimate ranges of +/–10%.

2. A(n) ______ ______ is a quantitative assessment of the likely amount or outcome.

3. Which cost-estimating technique requires the most detail?

4. The approved version of the time-phased project budget, excluding management reserves, is the ______ ______.

5. The project budget is composed of the ______ ______ and the ______ ______.

6. Where do you record the information on how you will plan, structure, and control project costs?

7. (True/False). A project that is using new technology will have a narrower range of estimates.

8. A weighted average estimate, also known as a PERT estimate, is represented by the equation ______.

9. The method of estimating that uses a scalable, mathematical model is ______ estimating.

10. The sum of all the budgets is the ______ ______ ______.

Answers

1 False. There is not usually enough information about the project and product scope to develop an estimate that is accurate to within +/–10%. *Read more in "Estimate Costs: Tools and Techniques."*

2 Cost estimate. Estimates are quantitative assessments of likely costs. They are not guesses, nor are they facts. *See the definition in "Estimate Costs: Inputs."*

3 Bottom-up estimating. Bottom-up estimating estimates the cost of individual work packages or activities. *You will find this information in "Bottom-up estimating."*

4 Cost baseline. The cost baseline can only be changed through formal change control procedures. *This information is in the section "Determine Budget: Outputs."*

5 Cost baseline and management reserve. The cost baseline includes projected expenditures; the budget includes a management. *Look over the information in "Determine Budget: Outputs."*

6 Cost management plan. The cost management plan contains information that defines how you will plan, manage, and control all aspects of the costs and budget for the project. You may see this referred to as the budget plan. *You can find more information on this in "Plan Cost Management."*

7 False. Projects with new or unproven technology have wider ranges of estimates. *See "Estimate Costs: Inputs."*

8 (O + 4M + P) / 6. *This equation is explained in the section "Three-point estimating."*

9 Parametric. Parametric estimating uses a statistical relationship to derive cost estimates. *See more about this in "Parametric estimating."*

10 Budget at completion. The budget at completion is also the cumulative planned value for the project. *You can find this definition in "Determine Budget."*

Plan Cost Management

Because the cost of a project is often the first thing that management is interested in, the budget for a project is one of the most important documents in the project management plan. The cost management plan describes units of measure, levels of accuracy, and variance thresholds, among other things, for the budget.

Cost management plan. A component of the project or program management plan that describes how costs will be planned, structured, and controlled.

Plan Cost Management: Inputs

When developing a cost management plan, you should reference the project charter and the project management plan. The project charter contains the summary level budget. The project management plan contains the scope and schedule baselines.

Enterprise environmental factors (EEFs) and organizational process assets (OPAs) play a big role in this process. The EEFs that are most influential include

- **Market conditions:** The ability to obtain resources at a reasonable rate
- **Published rate information:** For example, rate guides for certain industries
- **Currency exchange rates** for international projects

There are sure to be processes and procedures associated with developing project estimates and budgets. Other organizational process assets that you can use include lessons learned and information from prior similar project budgets.

Plan Cost Management: Tools and Techniques

Expertise from cost estimators, finance staff, and people with knowledge of the specific discipline and industry are often called on to analyze decisions, such as

- Whether to make or buy components
- Whether to buy or lease equipment
- Which financial metrics to use to make decisions — such as net present value (NPV), breakeven point, payback period, or discounted cash flow

The financial metrics are reviewed in Book II, Chapter 1.

Plan Cost Management: Outputs

The cost management plan includes a description of how costs will be estimated, budgeted, and controlled. It defines the methods and techniques used throughout the project. Some common content includes

- **Planning information**
  - *How costs will be recorded:* This could be hours, euros, yen, dollars, or some other metric.
  - *The detail level of cost reporting:* This defines whether you will report in 100s of dollars, or 1000s of dollars, or some other increment.
  - *Determining which costs will be tracked on the project:* Many organizations don't track the costs of internal resources, such as people, equipment use, supplies and so forth. On the other hand, if the project is being done under contract, labor will be tracked and billed at a specified rate — and perhaps an overhead rate will be assessed to account for indirect costs, such as overhead, executive salaries, and the like. Another example is determining whether capital equipment will be charged to the project or depreciated as part of the organization's operations.
  - *Systems used to track and report costs and also establish the links between cost and other artifacts and systems:* For example, this defines whether costs are reported using the work breakdown structure (WBS) numbering structure or the company's accounting codes. I discuss the WBS numbering structure in Book III, Chapter 2.
- **Executing information**
  - *How and when cost information is collected:* Your organization may have an automated system that allows the project manager (PM) to enter the costs for resources and assign those costs to a specific WBS item, or you may have to manually review monthly invoices to determine project costs. Some organizations track costs weekly, others monthly. Whichever situation you find yourself in, you should document the expectations in the cost management plan.
  - *How you will measure scope and budget performance:* This is most commonly used in EV management, but defining measurement methods upfront helps reduce surprises for any project. For example, you can define whether you will collect costs weekly and compare them against progress, or when a deliverable is complete, or whether to use interim deliverable milestones to track costs.
  - *When to record project costs for procured items:* Should costs be recorded when the order is placed? Delivered? Used? Invoiced? Paid? Most organizations have accounting policies in place that define when to record costs for operations, but you will need to determine

when to record them for project tracking up front to ensure reporting consistency.

- **Monitoring and controlling information**
  - Information and metrics to be collected and reported
  - Reporting format
  - Control thresholds
  - Forecasting techniques

The *PMBOK Guide* references the information in this section as a "cost management plan." However, the exam specification that the exam is built from calls this a "budget plan." Be prepared to see questions referencing either term on the exam.

Estimate Costs

Estimating how much everything will cost on a project can be very challenging. Unless you have a fixed price quote for work or materials, your costs are likely to evolve and change. When a project is initiated (see Book II, Chapter 2 on project initiation), you won't have much detail, so your cost estimates will not be very accurate. However, as you develop more detailed information, you will get more accurate cost estimates.

Developing, refining, and updating cost estimates is an iterative and ongoing process throughout the project. You need to include information from many other processes:

- Create WBS
- Develop Schedule
- Plan Human Resources
- Identify Risks

For smaller projects, the processes of estimating costs and determining the budget are completed at the same time. However, for larger projects, these are separate and more detailed processes.

Estimate. A quantitative assessment of the likely amount or outcome. Usually applied to project costs, resources, effort and durations and is usually preceded by a modifier (i.e., preliminary, conceptual, feasibility, order-of-magnitude, definitive). It should always include some indication of accuracy (for example, +/– *n* percent).

Estimate Costs. The process of developing an approximation of the monetary resources needed to complete project activities.

Estimate Costs: Inputs

You use the cost management plan to determine the level of accuracy and units of measure to use for estimating costs. Estimating the cost of the project starts with well-defined scope. For that, you need the scope baseline. Your scope statement tells you any constraints, such as a predetermined budget, set delivery dates, or limited resources. The WBS defines all the deliverables, but the WBS dictionary has the technical details and resources associated with those deliverables. This can include necessary licenses, permits, safety issues, and so on. More information on the scope baseline, WBS, and WBS dictionary is in Book III, Chapter 2.

The project schedule contains the information from the Estimate Activity Resources and Estimate Activity Durations processes. The project schedule — along with the human resource plan, which contains staffing information, such as hourly rates (see Chapter 3 of this minibook for more on the human resource plan) — are two important components in estimating costs accurately.

The risk register provides two types of costs:

- **Costs associated with specific risks:** Can include the cost to mitigate a risk, purchase a bond or insurance, or provide some other appropriate risk response.
- **Costs associated with contingency:** Used to ensure the project doesn't overrun the budget by setting aside funds to account for uncertainty and unidentified risks.

See more information about risk in Book V, Chapter 1.

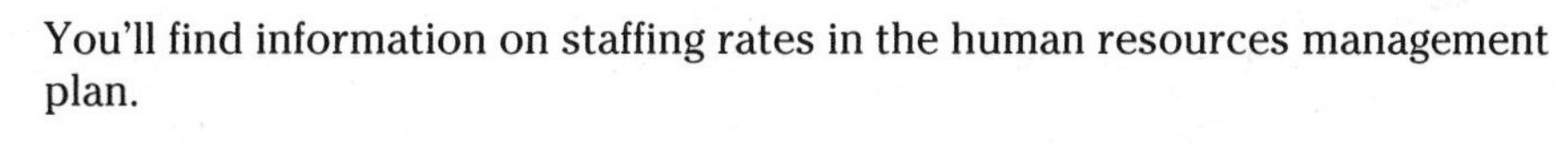

You'll find information on staffing rates in the human resources management plan.

Market conditions can have a significant impact on a project's costs, such as

- **Availability of resources:** Scarce human resources or materials will drive up costs.
- **Interest rates:** The cost of borrowing money and the availability of money will influence project choices and estimates.

In some industries, databases or publications offer market rates for resources. For example, construction costs are fairly stable, and you can find a lot of information on costs for material, labor, equipment, and so forth.

Information on past projects is really useful when estimating costs. However, take care that the information is current and relevant. Cost information for a project you completed five years ago is most likely no longer relevant.

Estimate Costs: Tools and Techniques

Part of the estimating process is looking at alternative project approaches. Sometimes, bringing in a full-time employee to fill a slot on the team is the best option; other times, going with contract labor is a better option. With equipment, you can compare the cost options of purchasing, leasing, or renting. You might want to look at the lifecycle cost of the product versus the project cost.

One of the axioms in estimating is that as you progress through the planning process, your estimates will get more accurate and have a narrower range. This is just common sense. As the scope is better defined, the costs can be better defined.

The *PMBOK Guide* doesn't state definitively the degree of accuracy that you should have for cost estimates based on where you are in the project lifecycle. The *PMBOK Guide* and the PMP have to apply to all industries. However, Table 1-1 shows some standard project-estimating accuracy ranges (Harold Kerzner, *Project Management: A Systems Approach to Planning, Scheduling, and Controlling,* Eleventh Edition [Wiley]).

Table 1-1 Standard Project-Estimating Accuracy Ranges

Type	*Range*	*Use*
Rough Order of Magnitude (ROM)	–25% to +75%	In the concept phase. Top down. Little information.
Budgetary	–10% to +25%	In the planning phase. Decomposed from top down. Some information.
Definitive	–5% to +10%	In production. Bottom-up. Detailed information.

Several variables can affect your range of estimates and the confidence level in the estimates (see Figures 1-1 and 1-2):

- Technology
- Experience
- Risk

Estimates have a narrow range and more confidence

Figure 1-1: Estimates with higher accuracy.

- Proven technology
- Experience with similar projects
- Low risk and uncertainty

Estimates have a wider range and less confidence

Figure 1-2: Estimates with lower accuracy.

- New or unproven technology
- Little or no experience with the type of work
- High degree of risk and uncertainty

Just like estimating durations, expert judgment in the form of team members and estimators is invaluable. These people can select the best method of estimating, and they bring their experience in how to save money and knowing which shortcuts end up costing more in the end.

You will obviously use some type of software to record your estimates. The simplest way is to use some kind of spreadsheet (such as Microsoft Excel) although many organizations use proprietary or off-the-shelf estimating software. Estimating software can run simulations, develop graphs and charts, and greatly simplify the estimating and budgeting processes.

You might be accountable for different types of costs on your project:

Direct Costs	Directly attributable to your project. Includes labor, material, travel costs, and so on.
Indirect Costs	Not directly attributable to your project. Includes overhead, management salaries, the legal department, and so on.

Analogous estimating

Analogous estimating uses expert judgment and historical information to develop cost estimates. This type of estimating is used in the earlier phases of a project to get an overall project cost although it can be used at any time in the project lifecycle and at any level of detail in the WBS. You start with a similar project and identify the variables that drive the cost. In cost estimates, some of the variables that are likely to drive cost are:

- Size
- Weight
- Complexity

For my running example of a childcare center, say that you're trying to get a high-level cost estimate for remodeling the space. You can look for information from a remodel that your organization recently did to compare that against the current project. If your company doesn't have that history, your contractor will surely be able to pull from his expertise and recent experience. The scenario might sound something like this:

> *We recently took 5,000 square feet of new space that hadn't been built out at all and put in a childcare center. That project ended up costing $550,000. But, for this project, we have to demo the existing space, so that will add about 10%. However, this project is only 4,000 square feet, so that's 20% less space.*

So, first you add the 10% for demo. That brings the cost to $605,000. Then you multiply that by 80% to get an analogous estimate of $484,000.

This is a relatively quick and simple way to estimate. As you fill in more details about the scope, the estimate will need to be re-examined, and a more accurate method will be appropriate.

Parametric estimating

Parametric estimating uses a statistical relationship based on past data to calculate an estimate. For the childcare center scenario, say that the general contractor rates this type of job at about $120 per square foot, and you have 4,000 square feet. That gives you an estimate of $480,000.

Parametric estimating is easy if you have a simple model, such as cost per square foot. It can get more complex, though, with the more variables you add. However, if you set up this kind of estimation model on a spreadsheet, it's relatively simple to change the parameters if your assumptions (say, the number of machines) or basis of estimates (cost per machine) changes. To use this method, the cost-estimating relationships (CERs) need to be scalable. In other words, if you are using cost per square foot, then the cost per square foot needs to remain the same whether the square footage is 10 or 10,000.

Bottom-up estimating

Bottom-up estimating is the most accurate form of estimating. However, you can employ this type of estimating only toward the end of the planning process when you have detailed information about the scope. This method

1. Determines the cost for each resource needed to create the deliverable
2. Sums all deliverables

3. Includes the contingency reserve

   Read about contingency reserve in the later section, "Determine Budget: Outputs."

4. Aggregates the total into a bottom-up estimate

Although bottom-up estimating is the most accurate type of estimate, it's also quite time consuming, and you can't do it until you have a significant level of detail for the deliverables.

Three-point estimating

When you have a lot of uncertainty, risk, or unknowns around a work package, you can use three-point estimating to give you a range and an expected cost. You collect three estimates based on the best case, most likely, and worst case scenarios.

- **Best case (optimistic):** Cost estimates play out while accurate, no-risk events occur, and the work takes only as long as estimated. This is represented as an *o* for "optimistic." Or you might see it notated as $\mathbf{c}_o$ for "cost optimistic."
- **Most likely:** Takes into account the realities of project life, such as needing extra parts or people, rework, things not going exactly as planned, and so forth. This is represented as an *m* for "most likely." You might see this presented as $\mathbf{c}_m$ for "cost most likely."
- **Worst case (pessimistic):** Assumes expensive resources, much rework, and delays in work getting accomplished. This is represented as a *p* for "pessimistic" or $\mathbf{c}_p$ for "cost pessimistic."

The simplest way to develop the expected cost, or $\mathbf{c}_e$ (cost expected), is to sum the three estimates and divide by three. You might see this referred to as a triangular distribution. However, that's not the most accurate way because you assume an equal probability that the best case, most likely, and worst case scenarios would occur — and that's not realistic. In reality, the most likely estimate has a greater chance of occurring than either the best case or the worst case scenarios. Therefore, you weight the most likely scenario to develop a weighted average. The most common way of calculating a weighted average is

$$\mathbf{c}_e = (\mathbf{c}_o + 4\mathbf{c}_m + \mathbf{c}_p) / 6$$

Notice that the numerator has six factors you are adding; therefore, the denominator to achieve the average is 6.

FOR THE EXAM

The PMP exam might refer to this as a Beta Distribution or PERT (Program Evaluation and Review Technique) estimating.

Suppose you're estimating costs to travel to a project site. You do some research on plane tickets; based on the time of year and how far in advance you purchase the tickets, you come up with some estimates. If you travel during normal business days (no holidays) and you purchase the ticket three weeks in advance, you can get a cost as low as $300 per round trip. This is the best case scenario. More likely, though, you won't book until two weeks prior to the trip, which will bump the cost to $450. However, in the past, you've had but 48 hours advance notice — and if this occurs during a holiday, you're looking at a cost of $1,200 per round trip. Using the weighted average, you determine your expected cost to be

$$(300 + 4(450) + 1200) / 6 = \$550$$

Table 1-2 summarizes the benefits and shortfalls of various methods of developing cost estimates.

Table 1-2 Comparing Cost Estimating Methods

Type	*Benefits*	*Shortfalls*
Analogous	Used if a limited amount of detailed information is available. Useful when the estimate must be delivered within certain time constraints.	Not as accurate as a bottom-up estimate. Can be used only when the projects are similar in fact not just in appearance.
Parametric	Useful if components are scalable. Useful if historical information on which the model is based is accurate. Quick.	Parameters must be quantifiable. Not as accurate as a bottom-up estimate. Computer program needed.
Bottom-up	Most accurate. Buy-in from the person doing the work. Used when the project is well defined.	Time consuming. Interaction costs may be overlooked. Contingency costs by task may inflate estimates.
Three-point	Used if there is a lot of uncertainty on the project. Provides a justification for cost reserve.	Time consuming. Many people have a hard time coming up with one estimate, much less three.

Reserve analysis for cost estimates

If your project is very complex or uses new and unproven technology, you need more reserves than if you had a simple project you've done many times before. You need to determine the appropriate amount, either in dollars or as a percent of the budget, to set aside for reserve. As you reduce the uncertainty, you can reduce the reserve.

Cost of quality

Cost of quality takes into consideration costs necessary to comply with quality requirements. These include prevention costs (such as training and more planning) and appraisal costs (such as test equipment and testing). Cost of quality also includes the costs associated with noncompliance, such as scrap, rework, warranty work, and so forth. Find more information about the cost of quality in the next chapter of this minibook.

Vendor bid analysis

A vendor bid analysis technique is used if you're outsourcing or procuring part of your project. You analyze the vendor bid, contract type, and incentive fees (if used) and then include that information in your cost estimates.

Additional techniques

Estimating software, spreadsheets, and simulation software can be useful to organize and review multiple cost estimates. To arrive at a viable range of outcomes it may be useful to engage a group of experts, in which case you are likely to need decision-making techniques such as the Delphi technique (described in Book V, Chapter 1).

Estimate Costs: Outputs

Activity cost estimates can be at a high level or a much more detailed level toward the end of the planning phase. Costs may be rolled into resource categories for accounting and reporting purposes. Common categories include

- Labor
- Equipment
- Material
- Supplies
- Travel
- Permits and licenses

- Facilities
- Contingency reserve
- Overhead

Along with the cost estimates, you should record your assumptions and the basis of estimates. Suppose that you're documenting supporting details for cost estimates for the eating area furniture for the childcare center. You'd document the following assumptions:

- No more than 30 children will be in the eating area at one time.
- All children can use the same size tables and chairs.
- Tables can seat 6 children comfortably.

Then you do your research on prices and find the following:

- Tables cost $250 each.
- Chairs cost $65 each.

The information on the number of children and the configuration are the assumptions, and the costs for the tables and chairs are the basis of estimates. Both pieces of information should be documented. If you make changes to the assumptions or the basis of estimates, costs will change.

You might want to indicate in your assumptions and basis of estimates the fixed costs and the variable costs. Fixed costs don't change based on volume. For example, office rent is the same whether you have 2 people using the office or 20, or whether they use it 40 or 100 hours per week. Comparatively, variable costs adjust based on volume. For example, whether you need 5 or 20 gallons of paint will affect the cost estimate for paint.

Based on developing your cost estimates, you might need to update your risk register and/or Assumption Log, or rebalance your scope to your estimated funding needs. The assumption log is discussed in Book III, Chapter 2. The risk register is introduced in Book V, Chapter 1.

Determine Budget

Your budget is the authorized funding for your project. In addition to the definition of this process, be familiar with the definition of *budget* and *budget at completion.*

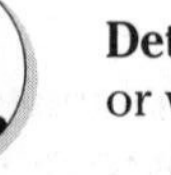

Determine Budget. Aggregating the estimated costs of individual activities or work packages to establish an authorized cost baseline.

Budget. The approved estimate for the project or any work breakdown structure component or any schedule activity.

Budget at completion (BAC). The sum of all the budgets established for the work to be performed.

To formulate the budget, you spread cost estimates across the schedule. This gives you a time-phased spending curve, often called an *S-curve.* It starts with looking at how scope, schedule, and cost relate.

Determine Budget: Inputs

You need numerous project documents and artifacts to create a reliable budget. You will want to apply the organization's budgeting policies and tools to keep the information organized. The following sections discuss the artifacts and documents by organizing them into scope, schedule, and cost categories.

Scope information

The scope baseline provides the obvious, which is the WBS and WBS dictionary that defines the detailed work for the project. However, the scope statement can have some very useful information. Remember that the scope statement documents project constraints. Many times, funding limitations are based on fiscal year budgets. For example, the project might have an overall cost estimate of 2.5 million, but only 1 million is available the first year, 1 million the second year, and the balance in the third year. Work done for the government often has funding limitations that restrict the expenditures of funds. You need to compare this information with information from the schedule and the cost estimates to develop an accurate budget.

Schedule information

Schedule artifacts include the project schedule, which has information on the planned start and finish dates for elements of the project scope. At the most detailed, you can see start and finish dates for activities. You can also see the dates for work packages and even control accounts. This can help you aggregate costs by work period.

You should also look at the resource calendars to see when people are available and when they are assigned to work. If you have to spread out work to accommodate funding limitations, you need to determine whether resources are available as needed.

Cost information

The cost management plan, cost estimates, and the basis of estimates are applied to the work packages and the schedule to develop the funding needs over time. You should look at agreements and contracts to determine when payment for goods and services are due. Review the risk register to determine how to aggregate risk response costs and to incorporate contingency reserves over time.

Determine Budget: Tools and Techniques

When building a budget, you need expert judgment in the form of team members and perhaps even finance folks, depending on the size and complexity of the budget. The main technique is *cost aggregation*. This will be coupled with reserve analysis and funding limit reconciliation. In some industries, you can use historical relationships to validate the budget curve. The following sections look at each of these a bit closer.

Cost aggregation

Cost aggregation is simply summing the costs for each work package to the control account up to the project level. You can aggregate this information by time period to see the scheduled spending per time period. Table 1-3 shows activities and costs for the playground installation for the childcare center. The second row from the bottom shows the weekly cost, and the bottom row shows the aggregation of costs so you can see a running total of planned expenditures.

Table 1-3 Cost Aggregation Example

	Estimate	*Week 1*	*Week 2*	*Week 3*	*Week 4*
Grade site	$2,500	$2,500			
Pour pad	$2,500		$2,500		
Install swings	$1,500			$1,500	
Install slide	$1,500			$1,500	
Install teeter-totter	$1,200			$1,200	
Lay sod	$1,500				$1,500
Plant trees	$600				$600
Weekly cost		*$2,500*	*$2,500*	*$4,200*	*$2,100*
Cumulative cost		**$2,500**	**$5,000**	**$9,200**	**$11,300**

Reserve analysis for determining the budget

Reserve analysis, as used in developing a budget, takes into consideration both contingency reserve and management reserve. This can be a tricky distinction, and not everyone agrees on the exact definition. The *PMBOK Guide* defines reserve and contingency reserve, but not management reserve. After the following definitions, I show some examples to elaborate the concepts.

Contingency reserve. Budget within the cost baseline or the performance measurement baseline that is allocated for identified risks that are accepted and for which contingent or mitigating responses are developed.

Reserve. A provision in the project management plan to mitigate cost and/or schedule risk. Often used with a modifier (for example, management reserve, contingency reserve) to provide further detail on what types of risk are meant to be mitigated.

Contingency reserve concerns risk identified in the risk register. It is used to reduce risk on the project by providing funds for specific deliverables, phases of the lifecycle, or the project as a whole. Contingency reserve is used to ensure that the project doesn't overrun the available funding. Contingency funds are included in the cost baseline and the funding requirements.

Using the childcare center example, assume that you set aside 10% of the budget for risk management. A week before the playground equipment is supposed to be installed, the playground equipment contractor calls to announce a delay in getting the slide delivered. The project manager could use contingency reserve to either find another supplier (even if the cost was a bit more), or perhaps expedite shipping and delivery, or maybe pay overtime to get it installed as fast as possible after delivery.

Management reserve is for unplanned, in-scope work. For example, say the plumbing contractor at the childcare center put in 20 feet of PVC pipe, and then the carpenter put up the drywall and painted everything only to discover a hairline crack in the pipe that was leaking and needed replaced. The plumber needs to take out the drywall, replace the pipe, and pay to have the drywall replaced and possibly repainted. This is in-scope work, but it was definitely not planned. Management reserve would be used to pay for that. Management reserve is not part of the baseline, but it is part of the funding requirements.

Another aspect of reserve analysis is deciding how to allocate it. Because installing a playground is a relatively low-risk endeavor, without many unknowns, you would probably put in only 5–10% contingency for unexpected costs. You might want to apply it evenly throughout the project, or assign 10% in the concept phase, 20% in the planning phase, 60% in the construction phase, and the remaining 10% at walk-through.

Funding limit reconciliation

When you first lay your cost estimates over time and aggregate the funds by time period, you should compare the results with any funding limitations identified in the scope statement or elsewhere. I discuss the scope statement in Book III, Chapter 2. This might require you to reschedule the work to meet the funding limitations. Usually, it necessitates extending the schedule to account for limited funding although sometimes funding must be spent by a certain date lest it be lost – and this might call for schedule acceleration.

Historical relationships

A good way to check the validity of your budget is to compare it with any historic data or industry data that show cost relationships. For example, organizations that do similar projects and use a defined lifecycle can tell you what percent of the budget should be spent in each lifecycle phase. You can compare the historic information with your project lifecycle to make sure that they're aligned. ***Note:*** You should be able to explain significant differences. If you need a refresher on lifecycles, see Book I, Chapter 3.

Determine Budget: Outputs

After you balance the scope, schedule, budget, risk, and funding limitations, you have a viable cost baseline, your project budget, and your funding requirements. You use that cost baseline to measure, monitor, and control your overall cost performance on the project.

When using EV (earned value) management, the cost performance baseline is referred to as the *performance measurement baseline.*

Cost Baseline. The approved version of the time-phased project, excluding any management reserves, which can be changed only through formal change control procedures and is used as a basis for comparison to actual results.

Performance measurement baseline (PMB). An approved integrated scope-schedule-cost plan for the project work against which project execution is compared to measure and manage performance. The PMB includes contingency reserve but excludes management reserve.

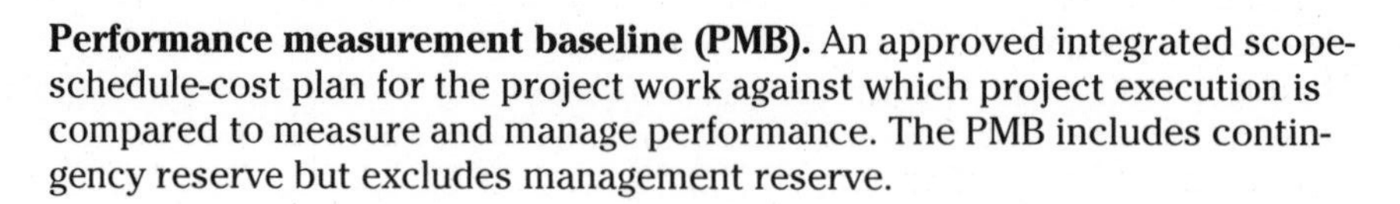

Figure 1-3 shows a cost baseline for the playground installation. The cost curve is based on the cost aggregation example in Table 1-3.

The difference between the cost baseline and the project budget is management reserves. You will measure performance against the baseline; however, you will need the management reserve as part of the project budget to address unforeseen risks.

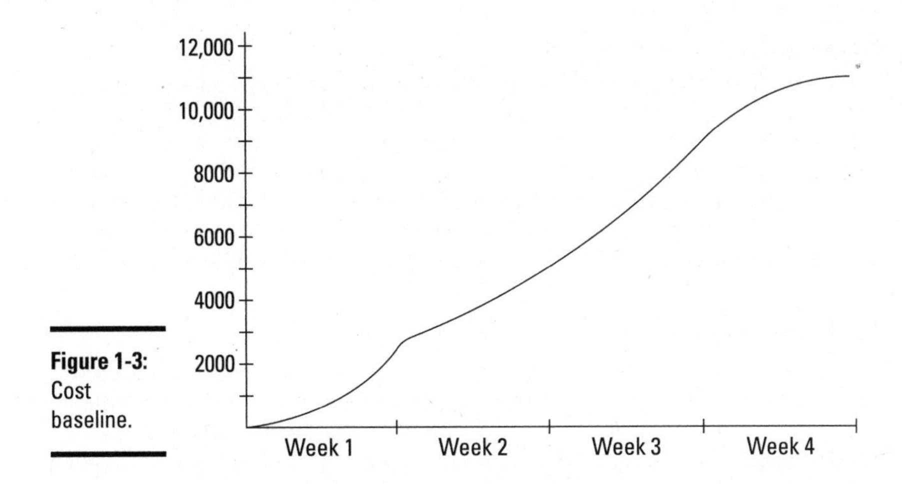

Figure 1-3: Cost baseline.

The project funding requirements outline the amount of total funding needed for the project. You might see them overlaid on the cost baseline for each time period (as shown in Figure 1-4). Although project expenditures usually occur relatively smoothly, funding often occurs in chunks. Figure 1-4 shows the cost baseline with funding occurring in a stair-step fashion.

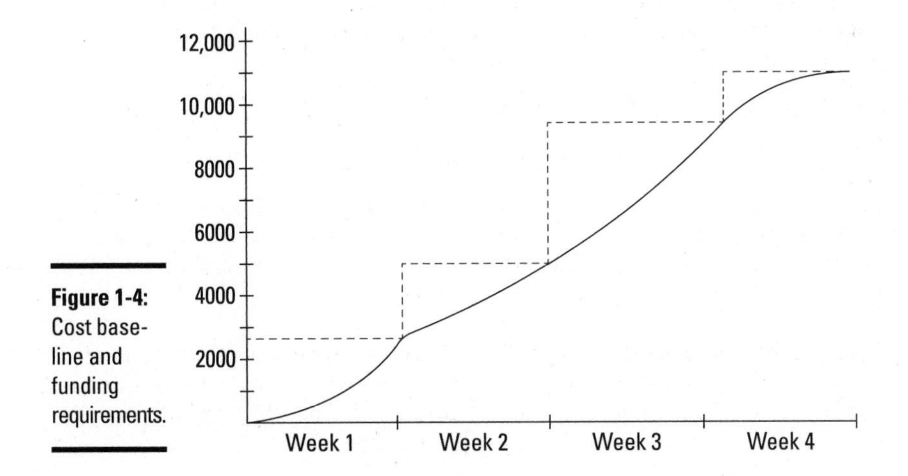

Figure 1-4: Cost baseline and funding requirements.

Another way of showing the funding needs is to show the build-up from work packages to control accounts to the cost baseline, then the project budget and, finally, the total funding requirements. Total funding requirements include the cost baseline + management reserve.

You can see in Figure 1-5 that the work in the WBS plus contingency reserves makes up the cost baseline. The addition of the management reserve determines the project budget.

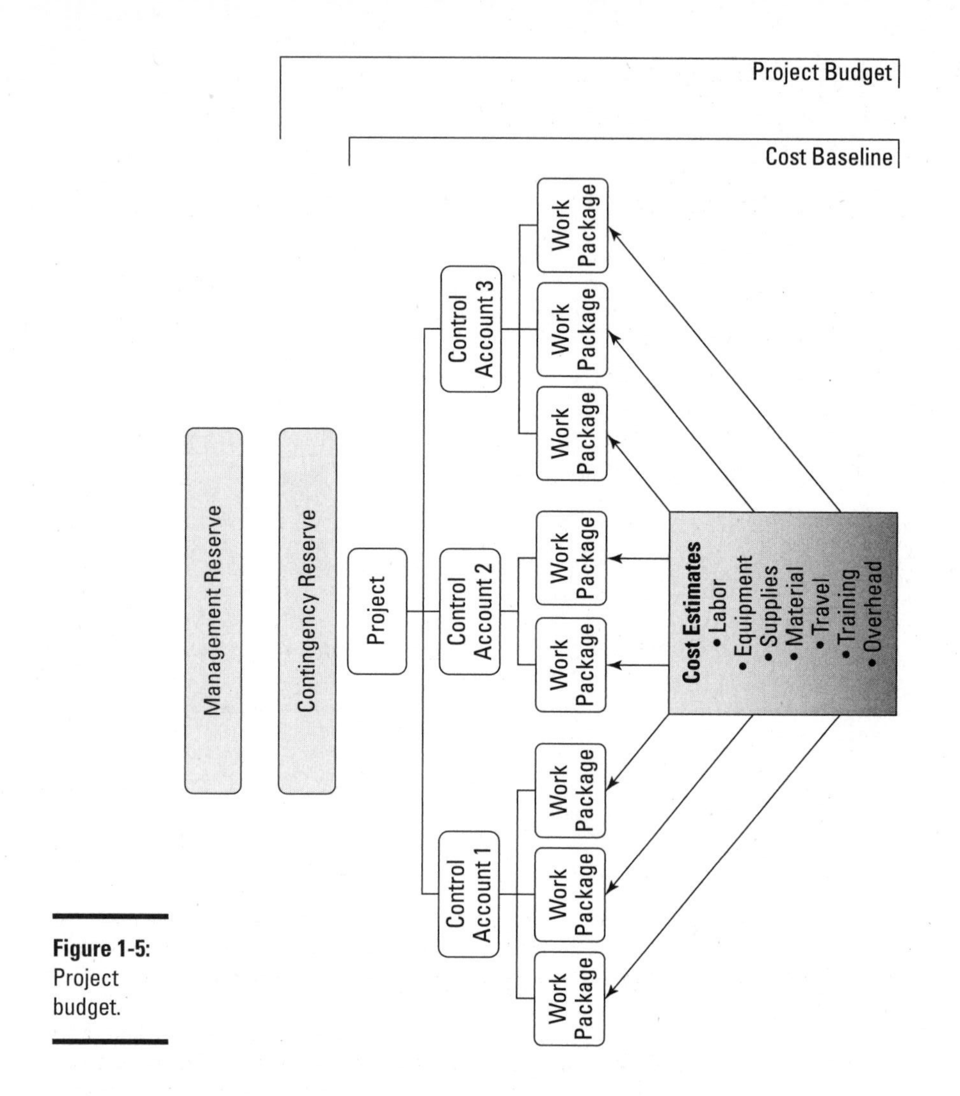

Figure 1-5: Project budget.

After the cost baseline and funding requirements are established, you might need to update your schedule, risk register, and other project documents.

Key Terms

Most of the terms in this chapter relate to estimating techniques and estimating accuracy. Quite a few terms relate to the cost baseline, too.

- ✦ Cost management plan
- ✦ Rough Order of Magnitude
- ✦ Budgetary estimate
- ✦ Definitive estimate
- ✦ Direct costs
- ✦ Indirect costs
- ✦ Analogous estimate
- ✦ Parametric estimate
- ✦ Bottom-up estimate
- ✦ Three-point estimate
- ✦ Budget
- ✦ Budget at completion
- ✦ Reserve
- ✦ Contingency reserve
- ✦ Management reserve
- ✦ Cost baseline
- ✦ Performance measurement baseline

Chapter Summary

Cost estimating and budgeting are two important processes in the planning process group. You need both of these processes to develop an effective cost baseline against which you will measure performance.

- ✦ Your cost estimates will get more accurate as you define your scope in more detail. In the beginning, you might have a rough order of magnitude estimate. Later, it evolves into a budgetary estimate. You will end up with a definitive estimate.
- ✦ Analogous estimating compares the current project with past, similar projects to develop a cost estimate.
- ✦ Parametric estimating uses a mathematical relationship to derive cost estimates.
- ✦ Bottom-up estimates decompose work to the work package level to determine the cost.

Chapter Summary

- Three-point estimates are used when there is a large degree of uncertainty associated with the estimate.
- Record your cost estimates in cost categories along with assumptions and a basis of estimates.
- A project budget allocates the cost estimates over time. The budget includes the cost baseline plus the management reserve.
- You need to balance your funding requirements with any funding limitations. Total funding requirements include the baseline, contingency, and management reserves.

Prep Test

Multiple Choice

1 **Which document sets out the format and establishes the activities and criteria for planning, structuring, and controlling the project's cost?**

A ❍ Activity cost estimates
B ❍ Basis of estimates
C ❍ Cost management plan
D ❍ Spend plan

2 **The type of estimate done in the beginning of a project with a range of –25% to +75% is**

A ❍ Rough Order of Magnitude
B ❍ Budgetary
C ❍ Engineering
D ❍ Definitive

3 **Which type of estimate uses expert judgment and historical information?**

A ❍ Parametric
B ❍ Analogous
C ❍ Three-point
D ❍ Bottom-up

4 **Which type of estimate uses a statistical relationship between historical data and variables, such as weight, size, and duration?**

A ❍ Analogous
B ❍ Three-point
C ❍ Parametric
D ❍ Bottom-up

5 **If you have a lot of uncertainty and risk associated with a particular work package, what type of estimate should you develop?**

A ❍ Analogous
B ❍ Three-point
C ❍ Parametric
D ❍ Bottom-up

6 The most accurate form of estimating is

- A ❍ Parametric
- B ❍ Analogous
- C ❍ Three-point
- D ❍ Bottom-up

7 Funds that cover unplanned in-scope work are called

- A ❍ Contingency reserve
- B ❍ Risk reserve
- C ❍ Management reserve
- D ❍ Risk response reserve

8 The authorized time-phased budget is

- A ❍ The project baseline
- B ❍ The cost baseline
- C ❍ The project management plan
- D ❍ The performance baseline

Scenario 1

You are installing 400 new computers and need to come up with a high-level estimate. You did a similar project last year. You look back at your records and find the following:

- **Each computer cost $675.**
- **Labor rates were $85 per hour.**
- **Each computer took 1 hour to install.**

Based on a vendor quotation, you estimate that the computers will cost $655 each. Labor rates are up by 10%. You estimate the time to install will be about the same. Using the analogous estimating technique, what is your cost estimate?

- A ❍ $299,400
- B ❍ $262,000
- C ❍ $296,000
- D ❍ $325,600

Scenario 2

Your organization is purchasing some new off-the-shelf software. You hired a consultant to do the integration with three existing applications. The consultant has given you the following information:

- **If the interfaces are relatively simple and the code is clean, it should take 50 hours.**
- **However, in his experience, something always goes wrong, so he thinks it will probably take 60 hours.**
- **And, if he runs into unforeseen problems, the interfaces don't work, and he has to write extensive coding workarounds, it will take closer to 130 hours.**

The consultant charges $100 per hour. What is the expected cost?

A ❍ $6,900
B ❍ $8,100
C ❍ $8,200
D ❍ $7,000

Answers

Multiple Choice

1. **C.** Cost management plan. The cost management plan describes the structure and criteria that will be used for cost planning, estimating, budgeting and reporting. See *"Plan Cost Management: Outputs."*
2. **A.** Rough Order of Magnitude. This measurement band can differ by industry, but it is a standard generic rough order of magnitude range. *Spend some time with "Estimate Costs: Tools and Techniques."*
3. **B.** Analogous. Analogous estimating uses expert judgment and information from past projects. *Go back to "Analogous estimating."*
4. **C.** Parametric. Parametric estimating uses mathematical models to develop cost estimates. *Review "Parametric estimating."*
5. **B.** Three-point. A three-point estimate accounts for risk and uncertainty. *Look into "Three-point estimating."*
6. **D.** Bottom-up. A bottom-up estimate is the most accurate estimate. It also takes the most time to prepare. *Check out the information in "Bottom-up estimating."*
7. **C.** Management reserve. Management reserve is used for project changes to scope and cost. It covers work that is in-scope, but unplanned. *See the content under "Reserve analysis for determining the budget."*
8. **B.** The cost baseline. This is the authorized budget for the project, allocated over time. *Check out "Determine Budget: Outputs."*

Scenario 1

A. $299,400. 400 computers × 655 = $262,000. 1 hour per computer install = 400 hours. The (old) rate of 85 × 1.1 = 93.5 hourly rate. 400 × 93.50 = $37,400. $262,000 + $37,400 = $299,400. *Go over "Parametric estimating."*

Scenario 2

D. $7,000. The three-point estimate with a weighted average will give you the expected cost. (50 + 4(60) + 130) / 6 = 70 hours. 70 × $100 = $7,000. *Go to "Three-point estimating."*

Chapter 2: Planning for Quality

Exam Objective

- **Review the project scope to determine the quality requirements and standards needed to meet stakeholder expectations.**

When talking about quality in project management, keep several things in mind. First, *project* quality is different from *product* quality. Project quality has to do with how you manage the project: For example, do you follow a methodology? Are your plans integrated and complete? Do you meet your schedule deliverables dates? Are you on budget? In contrast, product quality is dependent upon the nature of the product. After all, product quality requirements for producing a concert or an event are very different from building a childcare center.

Another thing to keep in mind is that the majority of the quality concepts used in project management come from a manufacturing environment. Therefore, many quality-management tenets are based on work done by J. Edwards Deming, Walter Shewhart, Philip Crosby, Joseph Juran, and other well-known quality pioneers. The PMP exam won't expect you to know which expert developed specific tools and axioms, nor will it expect you to know the details of any proprietary methodology, such as TQM, CMMI, or Six Sigma. However, you are expected to have a basic understanding of quality principles, including how they relate to project management.

In addition to the basic quality principles, you also have to know some simple statistics. Don't worry; you aren't going to have to conduct a chi-square test or do any regression analysis. However, you need to understand normal distributions and standard deviations.

In this chapter, I discuss basic quality concepts and definitions, then move into some simple statistics, and conclude by going over the information from the Plan Quality Management process in the *PMBOK Guide*.

Quick Assessment

1. When investing in quality, you want to make sure that you're getting more out of the investment than you're putting into it. One technique that you can employ to ensure this is a(n) ______ ______ ______.

2. A(n) ______ ______ is used to determine whether a process is stable or has predictable performance.

3. (True/False). The mode is the point where 50% of the results are greater, and 50% of the results are less.

4. A(n) ______ is a very specific operational definition that describes a project or product attribute.

5. (True/False). Quality should be planned in, not inspected in.

6. ______ is a category assigned to products or services having the same functional use but different technical characteristics.

7. What is the PERT equation?

8. Assuming a normal distribution, a cumulative distribution of the mean $+1\sigma$ represents what percent of the outcomes?

9. If you want to determine whether a product conforms to the intended result, which method of sampling would you use?

10. Which document provides instructions for optimizing a process and establishes targets for improvement?

Answers

1 Cost-benefit analysis. A cost-benefit analysis compares the investment in quality for a product or process with the expected benefit. *For more on cost-benefit analysis, see the "Plan Quality: Tools and Techniques" section.*

2 Control chart. A control chart plots the performance of a process. Results that fall within +/–3 standard deviations from the mean are said to be "in control." *You can find more information on this in the "Seven basic quality tools" section.*

3 False. The *mean* is the point where 50% of the results are greater, and 50% of the results are less. The *mode* is the most frequent point. *Look over the information in the "Basic Statistics" section.*

4 Metric. Metrics are very specific definitions used to measure project or product attributes. *See more about this in the "Plan Quality Management: Outputs" section.*

5 True. One of the axioms in project management is that quality should be planned in, not inspected in. *Find this in the "Basic Quality Concepts" section.*

6 Grade. Grade is different than quality. *Read more about the distinction in the "Basic Quality Concepts" section.*

7 The PERT equation is (O + 4M + P) / 6. *You can find this in the "Basic Statistics" section.*

8 84%. This represents 50% (mean) plus one standard deviation (34%). *Find out more about cumulative distributions in the "Basic Statistics" section.*

9 Attribute sampling. Attribute sampling determines whether a result conforms. Variable sampling determines the degree of conformance. *You can review this information in the section "Statistical sampling."*

10 Process improvement plan. *Read more about the process improvement plan in the "Plan Quality Management: Outputs" section.*

Basic Quality Concepts

Modern quality management focuses on *customer satisfaction,* which is generally defined as conformance to requirements and fitness for use. In other words, the product, process, and project meet the requirements, and the end result is used and useful. Certainly, when talking about *product* satisfaction, the focus is on the customer; however, *project* satisfaction needs to take into consideration the project team, the sponsor, vendors, regulatory entities, and other project-specific stakeholders. Therefore, when I address "project quality management," I prefer to focus on stakeholder satisfaction. It's important that all stakeholders are satisfied, not just the customer. In this sense, quality management is very integrated with collecting requirements and planning stakeholder management.

Another fundamental tenet is that quality should be planned, designed, and built in, rather than inspected in. A project is generally less expensive if you go into it preventing mistakes from happening rather than correcting those mistakes later on in the project's lifecycle.

Part of quality management is continuous improvement. This goes for product and project quality. The underlying basis for quality improvement is the plan-do-check-act cycle that Walter Shewhart developed and J. Edwards Deming refined and publicized in the 1950s. Figure 2-1 summarizes the plan-do-check-act cycle.

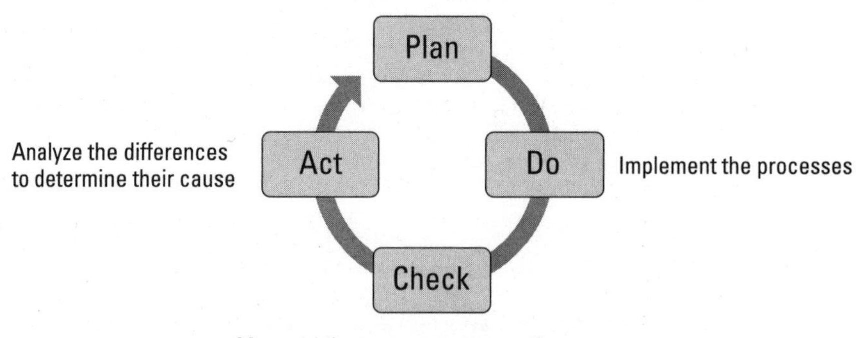

Figure 2-1: Plan-do-check-act cycle.

Much of the capability to significantly improve a product or process is dependent upon an investment in quality. This type of investment is usually done outside the project. Typically, management is responsible for the investment and providing the resources and organizational support for quality management. Examples include bringing proprietary methods (such as Capability Maturity Model Integration; CMMI) into the organization, or investing more in appraisal and analysis versus defect repair.

One of the aspects of quality you need to be familiar with is the distinction between *quality* and *grade.*

Quality. The degree to which a set of inherent characteristics fulfills requirements.

Grade. A category or rank used to distinguish items that have the same functional use (say, a hammer) but do not share the same requirements for quality (say, different hammers may need to withstand different amounts of force).

For my running example of a childcare center, you can compare quality and grade by the selection process used to choose a secure entrance for the facility. One vendor, Secure Source, proposes using a security system with cameras, retinal scans, infrared beams at the windows, a double-door entry system, and panic buttons that are directly wired to Secure Source.

Another vendor, Breach Proof, proposes using a double door with a badge swipe machine for entry. This would be bolstered with a computer application called Guardian that records entry and exit times by person as well as authorized drop-off and pick-up persons.

You do some research on both companies and find the following reviews for Secure Source:

> *"We used Secure Source, and I got caught in between the double doors with my daughter. They couldn't get us out for 2 hours."*
>
> *"The retinal scanners keep going off line, and we have to shut down and reboot the system to get them to reset."*
>
> *"When we called the hotline to test the responsiveness, we were put on hold!"*

Then you do some research on Breach Proof and see the following reviews:

> *"When I called, they picked up right away. The people were very helpful, and their response time was excellent."*
>
> *"The Guardian system is wonderful! It is so easy to use. It not only keeps the facility secure, it helps me plan my staffing!"*

These examples demonstrate that while Secure Source is high grade (it has lots of features and functions), it is low quality (doesn't meet the criteria of "fit for use"). On the other hand, the Breach Proof proposal is lower grade, but it is fit for use. In other words, it is higher quality because it meets the needs, doesn't break down, and is used — and useful.

Another distinction you need to know is the difference between accuracy and precision.

Accuracy. Within the quality management system, accuracy is an assessment of correctness.

Precision. Within the quality management system, precision is an assessment of exactness.

Here's a scenario for the childcare center example. The foreman is working with two new apprentices. He needs to frame some windows. He tells the apprentices he needs 24 boards that are four feet long, and each apprentice should cut 12 boards.

The foreman comes back and checks the results. One apprentice, Ryan, has his boards lined up; even without measuring, the foreman can tell that they are different lengths. He tells Ryan that he needs to work on his precision so that all the boards are the same length.

Next, the foreman looks at Seth's work. At first, he is very pleased. All the boards are lined up against the wall, and they are all the same length. He thinks this is very good. However, after the foreman measures the boards, he finds they are all 46.75" — not the 48" he asked for. So, although the measurements are precise, they're not accurate.

If you remember the preceding two scenarios, you'll do fine answering questions about grade, quality, accuracy, and precision on the exam.

You might come across a few other concepts on the exam:

- **Total Quality Management (TQM):** The practice of TQM focuses on organizations always looking for ways to improve the quality of their products and processes.
- **Continuous Quality Improvement (CQI):** Like TQM, this practice also looks to improve the quality of products and processes, but it focuses on continuous incremental improvements. You may also hear this referred to as *Kaizen,* the Japanese word for improvement.

Basic Statistics

For the PMP exam, you need to know some terminology, measurements, and concepts in distribution. First, look at some definitions.

Probability distribution. A mathematical or graphical representation that represents the likelihood of different outcomes from a chance event.

Normal distribution. The frequently encountered bell-shaped distribution; the mean, median, and mode are the same value. Also known as a *bell curve* or a *Gaussian distribution.*

Cumulative distribution. A way to graph any distribution to show the probability that a given value and less (or more) will be achieved.

Mean. Also called the expected value, mean is the average of all data points. Mean may be computed as a simple average or a weighted average, based on a specific type of probability distribution, or by using a simulation.

Median. The point in the distribution where 50% of the results are above the value, and 50% of the results are below the value.

Mode. The most frequent data point.

Triangular distribution. A continuous distribution that is calculated by using three discrete variables or data points: *optimistic, pessimistic,* and *most likely.* They are not weighted in calculating the mean.

$$\frac{Optimistic + Most\ likely + Pessimistic}{3}$$

PERT distribution. A continuous distribution is calculated by using three discrete variables: *optimistic, pessimistic,* and *most likely,* of which *most likely* is weighted in calculating the mean.

$$\frac{Optimistic + 4\ Most\ likely + Pessimistic}{6}$$

For the exam, all questions are based on a normal distribution. Figure 2-2 shows a normal distribution curve.

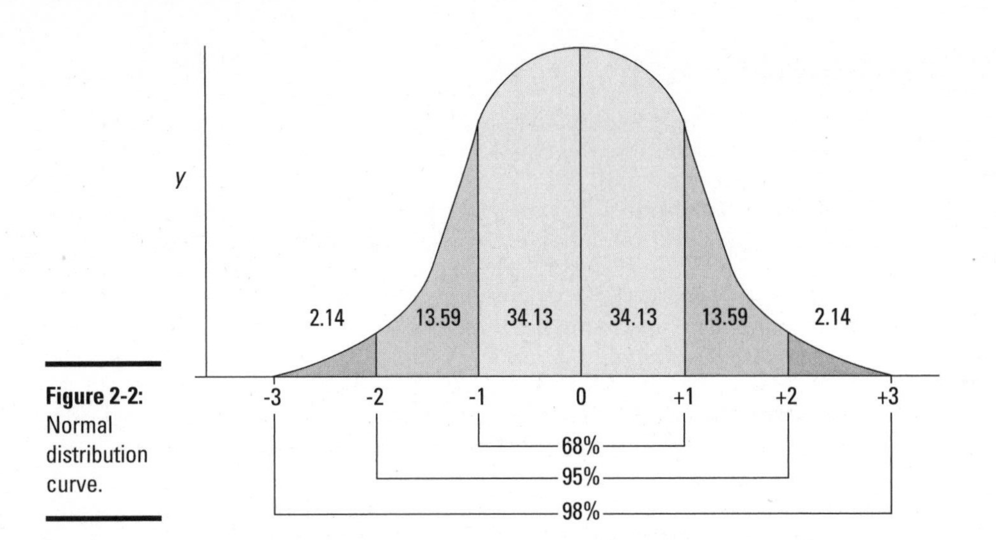

Figure 2-2: Normal distribution curve.

In a normal distribution, the mean, median, and mode are all the same. In Figure 2-2, that is the highest point of the curve. For a normal distribution, you're looking at two aspects: the mean and the standard deviation. Standard deviation represents the distance a given point is from the mean. It is also called *sigma,* or *s.* Here is a more technical definition:

Standard deviation. A measure of the range of outcomes, the average difference from the mean, calculated as the square root of the variance. The symbol for standard deviation is σ.

The basic equation for computing standard deviation is

$$\sqrt{\sum \frac{(x - mean)^2}{n-1}}$$

For the purposes of the PMP exam, you can use a shortcut. It works only for normal distributions, but because that's all the PMP exam uses, you should be okay. The shortcut is

(pessimistic – optimistic) / 6

Basically, the mean shows the height of the curve, and the standard deviation determines the width of the curve. A narrow curve has a relatively low standard deviation. See Figure 2-3 for an example of a narrow distribution. A flatter distribution has a relatively greater standard deviation.

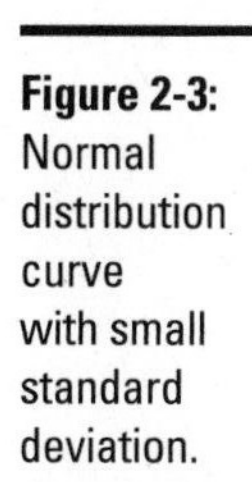

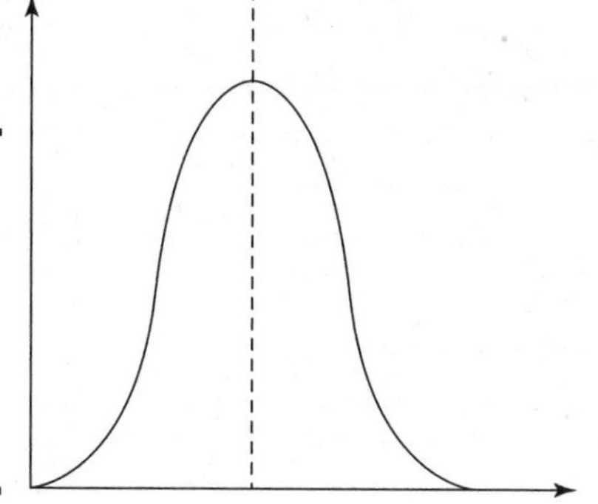

Figure 2-3: Normal distribution curve with small standard deviation.

See Figure 2-4 for a wide distribution.

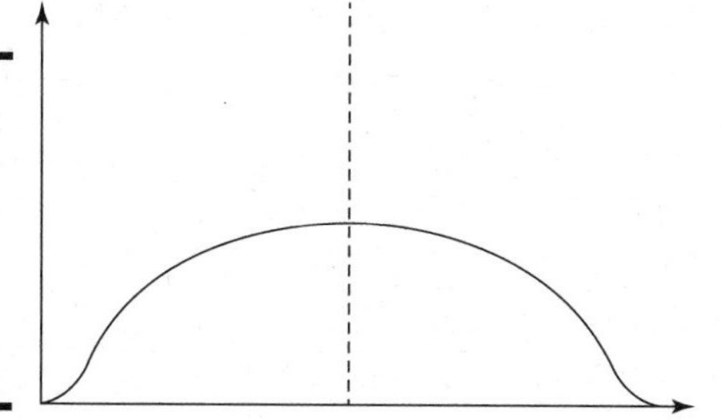

Figure 2-4: Normal distribution curve with a large standard deviation.

Generally, measurements are assessed by the number of standard deviations they are from the mean. In a normal distribution

- ✦ 68.3% of the data points fall within 1 standard deviation.
- ✦ 95.5% of the data points fall within 2 standard deviations.
- ✦ 99.7% of the data points fall within 3 standard deviations.

Thus, for a normal distribution, almost all values lie within 3 standard deviations of the mean.

You need this information for quality, cost-estimating, duration-estimation, and risk questions on the PMP exam. Here's a quick example about project quality where you're reviewing the quality of the duration estimates.

A team member estimates that Task A will most likely be finished in 30 days. The best case scenario is that it could be finished in 24 days, and the worst case scenario is that it would take 36 days. You would like estimates for expected completion. Based on this information, you want to know the answer to this question:

What is the probability that you will finish the task in 28–32 days?

To answer this question, take the following steps:

1. **Calculate the mean (expected value) by using the PERT distribution equation.**

   $(24 + 4(30) + 36) / 6 = 30$

2. **Calculate the standard deviation by using the short formula.**

   $(36 - 24) / 6 = 2$

3. **Add and subtract the standard deviation value to and from the mean.**

   $+/-1\sigma$ is 28–32 days, which represents 68%.

   So, you can reliably estimate a 68% chance that the activity will be finished within 28–32 days.

Here is one more piece of information you need to know: cumulative distribution. Remember that cumulative distribution is a way to show the probability that a given value and less (or more) will be achieved. In a cumulative distribution, you will see the following:

- 0.15% of the data points fall between 0 and -3σ from the mean.
- 2.25% of the data points fall between 0 and -2σ from the mean.
- 16% of the data points fall between 0 and -1σ from the mean.
- 84% of the data points fall between 0 and $+1\sigma$ from the mean.
- 97.75% of the data points fall between 0 and $+2\sigma$ from the mean.
- 99.85% of the data points fall between 0 and $+3\sigma$ from the mean.

Using the same question *(What is the probability that you will finish the task in 28–32 days?)*, calculate the probability of finishing in 32 days or less.

This question, though, is asking about the cumulative probability of all the values of 32 days or less. In Step 1 of the preceding list, the mean (the point in a normal distribution that 50% of the results are above or below) was 30 days. The standard deviation was 2. Take these steps to solve the problem:

1. 30 days (the mean) +1σ (2 days) = 32 days.
2. Looking at the preceding information, you can see that 84% of the results fall between 0 and +1σ from the mean.

Therefore, you can reliably estimate an 84% chance that the task will be finished in 32 days or less.

Because 68% of all results are +/–1σ from the mean, if you are trying to determine the percent that is just +1σ or just –1σ, you divide 68% by 2 to get 34%. To get the cumulative distribution, you start with the mean of 50% and add 34% to show the cumulative value for +1σ:

$$50\% + (68\% / 2) = 84\%$$

You can subtract 34% to get the cumulative value for –1σ:

$$50\% - (68\% / 2) = 16\%$$

You follow the same method for 2σ using 95.5% divided by 2, and for 3σ using 99.7% divided by 2.

Phew! With the math part done, it's time to move on to planning for quality.

Plan Quality Management

Planning for quality means identifying the quality standards you need for both the product and the project. You should plan for project and product quality throughout the project-planning phase.

Plan Quality Management. The process of identifying quality requirements and/or standards for the project and product, and documenting how the project will demonstrate compliance.

PMI takes the position that delivering more quality than is required is inappropriate. PMI views quality as "meeting the requirements." Delivering better quality or grade is considered "gold plating" and is frowned upon because gold plating uses time and resources usually at additional cost to add features and functions that are not necessary. Keep that in mind when planning for quality management.

Plan Quality Management: Inputs

A lot of the product quality planning happens concurrently while developing the project management plan. For example, as you plan for scope and requirements management and gather requirements, you're looking at performance, reliability, and maintainability requirements (and so forth). These are all related to product quality. As you create the scope statement, the work breakdown structure (WBS), and the WBS dictionary, you will find additional information about product quality. In fact, product scope and product quality are so tightly linked that on smaller, less-complex projects, they aren't really differentiated.

Many other inputs are used to plan for project quality. For example, you use the schedule and cost baselines to determine the quality of the project performance. The risk register can identify events that can negatively impact project or product quality. The stakeholder register documents stakeholders with an interest or impact on quality management.

Many products have standards and regulations that need to be followed for compliance or marketability reasons. Building codes are an example of regulations that affect the quality-planning process. Computer hardware configurations — such as USB ports, pin configurations, and the like — are examples of standards that affect the marketability of a product and that need to be considered when planning for product quality.

Your company policies often define processes that must be followed to ensure project and product quality. A key piece of information you can reference is the organization's quality policy (assuming that one exists), which you can use as a foundation to develop a project-quality policy.

Plan Quality: Tools and Techniques

When planning for project and product quality, you want to be able to assess the cost of conforming to the quality requirements with the consequences of nonconformance. For example, if you're building a staging area to hold equipment, material, and supplies, you need to meet building codes, but doing more than that is probably overkill. However, if you're building a corporate boardroom, you definitely want higher quality standards. The cost of upgrading the requirements for the staging area would outweigh the benefits, but the benefit of higher-quality requirements for the corporate boardroom would outweigh the costs (within reason). Therefore, when you look at the cost of quality, you always want to keep in mind the cost-benefit analysis of the investment in quality.

Cost-benefit analysis. A financial analysis tool used to determine the benefits provided by a project against its costs.

Cost of quality

The two aspects to the cost of quality are

- **Cost of conformance:** The cost of not allowing defects to occur. In other words, what are all the costs associated with having an acceptable end result?
- **Cost of nonconformance:** The cost of failure.

Cost of quality. A method of determining the costs incurred to ensure quality. Prevention and appraisal costs (cost of conformance) include costs for quality planning, quality control (QC), and quality assurance to ensure compliance to requirements (that is, training, QC systems, and so on). Failure costs (cost of nonconformance) include costs to rework products, components, or processes that are noncompliant, costs of warranty work and waste, and loss of reputation.

Cost of conformance

Costs of conformance are generally broken into two categories: prevention costs and appraisal costs.

Prevention costs are associated with not allowing defects to occur. Some common prevention costs are

- **Training:** Can include training on equipment, training in a quality methodology, or any kind of skill or knowledge needed to perform a role effectively.
- **Robust processes and documentation:** Having documented processes that reduce the variability of outcomes helps ensure quality outcomes. This can include policies, procedures, work instructions, checklists, technical manuals, and so forth.
- **Appropriate tools and equipment:** Having the right tools. You can't expect a valid schedule for a complex project if you're working in a word processing program.

In addition, you need to have the time to do the job right the first time.

Appraisal costs are associated with measuring results. This includes costs such as

- **Testing:** This can include software testing, a process walk-through, trying to break the product, and so on.
- **Inspections:** Inspections include measuring, observing, and reviewing data.

- **Test equipment calibration:** If you have test equipment (such as scales and thermometers), you need to make sure the test equipment is accurate and reliable.
- **Independent validation:** Getting an outside opinion or consultation is a form of appraisal cost. In fact, in many industries, this is considered a best practice.
- **Quality assurance:** Quality assurance comprises making sure that quality processes are being followed and are effective. It can include a quality audit.
- **Quality control:** Quality control is taking measurements and comparing them with the quality requirements to ensure the quality requirements are being met.

Cost of nonconformance

The costs of nonconformance are basically the cost of failure: internal and external failure costs.

Internal failure is a problem that the project team finds. Internal costs consist of

- **Scrap material:** This type of cost can include new parts as well as costs incurred to repair broken parts and keeping extra inventory on hand.
- **Rework:** The work to repair broken or malfunctioning products.
- **Root cause analysis:** Costs associated with discovering where and why the defect occurred as well as correcting the process that allowed it to occur.

External failure costs can get much higher. An *external failure* is not found by the project team. The defect is usually found by the customer. Although external failure costs are not typically absorbed by the project, they do affect the organization — sometimes, quite a bit. External failure costs include all the costs of internal failure plus the following:

- **Warranty:** This includes the shipping to and from the customer, or replacement of the part of product. It has incremental costs of help desks or customer support phone lines. In some cases, this entails sending technicians to the customer site to repair or replace the malfunctioning product.
- **Lawsuits:** In some circumstances, product failure will result in a lawsuit. At the very least, this entails the cost of legal representation. Of course, product recalls and class action suits can get extremely expensive.
- **Loss of business and goodwill:** If you release products that are prone to breaking or that aren't effective, it won't be long before you lose customers. And as we all know, word of mouth can allow bad experiences with your company to spread fast!

Evaluate the costs of conformance with the costs of nonconformance by using a cost-benefit analysis.

Benchmarking

When planning your quality parameters, you might want to look at best in class or best outcomes from other projects, and use those as a target. This is *benchmarking*. The childcare center example could benchmark customer satisfaction ratings for the site.

Design of experiments

This technique is used to optimize a product or a process. It entails working with multiple variables to find the best possible combination. For the child-care center example, the kitchen crew might try to optimize a menu with a healthy treat for snack time by adjusting ingredient ratios, cooking time, and cooking temperature to find the best interaction of these variables.

Statistical sampling

To determine whether a group of deliverables meets the quality requirements, you don't have to test every single one. In many circumstances, you can test a sample of them and determine the viability of the entire group based on the outcome of the sample. Say the Project Management Office Director wanted to determine how well all the project managers are following the change control policies. If 15 project managers were managing 42 projects, the director could randomly select five change control logs from different project managers for different projects and infer the performance of the rest of the projects based on the results of those five change control logs.

When sampling, you can employ

- **Attribute sampling:** Indicates whether the result conforms. For example, the light is on or off.
- **Variable sampling:** Indicates the degree to which the result complies as rated on a continuous scale. For example, if the desired measurement is 200°, a sample at 196° is 98% of the desired measurement.

During the planning process, you identify the items to be sampled, the number sampled, and the criteria for sampling.

Seven basic quality tools

There are seven quality tools, known as the "7QC tools" in quality management circles. I discuss each tool in greater detail in the chapter on controlling quality in Book VIII. For now, I give you a brief description of each tool.

Cause and effect diagram: Used to identify the root causes or contributors to a problem, error, or defect. The problem statement is the effect and the possible contributing factors are the causes. For example, a failure in a system integration test could be due to

- ✦ Improper coding
- ✦ Unskilled coder
- ✦ Inappropriate environment
- ✦ Inappropriate test script
- ✦ Insufficient bandwidth

The preceding are just a few examples. And each cause can be further explored for a more elaborate cause-and-effect diagram, also known as a "fishbone" diagram (because when drawn, it looks like a fish) or an "Ishikawa" diagram (named for the person who developed it). See Book VIII, Chapter 2 for more on cause-and-effect diagrams.

Flowcharts. A flowchart can help you see the relationship between the process steps. You can use this information to optimize the process and to see where problems and defects can occur. Flowcharts are useful in process improvement projects or to document any process.

Checksheets. Used to ensure that a series of steps are followed consistently. Checksheets (also known as "tally sheets") can be used to organize data around a quality problem. For example, you can tally the number of times that a specific cause is the source of a defect, and then use that when creating a histogram or Pareto chart to prioritize quality problems.

Pareto diagrams. A vertical bar chart that creates a graphic display of events (such as causes of defects or types of defects) in descending order. The objective is to rank problems based on the frequency of occurrence to determine the order in which to resolve them. See Book VIII, Chapter 2 for more on Pareto diagrams.

Histograms. A vertical bar chart (like the Pareto diagram), but a histogram is arranged to show the shape of distribution of an event: for example, the shape of distribution of calls coming into a call center. It can show the spread of results *(dispersion)* and the median (or mean or mode). See Book VIII, Chapter 2 for more on histograms.

Control charts. Used to determine whether a process is stable and predictable. The planned value of a process is the centerline. For many processes, the upper and lower control limits are +/–3 standard deviations from the plan, or the mean, depending on the circumstances. The upper and lower specification limits are the limits specified in the quality requirements. If a measurement is getting close to the control limit, you should take action to get it back toward the midline. Here are the definitions from the *PMBOK Guide:*

> ***Control chart.*** A graphic display of process data over time and against established control limits, and that has a centerline that assists in detecting a trend of plotted values toward either control limit.
>
> ***Control limits.*** The area composed of three standard deviations on either side of the centerline, or mean of a normal distribution of data plotted on a control chart that reflects the expected variation in the data.
>
> ***Specification limits.*** The area, on either side of the centerline, or mean, of data plotted on a control chart that meets the customer's requirements for a product or service. This area may be greater than or less than the area defined by the control limits.

Although control charts were developed to track manufacturing and repetitive processes, they can be used to track defects, cost and schedule variance, or any other predictable event on a project. For example, it is predictable that you will have cost and schedule variances on your project. However, you want to make sure they are within an allowable limit. You can track the variances using a control chart to spot trends and to monitor the quality of cost and schedule performance.

When planning for quality, establish the items that you will measure via a control chart and also set the upper and lower control limits as well as upper and lower specification limits.

Scatter diagrams. An X,Y matrix that plots the relationship between two variables to determine whether a relationship exists: for example, the number of hours worked in a week and the number of errors made. A positive correlation would show that the more hours were worked, the more errors per hour occurred.

Each of these seven basic quality tools can be used in the Control Quality process. During the planning process, the team meets and determines which tools to use, the parameters and measurements that should be used, and under which circumstances they will be used.

Additional quality planning tools

While identifying the quality requirements, you can use other project management tools, such as the following:

- Brainstorming
- Force field analysis
- Nominal group technique

In addition, you can use a number of proprietary techniques (particularly if they're used by your organization), including CMMI, Six Sigma, TQM, and so forth.

Plan Quality Management: Outputs

The output of all this work is a quality management plan, which is a component of the overall project management plan, describing how you plan to conduct the various quality processes on your project. In particular, it should address

- Roles associated with quality management
- Responsibilities associated with the roles
- Quality assurance approach
- Techniques and measurements used for quality control
- Plans for quality improvement activities

When planning for quality control, you need to establish very detailed descriptions of what you will be measuring and what the acceptable measurements are: in other words, metrics. A *metric* is a measurement or definition that describes in very specific terms what something is and how it will be measured.

You can create checklists for processes to ensure that the proper steps are carried out in the proper order. Another use for checklists is to help audit the process or for a quality control person to use to monitor results.

When working on a process-improvement project, or if part of your project charter includes instructions to improve the processes used for a project, you will include a process-improvement plan as well. Contents for the process-improvement plan include

- Process description
- Process metrics
- Targets for improvement
- Improvement approach
- Flowchart of the current process (sometimes called the "as-is process")

Key Terms

Several new terms in this chapter for the quality processes (Plan Quality Management, Perform Quality Assurance, and Control Quality) are important for you to know. Later in this book, you will see these terms used in the remaining two quality processes.

- Quality
- Grade
- Accuracy
- Precision
- Probability distribution
- Normal distribution
- Cumulative distribution
- Mean
- Median
- Mode
- Triangular distribution
- PERT distribution
- Standard deviation
- Cost-benefit analysis
- Cost of quality
- Cause-and-effect diagram
- Flowcharts
- Checksheets
- Pareto diagrams
- Histograms
- Control chart
- Control limit
- Specification limit
- Scatter diagrams
- Design of experiments
- Statistical sampling
- Metric

Chapter Summary

The Plan Quality Management process introduces the fundamental concepts in quality. Many of them appear to focus on product quality, but they also apply to project quality.

- Quality should be planned in, not inspected in.
- Quality and grade are not the same.
- Accuracy and precision are not the same.
- On a normal distribution curve, 68% of the results will fall within +/–1 standard deviation. 95.5% will fall within 2 standard deviations, and 99.7% will fall within 3 standard deviations.
- Conduct a cost-benefit analysis to determine the best approach for the cost of quality. The cost of quality includes costs of conformance (prevention and appraisal) and costs of nonconformance (internal failure and external failure).
- During quality planning, you determine the techniques you will use to measure quality and the appropriate metrics.

Prep Test

Multiple Choice

1 **A car with many features is said to be high ______. If those features don't work very well, it is said to be low ______.**

A ❍ Quality, grade
B ❍ Quality, standards
C ❍ Grade, quality
D ❍ Fidelity, grade

2 **The point where 50% of the results are above the center point and 50% of the results are below the center point is the**

A ❍ Mode
B ❍ Median
C ❍ Mean
D ❍ Standard deviation

3 **When analyzing the duration estimates for a project deliverable, you review prior projects to get some historical information. Based on that information, you determine the mean duration is 18 days and that the standard deviation is 2. If you estimate the duration at 20 days, how likely are you to meet that date or deliver early?**

A ❍ 50%
B ❍ 95%
C ❍ 84%
D ❍ 34%

4 **You have a budget of $1,550,000. Your sponsor told you to trim the budget. You look at your estimates, reserve, assumptions, and basis of estimates. You tell him that if you reduce your budget to $1,450,000, you have a 50/50 chance of making it. Your standard deviation is $100,000. He says that isn't good enough, and you need to drop the budget to $1,350,000. How likely are you to achieve that budget without reducing scope?**

A ❍ 16%
B ❍ 34%
C ❍ 84%
D ❍ 2.5%

5 **Your organization has an initiative to attain Level 3 CMMI this year. You have a new team member who is very smart, but she's not been through training on CMMI, and you need to make sure everyone is up to speed. From a quality perspective, training the new employee is**

A ❍ Prevention cost
B ❍ Appraisal cost
C ❍ Internal failure cost
D ❍ External failure cost

6 **Identifying industry best practices to measure your results against is an example of**

A ❍ Networking
B ❍ Brainstorming
C ❍ Appraisal costs
D ❍ Benchmarking

7 **Part of your project is training 500 people how to use a new process. You know that you have to produce 500 training manuals. You want to make sure that they're all correct, but you don't want to inspect each one. What's a good technique to use?**

A ❍ Design of experiments
B ❍ Benchmarking
C ❍ Statistical sampling
D ❍ Flowcharting

8 **To set up a system to make sure the same steps are followed each time a process is conducted, you should create a**

A ❍ Quality management plan
B ❍ Process improvement plan
C ❍ Checklist
D ❍ Metric matrix

Scenario 1

You're developing components for a lightweight piece of equipment. Each component has to weigh between 5.2 pounds and 5.6 pounds. You weigh each piece to ensure that all comply with the requirements. Also, once per month, you have someone come in to calibrate the scale.

1 **You check the weights and see that all the components are between 5.37 and 5.39 pounds. This indicates that the components' weight is very**

- **A** ❍ Precise
- **B** ❍ Accurate
- **C** ❍ Tight
- **D** ❍ Predictable

2 **One month, you discover that the scale is off by 8 ounces. This means that the measurements from the previous month are at risk of not being**

- **A** ❍ Precise
- **B** ❍ Accurate
- **C** ❍ Validated
- **D** ❍ Standard

3 **The cost of having the scale calibrated is**

- **A** ❍ Preventive
- **B** ❍ Appraisal
- **C** ❍ Internal failure
- **D** ❍ External failure

Answers

Multiple Choice

1 **C.** Grade, quality. Lots of features indicates high grade. Features that don't work too well are low quality. *Go over the information in "Basic Quality Concepts."*

2 **C.** Mean. The mean is the average where half the measurements are greater, and half are less. *Take a look at "Basic Statistics."*

3 **C.** 84%. Using a cumulative distribution, the mean plus 1 standard deviation is 84%. *Check out "Basic Statistics."*

4 **A.** 16%. Using a cumulative distribution, the mean minus 1 standard deviation is 16%. *Go over "Basic Statistics."*

5 **A.** Prevention cost. Training is a prevention cost. *Review "Cost of quality."*

6 **D.** Benchmarking. Benchmarking can include setting targets using best practices, best in class, or results from inhouse projects. *Look into "Benchmarking."*

7 **C.** Statistical sampling. This allows you to check a select number of training materials and infer the quality of all the training materials. *Look at "Statistical sampling."*

8 **C.** Checklist. A checklist facilitates following the same steps each time you do a process. *Read "Plan Quality Management: Outputs."*

Scenario 1

1 **A.** Precise. There is little scatter or variation in the measurements; therefore, they are precise. *Review "Basic Quality Concepts."*

2 **B.** Accurate. Measurements done by a scale that was not calibrated correctly are not accurate. *Return to "Basic Quality Concepts."*

3 **B.** Appraisal. Equipment, measurement, and maintenance of the equipment are appraisal costs. *Look at the information in "Cost of quality."*

Chapter 3: Identifying Your Team Members

Exam Objective

- **Develop roles, responsibilities, and an organizational structure as part of the human resource management plan to help manage project staff.**

When planning a project, we spend much of the time trying to figure out what the project is and what it isn't. Then we bury our heads in the schedule and the budget trying to figure out how to make it all work. The key, though, to making it all work is the project team. If you have team members with the right skills, committed to the project objectives, and who work well together, you're already on the path to success.

In this chapter, I look at the different kinds of project roles and responsibilities, how to effectively organize and structure your team, and how to plan for project staffing.

Quick Assessment

1. Which process is associated with identifying and documenting project roles, responsibilities, and required skills; reporting relationships; and creating a staffing management plan?

2. The group of people responsible for the leadership activities and initiating, planning, executing, monitoring and controlling, and closing the project phases is the _____ _____ _____.

3. Which tool illustrates the connection between the work packages and project team members?

4. Where would you document your strategy for acquiring and releasing team members?

5. The *PMBOK Guide* talks about a particular type of responsibility assignment matrix called a RACI chart. What does the C in RACI stand for?

6. The _____ provides the financial resource for the project and approves the project charter.

7. Which organizational structure gives the project manager the most authority?

8. The _____ _____ _____ is a hierarchically organized depiction of the project organization arranged to relate the work packages to the performing organizational units.

9. _____ defines the work the person in a particular role is expected to perform.

10. (True/False). Project managers have managerial authority over team members in a matrix organization.

Answers

1 Develop Human Resource Plan is the process of identifying and documenting project roles, responsibilities, and required skills; reporting relationships; and creating a staffing management plan. *For more on this, see "Plan Human Resource Management."*

2 Project management team. This team comprises the people responsible for initiating, planning, executing, monitoring and controlling, and closing the project phases. *You can find information about this in the "Plan Human Resource Management" section.*

3 A responsibility assignment matrix demonstrates the relationship between work packages and project team members. *This is explained in the section "Matrix charts."*

4 A staffing management plan is where you document your strategy for acquiring and releasing project team members. *You will find more detail in "Plan Human Resource Management: Outputs."*

5 The C in *RACI* chart stands for *Consult. Check out the information in "Matrix charts."*

6 The sponsor provides the financial resources for the project and approves the project charter. *This is described in the "Plan Human Resource Management" section.*

7 The projectized organizational structure gives the project manager the most authority. *Read about this in the "Plan Human Resource Management: Inputs" section.*

8 The organizational breakdown structure shows the organizational structure and how it relates to the work packages in the WBS. *This is described in "Hierarchy charts."*

9 Responsibility defines the work the person in a particular role is expected to perform. *Go to the "Text formats" section for more information.*

10 False. The functional manager has managerial authority in a matrix organization. *You can find information about this in the "Plan Human Resource Management: Inputs" section.*

Plan Human Resource Management

Much of human resource planning centers around identifying roles and responsibilities of team members and the organizational structure for the team.

DEFINITION

Plan Human Resource Management. The process of identifying and documenting project roles, responsibilities, required skills, reporting relationships, and creating a staffing management plan.

I start by identifying three important roles and describe how they support the project.

DEFINITION

Sponsor. The person or group that provides the financial resources, in cash or in kind, for the project.

Project manager. The person assigned by the performing organization to lead the team that is responsible for achieving the project objectives.

Project management team. The members of the project team who are directly involved in project management activities. On some smaller projects, the project management team may include virtually all the project team members.

Project team. A set of individuals who support the project manager in performing the work of the project to achieve its objectives.

Table 3-1 lists key roles and responsibilities per role.

Table 3-1 Key Project Team Roles

Role	*Responsibilities*
Sponsor	Provides the initial high-level requirements and information about the project
	Provides financial resources
	Approves the project charter
	Determines the priority among project constraints
	Approves major changes to the project
	Approves the baselines
	Monitors project progress
	Champions the project at the executive level
	Resolves conflicts outside the project manager's authority
	Provides mentoring and coaching to the PM as appropriate
	Manages corporate politics that could impact the project
	Reviews all variances outside the acceptable variance threshold

Role	*Responsibilities*
Project manager	Accountable for meeting all project objectives Develops plans to achieve project objectives Manages the project team to produce results Establishes systems to manage change Keeps the project on schedule and within budget Manages risk Collects project data and reporting progress Establishes an environment that supports team members in performing their roles Manages stakeholder expectations
Project management team	Provides leadership for particular aspects of the project Provides insight to the project manager Assists in managing the project through the project lifecycle
Project team	Assists in planning activities Provides information to create the work breakdown structure (WBS), schedule, cost estimates, and quality requirements Conducts activities as assigned Assists in identifying and responding to risk Applies knowledge and skills to project activities Participates in team meetings

Certain fundamental tenets are involved in managing a project, including

- **Project managers often don't have position authority over team members, such as in a functional or matrix organization.** In these situations, project managers must use their influence and negotiation skills to accomplish work.
- **Project managers must operate with the utmost integrity, demonstrate ethical and professional behavior at all times, and require their team members to do the same.**
- **Things change.** Promised resources won't always be available, skill sets don't always match what you need, and some projects might have higher priority. Project managers have to be flexible and adaptable while not losing sight of the end goal.

Plan Human Resource Management: Inputs

The first step in planning how to optimize your team is reviewing the resource requirements developed as a result of the Estimate Activity

Resources process. These are compared with available internal resources and marketplace conditions to make a determination whether internal resources should be used or external resources will be needed.

You'll want to consult the project management plan for information on the project lifecycle so that you can identify the skill sets you're likely to need in each phase and how work will be conducted. As you figure out how to organize your team, take into consideration the environment in which you work. Are you in a functional, matrix, or project environment? This information will tell you how much authority you are likely to have and how much influence you will have when it comes to setting up your team organizational structure. You may want to review the information on organizational structures in Book I, Chapter 3. Here are the definitions of each type of organizational structure.

Functional organization. A hierarchical organization where each employee has one clear superior, and staff are grouped by areas of specialization and managed by a person with expertise in that area.

Matrix organization. Any organizational structure in which the project manager shares responsibility with the functional managers for assigning priorities and for directing the work of persons assigned to the project.

Projectized organization. Any organizational structure in which the project manager has full authority to assign priorities, apply resources, and direct the work of persons assigned to the project.

You also want to look at project organizational structures from prior projects and any existing roles and responsibility descriptions.

Assume that you are working in a matrix environment unless the question is phrased otherwise.

Plan Human Resource Management: Tools and Techniques

I recommend networking and talking with team members and other project managers to get their expertise as input for effective organizational structures. Also, keep in mind organizational theories on motivation. You will want to assess what motivates individual team members. After all, some team members will be motivated by having a position of responsibility on the team, and others might be so overworked that they will be demotivated by taking on extra work.

You can document team roles, responsibilities, and structure in different ways. Three of the most common are hierarchy charts, matrix charts, and text formats. I describe each in a bit more detail and show you some samples.

Assume that you have a large project team consisting at least 50 or more people. You won't see questions that assume a 6-member team, so if you're used to managing projects with small teams, you have to adjust your thinking.

Hierarchy charts

Hierarchy charts are like organizational charts. You usually see them with the project manager at the top, with a subordinate project management team layer, and beneath that the project team layer. See Figure 3-1.

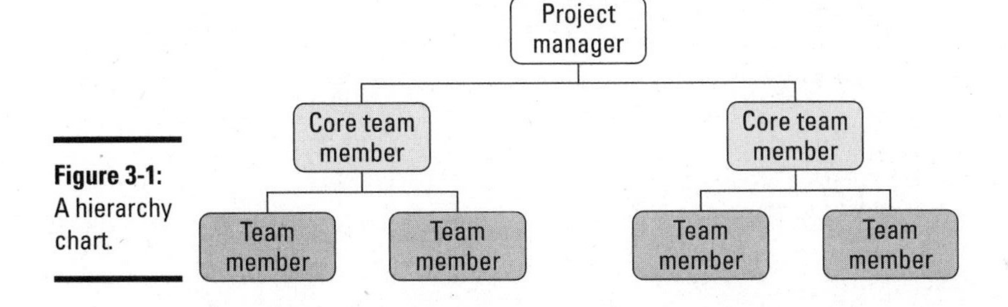

Figure 3-1: A hierarchy chart.

Another type of hierarchy chart is an *organizational breakdown structure* (OBS). This shows the organization of the team and is used to intersect with the WBS. The layer under the project manager is the control account manager. The control account manager manages team members who work on specific work packages in the WBS.

Organizational breakdown structure (OBS). A hierarchical representation of the project organization that illustrates the relationship between project activities and the organizational units that will perform those activities.

Figure 3-2 shows an OBS.

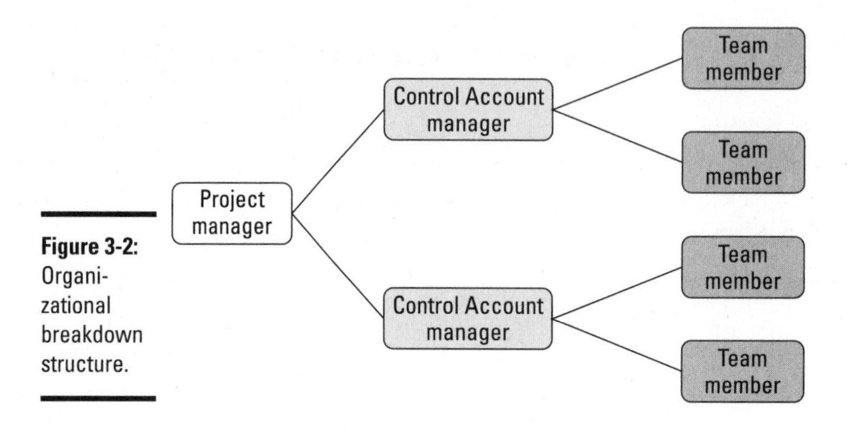

Figure 3-2: Organizational breakdown structure.

A third type of hierarchy chart is a resource breakdown structure, as shown in Figure 3-3.

Resource breakdown structure (RBS). A hierarchical representation of resources by category and type.

An RBS is used in resource-leveling schedules and to develop a resource-limited schedule, and that can be used to identify and analyze human resources as well as material and equipment.

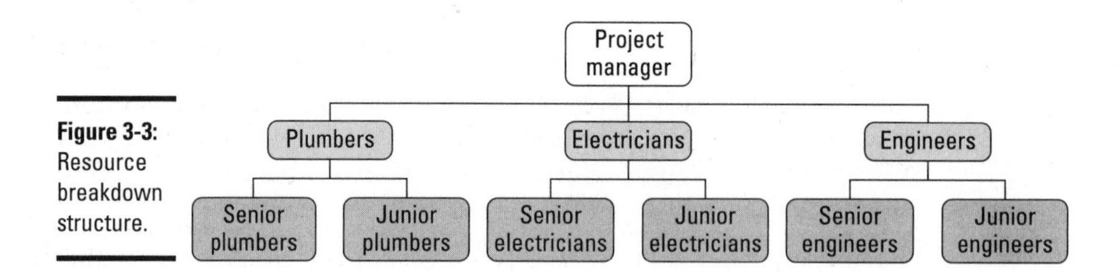

Figure 3-3: Resource breakdown structure.

Matrix charts

Matrix charts show how team members are used on each deliverable. A responsibility assignment matrix (RAM) is the most common form of a matrix chart.

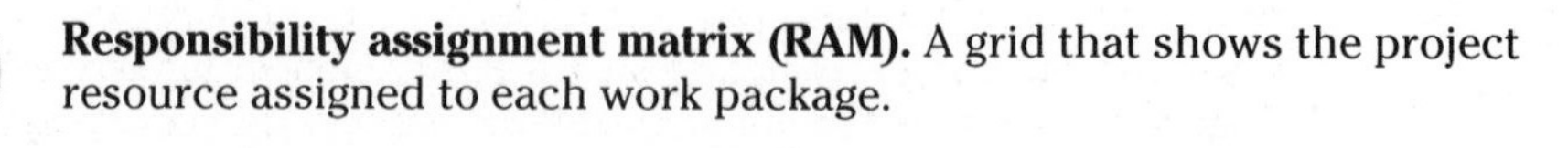

Responsibility assignment matrix (RAM). A grid that shows the project resource assigned to each work package.

Table 3-2 shows a RAM.

Table 3-2 Responsibility Assignment Matrix (RAM)

	Resource 1	*Resource 2*	*Resource 3*	*Resource 4*
Deliverable 1	A	R	R	I
Deliverable 2	C	R	A	R
Deliverable 3	I	I	A	C
Deliverable 4	C	A	I	R

The matrix chart in Table 3-2 is similar to that shown in the *PMBOK Guide.* It, too, uses a RACI format:

- R: Responsible
- A: Accountable
- C: Consult
- I: Inform

You don't have to use the same format. Some people use an ARIS chart, where ARIS stands for Accountable-Responsible-Inform-Sign-off. Use whatever works for you on your projects.

Text formats

Text formats describe roles and responsibilities, authority, and competencies.

Role. The position on the team. It describes the type of work that needs to be done, such as writer, programmer, or electrician. A role usually coincides with a job title.

Authority. The right to make and approve decisions. The person in the role of the contract administrator is usually the only person who has the authority to enter into or change a contract.

Responsibility. The work the person in a particular role is expected to perform. The person with the role of an editor is responsible for reviewing all written content, ensuring that it conforms to the editorial guidelines and is easily understandable.

Competency. Describes the skill or skill level of an individual. A Junior Plumber has the competencies to lay pipe and connect pipe following a set of blueprints. A Senior Plumber can actually design the plumbing to comply with standards and regulations.

The thought and effort put into organizing your team and thinking through the roles and responsibilities will be reflected in the human resource management plan.

Plan Human Resource Management: Outputs

The human resource management plan is part of the overall project management plan. It has three components:

- Roles and responsibilities
- Project organization charts
- Staffing management plan

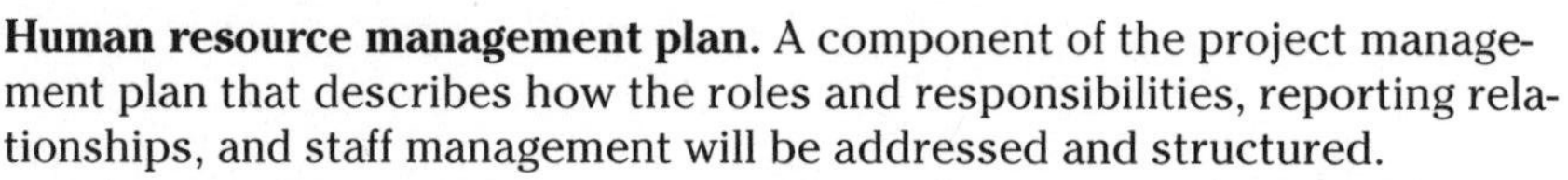

Human resource management plan. A component of the project management plan that describes how the roles and responsibilities, reporting relationships, and staff management will be addressed and structured.

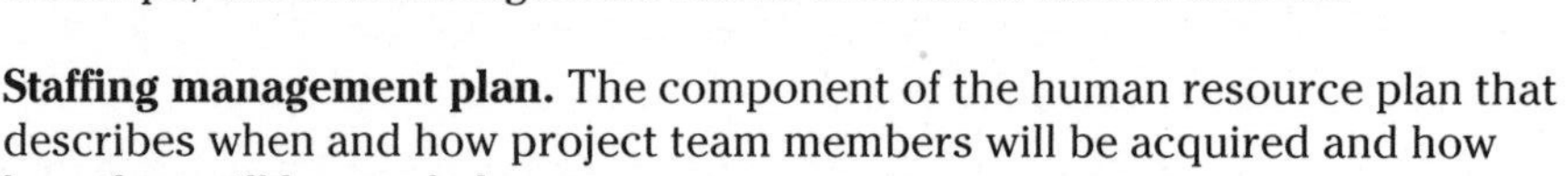

Staffing management plan. The component of the human resource plan that describes when and how project team members will be acquired and how long they will be needed.

You can distribute roles and responsibilities (which I define in the earlier section on text formats) to team members along with a RAM so that all team members can see specifically how they contribute to the project as well as how their roles interface and collaborate with other roles on the team.

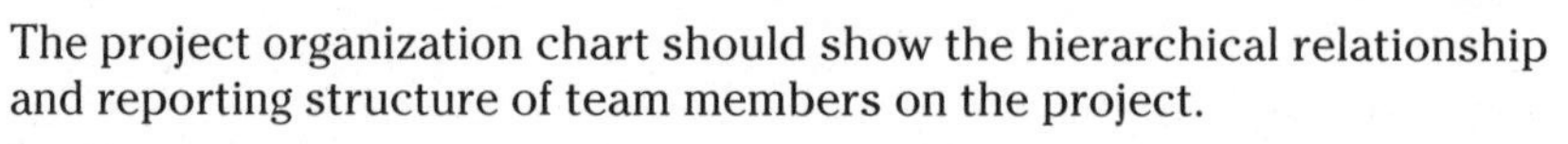

The project organization chart should show the hierarchical relationship and reporting structure of team members on the project.

The staffing management plan covers issues associated with staffing the project. It can include sections on

- **Staff acquisition:** How team members will be brought onto the team. For example, you might use different methods for bringing on team members, depending upon whether they're employees or contractors. Part of staff acquisition is determining how to orient new team members. Also, consider whether staff will be co-located in one location or remotely.
- **Resource calendars:** The number of labor units a team member or a group of team members will be working. The calendar can show hours in a week, days in a month, or whatever time scale is appropriate to the project. You can create a resource histogram that shows whether specific resources, or groups of resources, are over-allocated during any time period.
- **Staff-release plan:** How team members will be released when their work is complete. The plan should address how to maintain the knowledge that the team member developed.

✦ **Training needs:** Are any specific licenses, skills, certificates, or other training needed for the project? If so, you should develop a plan that demonstrates how to accomplish this.

✦ **Recognition and rewards:** How you motivate and recognize outstanding achievements and reward team members throughout the project.

Recognition and rewards can be good for team morale. You should recognize outstanding achievements and reward team members throughout the project. Take time during planning to set the criteria and timing for formal rewards and recognition. In addition, consider the factors that motivate team members. Here is a list of common motivators that you should keep in mind.

- *Being appreciated:* Whether you deliver the thank-you in person, or with a written note and a Cc to their boss and their personnel file, people are motivated when they know their work is appreciated.
- *Recognition:* Taking time in the team meeting to recognize excellent work is a nice way to recognize team members. It is even better if their boss or the sponsor is present.
- *Rewards, awards, and prizes:* Such incentives can be as simple as company logo-wear or a gift certificate to more substantial monetary awards.

✦ **Safety and compliance:** Are there safety or other compliance regulations that need to be met and documented as part of the project? If so, document the strategy for conforming to the regulations.

Key Terms

The definitions of the key roles in the project are important. The terms and concepts in this chapter are used in the executing processes later in the book, too.

✦ Sponsor

✦ Project manager

✦ Project management team

✦ Project team

✦ Organizational breakdown structure

✦ Resource breakdown structure

✦ Responsibility assignment matrix

✦ RACI chart

✦ Role

- Authority
- Responsibility
- Competency
- Human resource management plan
- Staffing management plan

Chapter Summary

This chapter examines planning the human resource aspects of managing the project. When I discuss executing the project work, I cover acquiring, developing, and managing the project team in more detail.

- The project sponsor provides funding for the project, sets high-level requirements, champions the project in the organization, and approves the charter and any major changes to the project. He also resolves escalated conflicts, provides mentoring, and reviews all variances outside the threshold.
- The project manager is accountable for meeting the project objectives; developing plans; managing the team; managing change; controlling the scope, schedule, and cost; managing risk; reporting progress; managing stakeholder expectations; and developing a supportive environment.
- The project management team assists in managing the project throughout the lifecycle.
- Project team members assist in planning, executing the work, providing status information, identifying and helping manage risk, and participating in team meetings.
- You can use hierarchy charts, matrix charts, and text formats to help plan your human resource needs. Hierarchy charts show the team organization structure. Matrix charts show how the deliverables and the team members relate. Text formats describe roles, responsibilities, authority, and competency.
- The human resource management plan contains the project organization chart, roles and responsibilities, and the staffing management plan.

Prep Test

Multiple Choice

1 **Which role on the project team is responsible for determining the priority among project constraints, approving major changes to the project, approving the baselines, and prioritizing project constraints?**

A ❍ The project manager
B ❍ The project sponsor
C ❍ The project management team
D ❍ The project team

2 **The project manager is accountable for all the following except**

A ❍ Developing plans to achieve project objectives
B ❍ Managing the project team to product results
C ❍ Establishing systems to manage change
D ❍ Championing the project to senior management

3 **If you want to create a chart that shows how various functions participate with work packages, you should create**

A ❍ An organizational breakdown structure
B ❍ A responsibility assignment matrix
C ❍ An organizational chart
D ❍ A RACI diagram

4 **Which tool shows the project resources by category and type?**

A ❍ A responsibility assignment matrix
B ❍ A resource histogram
C ❍ A resource breakdown structure
D ❍ An organizational breakdown structure

5 **If you want to create a matrix that shows the intersection of the organizational breakdown structure and the work breakdown structure, you would create**

A ❍ A responsibility assignment matrix
B ❍ A resource histogram
C ❍ A resource breakdown structure
D ❍ A roles and responsibilities chart

6 In a RACI chart, the A stands for

A ❍ Authority
B ❍ Acceptance
C ❍ Accountable
D ❍ Action

7 As you describe the roles and responsibilities of team members, you document the level of authority that each role has. In this context, "authority" means

A ❍ The person will be doing the actual work.
B ❍ The person will sign off on the completed deliverable.
C ❍ The person has overall accountability for the outcome.
D ❍ The person has the right to make and approve decisions.

8 You're documenting a structure for allocating bonuses based on performance. The bonus structure is part of

A ❍ The performance management plan
B ❍ The human resource development plan
C ❍ The rewards and recognition strategy
D ❍ Team performance assessment

9 All the following are components of the human resource management plan except

A ❍ The staffing management plan
B ❍ The team performance plan
C ❍ Roles and responsibilities
D ❍ Project organization charts

Scenario 1

Sara is a new member on your team. She will help with the scheduling. She has four years of experience using scheduling software, but she hasn't used the brand that your company uses. You need to send her to a two-week training course. The training plan should be updated to accommodate this change.

1 The training plan is part of the

A ❍ The staffing management plan
B ❍ The project management plan
C ❍ The roles and responsibilities
D ❍ The resource management plan

2 You would document Sara's role and reporting relationship in

A ❍ The staffing management plan
B ❍ The project management plan
C ❍ The human resource management plan
D ❍ The resource management plan

Answers

Multiple Choice

1. **B.** The project sponsor. This role is responsible for prioritizing constraints and approving all aspects of the project management plan. *See "Plan Human Resource Management."*
2. **D.** Championing the project to senior management. The liaison/champion role the project sponsor plays is important to project success. *Go over "Plan Human Resource Management."*
3. **A.** An organizational breakdown structure. This shows how functions relate to and work on work packages. *Check out "Hierarchy charts."*
4. **C.** A resource breakdown structure. This shows resources by category and type. *Look into "Hierarchy charts."*
5. **A.** A responsibility assignment matrix. The responsibility assignment matrix shows the intersection of the OBS and the WBS. *Go over "Matrix charts."*
6. **C.** Accountable. The A stands for Accountable. *Review information in "Matrix charts."*
7. **D.** The person has the right to make and approve decisions. Authority means the person has the right to make and approve decisions. *Look at "Text formats."*
8. **C.** The rewards and recognition strategy. The bonus structure is part of the rewards and recognition strategy that's part of the staffing management plan. *Dig into "Plan Human Resource Management: Outputs."*
9. **B.** The team performance plan. The team performance plan isn't part of the human resources plan; all other elements are. *Go back over "Plan Human Resource Management: Outputs."*

Scenario 1

1. **A.** The staffing management plan. The staffing management plan includes information on training. *Peruse "Plan Human Resource Management: Outputs."*
2. **C.** The human resource management plan. The human resource plan defines the roles, responsibilities, and reporting relationships. *Check out "Plan Human Resource Management: Outputs."*

Chapter 4: 90 Percent of Your Job Is Communication

Exam Objective

- **Use stakeholder requirements and the project organizational structure to create a communication plan that will help manage the flow of project information.**

The title of this chapter might seem provocative to you, but if you think about it, you spend the vast majority of your time communicating. Here are some ways how project managers communicate:

- Active listening
- Team meetings
- Conversations
- Status reports
- Memos
- Brainstorming
- Problem solving
- Presentations

I would go so far as to say that you're always communicating, even when you think you aren't. Think about all the nonverbal cues you send: posture, facial expression, tone of voice, a raised eyebrow, avoiding eye contact. All these methods of communication make up a significant portion of the message you're conveying.

The information in this chapter is partly technical in that it deals with techniques, outputs, and so forth. However, some of the information covers the interpersonal aspects of communication, such as listening, cultural sensitivity, and communication styles. Both sides of the equation are important because lack of communication and poor communication are significant factors in whether your project succeeds or fails.

Quick Assessment

1. If one of your team members says his deliverables are coming along fine while he looks down and shakes his head, what types of communication are you receiving?

2. Progress reports, status reports, and white papers are examples of what type of communication?

3. If you have five people on your team, you have ______ communication channels.

4. Who is responsible for making sure that a message is received in its entirety?

5. If you need to make sure your team members all get the latest update, are you more likely to use push or pull technology?

6. Which of the following will provide the most complete message: a note jotted on a sticky pad, a hallway conversation, or a phone call?

7. To identify people with whom you will communicate, you should review your ______ ______.

8. Where would you find templates for agendas, reports, and other project documents?

9. (True/False). Finding multiple ways to explain complex concepts only confuses things further.

10. Providing the right information, in a timely fashion, in a format that works for people is ______ communication.

Answers

1 Verbal and nonverbal. The response of "Fine" is verbal communication, but looking down and shaking one's head is nonverbal. *For more on this, see "Words, tone, and body language."*

2 Formal written. All these are formal communication, and they are all in a written format. *Look over "Formal and informal, written and verbal."*

3 10. (5 (5 – 1)) / 2 = 10. *See the information in the "Communication requirements analysis" section.*

4 Receiver. The receiver is responsible for making sure that the entire message was received. *I discuss this in "Communication models."*

5 Push. You are more likely to use push technology because you are sending it to the team. *You will find this information in "Communication methods."*

6 Hallway conversation. In a face-to-face conversation, you have benefit of body language, tone of voice, and words to convey a full message. *Review the information in the "Words, tone, and body language" section.*

7 Stakeholder register. Your stakeholder register has a list of all the project stakeholders and their expectations. This will help you identify who needs what type of communication and the appropriate frequency. *Review "Plan Communications Management: Inputs."*

8 The communications management plan. The communications management plan contains all the information on how communication will be managed and delivered for the project. *See "Plan Communications Management: Outputs."*

9 False. Finding various ways to communicate complex concepts increases comprehension. *Look at the information under "Communication skills."*

10 Effective. You want to make sure your communication is effective and people get the relevant information in a timely manner. *You will find information on effective and efficient information under "Plan Communications Management."*

Communication Building Blocks

Before looking at the process of planning communication, I want to cover basic communication concepts to not only lay the groundwork for communication planning, but also make sure that you know this information for the exam.

Formal and informal, written and verbal

Communication occurs throughout a project in all kinds of ways. Much communication is informal, including hallway conversations, cubicle conversations, and networking. These are all examples of informal verbal communication.

Formal verbal communication occurs with presentations or briefings to the steering committee, customer, or sponsor. Your kick-off meeting and team status meetings are additional examples of formal verbal communication.

However, verbal communication isn't the only way we communicate. A lot of communication on a project is written. This can be formal, such as contracts, status reports, defect lists, project plans, and project documents. Written communication can also be informal, such as a brief note to a team member, an inquiry via e-mail, or a follow-up reminder that something is due soon.

Table 4-1 compares these methods.

Table 4-1 Formal, Informal, Written, and Verbal Communication

	Formal	*Informal*
Verbal	Presentations Project reviews Briefings	Conversations Ad hoc discussions Brainstorming
Written	Progress reports Reports Project charter Project management plan Project documents	Notes E-mail Instant messaging Texting

Taking time to plan how to communicate effectively and efficiently will pay off in the end because your stakeholders will be informed of what is happening in your project and won't come asking you for status and other information.

Plan Communications Management. The process of developing an appropriate approach and plan for project communications based on stakeholder's information needs and requirements, and available organizational assets.

Plan Communications Management: Inputs

To determine who needs what information and how to give it to them, the first step is identifying your audience. You do that with the stakeholder register. The stakeholder register lists all the people who are affected by, or can affect, your project. I talk about the stakeholder register in Book II, Chapter 3.

Use the project management plan to identify the life cycle to determine the types of communication and the stakeholders for each phase in the life cycle.

Scrutinize your company's templates for reporting formats, presentation templates, and other assets that can help you get the right information to people. Often, using information from prior projects can be helpful. For example, maybe another project manager put together a great kick-off meeting presentation that you could customize to your needs.

You will be limited by your organization's infrastructure, such as its systems, presentation equipment, and communication capabilities.

Plan Communications Management: Tools and Techniques

Getting the word out effectively means analyzing your audience and your environment. Additionally, you want to select the most effective method of communication. I look at these and a communication model in this section.

Communication requirements analysis

As you review the stakeholder management register, compare it against your organization's infrastructure and assets to help determine the best communication approach. You might also want to look at your project and the company organization charts. Analyze what information is internal and what information needs to go outside the organization. Also consider whether stakeholders are in one location or many locations.

The more people you communicate with, the more opportunity there is for miscommunication. A mathematical model shows the relationship between the number of people and the number of communication channels (or *paths*):

$$(N(n-1)) / 2$$

where n is the number of people.

See how this plays out. If you have five people (as shown in Figure 4-1), here's how to calculate the number of communication channels you have:

$$(5(5-1)) / 2 = 10$$

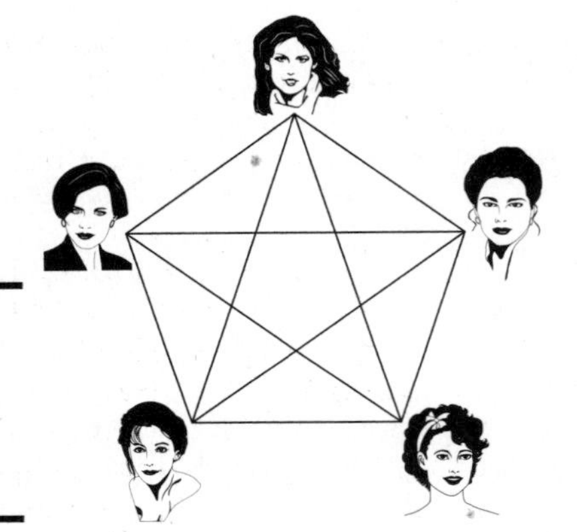

Figure 4-1: Five communication channels.

Now see what happens when you add three more people. You might think you have three more channels, or even six more channels. However, you actually have 18 more communication channels! (See Figure 4-2.)

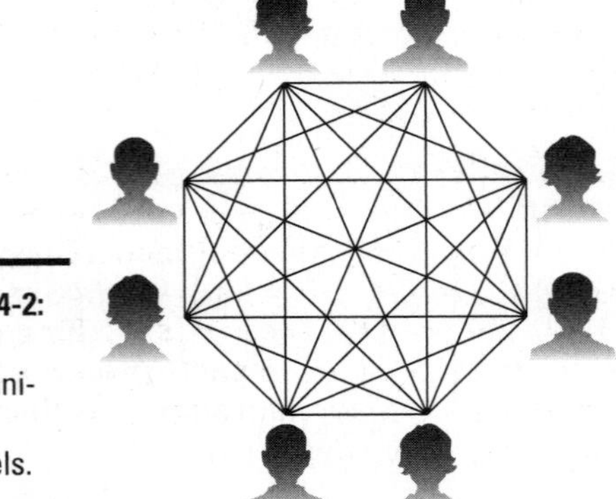

Figure 4-2: Eight communication channels.

The equation is now

$$(8(8-1)) / 2 = 28$$

Think about it this way: There are 28 ways for people to interpret the information — and that means 28 ways for your message to get misinterpreted. Add another four people to the team, and that number increases to 66! This is another reason why communication has to be effective and efficient!

Communicate only essential information that contributes to success, or where lack of communication would be detrimental.

Technology

The technology you have available is one of those enterprise environmental factors (EEFs) you have to take into consideration, especially if you have a team with internal team members and external contractors. Also, consider whether people are centrally located or geographically dispersed. Here are some technology factors that will shape your communication plan.

- **Urgency:** Determine whether stakeholders need information immediately or can wait. If you are working on a construction project in a hazardous environment, such as an area prone to hurricanes or tornadoes, you need the ability to communicate immediately with the construction site and the workers who could be impacted.
- **Technology availability:** Assess whether your organization has the technology and systems in place to support your communication strategy. Look at whether you will need significant changes or modifications to the current infrastructure. A project that requires some of the staff to work remotely for several days would require the staff to have laptops. If they are normally in the office full time and have only desktop computers, consider the matter upfront.
- **Ease of use:** You can set up a really cool website to communicate with your team. It might have document storage, messaging capability, version control, and all sorts of neat functionality, but if it's not intuitive to the audience and easy to use, no one is going to use it. When it comes to communication, remember: Keep it simple!
- **Expected staffing:** Check that everyone has the same platform or the same access to information. This is particularly relevant when working with contractors, who might work on a very different technology platform. For example, say you hire a marketing firm for part of your project; that firm uses Apple computers, but your firm uses PCs. Staffing your project with members from the marketing firm impacts project communication. You also have to determine what information to share with them versus what is proprietary.
- **Duration:** For projects that are three years or longer, you can count on at least some of your communications technology changing. You might not know how it will change, but it would be wise to keep that in mind.

With smartphones and tablet computers rapidly evolving with new applications, predicting how people will communicate in the future is difficult!

- **Project environment:** The environment can be as simple as part of the team being virtual, or it can include more complex factors such as team members located in different time zones, countries, or even extreme geographic locations, such as in the Arctic Circle or the Mojave Desert.

Communication models

The PMP exam uses a standard sender-receiver communication model. Look over Figure 4-3 as I walk you through the different components of the model.

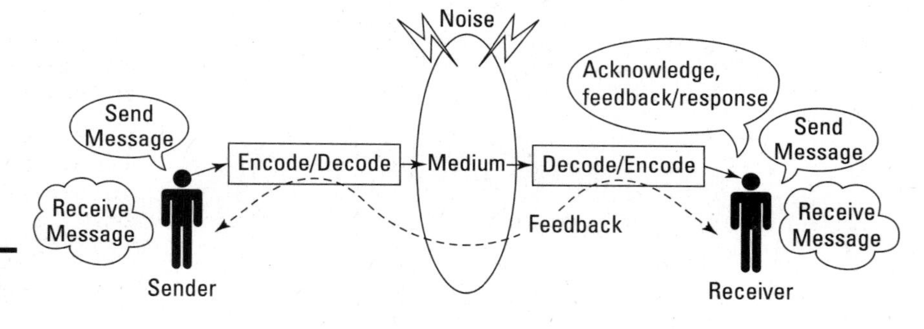

Figure 4-3: Communication model.

- **Sender:** Who conveys a message and is responsible for making the content clear and complete. The sender is also responsible for confirming that the receiver understands the message correctly.
- **Encoding:** Translating ideas into language, usually written or verbal language.
- **Message:** The output of encoding.
- **Medium:** The means of conveying the message. Sometimes the medium is referred to as the *channel.*
- **Noise:** Anything that interferes with the transmission of the message, including static, distractions, preconceptions and stereotypes, cultural norms, malfunctioning transmitting equipment, or anything that deteriorates or causes a barrier to successful transmission.
- **Decoding:** Translating the message into meaningful thoughts and ideas.

- **Receiver:** The recipient of the message, responsible for decoding the message and providing feedback. The receiver is responsible for making sure that the entire message is received and understood by encoding a message back to the sender conveying that.
- **Acknowledge:** Confirming receipt of the information. Acknowledging receipt does not imply agreement, but only receipt.
- **Feedback/response:** After the communication has been received and understood, the receiver may send a message with thoughts and ideas about the message.

Communication methods

Communication methods include push, pull, and interactive communication:

- **Push:** Communication sent to receivers, comprising a sender, medium, and message. It does not necessarily reach the receiver for decoding. This includes memos, e-mails, reports, voice mail, and so forth.
- **Pull:** Information sought by the receiver. In other words, the receiver actively searches for the information. This can include a team member going to an intranet to find communication policies or templates, running Internet searches, and using online repositories.
- **Interactive:** Sender and receiver exchanging information. This occurs in conversation, phone calls, meetings, and the like. This is the most effective form of communication.

The most common form of interactive communication is meetings. What project would be complete without meetings? We have meetings to plan, communicate status, problem-solve, make decisions, collect lessons learned, and for a variety of other reasons.

With today's distributed workforce, meetings can be held in person, over the phone, or via connecting computer technology. Most meetings have an agenda, notes, and/or meeting minutes that are distributed to meeting attendees. The ability to effectively facilitate communication and manage meetings is a valuable skill for project managers. I'm sure you've been to too many meetings where there was not agenda, or the agenda wasn't followed, or someone took the meeting in an entirely different direction than was planned.

REMEMBER

Staying on track is essential for productive meetings.

Plan Communications Management: Outputs

The communications management plan is a component of the project management plan. It documents the results of stakeholder information needs, available technology, and methods of communication.

Communications Management Plan. A component of the project, program, or portfolio management plan that describes how, when, and by whom information about the project will be administered and disseminated.

A simple version of the communications management plan is shown in Figure 4-4.

COMMUNICATIONS MANAGEMENT PLAN

Project Title: ______________ Date Prepared: ______________

Message	Audience	Method	Frequency	Sender

Term or Acronym	Definition

Communication Constraints or Assumptions:

Attach relevant communication diagrams or flowcharts.

Figure 4-4: Sample communications management plan.

A more complete plan would include additional elements, including

- ✦ Resources and budgets associated with communications
- ✦ Glossary and abbreviation list
- ✦ Communication flowcharts
- ✦ Communication constraints
- ✦ Templates for agendas, reports, minutes, and so forth

As necessary, update the stakeholder register and schedule with the communication strategy.

Key Terms

Most of the terms in this chapter are general communication terms and are not project management–specific. Many chapters rely heavily on glossary terms; however, this chapter is general, and most of these terms are not in the glossary.

- ✦ Sender
- ✦ Receiver
- ✦ Encoding
- ✦ Decoding
- ✦ Medium
- ✦ Message
- ✦ Noise
- ✦ Push communication
- ✦ Pull communication
- ✦ Interactive communication
- ✦ Communications management plan

Chapter Summary

A lot of the information in this chapter deals with communication principles. You will need a cursory knowledge of general communication principles, as presented here, to do well on the exam. The primary project-specific

pter Summary

nformation is how you summarize all the communication needs in a communications management plan.

- Communication can be formal or informal, and written or verbal. There is a time and a place for each kind of communication.
- Communication can be vertical or horizontal in the organization. It can also be internal or external, and official or non-official.
- Communication takes place in not only what we say but in how we say it (our tone). Communication also takes place in nonverbal ways, such as facial expressions and body language.
- Effective communication requires good listening and speaking skills.
- The more communication channels you have, the more complex communication becomes. The equation for this is $(N\,(n - 1))\,/\,2$.
- The standard communication model includes a sender and receiver, encoding and decoding, and the message and medium. The message can be affected by noise.
- You can push out communication or pull it in. You can also have interactive communication.
- The communications management plan documents who will receive information, what they will receive, how it will be delivered, and who is responsible for retrieving the information.

Prep Test

1 **Briefing your sponsor and the executive team on the status of your project is what type of communication?**

A ❍ Formal, written
B ❍ Informal, written
C ❍ Formal, verbal
D ❍ Informal, verbal

2 **If you have a routine request, you can convey it via ______. However, for complex topics, it is best to ______.**

A ❍ A one-on-one meeting, document it in a memo
B ❍ A briefing, write an e-mail
C ❍ A phone call, write a memo
D ❍ An e-mail, meet face to face

3 **Reviewing the company organizational charts, the team's geographic dispersion and the internal and external audiences are all part of**

A ❍ A project organizational structure
B ❍ Stakeholder analysis
C ❍ A communications management plan
D ❍ Analyzing communication requirements

4 **Your core project team has just expanded from four people to six. How many more communication channels do you have?**

A ❍ 9
B ❍ 6
C ❍ 15
D ❍ 4

5 **A team with nine people has how many communication channels?**

A ❍ 18
B ❍ 81
C ❍ 72
D ❍ 36

6 **The person responsible for confirming that the receiver understood the message correctly is**

A ❍ The encoder
B ❍ The sender
C ❍ The decoder
D ❍ The receiver

7 **_____ is translating ideas into language.**

A ❍ Encoding
B ❍ Decoding
C ❍ Interpreting
D ❍ Sending

8 **In a communication model, preconceptions and stereotyping are considered**

A ❍ Inappropriate
B ❍ Irrelevant
C ❍ Normal
D ❍ Noise

9 **Setting up a team website so that team members can retrieve information as needed is used for which type of communication?**

A ❍ Pull
B ❍ Push
C ❍ Interactive
D ❍ Dynamic

10 **Where would you find a glossary of terms for the project?**

A ❍ In the document library
B ❍ In the configuration management plan
C ❍ In the communications management plan
D ❍ In the training plan

Answers

1 **C.** Formal, verbal. The briefing is verbal, and the sponsor and executive team necessitate formal communication. *Look at the information in "Formal and informal, written and verbal."*

2 **D.** An e-mail, meet face to face. E-mail is good for routine information, but meeting face to face is best for complex topics. *Check into "Formal and informal, written and verbal."*

3 **D.** Analyzing communication requirements. *See the information in "Communication requirements analysis."*

4 **A.** 9. With four people, you have six channels. With six people, you have 15 channels. The difference is 9. *See the information in "Communication requirements analysis."*

5 **D.** 36. (9 (9 – 1) / 2) = 36. *See the information in "Communication requirements analysis."*

6 **B.** The sender. The sender is responsible for sending the message and for confirming that it was understood correctly. *Look at "Communication models."*

7 **A.** Encoding. Encoding is interpreting ideas into language. *Review "Communication models."*

8 **D.** Noise. Preconceptions and stereotyping are noise that interferes with communication. *Go over "Communication models."*

9 **A.** Pull. Pull communication is setting information up so that people can retrieve it as needed. *Look at "Communication methods."*

10 **C.** In the communications management plan. The communications management plan can contain a glossary of terms and abbreviations. *Go over "Plan Communications Management: Outputs."*

Book V

Planning for Risks, Procurement, and Stakeholder Management

Probability and Impact Matrix*

Very High					
High					
Medium					
Low					
Very Low					
	Very Low	Low	Medium	High	Very High

* This is a sample matrix for one project objective. The shading shows a balanced matrix that indicates ranking of High, Medium, or Low of risks based on the probability and impact scores. The darkest shade indicates high risks, the mid-shade indicates medium risks, and the light shade is for low risks.

Check out the article on the importance of stakeholder management at www.dummies.com/extras/pmpcertificationaio.

Contents at a Glance

Chapter 1: Identifying What Could Go Wrong

Exam Objective

- **Create a risk management plan that provides guidance for identifying, analyzing, prioritizing, and developing response strategies to manage uncertainty throughout the project.**

Risk is centered on the concept of uncertainty. When uncertainty can lead to negative effects on your project, that's a *threat.* Comparatively, when uncertainty can lead to positive effects on your project, that's an *opportunity.* And face it: Projects will never have the same degree of certainty that day-to-day operations have. Therefore, spend some time thinking about how to proactively address uncertainty. After all, that's what project risk management is all about — planning how to get in front of the uncertainty and reduce it. As for the uncertainty that you can't reduce, you can at least think about and develop an approach for handling it.

Five distinct processes are associated with risk in the planning process group:

- **Planning for risk management:** Defining how you approach the risk management process, including the techniques, methods, and degree of rigor that you will apply.
- **Identifying risks:** Taking a methodical approach to finding all the events that could cause your project to not meet one or more objectives.
- **Qualitative analysis:** After risks are identified, determining the probability and impact of the event. This step helps you prioritize your time so that you can address the risks that pose the greatest threat to your project.
- **Quantitative analysis:** Using quantitative tools that help you conduct the analysis. Some risks need to have a greater degree of analysis to determine their impact. In addition, this process helps you figure out how likely you are to meet specific schedule and budget objectives.
- **Planning responses:** Develop proactive responses. It isn't enough to identify and analyze risks; you need to determine what to do about them.

Risk management can be fairly technical. Some of the topics in this chapter will be among the most challenging on the exam, but given some time and effort, you will be up for the challenge!

Quick Assessment

1 The willingness to accept varying degrees of risk is called _____ _____.

2 If you were to develop a structure to categorize and organize risks in a framework, you would be developing a(n) _____ _____ _____.

3 The _____ _____ contains the outcomes of all the risk management processes as they are conducted.

4 Risks that are considered low impact and low probability are considered low priority. These should be kept on a(n) _____ _____.

5 To graphically depict various scenarios and the average outcome of each scenario given the likelihood and the associated values, you would create a(n) _____ _____.

6 If an organization wants to ensure that an opportunity is realized, what response strategy should it use?

7 Which document describes the risk roles and responsibilities and the risk methodology you will use on a project?

8 SWOT analysis stands for _____, _____, _____, and _____.

9 When calculating expected monetary value, you multiply the _____ of each scenario times the _____ _____ associated with each outcome.

10 The _____ _____ uses a group of anonymous experts to identify risks to a project.

Answers

1 Risk tolerance. Organizations that are comfortable with a lot of risk are said to be "risk tolerant." Those that aren't are "risk averse." *For more information on this topic, see "Projects Breed Uncertainty."*

2 Risk breakdown structure. A risk breakdown structure (RBS) is similar to a work breakdown structure (WBS), but it organizes and decomposes risk categories instead of deliverables. *The RBS is discussed in "Plan Risk Management: Outputs."*

3 Risk register. The risk register is started when you begin to identify risks. It is expanded to include the risk rating, response, triggers, and other relevant information. *You can find information on the risk register in "Identify Risks: Outputs."*

4 Watch list. Low-priority risks should be watched to see whether the probability or impact changes, but you don't need to come up with a defined response for them. *I discuss the watch list in "Perform Qualitative Risk Analysis: Outputs."*

5 Decision tree. A decision tree creates a graphic illustration of the information developed in an EMV equation. *Look over the information in the "Decision tree" section.*

6 Exploit. To take advantage of an opportunity and ensure that it occurs, you exploit that opportunity. *See the discussion in "Plan Risk Responses: Tools and Techniques."*

7 Risk management plan. The risk management plan defines how you will address risk on a project. It includes roles, responsibilities, and the methodology. *To read more about what is included in a risk management plan, go to the section "Plan Risk Management: Outputs."*

8 Strengths, weaknesses, opportunities, and threats. This is used to assess strengths and weaknesses in the organization and opportunities and threats in the environment. *You can read about this in "Risk identification analysis."*

9 Probability, monetary value. This gives you the expected monetary value of each outcome. *You can read more about this in "Expected Monetary Value (EMV)."*

10 Delphi technique. The anonymity encourages more honest and creative feedback when identifying risks. *This is discussed in more detail in the section "Gathering information."*

Projects Breed Uncertainty

Projects are fraught with uncertainty. Many times, there is no historic information to help develop duration and cost estimates, so you're uncertain about the project schedule and budget. You often don't know exactly who will be on your team, or whether they'll be available when you need them, and whether they have appropriate skill sets. In many cases, projects are initiated to solve a problem, but there is no clear solution. Sometimes the problem itself isn't clearly defined. Therefore, project scope is uncertain. Risk management attempts to reduce that uncertainty to an acceptable level.

In risk management, you try to reduce or eliminate the probability and impacts of threats while increasing the probability and impact of opportunities. Risk carries with it its own vocabulary. Here are some key terms you need to know.

Risk. An uncertain event or condition that if it occurs, has a positive or negative effect on one or more project objectives.

Threat. A risk that will have a negative impact on one or more project objectives.

Opportunity. A risk that will have a positive impact on one or more project objectives.

Risk tolerance. The degree, amount, or volume of risk that an organization or individual will withstand.

Risk appetite. The degree of uncertainty an entity is willing to take on, in anticipation of a reward.

Project objectives are identified in the project charter. For purposes of the exam, the objectives usually center on the scope, schedule, quality, and budget objectives.

Risks can be known or unknown. A *known risk* is one that you can identify, analyze, and develop a response for. Consider the following example of a known risk, using my running example of a childcare center:

> A piece of playground equipment is on back order and may not be available before the childcare center is scheduled to open. You can develop several responses to that risk. You can find another supplier, change the piece of equipment, open without it, see whether you can pay to expedite the process, or any other of a myriad of options.

Now, consider this example of an unknown risk:

> The three electricians went out to lunch and ate meat that was undercooked and contaminated with E. coli. They were all unable to work for three days, leading to a schedule delay.

There really is no way you can plan for this kind of event. Schedule and cost reserves are usually set aside for unknown risks.

Project risk management is the least mature practice in project management. Many projects have no real risk management plan, and their approach to managing risk is limited to identifying five or so things that could go wrong and discussing them every so often. Granted, a lot of risk management occurs that's not documented. Overall, though, there is much room for improvement.

You should assume that you have a large project and ample time to plan for risk management. If you're not used to an environment like this, you might need to spend significant time studying this chapter.

Plan Risk Management

Planning for the unknown is challenging, to say the least, and probably one of the reasons why people don't spend as much time on risk management as they should. However, just because it's hard doesn't mean that it isn't worthwhile.

Plan Risk Management. Defining how to conduct risk management activities for a project.

Here are some basic tenets to keep in mind about planning for risk:

- The amount of risk management planning should be commensurate with the amount of uncertainty and the degree of criticality of the project. Projects that are similar to prior projects and that are not complex need less risk management than complex projects with new and emerging technology and that have a high impact on the success of the organization.
- Risk management should begin very early on in the project and continue until the project is closed.
- To elevate the importance of risk management on a project, sufficient time, resources, and budget need to be allocated to the risk management process.

Plan Risk Management: Inputs

Risk management planning needs to be consistent with the project's approach for scope, schedule, cost, and quality. Therefore, you should consider at least the following information from the project management plan: scope management plan, schedule management plan, cost management plan, and quality management plan as you determine how to address risk. Look at how these various plans affect your risk management planning.

If you have a project with a very tight delivery time frame, and yet you have no schedule management plan (or one that is simple or not well defined), you need to account for the lack of attention to schedule management in your risk planning. However, if you have a robust schedule management plan that includes contingency reserves, a detailed approach to analyzing the progress on critical and near-critical paths, sufficient scheduling software, and people skilled in developing schedules, your risk management plan won't need to focus as heavily on the schedule aspect as you plan for risk.

The scope statement contains information about the types of deliverables and the associated acceptance criteria. A well–thought-out scope statement means less uncertainty — and, therefore, less risk associated with the scope and quality of the product and the project.

In organizations that practice risk management, plenty of tools and documentation are available that can help you. For example, there might be templates for probability and impact matrices and risk registers. Or, definitions for high, medium, and low risks may already exist, so you won't need to develop them on your own.

As you plan how to handle risk, keep in mind your organization's risk tolerance. Government or regulated agencies are bound to be risk averse and cannot take risks with the public's welfare or interests. Conversely, remember the Dot-Com boom in the 1990s? Those companies were indeed risk-seekers. They could see only the upside, taking tremendous risks — and, for a while, reaping tremendous rewards. However, many of those organizations paid the price for their risk taking by going out of business.

Plan Risk Management: Tools and Techniques

Analyzing stakeholder risk tolerances and the high-level project risk exposure will help determine the appropriate approach for risk management. A project with high risk exposure, or with stakeholders who are risk averse, will require more risk management than a project with low risk exposure or stakeholders with a high risk tolerance.

You will meet with your team, risk experts, and technical experts to determine the best approach for risk management. If your organization doesn't have risk management templates or definitions for probability and impact, you and your team will develop these as part of risk management planning. If your organization does have these key definitions and tools, you'll spend this time customizing them for your project.

Plan Risk Management: Outputs

Your risk management plan is a subsidiary plan of the overall project management plan. It describes how risk identification, analysis, and response planning will be conducted. It should be tailored to the needs of the project.

Risk management plan. A component of the project, program, or portfolio management plan that describes how risk management activities will be structured and performed.

Information in the risk management plan varies by application area and project size. The risk management plan is different from the risk register that contains the list of project risks, the results of risk analysis, and the risk responses.

The risk management plan and the risk register are sometimes confused. I discuss the risk management plan later and the risk register in the section "Identify Risks: Outputs."

The *PMBOK Guide* provides a list of some of the elements that should be included in the risk management plan, such as

- **Methodology:** Define the approach, tools, and data that you use to manage risk.
- **Roles and responsibilities:** Describe the role that various stakeholders have for managing risk. This can include a risk manager for very large projects, or the responsibility that each team member has with regard to risk management.
- **Budgeting:** Estimate the funds needed for risk identification, analysis, and response. Also, define the approach for allocating, using, and recording contingency funds.
- **Timing:** Identify the risk management activities that need to be added to the schedule and cite how often they will occur. Define the approach for allocating, using, and recording contingency for the project schedule.
- **Risk categories:** Identify the major categories of risk on the project and decompose them into subcategories. The *PMBOK Guide* has an example of an RBS using technical, external, organizational, and project

management as the main categories. These are then further decomposed to the level that makes sense for the project. Some branches may have two levels, and others may go down further. You can also categorize risks by objectives, such as scope, schedule, cost, quality, or stakeholder risks. These would then be further decomposed. These are not the only approaches to developing an RBS, though. You should develop one to meet the needs of your project.

✦ **Definitions of probability and impact:** To analyze risks effectively, use a common method of rating the probability of an occurrence and the impact if it does occur.

✦ **Probability and impact matrix:** Include a probability and impact matrix (PxI matrix) to rate risks as a high, medium, or low risk. Figure 1-1 shows a sample probability and impact matrix that's balanced. The low, medium, and high rankings are relatively balanced, as opposed to having more squares indicating high risk, as a risk-averse organization might show. The PxI matrix will be applied in the section, "Perform Qualitative Risk Analysis: Tools and Techniques."

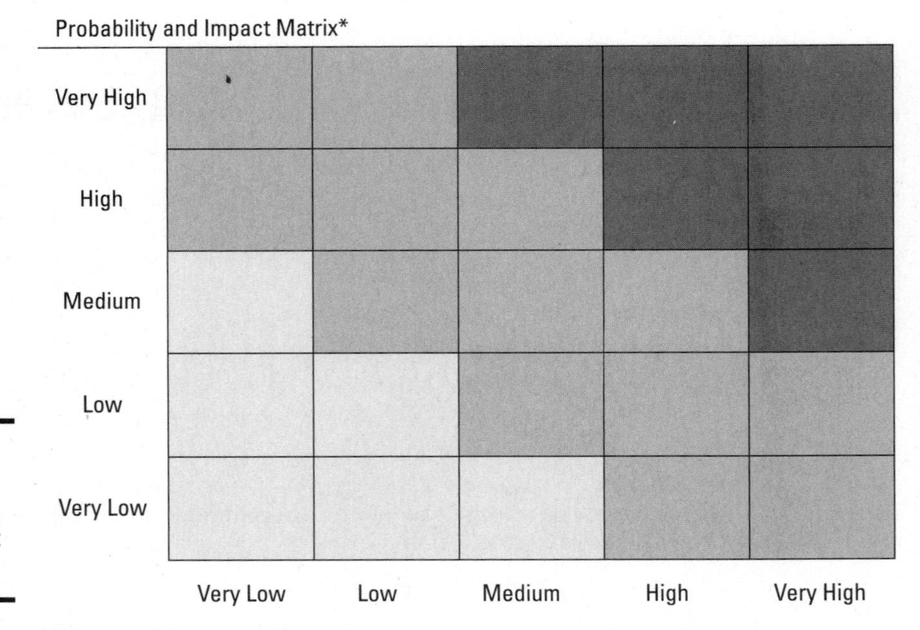

Figure 1-1: Sample probability and impact matrix.

As part of establishing your definitions for probability and impact, you are, in essence, defining your thresholds for action. A *threshold* defines the point where you need to take action. By identifying the combination of probability and impact that defines an event as a low, medium, or high risk, you're stating when you can merely observe the event compared with taking action to minimize the event compared with needing to avoid the event altogether.

- **Revised stakeholder tolerances:** If needed, update your risk tolerances as viewpoints that might have shifted while compiling the risk management plan.
- **Reporting and tracking formats:** Describe how risks will be recorded and reported during the project. This can include a sample risk register, sample risk data sheets, and risk analysis templates.

Whew! That is a lot of information! But remember, risk management is the least well-practiced discipline in project management. Having a robust risk management plan helps you integrate good risk management practices into your project.

Why it's important to define probability and impact

Joe might define an event as high probability if its chance of occurring is greater than 50%. Marie might say that 50% is a medium probability, and to reach the high threshold, it has to have greater than 80% probability of occurring.

The same can be said about impact. On a small project, you can define impact for any objective. In other words, you don't differentiate the project objectives. For larger projects, you might spend time defining the high, medium, and low impacts for scope, schedule, cost, and quality. As I mention earlier in the chapter, the risk management process should mirror the complexity and criticality of the project.

When establishing definitions for probability and impact, you can use a cardinal (numeric) scale or an ordinal (descriptive) scale. A cardinal scale might rank probability as

- 0%–20%
- 21%–40%
- 41%–60%
- 61%–80%
- 81%–100%

An ordinal scale could rank probability as

- Very low
- Low
- Medium
- High
- Very high

You can use the same approach for rating impacts as very high, high, medium, and so on, or cardinally, such as on a scale of 1–10 or 1–5.

Risk category. A group of potential causes of risk.

Risk breakdown structure (RBS). A hierarchical representation of risks according to their risk categories.

Probability and impact matrix (PxI matrix). A grid for mapping the probability of each risk occurrence and its impact on objectives if that risk occurs.

The *PMBOK Guide* presents one approach to the risk management plan. Of course, there are others. Ultimately, the needs of the project determine what should be in your risk management plan.

When answering questions in risk management, always keep in mind that prevention is preferred over reaction.

Identify Risks

Identifying risks is everyone's job. Even though the risk management plan defines roles and responsibilities for risk management, everyone should be on the lookout for events that could negatively affect the project as well as opportunities to improve project performance. Think about it as a sailor in a crow's nest with a telescope, constantly sweeping the horizon for perils.

Identify Risks. Determining which risks may affect the project and documenting their characteristics.

Risk identification and the subsequent analysis and response take place throughout the project.

Identify Risks: Inputs

To do a thorough job in identifying risks, you need to look at all the elements in the project management plan and all the other project documents as well as environmental factors associated with the project.

Planning takes place throughout the project, as does risk management. Not all project management plan components or project documents are available at the beginning of the project. As they become available, though, they should be referenced for sources of risk.

The four categories of documents you can look at are

- ✦ Project management plan elements (Chapter 3 in this minibook)
- ✦ Project documents (Chapter 3 in this minibook)

- Enterprise environmental factors (EEFs) (Book I, Chapter 2)
- Organizational process assets (OPAs) (Book I, Chapter 3)

Here is a list of the relevant information from each category.

- **Project management plan elements**
  - Risk management plan
  - Cost management plan
  - Schedule management plan
  - Quality management plan
  - Human resource management plan
  - Scope baseline
  - Schedule baseline
  - Budget
- **Project documents**
  - Project charter
  - Stakeholder register
  - Cost estimates
  - Duration estimates
  - Network diagram
  - Assumption log
  - Issue log
  - Performance reports
  - Earned value reports
  - Resource requirements
  - Procurement documents
- **Enterprise environmental factors (EEFs)**
  - Benchmarks
  - Industry information
  - Studies, white papers, and research
  - Risk attitudes
- **Organizational process assets (OPAs)**
  - Risk registers from past projects
  - Lessons learned

I know that seems like quite the laundry list. However, risk can come from any aspect of the project. That's why it is important to review all project management plan elements, project documents, and the project environment to get a full understanding of the risks on your project.

Identify Risks: Tools and Techniques

With all this information to review, the main techniques you will use are to analyze, compare, and contrast the documentation. If you see any inconsistencies, record that as a risk. For example, if your Assumption Log states that you will have an independent third-party vendor perform product testing but your budget doesn't account for the associated costs, you have inconsistencies among your project documents. This will cause you either to overrun your budget, or perhaps to not have the quality review by a third party that you need to ensure an unbiased assessment of the product.

If the plans and documents that you review are incomplete or of poor quality, that's also a risk.

Gathering information

As I mention earlier, risk identification is everyone's job. Some easy ways to identify risks include holding a brainstorming session with your project stakeholders. You can also conduct individual and group interviews. A more formal method of gathering information is using the Delphi technique.

The Delphi technique

I present the Delphi technique in Book III, Chapter 2 as a technique for collecting requirements. It can also be used to identify risks.

Delphi technique. An information-gathering technique used as a way to reach a consensus of experts on a subject. Experts on the subject participate in this technique anonymously. A facilitator uses a questionnaire to solicit ideas about the important project points related to the subject. The responses are summarized and re-circulated to the experts for further comment. Consensus may be reached in a few rounds of this process. The Delphi technique helps reduce bias in the data and keeps any one person from having undue influence on the outcome.

For identifying risks, follow these steps:

1. **Describe the project or the aspect of the project you want to identify risks for.**
2. **Select a panel of experts, who should remain anonymous throughout the process.**

3. **Send out background information on the project along with a questionnaire to each expert participant.**
4. **The facilitator compiles information returned from the experts, filtering out irrelevant content and content that can lead to loss of anonymity.**
5. **The facilitator sends out the compiled and cleaned responses to the questionnaire for the experts to comment on.**

   They can comment on individual observations or on the observations of the group as a whole.

   As a result of the comment process, people may want to modify their input.
6. **Several iterations of the analysis, response, and discussion take place until consensus is reached or until there is no more movement on the outcome.**

The Delphi technique is useful because the anonymity encourages more honest and creative feedback. Studies have found that groups of individual experts that come to consensus have a strong forecasting ability.

Root cause analysis and diagramming techniques

Another information-gathering technique is *root cause analysis,* which seeks to find the underlying source of a problem and then identify preventive actions. A root cause analysis can include diagramming techniques.

Root cause analysis. An analytical technique used to determine the basic underlying reason that causes a variance or a defect or a risk. A root cause may underlie more than one variance, defect, or risk.

Some of the more common diagramming techniques include

- ✦ Cause and effect diagrams (also known as fishbone or Ishikawa diagrams)
- ✦ Process flow charts or system diagrams
- ✦ Influence diagrams that show relationships among variables

Many of the diagramming and analysis techniques are similar to techniques you see in quality management. For quality, you're looking at how to keep defects out of your product and project. This is closely related to risk management, which looks at what could go wrong and how to prevent it.

Risk identification analysis

Various types of analysis are helpful in risk identification:

- **Checklist analysis:** This type uses a risk checklist. The problem with this approach is that after people complete the checklist, they might infer that they're done with risk identification. A checklist should be only a starting point, not an ending point.
- **Assumptions analysis:** This type reviews the documented assumptions for accuracy, stability, consistency, and completeness.
- **SWOT analysis:** SWOT (Strengths, Weaknesses, Opportunities, and Threats) analysis comprises
  - *Internal organizational analysis* to identify internal strengths and weaknesses that can help or hinder the organization
  - *External environment analysis* to identify opportunities and threats in the market or among competitors

Internal or external experts can complete the preceding techniques. Some experts have information on the specific technology being used, others have experience in similar projects, and still others are familiar with the market.

Identify Risks: Outputs

The risk register is started as an output of this process. However, you will add to it as you analyze your risks and develop responses to them. Initially, you're documenting your risks.

Documenting a risk statement like, "The budget is at risk" is not acceptable. That gives very little information to work with when addressing the risk. The following risk statements are much better:

> *Because the cost to install security cameras in the childcare center is greater than anticipated, there is a risk we will overrun the budget.*
>
> *The city might not approve the plans, thus causing a schedule delay.*
>
> *A team member might be reassigned to a higher priority project, thus causing a schedule delay.*

All risk statements start with the cause and then define the effect. The approach to describing the risk event is different, but both approaches provide something to work with when deciding how to analyze and respond to the risk. At this point in time, you might already know how you're going to respond to the risk event. In that case, you can enter a potential response in the risk register. However, it's a good practice to get a robust list of risks, analyze them, and then develop responses because a group of risks can often be addressed by one response. Your risk register will follow you throughout the rest of the risk management processes.

Risk register. A document in which the results of risk analysis and risk response planning are recorded.

The risk register details all identified risks, including description, category, cause, probability of occurring, impact(s) on objectives, proposed responses, owners, and current status.

The risk management plan describes how risk management will be structured and performed on the project. It is a management document. The risk register keeps track of identified risks, their ranking, responses, and all other information about individual risks. It is a tracking document.

Because you are progressively elaborating your project plan elements and your project documents, you will also progressively elaborate your risk register. As more is known about the project, existing risks can be further elaborated, and new risks will be identified.

Perform Qualitative Risk Analysis

If you did a thorough job identifying and documenting risks, you will have quite an intimidating list of things that could go wrong. Many people think, "Why bother? I don't have time to address all these. If I did, I wouldn't have time to manage the project." And that's precisely why you should take the next step of conducting a *qualitative analysis,* which is just fancy terminology for determining the probability and impact of each event and then ranking the risks based on that determination. At that point, about 80 percent of your risks will remain on a watch list. You should take a proactive approach toward the remaining 20 percent.

Perform Qualitative Risk Analysis. Prioritizing risks for further analysis or action by assessing and combining their probability of occurrence and impact.

Perform Qualitative Risk Analysis: Inputs

The main ingredients you need to begin the process are the risk register, scope baseline, risk management plan, and any historical information you can get your hands on. The risk management plan has good information to assist you in this process:

- Roles and responsibilities for the analysis process
- Risk categories you use to group similar risks
- Definitions of probability and impact, which can be inclusive of all objectives or a definition of impact for each objective

- A probability and impact (PxI) matrix template
- Documentation of the risk tolerance level — overall or for each objective — that can include a prioritization of the objectives and project constraints

Perform Qualitative Risk Analysis: Tools and Techniques

The primary technique for analyzing and prioritizing risks is a PxI analysis that is later charted on a PxI matrix.

To conduct a PxI assessment, you start with the risk statement (see "Identify Risks: Outputs") in the risk register. You might interview the team member with the most information about the risk or do some research to understand the risk. For complex and technical projects, you might call in a subject matter expert or conduct a risk workshop or survey. The outcome is rating the likelihood (probability) of the event occurring as well as the impact if the event occurs. This information is entered into the risk register and the PxI matrix.

Look at how this process would be applied using the three risks identified for the childcare center example:

For this example, the date is July 6; assume the following information:

- *Because the cost to install security cameras in the childcare center is greater than anticipated, there is a risk we will overrun the budget.*

  Ten cameras are planned for installation around the childcare center and the playground. Each camera is estimated to cost $250. However, the camera model that was estimated is no longer available, and the new model costs $310 each. Reducing the number of cameras, though, will compromise the security and is thus an unacceptable trade-off.

- *The city may not approve the plans, thus causing a schedule delay.*

  You interviewed the contractor, who stated that of the last ten childcare centers he built, the city sent back plans on four. The time to resubmit and get approval ranged from 14–35 days. You submitted your plans on June 30. The city has a 30-day time frame to get back to you.

- *A team member may be reassigned to a higher priority project, thus causing a schedule delay.*

  You heard that your team member in charge of security might be pulled off the project and replaced by someone who is new to the company and without the same experience level. You don't have confirmation, though.

Table 1-1 shows a PxI matrix, with the probability and impact by objective filled out. The table uses a cardinal rating of 1–5 for both probability and impact.

Table 1-1 Sample PxI Matrix

ID	*Statement*	*Probability*	*Impact*				*Score*
			Scope	*Schedule*	*Cost*	*Quality*	
1	Because the cost to install security cameras in the childcare center is greater than anticipated, there is a risk we will overrun the budget.	5	None	None	1	None	5
2	The city may not approve the plans, thus causing a schedule delay.	2	None	3	3	None	12
3	A team member may be reassigned to a higher priority project, thus causing a schedule delay.	2	1	2	None	2	10

The score is determined by multiplying the probability times the impact. If multiple objectives are impacted, you add the scores. For example, if you look at the risk of the city not approving the plans, you multiply

$$(2 \times 3) + (2 \times 3) = 12$$

Include a section for comments on your risk register. For the information in Table 1-1, you would expect to see an explanation on the score, as shown in Table 1-2.

Table 1-2 Risk Register Score Explanations

ID	*Statement*	*Comments*
1	Because the cost to install security cameras in the childcare center is greater than anticipated, there is a risk we will overrun the budget.	The cameras have gone up in price. We can't get them at a lower rate. The overall cost impact is $600. This is a minimal impact to the overall budget and will be funded by contingency reserve.
2	The city might not approve the plans, thus causing a schedule delay.	If the city delays the permits or we have to rework the plans, we will need to pay overtime to crash the schedule. This will impact our schedule by needing to fast-track some activities and add overtime on others. Thus, the schedule and budget are both impacted.
3	A team member may be reassigned to a higher-priority project, thus causing a schedule delay.	At this point, the team member being reassigned is only a rumor, so we are rating probability as a 2. However, if he is reassigned, there might be some rework and quality issues because the replacement is not as experienced.

At this point, responses are set for some cases (such as fast-tracking the schedule and working overtime), but the responses aren't formally outlined. When planning responses, you might apply multiple responses, or you might use a response that impacts multiple risks. At this point, you're only analyzing the risks.

The PxI matrix in Figure 1-2 is for the schedule objective. It demonstrates how risks would be plotted if you were looking only at schedule impacts. You would have one of these for all objectives.

Schedule Impact					
5					
4					
3		#2			
2		#3			
1					
	1	2	3	4	5
	Event Probability				

Figure 1-2: PxI matrix for the schedule objective.

If you're not rating each objective individually, you would obviously have just one matrix that combines impact scores.

The PxI matrix in Figure 1-2 is called a "5 x 5" (5 by 5) because it rates risks in five grades of probability and five grades of impact. You can use a 3 x 3, 10 x 10, 5 x 7, or whatever configuration you want. Most people use an odd number, but beware of too many risks congregating in the middle cell. Try to keep the middle cell empty so you can have a more definitive rating.

When assessing risks, take into consideration the urgency of the situation. Given that the date is July 6, the plans have been submitted to the city for approval, and the approval is due in three weeks, that is your most urgent risk. Even if it didn't have the highest score, you might consider moving this up your list for responses based on the near time frame.

Another technique to apply is determining the data quality. This means that you can perform a good risk assessment only if you have quality data. In other words, Garbage In, Garbage Out.

After analyzing the risks, you may find that you have groups or categories of risks, such as technical risks, requirements risks, schedule risks, and so on. Categorizing risks can help you later when developing responses because you can develop one response that will be effective for several risks.

Perform Qualitative Risk Analysis: Outputs

Based on your analysis, you update the risk register with the probability, impact, score, and comments, as shown in the preceding sections. Based on the scores and your urgency assessment, prioritize your risks. Some risks will require further analysis, and those go into the quantitative risk analysis process that I cover next. Some risks don't need further analysis, and you can work with your team to develop responses; I cover risk responses later in this chapter. However, most risks go on a "watch list," and you check the probability, impact, and urgency on watch list risks throughout the project. If any of those factors change, you might need to escalate the risk and develop a risk response. Or, if the event passes without occurring, the probability drops to 0, and the risk is closed. The watch list isn't a separate list; it just means you are not taking the time to develop a risk response, other than to "watch" the risk.

Perform Quantitative Risk Analysis

Not all projects need to conduct a quantitative risk analysis. That is usually reserved for the mega-projects. Remember, though, the PMP exam assumes you have a large project, so you need to be familiar with the techniques in this section.

Perform Quantitative Risk Analysis. Numerically analyzing the effect of identified risks on overall project objectives.

As the name implies, the techniques in this process are quantitative: In other words, you have to do the math! If you're math-phobic, review this part of the book enough times to develop a comfort level with the concepts.

The purposes of performing quantitative analysis are to

- ✦ Perform a deeper analysis on those risks that can potentially and substantially impact a project objective.
- ✦ Determine the likelihood of meeting cost and schedule objectives and provide a range of outcomes.
- ✦ Determine realistic schedule and budget targets given the project risks.
- ✦ Provide a method to quantify some of the uncertainty in the project to make better decisions.

If you're engaging in this process, you should do it both before and after you develop risk responses. You should expect to see the overall project risk drop significantly after applying risk responses.

Perform Quantitative Risk Analysis: Inputs

You need several components of the project management plan to conduct a quantitative risk analysis:

- ✦ Schedule management plan
- ✦ Cost management plan
- ✦ Risk management plan

Of course, you also need your risk register with your prioritized risks and any organizational or external information you can use to better understand the nature of the high risks.

Perform Quantitative Risk Analysis: Tools and Techniques

The first step to quantifying uncertainty is to get more information. This is generally done via research and interviewing subject matter experts. Because quantitative risk analysis is associated with the schedule and cost objectives, focus on those estimates. Assume that you're gathering cost estimates to determine whether a budget of $2.5 million is sufficient for the childcare center. Here are the steps you would take:

1. **Revisit your cost estimates and get an optimistic, a pessimistic, and a most-likely estimate for each WBS element.**
2. **Sum the optimistic, pessimistic, and most-likely estimates for the project as a whole.**
3. **Document your assumptions, basis of estimates, and rationale for each set of estimates.**
4. **Apply the PERT equation to the estimates.**

   This gives you an expected cost for each element and the project as a whole.
5. **Use software to create a probability distribution of the values.**
6. **Compare the sum of the most likely estimates with the sum of the expected value estimate.**

The PMP exam will use the PERT (Program Evaluation and Review Technique) equation that I discuss in the chapters on duration and cost estimating (Book III, Chapter 3, and Book IV, Chapter 1). That equation is

(optimistic + 4 (most likely) + pessimistic) / 6

You'll almost always find the sum of the most likely to be significantly less than the sum of the expected value. And because the expected value is the 50% probability figure, you will discover that your "most likely" estimate is not very likely at all!

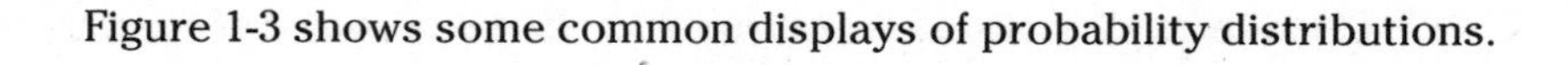

Figure 1-3 shows some common displays of probability distributions.

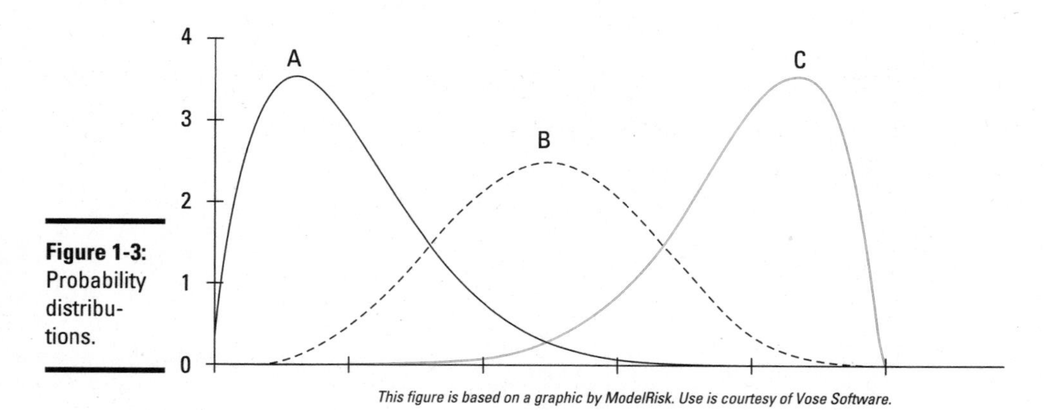

Figure 1-3: Probability distributions.

This figure is based on a graphic by ModelRisk. Use is courtesy of Vose Software.

The three curves represent three different scenarios. Curve A indicates that the optimistic and most likely estimates are close together and that the pessimistic estimate is significantly greater. Curve B indicates that all three values are evenly distributed. Curve C indicates that the optimistic value is significantly less than the most likely and pessimistic values, which are close together.

Curve A is a common occurrence because generally, the best case scenario and most likely are not that far off. However, if things really go wrong, the worst case scenario can be really bad! In Curve A, your expected value will be higher than your most likely value.

Scenarios, modeling, and simulations

Before getting too deep in this section, look at some key definitions.

Sensitivity analysis. A quantitative risk analysis and modeling technique used to help determine which risks have the most potential impact on the project. It examines the extent to which the uncertainty of each project element affects the objective being examined when all other uncertain elements are held at their baseline values. The typical display of results is in the form of a tornado diagram.

Expected Monetary Value (EMV) analysis. A statistical technique that calculates the average outcome when the future includes scenarios that may or may not happen. A common use of this technique is within decision tree analysis.

Decision tree analysis. A diagramming and calculation technique for evaluating the implications of a chain of multiple options in the presence of uncertainty.

Simulation. A simulation uses a project model that translates the uncertainties specified at a detailed level into their potential impact on objectives that are expressed at the level of the total project. Project simulations use computer models and estimates of risk, usually expressed as a probability distribution of possible costs or durations at a detailed work level, and are typically performed by using Monte Carlo analysis.

I explain each technique in a bit more detail.

Sensitivity analysis

You use a sensitivity analysis to see which variables have most impact on a project objective. You can develop what-if models or simulations to see the impact of a risk on either the budget or the schedule. Many times, the outcomes are graphed in a tornado diagram. Figure 1-4 shows the impact of various events on the schedule.

A tornado diagram has the following characteristics:

- The longer the bar, the more sensitive the project objective is to the risk.
- The risks are presented in descending order, with the largest impact on the top and the least impact on the bottom.
- It allows the team to focus on those risks with the greatest impact on a project objective.

A tornado diagram isn't the only way you can display information, but it is a common choice. You can also run a what-if scenario for your schedule (or budget) to see the impact of a risk event on the overall schedule or budget.

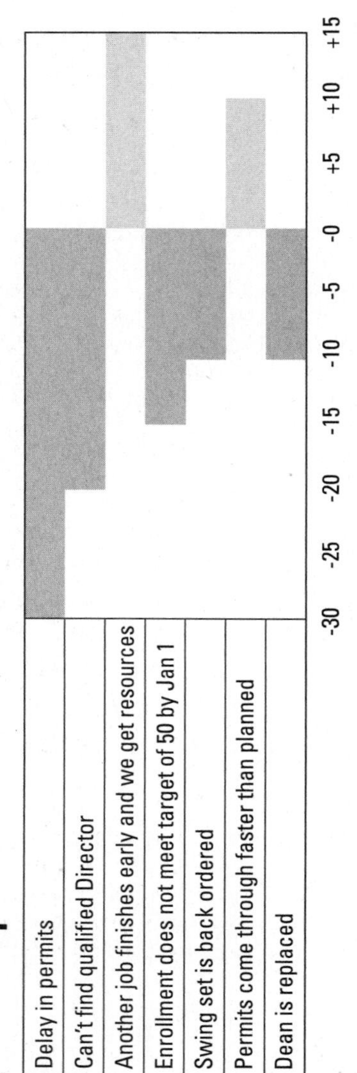

Figure 1-4: Sensitivity analysis for schedule.

Expected Monetary Value (EMV)

To determine the expected monetary value of a risk or a decision, do the following:

1. Identify the scenarios that could occur.
2. Determine the probability of each scenario.

3. Determine the monetary value associated with each outcome.
4. Multiply the probability times the monetary value of each outcome.
5. Sum the outcomes to get the expected monetary value of the risk or decision.

Note that none of the scenarios might occur: You're simply trying to get an average outcome given the uncertainty of the environment.

Consider this example. You're trying to decide whether to purchase software and customize it or to develop it inhouse. If you develop inhouse, you risk losing resources to other projects because there is a 50/50 chance that you'll lose 40% of your staff. If you keep your staff, developing software will cost $172,000. If you lose staff, you have to hire outside contractors, and developing software will cost $208,000. To calculate the expected value, add the values of each alternative; see the results in Table 1-3.

Table 1-3 EMV for Resource Availability Scenarios

Risk Event Alternative	*Probability*	*Cost*	*Expected Monetary Value (EMV)*
Keep staff	50%	$172,000	$86,000
Lose staff	50%	$208,000	$104,000
Expected Monetary Value			**$190,000**

If you purchase ready-made software, though, you have risk related to customization. There is a 60% chance that you will have to do only a little customization, which would bring the total cost to $152,000. And there is a 40% chance that you will have to do a lot of customization, which would bring the total cost to $188,000. To calculate the expected value, add the values of each alternative (see Table 1-4).

Table 1-4 EMV for Software Customization Scenarios

Risk Event Alternative	*Probability*	*Cost*	*Expected Value*
Little customization	60%	$152,000	$91,200
Much customization	40%	$188,000	$75,200
Expected Monetary Value			**$166,400**

Your decision would be to purchase software because the cost is lower. As you can see, EMV can be calculated easily in a spreadsheet or a table. More often, it is displayed as a decision tree, as I discuss next.

In an EMV analysis, opportunities are usually expressed as positive values, and threats are expressed as negative values.

Decision tree

Figure 1-5 uses the same information as in Table 4-1, but it depicts it graphically.

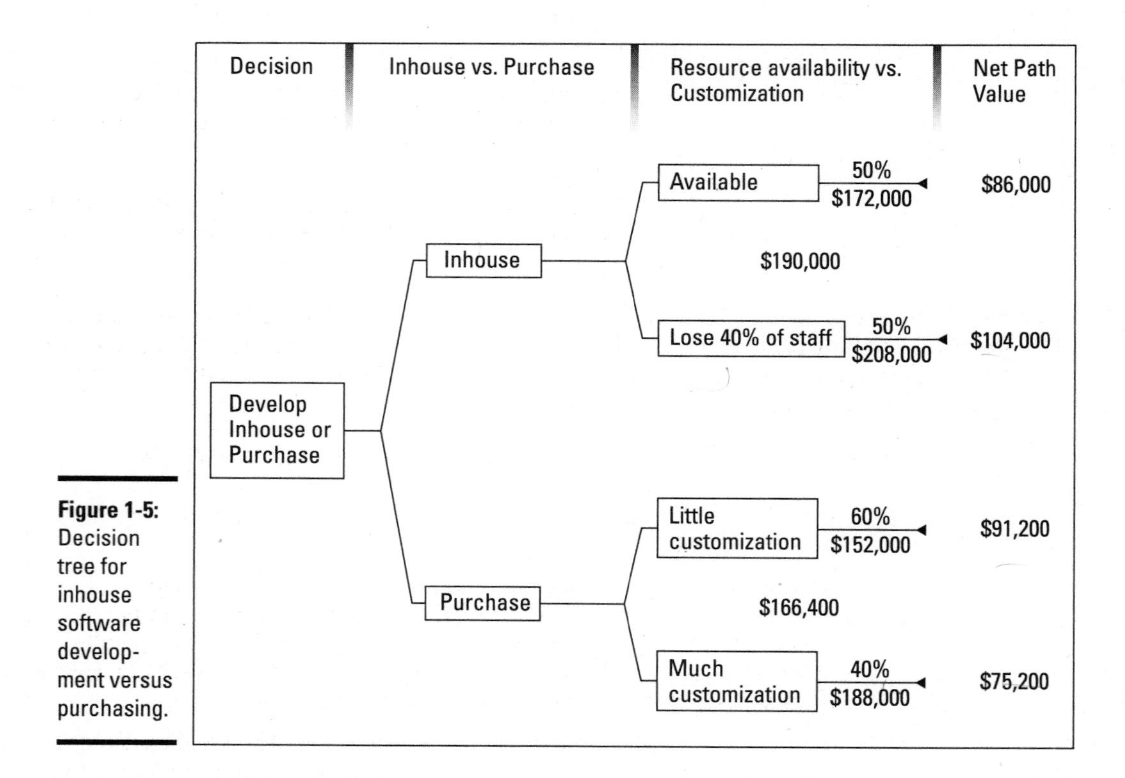

Figure 1-5: Decision tree for inhouse software development versus purchasing.

A decision tree is a simple way to get a visual display of the uncertainty and the various decision options for project risks.

Simulation

Most risk simulations use software to run thousands of possible iterations and come up with a probability distribution of the results. Here are the steps involved.

1. **Start with multiple estimates (optimistic, pessimistic, and most likely) for each work package and enter them into the software.**

   Assume duration estimates for our example.

2. **Enter the number of iterations you want the software to run.**

   Usually, 1,000–5,000 is sufficient without becoming overkill.

3. **Run the simulation.**

   The computer takes random amounts from the range of duration estimates for each work package and produces a probability distribution.

4. **Analyze the information.**

   The data show the likelihood of hitting a particular schedule target and tell you how much time you need to achieve 80% confidence (or 50%, or whatever level you want).

Monte Carlo simulation. A process that generates hundreds or thousands of probable performance outcomes based on probability distributions for cost and schedule on individual tasks. The outcomes are then used to generate a probability distribution for the project as a whole.

Figure 1-6 shows a Monte Carlo simulation that was run 1,000 times.

- The x-axis shows the total duration in days. For this example, the duration range is 23–37 days.
- The y-axis on the left shows the number of occurrences a specific total duration occurred. You use this axis with the bars that indicate the number of times the simulation showed the duration of a specific number of days. Rarely was the duration 23 days or 27 days. There were more than 140 instances when the duration was 30 days.
- The y-axis on the right shows the cumulative (overall) likelihood that a cumulative duration will occur. Use this with the line that indicates the cumulative likelihood the total duration will come in at or under a specified duration. You can see the line intersects the bar for 30 days at the 50% likelihood point. This is the expected duration: 50% of the time, the duration will be greater than 30 days; 50% of the time, it will be less than 30 days.

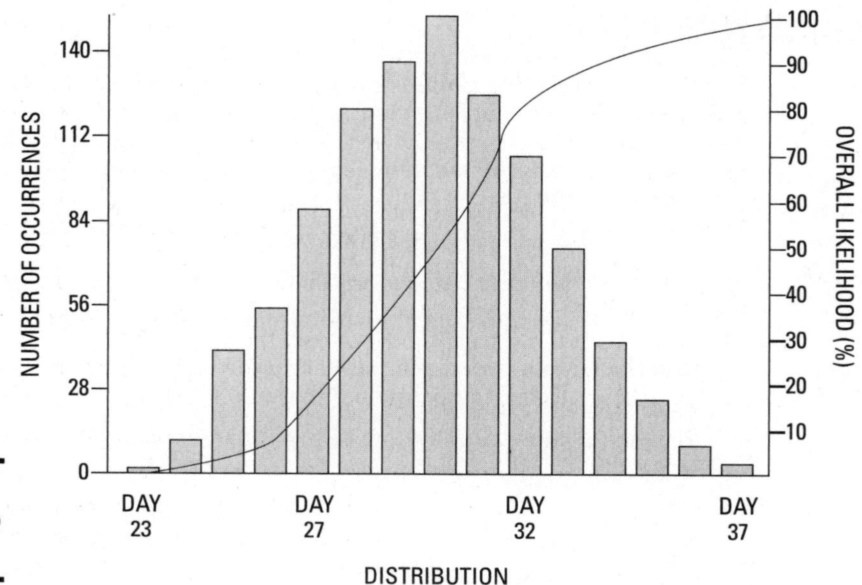

Figure 1-6: Monte Carlo simulation.

Courtesy of Pritchard Management Associates, Frederick, MD.

If you were using this information to determine the amount of time you needed for the work and you wanted an 80% confidence rating, you would select 32 days.

For this process, you must employ expert judgment. Expert judgment is needed to get the range of estimates, convert them to probability distributions, conduct a sensitivity analysis, determine event outcomes for decision trees, and conduct a simulation.

Perform Quantitative Risk Analysis: Outputs

What does all this work get you? Well, for starters, it gets you quantified information on those risks that pose the greatest risk to your project. EMV, decision trees, and PERT analysis can help with that. It helps you understand which risks will have the greatest impact to your project. You can use a sensitivity analysis to get that information. A simulation will tell you the likelihood of meeting cost and schedule objectives. You can also use the simulation to note project performance trends. For example, if you run the simulation once per quarter and find that the probability of hitting your budget target is progressively going down, you'll want to take some corrective action.

Plan Risk Responses

Your risk register should now be updated with a prioritized list of risks. During the process of planning risk responses, you will determine the most appropriate responses to risks and assign an accountable person to manage each risk.

Plan Risk Responses. Developing options and actions to enhance opportunities and to reduce threats to project objectives.

Keep in mind several key points when planning risk responses:

- **Responses need to be appropriate to the significance of the risk.** A low risk doesn't require a lot of time and effort to develop a response.
- **Responses need to be cost effective.** Don't spend more money to respond to a risk than the value of the event itself.
- **Responses should be realistic given the environment.** If your project is fairly low in priority in the project portfolio, don't expect people to drop what they're doing to respond to a minor risk.
- **Risks need to be assigned to someone to manage.** Without an accountable person to watch for the event, implement proactive responses, and notice when changes in the environment affect the risk, you can't expect to be able to respond effectively.
- **All parties need to agree on the approach for managing a risk.** If you think a vendor should take steps to reduce the probability of a risk event, make sure that the vendor agrees to take those steps.
- **Responses need to be timely.** Whenever possible, actions should be based on a proactive solution, not a reactive response.

Many risk events will have multiple responses. These responses will likely show up in components of the project management plan. For instance, you might need to put activities into the schedule to avoid or mitigate certain events. You might also need to add funds to accommodate transferring the risk to a vendor.

Plan Risk Responses: Tools and Techniques

The risk management plan defines the thresholds and probability and impact combinations that require action. You use this information along with the information in the risk register to begin developing responses.

The four categories for negative risk (threat) responses are

- ✦ Avoid
- ✦ Transfer
- ✦ Mitigate
- ✦ Accept

Risk avoidance. A risk response strategy whereby the project team acts to eliminate the threat or protect the project from its impact.

Risk transference. A risk response strategy whereby the project team shifts the impact of a threat to a third party, together with ownership of the response.

Risk mitigation. A risk response strategy whereby the project team acts to reduce the probability of occurrence or impact of a risk.

Risk acceptance. A risk response strategy whereby the project team decides to acknowledge the risk and not take any action unless the risk occurs.

When avoiding a risk, you're taking actions that eliminate the threat. For instance, if you have uncertainty associated with a deliverable, you can do more research to eliminate the uncertainty. If you have multiple schedule risks, you can extend the schedule to avoid the schedule constraint putting the delivery date at risk. For risks associated with technology, you might be able to find a proven or less-risky technology.

Transferring risk usually equates to spending money to give the risk management to another party. This can include insurance and contracts. Consider an insurance policy: You pay an insurer to absorb the financial risk of an uncertain event. If the event occurs, it is still your problem: The insurance company merely foots the bill.

The same is true for transferring risk to a vendor, who might be better qualified to manage the risk. If the vendor isn't effective, though, you're still on the hook for the result.

Mitigation tries to reduce or eliminate the probability of an event occurring, or the impact if it does. You can do iterative development and prototyping, run additional tests, or have redundant systems to mitigate the probability of an event or the impact of the event.

Acceptance can be passive: In other words, you do nothing. If the event occurs, you deal with it in the moment. Acceptance can also be active: For example, you can have a contingency plan. If the event occurs, you take specified actions. A common acceptance strategy is to have contingency time or budget to absorb overruns for unknown events.

Look at some of the risks identified for the childcare center example. Table 1-5 shows just the ID, risk statement, and response. A full risk register would include the probability, impact, score, response owner, and other relevant information.

Table 1-5 Risks and Responses

ID	*Statement*	*Response*
1	Because the cost to install security cameras in the child-care center is greater than anticipated, there is a risk we will overrun the budget.	**Accept.** This is a minimal impact to the overall budget and will be funded by contingency reserve.
2	The city might not approve the plans, thus causing a schedule delay.	**Mitigate.** Follow up with the city once per week. If it appears there is an issue, begin a corrective action immediately and submit it to reduce multiple cycles of submissions. This has a cost implication, but the permits are a critical factor, so we will accept the cost variance.
3	A team member might get reassigned to a higher-priority project, thus causing a schedule delay.	**Accept with a contingency plan.** We have no ability to influence staff reassignments. However, if this seems likely to occur, we will have the leaving employee work with the new employee for a week to make sure she is up to speed on remaining work.
4	Because we don't have a network or experience hiring childcare staff, we might not be able to find qualified candidates, thus causing degradation in the quality of care.	**Transfer.** We will outsource the hiring to a firm that specializes in childcare staffing.
5	If the enrollments are not at 50 by January, we will be operating at a loss, causing a budget overrun.	**Mitigate.** We will have an enrollment campaign for the center. If we don't have 50 enrollments by November 1, we will give incentives for enrollments prior to December 1.
6	Because the swing set is not in stock, we needed to place a back order, causing a potential schedule slip.	**Avoid.** We will redesign the playground to use a different model swing set that is in stock.

Opportunity management

There is a completely different, but related, set of responses for opportunities. I haven't really talked much about opportunity management, so I address it briefly here.

Opportunity. A risk that will have a positive effect on one or more project objectives.

Identifying opportunities

You can use the same techniques for identifying opportunities as you do for identifying threats. Here are some examples of opportunities:

> *Because Joanne is being replaced, there is an opportunity to have John work on our project. John has a higher skill set than Joanne, so we can complete the work ten days early.*
>
> *By combining an order for supplies with other projects and departments in the organization, we can reduce the cost by 15%.*
>
> *If we outsource the requirements gathering, we can reduce the work package duration by three weeks.*

Opportunity analysis

You then list those opportunities in the risk register and perform a probability and impact assessment on them. The impact looks at the objective it affects and the degree of impact. You can use a mirror approach to your probability and impact matrix for risks. When ranking opportunities, look for those opportunities with the highest impact and the highest probability and rank those at the top of the list. It is unusual to put opportunities through a quantitative risk analysis; therefore, you will not need to do that for the exam.

Opportunity responses

Here are the four responses for opportunities, a description of each, and an example of how they can be applied:

- **Exploit.** Take steps to ensure that it's realized. This is the counterpart to avoiding a risk. If you wanted to exploit the opportunity to save money on supplies, you would approach the other project managers and functional managers to coordinate ordering and purchasing. By taking the initiative and moving ahead, you are ensuring that you will benefit from the opportunity.
- **Share.** You share an opportunity when you don't have the ability to take advantage of the situation yourself. You find someone to work with to be able to reap the rewards. This is the counterpart to risk transfer. For example, if your company wanted to bid on a contract because it's a good

fit for the engineering aspect of the contract but weak in the construction aspect, your company could approach a construction firm and offer to partner with it on the bid. By sharing the opportunity of combining each organization's strengths, you have a better chance to win the bid.

✦ **Enhance.** Increase the probability that the opportunity will occur, or the benefit (impact) if it does. This is similar to mitigating a risk. Using the earlier hypothetical opportunity of replacing Joanne with John, you could approach John's manager directly and see about negotiating for him. This proactive approach will improve your chances of obtaining John, although it won't guarantee them.

✦ **Accept.** This is the same for opportunities and risks. This is a passive approach. If the opportunity presents itself, you will take advantage of it, but you are not proactively pursuing the opportunity.

More information about risk responses

As you go through the risk register to develop responses and assign an accountable person to manage them, you will discover that you should apply multiple responses to certain risks. For example, you might transfer the search for the director of the childcare center to a staffing agency, or you could post the position internally and on job-search boards. Thus, you are transferring and mitigating.

Using this same example, if the staffing agency doesn't come through, you're still in a bind of not having a director. In addition, you might have additional risks associated with outsourcing. For example, if you were initially planning on doing this work inhouse, but you decide to outsource it, you now have more expenses, which equates to a risk for your budget — and that is a secondary risk.

Secondary risk. A risk that arises as a direct result of implementing a risk response.

You have to treat the secondary risk as a new risk and put it through the analysis and response processes. For a situation like this, you would likely accept the residual risk and develop a contingency plan. One step further, you could also identify a risk trigger stating that if you don't have at least three candidates identified by November 15, you will have the lead educator and the operations manager split the duties associated with the director's role.

Sometimes, a response to one risk can serve to reduce the severity of several other risks.

Plan Risk Responses: Outputs

By this point, you should have a robust risk register. After the responses are taken into consideration, you want to reassess the probability and impact of the risk events and the overall risk to the project. If you ran a Monte Carlo simulation to determine the likelihood of meeting cost and schedule objectives (see the earlier section "Simulation"), you should re-run it now. The sample risk register in Figure 1-7 will give you an idea of the information you should have after this process is complete.

In addition to the information in the risk register, you likely will have the following information:

- Trigger conditions
- Residual risks
- Fallback plans
- Workarounds
- Contingency reserves

Trigger conditions. An event or a situation that indicates that a risk is about to occur.

Residual risk. A risk that remains after risk responses have been implemented.

Workaround. A response to a threat that has occurred, for which a prior response had not been planned or was not effective. (A workaround is distinguished from a contingency plan in that a workaround is not planned in advance of the occurrence of the risk event.)

Contingency reserve. Budget within the cost baseline or performance measurement baseline that is allocated for identified risks that are accepted and for which contingent or mitigating responses are developed.

Fallback plan. Include an alternative set of actions and tasks available in the event that the primary plan needs to be abandoned because of issues, risks, or other causes.

Contingency reserve should be included in the schedule and the budget. It is commonly derived as a percent of the residual risk for the overall project.

If your contingency plans aren't effective, you have two options:

- **Use a fallback plan** when the contingency response is not adequate.
- **Create a workaround,** which is an unplanned response to an event.

RISK REGISTER

Project Title: ____________ Date Prepared: ____________

Risk ID	Risk Statement	Probability	Impact				Score	Response
			Scope	Quality	Schedule	Cost		
Identifier.	*Description of the risk event or circumstance.*	*Likelihood of occurrence.*	*Impact on each objective if it does occur.*				*Probability × impact.*	*Description of planned response strategy to the risk event.*

Revised Probability	Revised Impact				Revised Score	Responsible Party	Actions	Status	Comments
	Scope	Quality	Schedule	Cost					
Likelihood after the response strategy.	*Revised impact on each objective after the response strategy.*				*Revised probability × impact.*	*Who will follow through on the risk and response.*	*Actions that need to be taken to address the risk.*	*Open or closed.*	*Any comments that provide information about the risk.*

Figure 1-7: Risk register after risk response planning.

Say you decide that if you don't have a director by December 15 and you aren't comfortable with the lead educator taking over part of the director's responsibilities, you could decide that as a fallback, you will delay the opening until the position is filled. On the other hand, say you hire the director, but two days before the center is scheduled to open, she decides to take another job. Now you're in the position of needing to work around the situation to find a way to make it work.

Many times, there is too much information on each individual risk to record in the risk register. Keeping a risk data sheet (as shown in Figure 1-8) to track this information by risk can be a good way to address this situation.

Based on all the work you did in planning risk responses, you will need to update several components of the project management plan as well as other project documents. Here is a list of places to start. Of course, the needs of the project will dictate which elements you need to update.

- WBS and WBS dictionary
- Schedule baseline
- Cost performance baseline
- Schedule management plan
- Cost management plan
- Quality management plan
- Procurement management plan
- Human resource plan
- Assumption logs
- Technical documentation

Your decision to transfer risk to a third party will probably create some secondary risks and will likely necessitate procurement activities. You need to make sure that those decisions are documented and that the activities and funding are allocated.

RISK DATA SHEET

Project Title: ____________ Date Prepared: ____________

<table>
<tr><td>Risk ID:
Risk identifier.</td><td colspan="7">Risk Description:
Detailed description of the risk.</td></tr>
<tr><td>Status:
Open or closed.</td><td colspan="7">Risk Cause:
Description of the circumstances or drivers that are the source of the risk.</td></tr>
<tr><td rowspan="2">Probability</td><td colspan="4">Impact</td><td rowspan="2">Score</td><td colspan="2" rowspan="2">Responses</td></tr>
<tr><td>Scope</td><td>Quality</td><td>Schedule</td><td>Cost</td></tr>
<tr><td>Qualitative or quantitative.</td><td colspan="4">Qualitative or quantitative assessment of the impact on each objective.</td><td>Probability x impact.</td><td colspan="2">Response strategies for the event. Use multiple strategies where appropriate.</td></tr>
<tr><td rowspan="2">Revised Probability</td><td colspan="4">Revised Impact</td><td rowspan="2">Revised Score</td><td rowspan="2">Responsible Party</td><td rowspan="2">Actions</td></tr>
<tr><td>Scope</td><td>Quality</td><td>Schedule</td><td>Cost</td></tr>
<tr><td>Qualitative or quantitative.</td><td colspan="4">Qualitative or quantitative assessment of the impact on each objective.</td><td>Probability x impact.</td><td>Person who will manage the risk.</td><td>Actions needed to implement responses.</td></tr>
<tr><td colspan="8">Secondary Risks:
Description of new risks that arise out of the response strategies taken to address the risk.</td></tr>
<tr><td colspan="8">Residual Risk:
Description of the remaining risk after response strategies.</td></tr>
<tr><td colspan="5" rowspan="2">Contingency Plan:
A plan that will be initiated if specific events occur, such as missing an intermediate milestone. Contingency plans are used when the risk or residual risk is accepted.</td><td colspan="3">Contingency Funds:
Funds needed to protect the budget from overrun.</td></tr>
<tr><td colspan="3">Contingency Time:
Time needed to protect the schedule from overrun.</td></tr>
<tr><td colspan="8">Fallback Plans:
A plan devised for use if other response strategies fail.</td></tr>
<tr><td colspan="8">Comments:
Any other information on the risk, the status of the risk, or response strategies.</td></tr>
</table>

Figure 1-8: Risk data sheet.

Key Terms

Risk management has its own set of vocabulary. There are quite a few terms to remember here, so make sure you are comfortable with them before taking the exam.

- Risk
- Threat
- Opportunity
- Risk tolerance
- Risk appetite
- Risk management plan
- Risk category
- Risk breakdown structure (RBS)
- Probability and impact matrix (PxI)
- Risk register
- Delphi method
- Root cause analysis
- Risk register
- Sensitivity analysis
- Expected Monetary Value (EMV)
- Decision tree analysis
- Simulation
- Risk avoidance
- Risk transference
- Risk mitigation
- Risk acceptance
- Opportunity
- Exploit
- Share
- Enhance
- Secondary risk
- Residual risk

- ✦ Triggers
- ✦ Workaround
- ✦ Contingency reserve
- ✦ Fallback plan

Chapter Summary

This complex section covers five planning processes. Some of the math in the quantitative analysis section can be intimidating, but I'm sure that if you go through it a few times, you'll do just fine.

- ✦ Risk management deals with the inherent uncertainty in projects. Risk can be negative (threats) or positive (opportunities).
- ✦ The degree of risk management you apply should be consistent with the complexity and criticality of the project. The risk management plan is used to document your approach to risk management on the project.
- ✦ You should look everywhere for events that can impact your project. Review all documents, interview all stakeholders, develop diagrams, and conduct an analysis to identify risk events. These are then documented in the risk register.
- ✦ Qualitative risk analysis helps prioritize risks. Risks are prioritized based on the probability of occurrence, the impact if they occur, and how soon they are likely to occur.
- ✦ The probability and impact (PxI) analysis and PxI matrix are used to plot risks. The PxI matrix, definitions, and rating should be tailored to meet the needs of your organization and project. Multiplying the probability by the impact gives you a risk score. Your risk score will help prioritize your risk list.
- ✦ Quantitative analysis is used to conduct further analysis on risks that can substantially impact a project objective. It can also be used to determine the likelihood of achieving cost and schedule objectives.
- ✦ Techniques used in quantitative analysis include
  - Sensitivity analysis
  - Interviewing
  - Creating probability distributions
  - Conducting an Expected Monetary Value (EMV) analysis
  - Creating a decision tree
  - Running a simulation

- To respond to threats, you can avoid, accept, transfer, or mitigate the threat. To respond to opportunities you can exploit, enhance, share, or accept the opportunity.
- You can develop risk triggers, contingency plans, and fallback plans for risks. Use contingency reserves of funding and time to reduce residual risks.

Prep Test

Multiple Choice

1 **Your approach to risk management on a project should be documented in which document?**

A ❍ Risk register
B ❍ Risk data sheet
C ❍ Risk management plan
D ❍ Risk breakdown structure

2 **What is a good way to develop a structure to systematically group risks?**

A ❍ Risk register
B ❍ Risk data sheet
C ❍ Risk management plan
D ❍ Risk breakdown structure

3 **The degree to which an organization is able to tolerate uncertainty on projects is**

A ❍ Risk averseness
B ❍ Risk avoidance
C ❍ Risk tolerance
D ❍ Risk seeking

4 **You pull together a group of subject matter experts. Some have expertise in risk, some in the technology your project is using, and some in project management. You keep the participants separated and anonymous and then send a questionnaire asking them what risks they think the project is most susceptible to. This goes on for several rounds until they reach consensus. What is this technique called?**

A ❍ Brainstorming
B ❍ Delphi technique
C ❍ Monte Carlo simulation
D ❍ Assumptions analysis

5 **Looking for risks from the perspective of external opportunities and threats and internal strengths and weaknesses is an example of**

- **A** ❍ A SWOT analysis
- **B** ❍ A root cause analysis
- **C** ❍ Directed brainstorm
- **D** ❍ Assumptions analysis

6 **Which technique helps determine which risks have the most potential impact on a project, and what type of diagram is used to depict this?**

- **A** ❍ EMV, a decision tree
- **B** ❍ Monte Carlo simulation, a probability distribution
- **C** ❍ Sensitivity analysis, a tornado diagram
- **D** ❍ Expert judgment, a decision tree

7 **All the following are responses to opportunities except**

- **A** ❍ Exploit
- **B** ❍ Enhance
- **C** ❍ Accept
- **D** ❍ Transfer

8 **Taking actions to reduce the probability or the impact of a threat is an example of**

- **A** ❍ Risk mitigation
- **B** ❍ Risk avoidance
- **C** ❍ Risk transference
- **D** ❍ Risk acceptance

9 **To respond to a risk of not having available staff inhouse to do some work, you decide to outsource the work to a vendor. Now you have a new risk that the vendor won't meet the tight delivery date. This new risk is an example of**

- **A** ❍ A workaround
- **B** ❍ A contingency plan
- **C** ❍ A secondary risk
- **D** ❍ A residual risk

Scenario 1

Use this PxI matrix to answer the following two questions.

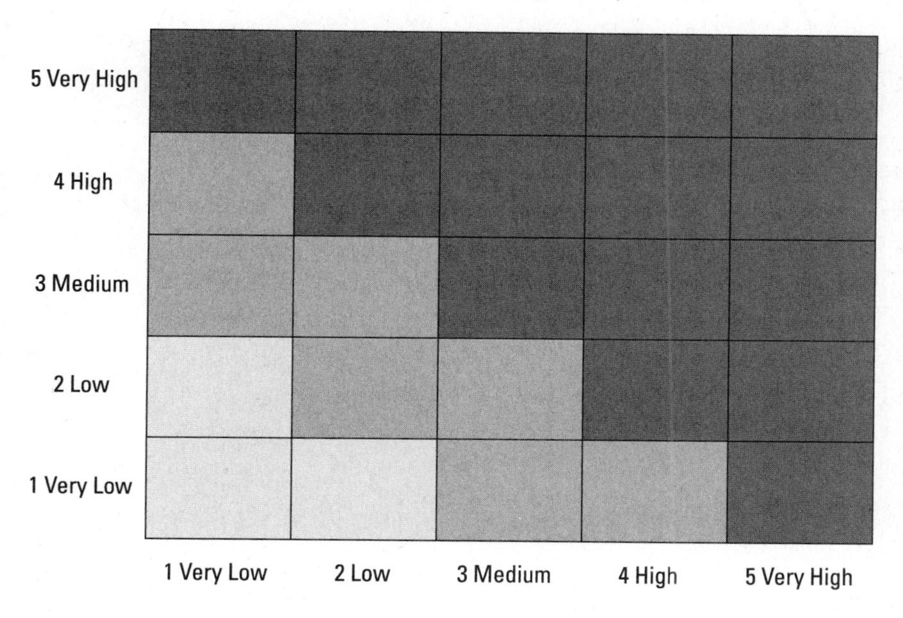

1 The PxI matrix represents an organization that is

A ❍ Risk averse
B ❍ Risk tolerant
C ❍ Risk neutral
D ❍ Risk taking

2 A risk that was ranked as high-high would have a risk score of

A ❍ 25
B ❍ 16
C ❍ 9
D ❍ 20

Scenario 2

Your company needs more space, and you're considering whether to relocate or build out existing space. Historically, there has been a problem with availability of furniture and equipment at your existing location. With a new location, you're concerned about the amount of build-out you'd have to do. You draw a decision tree to represent the possible outcomes.

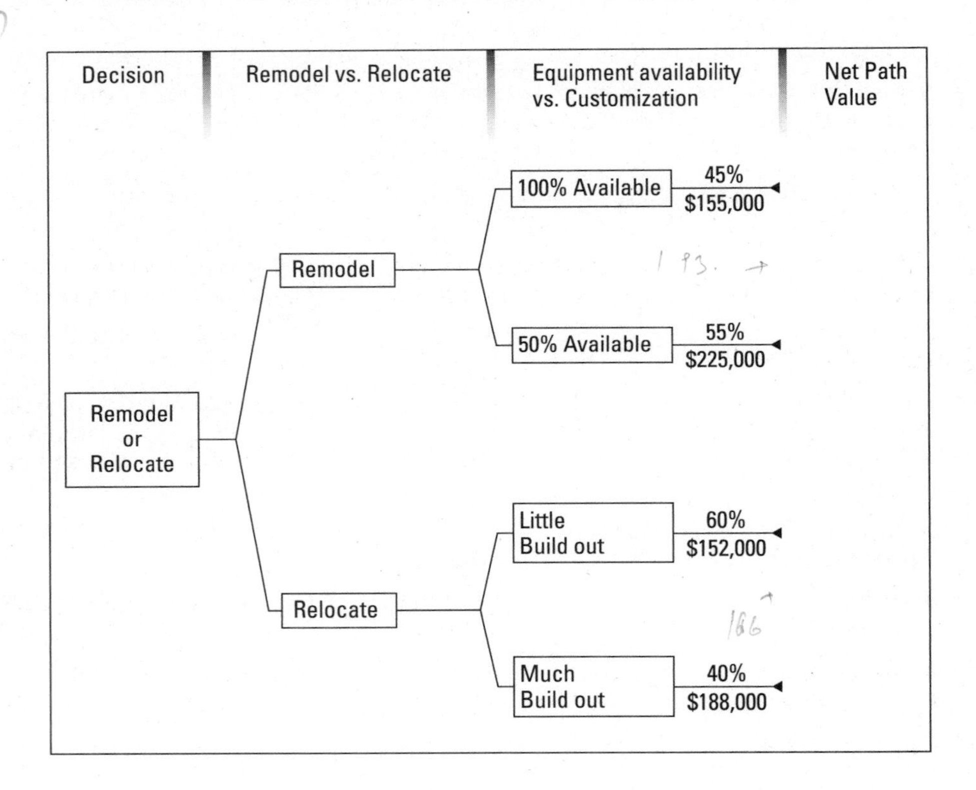

1 **What is the value of the remodel, and what is the value of the relocation?**

A ❍ Remodel = $193,500, relocation = $166,400

B ❍ Remodel = $380,000, relocation = $340,000

C ❍ Remodel = $190,000, relocation = $170,000

D ❍ Remodel = $195,400, relocation = $165,200

Answers

Multiple Choice

1 **C.** Risk management plan. A risk management plan describes how risk management will be structured and performed on the project. *Review "Plan Risk Management: Outputs."*

2 **D.** Risk breakdown structure. A risk breakdown structure provides a structure that ensures a comprehensive process of systematically identifying risks. *Check out "Plan Risk Management: Tools and Techniques."*

3 **C.** Risk tolerance. Risk tolerance refers to the amount of risk a person or an organization is willing to tolerate. *Look at "Projects Breed Uncertainty."*

4 **B.** Delphi technique. The Delphi technique works with a group of anonymous experts to reach consensus. *Go over "Identify Risks: Tools and Techniques."*

5 **A.** A SWOT analysis. A SWOT analysis looks outside and inside an organization for threats. *Read "Identify Risks: Tools and Techniques."*

6 **C.** Sensitivity analysis, a tornado diagram. A sensitivity analysis helps determine which risks have the most potential impact on a project, and the tornado diagram is a visual display of the information. *See the information in "Sensitivity analysis."*

7 **D.** Transfer. Transfer is the only option that is used for threats. *Check "Plan Risk Responses: Tools and Techniques."*

8 **A.** Risk mitigation. Mitigation seeks to reduce the probability and/or the impact of a threat. *Go over "Plan Risk Responses: Tools and Techniques."*

9 **C.** A secondary risk. A secondary risk is the result of implementing a risk response. *Look at "Plan Risk Responses: Tools and Techniques."*

Scenario 1

1 **A.** Risk averse. There is more dark-gray than any other shade. *Review "Plan Risk Management: Outputs."*

2 **B.** 16. High = 4. 4 × 4 = 16. *Review "Perform Qualitative Risk Analysis: Tools and Techniques."*

Scenario 2

1 **A.** Remodel = $193,500, relocation = $166,400. The sum of the remodel is (45% × $155,000) + (55% × $225,000) = $193,500. The sum of the relocation is (60% × $152,000) + (40% × $188,000) = $166,400. *Go back over "Perform Quantitative Risk Analysis: Tools and Techniques."*

Chapter 2: Getting Help — Procuring Project Scope

Exam Objective

- **Review the project scope and schedule to determine what, if any, scope or resources will need to be procured.**

Project procurement concerns purchasing project scope. This knowledge area can be approached from the perspective of the buyer or the seller. The buyer needs to carefully consider which parts of the project scope to buy, which must be made inhouse, and which parts to make or buy.

Procurement can take place any time during the project life cycle although the identification of which items will ultimately be procured is generally made early, during scope definition. After the work breakdown structure (WBS) is decomposed to deliverables, it can be used to determine the "make or buy" decisions.

Procurements other than readily available commercial goods are executed with a contract. Sometimes that contract is called an agreement, a purchase order (PO), a subcontract, or an understanding. However, because it is a legal document, a contract obligates the seller and the buyer to perform in specific ways. Therefore, there is usually input or oversight by each organization's legal department and/or purchasing department.

When a project procures product scope from outside the organization, the contract management work associated with administering the procurement and the contract needs to be integrated with the other project work. The development and delivery schedule of the buyer and seller need to integrate, the quality requirements need to be aligned, risks associated with the procured items need to be addressed, and communication between the buyer and the seller needs consensus. Thus, contract management can be a complex process, particularly for large procurements. It gets even more complex when multiple vendors are involved on a project. Therefore, careful upfront planning and analysis are imperative to ensure a smooth integration of all stakeholders.

Quick Assessment

1. Name three reasons to purchase scope.

2. Which type of contract has the least amount of risk for the purchaser?

3. A(n) _____ _____ _____ contract has aspects of a fixed price and a cost-reimbursable contract.

4. The _____ _____ _____ documents the approach to managing the bid process and administering the contract.

5. A(n) _____ _____ _____ is used when the buyer is looking for a solution as opposed to just shopping for the best price.

6. A mutually binding agreement that obligates the seller to provide the specified product or service or result and obligates the buyer to pay for it is a(n) _____.

7. (True/False). You should consider risk when you are determining whether to procure something for the project.

8. If you are setting up a weighted scoring model, and the weight of the criterion is .4 and the score is 3, what would the rating be?

9. Understanding of need, overall cost, and management approach are all examples of _____ _____ _____.

10. Which type of contract has a point of total assumption?

Answers

1. Reasons to purchase scope include cost, availability of skills, small volume requirements, limited inhouse capacity, transferring risk, maintaining supplier relations, and readily available goods. *For more, see "Plan Procurements: Tools and Techniques."*

2. A firm fixed price contract has the least risk for the buyer. *This is discussed in the "Fixed price contracts" section.*

3. A time and material contract has aspects of both fixed price and cost-reimbursable contracts. *Time and material contracts are discussed in the "Time and material contracts" section.*

4. The procurement management plan documents the approach for managing the bid process and the contract administration. *Read about the procurement management plan in the "The procurement management plan" section.*

5. A request for proposal is used when the buyer is more interested in a proposed solution rather than just price. *Look over the information in "Procurement documents."*

6. Contract. *You will see contracts discussed in "Procurement Basics."*

7. True. A risk response for some risks is to transfer the risk via a contract. *See the information in "Plan Procurement Management: Inputs."*

8. 1.2. The weight times the score equals the rating. *Learn more about this in the "Source selection criteria" section.*

9. Source selection criteria. All those elements are used to determine the best proposal for the procurement. *You can see more about this topic in "Source selection criteria."*

10. Fixed price incentive fee (FPIF). This is the only contract type that has a point of total assumption. *Read more about it in "Fixed price contracts."*

Procurement Basics

Because procurements deal with contractual relationships, I want to start by defining a contract.

Agreements. Any document or communication that defines the initial intentions of a project. This can take the form of a contract, memorandum of understanding (MOU), letters of agreement, verbal agreements, e-mail, and so on.

Contract. A mutually binding agreement that obligates the seller to provide the specified product or service or result and obligates the buyer to pay for it.

For a contract to be valid, there must be mutual agreement between the parties. In other words, you need an offer, acceptance of the offer, and *consideration* (in this context, the fancy legal term for payment or money). Contracts must have a legal purpose, and must be entered into by someone with capacity or delegated procurement authority, usually a contracting officer.

Exam questions dealing with this knowledge area assume that the procurement is large and based on a contract. Although it's true that you can purchase labor and supplies, you should address these questions as if you were purchasing something significant: say, more than $1 million. Also, questions on the exam assume that you are in the role of the buyer.

Plan Procurement Management

For some projects, you won't have any procurements. In that case, you won't need the processes in this knowledge area. However, most large projects have at least a few procurements.

Procurements involve a relationship between the buyer and the seller. You may see the seller referred to as

- Contractor
- Subcontractor
- Vendor
- Service provider
- Supplier

The buyer may be referred to as

- Client
- Customer
- Acquiring organization
- Purchaser
- Service requestor

Plan Procurement Management. Documenting project procurement decisions, specifying the approach, and identifying potential sellers.

Plan Procurement Management: Inputs

Many individual elements that make up the project management plan need to be taken into consideration when planning what to purchase, when to purchase, and how much to purchase. At a minimum, review the following project plan elements and project documents:

- Scope baseline
- Requirements documentation
- Activity resource requirements
- Project schedule
- Activity cost estimates
- Risk register
- Stakeholder register

In addition, consider risk (discussed in the preceding chapter). As I mention there, one risk response is to transfer risk. The decision to transfer risk via a contract is an input to this process. Therefore, review the risk register and any risk-related contract decisions.

Enterprise environmental factors (EEFs) play a big role in this process. In particular, you will want to have information about

- Availability of goods and services in the marketplace
- Marketplace conditions
- Potential suppliers and their past performance and reputation
- Any specific local requirements, regulations, or restrictions

For large procurements, the purchasing department will usually have template contracts as well as a set of policies and procedures that you have to follow. For complex procurements, or if you have multiple vendors, you should have a specific person from the contracts or purchasing department assigned to your team.

Picking the right contract type

Contract types are organizational process assets (OPAs). The type of contract you select can increase or reduce your risk. The objective in selecting a contract type is to select a contract that shares the risk between the buyer and the seller appropriately while providing sufficient incentive for the seller to perform.

The three basic families of contracts are

- Fixed price
- Cost-reimbursable
- Time and material

You can enhance these contract types with incentive fees or fixed fees. The terms *cost, fee,* and *price* are used precisely in procurements. The following definitions describe how contract terminology is used:

- **Fee:** Profit, in the contracting world
- **Cost:** The amount of funds it takes to complete the work
- **Price:** Cost plus the fee

Fixed price contracts

Fixed price contracts are favored when the scope of the project is clearly defined and is not subject to change. With this type of contract, the seller is required to finish the work, regardless of the final price. Therefore, the majority of the cost risk is on the seller. There are several types of fixed price contracts. After some definitions, I talk about the firm fixed price and fixed priced incentive fee contracts.

Fixed price contract. A type of contract that sets a fixed total price for a defined product or service to be provided. Fixed price contracts may also incorporate financial incentives for achieving or exceeding selected project objectives, such as schedule delivery, dates, cost and technical performance, or anything that can be quantified and subsequently measured.

Firm fixed price (FFP) contract. A type of fixed price contract where the buyer pays the seller a set amount (as defined by the contract), regardless of the seller's costs.

Fixed price incentive fee (FPIF) contract. A type of contract where the buyer pays the seller a set amount (as defined by the contract), and the seller can earn an additional amount if the seller meets defined performance criteria.

Fixed price with economic price adjustment (FP-EPA) contract. A type of contract that is used when the seller's performance period spans a considerable period of years. It is a fixed price contract with a provision allowing for predefined final adjustments to the contract price due to changing conditions, such as inflation, cost increases, or decreases for commodities. The EPA clause must relate to a reliable financial index that is used to adjust the final price.

About fees

In procurement jargon, the word *fee* is synonymous with *profit.* The fee is what the seller receives after all the costs have been paid. A fixed fee remains the same regardless of the level of performance on the contract. Fixed fees usually are used on cost-reimbursable contracts. Incentive fees can be used to stimulate performance on schedule, technical, quality, cost, or other types of performance. They can be used to motivate the seller to deliver early or to reach performance or quality standards. Award fees are based on a broad set of subjective criteria. They are used on cost-reimbursable contracts.

Firm fixed price

Most buyers prefer a firm fixed price contract because they know the price upfront. The buyer and the seller agree on a price for the work. The price remains the same unless there is a scope change. All risk for cost growth is on the seller. However, this isn't always the best choice, particularly if the project scope is still evolving or subject to change.

Fixed price incentive fee

Fixed price incentive fee (FPIF) contracts establish a price ceiling and build in an incentive fee (profit) for cost, schedule, or technical achievement. The term "fixed price" can be misleading. When the buyer is incentivizing cost performance, the buyer and seller establish a cost target, a target fee, and a share ratio, such as 80/20, 70/30, or something similar. Cost performance below the target cost earns an incentive fee. Cost performance above the target cost means the seller relinquishes some of the target fee.

When a contract has a share ratio for an incentive fee, the first number is what the buyer keeps, and the second number is what the seller keeps. Both numbers must total 100%. A 70/30 share ratio means that if the actual cost comes in under-target by $20,000, the buyer keeps $14,000 (70% of 20,000), and the seller gets the remaining $6,000.

Here's an example. Say you have a contract with a target cost of $400,000, a price ceiling of $460,000, a target fee of $40,000, and an 80/20 share ratio. In this case, the price ceiling is the fixed price part. Regardless of the total cost, the buyer won't pay more than $460,000. However, if the seller delivers the scope for less than $400,000 (target price), the seller gets the target fee of $40,000 plus 20% of the amount less than $400,000. However, if the cost is greater than $400,000, the $40,000 fee is reduced by 20% of the amount over $400,000.

See how this plays out if the actual cost is $425,000.The incentive fee would be calculated as follows:

((Target cost – actual cost) × share ratio) + target fee

((400,000 – 425,000) × .2) + 40,000

(–25,000 × .2) + 40,000 = 35,000

Therefore, the total price of the contract would be

$425,000 + $35,000 = $460,000

In this case, the price came in right at the ceiling. If the actual price had been more, the ceiling would have stayed at $460,000, and the seller would have started to lose some of his fee. The point at which the seller hits the dollar amount where he has to give back some of the fee is the *point of total assumption.*

This concept of the point of total assumption is something that started showing up on the PMP exam a few years ago. It is not in the *PMBOK Guide.* Likely, only one or two questions mention it. It is found only on FPIF contracts.

Cost-reimbursable contracts

Cost-reimbursable contracts are used when the scope of work isn't well defined or is subject to change. This is useful for research and development work. With this type of contract, the buyer must reimburse the seller for legitimate costs associated with completing the work, plus a fee. The buyer and seller agree to a target cost upfront, and fees are calculated from that target cost. The three main types of cost-reimbursable contracts are

- ✦ Cost plus fixed fee
- ✦ Cost plus incentive fee
- ✦ Cost plus award fee

After some definitions, I'll walk you through a comparison calculation of a cost plus fixed fee and a cost plus incentive fee.

Cost-reimbursable contract. A type of contract involving payment to the seller for the seller's actual costs, plus a fee typically representing the seller's profit. Cost-reimbursable contracts often include incentive clauses where if the seller meets or exceeds selected project objectives, such as schedule targets or total cost, then the seller receives from the buyer an incentive or bonus payment.

Cost plus fixed fee (CPFF) contract. A type of cost-reimbursable contract where the buyer reimburses the seller for the seller's allowable costs (allowable costs are defined by the contract) plus a fixed amount of profit (fee).

Cost plus incentive fee (CPIF) contract. A type of cost-reimbursable contract where the buyer reimburses the seller for the seller's allowable costs (allowable costs are defined by the contract), and the seller earns its profit if it meets defined performance criteria.

Cost plus award fee (CPAF) contract. A type of cost-reimbursable contract where the buyer reimburses the seller for the seller's allowable costs (allowable costs are defined by the contract), but the majority of the fee is earned based only on the satisfaction of certain broad subjective performance criteria defined and incorporated into the contract.

A fixed fee puts more risk on the buyer because the seller gets the same fee regardless of the capability to meet the target cost. Here is an example of how a cost plus fixed fee calculation would work.

Assume that the target cost is $300,000, and the fixed fee is $20,000.

Project	*Final Cost*	*Fixed Fee*	*Total Price*
Project 1	$280,000	$20,000	$300,000
Project 2	$300,000	$20,000	$320,000
Project 3	$320,000	$20,000	$340,000
Project 4	$350,000	$20,000	$370,000

Now look at the same scenario with a cost plus incentive fee with an 80/20 share ratio.

Like a fixed price incentive fee, the incentive percentage is applied to the difference between the target cost and the actual cost. By coming in under the target cost, the seller receives 20% of the difference between target and actual costs.

In Project 1, 80% of the cost savings between $300,000 and $280,000 remains with the buyer, and 20% (or $4,000) goes to the seller as an incentive, in addition to the $20,000 fee.

Project	*Final Cost*	*Calculation*	*Total Fee*	*Total Cost*
Project 1	$280,000	$20,000 + [(300,000 – 280,000) × 20%]	$24,000	$304,000
Project 2	$300,000	$20,000 + [(300,000 – 300,000) × 20%]	$20,000	$320,000
Project 3	$320,000	$20,000 + [(300,000 – 320,000) × 20%]	$16,000	$336,000
Project 4	$350,000	$20,000 + [(300,000 – 350,000) × 20%]	$10,000	$360,000

Sometimes, the fee is expressed as a percentage of the target cost. For example, the target cost is $300,000, and the fee is 10%, so the fee target is $30,000. The fee is *not* a percentage of the actual cost; it's a percentage of the target cost.

Time and material contracts

Time and material (T&M) contracts are generally used for smaller contracts when there is not a firm scope of work or the work is for an indefinite period. Hourly labor rates and material rates are agreed to upfront (this is the fixed part of the contract), but the amount of time and material are subject to the needs of the job or the buyer. Generally, expenses are reimbursed at cost. Many times, this type of contract is used until the scope of work can be well defined. It may include a not-to-exceed amount.

Time and material (T&M) contract. A type of contract that's a hybrid contractual arrangement containing aspects of both cost-reimbursable and fixed price contracts. Time and material contracts resemble cost-reimbursable type arrangements in that they have no definitive end because the full value of the arrangement is not defined at the time of the award. Thus, time and material contracts can grow in contract value as if they were cost-reimbursable–type arrangements. Conversely, time and material arrangements can also resemble fixed price arrangements. For example, the buyer and seller preset the unit rates, when both parties agree on the rates for the category of senior engineers.

Plan Procurements: Tools and Techniques

The techniques you will apply in this process are

- ✦ Determine which items you will make inhouse and which you will procure from an outside source.
- ✦ Conduct market research to identify the technology and resource availability.

Of course, any time you are working with procurements, you will need some expertise in the form of procurement or contracting specialists. Make sure you have someone on your team who can help you with the legal and contractual issues.

To make or buy: That is the question

Of the many things to consider when deciding to procure project scope, some decisions are obvious. For example, you might procure goods if your organization doesn't have the skills necessary to develop the product. Or, in other cases, you might have the skills but not the capacity, or you don't have enough resources to get the work done in a timely manner.

Sometimes, the reasons to keep work inhouse are fairly obvious. For example, if the item you need is your organization's core competency — a fundamental knowledge or an ability that the organization possesses — you have the resources, and you can do it efficiently and inexpensively. Perhaps proprietary reasons determine keeping work inhouse.

The following table summarizes standard reasons to make or buy scope:

Reasons to Make	***Reasons to Buy***
Less costly	Less costly
Use existing capacity	Use supplier skills
Maintain direct control	Small volume requirement
Maintain design secrecy	Limited inhouse capacity
Develop a new competency	Maintain supplier relations
Company's core competency	Transfer risk
Available staff	Readily available

For certain products or services, you may have the option to keep the work inhouse or to outsource it. You will want to do some market research to help you make a good decision.

Market research

For those deliverables or services that can be either purchased or developed inhouse, market research can be used to help determine the market conditions that will inform your make-or-buy decision. For deliverables or services that you know you will purchase or outsource, market research can help you identify emerging technologies, qualified vendors, and alternative approaches.

Information gathered from market research can help refine the information in the statement of work (SOW), the procurement management plan, and the source selection criteria.

Plan Procurements: Outputs

After deciding which elements to make and which to buy and selecting the contract type, you can document your procurement management plan, develop procurement documents and the SOW, and define your source selection criterion.

The procurement management plan

A component of the overall project management plan, the *procurement management plan* describes how all facets of the procurement will be conducted. For small projects with simple purchases, a paragraph in the project management plan will suffice. For complex procurements, or when a project has numerous procurements or high-risk procurements, the plan should be more detailed and robust. The following components are fairly common for a procurement management plan, but obviously, the needs of the project will dictate the contents:

- Type of contract for each procurement
- Roles, responsibilities, and limits of decision-making authority on procurements
- Relevant policies, procedures, guidelines, and templates
- Strategy for managing and integrating multiple procurements
- Strategy for integrating procurements into the rest of the project
- Procurement assumptions and constraints

- ✦ Strategy for handling long lead items
- ✦ Procurement milestones for each procurement
- ✦ Reporting requirements for sellers
- ✦ Required bonds, warranties, insurance, licenses, and permits
- ✦ Format for the SOW
- ✦ How and if independent cost estimates will be used
- ✦ A list of prequalified sellers
- ✦ Selection criteria and weighting
- ✦ Processes for managing contracts
- ✦ Process for procurement audits
- ✦ Risk management issues

Figure 2-1 shows a sample procurement management template.

The source selection criteria listed in the procurement management plan will be used to score seller proposals and should be specific to the item(s) being procured. Here are some items to keep in mind while you establish source selection criteria:

- ✦ Understanding of need
- ✦ Overall cost (includes operating and maintenance costs)
- ✦ Financial capacity
- ✦ Technical capability and approach
- ✦ Management approach
- ✦ Risk sharing
- ✦ Production capacity
- ✦ Business type (for example, women- or minority-owned or small business)
- ✦ Past performance and references
- ✦ Warranty
- ✦ Intellectual property and proprietary rights

PROCUREMENT MANAGEMENT PLAN

Project Title: ______________________ **Date Prepared:** ______________________

Procurement Authority:

Describe the project manager's decision authority and limitations, including at least: budget, signature level, contract changes, negotiation, and technical oversight.

Roles and Responsibilities:

Project Manager:	Procurement Department:
1. *Define the responsibilities of the project manager and their team.*	1. *Describe the responsibilities of the procurement or contracting representative and department.*
2.	2.
3.	3.
4.	4.
5.	5.

Standard Procurement Documents:

1. *List any standard procurement forms, documents, policies, or procedures relevant to procurements.*
2.
3.
4.
5.

Contract Type:

Identify the contract type, incentive or award fees, and the criteria for such fees.

Bonding and Insurance Requirements:

Define bonding or insurance requirements that bidders must meet.

Selection Criteria:

Weight	Criteria
Identify selection criteria and their relative weighting. Include information on independent cost estimates if appropriate.	

Procurement Assumptions and Constraints:

Identify and document relevant assumptions and constraints related to the procurement process.

Figure 2-1: Sample procurement management plan.

Source selection criteria

The criteria that are essential to being able to perform the contract are screening criteria. If a proposal doesn't demonstrate that the seller meets the criteria, then the seller is screened out of the process. Examples include needing specific licenses, having a minimum number of years of experience, or being financially sound. U.S. federal government contracts require that the source selection criteria be published. However, many commercial procurements do not publish the selection criteria.

Some criteria can be set up as a weighting system. In this case, you identify the most relevant criteria and then weight them relative to one another. Here are the steps involved, along with a simple example:

1. **Establish the criteria you will evaluate proposals against.**

   For this scenario, you decide on cost, references, and schedule.

2. **Rank the criteria in order of importance.**

   You decide on schedule, cost, and then references.

3. **Establish a relative numeric weight for each criterion.**

   - Schedule = 50%
   - Cost = 30%
   - References = 20%

4. **Determine how you will objectively score proposals.**

   Table 2-1 shows how proposal information might be scored.

Table 2-1 Proposal Weighting Criteria

	1	*2*	*3*	*4*	*5*
Schedule	Can't deliver in April	Can deliver by April 30	Can deliver by April 20	Can deliver by April 10	Can deliver by April 1
Cost	Costs more than $120K	Costs between $110–$120K	Costs between $105–$110K	Costs between $100–$105K	Costs less than $100K
References	No references	More than one mediocre reference	Up to two great references	More than two great references	All references were great

5. **Score the proposal.**

   You determine scores by comparing the information in the seller's proposal against the Proposal Weighting Criteria.

6. **Multiply each vendor's scores by its weight to get a rating, and then sum the ratings.**

   Table 2-2 shows the calculations.

Table 2-2 Proposal Scores and Ratings

	Weight	*Company A*		*Company B*		*Company C*	
		Score	*Rating*	*Score*	*Rating*	*Score*	*Rating*
Schedule	.5	4	2	3	1.5	4	2
Cost	.3	5	1.5	3	.9	4	1.2
References	.2	4	.8	4	.8	3	.6
Total			**4.3**		**3.2**		**3.8**

7. **Select the proposal with the highest total rating.**

Procurement statement of work

The *procurement statement of work* (SOW) is a narrative description of the work to be done. It describes the deliverables in sufficient detail to allow sellers to determine whether they can complete the work, but it doesn't define how the work must be done. The SOW can be very simple or very complex, depending on the needs of the project. Because it is the meat of the contract, it needs to be clear, concise, and not open to interpretation.

You might see the following types of elements in a procurement SOW:

- Specifications
- Performance requirements
- Support work, such as training and documentation
- Quality requirements
- Reporting requirements

The specifications, performance requirements, and support work will be defined and elaborated as part of the project scope definition (discussed in Book III, Chapter 2). The quality requirements are defined as part of the Plan

Quality Management process (Book IV, Chapter 2). Reporting requirements should mirror the reporting needs for the overall project. Planning for communication and reporting is discussed in Book IV, Chapter 4.

Procurement documents

Procurement documents make up the package you send out to potential sellers. This package can be called a *bid, tender,* or *quotation* when the primary deciding factor is price. When the buyer is looking for a technical solution and is weighing factors other than price, you might hear the term *proposal.* Common terms for procurement documents are

- Request for Quote (RFQ)
- Invitation for Bid (IFB)
- Request for Proposal (RFP)
- Invitation for Negotiation
- Tender Notice

The procurement documents contain the SOW, instructions on how and when to respond, and any required contractual provisions.

Key Terms

Procurement and contracting have their own language. Many terms here have specific meanings when applied to contracting. Make sure you are familiar with how these words are used in the context of project procurements.

- Agreement
- Contract
- Fee
- Cost
- Price
- Fixed price contract
- Firm fixed price (FFP)
- Fixed price incentive fee (FPIF)
- Fixed price with economic price adjustment (FP-EPA)
- Cost-reimbursable contract
- Cost plus fixed fee (CPFF)

- Cost plus incentive fee (CPIF)
- Cost plus award fee (CPAF)
- Time and material (T&M) contract
- Procurement management plan
- Screening criteria
- Weighting criteria
- Procurement statement of work (SOW)
- Procurement documents
- Request for proposal (RFP)
- Request for quote (RFQ)

Chapter Summary

Here are the main ideas to take away from this chapter.

- For purposes of the PMP exam, procurements are large and complex, requiring knowledge of contracts and legal terms.
- Procurements need to be integrated with the nonprocured project work, other procurements, and the organization's operations.
- The three basic families of contracts are fixed price, cost-reimbursable, and time and material. You can include an incentive fee on fixed price and cost-reimbursable contracts. Cost-reimbursable contracts can also have a fixed fee or an award fee.
- The price of procurement is the cost plus the fee. Price = Cost + Fee
- Fixed fee contracts are favored when the scope of the project is clearly defined and not subject to change. Fixed fee contracts include firm fixed price (FFP), fixed price incentive fee (FPIF), and fixed price with economic price adjustment (FP-EPA).
- Cost-reimbursable contracts are used when the scope of work is not well defined or is subject to change. The three main types of cost-reimbursable contracts are cost plus fixed fee (CPFF), cost plus incentive fee (CPIF), and cost plus award fee (CPAF).
- Time and material (T&M) contracts are generally used for smaller contracts when there is not a firm scope of work, or when the work is scheduled for an indefinite period.

- A "make or buy" assessment will let you know which items you *must* buy, items you *must* make, and those items you can make or buy.
- The procurement management plan describes how all facets of the procurement are to be conducted.
- The procurement statement of work describes what will be purchased but not how it will be developed.

Prep Test

Multiple Choice

1 **Which of the following is a reason to procure scope?**

A ❍ Maintain direct control.
B ❍ Maintain design secrecy.
C ❍ Small volume requirement.
D ❍ Develop a new competency.

2 **Which type of contract places the most risk on the buyer?**

A ❍ FFP
B ❍ FPIF
C ❍ CPIF
D ❍ CPFF

3 **Which type of contract allows for a final adjustment to price because of inflation or changes in the cost of commodities?**

A ❍ FP-EPA
B ❍ FPIF
C ❍ CPFF
D ❍ T&M

4 **The point at which the seller has to give back some of the fee is called**

A ❍ The refund point
B ❍ The point of absorption
C ❍ The point of total assumption
D ❍ The fee assumption point

5 **You just won a contract to provide a telecommunications infrastructure to a large company with several locations. You have a cost plus fixed fee (CPFF) contract. The target cost is $200,000. The target profit is 10%. The final costs come in at $150,000. What is the total price for the contract?**

A ❍ $170,000
B ❍ $150,000
C ❍ $200,000
D ❍ $220,000

6 **You're doing the close-out for a project to design an airport. The contract is a cost plus incentive fee (CPIF) contract. The target cost is $200,000, with a 10% target profit. The final cost was $180,000. The incentive split is 80/20. How much is the total contract price?**

A ❍ $200,000
B ❍ $196,000
C ❍ $184,000
D ❍ $204,000

7 **Which document records a narrative description of work for a procurement?**

A ❍ A statement of work
B ❍ A procurement management plan
C ❍ Contract terms and conditions
D ❍ The scope statement

8 **If you have a complex procurement that isn't well defined and you're looking for a vendor to solve the problem and come up with a solution, what is the best type of bid document to prepare?**

A ❍ RFP
B ❍ IFB
C ❍ RFQ
D ❍ IFN

Scenario 1

Use the following table to answer Questions 1 and 2.

		Company A		*Company B*		*Company C*		*Company D*	
	Weight	*Score*	*Rating*	*Score*	*Rating*	*Score*	*Rating*	*Score*	*Rating*
Schedule	0.6	4		3		4		2	
Cost	0.25	3		3		5		4	
References	0.15	4		4		3		3	
Total									

1 **What is the total for company A?**

A ❍ 4.1
B ❍ 3.75
C ❍ 11
D ❍ 3.15

2 **Which company should be selected based on the weighted scoring?**

A ❍ Company A
B ❍ Company B
C ❍ Company C
D ❍ Company D

Answers

Multiple Choice

1 **C.** Small volume requirement. If you need only a few items, it's best to procure rather than manufacture. *Review the section "Plan Procurements: Tools and Techniques."*

2 **D.** CPFF. A cost plus fixed fee contract reimburses the seller for expenses, and the fee does not change based on performance. *Look at "Cost-reimbursable contracts."*

3 **A.** FP-EPA. A fixed price economic price adjustment contract allows for adjustment because of changes in price based on an agreed-upon index. *Go to "Fixed price contracts."*

4 **C.** The point of total assumption. The point of total assumption is where the seller starts to return some of the fee. *Look at "Fixed price contracts."*

5 **A.** $170,000. The cost was $150,000. The fee was fixed at 10% of the target: that is, $20,000. Thus, the cost plus the fee is $170,000. *See the information in "Cost-reimbursable contracts."*

6 **D.** $204,000. The final cost is $180,000. The target cost is $200,000 with a 10% target fee, or $20,000. The 20% share ratio is (200,000 – 180,000) × 20% = $4,000. Therefore, the final price is $180,000 + 20,000 + 4,000 = $204,000. *Check out "Cost-reimbursable contracts."*

7 **A.** A statement of work. The procurement statement of work (SOW) has a narrative description of the work that needs to be done. *You will find information on the SOW in the section on "Procurement statement of work."*

8 **A.** RFP. An RFP is used for proposals that don't have a firm scope and need help solving a problem. *This is discussed in "Procurement documents."*

Scenario 1

1 **B.** 3.75. The score for schedule is 2.4. The score for cost is .75. The score for references is .6. This sums to 3.75. *You can review this information in "Source selection criteria."*

2 **C.** Company C. The score for A is 3.75, the score for B is 3.15, the score for C is 4.1, and the score for D is 2.65. C has the highest score. *Review "Source selection criteria."*

Chapter 3: Who Are All These People? Planning Stakeholder Management

Exam Objective

- **Perform stakeholder management planning to ensure effective engagement of stakeholders throughout the project.**

Many a project has met its demise by failing to manage stakeholders effectively. When I introduce the process of identifying stakeholders in Book II, Chapter 3, I discuss how to conduct a stakeholder analysis to assess how much influence each stakeholder has on a project and whether that influence was favorable toward the project — or not so favorable.

In this chapter, I show you how to manage stakeholders and their level and type of engagement on a project. You'll probably encounter some stakeholders whom you want to encourage to support your project, and you'll likely also find others whom you'll be happy with if they just don't actively resist your project.

Because of the potential numerous stakeholders with a wide range of influence, it is imperative to engage in careful upfront planning to ensure effective engagement of all stakeholders.

Quick Assessment

1 Name three components of the project management plan that can be helpful in planning stakeholder management.

2 Which element of the project management plan identifies project team reporting structure that can be used for managing stakeholders?

3 Organizational culture is an example of a(n) _____ _____ _____ that influences your stakeholder management plan.

4 The stakeholder register from a prior project is an example of a(n) _____ _____ _____ that can help you create a stakeholder management plan.

5 Meeting with people who have technical experience in your project's technical field is an example of _____ _____ _____.

6 A stakeholder who is ambivalent about your project is said to be _____.

7 A stakeholder who has no knowledge of your project is classified as _____.

8 In which document would you record your strategy for management stakeholder involvement?

9 The main tool you have to influence stakeholders is _____.

10 (True or False). An external vendor on your project is a stakeholder.

Answers

1. Project life cycle, schedule, communications management plan. Components of the project management plan that are helpful in planning stakeholder management include the project life cycle, schedule, communications management plan, procurement management plan, quality management plan, and human resources management plan. You may come up with a different list. All aspects of the project management plan should be reviewed during the Plan Stakeholder Management process. *For more, see "Plan Stakeholder Management: Inputs."*
2. Human resources management plan. The human resources management plan contains the project team resources, their roles and responsibilities, reporting structure, and the staffing management plan. *This is discussed in the "Plan Stakeholder Management: Inputs" section.*
3. Enterprise environmental factor. Organizational culture is an enterprise environmental factor that limits your options when developing a stakeholder management plan. See the *"Plan Stakeholder Management: Tools and Techniques" section.*
4. Organizational process asset. One of the organizational process assets that you can use from a previous project is the stakeholder register. *Read about the organizational process assets in the "Plan Stakeholder Management: Inputs" section.*
5. Utilizing expert judgment. Meeting with people who have expertise in the technical field is an example of utilizing expert judgment. *Look over the information in the "Plan Stakeholder Management: Tools and Techniques" section.*
6. Neutral. *I discuss stakeholder categories in the "Plan Stakeholder Management: Tools and Techniques" section.*
7. Unaware. *See the information in the "Plan Stakeholder Management: Tools and Techniques" section.*
8. Stakeholder management plan. The stakeholder management plan is used to document your approach to managing stakeholder engagement. *Learn more about this in the "Plan Stakeholder Management: Outputs" section.*
9. Communication. Communication is the best method to work with stakeholders and manage their engagement level. *You can see more about this topic in "Plan Stakeholder Management: Outputs."*
10. True. A stakeholder is an individual, a group, or an organization that may affect, be affected by, or perceive itself to affected by a decision, an activity, or an outcome of a project. *Read more about it in "Plan Stakeholder Management: Inputs."*

Plan Stakeholder Management

As you plan on how best to manage stakeholder engagement, you will want to consider

✦ Which stakeholders are active in each phase of the project lifecycle

✦ Whether a stakeholder is a supporter of your project or a resistor

✦ The information each stakeholder needs and the best way to impart that information

Plan Stakeholder Management. Developing appropriate management strategies to effectively engage stakeholders throughout the project lifecycle, based on the analysis of their needs, interests, and potential impact on project success.

Plan Stakeholder Management: Inputs

You should consider each component of the project management plan to help you plan for effective stakeholder engagement. For example:

✦ **Project lifecycle:** Informs you about the activities, processes, expertise, deliverables, and approvals needed in each phase of the project. Traditional waterfall lifecycles require a different method of engaging stakeholders than an agile lifecycle.

✦ **Schedule:** Identifies which resources will be active in the project at any given time.

✦ **Communications management plan:** Describes who needs information, the type of information they need, and when they need it.

✦ **Procurement management plan:** Identifies vendors, contractors, and other external stakeholders that you will need to determine how best to work with.

✦ **Quality management plan:** The quality management plan can highlight quality requirements, measurements, and techniques that may require special attention, such as sending quality results to external regulatory agencies or to an external customer.

✦ **Human resource management plan:** Identifies the project team resources, reporting relationships, and roles and responsibilities.

The stakeholder register records stakeholder identification information and the stakeholder category, such as supporter, neutral, or resistor. You will use the register to create a stakeholder engagement assessment.

The organizational culture and politics are very influential in how you can manage stakeholder engagement. For instance, in a highly bureaucratic organization, you need to make sure you have plenty of documentation as well as a communications management plan that takes into consideration the multiple layers of information and approval. Conversely, in a lean and flat organization, stakeholder engagement may be much less formal.

Reviewing lessons learned, stakeholder registers, and stakeholder management plans from prior projects can help you create an effective stakeholder management plan for the current project.

Plan Stakeholder Management: Tools and Techniques

To create an effective stakeholder management plan, you need to meet with people with expertise in several areas:

- **Technical:** People with expertise in the technical fields involved in the project can help you understand the stakeholders who will be involved during each phase of the lifecycle, what their concerns will be, and how they can contribute to the project.
- **Management:** Management can let you know the types of reports that are needed and provide insight into senior management concerns as well as some of the politics you need to be aware of to manage stakeholders effectively.
- **Previous project managers or team members:** People who have worked on similar projects will be able to tell you where the pitfalls are and what to watch out for on the project. They can provide valuable advice and inform you of techniques that were effective in the past.

Analyzing the current level of stakeholder engagement and the desired level of stakeholder engagement is a useful way to start developing a stakeholder management plan. You can start with the power/support grid (see Book II, Chapter 3) and note the current category of each stakeholder to determine whether you want to take steps to increase that stakeholder's support for your project.

Another technique for mapping stakeholder engagement is to classify each stakeholder, each stakeholder's current level of engagement, and the desired level of engagement. One way of assessing engagement is the following:

- **Unaware:** The stakeholder is not aware of the project nor its outcomes.
- **Resistant:** The stakeholder is aware of the project but does not support it.
- **Neutral:** The stakeholder is ambivalent about the project and its outcomes.

- **Supportive:** The stakeholder feels favorably about the project and its outcomes.
- **Leading:** The stakeholder is actively engaged in promoting the project.

You can document the steps that you will take to move stakeholders from resistant to neutral or unaware to supportive (and so forth) in a matrix called a Stakeholder Engagement Assessment Matrix. Table 3-1 shows a sample Stakeholder Engagement Matrix that documents the stakeholder classification before (B) and after (A) the stakeholder engagement strategies are employed.

Table 3-1 Sample Stakeholder Engagement Matrix

Stakeholder	*Unaware*	*Resistant*	*Neutral*	*Supportive*	*Leading*
Manny	B			A	
Jocelyn		B	A		
Jamie				B	A
Kim	B		A		

Table 3-1 shows that prior to implementing a stakeholder management strategy, Manny was unaware of the project, and that the desired outcome is that after the plan is implemented, he will be supportive. Jocelyn is resistant, and the desired "after" classification is neutral. This type of matrix can be recorded as part of the stakeholder management plan, or it can be used to develop the approach documented in the stakeholder management plan.

Plan Stakeholder Management: Outputs

The strategies and steps you take to engage stakeholders effectively are documented in a stakeholder management plan, which is a component of the project management plan.

A stakeholder management plan can be very high-level. For example, you can develop a strategy based on the grid cell that you placed your stakeholders when analyzing their engagement: say, how to move a stakeholder from high power/low support to high power/high support. If you used the stakeholder analysis model of unaware up through leading, you can document strategies and steps to get from neutral to supportive or even leading.

For the running childcare center example, you might develop different strategies for internal stakeholders (such as the sponsor, team members, and employees) than you would for external stakeholders (such as vendors and the city).

You can also assess strategies depending on the type of role, such as leader, supporter, and neutral. The needs of the project will help you determine the best approach. The four things to remember about developing stakeholder engagement strategies are the following:

- **Be proactive.** Take time upfront to determine how to make the most of your supportive stakeholders and also how to minimize the potential damage from your resistor stakeholders.
- **Be sensible.** Some of your strategies may be politically sensitive. Use discretion on what you write down versus how much you consider as a public document.
- **Use communication.** The main tool with which to influence stakeholders and manage their expectations is communication. Information from the stakeholder engagement plan strategy will feed into the communications management plan (see Book IV, Chapter 4) and managing stakeholder engagement (see Book VI, Chapter 3).
- **Gain support.** Ensure your stakeholders' expectations align with the project and identify strategies to engage stakeholders in supporting your project.

Figure 3-1 shows a sample stakeholder management plan template.

STAKEHOLDER MANAGEMENT PLAN

Project Title:__________ Date Prepated: __________

Stakeholder	Unaware	Resistant	Neutral	Supportive	Leading

C= Current level of engagement D= Desired level of engagement

Stakeholder	Communication Needs	Method/Medium	Timing/Frequency

Pending Stakeholder Changes

Page 1 of 2

Figure 3-1: Sample stakeholder management plan.

STAKEHOLDER MANAGEMENT PLAN

Stakeholder: Relationships

Stakeholder Engagement Approach

Stakeholder	Approach

Page 2 of 2

You likely will need to circle back and make some updates to your stakeholder register, communications management plan, and other project management plan components and the documents.

Key Terms

I go over some stakeholder management terms at the end of the chapter on Identifying Project Stakeholders (Book II, Chapter 3). There are a few new terms in this chapter associated with classifying stakeholder engagement:

- Unaware
- Resistant
- Neutral
- Supportive
- Leading
- Stakeholder management plan

Planning summary

Books III, IV, and V are all about planning. The planning process group makes up 24 percent of the questions on the test; in other words, there will be 48 planning questions. For these questions, you will need to be adept at the following techniques:

Planning for change	Book III, Chapter 1
Planning the project	Book III, Chapter 1
Gathering requirements	Book III, Chapter 2
Creating a WBS	Book III, Chapter 2
Defining scope	Book III, Chapter 2
Estimating duration, costs, and budgets	Book III, Chapter 3; Book IV, Chapter 1
Planning quality	Book IV, Chapter 2
Planning for resources	Book IV, Chapter 3
Planning communications	Book IV, Chapter 4
Planning for risk	Book V, Chapter 1
Planning for procurement	Book V, Chapter 2

You will also need to know the elements of and the purpose of the following:

Change management plan	Book III, Chapter 1
The project management plan	Book III, Chapter 1
Quality management plan	Book IV, Chapter 2
Communication management plan	Book IV, Chapter 4
Risk management plan	Book V, Chapter 1
Procurement management plan	Book V, Chapter 2

er Summary

Here are the main ideas to take away from this chapter.

- You need to review all elements of the project management plan, along with the stakeholder register, to determine the best way to manage stakeholder engagement throughout the project life cycle.
- Enterprise environmental factors, such as organizational structure and politics, influence how you can manage stakeholder engagement.
- Seek expert guidance to determine current and desired future engagement levels of stakeholders.
- Document your strategy in a stakeholder management plan.

Prep Test

Multiple Choice

1 **Which element of the project management plan will help you identify requirements or measurements that need to be sent to outside agencies or external customers?**

- **A** ❍ Procurement management plan
- **B** ❍ Communications management plan
- **C** ❍ Quality management plan
- **D** ❍ Project life cycle

2 **Which input records information on stakeholder identification information and their category?**

- **A** ❍ Enterprise environmental factors
- **B** ❍ Stakeholder register
- **C** ❍ Stakeholder management plan
- **D** ❍ Lessons learned

3 **Which two enterprise environmental factors should you pay special attention to when developing your stakeholder management plan?**

- **A** ❍ Organizational culture and politics
- **B** ❍ Politics and market environment
- **C** ❍ Organizational culture and lessons learned
- **D** ❍ Information from prior projects and politics

4 **A stakeholder who does not support your project is classified as**

- **A** ❍ A detriment
- **B** ❍ Neutral
- **C** ❍ A resistor
- **D** ❍ A threat

5 **Which stakeholder classification actively promotes a project?**

- **A** ❍ Supportive
- **B** ❍ Proactive
- **C** ❍ High interest/high influence
- **D** ❍ Leading

6 **Jared has been asking for a faster network for the past 18 months. You are leading a project to upgrade the network to the latest technology. This will increase the speed and reliability. Which classification of stakeholder is Jared considered?**

A ❍ Leader
B ❍ Neutral
C ❍ High opportunity
D ❍ Supportive

7 **You are leading a project to replace the phone system and the Acme Voice Network vendor to install a new phone system with the latest technology. This will increase the speed and reliability of your data and voice networks. Which classification of stakeholder is Acme Voice Network considered?**

A ❍ A resistor
B ❍ A follower
C ❍ Neutral
D ❍ Unaware

8 **If you have a complex procurement that isn't well defined and you're looking for a vendor to solve the problem and come up with a solution, what type of stakeholder is the vendor?**

A ❍ A resistor
B ❍ A follower
C ❍ Neutral
D ❍ A supporter

Scenario 1

Use the following table to answer Questions 1 and 2.

Name	*Unaware*	*Resistant*	*Neutral*	*Supportive*	*Leading*
John		B		A	
Lulu			B	A	
Tessa				B	A
Avery		B	A		

1 **Which stakeholder will need the most work, according to the table?**

A ❍ John
B ❍ Lulu
C ❍ Tessa
D ❍ Avery

2 **Who will help you champion the project?**

A ❍ John
B ❍ Lulu
C ❍ Tessa
D ❍ Avery

Answers

Multiple Choice

1. **C.** Quality management plan. A quality management plan contains quality requirements that may need specific stakeholder input or review. *Review the section "Plan Stakeholder Management: Inputs."*
2. **B.** Stakeholder register. The stakeholder register lists stakeholder identification information and their category. *Look at "Plan Stakeholder Management: Inputs."*
3. **A.** Organizational culture and politics. Organizational culture and politics both limit your options for managing stakeholders. *Go to "Plan Stakeholder Management: Inputs."*
4. **C.** A resistor. Resistors are aware of your project but do not support it. *Look at the "Plan Stakeholder Management: Tools and Techniques" section.*
5. **D.** Leading. Leading stakeholders take an active role in championing and promoting your project. *See the information in the "Plan Stakeholder Management: Tools and Techniques" section.*
6. **D.** Supportive. Jared feels favorably about the project. *Check out "Plan Stakeholder Management: Tools and Techniques."*
7. **A.** A resistor. The vendor who is being replaced is likely not in support of your project to bring in a new vendor and new technology. *You will find information on the stakeholder engagement matrix in the section on "Plan Stakeholder Management: Tools and Techniques."*
8. **D.** A supporter. A vendor that is helping you solve a problem feels favorably about the project and is supportive of it. *This is discussed in the "Plan Stakeholder Management: Tools and Techniques" section.*

Scenario 1

1. **A.** John. This matrix shows that you expect to move John from resistant to supportive. That generally requires more work than moving from resistant to neutral. *You can review this information in the "Plan Stakeholder Management: Tools and Techniques" section.*
2. **C.** Tessa. A leader helps champion and promote your project. *Review the "Plan Stakeholder Management: Tools and Techniques" section.*

Book VI

Managing Your Project

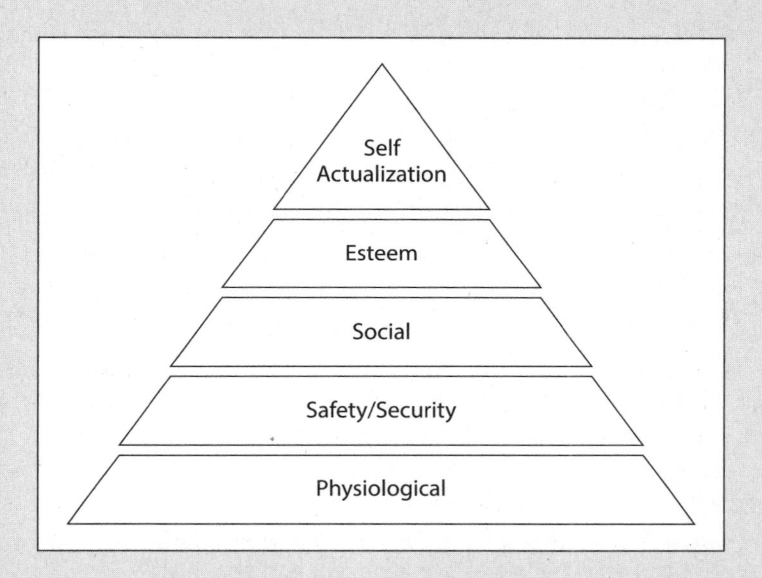

For more, read the article on executing knowledge and skills at `www.dummies.com/extras/pmpcertificationaio`.

Contents at a Glance

Chapter 1: Managing the Work and Assuring Quality

Exam Objectives

- **Execute project activities defined in the project management plan to create project deliverables on time and within budget.**
- **Follow the change management plan with regards to processes and procedures and implement approved changes.**
- **Actively employ risk management techniques as documented in the risk management plan to minimize the impact of risk on the project.**
- **Follow the quality management plan, using appropriate tools and techniques to assure work and scope meet the quality requirements and standards.**

At this point, you move from the planning processes into the executing processes. You are now implementing your project management plan. The executing processes are where the majority of the project work occurs. As such, it is also the most reliant upon the nature of the work being performed. Therefore, there isn't a lot of specific guidance I can give you, nor is there a lot of specific information that PMI can test on. Nonetheless, these questions account for 30 percent of the exam questions. In other words, 60 questions on the exam will be from the eight processes in the Executing process group.

This chapter starts off with a look at the cross-cutting knowledge and skills you are most likely to employ in the Executing process group. Then I move into the Direct and Manage Project Work process. That process is integrative and pulls together all the work from the other processes to create the project deliverables.

Next, you review the Perform Quality Assurance process. This can be a misunderstood process. I like to think of it as the "management" part of quality management. Oftentimes, this process is not done within the project team. There might be a separate department — such as Quality Management or Quality Improvement — that acts as a third party to conduct quality audits.

The heart of this process is about auditing the performance of the project and then ensuring that the team is using the policies, procedures, methods, and techniques identified in the quality management plan. The intention is to improve the performance of the project, the processes used in the project, and the product.

Quick Assessment

1 Approved changes are implemented in which process?

2 Change requests include corrective actions, ______ ______, and defect repairs.

3 To rank options for process improvement in order from most impactful to least impactful, what type of chart would you use?

4 Looking for ways to remove nonvalue-adding activities is part of ______ ______.

5 (True/False). Process improvement is part of the Perform Quality Control process.

6 (True/False). Quality audits can be used to communicate best practices throughout the organization.

7 Documented direction for executing the project work to bring expected future performance of the project work in line with the project management plan is called ______ ______.

8 Determining whether the quality metrics identified in the quality management plan are appropriate for the project is part of which process?

9 In Perform Quality Assurance, you would use a(n) ______-______ ______ to determine whether the cost to improve a process is worth it.

10 A permission and direction, typically written, to begin work on a specific schedule activity or work package or control account is known as ______ ______.

Answers

1. Direct and Manage Project Work. Changes are authorized in the Perform Integrated Change Control process and implemented in the Direct and Manage Project Work process. *Read more about this in "Direct and Manage Project Work."*

2. Preventive actions. Preventive actions are a type of change request. *You can read about this in "Direct and Manage Project Work: Inputs."*

3. Pareto chart. A Pareto chart ranks options for process improvement in order from most impactful to least impactful. *Look over the information in "Perform Quality Assurance: Tools and Techniques."*

4. Process improvement. Process improvement can improve project performance by identifying nonvalue-adding activities. *This is explained in the section on "Process analysis."*

5. False. Process improvement is part of the Perform Quality Assurance process, not the Perform Quality Control process. *You will see this in the section on "Process analysis."*

6. True. Quality audits can be used to communicate best practices or suggest improvements. *Quality audits are discussed in the section "Quality audits."*

7. Corrective action. Corrective action is a type of change request. *I discuss this in "Direct and Manage Project Work: Inputs."*

8. Perform Quality Assurance. Part of quality assurance is making sure the metrics you are using are appropriate and effective. *Look over the information in Table 1-2: How Quality Assurance Monitors Project Quality.*

9. Cost-benefit analysis. It is not useful to spend more improving a process than the benefit it will provide. *This is discussed in "Perform Quality Assurance: Tools and Techniques."*

10. Work authorization. Work authorization is given to start work on a deliverable or activity during project execution. *I discuss this in the section "Direct and Manage Project Work: Tools and Techniques."*

Knowledge and Skills for the Executing Processes

Because the majority of the project work is completed in this process group, you will need to employ a lot of the cross-cutting knowledge and skills. Think about how the following can be used as you learn the information in this minibook:

- ✦ Active listening
- ✦ Conflict resolution techniques
- ✦ Cultural sensitivity and diversity
- ✦ Decision-making techniques
- ✦ Facilitation
- ✦ Information management tools, techniques, and methods
- ✦ Leadership tools and techniques
- ✦ Negotiating
- ✦ Oral and written communication techniques, channels, and applications
- ✦ Presentation tools and techniques
- ✦ Prioritization/time management
- ✦ Problem-solving tools and techniques
- ✦ Relationship management
- ✦ Targeting communications to intended audiences (for example, team, stakeholders, and customers)
- ✦ Team motivation methods

Questions in the Executing process group account for 30 percent of the exam. Although there will be many questions about the tools, techniques, and outputs, there will also be quite a few questions about the cross-cutting skills!

Direct and Manage Project Work

Carrying out the work in the project management plan is all about integrating the various plans and activities of the project. A lot of your time is spent analyzing information and coordinating your team members' actions. While managing the work, you need to be flexible and nimble to respond appropriately to the day-to-day situations, issues, and risks that arise. You will have to call on your interpersonal skills to be an effective leader. During this process, you will also be implementing approved changes to the project management plan. The process of getting changes approved is in the Monitoring and Controlling process group. After the changes are approved, they are implemented in this process.

Direct and Manage Project Work. Leading and performing the work defined in the project management plan and implementing approved changes to achieve the project's objectives.

Notice that there are no processes in the Executing process group for scope, schedule, cost, or risk. (For a list of the processes in the Executing process group, see Book I, Chapter 4.) The underlying assumption is that these are so tightly connected that they are the nexus of the Integration process of Direct and Manage Project Work. In the start of the planning processes, you can plan your scope independent of your schedule and cost, but you can't execute scope independent of the schedule or the budget or risk events. Therefore, you can consider this Integration process the direct intersection of those knowledge areas and all the others as well. Table 1-1 shows the execution activities you will be conducting arranged by knowledge area.

Table 1-1 Executing Activities

Scope	Creating deliverables Meeting project requirements Providing information on deliverable status Requesting scope changes Repairing any defective products or results Implementing corrective or preventive actions regarding deliverables
Time	Performing activities as defined in the schedule Refining duration estimates Providing status information on the duration and forecasts for completion dates Requesting changes to the schedule Implementing corrective or preventive actions regarding the schedule
Cost	Committing costs Expending resources Tracking cost information Providing status information regarding expenses committed and incurred Refining cost estimates Providing forecast information for future expenditures Requesting changes to the budget Implementing corrective or preventive actions regarding the budget

(continued)

Table 1-1 *(continued)*

Quality	Ensuring the quality process is being implemented as planned Ensuring the planned quality process is effective Implementing quality audits Sharing good practices Identifying and documenting quality gaps Improving process effectiveness Requesting changes to the quality process
Human Resources	Acquiring project staff Training team members Managing team performance Enhancing and improving team performance Mentoring and coaching team members Providing feedback to team members Problem solving Resolving conflicts
Communication	Reporting work performance results Distributing information as indicated in the communications management plan Documenting and distributing lessons learned
Risk	Implementing risk response plans Providing information regarding risk status Managing resources assigned to risk activities
Procurement	Releasing procurement documents Conducting bid conferences Applying source selection criteria Awarding contracts
Stakeholders	Interfacing with internal and external stakeholders Managing stakeholder engagement Resolving issues

You can see that even though there isn't any specific information about the product, you are doing a heck of a lot of product work as well as project work! If you use this table to help you conceptualize all the work of the project, you can better understand the context of questions on the exam.

Direct and Manage Project Work: Inputs

Most of what you work with when creating deliverables is following the guidance of the project management plan, which is an important input to this process. You are subject to the organizational processes and constraints. The most common ones to keep in mind are

- ✦ Organizational policies
- ✦ Procedures
- ✦ Work guidelines
- ✦ Information from past projects
- ✦ Organizational infrastructure
- ✦ Information systems

Approved change requests are also inputs to the Direct and Manage Project Work process. The *PMBOK Guide* uses the term "change request" as an umbrella to encompass not only a request to change some aspect of the product or project, but also corrective action, preventive action, and defect repairs. There are specific definitions for each of those terms.

DEFINITION

Change Request. A formal proposal to modify any document, deliverable, or baseline.

Corrective Action. An intentional activity that realigns the performance of the project work with the project management plan.

Preventive Action. An intentional activity that ensures that the future performance of the project work is aligned with the project management plan.

Defect. An imperfection or deficiency in a project component where that component does not meet its requirements or specifications and needs to be either repaired or replaced.

Defect Repair. An intentional activity to modify a nonconforming product or product component.

You will generally see change requests as an output from the Monitoring and Control processes, and some of the Executing processes. They are inputs to the Perform Integrated Change Control process, where they are analyzed to determine whether they should be accepted, rejected, or deferred. The Direct and Manage Project Work process is where the approved change requests come to be implemented. Figure 1-1 shows where change requests come from.

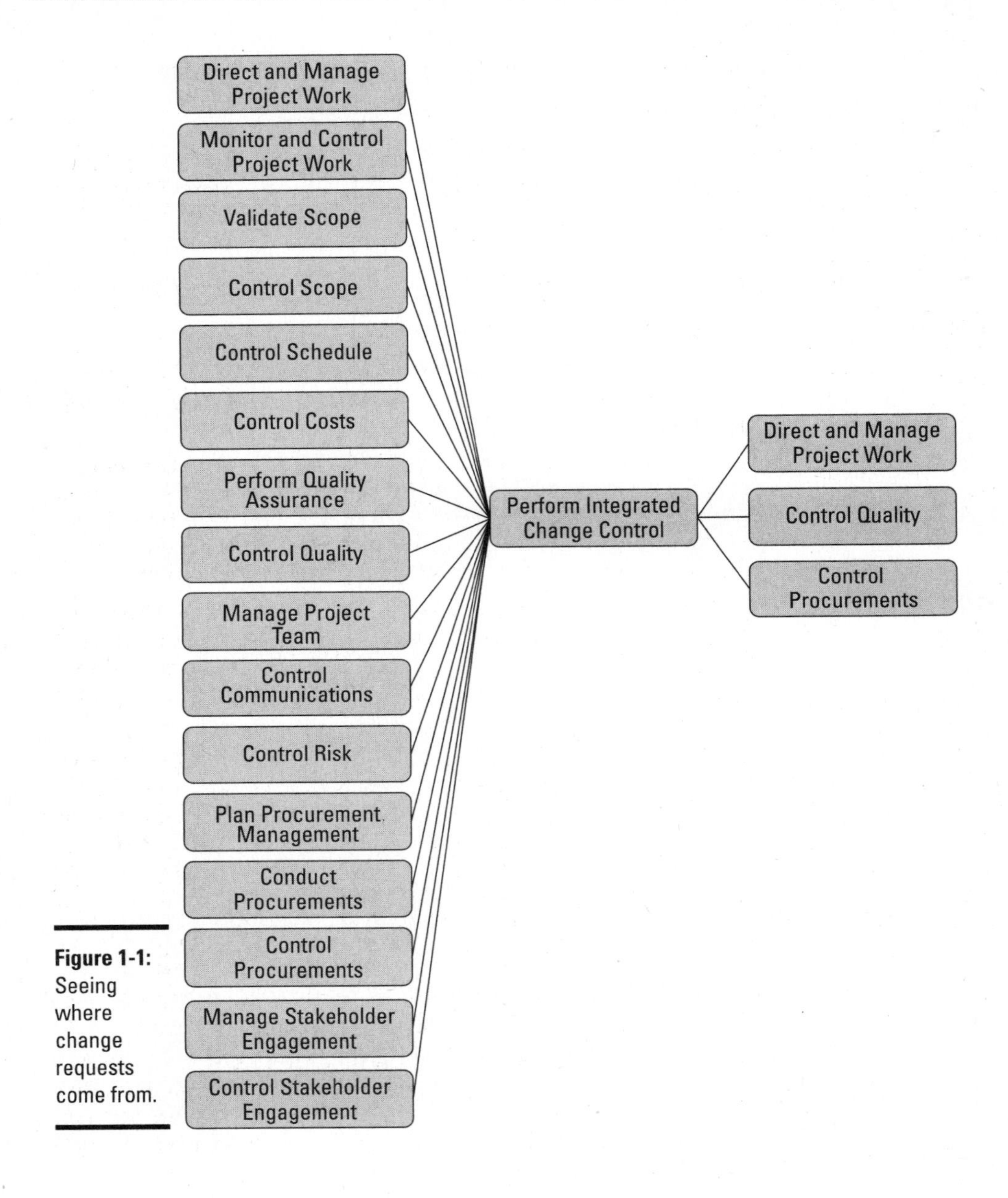

Figure 1-1: Seeing where change requests come from.

Direct and Manage Project Work: Tools and Techniques

The work in this process is accomplished by the expert judgment on your team. Your team members, including any vendors, have the technical expertise and experience to complete the work. You will also use the supporting information systems to accomplish work.

As the project manager, you'll be busy applying your expertise with the following types of activities:

- **Implementing policies and procedures:** All work needs to be accomplished according to company policy. Think about safety policies, quality policies, human resource policies, and the like.
- **Making sure team members have work authorization and are using approved methods of accomplishing work:** If you think about managing a large project with multiple vendors doing work, you want to make sure that you maintain visibility and control of when work starts and how it progresses. A work authorization system is designed to do that.

Work Authorization: A permission and direction, typically written, to begin work on a specific schedule activity or work package or control account. It is a method for sanctioning project work to ensure that the work is done by the identified organization, at the right time, and in the proper sequence.

- **Ensuring a common understanding of the work:** One of the most frustrating events that can happen on a project is to have team members doing their best to meet the project objectives but not having the same understanding of what that means. Part of your job is to make sure everyone has the same understanding of the work that needs to be done and also that everyone understands the prioritization of the work so they can manage their time effectively.
- **Enabling:** A big part of your job is enabling the team members to perform their work. This includes removing barriers, solving problems, and fostering communication among team members.
- **Managing interfaces:** A large project has many interfaces, both internal as well as outside the organization. Internal interfaces can include interfacing with operations, with other projects, and inside the project. External interfaces can be almost anything from regulatory and government agencies to the public to suppliers.
- **Implementing risk management actions:** While executing the project, you will implement planned risk responses, such as taking mitigating actions or transferring risk via procurement. You may also need to implement a contingency plan if a risk event occurs.

- **Making decisions:** Regardless of the decision-making process you use, your job is to make decisions that impact the project. Most project managers will consult with their team members and interview stakeholders before making decisions, but a big part of your everyday job is making decisions, whether they are little decisions or major decisions that impact the entire project.

Use a decision log to keep track of your decisions. It can be frustrating to make a decision in a team meeting and then revisit the same decision months later because no one can remember what the team decided on. A decision log tracks the decision, the impacted parties, the date, and any comments. It can also log approval if the decision needs buy-in from other stakeholders.

Meetings are an integral part of any project. You hold meetings to both inform stakeholders and to get information from them. You can hold meetings to brainstorm, evaluate options, and resolve problems and issues. You can also use meetings to make decisions about the product or the project.

Best practices for meeting management include

- Make sure that all the appropriate stakeholders and decision makers are at the meeting.
- Communicate the purpose of the meeting.
- Have an agenda.
- Manage participation so that all meeting attendees have time to interact, ask questions, discuss options, and so forth.
- Take notes or minutes.
- Document and follow up on action items and issues.

Direct and Manage Project Work: Outputs

The outputs of executing the project work are fairly logical. You have your deliverables and the work performance data. You can see in Figure 1-2 that work performance information is an input to nine Monitoring and Controlling processes.

Some specific definitions are associated with deliverables and work performance information. Take a look at them to make sure you understand what PMI means by these terms.

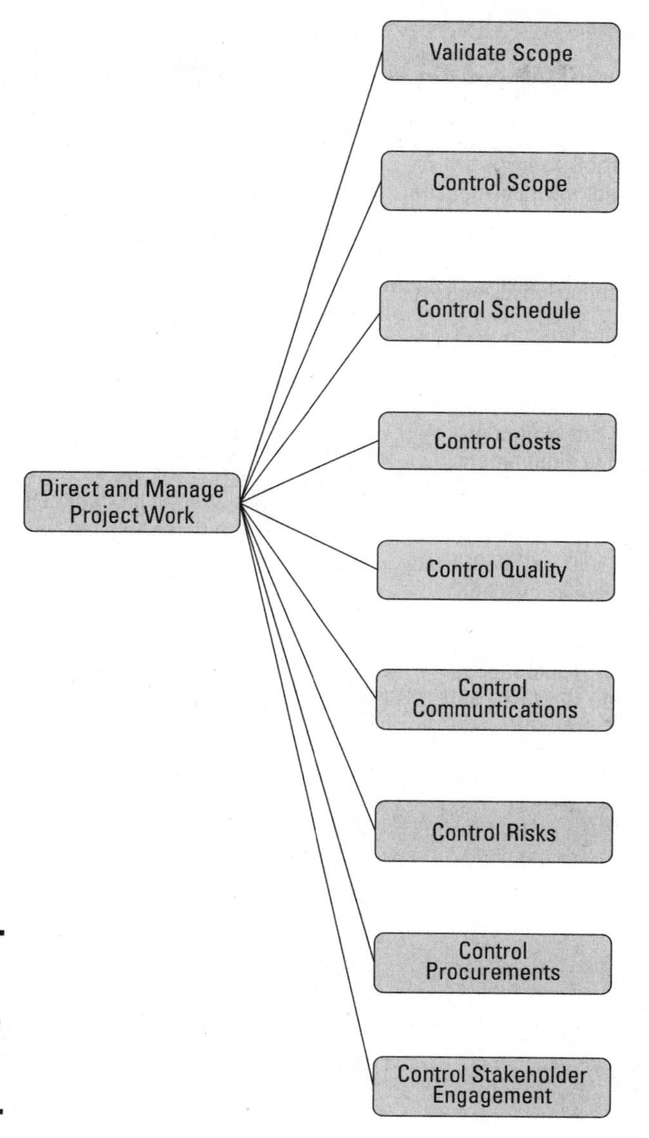

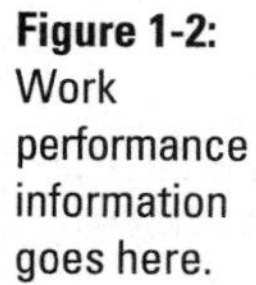

Figure 1-2: Work performance information goes here.

Deliverable. Any unique and verifiable product, result, or capability to perform a service that is required to be produced to complete a process, phase, or project.

Product. An artifact that is produced, is quantifiable, and can be either an end item in itself or a component item. Additional words for products are *material* and *goods.*

Result. An output from performing project management processes and activities. Results include outcomes (for example, integrated systems, revised process, restructured organization, tests, trained personnel, and so on) and documents (for example, policies, plans, studies, procedures, specifications, reports, and so on).

Work Performance Data. The raw observations and measurements identified during activities being performed to carry out the project work.

You might have change requests, depending on how the work is going, and you will update components of the project management plan and project documents. Change requests that are a result of this process can address project or product issues. You might see a change request to revise work instructions, the schedule, scope, budget, or requirements. It's common to see requests for preventive and/or corrective actions as a result of this process.

Perform Quality Assurance

Quality assurance is sandwiched between Plan Quality Management and Control Quality. In reality, the flow is different. First, you plan the quality processes, policies, techniques, methods, and metrics. Then, using the tools in quality control, you measure the results by using the identified tools, techniques, and methods to see whether they comply with the identified metrics. In quality assurance, you're identifying whether the process is working — and if there are ways to improve it. Table 1-2 summarizes this flow.

Table 1-2 How Quality Assurance Monitors Project Quality

Plan Quality Management	*Control Quality*	*Perform Quality Assurance*
Identifies the policies and procedures used on the project		Are we using those policies and procedures? Are they appropriate?
Identifies the quality processes used on the project		Are we using those processes? Are they appropriate?

Plan Quality Management	Control Quality	Perform Quality Assurance
Identifies the tools and techniques used to measure quality	Measure using the identified tools and techniques.	Are these the right tools and techniques?
Identifies the metrics and measurements for the product and project	Compare the measurements with the metrics.	Are the metrics appropriate? If there are variances, what is the cause?
	Identify gaps in planned versus actual measurements.	Can we improve our policies, procedures, tools, techniques, or methods?
		Develop corrective action plans for problem areas.
		Communicate areas that work.

Perform Quality Assurance. Auditing the quality requirements and the results from quality control measurements to ensure that appropriate quality standards and operational definitions are used.

Quality assurance is predominately concerned with improving processes, which will lead to improved results. Therefore, much of the information in this chapter focuses on process performance, analysis, and improvement.

The intent of performing quality assurance is to provide confidence that the processes, products, deliverables, and data are sound and will meet the documented requirements and specifications.

Perform Quality Assurance: Inputs

Inputs for the Perform Quality Assurance process come from the project management plan, the Plan Quality Management, and the Control Quality processes. Here are brief descriptions of the inputs:

- **Quality management plan:** Describes the quality assurance approach, including processes, procedures, methods, and tools that will be used for quality assurance. For more on the quality management plan, see Book IV, Chapter 2.
- **Process improvement plan:** The Perform Quality Assurance process is the umbrella for improving processes for the organization and the project.

- **Quality metrics:** The specific measurements that a project, product, service, or result needs to meet to be considered in compliance. Metrics can also describe the measurement process or tool used to measure the outcome. You can read up on quality metrics in Book IV, Chapter 2.
- **Quality control measurements:** The outcomes from the measurements taken in the Control Quality process (see Book VIII, Chapter 2).

Perform Quality Assurance: Tools and Techniques

The same tools and techniques introduced in Plan Quality Management (see Book IV, Chapter 2) and that will show up in Control Quality (see Book VIII, Chapter 2) can help in this process. The difference is that here, they are predominately process-oriented rather than product- or project-oriented. Table 1-3 shows how tools and techniques are applied to assure quality.

Table 1-3 Tools and Techniques in Quality Assurance

Tools/Techniques	*How It Is Used*
Cost-benefit analysis	Determine whether cost to improve a process is worth the benefit.
Cost of quality	Determine whether you can invest in prevention costs to reduce the cost of failure.
Control charts	If you have unexpected, negative, or erratic trends in measurements from the control charts, the process should be analyzed for improvement opportunities.
Benchmarking	Benchmark process-improvement goals to improve process results.
Design of experiments	Identify multiple variables in the process that can be modified in conjunction with one another to improve a process.
Statistical sampling	Conduct a random audit of process documentation or quality control documentation to determine whether the appropriate processes and procedures are being employed.
Flowcharting	Create a flow chart of a process to find redundant work or steps that don't add value.
Cause-and-effect diagrams	Use to determine the drivers of process problems and identify areas where you can make adjustments to improve performance.
Histograms	Quantitatively identify the impact of each source of errors or defect.

Tools/Techniques	*How It Is Used*
Pareto charts	Rank those areas with the least-favorable outcomes to apply corrective action to those areas first.
Run charts	Identify trends in performance. Negative trends should be analyzed for corrective actions.
Scatter diagrams	Look at how two independent variables relate. You may be able to modify one variable to improve the results of a second variable.
Inspection	Inspect a process to determine whether it's functioning optimally.

In addition to the tools and techniques listed in Table 1-3, the additional quality management tools in Table 1-4 may be of use.

Table 1-4 Additional Quality Management Tools and Techniques

Tools/Techniques	*How It Is Used*
Affinity diagrams	Group similar ideas for example causes of defects.
Process decision program charts (PDPC)	Identify the steps necessary to achieve a goal and how those steps can lead to a failure in attaining the goal.
Interrelationship diagraphs	Show how relationships among multiple systems or entities interact.
Tree diagrams	Used to decompose systems and show parent-child relationships. A WBS is an example of a tree diagram.
Prioritization matrices	Identify key issues and alternatives that can be prioritized by using a weighting system to rank alternatives and solutions.
Activity network diagrams	Shows activities in the order in which they occur: a version of a schedule network diagram.
Matrix diagrams	Shows the strength of relationships between variables, using rows and columns that intersect.

Quality audits

Quality audits are used to perform a structured review of the project to determine whether the team is complying with project and organization policies, procedures, and processes. Those areas not in compliance will result in some type of deficiency report. The team will then develop a corrective action plan and assign someone to implement the plan and follow up on the deficiency report.

For those areas in compliance, no action is needed. For those areas that are performing well, the audit team may identify the good or best practices being employed and share them throughout the organization so other teams can improve their performance as well.

Quality audit example

To see how a quality audit could occur on a project, I use my running child-care center example. During the project, the quality assurance department announced that it would be auditing the project, specifically interested in safety, procurement, and project management practices. Here's the setup:

> *On the first day of the audit, Quentin (from Quality Assurance) walked around the site with George, the foreman. Quentin had a checklist of safety policies and procedures that he wanted to ensure were being followed. He also walked around and looked at all the equipment and the workers to make sure that the job site was safe and secure. He found one instance where a cord for a piece of equipment was not properly coiled. He also noted that some of the material was not stored properly. This was noted, and the foreman corrected it immediately.*
>
> *Next, Quentin checked the safety log and noted only one incident of a cut finger. The cut did not require stitches or transport to urgent care. The incident was properly logged.*
>
> *On the second day, Quentin asked to see all the procurement documentation. He reviewed the bid documents, the source selection score sheets, the statement of work, status reports, and invoices. There were three instances where a contractor was late with a deliverable, but the job was currently on time. Therefore, no corrective actions were noted.*
>
> *On the third day, Quentin reviewed the project documentation. He noted that all the documentation was complete and in good order. The cost variances were acceptable (–3%), and the project was on schedule. In addition, there were very few change requests. He interviewed the project manager and noted that he usually saw significantly more change requests. The project manager replied that he had spent more time than usual gathering stakeholder requirements. Then he had a meeting with the parents and showed them drawings of the childcare center. The contractor and architect attended the meeting. There were a few requested changes, which were incorporated into the plans. Quentin seemed very pleased with this process. He noted that this was a good practice and that he would share it with other project managers.*

Process analysis

Because Perform Quality Assurance is concerned with process improvement, I take a brief moment here to discuss how the process improvement flows. The process improvement plan is developed in the Plan Quality Management process. It should contain at least the following information:

- ✦ Existing process description
- ✦ Current process metrics
- ✦ Targets for improvement
- ✦ Approach for improvement
- ✦ Flow of the existing process

In the Perform Quality Assurance process, the target process is analyzed, and alternative approaches for improvement are identified. As a result of the analysis, the best alternative is selected, and a flow of the new process is developed. At that point, a change request is generated. If approved, the new process is implemented. Figure 1-3 shows how the three steps work together.

Think of process improvement as *Kaizen,* the Japanese philosophy that focuses on the continuous improvement of processes.

Perform Quality Assurance: Outputs

The intended outcome of quality audit and process improvement activities is to reduce the cost of quality and/or to increase customer satisfaction. Any corrective actions identified in quality audit, as well as any opportunities to improve processes, will go through the Integrated Change Control process. Change requests can take the form of

- ✦ Changing a policy
- ✦ Changing a procedure
- ✦ Changing a process
- ✦ Corrective action
- ✦ Preventive action
- ✦ Changing the quality management plan

Depending on the results of the Perform Quality Assurance process, you may also need updates to the project management plan, project documents, and the organizational process assets.

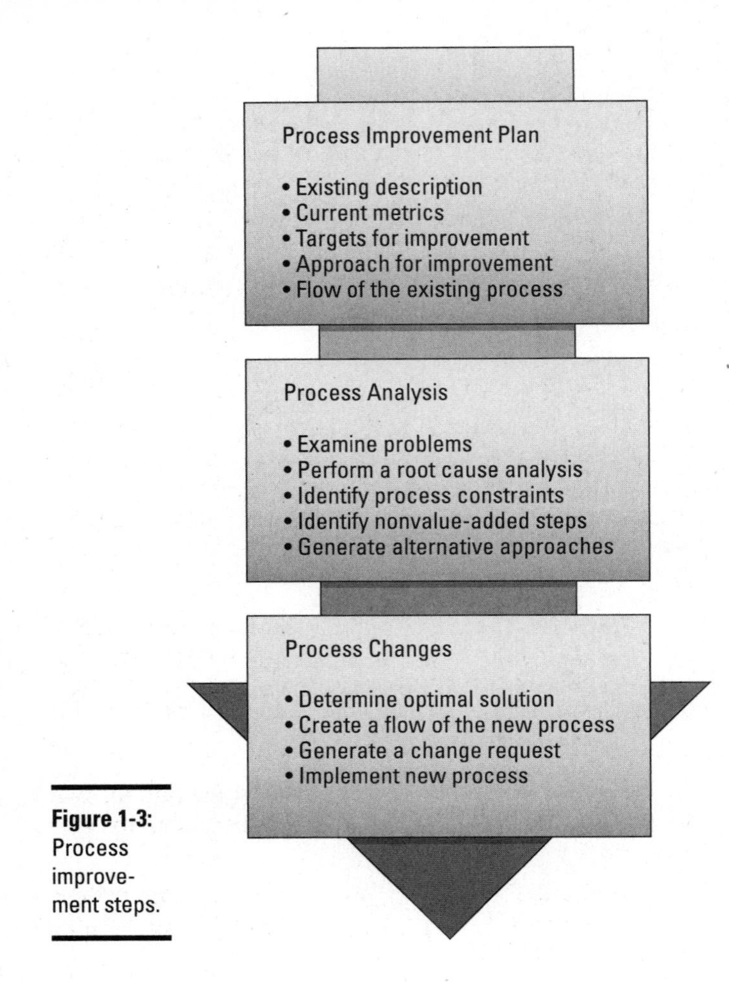

Figure 1-3: Process improvement steps.

Key Terms

Many of these terms are used throughout this book and Books VII and VIII, where I discuss monitoring and controlling. Therefore, you need to understand these terms well enough to be able to explain them and use them in context.

- Direct and Manage Project Work
- Change request
- Corrective action

- ✦ Preventive action
- ✦ Defect
- ✦ Defect repair
- ✦ Work authorization
- ✦ Deliverable
- ✦ Product
- ✦ Result
- ✦ Work performance information
- ✦ Perform Quality Assurance
- ✦ Quality audit
- ✦ Process analysis

Chapter Summary

This chapter is the foundation for doing the project work of creating deliverables and results. The chapter also discusses ways to ensure that the project processes are operating as designed. The executing concepts are relatively simple, but because they make up the backbone of a project, you need to be comfortable with them.

- ✦ The majority of the project work is performed in the Direct and Manage Project Work process. It combines the executing function for scope, schedule, cost, and risk knowledge areas.
- ✦ The team uses the organizational policies, procedures, work guidelines, information from past projects, the organizational infrastructure, and information systems to perform its work.
- ✦ Direct and Manage Project Work is where approved change requests are implemented. Change requests can include preventive actions, corrective actions, and defect repairs.
- ✦ As a project manager, you're following organizational policies while supporting your team, managing stakeholders, and making decisions.
- ✦ As a result of the work, the team produces deliverables, work performance information, and change requests, and updates the project management plan and project documents.
- ✦ Quality assurance monitors whether quality policies and procedures are being used as intended.

Summary

✦ Perform Quality Assurance is concerned with process more than the product. The process uses information from quality control measurements to determine whether the quality processes are effective.

✦ Quality audits can result in corrective actions and can also be used to share best practices across the organization.

✦ Process analysis seeks to find ways to improve process effectiveness and efficiency.

Prep Test

1 **Examining process problems and conducting a root-cause analysis is part of**

A ❍ Process changes
B ❍ Process improvement
C ❍ Process analysis
D ❍ Process implementation

2 **Creating deliverables is part of which knowledge area?**

A ❍ Communication
B ❍ Human resources
C ❍ Risk
D ❍ Scope

3 **Approved change requests are an input to Direct and Manage Project Work. In which process are they approved?**

A ❍ Perform Integrated Change Control
B ❍ Any control process
C ❍ Monitor and Control Project Work
D ❍ Perform Quality Control

4 **A documented direction to perform an activity that can reduce the probability of negative consequences associated with project risks is known as**

A ❍ Defect repair
B ❍ Preventive action
C ❍ Corrective action
D ❍ A change order

5 **An artifact that is produced, is quantifiable, and can be either an end item in itself or a component item is a(n)**

A ❍ Deliverable
B ❍ Product
C ❍ Result
D ❍ Artifact

6 **In which process would you measure product results to determine whether they conform to quality requirements?**

A ❍ Plan Quality
B ❍ Improve Quality
C ❍ Perform Quality Assurance
D ❍ Control Quality

7 **In which process do you determine whether measurement metrics are appropriate?**

A ❍ Plan Quality
B ❍ Perform Quality Improvement
C ❍ Perform Quality Assurance
D ❍ Control Quality

8 **If you wanted to determine whether investing in more rigorous prevention costs would result in less rework and scrap, and ultimately be more cost effective, which tool would you use?**

A ❍ Cost of quality
B ❍ Benchmarking
C ❍ Cause-and-effect diagram
D ❍ Statistical sampling

9 **To identify the root cause of a problem in a process, which tool would you use?**

A ❍ Cause-and-effect diagram
B ❍ Design of experiments
C ❍ Pareto diagram
D ❍ Control charts

10 **Which technique is used to perform a structured, independent review to determine compliance with policies and procedures?**

A ❍ Inspection
B ❍ Quality audit
C ❍ Cause-and-effect diagram
D ❍ Statistical sampling

Answers

1. **C.** Process analysis. Examining process problems and their root cause are part of process analysis. *Check out "Process analysis."*

2. **D.** Scope. The scope processes define the deliverables for the project via the processes of collecting requirements and creating a WBS. *Review Table 1-1: Executing Activities.*

3. **A.** Perform Integrated Change Control. Change requests are analyzed, and a decision is made in the Perform Integrated Change Control process. *Look at "Direct and Manage Project Work: Inputs."*

4. **B.** Preventive action. Preventive action is a documented direction to perform an activity that can reduce the probability of negative consequences associated with project risks. *Check out the definitions in "Direct and Manage Project Work: Inputs."*

5. **B.** Product. An artifact that is produced, is quantifiable, and can be either an end item in itself or a component item is a product. *Review the definition in the "Direct and Manage Project Work: Outputs" section.*

6. **D.** Control Quality. Control Quality is where you take measurements to ensure compliance with the plan and metrics. *Take a look at Table 1-2: How Quality Assurance Monitors Project Quality.*

7. **C.** Perform Quality Assurance. Perform Quality Assurance is where you determine whether the metrics you're using are appropriate. *Review Table 1-2: How Quality Assurance Monitors Project Quality.*

8. **A.** Cost of quality. The cost of quality would help you identify whether the costs associated with prevention are more cost effective than the costs associated with internal failure. *Check out Table 1-3: Tools and Techniques in Quality Assurance.*

9. **A.** Cause-and-effect diagram. A cause-and-effect diagram can help you identify the root cause of a problem. *Go over Table 1-3: Tools and Techniques in Quality Assurance.*

10. **B.** Quality audit. A quality audit is a structured independent review to determine compliance with policies, processes, and procedures. *Look at the information in the "Quality audits" section.*

Chapter 2: Managing the People Side of Your Project

Exam Objectives

- **Acquire and manage project resources, both internal and external, to execute the project. Follow the procurement management plan to acquire external resources.**
- **Employ leadership, training, motivating, mentoring, and other interpersonal skills to maximize team performance.**

Executing the project is where the real skills in managing, leading, and working with people come into play. The interpersonal skills that you need to successfully acquire, develop, and manage the team are described in this chapter. Of course, they're deployed throughout the project, but because the majority of the work occurs during the execution, those skills and processes are outlined here.

Unlike many of the other processes, the processes in this chapter are more concerned with people rather than deliverables. Some skills that you're most likely to use include

- Negotiating
- Communicating
- Team building
- Developing trust
- Influencing
- Motivating
- Resolving conflict
- Leading
- Making decisions

In addition to these skills, I also discuss management styles and power. There's a lot to cover!

Quick Assessment

1 To take advantage of expertise in a different location and to incorporate people who work at home, you should establish a(n) _____ _____.

2 Herzberg developed a theory based on hygiene and _____ factors.

3 The five distinct phases of team building are forming, _____, _____, performing, and adjourning.

4 Someone who is published in his or her field and trains others has _______ power.

5 "It's my way or the highway" demonstrates which style of conflict management?

6 As you acquire your project team, you will want to reference the component of the human resource plan that documents the role, authority, responsibility, and competency for each position on the project team. Where would you find this information documented?

7 (True/False). Paraphrasing and summarizing someone's message is an indication of disrespect because it infers a lack of communication skills.

8 ERG is a motivation theory. What does the "R" stand for?

9 A project team that is all in one physical location is said to be _____. This is also known as a(n) _____ matrix.

10 If you are having a conflict with a team member, is it best to let things settle down for a while, confront the situation directly, or set up an intermediary to discuss the situation?

Answers

1 Virtual team. A virtual team allows you to bring a broad range of skills and diversity to the team. *For more on this topic, see "Acquire Project Team: Tools, Techniques, and Outputs."*

2 Motivation. Herzberg developed the Motivation-Hygiene Theory. *You can read up on several motivation theories in the section on "Interpersonal skills."*

3 Storming, norming. Bruce Tuckman developed this model for team building. *Read about it in "Interpersonal skills."*

4 Expert. A published person who trains others has expert power. The person might or might not have position power, but at the very least she has expert power. *Read about the types of power in the section on "Power."*

5 Forcing. "It's my way or the highway" demonstrates a forcing style of conflict management where the person enforcing the decision is not open to collaboration or compromise. *Conflict management is covered in "Resolving conflict."*

6 Roles and responsibilities. The human resource plan, which includes roles and responsibilities, is an input to the Acquire Project Team process. *Read about this in the section "Acquire Project Team: Inputs."*

7 False. Paraphrasing and summarizing a message is part of active listening, which is considered a key interpersonal skill. *For more on active listening, go to the section "Interpersonal skills."*

8 Relatedness. ERG stands for Existence, Relatedness, and Growth. *Read more about this topic in "Interpersonal skills."*

9 Co-located, tight. Co-location and a tight matrix are ways of indicating that there are no virtual team members and everyone on the team is in the same physical location. *This is discussed in "Co-location."*

10 Confront the situation directly. The Code of Ethics and Professional Conduct states that we should confront a conflict directly but still be professional and respectful. *Look over the information in "Resolving conflict."*

Acquire Project Team

Acquiring your project team is all about bringing team members onto your project team. This can include internal and external resources. Of course, if you are using external resources, you will need to follow your procurement management plan (see Book V, Chapter 2). I discuss how to conduct a procurement to bring external resources onto your team in the next chapter of this minibook.

Acquire Project Team. Confirming human resource availability and obtaining the team necessary to complete project activities.

The PMP exam assumes that you're working on a large project. For a large project, you would have a core group of people helping to plan the project. After the plans are finalized, you bring on the hundreds of resources needed to complete the work. In other words, you would staff the team as part of executing the project. Obviously, for a small project, the group responsible for planning the work would also be doing the work, so acquiring the team would occur very early in the planning phase.

Acquire Project Team: Inputs

Think back to the information you put together for your human resource management plan (see Book IV, Chapter 3). This is where much of that information will be used. The main components of the human resource management plan are

- **Roles and responsibilities:** This component of the human resource management plan documents the role, authority, responsibility, and competency for each position on the project team.
- **Project organization charts:** This component describes the reporting relationships on the team. You might see a hierarchy chart or a responsibility assignment matrix (RAM) here. There is an example of a RAM in Table 3-2 of Book IV, Chapter 3.
- **Staffing management plan:** This component includes
  - *Staff acquisition:* Describes how you will bring new team members on board, both from within the organization and external to the organization
  - *Resource calendars:* Identifies when specific roles are planned to be used; can include histograms
  - *Staff release plan:* Describes how team members will be released from the team

- *Training needs:* Identifies those parts of the work that will require training
- *Recognition and rewards:* Defines criteria for rewards and recognition
- *Compliance.* Describes any licensing, permitting, or other regulatory or compliance requirements
- *Safety:* Defines any safety rules and policies applicable to the project

In addition to the information from the human resource management plan, you are constrained by the project environment and resource availability in your organization. The process and ability to acquire resources will be significantly influenced by whether you work in a project-oriented culture, a matrix environment, or a functionally driven environment. You will also need to be mindful of the human resource policies and procedures you will need to follow.

Acquire Project Team: Tools, Techniques, and Outputs

In some situations, you will have pre-assigned resources. This might occur because your organization bid on a proposal and submitted resumes of the promised resources as part of the bid. However, in most cases, you have to negotiate with functional managers, resource managers, and other project managers.

Negotiation

You should negotiate for those team members who have the skill sets you identified in your RAM or other planning documents. This might mean that you're not necessarily looking for the most-skilled resource but rather a resource that meets your needs. A highly skilled resource is always nice to have on the team, but if you don't have work that requires those skills, you're paying for a level of competency you don't need. Also, a highly skilled resource person may get bored easily and look for something more interesting to do.

If, on the other hand, you get someone with a lower level of competency, you might have issues with the schedule, your quality requirements, and rework. In some situations, you might need to go outside the organization to acquire the skills you need. If you didn't plan for this upfront, you could overrun the budget; therefore, your ability to negotiate and influence are important in this process.

Virtual teams

One way of taking advantage of resources that have the skills you need is to incorporate them as a virtual team member. In other words, this team member isn't co-located with you or the rest of the team. Some benefits to using virtual team members include

- ✦ They might have the skills you need that aren't available locally.
- ✦ They might cost less than going outside the organization.
- ✦ You can take advantage of employees who work at home because of disabilities, personal reasons, or telecommuting policies.
- ✦ Travel costs can be reduced.

PMI uses the term *co-located* or *tight matrix* to indicate that team members are in the same office.

However, when you establish a virtual team, spending extra time on communications is critical. You want people to feel connected even though they don't get to see each other. In addition, when you can't read someone's body language, you miss some good communication cues, so establishing as many communication channels as necessary to reduce the opportunities for misunderstandings is important.

Have some type of regular face-to-face interaction, even if only a few times per year. Nothing can replace the relationships you build when you can sit across from someone and solve a problem or discuss an issue. Using telephone, web conferencing, e-mail, and faxes is good for addressing routine situations, but to build a team and to solve complex problems, being in a room together is best.

If you aren't able to negotiate for onsite or virtual team members, you will need to acquire them from outside the organization. This can be as simple as bringing in an external subject matter expert, or as complex as outsourcing the capabilities of an entire department.

Multicriteria decision analysis

Sometimes you will have to choose between a potential team member who has experience and expertise but little time and poor teamwork skills, and a potential team member with less experience but more time and a better attitude. In this type of circumstance, evaluate which criteria are more important on your project to help you make the best staffing choices. Some common criteria to consider include

- ✦ Availability
- ✦ Cost

- Experience
- Desire to work on the project
- Competencies
- Attitude
- Geography
- Flexibility of skill set

After you have your team members identified, you make team assignments, create a team directory, and then update the resource calendars and human resource management plan as necessary.

The Code of Ethics and Professional Conduct states that as a project manager, we do not discriminate against others based on, but not limited to, gender, race, age, religion, disability, nationality, or sexual orientation. You might see this standard referenced on a question about acquiring team members.

Develop Project Team

Here are two aspects to developing your team:

- Developing team member competencies and skills
- Developing the team as a whole by getting individuals to work together, thereby improving project performance

Develop Project Team. Improving the competencies, team member interaction, and the overall team environment to enhance project performance.

The intended outcomes of developing the project team and creating a team culture include

- Improved feelings of trust
- Higher morale
- Lower conflict
- Increased productivity
- Collaboration
- Higher cooperation
- Sharing knowledge and experience
- Leveraging cultural differences

The exam blueprint specifically mentions skills and knowledge in the areas of cultural sensitivity and diversity. The Code of Ethics and Professional Conduct (see Book IX, Chapter 2) states that project managers should inform themselves about the norms and customs of others and avoid engaging in behaviors that could be considered disrespectful.

Develop Project Team: Inputs, Tools, and Techniques

The human resource management plan, resource assignments, and resource calendars are inputs for developing the project team.

To support and develop your project team, you will need to find ways to inspire and motivate team members as well as build, maintain, and lead the team toward the desired outcome.

A big part of being successful managing a project is utilizing good interpersonal skills. You might hear this referred to as "soft skills" or "people skills." In my opinion, having good interpersonal skills is one of the most important requirements for being a project manager.

Interpersonal skills

The *PMBOK Guide* lists interpersonal skills as a tool and technique for this process. Leading, team building, and motivating are three of the most important interpersonal skills you can demonstrate to develop a high-functioning team.

Leadership

Leadership means different things to different people. When developing a team, here are some key behaviors you should demonstrate:

- **Vision:** You have to have a clear vision of what you want to accomplish and how you want the team to contribute to that vision. Part of this entails communicating the vision clearly, and part is influencing the team in supporting and owning the vision. This can include letting team members know what's in it for them if they support the vision.
- **Trust:** There are two aspects of trust in this process. The first is that team members have to trust that you have the skills and abilities to lead them through the project. The second is that they have to trust that you will support them, remove barriers, and empower them.

The Code of Ethics and Professional Conduct states that we strive to create an environment in which others feel safe to tell the truth.

- **Communication:** Earlier, I mention that communicating the vision clearly is important. Another aspect of communication is the way you communicate. You need to match your communication style to the needs at hand. Sometimes this means being clear and concise; other times, it means listening or being empathetic. Your ability to communicate appropriately will make a big difference in your ability to lead effectively.
- **Active listening:** Many people consider listening part of communication, but because it is such an important skill in project management, I am listing it separately. Active listening should include
  - Making eye contact, facing the person speaking, and having an open posture, such as not crossing your arms or legs
  - Giving the speaker your full attention without distractions or planning your response
  - Paraphrasing, summarizing, and/or clarifying the message to ensure you understand the message correctly
  - In situations where you're talking with someone who is emotional, you should empathize with the person, indicating that you understand what he is feeling

Training

The human resource plan identifies areas that may require training. Of the many different options for training, some are

- Classroom
- Online
- Mentoring
- On-the-job
- Coaching

Team building

Team building should be done early, and it should be done often. Some team building is formal, such as a retreat. Other team building is informal, such as going out for lunch, or starting a meeting by asking everyone present to share a little known fact about herself or telling something she is proud of. The intention is to get people comfortable working together effectively.

To form an effective team, people need to trust and respect the other team members and understand how to work well with them. Bruce Tuckman is a psychologist who conducted research in group dynamics. He developed a ladder (shown in Table 2-1) that describes the various stages of team building.

Table 2-1 Stages of Team Building

Phase	*Description*
Forming	The team first comes together. Members get to know each other's name, position on the team and department, and other pertinent background information. This might occur in the kick-off meeting.
Storming	Team members jockey for position on the team. This phase is where people's personalities, strengths, and weaknesses start to come out. There might be some conflict or struggle as people figure out how to work together. Storming might go on for some time or pass relatively quickly.
Norming	The team starts to function as a team. At this point, members know their places on the team and how they relate to and interface with all the other members. They are starting to work together. There might be some bumps in the road, but these are resolved quickly, and the team moves into action.
Performing	The team becomes operationally efficient. This is the mature team stage. Teams that have been together for awhile are able to develop a synergy. By working together, members accomplish more than other teams and produce a high-quality product.
Adjourning	The team completes the work and moves on to other projects. If the team has formed a good relationship, some members might be sad about leaving the team.

The intended outcome is for the team to develop a synergy and a relationship in which members can solve problems and perform work more effectively and efficiently.

Motivating

Motivation entails influencing people to perform certain actions. After all, not everyone is motivated by the same type of reward. Much research has been conducted as to what motivates people. As such, theories abound.

The following motivation theories appear most often on the PMP exam, and I describe each in a more detail.

- McGregor's Theory X and Theory Y
- Herzberg's Motivation-Hygiene Theory

- Maslow's Hierarchy of Needs
- ERG Theory
- McClelland's Theory of Needs
- Vroom's Expectancy Theory

Theory X and Theory Y

As proposed by Douglas McGregor, Theory X and Theory Y describe two different types of workers and how they should be managed. Theory X states that management believes that workers will do as little as possible to get by, and thus need a great deal of direction. Theory Y states that management believes that workers are interested in doing their best and, given the freedom, will perform well. Table 2-2 compares the two.

Table 2-2 Theory X and Theory Y

Theory X	*Theory Y*
The average worker has an inherent dislike of work and will avoid it if possible.	The average worker wants to be active and finds the physical and mental effort on the job to be satisfying.
Because of their dislike for work, most people must be controlled before they will work hard enough.	The greatest results come from willing participation, which will tend to produce self-direction toward goals without coercion or control.
The average worker prefers to be directed and dislikes responsibility.	The average worker seeks the opportunity for personal improvement and self-respect.
The average worker is not ambitious, and desires security above everything else.	Imagination, creativity, and ingenuity can be used to solve work problems by a large number of employees.

Motivation-Hygiene Theory

Frederick Herzberg believed that the two aspects to the work environment are hygiene and motivation. He stated that hygiene factors (detailed in the following table) don't motivate a worker to perform. However, the way they are implemented — or not implemented — can lead to employee dissatisfaction. On the other hand, motivation factors lead to higher individual performance. Table 2-3 shows examples of hygiene and motivation factors.

Table 2-3 Motivation-Hygiene Theory

Hygiene Factors	*Motivation Factors*
Policies	Achievement
Administration	Recognition
Working conditions	Growth
Salary	Advancement
Status	Interest in the job
Supervision	Job challenge
Security	

Maslow's Hierarchy of Needs

One of the most well known of all motivation theories is Maslow's Hierarchy of Needs; see Figure 2-1. This theory states that human beings have basic needs and that we need to meet lower-level needs before we can move onto the next level of needs. This theory is shown as a pyramid.

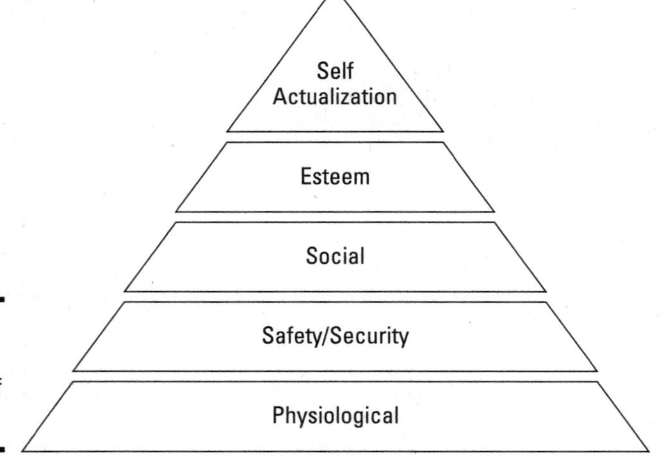

Figure 2-1: Maslow's Hierarchy of Needs.

ERG Theory

ERG Theory is similar to Maslow's Hierarchy of Needs, but it focuses on existence, relatedness, and growth needs. Figure 2-2 shows the ERG hierarchy.

- ✦ Existence includes the needs for food, drink, shelter, and safety.
- ✦ Relatedness needs include the need to feel connected to other individuals or a group. Relatedness needs are fulfilled by establishing and maintaining relationships.
- ✦ Growth needs are fulfilled by personal achievement and self-actualization.

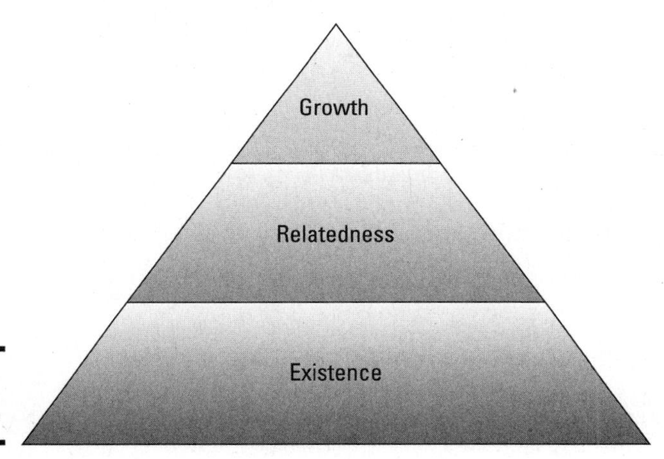

Figure 2-2: ERG Theory.

McClelland's Theory of Needs

David McClelland posited that people are motivated by power, achievement, or affiliation, and that how you manage a person is different based on what motivates that individual. Table 2-4 compares McClelland's three motivational drives.

Table 2-4 Theory of Needs

Need	*Behavior*
Power	These people like to organize, motivate, and lead others. Rewards should be focused on giving them more responsibility.
Achievement	These people are result oriented. They like to reach a goal and be recognized for it. They like challenges that are reasonable.
Affiliation	These people seek acceptance and belonging. They like being part of a team.

Vroom's Expectancy Theory

Victor Vroom states that "intensity of work effort depends on the perception that an individual's effort will result in a desired outcome." Employees are motivated when they believe the following:

- Putting in more effort will yield better job performance.
- Better job performance will lead to organizational rewards, such as an increase in salary or benefits.
- These predicted organizational rewards are valued by the employee.

The theory supports the concept of the reward being tied to performance, and ensuring that the reward is what the employee wants. It emphasizes the links between behavior, rewards, and the organization's goals (see Figure 2-3).

Figure 2-3: Expectancy Theory.

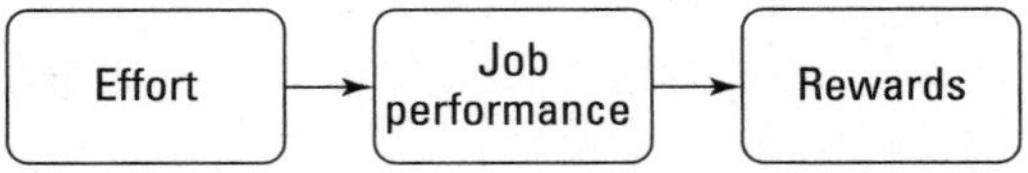

Ground rules

It is useful to establish ground rules in the beginning of the project to set expectations on how people should interact with each other. Some key items to include are

- How decisions will be made
- How the team will communicate with each other
- How conflicts will be addressed
- Meeting guidelines (only one person talks at a time; no side conversations)

Some teams use a team operating agreement to document their team approach. A team operating agreement might include the team's values and principles, meeting guidelines, and direction on when decisions can be revisited. It should be signed by all team members. If you have a large team, you might want to use it for the project management team only. See Figure 2-4 for an example of a team operating agreement form.

TEAM OPERATING AGREEMENT

Project Title: ____________________ Date Prepared: ________________

Team Values and Principles:

Meeting Guidelines:

Communication Guidelines:

Decision-Making Process:

Conflict Management Approach:

Figure 2-4: Sample team operating agreement.

Co-location

Co-location can help build team camaraderie by having all the team members in the same location. This facilitates communication, problem-solving, issue resolution, and relationship building. If having the team all in one place isn't feasible, sometimes having a team meeting room where the team has its status meetings and stores project documentation is a good substitute.

Rewards and recognition

Rewards and recognition are separate from, but closely tied to, motivating. You have to know what motivates folks to reward them appropriately. According to McClelland, someone who is motivated by affiliation won't feel rewarded if you give her more responsibility. However, someone who is motivated by challenges or power will feel rewarded by receiving more responsibility.

Oftentimes, project managers don't have the capability to give or withhold raises, but sometimes they have perks at their disposal or the capability to hand out bonuses. For example, they may be able to give out company logo wear or gift certificates to local restaurants.

Keep these key points in mind that apply regardless of what motivates people:

- ✦ Reward only that behavior you want to see more of, such as meeting a milestone because the work was well planned and executed — not because heroics and overtime were needed to meet it because the work wasn't well planned.
- ✦ In general, win-win rewards are better than win-lose rewards. For example, rewarding the team for pulling together to overcome a challenge is a win-win because everyone worked together and everyone gets rewarded. Comparatively, a reward for the team member of the month means that if one person wins, others lose. Win-win creates collaboration; win-lose creates competition.

The Code of Ethics and Professional Conduct (see Book IX, Chapter 2) specifically states that project managers should not reward or punish based on personal considerations, including but not limited to, favoritism, nepotism, or bribery.

Develop Project Team: Outputs

A *team performance assessment* looks at how the team is performing. This is different than a team member performance assessment that measures how a specific team member is performing. I cover team member performance assessments shortly. The team performance assessment should measure both technical achievement and interpersonal competencies.

Technical achievement looks at the scope and quality that have been produced by the team as well as whether the project is on time and on budget. Interpersonal competencies look at the team's ability to communicate effectively, how well members collaborate, how they are doing making decisions and resolving conflicts, and their overall morale. Another aspect that you can look at is how well they work together and whether some team synergy is developing. You should document areas that need improvement and develop a strategy to improve underperforming areas.

The Develop Project Team process and the Manage Project Team process are the only processes that update the environmental factors. They update the skill sets of individual team members.

Manage Project Team

Managing the team has a different focus than developing the team. Developing the team is more team-focused, and managing the team is more team member–focused.

Manage Project Team. Tracking team member performance, providing feedback, resolving issues, and managing changes to optimize project performance.

Manage Project Team: Inputs

Looking at the team performance assessment and the work performance reports can help you determine where the trouble spots are in the project. Work performance reports (see more about these in Book VIII, Chapter 2) provide information about the project status for scope, quality, schedule, cost, risks, and issues. The team performance assessments will tell you whether the team is working together well or whether there are pockets of conflict and dysfunction.

In addition to the team and work performance reports, you're going to get your best information by walking around, talking with team members, and observing behavior. Of course, this is a bit more difficult with virtual teams. That just means you have to make a concerted effort to reach out and touch base with virtual team members to see what's happening with them.

You aren't going to be able to tell whether something is bothering a team member from individual progress reports: All you're going to get is status. To get a feel for what is worrying the team member, what barriers he is encountering, and where you can step in and help, you have to get out from behind your desk and talk to people face to face. Some team members might think that you're being nosy or hovering, but to be effective, you need to see for yourself what's happening.

The issue log contains information that you can use to identify whether a team member's behavior is causing issues and to track team member progress on issue-resolution activities.

Manage Project Team: Tools and Techniques

Observing team member interaction with each other and with customers gives you a good idea of the team member attitude and team work. One-on-one conversations (even casual ones) can tell you a lot about morale, motivation, points of pride, and sources of conflict.

On very large projects, you'll probably be responsible for submitting a performance appraisal for team members. On medium or small projects, this can be a more informal process. The team member's manager might ask you for formal or informal feedback about the team member. Either way, look for ways to provide constructive feedback that can help the team member improve performance. Some topics include

- Training that will help build skills
- Goals for professional development
- Clarifying or modifying roles and responsibilities
- Resolving any workplace issues

Be careful about how you approach performance appraisals. Many policies and procedures and even union constraints control how you communicate with someone about his job performance.

Resolving conflict

Conflict is a natural event on projects. Many stakeholders have differing needs that can lead to conflict. If you add tight time frames and the pressure of working on a critical project, tempers can flare.

Conflict management on the PMP exam

There are quite a few standards from the Code of Ethics and Professional Conduct that can be referenced on the exam when discussing conflict. All the standards are covered in Book IX, Chapter 2, but here is a list of topics that refer specifically to conflict:

- We listen to others' points of view, seeking to understand them.
- We approach directly those persons with whom we have a conflict or disagreement.
- We conduct ourselves in a professional manner, even when it is not reciprocated.
- We do not act in an abusive manner toward others.

Many people shy away from conflict. However, when handled appropriately, conflict can be constructive. You can actually reach a better understanding of the project and find better ways of performing work. The key is involving the team in problem-solving techniques. Three behaviors will help the team stay focused on resolution instead of escalation:

- **Keep the conversation open.** Make sure to foster open communication. Team members need to state their positions and why they feel that way. Withholding information is counterproductive.
- **Focus on the issues.** To keep things constructive, people need to focus on the facts surrounding the conflict. Blame, conjecture, and assumptions are contrary to good problem-solving. Don't let people focus on personalities or "he said, she said" type of behavior.
- **Focus on the present.** Sometimes people bring baggage with them. Treat each conflict and situation separately. Resolving a conflict is not the time to rehash past problems.

Causes of conflict

With so much uncertainty on projects, there is ample opportunity for conflict. In reality, though, you can group most conflicts into the following seven categories, which I list by frequency of occurrence.

1. Schedule
2. Priorities between the objectives
3. Scarce resources
4. Technical approach
5. Administrative procedures
6. Cost
7. Personality

Sometimes personality is the main problem, but if you look deeper, you will see the underlying cause is usually one of the other six issues, and the personality issues just exacerbate the problem.

Managing conflict

For the exam, you will need to know the following six approaches to resolve conflict, as shown in Table 2-5. The Approach column has the name or label you will see on the exam. The Description column is a brief definition. The Situation column describes when the approach is most useful.

Some conflict management approaches have multiple labels, so be prepared to respond to either label on the exam.

Table 2-5 Conflict Management Styles

Approach	*Description*	*Situation*
Confronting/ Problem-solving	Confronting the conflict together as a problem to be solved	When you have confidence in the other party's ability to problem-solve When the relationship is important When you need a win-win solution
Collaborating	Win-win through collaborating and meeting to resolve issues	When there is time and trust When the objective is to learn When you want to incorporate multiple views When there is time to come to consensus
Compromising	Looking for some degree of satisfaction for both parties	When there is a willingness to give and take When both parties need to win When you can't win When an equal relationship exists between the parties in conflict When the stakes are moderate To avoid a fight
Smoothing/ Accommodating	Emphasizing areas of agreement and de-emphasizing areas of conflict	To reach an overarching goal To maintain harmony When any solution will be adequate When you will lose anyway To create goodwill
Forcing	Win-lose; imposing the resolution	When you are right In a do-or-die situation When the stakes are high To gain power If the relationship is not important When time is of the essence
Withdrawal/ Avoiding	Retreating from the situation; having a cooling-off period	When you can't win When the stakes are low To preserve neutrality or reputation If the problem will go away on its own

In general, the best approaches are the collaborating and confronting/problem-solving. Forcing is usually considered the least desirable approach. Confronting doesn't mean being confrontational: Rather, it means confronting the problem rather than avoiding it.

Decisions and problem-solving

One of the more important roles of the project manager is making decisions and solving problems. I have seen many situations where the project manager's inability to solve a problem or unwillingness to make a decision has negative impacts on the project. Look at some of the methods used to make decisions and solve problems and the factors that influence methods, and then take a look at a model you can use when managing your projects.

The Code of Ethics and Professional Conduct states that as project managers, we need to demonstrate transparency in our decision-making process.

Styles and influences

You will notice that decision-making and problem-solving styles are similar to conflict-resolution styles:

- **Command:** Used when time is of the essence. This is similar to a forcing conflict-management style and used in the same types of situations.
- **Consultation:** Used when you need input and information to make an informed decision. One person is still making the decision, but she seeks input prior to making the decision.
- **Consensus:** Used when you need buy-in from the people involved. In some cases, the team will agree to a majority or plurality voting block to come to a decision.
- **Random:** Like a coin toss. It is used when any solution is fine.

The style you use will depend upon the factors involved:

- **Time constraints:** If time is of the essence, you might need to use a command or random method. Consultation and consensus take more time.
- **Trust:** If you trust the people involved in making the decision, or if you need to build trust, you should use a consultation or consensus model.
- **Quality:** Consensus decisions tend to lead to better decisions. Random decisions are least likely to lead to a good decision.
- **Acceptance:** If you need to have acceptance, you are best served by using a consensus style. You might be able to use a consultative style and still gain acceptance.

Problem-solving model

You can use the following model (also shown in Figure 2-5) for either solving a problem or making a decision.

1. **Define the problem.** Clearly define the problem or decision. Many times, groups of people are unable to solve a problem because they aren't clear what they are trying to solve, or they're solving different problems from one another. You should be able to clearly articulate the problem or decision in a few concise sentences.
2. **Define solution criteria.** Define the important factors in reaching a decision. Is time the driver? Is technical performance the more important element? You might want to set up a weighted scoring mechanism similar to the one in Book V, Chapter 2, for procuring project scope.
3. **Brainstorm options.** You and your team should consider various options as well as the implications and risk associated with each.
4. **Choose an option.** Define the pros and cons of each option and apply the decision-making criteria to your alternatives. This should give you a decision.
5. **Evaluate the result.** You can evaluate the effectiveness of your decision-making and problem-solving process at the end of the process. Several weeks later, you might want to reconvene and determine whether the decision or problem resolution was effective.

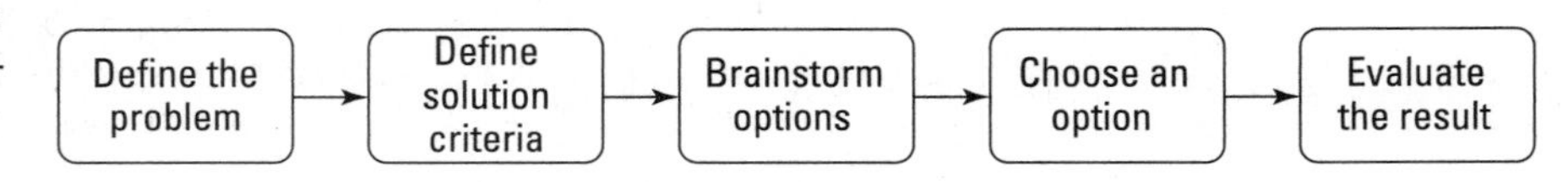

Figure 2-5: A problem-solving model.

Influence

Influence is the ability to compel people to behave or think in a certain way. Because project managers often don't have a lot of power or authority, they often need to use their influence. You can influence stakeholders by your knowledge, charisma, trust, or reputation.

- **Knowledge:** In many instances, project managers have significant knowledge about the project and the details involved in the project. That knowledge can influence stakeholders to follow your lead.
- **Charisma:** Sometimes, people follow a person because of her charm, energy, or effect on others.

✦ **Trust:** When stakeholders don't have all the facts but they trust you based on experience, they might go along with what you want.

✦ **Reputation:** You've heard the notion, "His reputation precedes him." Sometimes having a good reputation is enough to influence people.

As a project manager, you have an ethical duty to influence only with integrity — not for personal gain! The Code of Ethics and Professional Conduct (see Book IX, Chapter 2, for more) specifically states, "We must make decisions and take actions based on the best interests of society, public safety, and the environment."

Power

Closely related to influence is the concept of power. *Power* is the ability to do or accomplish something. Project managers have different types of power depending on the organizational structure, the project, and the project manager. Table 2-6 shows the types of power and a description of each.

Table 2-6 Types of Power

Power Type	*Description*
Formal/ Position	Based on your role as a project manager. It is defined in the project charter and the organizational chart. This is also called *legitimate power.*
Expert	Based on what you know. Subject matter experts and team members have expert power for their portion of the project. There may be people who outrank them in position power, but these people may have a greater influence on an outcome because of their expertise.
Reward	The ability to give people something they desire. This can be a raise, good review, or good assignment.
Penalty	The ability to take away or withhold something people want. This can include not giving a bonus or not giving a recommendation to someone.
Referent	There are two types of referent power. One type is personality- and charisma-based. The other is based on whom you know, or whom you are associated with: *affiliation.*

Here are examples of each type of power:

✦ **Position power:** Because you are the project manager, you have the position power defined in the project charter to resolve team conflicts, determine the project organizational structure, and define the change control system for the project.

✦ **Expert power:** The system engineer on your project has 25 years of experience. He knows how to set up a requirements-gathering process and a testing and verification process for the project you're managing. Therefore, you allow him to make those technical decisions.

✦ **Reward/penalty power:** The resource manager assigns resources to your team. She has the reward power to give you really good resources or the penalty power to assign unproven or problematic resources.

✦ **Referent power:** The two types of referent power are

- *Personality:* Your lead scheduler is a really funny person, always smiling and with something nice to say to everyone. People want to be around him and usually follow what he has to say because they like his personality. This is a type of charismatic referent power.
- *Affiliation:* The administrative assistant on your project is married to the Chief Operating Officer. Because you don't want her to say anything bad about you to her husband, you're always polite. She has power based on affiliation.

At different times in the project, you're likely to use different types of power, and you're likely to be affected by different types of power. Like influence, you should always use your power for the good of the project and the good of the organization.

The Code of Ethics and Professional Conduct states that as project managers, we do not exercise the power of our expertise or position to influence the decisions or actions of others in order to benefit personally at their expense.

Management styles

There are many different styles of leading and managing. Throughout the project, you will use many — if not all — the styles. It really depends on the team members, the team experience, the organization's culture, and your own skill.

There are a lot of terms used to convey specific meanings. If you aren't familiar with the terms and how they are used, you will have a difficult time with this part of the exam. After you know the vocabulary, it's fairly easy to do well.

- **Analytical:** Based on technical knowledge of a situation. Finding facts and making decisions based on reasoning.
- **Autocratic:** Top-down style where the leader makes the decisions, and everyone else follows.
- **Bureaucratic:** Procedure and process driven. Management is based on following the rules and guidelines.
- **Charismatic:** Management based on an influential personality.
- **Coaching:** Helping others to achieve their outcomes.
- **Consensus:** Getting everyone's input and having the group come up with the decision or solution.
- **Consultative:** Getting everyone's input. This can mean that the project manager does what the team wants, or it can mean that the project manager gets everyone's input before making the decision (consultative-autocratic).
- **Delegating:** The project manager working with the team to identify the work that needs to be done and then delegating the work to team members.
- **Democratic:** Also known as *participatory management.* The team comes up with the approach and owns the outcome.
- **Directive:** Similar to an autocratic style. The manager makes the decisions and tells the team what to do.
- **Driving:** Similar to directive but with more of an urgent edge. The edge may be based on time constraints or a competitive nature.
- **Facilitating:** Working with the group to lead its members to develop a decision or resolution.
- **Influencing:** Using team building and teamwork to encourage the team to achieve the results.
- ***Laissez-faire:*** Hands-off management. The leader is available as needed but allows the team to manage itself.
- **Supportive:** Providing assistance as needed to achieve the project objectives. More hands-on than *laissez-faire.*

Manage Project Team: Outputs

The outcome of managing the team is mostly documentation updates. These include

- Skill sets for individual team members (an enterprise environmental factor [EEF] as described in Book I, Chapter 2)
- Input to team member performance appraisals (an organizational process asset update [OPA] as described in Book I, Chapter 3)
- Project management plan components, such as the human resource plan

- Change requests for staffing
- Project documents, such as issue logs

Issue. A point or matter in question or in dispute, or a point or matter that is not settled and is under discussion or over. There are opposing views or disagreements.

Issue log. A project document used to document and monitor elements under discussion or in dispute between project stakeholders.

An issue log is a good tool to use to track and manage issues. Common fields in an issue log include

- Issue ID
- Category
- Issue
- Impact on objectives
- Urgency
- Responsible party
- Actions
- Status
- Due date
- Comments

Key Terms

This chapter holds a whole lot of terms, not all of which are in the glossary. Still, you need to know them to do well on the exam.

- Acquire Project Team
- Develop Project Team
- Manage Project Team
- Forming
- Storming
- Norming
- Performing
- Adjourning

- Theory X
- Theory Y
- Hygiene factors
- Motivating factors
- Hierarchy of Needs
- Theory of Needs
- Expectancy Theory
- Confronting/problem-solving
- Collaborating
- Compromising
- Smoothing/accommodating
- Forcing
- Withdrawal/avoiding
- Command
- Consultation
- Consensus
- Random
- Formal/position power
- Expert power
- Reward power
- Penalty power
- Referent power
- Analytical
- Autocratic
- Bureaucratic
- Charismatic
- Coaching
- Consensus
- Consultative
- Delegating
- Democratic
- Directive

- Driving
- Facilitating
- Influencing
- *Laissez-faire*
- Supportive
- Issue

Chapter Summary

If you've been studying the technical side of project management and the project management plan components, much of what is in this chapter will be new to you. However, with some studying, I am sure you will master it!

- Some of your resources will be preassigned, and you will have to negotiate for others. Some of your resources might be virtual, working from home, or in distant locations.
- Applying leadership when developing your team entails communicating your vision of the project, developing trust with the team, and communicating appropriately.
- Team building should be done early and often. The five stages to team development are forming, storming, norming, performing, and adjourning.
- You need to be familiar with several motivational theories for the exam:
  - Theory X and Y
  - Hygiene and Motivation
  - Hierarchy of Needs
  - Theory of Needs
  - Expectancy Theory
- Rewards and recognition should be based on good behavior and should be something that is important to the team member.
- Assessing the team means analyzing how the members are performing as a group. Assessing a team member means looking at her technical and interpersonal skills.
- You will encounter conflict on your project. The six techniques for resolving conflict are
  - Confronting/problem-solving
  - Collaborating

- Compromising
- Smoothing/accommodating
- Forcing
- Withdrawal/avoiding

✦ Decision-making and problem-solving styles include

- Command
- Consultation
- Consensus
- Random

✦ The types of power are

- Formal/position
- Expert
- Reward
- Penalty
- Referent

✦ Many different management styles are at your disposal, depending upon the situation and the experience of the team.

Prep Test

1 **All the following are benefits of virtual teams except**

A ❍ Less travel expenses
B ❍ Utilizing employees who work from home
C ❍ Increased communication
D ❍ Using skill sets from employees inside and outside the organization

2 **Which interpersonal skill are you most likely to use while developing the project team?**

A ❍ Motivating
B ❍ Political savvy
C ❍ Negotiating
D ❍ Problem-solving

3 **Jan and Becky are arguing about who should have the final sign-off on a component of a deliverable. What stage of team development are they likely in?**

A ❍ Forming
B ❍ Storming
C ❍ Norming
D ❍ Performing

4 **Your project team has worked together for the past 14 months. The team has set up good processes, has a really nice synergy, and can accomplish its work more efficiently than most other teams. What stage of team development is the team in?**

A ❍ Forming
B ❍ Storming
C ❍ Norming
D ❍ Performing

5 **"The average worker is not ambitious and desires security above everything else." This statement is reflective of which of the following motivational theories:**

A ❍ Theory X
B ❍ Expectancy Theory
C ❍ Hygiene factors
D ❍ Theory of Needs

6 **Which of the following is a hygiene factor?**

- **A** ❍ Achievement
- **B** ❍ Recognition
- **C** ❍ Security
- **D** ❍ Job challenge

7 **People who like to organize, motivate, and lead others have a need for**

- **A** ❍ Power
- **B** ❍ Achievement
- **C** ❍ Security
- **D** ❍ Affiliation

8 **Which of the following creates the most conflict on projects?**

- **A** ❍ Scarce resources
- **B** ❍ Technical approach
- **C** ❍ Cost constraints
- **D** ❍ Schedule issues

9 **The most effective method of conflict resolution is**

- **A** ❍ Compromising
- **B** ❍ Confronting
- **C** ❍ Avoiding
- **D** ❍ Accommodating

10 **If you need to maintain harmony in the relationship and build goodwill, you should use which method of conflict resolution?**

- **A** ❍ Compromising
- **B** ❍ Confronting
- **C** ❍ Avoiding
- **D** ❍ Accommodating

11 **You have to make a decision about how to work with a stakeholder on your project. You call your project management team together and discuss the situation. You want to make sure everyone is in agreement with the decision. Ultimately, the team will vote and make the final decision. What decision-making style are you using?**

- **A** ❍ Command
- **B** ❍ Consultation
- **C** ❍ Consensus
- **D** ❍ Random

12 **Your team is discussing how to roll out an upgrade to some new software. It is a collegial discussion. Ultimately, you decide to go with the approach that George suggested. He has done this type of roll-out several times and has more experience than anyone else on the team. Which type of power and influence does George have?**

A ❍ Expert
B ❍ Position
C ❍ Referent
D ❍ Reward

13 **You are talking with Marjorie about her role on the team. You know she has experience and that she is looking to move up in the organization. You tell her that if she does a good job over the next couple of months, you will make sure she gets some cross-training and more responsibility on the project. In addition, you will be happy to put in a good word with her boss. Which type of power are you demonstrating?**

A ❍ Expert
B ❍ Reward
C ❍ Penalty
D ❍ Referent

14 **Your team has worked together before, and the members are all competent in their roles. As the project manager, you guide them in the process and assist them in coming to decisions, but you are not heavy-handed. They do most of the decision making themselves. Which type of management style are you using?**

A ❍ Consensus
B ❍ *Laissez-faire*
C ❍ Facilitating
D ❍ Charismatic

Answers

1. **C.** Increased communication. Increased communication is a requirement for virtual teams, not necessarily a benefit. *Look at "Acquire Project Team: Tools, Techniques, and Outputs."*
2. **A.** Motivating. You are most likely to use motivating. The other options are interpersonal skills, but they're not as likely to be used while developing the project team. *Check out "Interpersonal skills."*
3. **B.** Storming. Jan and Becky are storming. They are experiencing conflict as they figure out how to work together. *Review "Interpersonal skills."*
4. **D.** Performing. Your team is performing. The members have developed a nice synergy working together. *Go to the "Interpersonal skills" section.*
5. **A.** Theory X. Theory X states that workers are not ambitious and need to be closely managed. *Review "Interpersonal skills."*
6. **C.** Security. Security is a hygiene factor. All the other answer choices are motivating factors. *Look at "Interpersonal skills."*
7. **A.** Power. People who are motivated by power enjoy leading and organizing others. *See "Interpersonal skills."*
8. **D.** Schedule issues. Schedule issues create the most conflict on projects. *Look into "Resolving conflict."*
9. **B.** Confronting. Confronting and collaborating are the most effective means of dealing with conflict. *Go over "Resolving conflict."*
10. **D.** Accommodating. Accommodating is the best way to maintain the relationship. *Review "Resolving conflict."*
11. **C.** Consensus. By leaving the decision to the team, you are employing a consensus decision-making style. *Take a look at the section on "Decisions and problem-solving."*
12. **A.** Expert. George has expert power because of his knowledge and experience. *Go over the "Power" section.*
13. **B.** Reward. Because you can give Marjorie what she wants, you have reward power. *Check out the information in the section "Power."*
14. **C.** Facilitating. Guiding and assisting is a facilitating management style. *Go over the section "Management styles."*

Chapter 3: Getting the Word Out to Stakeholders and Contractors

Exam Objectives

- **Ensure a common understanding by setting expectations in accordance with the project plan to align the stakeholder and team members.**
- **Minimize the impact of issues with the project schedule, cost, and resources by using the issue register to manage issues and assign corrective actions.**
- **Implement the procurement of project resources in accordance with the procurement plan.**

When I discuss communications in the planning chapter (Book IV, Chapter 4), I state that 90 percent of the project manager's job is communication. This chapter looks at the process of managing communications according to the project management plan.

Of special interest when communicating is managing stakeholder engagement. This can include negotiating, listening, addressing issues, and influencing. You significantly increase the likelihood of project success by actively managing stakeholders, their expectations, and their engagement level.

Both processes rely heavily on effective communication skills. Therefore, in this chapter, I talk about how to communicate effectively as well as what blocks effective communication. Because a large part of your communication takes place in meetings, I also spend some time discussing how to run effective meetings.

Another key part of getting the word out and engaging stakeholders is making sure that potential sellers have a chance to bid. I talk about the two parts of conducting procurements: seeking proposals and awarding a contract.

Quick Assessment

1 ______ ______ is used to distribute project performance and status information.

2 Which component of the project management plan is used to provide guidance for distributing performance reports?

3 Who is responsible for stakeholder engagement management?

4 Building trust, resolving conflict, and active listening are examples of ______ ______ that are used to manage stakeholder engagement.

5 Facilitating consensus, negotiation, and influencing people are examples of ______ ______ that are used to manage stakeholder engagement.

6 A(n) ______ ______ is used to make sure that all sellers have the same information.

7 (True/False). You can use an RFI to gather information before sending out an RFP.

8 (True/False). You can negotiate contract terms and conditions.

9 (True/False). To improve communication, you should use simple language and redundancy.

10 A(n) ______ is a point or matter in question or in dispute.

Answers

1 Performance reporting. Performance reporting is used to distribute project performance and status information. *Read more about this in "Performance reporting."*

2 Communications management plan. The communications management plan provides guidance on who needs information, when they need it, and how it will be provided. *You can read more about the plan in "Manage Communications."*

3 Project manager. The project manager is responsible for engaging and managing stakeholders. *Take a look at how project managers manage engagement in the section "Manage Stakeholder Engagement."*

4 Interpersonal skills. In addition to these interpersonal skills, you will also use management skills and communication methods. *Look at "Manage Stakeholder Engagement: Tools and Techniques" to learn more about this topic.*

5 Management skills. Management skills are important in providing information, managing meetings, and maintaining good relationships with stakeholders. *They are discussed more in the section on "Manage Stakeholder Engagement: Tools and Techniques."*

6 Bidder conference. A bidder conference is used to ensure a fair process by making sure all sellers have the same information and to also answer questions that bidders may have. *You can read more on this in the "Bidder conferences" section.*

7 True. An RFI can be used to understand the abilities of the potential bidders before releasing an RFP. *This is discussed in the sidebar "Doing the two-step."*

8 True. You can negotiate almost anything in an agreement, including place of delivery, payment schedules, and terms and conditions. *Negotiating is discussed in the "Negotiating the contract" section.*

9 True. Simple language and redundancy increase the likelihood that your message will be understood correctly. *Read more in "Manage Communications: Tools and Techniques."*

10 Issue. An issue can also be a matter that is not settled and is under discussion. *I talk about issues in "Manage Stakeholder Engagement: Outputs."*

Manage Communications

Obviously, you're communicating throughout the entire project lifecycle. The communications management plan is started early in the project (see Book IV, Chapter 4 for more information), and after that, it provides guidance on what information should be communicated, to whom, how often, when, and in what format. Managing communications is concerned not only with following the communication management plan but also with responding to stakeholder requests for additional information or clarification of information.

Manage Communication. Creating, collecting, distributing, storing, retrieving, and the ultimate disposition of project information in accordance to the communications management plan.

In Book IV, Chapter 4, I cover the basic sender-receiver model that will be employed throughout the project. Keep that model in mind as I cover information on managing communication.

The inputs to the process are (of course) the communications management plan (part of the project management plan), work performance reports, influencing factors such as organizational culture or regulatory requirements, and any organizational process assets that can help you, such as information from past projects and communication templates.

Manage Communications: Tools and Techniques

In Book IV, Chapter 4, I talk about formal and informal communication and written and verbal communication. Here is where that is applied. Table 3-1 is a refresher. It includes examples of when each type of communication can be applied.

Table 3-1 Types of Communication

Method	*When to Use*	*Examples*
Formal written	Complex issues, virtual teams, political situations	Reports, presentations, contracts, white papers
Formal verbal	Corrective action, negotiations, critical issues	Presentations, team meetings
Informal written	Day-to-day management, routine maintenance	Memos, notes, e-mails
Informal verbal	Routine management, building relationships, gathering information	Conversations, management by walking around, brainstorming

Communication technology and methods

Following is a list of communication technology and methods. When selecting communications technology, remember that not everyone has the same degree of technological knowledge or equipment. For example, a contractor to develop media presentations may work with Apple machines, but the buyer may work with PCs. Baby Boomers may not be familiar with social media, whereas Generation Y users are usually very comfortable with all kinds of electronic communication.

When choosing a communication method, keep in mind the guidelines given in Table 3-1.

- Meetings
- Presentations
- One-on-one conversations
- Memos
- E-mails
- Web pages
- Videoconferencing
- Teleconferencing
- Web conferencing
- Intranets
- Filing systems
- Portals
- Collaborative work tools
- Text messaging

The most effective project managers are those who are good communicators. Project managers who communicate effectively to team members, senior management, functional managers, and any other stakeholders will have better outcomes than those who don't.

When communicating with someone, remember these simple techniques to help make your communication effective:

- Seek feedback.
- Establish multiple communication channels.
- Use face-to-face communication when possible.

- Be aware of the receiver's body language and expressions.
- Communicate at the proper time.
- Reinforce words with actions.
- Use simple language.
- Use redundancy.

Information management systems

Creating, collecting, distributing, storing, and retrieving require some type of information management system. The larger and more complex the project, the more robust the information management system needs to be. Some aspects of the information management system will use hard-copy documents. I always keep a hard-copy project notebook where I store memos, meeting minutes, external communications, and information I need on a regular basis, such as the latest schedule.

Electronic communications management includes e-mail, web information, electronic reports, and so forth. Electronic communications tools include everything from web meeting tools, portals, scheduling software, collaboration tools, and other electronic interfaces, depending on the needs of the project.

Performance reporting

Performance reporting is a specific type of communication. Performance reporting entails collecting and analyzing information on the project baselines and the actual results and comparing the variances in order to communicate current and forecasted project status.

Figure 3-1 shows an example of a project performance report.

There are several cross-cutting skills that are relevant to the Manage Communications process:

- Oral and written communication techniques, channels, and applications
- Presentation tools and techniques
- Information management tools, techniques, and methods
- Targeting communications to intended audiences

PROJECT PERFORMANCE REPORT

Project Title:________________ Date Prepared: ________________

Project Manager:________________ Sponsor: ________________

Accomplishments for This Reporting Period:

1. *List all work packages or other accomplishments scheduled for completion this period.*
2.
3.
4.
5.

Accomplishments Planned but Not Completed This Reporting Period:

1. *List all work packages or other accomplishments scheduled for this period but not completed.*
2.
3.
4.

Root Cause of Variances:

For any work that was not accomplished as scheduled, identify cause of the variance.

Impact to Upcoming Milestones or Project Due Date:

For any work that was not accomplished as scheduled, identify any impact to upcoming milestones or overall project schedule. Identify any work currently behind on the critical path or if the critical path has changed based on the variance.

Planned Corrective or Preventive Action:

Identify any actions needed to make up schedule variances or prevent future schedule variances.

Funds Spent This Reporting Period:

Record funds spent this period.

Root Cause of Variances:

For any expenditures that were over or under plan, identify cause of the variance. Include information on labor variance versus material variances.

Page 1 of 2

Figure 3-1: Project Performance Report.

PROJECT PERFORMANCE REPORT

Impact to Overall Budget or Contingency Funds:

For cost variances, indicate impact to the overall project budget or whether contingency funds must be expended.

Planned Corrective or Preventive Action:

Identify any actions needed to recover cost variances or prevent future schedule variances.

Accomplishments Planned for Next Reporting Period:

1. *List all work packages or accomplishments scheduled for completion next period.*
2.
3.
4.

Costs Planned for Next Reporting Period:

Identify funds planned to be expended next period.

New Risks Identified:

Identify any new risks that have arisen this period. These risks should be recorded in the Risk Register as well.

Issues:

Identify any new issues that have arisen this period. These issues should be recorded in the Issue Log as well.

Comments:

Record any comments that add relevance to the report.

Manage Communications: Outputs

As a result of all the meetings and communicating, you will have updated project information, such as

- **Stakeholder communications:** Information communicated to stakeholders, such as issue resolution and approved changes, as well as feedback from stakeholders, such as product-related queries and process information
- **Project reports:** Status reports, issue logs, lessons learned, and closure reports
- **Project presentations:** Information from presentations made to project stakeholders
- **Project management plan updates:** Updates to any project baseline
- **Project document updates:** Schedule updates, issue log updates
- **Project records:** Correspondence, memos, and minutes
- **Lessons learned:** Causes of issues and the reasons for choosing corrective actions

Manage Stakeholder Engagement

The larger your project, the more time you will spend managing stakeholders and their engagement level, and the more critical this process is to the success of your project. Imagine a project with city and county government, the public, the department of transportation, police, and various and sundry other stakeholders. Do you think that you're going to spend your time looking at a schedule? No. You're going to spend your time juggling the various needs and interests of all these very influential stakeholders!

The cross-cutting skill of relationship management is particularly relevant to the Manage Stakeholder Expectations process.

To maintain satisfied stakeholders, you want to do three things:

- **Engage stakeholders.** Talk to your stakeholders throughout the project to ensure a common understanding of the project scope, benefits, and time and cost estimates. You will want to ensure their continued support of the project.
- **Actively manage stakeholder expectations.** You can do a lot of this by seeking stakeholder input while you're planning the project. The project management plan and the project documents are written records that

communicate all aspects of the project. These are an effective method of managing expectations. I discuss the project management plan and the project documents in Book V, Chapter 3.

- **Address stakeholder concerns before they escalate.** You might need to have individual conversations with some stakeholders to ensure that they understand situations, such as why the scope they wanted is not part of the project, why they can't have what they want in the time frame they want it, or why you require their staff for specific periods of time. By addressing concerns before they become issues, you will save a lot of time and hassle.
- **Clarify and resolve issues in a timely manner.** If a stakeholder has a concern that rises to the level of an issue that you need to document and address, do so as soon as is reasonable. Sometimes, this results in a change request to alter the schedule, the scope, or the resources. Change requests are discussed in Chapter 1 of this minibook.

Manage Stakeholder Engagement. Communicating and working with stakeholders to meet their needs/expectations, addressing issues as they occur, and fostering appropriate engagement in project activities throughout the project lifecycle.

Managing stakeholders can get very political. Make sure you know whom you are talking to and what their agenda is!

Manage Stakeholder Engagement: Inputs

During project planning, you create a stakeholder management plan that you will use and update throughout the project. Because your main method of managing expectations is communication, you will use your communication management plan as well. (See Book IV, Chapter 4 for more.)

It would be nice to assume that everything will go smoothly and as planned, but because this never happens on projects, you also need a change log. Many change logs are based on templates or information from past projects — in other words, organizational process assets (OPAs).

Manage Stakeholder Engagement: Tools and Techniques

The communication skills I discuss earlier in this chapter are applied when managing your stakeholders. As you manage stakeholders, pay particular attention to their needs, promoting open communication and building trust.

You can build trust by employing active listening. For more on active listening, see Book VI, Chapter 2. The nature of projects is that they have changes along the way. Some stakeholders will be resistant to the changes, but you have to help them overcome their resistance. You will also use conflict resolution skills during this process. For a refresher on conflict resolution, see Book VI, Chapter 2.

Some interactions with stakeholders will be in one-on-one meetings. Other times, you will be speaking to a large group and making presentations. Still others will require you to communicate via report or other written methods. All these situations are considered management skills.

Manage Stakeholder Engagement: Outputs

An issue log is a key output that documents an issue and the potential impact. It can include an indicator of the urgency of the situation and the person accountable for resolving the issue as well.

Issue. A point or matter in question or in dispute, or a point or matter that is not settled and is under discussion or over which there are opposing views or disagreements.

Working through issues

Working through issues requires communication skills, interpersonal skills, and management skills. I discuss these skills in various places throughout this book, so to make the information more meaningful, I am going to use my running example of the childcare center to demonstrate each of the skills. I use the parents, the human resources department, and vendors as the primary stakeholders.

For purposes of this example, I assume that the stakeholder register has the following information. For a refresher on the stakeholder register, go to Book II, Chapter 3.

Name	***Role***	***Power***	***Support***	***Function***
Parents	Supporter	M	H	End User
HR department	Supporter	H	H	Staffing
Project vendors	Supporter	M	H	Build-out

M = medium. H = high.

Assume the communications management plan has the following information:

Audience	***Message***	***Method***	***Frequency***	***Sender***
Parents	Send milestone status information	Newsletter	Monthly	PM
	Send changes to scope or schedule	Newsletter	Monthly	PM
HR department	Receive HR progress reports	Progress report forms	Bi-monthly	HR team lead
	Send project status reports	Status reports	Monthly	PM
	Send changes	Change logs	As needed	PM
Project vendors	Receive vendor progress reports	Progress report forms	Weekly	Vendor
	Send plans	Blueprints	As approved	Facilities
	Send changes	Change logs	As needed	PM

Assume that it's November 1. The childcare center is due to open on January 1. You have the following situations documented in your issue log:

Issue	***Impact***
The contractor has discovered that the sprinkler system in the childcare center space is not up to the new codes that went into effect this year. The water pressure is not high enough, and the flow rate is too low. He has submitted a change request to bring the system up to code.	The cost will be $15,000. He will bring in additional workers to complete the work so there will not be a schedule slip.
The staffing for the executive director and the childcare staff is running behind. By this time, they should have had 4 resumes for the executive director and 60 for the childcare staff. They only have 2 for the executive director and 50 for the childcare staff. In addition, they should have had 15 signed contracts for childcare staff, but they have only 10.	This could lead to a schedule slip if there isn't enough staff to open the center.

Issue resolution for the childcare center

To resolve these issues, you'll need to meet with various stakeholders and employ communication, interpersonal, and management skills.

Contractor issue resolution

To deal with issues with the contractor, you convene a meeting with the contractor, the head of facilities, the maintenance supervisor, and yourself to discuss options. The maintenance supervisor says that his staff can handle the sprinkler issue, thereby saving the $15,000 for the change order. You all review the remaining scheduled work to find a way to resequence the work so that the maintenance staff isn't working in the same location as the contractor's staff. By looking at a detailed network diagram and resource histogram, you figure out that by doing some of the work after hours, some on weekends, and rearranging the sequence of the contractor's work, you can have the sprinkler system up to code within ten days and not lose any time on the schedule. This scenario demonstrates collaboration, problem-solving, and negotiation.

Staffing issue resolution

Your next meeting is with the team leader for the human resources department. You ask her why the staffing schedule is slipping. She states that in order to staff the center with licensed childcare workers, you have to pay them more. It is a safety and quality risk to hire staff that aren't licensed, even if they have experience and have met the Department of Justice requirements.

You both agree that if you do hire only licensed staff, then the operating costs will be higher, and per Morgan Cuthbert (sponsor), the higher cost will have to be passed on to the parents. The increased cost works out to about $15 per week, per child. You know that this increased fee will result in some unhappy parents and possibly lower enrollments.

You and the team leader discuss options as alternatives to the higher cost, such as reducing the number of hours that the childcare center is open and changing the ratio of childcare staff to children. Because the staff licensing issue represents a change to the project scope, the sponsor (Morgan Cuthbert) has asked you to meet with the parents to discuss impact.

You ask the team leader to accompany you to the meeting with the parents so she can help them understand the issues and participate in the issue resolution. She agrees. This scenario demonstrates problem-solving and active listening.

Talking to the parents

Although the communication plan states that scope changes would be communicated via newsletter, you believe you need to seek the parents' input, and so you schedule a meeting in the company auditorium. You work with the human resources team leader to put together a slide presentation that outlines the issues and options.

The day of the meeting, about 45 parents show up. After welcoming them to the meeting, you begin your presentation. None of the parents are happy with the proposed price increase of $15 per week. The audience is split about needing all licensed staff members. You switch your role from presenter to facilitator and keep the discussion focused and resolution oriented.

At the end of the meeting, the parents agree to the following:

- They will accept a staff-per-child ratio of 1:7 instead of 1:6.
- All caregivers will be licensed.
- The center opening time of 6 a.m. will be changed to 6:30 a.m.

All these accommodations will allow the center to open with the original rates.

The group agrees to try this arrangement for three months. At that point, they will meet with the Executive Director and discuss whether they want to negotiate a different arrangement. As the parents walk out, some of them stop to shake your hand and thank you for facilitating the meeting. This scenario demonstrates overcoming resistance to change, presentation skills, public speaking, negotiating, and building trust.

The common outputs from the Manage Stakeholder Engagement process are updates to project documents and the project management plan, change requests, and updates to project records.

One of the exam objectives in the Monitoring and Controlling process group states that you use the issue register to manage issues and assign corrective action, which is why I have included it in this section, because Manage Stakeholder Engagement is an Executing process. Wherever you see this type of question, the important point is to document issues in an issue register (also known as an issues log), determine the appropriate action, and assign it to someone to follow up with the resolution.

Conduct Procurements

Conducting procurements is where you make sure your potential customers have an opportunity to bid in fairness. The three aspects to conducting procurements are

- Sending out the bid documents to qualified sellers
- Applying the source selection criteria to the bids
- Selecting a seller

These aspects overlap in places. In the following sections, I present each aspect separately.

Conduct Procurements. Obtaining seller responses, selecting a seller, and awarding a contract.

Conduct Procurements: Inputs

Your make-or-buy decisions as well as information from select project documents — such as the risk register that contains risk-related contract decisions — are a starting point for conducting procurements.

The procurement management plan provides information that guides the bid and award process. For the bid process, it identifies the various roles and responsibilities as well as the procurement documents that will be used. Roles and responsibilities can include

- Who manages the bidder conferences
- Who sits on the selection committee
- Who negotiates with sellers
- Who has authority to sign contracts

If you need, review the following types of procurement documents in Book V, Chapter 2:

- Request for Quote (RFQ)
- Invitation for Bid (IFB)
- Request for Information (RFI)
- Request for Proposal (RFP)

The procurement statement of work (defined in Book V, Chapter 2) describes the goods or services required in enough detail so that prospective bidders can decide whether to bid.

Many times, the contracting department or procurement department will have lists of qualified sellers or sellers who have worked with the organization. This information can cut down the time you spend looking for qualified sellers, and it can also steer you clear from sellers who performed poorly in the past.

There are some instances when you don't need to compete for a bid:

- **Sole source:** There is only one provider in the market. This may be because of high entry costs (such as a utility company) or because a certain company owns a patent.
- **Single source:** You decide you want to work with a particular contractor. You may have had a good relationship in the past, he may be familiar with your business, or you held a similar competition in the near term past. If the seller has specific, unique qualifications, you may choose him without competition as well.

Sole source. A condition that can exist when there is only one source for a given product, and the buyer is thus forced to procure from only that source.

Single source. A condition that occurs when there are multiple qualified sources for a given product, but the buyer or project elects to place an order from only one seller, thus waiving the opportunity to hold a competition.

—*Project Procurement Management. Quentin W. Fleming. FMC Press. 2003.*

After bidders respond to the procurement documents, you will apply the source selection criteria that you developed in the planning process to the seller proposals.

Conduct Procurements: Tools and Techniques

If the procurement department doesn't have a list of qualified sellers, you might need to do some research to find candidates to send the procurement documents to. An Internet search or advertising in trade publications are common methods of generating interest in the bid process.

By law, all government agencies, as well as county, state, and federal governments, are required to publicize bids as well as the evaluation criteria used to award the contract. You can sign up to be notified of pending government bid opportunities.

Bidder conferences

A bidder conference — also known as a vendor conference or contractor conference — is a meeting between the buyer and the prospective sellers to ensure that everyone bidding has all the information needed to submit proposals. Most times, bids are done in person at the seller's site, a hotel, or conference center, or the site where the work will take place. However, it is becoming more common to hold bidder conferences virtually by using conference calls or web meetings.

The Code of Ethics and Professional Conduct has two standards that are applicable to bidder conferences:

- We provide equal access to information to those who are authorized to have that information.
- We make opportunities equally available to qualified candidates.

Applying selection criteria

For awarding a contract, the procurement management plan has the selection criteria, the contract type, and bonding and insurance requirements. As I discuss in Book V, Chapter 2, the different types of contracts are

- Firm fixed price (FFP)
- Fixed price incentive fee (FPIF)
- Fixed price-economic price adjustment (FP-EPA)
- Cost plus fixed fee (CPFF)
- Cost plus incentive fee (CPIF)
- Cost plus award fee (CPAF)
- Time and materials (T&M)

After the seller proposals come in, you apply the source selection criteria developed in the planning process. For complex procurements, you might have a source selection board that goes through all the proposals and applies the criteria. The source selection board needs someone with the required technical expertise ("expert judgment" in PMP-speak) to read through the proposals and rate them from a technical perspective. Complex procurements may also use an independent estimate as a benchmark or a "should cost" estimate to evaluate proposals.

Conflicts of interest

The Code of Ethics and Professional Conduct (see Book IX, Chapter 2) has several standards concerning fairness that apply to awarding a contract. The intent behind these standards is to disclose conflicts of interest and make sure that procurements and contracting situations are conducted with integrity. The fairness standards in the Code include the following:

- We constantly reexamine our impartiality and objectivity, taking corrective action as appropriate.
- We proactively and fully disclose any real or potential conflicts of interest to the appropriate stakeholders.
- When we realize that we have a real or potential conflict of interest, we refrain from engaging in the decision-making process or otherwise attempting to influence outcomes, unless or until
  - We have made full disclosure to the affected stakeholders.
  - We have an approved mitigation plan.
  - We have obtained the consent of the stakeholders to proceed.

Negotiating the contract

After the field is narrowed to one seller or a few potential sellers, the negotiations begin. You can negotiate everything. Here is a partial list of some items you might want to negotiate:

- Price
- Award structure
- Schedule
- Place of delivery
- Terms and conditions
- Authority to make changes
- Technical solutions
- Proprietary rights
- Maintenance and support fees
- Payment schedule

The Code of Ethics and Professional Conduct states that as professionals, we negotiate in good faith and that we respect the property rights of others. In addition, the cross-cutting skill of negotiating is likely to be integrated into questions regarding contract negotiation on the exam.

After everything is agreed to, you can put together the contract.

Because a contract is a legal document, it often takes a significant amount of time to finalize. In the meantime, both parties want work to start. You can use a letter contract to start work until the contract is signed. A letter contract lays out the general agreement, but it specifies a time limit: usually, 30 days. The letter agreement states the work that will be done and outlines the payment structure for the time that the agreement is in place. This allows work to begin before the legal eagles are done dotting all the i's and crossing all the t's.

Before signing a contract you, or someone on your team with appropriate expertise, should review the potential vendor site to determine its readiness to perform the work. This can be called a "readiness review." Common items to review include

- ✦ Are the staff in place or available quickly to begin work?
- ✦ Is all the necessary equipment maintained and operational?
- ✦ Is there sufficient upfront funding to initiate operations?
- ✦ Are all needed procedures, training, and processes in place?
- ✦ Are a quality program, risk management process, and change control process in place?

Sometimes projects start late because the buyer assumes the items in the preceding list are in place and ready to go on Day 1, but the seller has those resources working on other jobs until the contract is signed.

Doing the two-step

It's not uncommon to have a two-step proposal process and a two-step award process. For Step 1 of the proposal process, the buyer may send out a Request for Information (RFI) to many potential sellers, asking questions about their business, their capacity, their capabilities, experience in the field, references, and the like. Based on the responses to the RFI, Step 2 entails sending the bid documents to a smaller pool of potential sellers.

For the two-step award process, the selection committee may set a cut-off score for proposals. The committee would rank all the proposals for Step 1, and only the proposals ranking higher than the cut score would move forward into negotiations.

Conduct Procurements: Outputs

After negotiations are finalized, the parties can sign an agreement. A simple purchase may be documented on a purchase order (PO) or a basic ordering agreement (BOA). More complex purchases will have contracts with multiple components and be quite complex and lengthy. The following are components that you could see in a contract:

- Statement of work (SOW)
- Schedule baseline
- Performance reporting
- Roles and responsibilities
- Cost, fee structure, and payment terms
- Product acceptance criteria
- Warranty, limitation of liability, and product support information
- Insurance and performance bond requirements
- Change request process
- Termination and alternative dispute resolution mechanisms

The legal term used to indicate a legal relationship is *privity.* If you sign a contract with a seller, you have *contract privity.* However, if the seller signs a contract with a subcontractor, you have no legal privity with the subcontractor.

Based on the contract, there may be changes and updates to other documentation, such as

- **Resource calendars:** You might have to add contractor resources and adjust the hours of inhouse resources.
- **Change requests:** Changes to the work, approach, and elements of the project management plan might require changes.
- **Project management plan updates:** The schedule baseline, cost baseline, scope baseline, staffing plan, and procurement management plan might require updates.
- **Project documents:** Requirements documentation, the stakeholder register and stakeholder management strategy, and the risk register might require updates.

Executing process group review

This minibook describes all the processes in the Executing process group. This information makes up 30 percent of the questions on the exam, or in other words, 60 questions. To do well on those 60 questions, you will need to know the tools, techniques, and outputs associated with the processes. You will also need to be proficient in the skills and knowledge associated with interpersonal skills. Many of the questions will integrate the information from the Code of Ethics and Professional Conduct. Expect to see questions that require knowledge and skills associated with the following:

For this topic	Turn to this section
✓ Creating project deliverables	Chapter 1, "Direct and Manage Project Work"
✓ Integrating scope, schedule, and cost	Chapter 1, "Direct and Manage Project Work"
✓ Decision-making	Chapter 1, "Direct and Manage Project Work: Tools and Techniques" Chapter 2, "Decisions and problem-solving"
✓ Applying quality standards	Chapter 1, "Perform Quality Assurance"
✓ Cultural diversity	Chapter 2, "Acquire Project Team"
✓ Resolving conflict	Chapter 2, "Manage Project Team"
✓ Active listening	Chapter 2, "Leadership"
✓ Motivating team members	Chapter 2, "Motivating"
✓ Negotiating	Chapter 2, "Acquire Project Team" Chapter 3, "Negotiating the contract"
✓ Managing and distributing information	Chapter 3, "Manage Communications"
✓ Presentations	Chapter 3, "Manage Communications"
✓ Solving problems	Chapter 2, "Decisions and problem-solving"
✓ Managing relationships and expectations	Chapter 3, "Manage Stakeholder Engagement"

Key Terms

Many of the communication, stakeholder, and procurement terms are introduced in Book IV, Chapter 4, and Book V, Chapters 2 and 3, where I talk about planning processes. In addition to all the terms in those chapters, you should also be familiar with the following terms.

- Issues
- Sole source
- Single source
- Privity
- Letter contract

Chapter Summary

Three separate processes are covered in this chapter: Manage Communications, Manage Stakeholder Engagement, and Conduct Procurements. Even though they are three separate processes, the concept of using communication to manage stakeholders (internal and external) is a common theme throughout each process.

- Managing Communications is about getting stakeholders the information they need. You follow the communications management plan and respond to unexpected requests for information.
- Managing stakeholder engagement is a critical component in project success. You need to use interpersonal and management skills.
- Proactively manage engagement and expectations to try and avoid situations escalating to the point of becoming an issue, but use an issue log to manage those situations that do end up as an issue.
- The two aspects to conducting procurements are sending bid documents to qualified sellers, and then applying the source selection criteria to the bids and selecting a seller.
- Sending bid documents entails identifying bidders and holding a bidder conference. Bidder conferences make sure that all bidders have the same information and sufficient information to respond to the bid documents.
- After the bids are submitted, you apply source selection criteria to determine the best candidate(s) to negotiate with. After negotiations are complete, you award and sign the contract.

Prep Test

1 **All the following are techniques that you can use to make your communication effective except**

A ❍ Seeking feedback
B ❍ Being aware of body language
C ❍ Using simple language
D ❍ Using acronyms and technical terms

2 **Which of the following is not a communication blocker?**

A ❍ Redundancy
B ❍ Stereotyping
C ❍ Selective listening
D ❍ Ignoring cultural differences

3 **Which statement is true about managing stakeholders' engagement?**

A ❍ They are open to change, so as long as you keep them informed, you should be fine.
B ❍ You need to spend time only with the ones who aren't supporters of your project.
C ❍ You should spend time working through concerns before they become issues.
D ❍ Face-to-face is the only reliable way to manage expectations.

4 **You've just been informed of a regulatory change that will impact your project. To whom should you communicate this?**

A ❍ The sponsor
B ❍ The project management team
C ❍ The people identified in the communications management plan
D ❍ Any stakeholders listed in the register

5 **All the following are important actions to take to keep your stakeholders satisfied except**

A ❍ Clarify and resolve issues in a timely manner.
B ❍ Address stakeholder concerns before they escalate.
C ❍ Actively manage stakeholder expectations.
D ❍ Make sure they receive team member status reports weekly.

6 **Which information in the procurement management plan is used to elicit bids from vendors?**

A ❍ Types of bid documents
B ❍ Types of contracts
C ❍ Source selection criteria
D ❍ Bonding requirements

7 **Which is not a method used to identify potential sellers?**

A ❍ Internet search
B ❍ Bidder conference
C ❍ Advertising
D ❍ Prequalified seller lists

8 **A two-step award process is**

A ❍ Sending an RFI for information and an RFQ for a quote at the same time
B ❍ First determining the seller pool and then finalizing the bid documents
C ❍ Used to narrow the field of proposals to those you will negotiate with
D ❍ Used when you want the contractor to start work but the contract isn't finalized

9 **You and the seller have agreed to terms. The selection and negotiation process was long and arduous, and you're both ready to go to work. Because the contract is lengthy and complex, the legal departments have been going back and forth. To start work before the legal department is done, you should create a**

A ❍ Basic ordering agreement
B ❍ Letter contract
C ❍ Purchase order
D ❍ Statement of work

10 **Information on the warranty and product support belongs in the**

A ❍ Contract
B ❍ Bid documents
C ❍ Selection criteria
D ❍ Statement of work

Answers

1. **D.** Using acronyms and technical terms. Using acronyms and technical terms can cause confusion. They are not effective communication tools. *Review "Communication technology and methods."*
2. **A.** Redundancy. Redundancy is a good communication technique, not a communication blocker. *Go over "Communication technology and methods."*
3. **C.** You should spend time working through concerns before they become issues. Spending time going over concerns before they become issues is a good way to manage stakeholders. *Check out "Manage Stakeholder Engagement."*
4. **C.** The people identified in the communications management plan. The communications management plan tells you who needs what information. *Look into "Manage Communications."*
5. **D.** Make sure they receive team member status reports weekly. Not all stakeholders should receive status or progress reports. Follow the communications management plan. *Go over "Manage Stakeholder Engagement."*
6. **A.** Types of bid documents. Bid documents are used to get bids. The other options are used for awarding the contract. *Review "Conduct Procurements: Inputs."*
7. **B.** Bidder conference. A bidder conference is used after potential sellers have been identified. *See "Bidder conferences."*
8. **C.** Used to narrow the field of proposals to those you will negotiate with. All the other options are used in a two-step bid process. *Go over the sidebar "Doing the two-step."*
9. **B.** Letter contract. A letter contract allows the contractor to start work before the final contract is signed. *See "Conduct Procurements: Tools and Techniques."*
10. **A.** Contract. The contract has the warranty and product support information. *Check out "Conduct Procurements: Outputs."*

Book VII

Controlling Scope and Schedule

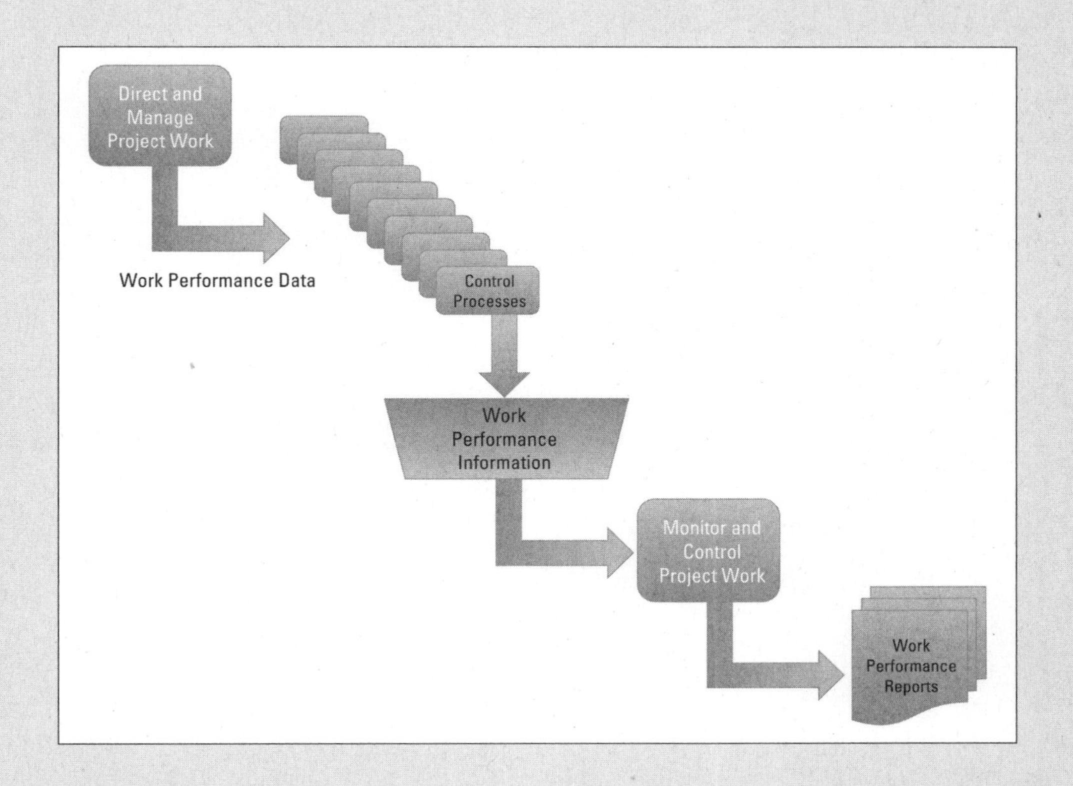

For more, take a look at the article on monitoring and controlling knowledge and skills at www.dummies.com/extras/pmpcertificationaio.

Contents at a Glance

Chapter 1: Monitoring, Controlling, and Managing Change

Exam Objectives

- **Measure project performance, identify and quantify variances, and determine appropriate preventive and corrective actions. Communicate status to stakeholders per the communication management plan.**
- **Ensure baseline integrity by updating the project management plan in response to approved changes and communicating those approved changes to the team.**

This chapter is the start of the Monitoring and Controlling processes. I start by looking at the integration process Monitor and Control Project Work, and then move into the integration process Perform Integrated Change Control. These processes use information from many of the other control processes as well as some of the Executing processes and even the integration planning process Develop Project Management Plan.

The Monitor and Control Project Work process looks at project performance overall and compares it against the project management plan (see Book III, Chapter 1). Other control processes look at specific aspects of the project performance, such as schedule, cost, or quality, and compare those performance aspects with specific components of the project management plan, such as the schedule baseline (see Book III, Chapter 3), cost baseline (see Book IV, Chapter 1), and quality metrics (see Book IV, Chapter 2). I get into each of those aspects of control in upcoming chapters in this minibook and in Book VIII.

Employing integrated change control ensures that your baselines are meaningful and up to date. It is what gives stakeholders confidence that your measurements are relevant and that you are in control of the project scope, schedule, cost, and quality.

As you read through this information, try and keep in mind the integrative nature of each process. Think about how it relates to the project as a whole rather than one specific knowledge area.

Quick Assessment

1. (True/False). Monitoring project work is about taking corrective action to ensure that the project stays within the threshold limits.

2. ______ ______ is compared with the ______ ______ ______ to discover the degree of variance.

3. The ______ ______ ______ determines the disposition of all change requests.

4. To provide a standardized, effective, and efficient way to centrally manage approved changes and baselines, you should use a(n) ______ ______ ______.

5. (True/False). Deferred changes are tracked in the Direct and Manage Project Execution process.

6. Crossing the ______ should trigger some action, such as generating an exception report.

7. Which process ensures that changes to the project are coordinated across all aspects of the project?

8. A(n) ______ ______ ______ is a collection of formal documented procedures that define how project deliverables and documentation will be controlled, changed, and approved.

9. (True/False). Preventive action is a type of change request.

10. In which process do you approve, disapprove, or defer requested changes?

Answers

1. False. Monitoring project work entails collecting information about the project, compiling and analyzing it, and communicating the status. Controlling is about taking corrective action. *Look over the content in "Monitoring versus controlling."*

2. Work performance information, project management plan. Work performance information communicates the work completed and in progress. The project management plan contains the baseline(s). *See "Monitor and Control Project Work" for more information on this topic.*

3. Change control board. The change control board reviews all change requests and determines whether the changes should be accepted, rejected, or deferred. *Read about the change control board in "Perform Integrated Change Control."*

4. Configuration management system. A configuration management system ensures there is a deliberate, defined method to manage product components and project documents. *Read about this in "Configuration management."*

5. False. Approved changes are implemented in the Direct and Manage Project Execution process. Deferred changes are pending until they are either approved or denied. *You will find more information about this in "Perform Integrated Change Control."*

6. Threshold. A threshold can apply to cost, schedule, or other project parameters. When a set value (threshold) is crossed, it means you need to take some kind of corrective or preventive action. *Look over "Monitor and Control Project Work: Tools and Techniques."*

7. Perform Integrated Change Control. Perform Integrated Change Control ensures that a change to the scope considers the impact to schedule, cost, quality, risk, and so forth, and that the change is reflected in all elements of the project management plan and the project documents. *This information is discussed in "Perform Integrated Change Control."*

8. Change control system. A change control system provides a structure to submit, analyze, decide, and communicate project changes. *Check out the information in "Perform Integrated Change Control."*

9. True. Both preventive and corrective actions are considered change requests. *See the information in "A Change Control process."*

10. Perform Integrated Change Control. The Perform Integrated Change Control process is where all change requests are analyzed and a decision is made about which action the team should take with regards to the change. *Look over Table 1-1: Monitor and Control Project Work versus Perform Integrated Change Control.*

Knowledge and Skills for the Monitoring and Controlling Processes

Monitoring and controlling project work takes place throughout the project. It begins as soon as you start to formalize plans, and it doesn't end until the last document is archived.

Monitoring and Controlling Process Group. Those processes required to track, review, and regulate the progress and performance of the project; identify any areas in which changes to the plan are required; and initiate the corresponding changes.

To master the monitoring and controlling processes, you need cross-cutting skills that help you gather, analyze, organize, and communicate information. You will also need to employ problem-solving skills as well as stakeholder management and decision-making skills. Keep the following list of cross-cutting skills in mind as you read through the information in this minibook and Book VIII.

- ✦ Data-gathering techniques
- ✦ Decision-making techniques
- ✦ Information management tools, techniques, and methods
- ✦ Leadership tools and techniques
- ✦ Oral and written communication techniques, channels, and applications
- ✦ Presentation tools and techniques
- ✦ Problem-solving tools and techniques
- ✦ Project management software
- ✦ Relationship management
- ✦ Stakeholder impact analysis
- ✦ Targeting communications to intended audiences

Questions in the Monitoring and Controlling process group account for 25 percent of the exam. Although there will be many questions about the tools, techniques, and outputs, there will also be quite a few that have to do with these cross-cutting skills!

Monitor and Control Project Work

This process uses information from the project management plan and the work performance information and compares the two.

Monitor and Control Project Work. Tracking, reviewing, and reporting the progress to meet the performance objectives defined in the project management plan.

To begin with, look at the difference between monitoring and controlling.

Monitoring versus controlling

When monitoring project work, you're performing the following activities:

- ✦ Collecting information about the project performance
- ✦ Providing forecasts for future work
- ✦ Tracking and analyzing risks
- ✦ Communicating the status of the project

When controlling the work, you are

- ✦ Comparing the information with the project management plan
- ✦ Compiling and analyzing the information
- ✦ Developing preventive action plans to keep the project within the variance thresholds
- ✦ Developing corrective action plans to bring the project back within the variance thresholds
- ✦ Recommending defect repairs for processes that allow poor performance
- ✦ Submitting change requests to implement the preventive and corrective actions, defect repairs, or other necessary changes

Here is how the *PMBOK Guide* Glossary defines these two terms.

Monitor. Collect project performance data with respect to a plan, produce performance measures, and report and disseminate performance information.

Control. Comparing actual performance with planned performance, analyzing variances, assessing trends to effect process improvements, evaluating possible alternatives, and recommending appropriate corrective action as needed.

Notice that many of these actions take place in other processes such as Control Risks (covered in Book VIII, Chapter 4), Control Quality (covered in Book VIII, Chapter 2), and other control processes. You can consider Monitor and Control Project Work the parent process to most of the other monitoring and control processes.

Monitor and Control Project Work: Inputs

Where does the information you are monitoring come from? Figure 1-1 shows how information about work performance migrates through the various project processes.

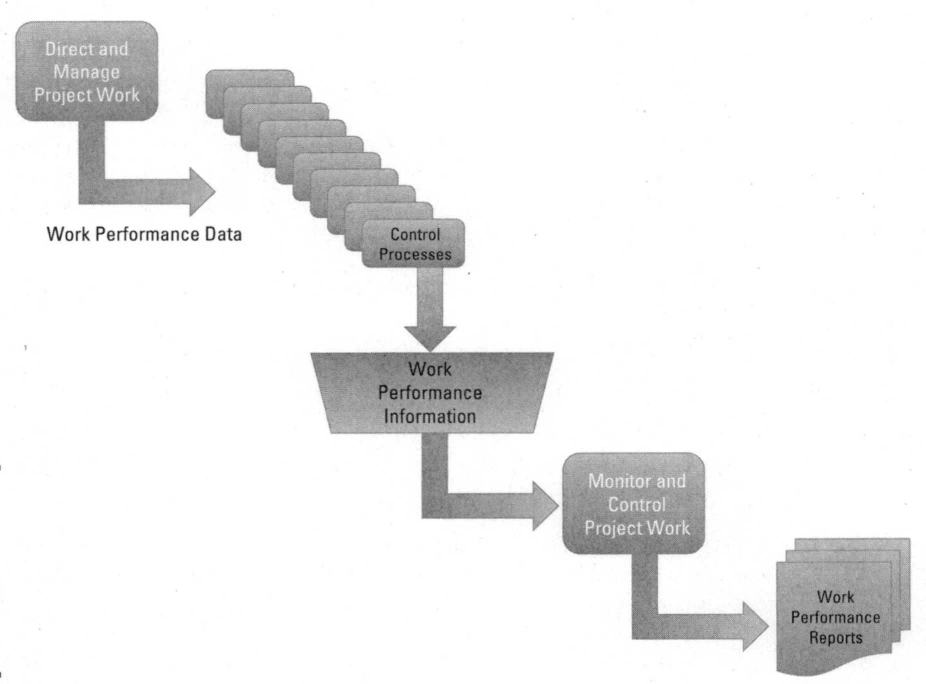

Figure 1-1: Where project performance information comes from.

Figure 1-1 breaks down into the following steps:

1. The team performs work to create project deliverables. The work takes place in the Direct and Manage Project Work process. The output from that process is work performance data.
2. Work performance data is an input into processes in the Monitor and Control process group:
   - Control Scope
   - Control Schedule
   - Control Costs
   - Control Communications
   - Control Risks
   - Control Procurements
   - Control Stakeholder Engagement
3. An output from each of the control processes is work performance information — the work performance data compared with the baseline and the variance thresholds.
4. Work performance information is an input to the Monitor and Control Project Work process in Project Integration Management. The work performance information is combined and analyzed to create work performance reports that describe the project status.

The definitions for the various stages of work performance are

Work Performance Data. The raw observations and measurements identified during activities being performed to carry out the project work.

Work Performance Information. The performance data collected from various controlling processes, analyzed in context and integrated based on relationships across areas.

Work Performance Reports. The physical or electronic representation of work performance information compiled in project documents, intended to generate decisions, actions, or awareness.

The inputs to compare actual project performance to the planned performance are the project management plan and the work performance information. You can see that the work performance information comes from controlling processes in scope, schedule, cost, and so forth. The work performance information is then compared with the project baselines and variance thresholds documented in the project management plan. The work performance information from scope, schedule, and cost has actual measurements, such as the dollar amounts spent, the deliverables actually completed, and so forth. Cost and schedule forecasts are also used when assessing the overall project performance.

The project management plan not only contains the project baselines, but also the thresholds for variance for each of the project objectives, including at least scope, quality, schedule, and cost.

Threshold. A cost, time, quality, technical, or resource value used as a parameter, and which may be included in project specifications. Crossing the threshold should trigger some action, such as generating an exception report.

Monitor and Control Project Work: Tools and Techniques

Monitor and Control Project Work not only involves identifying variances but also determining whether the variance is acceptable, what caused the variance, and what (if anything) you should do about it. This is where expert judgment is useful. Expertise is used to analyze performance, pinpoint the cause of variances, and determine the appropriate actions to address performance variances. You can use a number of techniques to analyze past and current performance and also forecast future performance.

Analytical techniques

When analyzing data, you should check the accuracy of the source data and make sure that schedule measurements and cost measurements are using the same scope information to report performance information. Analyze what the combined schedule and cost information tells you. Look at a few examples of reviewing cost data:

- **Over budget, ahead of schedule**

  This state could mean that you're accomplishing work faster than expected, so you're spending funds faster than expected. This is fine if you're actually spending the same amount you budgeted for the work; you're just doing it earlier than you planned.

  This could also mean that you're spending money to expedite work. In other words, you're crashing your schedule to finish quicker. (Read about crashing schedules in Book III, Chapter 3, and Book VII, Chapter 3.) This might be okay, depending on the priorities for the project. If you're trying to get to market as soon as possible and the sponsor or client is willing to spend more to get there faster, you're in good shape.

- **Over budget, behind schedule**

  This isn't good. You might have underestimated, or maybe you're not doing a good job managing the project.

  This could also mean that a risk event occurred, and you had to spend money and take time to respond to the situation.

- **Under budget, ahead of schedule**

  This might be the most suspicious of all situations. It rarely happens, so the results should be scrutinized to see whether the cost and schedule estimates were padded, or perhaps you have an error in the numbers.

- **Under budget, behind schedule**

  Most likely, your project is starved for resources. You're under budget because your labor costs are lower than expected, but you're behind schedule because you don't have the manpower to accomplish the work as planned.

From these examples, you can see that you're looking at combined information to understand the cause of any variances and understand the implications of the variances.

Another source of information you should review is the status of your cost and schedule reserves. If your project is 30 percent complete but you've spent 60 percent of your reserves, you should understand the implications for your project. Perhaps the first 30 percent was the riskiest, and the remaining 70 percent is relatively risk free. In this circumstance, your remaining reserve should be sufficient. However, if the majority of the uncertainty in your project is likely to be toward the end, then it's a fair assumption that you will overrun your budget.

Forecasting

Good performance reports include cost and schedule forecasts along with the supporting data to explain the forecasts.

Forecast. An estimate or prediction of conditions and events in the project's future based on information and knowledge available at the time of the forecast. The information is based on the project's past performance and expected future performance, and includes information that could impact the project in the future, such as estimates at completion and estimate to complete.

Of the several different methods of forecasting available, the main three to look at are

- Time series
- Regression analysis
- Expert opinion

Time series

A *time series* forecasting method uses a model to predict performance based on past performance. In general, time series forecasting is more accurate for a short-term forecast for which future events are expected to be similar to the recent past. Predictions get less accurate the further in the future they fall. Another consideration with time series forecasting is whether the work or the environment for the future work is different from the past work. If so, time series forecasting is not the best method.

In Book VIII, Chapter 1, I discuss the earned value (EV) cost forecasting methods of estimate to complete (ETC) and estimate at completion (EAC). These are a form of a time series method. In other words, EAC and ETC take information from the past and project it into the future. Another time series method is trend analysis. Trend analysis (see Figure 1-2) entails plotting the progress for past reporting periods and then projecting future performance assuming the same trend continues. Figure 1-2 shows a trend chart that shows a cost forecast based on multiple scenarios.

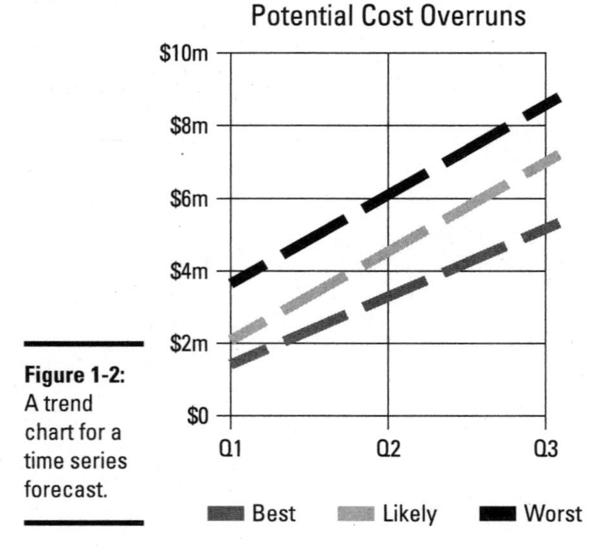

Figure 1-2: A trend chart for a time series forecast.

Regression analysis

Regression analysis looks at the relationship among variables that cause fluctuations in outcomes. You assume the budget is the dependent variable and then that resource skills, availability, and cost are independent variables. You are looking to see the expectation of achieving the budget based on changes in each independent variable.

Expert opinion

With this method, a person (or group) estimates cost or schedule performance; this estimate is based on knowledge and expert opinion. Experts may develop probability estimates or build models based on various scenarios. Sometimes this method seems as if it's based on intuition or an educated guess. However, many times, you can't really quantify the knowledge that experience brings. A bottom-up estimate by an expert can oftentimes be the most accurate method of forecasting.

Other forecasting methods

Other forecasting methods include running simulations and probabilistic forecasts (a forecast based on a probability distribution). In reality, using multiple methods will end up with the best results.

The *PMBOK Guide* mentions many analytical techniques, including fault tree analysis, failure mode effect analysis (FMEA), and grouping methods. Don't worry! You don't have to know and understand all those methods of forecasting. You should just understand the basic ideas that you can use the past performance, variables that drive the future, or expert judgment to develop a forecast.

One way of documenting variances is by using a simple variance analysis form, like the one shown in Figure 1-3.

VARIANCE ANALYSIS

Project Title: ______________________ Date Prepared: ______________________

Schedule Variance:

Planned Result	Actual Result	Variance
Identify the work planned to be accomplished.	*Identify the work actually accomplished.*	*Identify the variance.*

Root Cause:
Describe the root cause of the variance.

Planned Response:
Describe the planned corrective action.

Cost Variance:

Planned Result	Actual Result	Variance
Record the planned costs for the work planned to be accomplished.	*Identify the actual costs for the work accomplished.*	*Identify the variance.*

Root Cause:
Describe the root cause of the variance.

Planned Response:
Describe the planned corrective action.

Quality Variance:

Planned Result	Actual Result	Variance
Describe the planned performance or quality measurements.	*Describe the actual performance or quality measurements.*	*Identify the variance.*

Root Cause:
Describe the root cause of the variance.

Planned Response:
Describe the planned corrective action.

Figure 1-3: A variance analysis form.

Monitor and Control Project Work: Outputs

By comparing the project management plan with the work performance information, the project manager can determine whether any change requests are required.

In context of reviewing performance, a change request can be

- Corrective action
- Preventive action
- Defect repair

These are defined in Book VI, Chapter 1. If a change request is initiated, it will go to the Perform Integrated Change Control process that I review next. Regardless of any changes requested, the project management plan and the project documents are updated to reflect the current project status.

Work performance reports

The three aspects of reporting performance are progress reporting, status reporting, and forecasting.

- **Progress reporting:** Identifies the activities and progress that have taken place since the last progress report. This includes the scope that has been completed, the schedule work that has been accomplished, costs that have been incurred, and any significant milestone achievements.
- **Status reporting:** Describes the state of the project overall. For example, a status report might indicate that you have accomplished 50 percent of the project work, spent 55 percent of the project funds, and are 20 months into a 36-month project.
- **Forecasting:** Attempts to predict future accomplishments for scope and schedule and future expenditures. A forecast report will often identify an updated finish date and an updated cost estimate. I detail forecasts shortly.

I start out by listing the types of information that you should have in a performance report, and then I talk about the different ways of presenting the information.

Performance report data

As I mention previously, the information in the reports is identified in the communication management plan. The information and the method of presentation will vary by audience. At the very least, all performance reports should include

- Work completed in the current period
- Work planned for completion but not complete, along with the reason(s) why
- Funds expended during the current period
- Any variance in the funds expended, along with the reason(s) why
- Any corrective or preventive actions taken
- Status of existing risks and issues
- Any new risks or issues
- Forecast for future schedule performance
- Forecast for future cost performance

I show you a simple performance report illustration in Book VI, Chapter 3. For more complete information, you might also want to report on

- Resource utilization variances
- Summary of changes requested and their status
- Any quality findings
- New and resolved assumptions

Reporting methods

In addition to the performance report I show you in Book VI, Chapter 3, you can develop more visual charts and reports, such as

- Trend charts
- Tabular
- Bull's eye charts

- Stop light charts
- Dashboards

Knowledge and skills in reporting procedures is one of the areas that will be tested on the exam. Work performance reports are the primary outputs that will be used to test your knowledge and skills for reporting procedures.

Here are some examples of the types of information you can find in work performance reports.

The chart in Figure 1-4 shows the trend of the cost performance index (CPI), which I explain in Book VIII, Chapter 1.

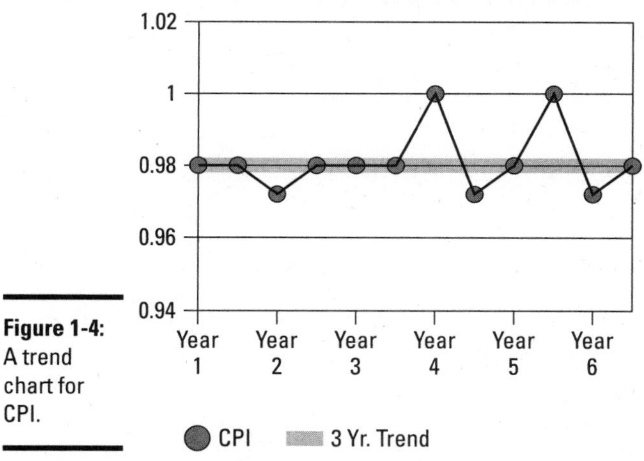

Figure 1-4: A trend chart for CPI.

Figure 1-5, a bull's eye chart, shows performance of the project by plotting the schedule performance index (SPI) and CPI. (See Book VIII, Chapter 1, for more discussion on SPI and CPI.) This chart shows that Project E is in the worst shape, while D and F are performing better than expected. Projects C and F are the closest to plan of all the projects.

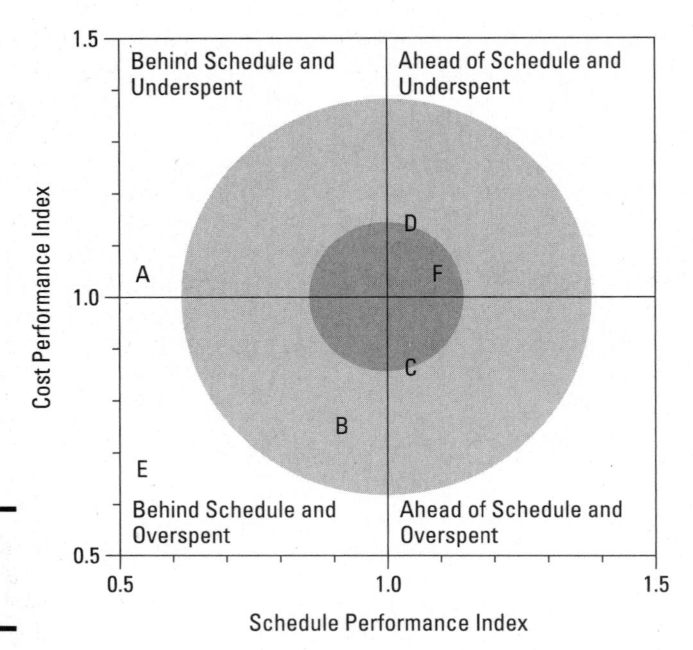

Figure 1-5: The bull's eye chart.

Some other types of charts include

- ✦ Stop light charts
- ✦ Dashboard reports
- ✦ S-curve

The stop light chart in Figure 1-6 indicates project status green (medium gray) if performing well within the threshold (0%–5% variance), yellow (light gray) if within the threshold but getting close to going beyond it (5%–10% variance), or red (dark gray) if over the threshold.

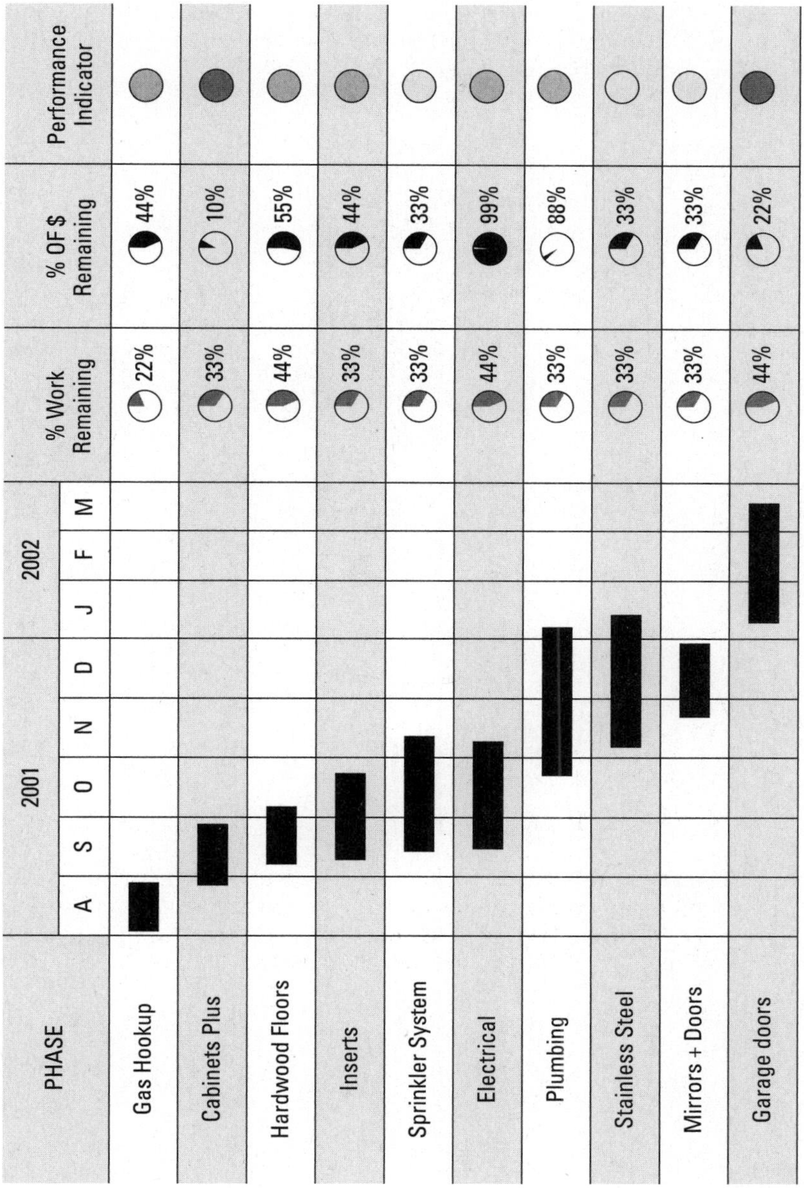

PHASE	2001					2002			% Work Remaining	% OF $ Remaining	Performance Indicator
	A	S	O	N	D	J	F	M			
Gas Hookup									22%	44%	
Cabinets Plus									33%	10%	
Hardwood Floors									44%	55%	
Inserts									33%	44%	
Sprinkler System									33%	33%	
Electrical									44%	99%	
Plumbing									33%	88%	
Stainless Steel									33%	33%	
Mirrors + Doors									33%	33%	
Garage doors									44%	22%	

Figure 1-6: Stop light chart.

The dashboard report shown in Figure 1-7 uses a series of gauges that show performance, using colors from a stop light chart or using other information to show performance.

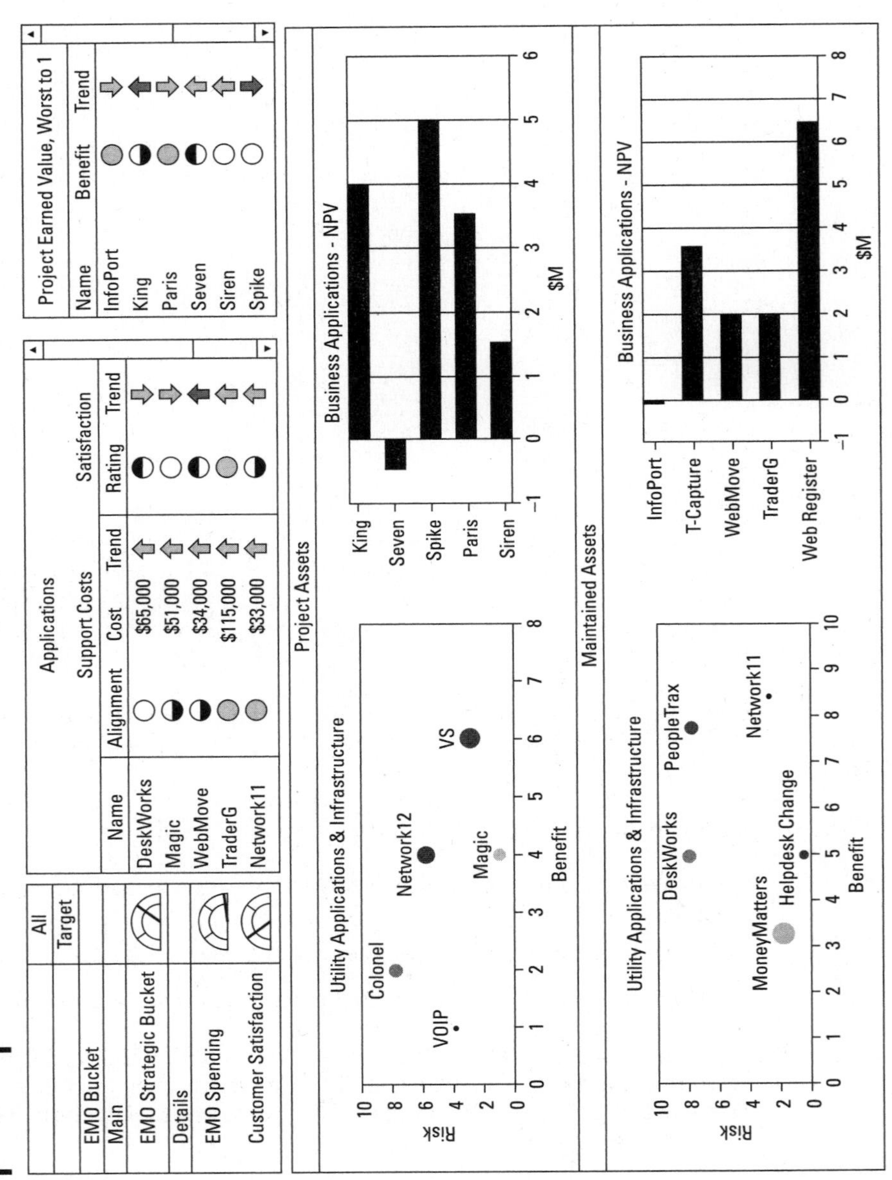

Figure 1-7: Dashboard report.

The S-curve in Figure 1-8 is a common way to compare the planned value (PV), earned value (EV), and actual cost (AC) data for a project using earned value management.

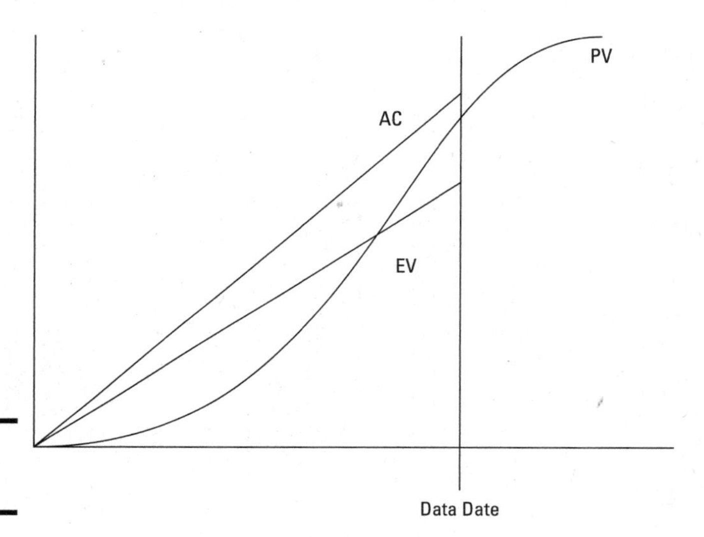

Figure 1-8: S-curve.

In general, graphics that highlight the outliers are useful for senior executives. The project manager and the team should look at detailed tabular reports and variance analysis reports to understand the reasons behind the outliers.

Depending on your work performance, you may need to update or change components in your project management plan or project documents.

The Monitor and Control Project Work process requires you to have knowledge and skills in the following areas to pass the exam:

- Project control limits (thresholds and tolerances for scope, schedule, cost, and quality)
- Project performance metrics (effort, duration, and cost)
- Controlling performance against the project management plan

The honesty standards in the Code of Ethics and Professional Conduct are more relevant to the Report Performance process than any other process. There are many ways to misrepresent information in a performance report or leave out information that could reflect poorly on the project. You are likely to see scenario questions that address honesty standards and performance reporting on the PMP. The following are honesty standards from the Code of Ethics and Professional Conduct:

- ✦ Earnestly seek to understand the truth.
- ✦ Be truthful in communication and conduct.
- ✦ Provide accurate information in a timely manner.
- ✦ Do not engage in or condone behavior that is designed to deceive others, including but not limited to, making misleading or false statements, stating half-truths, providing information out of context or withholding information that, if known, would render statements as misleading or incomplete.

Taking responsibility for project performance

More than any other process, the Monitor and Control Project Work process is where you determine whether you are fulfilling your obligations to deliver project scope, with the agreed-upon quality, in a timely manner, for the agreed-upon budget.

If you cannot fulfill your commitments, you have an obligation to take ownership and make corrections as needed. Taking ownership applies to you as a project manager and to your team members as well. The project manager and the team members need to be accountable for any issues arising from errors or omissions in the project.

The following responsibility standards from the Code of Ethics and Professional Conduct are applicable to all the project management processes; however, they are particularly relevant in the Monitoring and Controlling process group.

- ✦ We fulfill the commitments that we undertake — we do what we say we will do.
- ✦ When we make errors or omissions, we take ownership and make corrections promptly. When we discover errors or omissions caused by others, we communicate them to the appropriate body as soon as they are discovered. We accept accountability for any issues resulting from our errors or omissions and any resulting consequences.

The sidebar "The project scheduler" shows how many of the responsibility standards from the Code of Ethics and Professional Conduct could be applied in a project situation.

The project scheduler

A few weeks ago, your project scheduler went on a leave of absence. Jill, your new scheduler, has been working on the project for four weeks. You are looking at the latest performance report and notice some errors in the network logic, certain baselines dates are different, and the reports don't seem reflective of what's really happening. You approach John, the PMO manager, who assigned Jill to your project. John informs you that Bill was originally scheduled to work on your project. However, he was pulled to work on a different project, and the only available resource was Jill. John sheepishly acknowledges that Jill is new, and he wasn't too sure about her skill set, but based on your issues, John agrees that Jill needs some additional training.

You, John, and Jill review past and current performance reports to determine the real status and identify corrective actions you need to take to get the project back on track. In your monthly performance report that you submit to the Project Portfolio Committee, you take responsibility for the variance and describe the actions you're taking to correct it.

This scenario demonstrates the following responsibility standards:

- We accept only those assignments that are consistent with our background, experience, skills, and qualifications.
- We uphold this Code and hold each other accountable to it.
- When we make errors or omissions, we take ownership and make corrections promptly. When we discover errors or omissions caused by others, we communicate them to the appropriate body as soon as they are discovered. We accept accountability for any issues resulting from our errors or omissions and any resulting consequences.

Perform Integrated Change Control

It's inevitable. You will have changes to your project. Change requests can come from anywhere. The *PMBOK Guide* shows a change request as an output from 16 different processes. The question, then, becomes whether you will manage them, or whether they will manage you. The structure you documented in the project management plan to manage change as well as the degree to which you adhere to that structure determines the answer to that question.

You will be managing changes to the project from inception until final closeout. You will have project changes, product changes, changes to plans, and changes to project documents. All need to be analyzed and a decision made whether to accept, reject, or defer the change.

Using my running childcare center example, here are some changes that could occur:

- **Project change:** The core team member from legal has taken another job, so you need to bring a new team member onto the project.
- **Product change:** To keep down costs, management decided to have one large playground instead of two separate playgrounds.
- **Project management plan change:** The schedule was just shortened by a month.
- **Project document change:** The city has a new regulation that impacts the childcare center. This is now a requirement that needs to be entered into the requirement documentation and the traceability matrix (see Book III, Chapter 2).

In Book VI, Chapter 1, I discuss the Direct and Manage Project Execution process. In that chapter is a figure that shows all the places a change request could come from — 14 different processes, in fact, that generate change requests. Perform Integrated Change Control is where all the change requests come for analysis and a decision on whether to approve the change requests. The approved changes get implemented; the others don't. Before getting into too much more detail, review some of the key definitions associated with this process and managing change.

Perform Integrated Change Control. Reviewing all change requests; approving changes and managing changes to deliverables, organizational process assets, project documents, and project management plan; and communicating their disposition.

Change Control. A process whereby modifications to documents, deliverables, or baselines associated with the project are identified, documented, approved, or rejected.

Change Request. A formal proposal to modify any document, deliverable, or baseline.

Change Control System. A set of procedures that describes how modifications to the project deliverables and documentation are managed and controlled.

Change Control Board (CCB). A formally chartered group responsible for reviewing, evaluating, approving, delaying, or rejecting changes of a project, and for recording and communicating such decisions.

In Book III, Chapter 1, I define some of the change management and configuration management terms. I also discuss the change control plan and the configuration management plan along with a sample of those plans. Perform Integrated Change Control is where those plans are put into action.

A Change Control process

Change control starts with a change request. Figure 1-9 shows an example of a change request.

CHANGE REQUEST

Project Title: ______________________ **Date Prepared:** ______________________

Person Requesting Change: ______________________ **Change Number:** __________

Category of Change *(Check a box to indicate the category of change.):*

☐ Scope ☐ Quality ☐ Requirements
☐ Cost ☐ Schedule ☐ Documents

Detailed Description of Proposed Change:

Describe change proposed.

Justification for Proposed Change:

Indicate the reason for the change.

Impacts of Change:

Scope	☐ Increase	☐ Decrease	☐ Modify
Description: *Describe the impact of the proposed change on the project or product scope.*			
Quality	☐ Increase	☐ Decrease	☐ Modify
Description: *Describe the impact of the proposed change on the project or product quality.*			
Requirements	☐ Increase	☐ Decrease	☐ Modify
Description: *Describe the impact of the proposed change on the project or product requirements.*			
Cost	☐ Increase	☐ Decrease	☐ Modify
Description: *Describe the impact of the proposed change on the project budget or cost estimates.*			
Schedule	☐ Increase	☐ Decrease	☐ Modify
Description: *Describe the impact of the proposed change on the schedule and whether it will cause a delay on the critical path.*			
Project Documents *Describe changes needed to project documents.*			

Page 1 of 2

Figure 1-9: A change request form.

CHANGE REQUEST

Comments:

Any comments that will clarify information on the change request.

Disposition ☐ Approve ☐ Defer ☐ Reject

Justification:

Justification for the change request disposition.

Change Control Board Signatures:

Name	Role	Signature

Date:

Page 2 of 2

Change requests can include corrective and preventive actions, as well as defect repairs.

The exam questions assume that you have a robust, documented Change Control process for your project, and also that the Change Control process handles changes to the product, project, and all project management plans and project documents.

Following a Change Control process requires a series of steps. You can refer to Figure 1-10 as I walk through each of them.

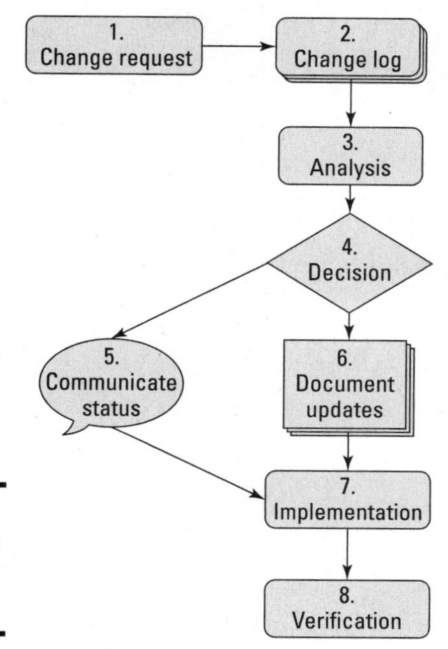

Figure 1-10: The Change Control process.

✦ **Change request:** A stakeholder fills out a change request. Change requests can come from any stakeholder on the project.

✦ **Change log:** Each change request is documented in a change log. The change log has information such as

- Change ID
- Category
- Description
- Submitted by
- Date submitted
- Status
- Disposition

At this point, the Status would be open, and the Disposition field would be blank.

✦ **Analysis:** You need to fully understand the impact of the change request across all areas of the project. This is where the project management plan comes in handy. Even if the change is not optional, you should still analyze and document the impact on all areas of the project.

- **CCB meeting:** The change request and the completed analysis go to the change control board. The CCB approves the change, denies the change, or defers the decision until more information is available. At this point, the Disposition field of the change control log is filled in. This is called the *change request status update* that is the output from the Perform Integrated Change Control process and an input to the Direct and Manage Execution and the Perform Quality Control processes.
- **Communication:** Approved changes are communicated to all impacted parties, and the change is implemented. If the change isn't approved, the stakeholder is advised of the reasons why the change was not approved.
- **Document updates:** For changes that are approved, the project management plan and the appropriate project documents are updated.
- **Implementation:** Implementation of approved changes is managed via the Direct and Manage Project Work process.
- **Verification:** All approved change requests are verified in the Control Quality process to ensure that they were implemented as approved.

Managing change, analyzing change, updating documents, and communicating about change all take time. You need to take into consideration that part of your time as a project manager, as well as part of your team members' time, will be taken up by these activities.

Everyone must follow the change control process, regardless of her position in the organization. If your sponsor or the customer demands a change, you may have to implement it, but you still have to submit a change request, log the change, analyze the impacts, and so forth.

The fairness standard "We apply the rules of the organization without favoritism or prejudice" from the Code of Ethics and Professional Conduct should be applied throughout the project, but you may find particular relevance when it comes to maintaining a rigorous change control process.

Configuration management

One of the areas you will have to be familiar with for the exam is configuration management. If you work on small projects, you might never have heard this term. It's kind of like change management on steroids.

I define configuration management system in Book III, Chapter 1, but I am repeating that definition here. I also want to look at some of the other definitions you will need to do well on these exam questions. The other definitions are not from the *PMBOK Guide.*

Configuration management system. A subsystem of the overall project management system. It is a collection of formal documented procedures used to apply technical and administrative direction and surveillance to

Identify and document the functional and physical characteristics of a product, result, service, or component

Control any changes to such characteristics

Record and report each change and its implementation status

Support the audit of the products, results, or components to verify conformance to requirements

It includes the documentation, tracking systems, and defined approval levels necessary for authorizing and controlling changes.

Configuration identification. Selection and identification of a configuration item provides the basis for which product configuration is defined and certified, products and documents are labeled, changes are managed, and accountability is maintained.

Configuration status accounting. Information is recorded and reported as to when appropriate data about the configuration item should be provided. This information includes a listing of approved configuration identification, status of proposed changes to the configuration, and the implementation status of approved changes.

Configuration verification and audit. Configuration verification and configuration audits ensure the composition of a project's configuration items is correct and that corresponding changes are registered, assessed, approved, tracked, and correctly implemented. This ensures the functional requirements defined in the configuration documentation have been met.

These definitions are admittedly pretty technical. The following example assumes that a donation was made for the childcare center to customize a van for transporting children on field trips to nearby locations, such as zoos, the library, and so on. This example shows how configuration management would be applied to the design and construction of the van for babies, toddlers, and children at the childcare center.

Configuration identification

During the design phase of building the van, you have lots of drawings of the various systems and parts that go into the van. As you elaborate and revise your ideas, you make changes to these drawings. As one design idea changes, it might affect the layout and design of other components.

You can see that the number of drawings and making sure that you have the right drawings are critical to keeping control of the project. To maintain control of the drawings, you decide to label all systems with an "alpha" code: The engine drawings start with an E, the transmission drawings with a T, the chassis drawings with a C, and so forth. Then you identify each part in the various systems and apply a number to them. Then you put a "build number" on each drawing to indicate whether it's in the concept phase, design phase, detail design phase, and so on. Each drawing has a date and time identifier at the bottom.

Now assume that you're in the detail design phase of building the vehicle. You identify the items that need to be included in this phase of the project as well as the information you want to record about those items. For example, you might want to have all the physical components listed along with their size, weight, material composition, and the supplier. By looking at the configuration control log, you should be able to identify this information — and also see whether and when changes to the items were submitted and also the disposition of those changes.

Configuration status accounting

During the production cycle of building the van, you find that a lot of changes keep coming through, and you need to keep retooling part of the production line. After you run some reports to determine where the changes are coming from, you find that they are coming from a particular branch within the drawing (engineering) tree. You use these reports and metrics to communicate production status.

Configuration verification and audit

When you build your prototype van, you want to make sure that the actual parts are consistent with what the drawings say should be in the vehicle. You also want to make sure that the system was used to document any changes to the parts.

The PMP exam usually (but not always) considers the change control system to be a part of the configuration management system. In practice, it may be that the configuration management system is part of the change control system. Read the questions carefully to determine which method the question is using.

The information in the Perform Integrated Change Control corresponds directly with the knowledge and skills that will be tested for change management techniques and integrated change control techniques.

Comparing Control Processes

So far, I have talked about two processes in the Project Integration Management knowledge area. Table 1-1 should help you understand the difference between them.

Table 1-1 Monitor and Control Project Work versus Perform Integrated Change Control

Monitor and Control Project Work	*Perform Integrated Change Control*
Comparing the project management plan with the actual project performance information	Identifying that a change has occurred or should occur
Providing forecasts for future work performance	Influencing the factors that create changes to ensure that changes are agreed upon and that the process is not circumvented
Tracking and analyzing project risks	Reviewing requested changes, including recommended corrective and preventive actions, analyzing the requests, and documenting the impact on the project
Ensuring that the appropriate risk responses are implemented	Approving, disapproving, or pending requested changes, corrective actions, and preventive actions
Recommending corrective and preventive action as well as defect repair so that actual performance is aligned with planned performance	Maintaining the integrity of the baselines by managing the related configuration management and planning documentation
Ensuring that accurate and timely progress information is available	Managing the approved changes

Key Terms

This chapter introduces vocabulary associated with monitoring and controlling the project work as well as managing change to the project.

- Monitor
- Control
- Threshold
- Forecast
- Time series
- Regression analysis
- Change control
- Change request
- Change control system
- Change control board (CCB)
- Change log
- Configuration management system
- Configuration identification
- Configuration status accounting
- Configuration verification and audit

Chapter Summary

In this chapter, I introduce the Monitoring and Controlling process group and discuss the cross-cutting skills you need to do well on the exam. Monitoring and controlling progress happens throughout the project to ensure the work is progressing according to plan. If changes to the plan are required, a Change Control process is followed to ensure the integrity of the baselines.

- Monitoring and Controlling Project Work comprises two parts: monitoring and controlling. Monitoring collects information and communicates project status. Controlling compares the project status information against the plan to determine whether a change request for preventive or corrective action should be submitted.

- Monitor and Control Project Work is a parent process to many of the other control processes. Performance measurements from Control Scope, Control Schedule, and Control Costs are combined with information from Direct and Manage Project Work to create a performance report.
- Work performance information is compared with the information in the project management plan to determine whether any action should be taken, other than updating the project management plan and the project documents.
- Reporting integrates information from controlling and executing processes and combines it into a report that provides an overview of the project's performance overall. Like with most controlling processes, reporting uses information from the baseline(s) to compare against actual results. Causes and responses to variances are explained in the performance reports.
- Forecasts use information from past performance, future drivers of performance, and/or expert judgment to predict future performance.
- Performance reports are distributed to the stakeholders identified in the communications management plan in the format indicated. Reports can be illustrated via reporting template, charts, tables, and graphics.
- Perform Integrated Change Control ensures the project baselines are valid and that only approved changes are integrated into the baselines. This process implements the change management plan and the configuration management plan.
- The Change Control process should include a change request, analysis, deliberation, and a decision. Those decisions should be communicated, and the approved changes will be implemented.
- Configuration management is used to provide direction and surveillance to project components, products, and documents. The three parts are identification, status accounting, and verification and audit.

Prep Test

Multiple Choice

1 **What is the process of tracking, reviewing, and reporting the progress to meet the performance objectives defined in the project management plan?**

A ❍ Perform Integrated Change Control
B ❍ Configuration Management
C ❍ Direct and Manage Project Work
D ❍ Monitor and Control Project Work

2 **Which of the following is an example of a monitoring activity?**

A ❍ Tracking and analyzing risks
B ❍ Fixing defects
C ❍ Developing preventive actions
D ❍ Submitting change requests

3 **Which process compiles status reports and puts them into a single document?**

A ❍ Monitor and Control Project Work
B ❍ Perform Integrated Change Control
C ❍ Direct and Manage Project Work
D ❍ Control Communications

4 **Variances that are within the ______ are considered acceptable.**

A ❍ Baseline
B ❍ Threshold
C ❍ Boundaries
D ❍ 10% range

5 **Reducing the budget by 3% is considered a**

A ❍ Project change
B ❍ Product change
C ❍ Project management plan change
D ❍ Project document change

6 **Approved changes are implemented in which process?**

A ❍ Monitor and Control Project Work

B ❍ Perform Integrated Change Control

C ❍ Direct and Manage Project Work

D ❍ Develop Project Management Plan

7 **What document is used to track the status of all changes?**

A ❍ A change request

B ❍ A change log

C ❍ A status update

D ❍ A change request control log

8 **Determining how you will manage version control on your project documents is an example of**

A ❍ A configuration management system

B ❍ Configuration identification

C ❍ Configuration status accounting

D ❍ Configuration verification and audit

Scenario 1

A team member has come to you with an idea to revise a work process. The new process will save time and increase quality. The idea for the new process looks good. The team member submitted a request and you worked with her to determine the impact to other processes. The CCB met and has a couple of follow-up questions for the team member to respond to before the CCB makes a decision.

1 **What is the first step in the change control process?**

A ❍ Implement the new process as part of the process improvement initiative.

B ❍ Analyze the impact of the change on other processes.

C ❍ Submit a change request.

D ❍ Bring the idea to the CCB.

2 **The CCB decided to ________ the change.**

A ❍ Defer

B ❍ Reject

C ❍ Accept

D ❍ Pend

Answers

Multiple Choice

1 **D.** Monitor and Control Project Work. The definition of Monitor and Control Project Work is "The process of tracking, reviewing, and regulating the progress to meet the performance objectives defined in the project management plan." *See "Monitor and Control Project Work."*

2 **A.** Tracking and analyzing risks. Tracking and analyzing risks is a monitoring activity. The others are control activities. *Look at "Monitoring versus controlling."*

3 **A.** Monitor and Control Project Work. Monitor and Control Project Work takes information from control processes and puts it into a single performance report. *Review the information in "Monitor and Control Project Work: Inputs."*

4 **B.** Threshold. Variances within the threshold are acceptable. *Check out "Monitor and Control Project Work: Inputs."*

5 **A.** Project change. Reducing the budget is a project change. You have to change the project management plan, but the change to the project is the driver, not the plan itself. *Go over "Perform Integrated Change Control."*

6 **C.** Direct and Manage Project Work. Approved changes are implemented in the Direct and Manage Project Work process. The output from Perform Integrated Change Control is "Change request status updates." The input shows up as "Approved change requests." *See the section "A Change Control process."*

7 **B.** A change log. A change log is used to enter and record the status of each change request. *Go back over "A Change Control process."*

8 **B.** Configuration identification. Determining how you will identify and control documents is configuration identification. *Review "Configuration management."*

Scenario 1

1 **C.** Ask the team member to submit a change request. The first step is to get a change request in the system. Then you can analyze it and bring it to the CCB. *Look at "A Change Control process."*

2 **A.** Defer. The CCB wants more information; therefore, it is deferring the change. *Check out "A Change Control process."*

Chapter 2: Controlling Project Scope

Exam Objectives

- **Measure project performance, identify and quantify variances, and determine appropriate actions. Communicate status to stakeholder per the communication management plan.**
- **Ensure baseline integrity by updating the project management plan in response to approved changes and communicating those approved changes to the team.**

You may recognize these exam objectives. After all, they're the same exam objectives from the previous chapter. In fact, the same exam objectives are used for the next chapter of this minibook as well as the first chapter of the following minibook. As project managers, we measure project performance for our scope, schedule, and cost. As part of measuring the performance, we identify variances and then determine what to do about them. By controlling scope, schedule, and cost, we ensure baseline integrity by updating our plans only in response to approved changes.

The two scope processes in the Monitoring and Controlling process group are Control Scope and Validate Scope. Control Scope ensures that only the work identified as being in-scope is delivered. In other words, it guards against scope creep. The scope baseline and the requirements are compared results as depicted in work performance data to ensure that all the approved scope is being delivered.

Validate Scope takes the deliverables that have been verified as correct in the Control Quality process and works with the customer or sponsor to inspect them for acceptance. After all the deliverables have been accepted, the project or phase moves into the closure processes.

I start this chapter by discussing the Validate Scope process and how deliverables flow through the project. Then I spend some time looking at the relationship between the various processes in the Monitoring and Controlling process group. The last section of this chapter focuses on controlling your project scope.

Quick Assessment

1 (True/False). Only those deliverables that have passed quality inspections are accepted by the customer.

2 Deliverables from the _____ _____ process are verified and become inputs to the Validate Scope process.

3 Which two planning processes have inputs to the Validate Scope process?

4 _____ _____ is the process of monitoring the status of the project and product scope and managing changes to the scope baseline.

5 A(n) _____ is a quantifiable deviation, departure, or divergence from a known baseline or expected value.

6 In which process do you formalize the acceptance of project deliverables?

7 Which method of inspection is used for requirements you can validate by visual inspection?

8 When seen in a control process, is variance analysis considered an input, a tool and technique, or an output?

9 Adding a new feature to a product without addressing the impact on the cost or schedule is called _____ _____.

10 (True/False). Implementing a contingency plan is an example of scope creep.

Answers

1. False. The customer may choose to accept deliverables that don't pass the quality control process. The customer may waive a requirement, or the deliverables might not have passed because they are better than the requirements. *Look over the information in the "Validate Scope" section.*

2. Control Quality. Deliverables from the Control Quality process are verified and become inputs to the Validate Scope process. *The section "The flow of deliverables" has more information about this question.*

3. Develop Project Management Plan and Collect Requirements. These two processes have planning documents and requirements documentation and information used in comparison with the work performance data and deliverables. *For more information, check out Figure 2-1 in "The flow of deliverables."*

4. Control Scope. The glossary definition of Control Scope is the process of monitoring the status of the project and product scope and managing changes to the scope baseline. *You can find this definition in "Control Scope."*

5. Variance. A variance is a quantifiable deviation, departure, or divergence from a known baseline or expected value. *Look at "Control Scope: Tools and Techniques."*

6. Validate Scope. Verified deliverables are inputs to the Validate Scope process. The deliverables are formally accepted by the sponsor, customer, or other authorized stakeholder in the Validate Scope process. *See "Validate Scope" for more information.*

7. Examine. There are four methods you can use in inspection. Examining a deliverable is used when you can visually confirm the requirement. *You can learn more about this in "Validate Scope: Tools, Techniques, and Outputs."*

8. Tool and technique. Variance analysis is a technique used in the Control Scope process. *Check out Validate Scope: Tools, Techniques, and Outputs."*

9. Scope creep. If you don't consider the impacts of a scope change on the schedule, cost, resources, risk, quality, and so forth, you are setting yourself up for challenges and disappointments. *Look at the information in "Creep versus change."*

10. False. Implementing a contingency plan is an example of a change in scope. *Read about this in "Scope change."*

Validate Scope

When I first heard the phrase "validate scope," I thought it meant that I needed to check with the stakeholders to make sure I had correctly heard what they wanted. Be forewarned, though: That's not what it means on the PMP exam! Rather, it means that you're receiving formal acceptance of project deliverables. The project charter (discussed in Book II, Chapter 2) identifies who can sign off that the project is complete. The project scope statement (discussed in Book III, Chapter 2) identifies criteria for completion.

Validate Scope. Formalizing acceptance of the completed project deliverables.

Another area where you could have trouble if you don't know the glossary terms is understanding the difference between *validation* and *verification.* These two terms can be used interchangeably or in very specific ways, depending on the industry in which you work. The PMP exam will say that verification means the product complies with requirements. Validation means the product meets the needs of the customer.

Verification. The evaluation of whether a product, service, or system complies with a regulation, requirement, specification, or imposed condition. It is often an internal process.

Validation. The assurance that a product, service, or system meets the needs of the customer and other identified stakeholders. It often involves acceptance and suitability with external customers.

Here is one other little nuance you should know about validating scope before you get into the meat of the process: Validate Scope and Control Quality are closely related. The difference is that the intent of Control Quality is to ensure that the deliverables are technically correct. The intent of Validate Scope is to obtain customer acceptance. This means that theoretically, you could have a deliverable that's not correct and doesn't pass quality control but might be accepted by the customer. The customer might waive a requirement or say the deliverable is good enough — or perhaps it isn't correct because you over-delivered. In all these situations, the deliverable is not correct, but it would be accepted.

In general, the Control Quality process is performed prior to validating scope.

The flow of deliverables

Figure 2-1 shows the flow of completed deliverables through various processes.

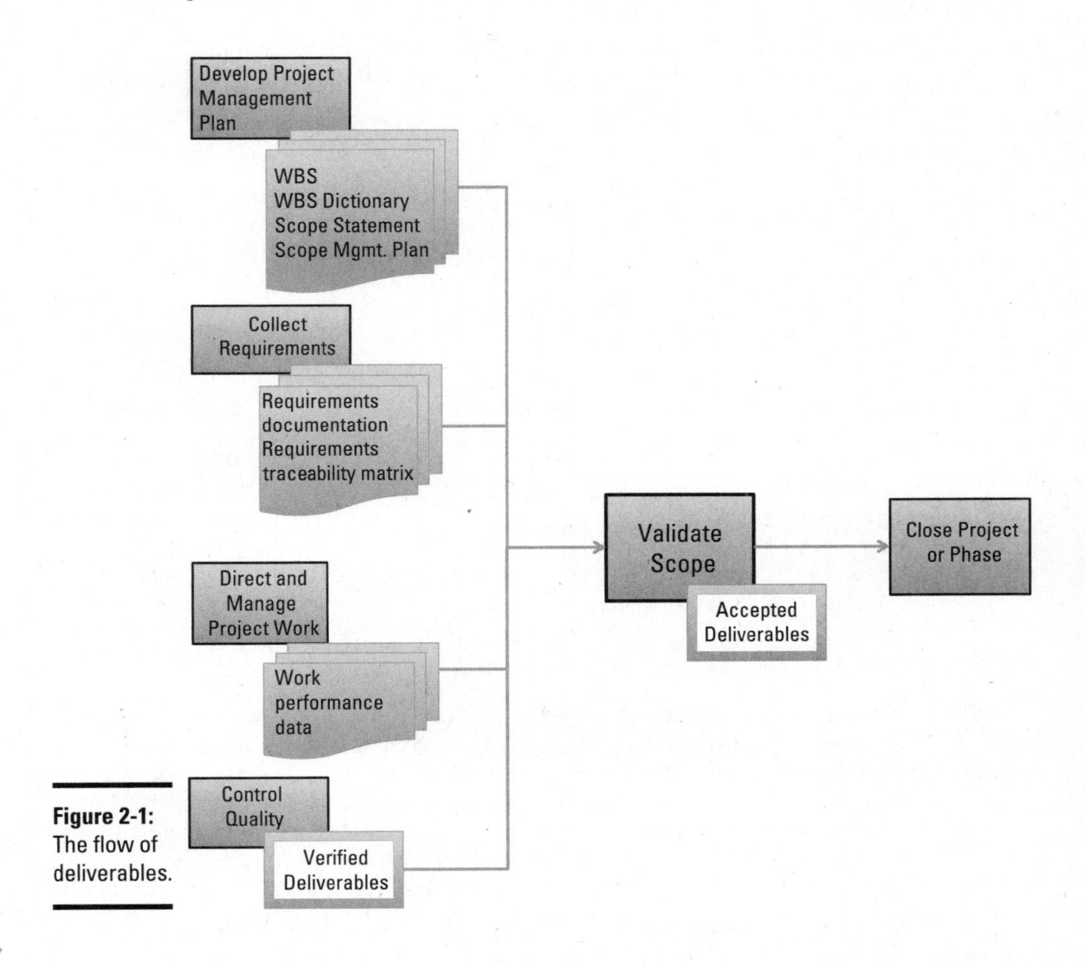

Figure 2-1: The flow of deliverables.

You can see how components from the project management plan and the Collect Requirements process are used along with the deliverables created from the Direct and Manage Project Work process that have been are verified in the Control Quality process. Those verified deliverables are ready for inspection in the Validate Scope process. After the deliverables are accepted, they are ready for close-out.

I want to stress an important point about the relationship between getting acceptance on the deliverables and closing the project or phase: You should perform scope validation throughout the project. You don't want to wait until the end of the project to show everything to the customer and hope that he likes it. You need to show deliverables along the way. The Close Project or Phase process occurs at the end of a phase when the customer accepts an entire set of deliverables and formally signs off that the phase is complete — or, in the case of the project, signs off that all deliverables are complete and accepted, and then the project can move into project closure.

Validate Scope: Inputs

To accept the deliverables, the customer should look at the scope baseline and the requirements. These documents contain all the detailed information about each deliverable. Each of the documents below is discussed in detail in Book III, Chapter 2. As a refresher, you would have the following information:

- **Scope management plan:** Contains information on how you will validate each deliverable
- **Scope statement:** Describes product deliverables and their acceptance criteria
- **Work breakdown structure (WBS):** Identifies all the deliverables
- **WBS dictionary:** Provides a detailed technical description of each deliverable in the WBS
- **Requirements documentation:** Lists all the technical requirements, product requirements, business requirements, and so forth
- **Requirements traceability matrix:** Links requirements to their origin and may have information on how the requirement will be verified

The project manager (or the delegated representative) should inspect the verified deliverables and/or the work performance data and compare them with the information in the documents listed in the preceding list.

Validate Scope: Tools, Techniques, and Outputs

The only technique used for validating scope is inspection. Inspection entails reviewing the deliverables to make sure they meet the stakeholder needs. There are many ways to do this:

- **Test.** For quantifiable requirements, you can measure. This is good for size, weight, and speed.
- **Examine.** For those requirements you can validate by a visual inspection, you can examine the deliverable.

- **Analysis.** This method is used if you can't see what is happening, but you can infer from the result that things work correctly.
- **Demonstration.** For deliverables that need to perform one or more steps, you can demonstrate the steps.

Take a look at how you could use each of these methods with my running childcare center example:

- You can test how the security system works by making sure the cameras cover the area you need and that the alarm company is notified when the perimeter is breached.
- You can examine the furniture and equipment to make sure that it's child-size and safe.
- You can analyze the enrollment software to see that it performs as promised.
- You can demonstrate that the security system cameras and motion detectors show up in the correct locations on the computer screens and that they correctly represent the physical layout of the childcare center.

As I mention earlier, you should conduct validation throughout the project. You can do it as deliverables are completed, at phase gates, or at milestones. For the childcare center, you could perform validation at the following points:

1. Meet with the parents to gather requirements.
2. After the blueprints are complete, show the parents how the blueprints meet the requirements.
3. Do a walk-through when the rough construction work is done to validate that construction is consistent with the blueprints.
4. Do a final walk-through to gain final acceptance that the final build-out is acceptable.

At each inspection, you would receive sign-off from a parent representative, the project team member in charge of engineering and construction, and the project manager. One tool that can help you is a Product Acceptance form, which can track verification information, such as

- Requirement
- Verification method
- Acceptance criteria
- Status
- Signature

You can set this up in a table like the form in Figure 2-2. That way, when all the deliverables are signed off, you can move to the Close Project or Phase process.

PRODUCT ACCEPTANCE FORM

Project Title: ____________ Date Prepared: ____________

ID	Requirement	Verification Method	Validation Method	Acceptance Criteria	Status	Sign-off
Identi fier.	*Describe the requirement.*	*Method of verifying the requirement is met.*	*Method of validating the requirement meets the stakeholder's needs.*	*Criteria for acceptance.*	*Accepted or not.*	*Signature of party accepting the product.*

Figure 2-2: A Product Acceptance form.

Those deliverables that meet the acceptance criteria are formally signed off by the customer. Those that don't will require a change request for defect repair. You should note why the deliverables were not accepted as well as the subsequent follow-up actions.

A defect repair is a type of change request. I define *defect repair* as "A formally documented identification of a defect in a project component with a recommendation to either repair the defect or completely replace the component."

Control Scope

Losing control of the project and product scope is the fastest way to get behind schedule and overrun your budget. Controlling the scope is challenging because stakeholders have differing ideas about what is in and out of scope, and senior managers and customers don't appreciate being told they can't have what they ask for. However, if you want to have any hope of a successful project, *you must control your scope!* That doesn't mean that your scope will never change — because it will. Rather, this means that *all changes must follow the change control process,* and all changes must take into consideration the impact on schedule, cost, quality, resources, risks, and so forth. I discuss the Perform Integrated Change Control process in the previous chapter. The following definitions will help frame my forthcoming discussion about the Control Scope process.

Control Scope. Monitoring the status of the project and product scope and managing changes to the scope baseline.

Scope Change. Any change to the project scope. A scope change almost always requires an adjustment to the project cost or schedule.

Scope Creep. The uncontrolled expansion to product or project scope without adjustments to time, cost, and resources.

Creep versus change

You can see by the preceding definitions that the difference between scope creep and scope change is addressing the impact of the scope change on the schedule, cost, and other aspects of the project.

Scope change

Start by looking at some of the common causes of scope changes:

- **External event:** Changes in the competitive environment or a new regulation can cause the team or the customer to reconsider the product scope.
- **Error in defining product scope:** If a requirement was left out in defining the scope originally, the scope will have to be changed to include the new requirement.
- **Error in defining project scope:** An error in defining the project scope, such as needed to employ specific procedures or processes, could entail changing the project scope.
- **Value-adding change:** Sometimes a team member finds a better way of accomplishing the work or determines how to improve quality by doing things differently.
- **Implementing a contingency plan or workaround:** If a risk event occurs and you need to take actions to respond to it, the actions could cause a change to either the project or product scope.
- **Customer sees the product and wants changes:** Some product development projects employ a life cycle that allows for iterative development as the customer and end users see interim deliverables. This is still a scope change, but the project team is planning for the design and the deliverables to evolve with each iteration.

Here's how each of these types of changes could be applied to the childcare center.

- **External event:** There are new regulations regarding water pressure and flow rate.
- **Error in defining the product:** The architect didn't lay out the HVAC system correctly to match the floor plan.
- **Error in defining the project:** The project manager didn't include the contractor in the weekly team meetings or include the weekly report templates the contractor will need to submit.
- **Value-adding change:** The general contractor comes by one morning and tells you he knows of a kitchen supply wholesaler that's going out of business, with appliances for less than wholesale and higher grade than the appliances you planned for the childcare center. This change improves performance and reduces cost.

- **Implementing a contingency plan or workaround:** In Book V, Chapter 1, I identify the following risk: "The city might not approve the plans, thus causing a schedule delay." If this risk did occur, the response was to mitigate the risk by following up weekly. If the risk occurred anyway, the contingency plan was to immediately start drawing up plans to resubmit. This is additional scope that would need to be incorporated into the project.
- **Customer seeing the product and wanting changes:** Assume that the parents come to the childcare center after the frame is completed but before any of the electric, plumbing, and HVAC work has been done. Some of the parents think it would be a good idea to increase the size of the playroom and decrease the size of the eating area. The contractor is on-site and says that could be done — and that he can give you an estimate for cost and schedule implications by the end of the week.

Scope creep

Now look at the other side of the equation: scope creep. No project is immune to the perils of scope creep. You have to be strong, have good scope definition, and have a good change control process to avoid it. Here are some common causes of scope creep:

- **Lack of change control:** If you don't have a well-defined change control system, you can't effectively control the project. It isn't enough to have a change control system, though. Stakeholders have to know about it, it can't be overly prohibitive to use, and you have to enforce it.
- **Not understanding the work needed to meet project objectives:** If you start working on a project before you understand all the work needed to meet the project objectives, you are likely to miss deliverables or miss the amount of work it takes to meet those deliverables.
- **Lack of communication:** Stakeholders can say what they want (encoding) — and in their heads, that message is very clear. However, in the decoding process, the receiver might have a completely different interpretation of what the stakeholder wants. By not using multiple modes of communication, using jargon, or assuming that you understand what the customer wants, you are leaving yourself open to misinterpretation of scope — and thus rework and scope creep — to deliver what the stakeholder wants.
- **Not saying no:** This applies to the project manager, sponsor, and team members. It can be scary and unpleasant to tell someone she can't have what she wants. Sometimes it seems easier to just give people what they want and deal with the schedule and cost overruns later. You must enforce the change control system. You don't have to be rude about it, but you must make sure it is followed! If you give in once, you will get walked over time and time again.

To prevent scope creep, follow these rules:

1. Fully define and document your scope.
2. Meet with your stakeholders and customers often to confirm that you all have the same understanding of scope.
3. Establish a change control system (see Book VII, Chapter 1) that includes
   - A change request form
   - A process to analyze the impacts of change requests
   - A change control board to discuss and determine the outcome of the change request
   - A method to communicate change request status (approved, denied, pended)
   - A procedure to update plans to incorporate approved changes
4. Document the scope using requirements, a scope statement, a WBS, and a WBS dictionary.
5. Get sign-off on the scope and baseline it.
6. Enforce the change control system.
7. Keep project documents up to date.

Control Scope: Inputs

To this point, I've talked quite a bit about the causes of change to project scope. Now I walk you through the process.

All control processes begin with the project management plan as an input. In the case of the Control Scope process, you will consider the following elements:

- **Scope baseline,** comprising the scope statement, WBS, and WBS dictionary
- **Scope management plan,** with a section describing how you will control project scope
- **Change control plan** that describes the overall project change control system
- **Configuration management plan** that describes how you will control the physical elements of the product
- **Requirements management plan** that describes how you will manage and control project requirements

In addition to the scope baseline, you will need information about the requirements — specifically, the requirements documentation and the requirements traceability matrix. If you need a refresher on these, check out Book III, Chapter 2.

Work performance data includes the deliverables that have started, their progress to date, and the deliverables that have been completed. You will also want to know the number of scope change requests and the status of those requests.

Control Scope: Tools and Techniques

The team takes the information from the inputs and performs a variance analysis. Take a minute and look at a few definitions.

Variance. A quantifiable deviation, departure, or divergence away from a known baseline or expected value.

Variance Analysis. A technique for determining the cause and degree of difference between the baseline and actual performance.

This is a fancy way of saying you are determining whether the scope you have is consistent with the scope that was planned. Variance analysis includes a technical as well as physical evaluation of the products. If you find a variance, you need to discover the degree of variance as well as the root cause. That information will help you determine whether you need to take any actions to resolve the variance.

Control Scope: Outputs

As a result of the variance analysis, you will have work performance information. The information is used to update your organizational process assets (OPAs), such as causes of variances and lessons learned. If your variances cross the threshold, you need to submit a change request for corrective or preventive actions or a defect repair. You might also need to update various elements of the project management plan, such as the scope baseline and probably the schedule and cost baselines as well, because a change in scope usually causes a change in schedule and cost. You may need to update your requirements information, too.

Data versus information

There is a difference between *work performance data* and *work performance information.* Work performance data is an output from the Direct and Manage Project Work process. Work performance data is the raw observations and measurements identified during activities being performed to carry out the project work. Work performance data is a generic term that can include

- Status of deliverables
- Implementation of change requests
- Corrective actions taken
- Preventive actions taken
- Status of defect repairs
- Forecasts for estimates to complete
- Percent of work actually completed
- Technical achievements
- Actual start and finish dates of schedule activities

Work performance information takes the baselines and compares them with the actual performance to develop contextualized measurements of progress. For example, work performance data might state that you have 8 of 10 widgets built, and the variance analysis shows that they are built correctly. Therefore, work performance information states that you are 80 percent complete with the work.

The ability to control performance to the project management plan is prevalent in many of the monitor and control processes. However, it all starts with managing the project scope effectively. Therefore, it is predictable that the test questions on the ability to manage the project plan will focus on the Control Scope process.

Key Terms

The following terms are used to validate and control changes to the project scope:

- Verification
- Validation
- Scope change
- Scope creep
- Variance
- Variance analysis

Chapter Summary

In this chapter, I look at validating that the product meets the needs of the customer. I also discuss how to control the project scope.

- Validating scope is about demonstrating to the customer or sponsor that the deliverables meet her needs. After validation is complete, the customer or sponsor should approve and sign off on the scope.
- Deliverables are created in the Direct and Manage Project Work process. They then go to Control Quality to ensure that they are correct. After they are verified as correct, deliverables go to the Validate Scope process for customer acceptance. When all deliverables are accepted, they go to the Close Project or Phase process.
- Inspection is how you prove the capabilities of deliverables. You can measure, examine, test, and demonstrate capabilities.
- Scope change is common on projects. Scope creep is changing the scope without addressing the effects on time, cost, resources, or other aspects of the project. Any change needs to go through the Perform Integrated Change Control process, and the impact on schedule, cost, and other objectives needs to be taken into consideration before implementing the change.
- To control scope, you compare the baseline and requirements with the results. By conducting a variance analysis, you will determine whether a variance exists — and if one does, whether you should submit a change request. You will end up with work performance information and updates to the project management plan, project documents, and organizational process assets.

Prep Test

1 **Making sure that the deliverables are built according to the requirements and specifications is part of**

A ❍ Validate Scope
B ❍ Control Scope
C ❍ Perform Quality Assurance
D ❍ Control Quality

2 **The objective of the Validate Scope process is to**

A ❍ Get sign-off on deliverables.
B ❍ Close out the project.
C ❍ Make sure all the deliverables meet the specifications.
D ❍ Make sure you understood the scope requirements correctly.

3 **Which is the proper sequence of events?**

A ❍ Control Quality, Direct and Manage Project Work, Validate Scope, Close Project or Phase
B ❍ Direct and Manage Project Work, Validate Scope, Control Quality, Close Project or Phase
C ❍ Direct and Manage Project Work, Perform Quality Assurance, Validate Scope, Close Project or Phase
D ❍ Direct and Manage Project Work, Control Quality, Validate Scope, Close Project or Phase

4 **The requirement states that the software must pull information from three different reports and then average the outcome and show the range and standard deviation. Which inspection technique should you use?**

A ❍ Test
B ❍ Examine
C ❍ Inspect
D ❍ Measure

5 **You hired a contractor to build a deck that holds your patio furniture, a grill, and a fire pit. The contractor is done with the job and asks you to come inspect the work before submitting a final bill. Which technique should you use to inspect the work?**

A ❍ Test
B ❍ Examine
C ❍ Demonstrate
D ❍ Measure

6 **Which of the following is not an output of the Control Scope process?**

A ❍ Organizational process asset updates
B ❍ Change requests
C ❍ Work performance data
D ❍ Project document updates

7 **Which of the following is a common cause of changes to scope?**

A ❍ Lack of communication
B ❍ Not understanding the work needed to meet project objectives
C ❍ Defining the work incorrectly
D ❍ Lack of a change control process

8 **Which of the following is a common cause of scope creep?**

A ❍ Not being able to say no
B ❍ A change in the marketplace
C ❍ Implementing a workaround
D ❍ A value-added change

9 **If you want to prevent scope creep, you should take a number of steps. Of the following steps, which would you do first?**

A ❍ Get sign-off on the scope and baseline it.
B ❍ Meet with stakeholders to affirm you have a common understanding of the scope.
C ❍ Enforce the change control system.
D ❍ Communicate changes.

10 **Which of the following is an example of work performance information?**

A ❍ Technical achievements
B ❍ Status of defect repairs
C ❍ 60% complete
D ❍ Actual start date

Answers

1. **D.** Control Quality. Control Quality is about making sure the deliverables are built correctly according to requirements and specifications. *Look at "Validate Scope."*
2. **A.** Get sponsor sign-off on deliverables. In Validate Scope, you want the customer or sponsor to accept and sign off on deliverables. *See "Validate Scope."*
3. **D.** Direct and Manage Project Work, Control Quality, Validate Scope, Close Project or Phase. That is the sequence of processes that occur with deliverables. *Review "The flow of deliverables."*
4. **A.** Test. Because you can't see what is happening, you have to infer, based on the result. This is an example of testing. *Check out "Validate Scope: Tools, Techniques, and Outputs."*
5. **B.** Examine. You can examine that the deck holds the furniture and grill and has a fire pit. *Look into "Validate Scope: Tools, Techniques, and Outputs."*
6. **C.** Work performance data. Work performance information is an input. *Review "Control Scope: Outputs."*
7. **C.** Defining the work incorrectly. Incorrectly defining the work is an error in defining product or project scope. The other answers are examples of what causes scope creep. *Go over "Scope change."*
8. **A.** Not being able to say no. One of the common causes of scope creep is not being able to say no to a customer, sponsor, or other stakeholder. The other options are common reasons for scope change. *Look at "Scope creep."*
9. **B.** Meet with stakeholders to affirm you have a common understanding of the scope. Having a common understanding of project scope upfront is the first step to preventing scope creep. *See the information in "Scope creep."*
10. **C.** 60% complete. All the other answers are examples of work performance data. *Review the sidebar "Data versus information."*

Chapter 3: Controlling Your Schedule

Exam Objectives

- **Measure project performance, identify and quantify variances, and determine appropriate preventive and corrective actions. Communicate status to stakeholders per the communication management plan.**
- **Ensure baseline integrity by updating the project management plan in response to approved changes and communicating those approved changes to the team.**

Controlling the schedule has similar exam objectives, inputs, and outputs to the Control Scope (see Book VII, Chapter 2) and Control Cost (see Book VIII, Chapter 1) processes. However, the tools and techniques are similar to the Develop Schedule process (see Book III, Chapter 3).

In the Control Schedule process, you determine the current schedule status of the project. Where variances exist, you need to understand the nature of the variances and what caused them. This allows you to respond appropriately. Where possible, try to influence those factors that cause variances, such as resource variances, scope creep, different productive rates, and so forth.

When changes are required to the schedule, make sure that they go through the change control process; then, update the schedule baseline to maintain baseline integrity.

Quick Assessment

1 (True/False). A schedule revision needs to go through the integrated Change Control process.

2 The ______ ______ ______ establishes criteria and the activities for developing and controlling the project schedule.

3 (True/False). A change in priorities is one of the reasons why project schedules slip.

4 What are the two types of schedule compression?

5 One way to optimize your schedule is to adjust ______ and ______.

6 Which scheduling technique should you use to analyze your utilization of buffer?

7 To assess how various situations can impact your project, you should use which scheduling technique?

8 If you want to shorten your schedule and you are willing to spend funds to do so, what schedule compression technique should you employ?

9 (True/False). An SPI of –.96 is a viable work performance measurement from the Control Schedule process.

10 Fast-tracking your schedule increases the possibility of ______.

Answers

1. False. A schedule change needs to go through the Perform Integrated Change Control process. A schedule revision does not. *You can find more information about schedule revisions in "Control Schedule: Inputs."*

2. Schedule management plan. The schedule management plan is the part of the project management plan that establishes criteria and the activities for developing and controlling the project schedule. *You can find information on the schedule management plan in "Control Schedule."*

3. True. A change in priorities is one of the reasons why project schedules slip; others include staffing variance and inaccurate estimating. *To see more reasons why schedules can slip, read up on "Control Schedule: Tools and Techniques."*

4. Crashing, fast-tracking. The two types of schedule compression you will be tested on are crashing and fast-tracking. *You can read about them in "Schedule compression."*

5. Leads, lags. Adjusting leads and lags can help you find the best approach for scheduling project work. *You can read about adjusting leads and lags in "Fast-tracking."*

6. Performance reviews. In addition to analyzing the utilization of buffer, performance reviews include trend analysis and earned value management. *Read more about this in the section "Performance reviews."*

7. Modeling techniques. Modeling techniques allow you to see how the schedule will be impacted based on uncertain future events. *You can learn more about this technique in "Modeling techniques."*

8. Crashing. Crashing generally costs money, whereas fast-tracking does not. *Check out "Schedule compression."*

9. False. You can't have a negative SPI. *You can read about work performance measurements in "Control Schedule: Outputs."*

10. Rework. Fast-tracking increases your risk for rework because you are overlapping activities that would normally be done in sequence. *Look over "Fast-tracking."*

Control Schedule

Your schedule is one of the most important documents you will produce. It is a key component in managing stakeholder expectations. It tells team members when they will be performing work, the type of work they will perform, whom team members will be working with, and how long the work should take. Your schedule also tells the customer when deliverables can be reviewed and when to expect a finished product. And the schedule lets management know when the project reviews are scheduled and how the team is doing in meeting its timelines.

However, as much time as you spend developing this very important document, you will spend even more time updating and controlling the schedule. This chapter is all about staying on schedule and influencing all the variables that could cause a schedule variance.

I start out with the process definition and a refresher on some of the terms associated with planning and developing the project schedule.

Control Schedule. Monitoring the status of the project activities to update project progress and manage changes to the schedule baseline to achieve the plan.

Schedule Model. A representation of the plan for executing the project's activities — including durations, dependencies, and other planning information — used to produce a project schedule along with other scheduling artifacts.

Project Schedule. An output of a schedule model that presents linked activities with planned dates, durations, milestones, and resources.

Schedule Baseline. The approved version of a schedule model that can be changed only through formal change control procedures and is used as a basis for comparison to actual results.

Schedule Management Plan. A component of the project management plan that establishes the criteria and the activities for developing, monitoring, and controlling the schedule.

The schedule baseline is your commitment to the sponsor and the customer about when to expect certain deliverables, phase gates, and due dates. The project schedule is what you use to manage the day-to-day project. The project schedule is likely to be adjusted on a fairly regular basis. The schedule baseline should change only in response to a change request that has gone through the Perform Integrated Change Control process.

Control Schedule: Inputs

As with most control processes, you start with the project management plan, work performance data, and organizational process assets (OPAs). For the Control Schedule process, you will also have specific schedule information, such as the project schedule, schedule data, and resource calendars. Here is how each input contributes to the process:

- **Project management plan:** This has two components you will use in this process:
  - *Schedule baseline:* Compare your planned progress with your actual progress.
  - *Schedule management plan:* The schedule management plan should identify the acceptable variances for schedule performance. For example, if you're behind on work that's not on the critical path, is that considered a variance? If you're ahead on the critical path, is that considered a variance? Under what circumstances can you use schedule reserves, and what process do you use to update the plan to show that?
- **Work performance data:** This tells you which activities have started, which have finished, and how far along you are for those activities that are in progress.
- **Project schedule:** This is the day-to-day schedule used to track and monitor project work.
- **Schedule data:** This refers to any and all project specific schedule information. For example, a resource histogram that shows the hours of work by team member per week, schedule reserve or schedule buffer utilization, network diagrams, milestone charts, and so forth.
- **Resource calendars:** If you have resources that work to different calendars, you will need information on individual calendars. You might have some resources that work 80 hours in 9 days, or resources in other countries that have different work hours and different holidays.
- **Organizational process assets:** These include the organizational policies, templates, and procedures you need to manage the project schedule.

TIP

You should be aware of a few scheduling nuances, such as the difference between a schedule change, a schedule revision, and a schedule update.

- A **schedule change** is based on a change request that's approved via the Perform Integrated Change Control process.

- A **schedule revision** may change the sequencing of activities, the resources on activities, the start and finish dates within an activity's float, or some other revision that doesn't impact the baseline schedule.
- A **schedule update** is when you enter status into your project schedule. For instance, you note that an activity started on a specific date and that it's now 50 percent complete.

Control Schedule: Tools and Techniques

Many of the techniques you will use to control the schedule are similar to those you used to develop the schedule. For a refresher on developing the schedule, you can review Book III, Chapter 3. Table 3-1 shows the techniques used in the Control Schedule process compared with the techniques used in the Develop Schedule process. The italicized techniques are similar or identical.

Table 3-1 Control Schedule versus Develop Schedule Techniques

Control Schedule	Develop Schedule
Performance reviews	Schedule network analysis
Project management software	Critical path method Critical chain method
Resource optimization techniques	*Resource optimization techniques*
Modeling techniques	*Modeling techniques*
Leads and lags	*Leads and lags*
Schedule compression	*Schedule compression*
Scheduling tool	*Scheduling tool*

Performance reviews

Performance reviews compare the baseline with the actual results. You can compare several elements to determine the progress. The following is a list of common elements you can compare:

- Planned start dates to actual start dates
- Planned finish dates to actual finish dates
- Planned duration to actual duration
- Planned effort to actual effort

In addition, your review should include determining the amount of buffer or float you have used compared against how far along you are in the project. For example, if you have 30 days of float for the project, you're halfway through, and you've used 21 days of float, that might be cause for concern. You are 50 percent done but have used 70 percent of the float. Float is used for critical path methodology, and buffer is used for critical chain methodology. You can refresh your memory on these scheduling methods by reviewing information in Book III, Chapter 3.

Performance reviews shouldn't just identify variances: They should also address the root cause of the variance and whether corrective or preventive actions are desired or even possible. Here are some of the common causes of schedule variances:

- **Staffing variances:** If you were planning to have specific resources available but they're not available, you might have a variance.
- **Change in priorities:** When you planned the project, it was considered a high-priority project. However, things changed. When your project is no longer high priority, your resources might be available for less time than you planned.
- **Inaccurate estimating:** If your duration estimates were too aggressive, you should expect a negative schedule variance.
- **Rate of work:** Some people work really fast, and others work really slowly. The rate of work can affect how quickly you get work done.
- **Scope creep:** Of course, if you add scope without analyzing the impact of budget and schedule, you will most likely be behind schedule.

A performance review can be as simple as reviewing your schedule and having the project management software identify variances, or it can be a very structured affair that includes the sponsor, the customer, and key vendors. These reviews can take several hours.

During the performance reviews, you should look at the current status as well as performance trends. Charts and graphs that forecast future schedule performance are a common method for assessing the schedule status. If the variance is negative and greater than your schedule threshold, you should consider various options for correcting the variances. It is common to present earned value (EV) data at performance reviews as well. I spend quite a bit of time going over EV in the next chapter, so I don't address it here other than to say that you may present schedule variance (SV) and schedule performance index (SPI) measurements as part of your variance analysis and performance review.

Resource optimization

Throughout the project, you may revisit your resource allocation among activities to try and optimize your resources. For example, you might move some resources to activities on the critical path if you're concerned that those activities won't finish on time. Or you might find that work is taking longer than expected, and some resources are working 60-hour weeks. In that case, you might reduce the amount of work that they're doing. Of course, this could have negative impacts, so you have to analyze your options and select the best one.

Modeling techniques

As the project progresses, your uncertainty in some areas will diminish, but it might increase in other areas based on the work performance. You can use what-if scenario analysis much the same way you do in planning by thinking through different scenarios that could affect the project and seeing what happens to the schedule based on those scenarios.

You can use this technique along with resource leveling to see the effect of shifting resources, adding resources, or reducing the amount of time that you're using specific resources. You can also use what-if scenario analysis when analyzing the impact of risk events to see the impact on a schedule if a specific risk occurs.

A specific type of modeling technique is a simulation that calculates the duration based on differing assumptions. A Monte Carlo simulation will use three different estimates (optimistic, most likely, and pessimistic) to account for uncertainty in the duration and resource estimates. The output of a simulation is a probability distribution for the project duration.

Leads and lags

If you're behind schedule, you may want to use leads to start successor activities before their predecessor activities are completed. For example, if the requirements gathering activities are taking longer than planned, you might start some of the preliminary design work before the final requirements documentation is complete.

Schedule compression

As you go through the project, you will probably need to find ways to compress some parts of the schedule because other parts took longer than expected. As I discuss in Book III, Chapter 3, the two main types of schedule compression are crashing and fast-tracking.

Crashing

Crashing looks for cost/schedule trade-offs. In other words, you're looking for ways to shorten the schedule by applying more resources or by spending more. The intent is to get the most schedule compression for the least amount of money. Some common ways of accomplishing this include

- ✦ Bringing in more resources
- ✦ Working overtime
- ✦ Paying to expedite deliverables

You want to crash only those activities on the critical path because that's the path that drives the duration of the project. Here is an example of how you would evaluate crashing activities on the critical path.

Assume you have a network path with five activities on it: Activity A, Activity B, and so on. The durations and the predecessor information in Table 3-2 have been given to you, and you can assume this information is accurate.

Table 3-2 Crashing Information

Task	*Duration*	*Predecessor*
A	4	None
B	6	None
C	3	A
D	1	B
E	2	C, D

You also have the following information about the costs to crash each activity.

- ✦ Task A costs $1,000.
- ✦ Task E costs $1,500.
- ✦ Task B is three times as expensive as Task A.
- ✦ Task C costs $2,400.
- ✦ Task D costs twice as much as Task A.
- ✦ To crash Task A and save 1 day, it will cost 50% more. It cannot be crashed more than 1 day.

- To crash Task B, it will cost $300 more per day, and it can be crashed up to 2 days.
- Task C can be crashed by 1 day for a cost of $600.
- Task D can be crashed by 1 day for a cost of $500.
- Task E cannot be crashed.

If you think about it, you can probably figure out how to solve this on your own. Still, here's a six-step method to solve this kind of problem:

1. **Create a table that shows the regular duration and crash duration, and the regular cost and crash cost for each activity. Then include a column that shows the crash cost per day.**

Task	Regular Duration	Crash Duration	Regular Cost	Crash Cost	Cost Per Day
A	4	3	1,000	1,500	500
B	6	5/4	3,000	3,300/3,600	300
C	3	2	2,400	3,000	600
D	2	1	2,000	2,500	500
E	2	2	1,500	n/a	n/a

   By looking at the table, you can see that the least-expensive activity to crash is Activity B, and you can crash that by either 1 day or 2 days.

2. **Draw a network diagram that corresponds to the network information you were given.**

   Figure 3-1 shows the network diagram. If you want a refresher on network diagrams, check out Book III, Chapter 3.

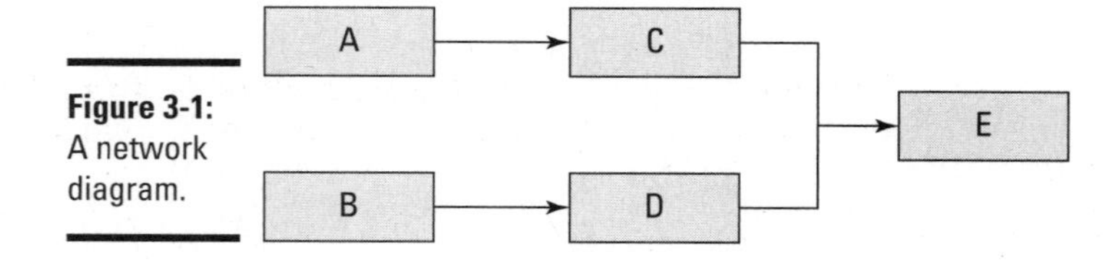

Figure 3-1: A network diagram.

3. **Fill in the regular and crash durations and the regular and crash costs according to the legend in Figure 3-2.**

   Figure 3-2 shows the network diagram with cost and schedule information.

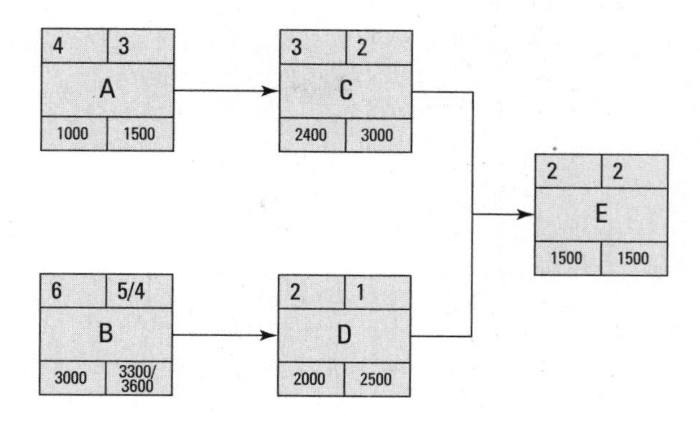

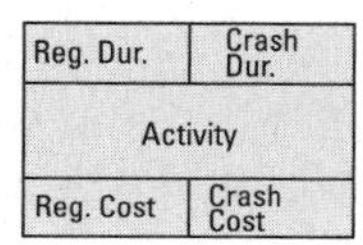

Figure 3-2: A network diagram with cost and schedule information.

4. **Add the durations for each path and determine the critical path.**

   The critical path in this example is BDE, with a duration of 10 days. (Book III, Chapter 3 shows you how to determine the critical path.)

5. **Start by crashing the least-expensive activity on the critical path until you have a new critical path.**

   In this example, you can crash Activity B for $300 for 1 day. Then both paths are 9 days.

6. **Continue this process until you reach the duration you need, or until you can't crash anymore.**

   For this example, you can crash the network down to 7 days for a total additional cost of $2,200.

The summary of this example is that the regular duration is 10 days, and the regular cost is $9,900. The fully crashed duration is 7 days, and the cost is $12,100.

You might see this type of question in the Planning section or the Control section. In both instances, you're looking to gain the most amount of time for the least amount of cost.

Fast-tracking

Fast-tracking shortens the schedule by overlapping activities that are normally done in sequence. One way of doing this is by changing the network logic adjusting your leads and lags and changing a finish-to-start (FS) activity to an FS with a lead or to a start-to-start (SS) with a lag. The method is the same as covered in Book III, Chapter 3.

Fast-tracking can increase your risk on the project and may necessitate rework. Make sure you understand the real relationship between activities when you fast-track!

Project management software and scheduling tool

Even though the *PMBOK Guide* lists project management software and the scheduling tool as two separate tools, they are essentially the same. Project management software can include more than just the scheduling tool: It can include budgeting and estimating software, resource management software, and so on. The point is that you have electronic tools to help you control your schedule.

The monitoring and controlling knowledge and skills that you should expect to see tested for the Control Schedule process include

- Project performance metrics: specifically, effort, duration, and milestones
- Variance and trend analysis techniques
- Performance measurement techniques, specifically, CPM, PERT, SPI, and SV

Control Schedule: Outputs

The outputs for this process are similar to those for the Control Scope process. The Control Schedule process includes schedule forecasts, but other than that, the differences lie in the types of data:

- Work performance information is usually earned value (EV) numbers for schedule variance and the schedule performance index (SPI).
- Change requests have to do with preventive and corrective actions to bring schedule performance in line with the baseline, or requesting a change to the schedule.
- Components of the project management plan that you could update include the schedule baseline, the schedule management plan, and the cost baseline.
- Project documents that could be updated include the schedule and the schedule data.
- Organizational process asset updates are based on causes of schedule variances.

Work performance information for the Control Schedule process can be easily abused to hide schedule variances. For example, if a team member is behind on a project activity but he plans to work overtime to catch up, he might not disclose that the activity is behind because he thinks he can correct it before anyone finds out. Another example is if an activity takes more effort than was forecast but the duration is not impacted by this extra effort, a team member may report that the original effort was sufficient. To avoid this type of behavior, you need to have clear reporting expectations in your schedule management plan.

Schedule forecasts predict future performance based on past performance and knowledge about upcoming events and risks that could impact future performance. Forecasts may be substantiated by using EV calculations as well.

The following honesty standards from the Code of Ethics and Professional Conduct relate to work performance measurements:

- ✦ We are truthful in our communications and in our conduct.
- ✦ We provide accurate information in a timely manner.
- ✦ We do not engage in or condone behavior that is designed to deceive others, including but not limited to, making misleading or false statements, stating half-truths, or providing information out of context or withholding information that, if known, would render our statements as misleading or incomplete.

Agile schedule control

If you are using an agile scheduling technique, you will take a different approach to controlling the schedule. The PMP exam doesn't test on agile techniques to any great degree, but you should have a basic knowledge of the concepts:

1. Compare the estimated work with the actual work delivered in a set time period (a *sprint*).
2. Based on stakeholder feedback, revise and update the backlog of work.
3. Conduct a retrospective review of the sprint to determine what worked and how to improve the process in the future.
4. Estimate the velocity of work for the iteration or time frame and compare it with the planned velocity.

The majority of the scheduling terms can be found in Book III, Chapter 3, where I first discuss scheduling. Some of those terms are reiterated here, and a few additional terms are introduced.

- Schedule model
- Project schedule
- Schedule baseline
- Schedule management plan
- Schedule change
- Schedule revision
- Schedule update
- Crashing
- Fast-tracking

Chapter Summary

This chapter covers the information you need to determine whether your schedule progress is acceptable or you need to take corrective or preventive actions to achieve your planned schedule performance.

- A great deal of your time with the schedule is spent managing and controlling it. You will need to revise the schedule, update the schedule, and maybe even change the schedule.
- Like the Control Scope and Control Cost processes, you will start by comparing work performance data against the baseline. You will perform a performance review to determine whether the schedule performance requires action. You can also use performance reviews to discuss schedule status with management. You might need to employ resource optimization techniques and modeling techniques to determine how best to revise the schedule. Fast-tracking, adjusting leads and lags, and crashing are options you can take to compress the schedule.
- Work performance information might indicate the need for a change request. And, of course, you will update the forecasts, organizational process assets, the project management plan, and project documents to document the progress to date.

Prep Test

Multiple Choice

1 **Resequencing the order of activities on a path without impacting a milestone or key deliverable date is an example of**

A ❍ A schedule revision
B ❍ A schedule update
C ❍ A schedule slip
D ❍ A schedule change

2 **A specific version of the schedule model used to compare actual results with the plan to determine whether preventive or corrective action is needed to meet the project objectives is the**

A ❍ Project schedule
B ❍ Performance measurement baseline
C ❍ Schedule baseline
D ❍ Schedule data

3 **Many variables can have an impact on your ability to meet your schedule. Which of the following is not one of the common reasons for causing a schedule slip?**

A ❍ Inaccurate duration estimates
B ❍ Scope creep
C ❍ Rate of work
D ❍ More costly resources

4 **You are concerned that one of the resources on your team will be pulled off and put onto another project. Your project sponsor has asked you what the impact on the schedule would be if that occurred. What technique should you use to determine the impact?**

A ❍ Variance analysis
B ❍ What-if scenario analysis
C ❍ Fast-tracking
D ❍ Resource leveling

5 **Based on some schedule revisions you made, Joe is now working 65 hours during Week 1, 12 hours during Week 2, and 30 hours during Week 3. What technique should you use to allocate Joe's time better?**

A ❍ Crashing
B ❍ Fast-tracking
C ❍ What-if scenario analysis
D ❍ Resource optimization

6 **You need to compress your schedule. You decide to test two software components at the same time instead of sequentially. In addition, you're changing the dependencies on some other tasks from a finish-to-start to a finish-to-finish with a lag. What type of technique are you using?**

A ❍ Crashing
B ❍ Fast-tracking
C ❍ Resource leveling
D ❍ What-if scenario analysis

Scenario 1

Use the following information for the next four questions. Be warned, though: Some of the information is the same as the example in the crashing section of the chapter, but not all of it! Start from the beginning and work the whole problem.

Assume you have a network path with five activities on it and the following information about the network.

Task	*Duration*	*Predecessor*
A	4	-
B	6	A
C	3	A
D	1	B
E	2	C

You also have the following information about the costs to crash each activity:

- Task A costs $1,000.
- Task E costs $1,500.
- Task B is three times as expensive as Task A.
- Task C costs $2,400.
- Task D costs twice as much as Task A.
- To crash Task A and save 1 day, it will cost 50% more. It cannot be crashed more than 1 day.
- To crash Task B, it will cost $300 more per day, and it can be crashed up to 2 days.
- Task C can be crashed by 1 day for a cost of $600.
- Neither Task D nor E can be crashed.

1 What is the regular time for this path?

A ❍ 8 days
B ❍ 9 days
C ❍ 10 days
D ❍ 11 days

2 What is the crash time for this path?

A ❍ 8 days
B ❍ 9 days
C ❍ 10 days
D ❍ 11 days

3 What is the regular cost for this path?

A ❍ $11,600
B ❍ $11,000
C ❍ $9,900
D ❍ $9,000

4 What is the crash cost for this path?

A ❍ $11,600
B ❍ $11,000
C ❍ $9,900
D ❍ $9,000

Answers

Multiple Choice

1 **A.** A schedule revision. Resequencing is a schedule revision. *Review "Control Schedule: Inputs."*

2 **C.** Schedule baseline. The schedule baseline is used to compare the plan against the actual results. *Look at "Control Schedule."*

3 **D.** More costly resources. More costly resources can cause a budget overrun, but not usually a schedule slip. *Go over "Performance reviews."*

4 **B.** What-if scenario analysis. A what-if scenario analysis will show how the schedule will be affected by losing the resources. *Check out "Modeling techniques."*

5 **D.** Resource optimization. Use resource optimization to even out Joe's schedule. *Review "Resource optimization."*

6 **B.** Fast-tracking. Doing activities in parallel instead of sequentially is an example of fast-tracking. *Look over "Fast-tracking."*

Scenario 1

1 **D.** 11 days. The regular time is 11 days. The critical path is ABD. *See "Crashing."*

2 **A.** 8 days. The crash time is 8 days. ABD can be crashed to only 8 days. Even though ACE can be crashed to 7 days, ABD will still drive the duration. *Check out "Crashing."*

3 **C.** $9,900. The regular cost with no crashing is $9,900. It is the sum of all the regular costs for the activities. *Go over "Crashing."*

4 **B.** $11,000. The crash cost is $11,000. You shouldn't crash Task C because you can't get the schedule any shorter by spending the additional $600. *Look at "Crashing."*

Book VIII

Controlling Cost, Quality, and More

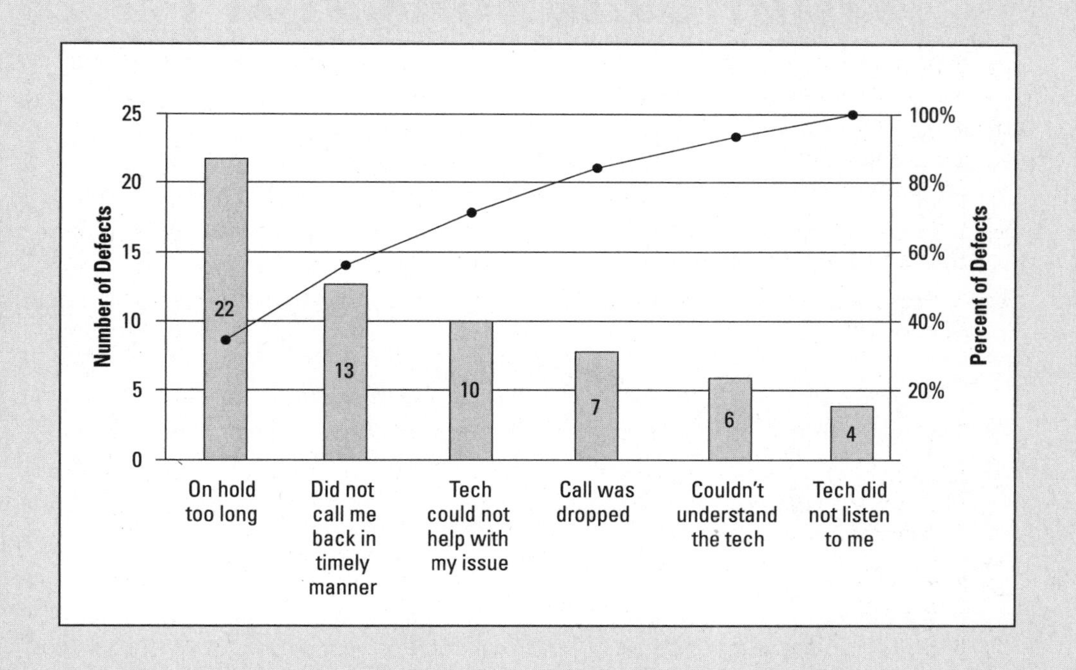

Check out the article on earned value basics at `www.dummies.com/extras/pmpcertificationaio`.

Contents at a Glance

Chapter 1: Controlling Cost and Using Earned Value

Exam Objectives

- **Measure project performance, identify and quantify variances, and determine appropriate preventive and corrective actions. Communicate status to stakeholders per the communications management plan.**
- **Ensure baseline integrity by updating the project management plan in response to approved changes and communicating those approved changes to the team.**

Like the Control Scope and Control Schedule processes, the exam objectives are concerned with measuring performance, correcting performance, and communicating that information. It also entails implementing only approved change requests.

Estimating, developing, and controlling the project budget is one of the highest-visibility activities that you do as a project manager. All the higher-up people want to know how you're doing according to budget. Because people often estimate as if everything will work perfectly, staying within the budget can be quite challenging.

When monitoring and controlling the budget, you need to make sure to compare the baseline cost for a deliverable or element of work with the actual cost. Don't fall into the trap of comparing how much you planned to spend to how much you have spent without taking into consideration what you got for what you spent! You have to monitor the performance to the money spent.

Controlling costs also consists of managing expenditures to stay within funding limitations as well as recording actual costs as they are incurred.

When you identify a cost variance, you should determine what caused it and what the appropriate response is. You might need to take corrective or preventive actions to stay within the cost threshold.

Finally, you need to update the budget to align with any changes to scope, schedule, quality, human resources, risk, and procurements.

Quick Assessment

1 The ______ ______ is the approved version of the time-phased project budget used to compare actual expenditures against planned expenditures to determine whether preventive or corrective action is needed to meet the project objectives.

2 The cost baseline is known as the ______ ______ ______ if you are using earned value techniques on your project.

3 Project funding requirements include funds for ______ and ______.

4 The sum of the planned value for all work packages is ______ ______ ______.

5 An indicator of how efficient you are performing against the budget is the ______ ______ ______.

6 (True/False). A positive cost variance says you have spent less than was budgeted for the work.

7 A work package that is valued at $5,000 with a fixed formula measurement method of 25/75 would receive credit for ______ after the work package is started.

8 EVM integrates ______, ______, and ______.

9 Which EVM measurement is used to forecast the remaining funds you need to complete the project?

10 The difference between the BAC and the EAC is the ______ ______ ______.

Answers

1 Cost baseline. The cost baseline will be used to measure cost performance on the project. You will compare this with the actual results to determine whether preventive or corrective action is required. *Read more in "Control Costs."*

2 Performance measurement baseline. The performance measurement baseline and cost baseline are essentially the same. *See the information in "Control Costs."*

3 Expenditures, reserves. You will manage your team to the cost estimates it provided. However, you will also require funding for reserves to account for unforeseen events, such as risks. *You can find more about project funding in "Control Costs: Inputs."*

4 Budget at completion. The budget at completion (BAC) is the total of all the estimates for the project. *The BAC is defined in "Earned Value Management."*

5 Cost performance index. The cost performance index (CPI) is the single most relevant indicator of the project's cost efficiency. *I discuss this in the section "Variances and indexes."*

6 True. A positive cost variance says you have spent less than was budgeted for the work. However, it doesn't say why. For example, you may have spent less because the original estimate was inflated. *I will talk about this in "Variances and indexes."*

7 $1,250. The fixed formula states that 25% of the value of the work should be credited when the work begins. Therefore, $1,250 is credited. *You can read about this in "Control Costs: Inputs" and Table 1-1: Fixed Formula Measurement Method.*

8 Scope, schedule, and cost. EVM gives you an integrated view of project progress by looking at scope, cost, and schedule performance. *There is quite a bit of information on earned value in "Earned Value Management."*

9 Estimate to complete (ETC). The ETC indicates the amount of funding you will need to finish the project. The equation is the BAC – AC. *Check out "Forecasting."*

10 Variance at completion. The variance at completion (VAC) tells you how much additional funding you will need to complete the project, over and above your budget at completion. *For more information, check out "Variance at completion."*

Control Costs

Cost overruns can be caused by so many different events. Here are some of the more common causes:

- **Inaccurate estimating:** The person estimating didn't know how to estimate, wasn't given enough time or information to develop a good estimate, or was asked to arbitrarily reduce the estimate.
- **Inappropriate estimating methods:** If you use cost estimates that are more than two to three years old, they won't be reliable. In addition, you need to select the correct estimating method, such as parametric, analogous, and so on. I cover estimating methods in Book IV, Chapter 1.
- **Unplanned, in-scope, work:** If you don't fully define your project and product scope, you might find work in there that you didn't identify during the planning process. You still have to do that work, but you don't have the budget for it.
- **Scope creep:** Adding or changing scope without taking into consideration that the cost impacts will cause you to go over budget.
- **Quality issues:** If you find a lot of defects and have more scrap and rework than planned, you will go over budget.
- **Change in resources:** If you plan resource rates at one amount and then get different resources that cost more, you will incur an overrun.
- **Risk event occurring:** Responding to identified risks, or developing a work-around for unidentified risks, can cost money that wasn't budgeted.
- **Contractor overrun:** A cost-reimbursable contract can require you to spend more than you had planned.
- **Lack of change control process:** If you don't have a process to identify, evaluate, vote on, and manage project changes, you will almost certainly go over budget because the scope will run amok, the schedule will never baseline, and people will tell you "it costs what it costs."

Given all those reasons for cost overruns, you can see why this process can be challenging. Before I delve into the details, I start out with the process definition and a refresher of some of the terms encountered when planning and developing the project cost estimates and budget.

Control Cost. Monitoring the status of the project to update the project costs and managing changes to the cost baseline.

Cost Baseline. The approved version of the time-phased budget, excluding any management reserves, which can be changed only through formal change control procedures and is used as a basis for comparison against actual results.

Performance Measurement Baseline. An approved integrated scope/schedule/cost plan for the project work against which project execution is compared to measure and manage performance. The PMB includes contingency reserve but excludes management reserve.

Cost Management Plan. A component of the project or program management plan that describes how costs will be planned, structured, and controlled.

The cost baseline is your commitment to the sponsor for project expenditures and reserves. The cost baseline should change only in response to a change request that has gone through the Perform Integrated Change Control process.

The phrase "performance measurement baseline" is used when earned value (EV) techniques are employed on the project. I discuss EV shortly.

Control Costs: Inputs

Like Control Scope and Control Schedule, the inputs consist of the project management plan, work performance data, and OPAs. In addition, the project funding requirements are also an input. I summarize the inputs in the following list:

- **Project management plan:** The two components you will use in this process are discussed in detail in Book IV, Chapter 1.
  - *Cost baseline:* Use this to compare planned expenditures against actual costs.
  - *Cost management plan:* The cost management plan should identify the acceptable variances for cost performance. For example, if you are over budget by 20% on a deliverable but under budget on the project overall, should you report the variance? Under what circumstances can you use reserve, and what process do you use to update the plan to show that? How do you measure cost performance for work that is in progress?

- **Work performance data:** This includes which activities have started and finished, which costs have been authorized, and which have been incurred. Work performance data is discussed in Book VI, Chapter 1.
- **Project funding requirements:** The periodic required funds for expenditures and reserves (see Book IV, Chapter 1).
- **Organizational process assets (OPAs):** Organizational policies, templates, and procedures you need to manage and report project costs.

One of the methods you use to determine how well you're performing is to look at the work performance data to determine how much work has been completed on work in progress. A common way of doing this is to ask the appropriate team member what the percent complete is. However, there are two problems with this approach: The first is that it's subjective and can be abused; and the second is that for short-term activities, it's time consuming. One way to reduce the time associated with recording progress is to set up a fixed formula for short-term activities, *short-term* being defined as spanning one to two reporting periods.

You select a ratio that adds up to 100%, such as 50/50, 25/75, or 20/80. When an activity starts, the first percentage is credited. When the activity is done, the remainder is credited. Using a 50/50 measure is the most aggressive, and 20/80 is the most conservative. Although percentage isn't a true measure of accomplishment — after all, it's only short-term — the overall performance equalizes quickly because of the short-term nature of the measurement method. Table 1-1 shows an example of each method.

Table 1-1 Fixed Formula Measurement Method

Measurement Method	*Activity Value*	*Measure 1*	*Measure 2*	*Total*
50/50	2,000	1,000	1,000	2,000
25/75	2,000	500	1,500	2,000
20/80	2,000	400	1,600	2,000

Some measurement methods are 0/100, meaning that no credit is allocated until the work is complete. However, using this method is appropriate only for small activities that span just one reporting period.

Control Costs: Tools and Techniques

The first technique in the Control Cost process is earned value management (EVM). This is a whole discipline in itself, so I spend significant time explaining this technique before moving onto additional techniques.

Earned value management

The PMP exam scratches the surface of EVM, but nonetheless, you should expect five or so questions on this topic. After you understand the underlying concept, it is quite simple.

EVM integrates scope, schedule, and cost in the planning, monitoring, and controlling disciplines. Although implementation of a full-scale EV system is quite complex, the following nine steps summarize what you need to know to understand the concept for the PMP.

1. Plan the work by using a work breakdown structure (WBS).
2. Identify resources and persons accountable for the work.
3. Schedule the work.
4. Estimate the costs.
5. Develop a performance measurement baseline.
6. Monitor the work against the baseline to determine variances.
7. Control the work to keep the project on schedule and on budget.
8. Manage changes to maintain the baseline integrity.
9. Develop forecasts for future performance.

Note that all these steps are consistent with good project management. In fact, there is a saying, "You can do good project management without using earned value, but you can't do earned value without using good project management."

Many terms are associated with EV as well as many abbreviations and acronyms. I introduce these terms and acronyms in chunks as I explain the concepts. And so you can really understand how this works and can be applied, I show you an example that will help the pieces fall into place.

Earned Value Management (EVM). A methodology that combines scope, schedule, and resource measurements to assess project performance and progress.

Planned value (PV). The authorized budget assigned to the scheduled work.

Earned value (EV). The measure of work performed expressed in terms of the budget authorized for that work.

Actual cost (AC). The realized costs incurred for the work performed on an activity during a specific time period.

Budget at Completion (BAC). The sum of all the budgets established for the work to be performed.

If you work for the federal (U.S.) government, or for a subcontractor for the government, you might be required to use EV on your projects. However, you might have heard different terms used. When the earned value technique was first used in the 1960s, the terms were "budgeted cost of work scheduled," "budgeted cost of work performed," and "actual cost of work performed." Since then, the terms "planned value," "earned value," "and actual cost" have been substituted for those terms. However, there are still pockets in government agencies, the Department of Defense (DoD), and their subcontractors that use the old terms. The following table shows the correlation.

Old Term	*Current Term*
Budgeted cost of work scheduled (BCWS)	Planned value (PV)
Budgeted cost of work performed (BCWP)	Earned value (EV)
Actual cost of work performed (ACWP)	Actual cost (AC)

Planning with EVM

To demonstrate how you plan your project by using earned value techniques, I use a simple story based on my running childcare center example. Assume that you met with the parents, and as part of the curriculum, they wanted the children to learn about gardens and growing food. The parents were willing to give up some space dedicated to the sandbox, and the designer for the outside area said that you could use part of the outside area originally set aside for landscaping to fit in with the garden.

The decision was made to have a low deck area that would have planter boxes for vegetables, fruit trees, and flowers. There will be some rock walkways and grassy areas along with a small fountain. This change in scope went through the change control process and was incorporated into the scope along with the budget. Because the change went in early in the process, there is no impact to the delivery date.

The first step is to create a WBS for this new work. You can see this in Figure 1-1.

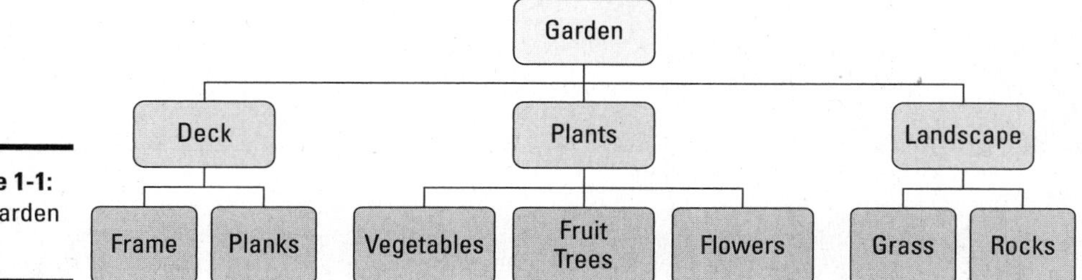

Figure 1-1: The garden WBS.

The schedule in Table 1-2 shows the activities, duration estimates, sequence of events, and the resources.

Table 1-2 Garden Schedule

ID	*Activity*	*Duration in Days*	*Predecessor*	*Resource*
1	**Deck**	10		Michael
2	*Frame*	4		Michael
3	Grade	1		Michael
4	Set posts	1	3	Michael
5	Set frame	2	4	Michael
6	*Planks*	6		Michael
7	Lay planks	3	5	Michael
8	Finish work	1	7	Michael
9	Stain deck	1	8	Michael
10	Seal deck	1	9	Michael
11	**Landscape**	4		José
12	*Vegetables*	3		José
13	Purchase vegetables	1	9	Larry
14	Plant vegetables	2	13	José

(continued)

Table 1-2 *(continued)*

ID	Activity	Duration in Days	Predecessor	Resource
15	*Trees*	4		José
16	Purchase trees	1	13SS*	Larry
17	Plant trees	3	16	Jorge
18	*Flowers*	4		José
19	Purchase flowers	1	13SS*	Larry
20	Plant flowers	3	19	John
21	**Hardscape**	12		Mark
22	*Sod*	3		José
23	Purchase sod	1	14	Larry
24	Plant sod	2	23	José
25	*Rocks*	3		Mark
26	Purchase rock	1	14	Larry
27	Fill in rock work	2	26	Mark

**SS = start-to-start*

The schedule shows that the deck work gets done first. On the last day of the deck work, the vegetables, trees, and flowers are to be purchased. The following two to three days, they will all be planted. After the vegetables are planted, the grass and rocks will be purchased. They will be planted, and the rock pathways will be laid over the next two days. To accomplish all the work, it should take three weeks. Figure 1-2 is another view of the schedule, using a bar chart, so you can see the flow of work.

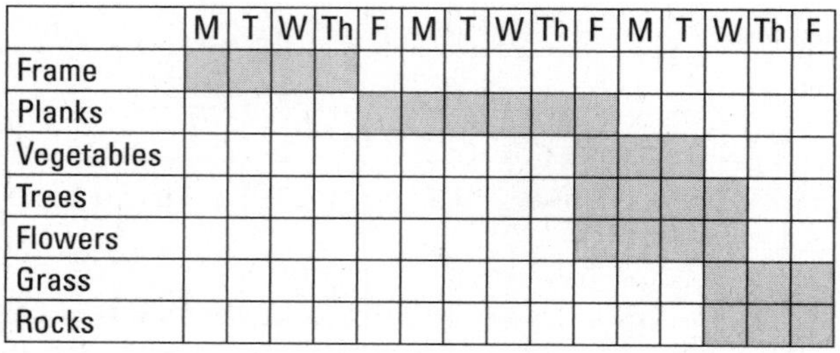

	M	T	W	Th	F	M	T	W	Th	F	M	T	W	Th	F
Frame															
Planks															
Vegetables															
Trees															
Flowers															
Grass															
Rocks															

Figure 1-2: Bar chart garden schedule.

The next step is to estimate the costs. Figure 1-3 shows the costs for each WBS work package. The estimates are inclusive of materials, supplies, and labor. It also shows when the costs planned are to be incurred.

	M	T	W	Th	F	M	T	W	Th	F	M	T	W	Th	F
Frame	600	600	600	600											
Planks					400	400	400	400	400	400					
Vegetables										500	500	500			
Trees										450	450	450	450		
Flowers										250	250	250	250		
Grass													500	500	500
Rocks													500	500	500
Weekly	600	600	600	600	400	400	400	400	400	1600	1200	1200	1700	1000	1000
Cumulative	600	1200	1800	2400	2800	3200	3600	4000	4400	6000	7200	8400	10100	11100	12100

Figure 1-3: The garden budget.

Notice that the cost per day is shown as well as the cumulative cost. This budget follows the schedule by showing that the deck will be done first, and then all the landscape and hardscape. The total cost estimate is $12,100. This total is the *budget at completion* (BAC).

Figure 1-4 is another way of looking at the information with the dollar amounts filled into the schedule. This is sometimes referred to as a dollarized schedule.

	M	T	W	Th	F	M	T	W	Th	F	M	T	W	Th	F
Frame	2,400														
Planks					2,400										
Vegetables										1,500					
Trees										1,800					
Flowers										1,000					
Grass													1,500		
Rocks													1,500		

Figure 1-4: Dollarized schedule.

At this point, you can create a performance measurement baseline, as shown in Figure 1-5.

The performance measurement baseline is also the planned value (PV) for the project. It integrates the scope, schedule, and cost. You will use this to compare your planned work against the work actually accomplished.

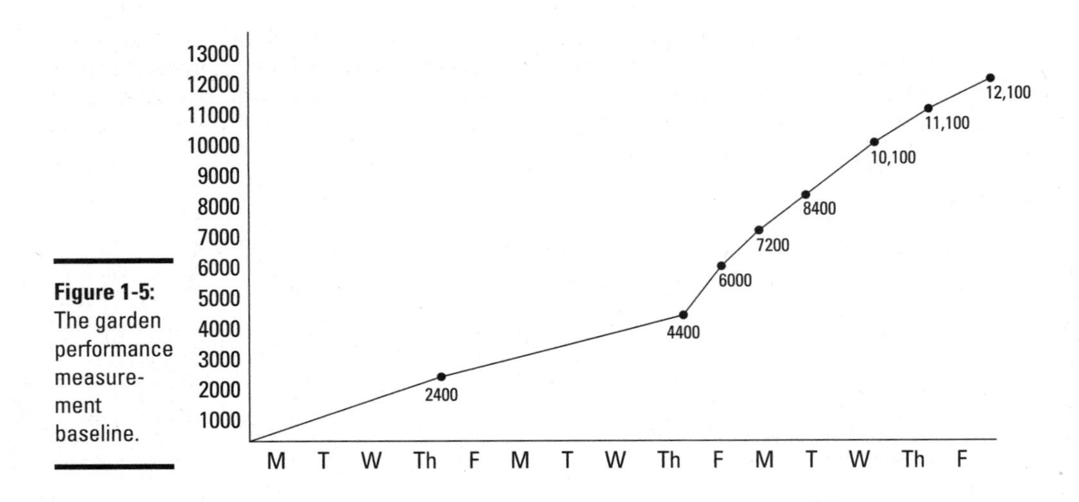

Figure 1-5: The garden performance measurement baseline.

Monitoring with EVM

After work on the project begins, you start tracking the work that was accomplished (EV) and the costs incurred to perform the work (AC). The earned value is the dollar value of the work actually accomplished, using the measurements set up with the planned value. In other words, the frame for the deck is valued at $2,400. If you're 50% complete, you've earned $1,200 worth of value.

Assume that at the end of Week 2, you're 100% complete with the frame and 80% done with the planks. You haven't yet ordered plants or landscape materials. Therefore, your EV numbers are as shown in Table 1-3.

Table 1-3 Garden Status as of Week 2

Work	*Planned Value*	*Percent Complete*	*Earned Value*
Frame	2,400	100	2,400
Planks	2,400	80	1,920
Vegetables	500	0	0
Trees	450	0	0
Flowers	250	0	0
Total	6,000		4,320

Notice that you haven't indicated expenses for the work done — only the PV and the EV. The actual cost is determined by totaling the invoices to see what has been paid. In this case, the invoices show that the frame cost $2,500, and the planks cost $2,300 so far. Now you can add the actual costs, as shown in Table 1-4.

Table 1-4 Earned Value Data at End of Week 2

Work	*Planned Value*	*Percent Complete*	*Earned Value*	*Actual Cost*
Frame	2,400	100	2,400	2,500
Planks	2,400	80	1,920	2,300
Vegetables	500	0	0	0
Trees	450	0	0	0
Flowers	250	0	0	0
Total	6,000		4,320	4,800

The next thing to look at is how the results compare against the planned results and to the costs. By looking at Table 1-4, you can intuitively figure out that things are not going well. It is fairly obvious that the project is earning less than planned and is also costing more than planned. With earned value techniques, you can make some simple calculations to quantify the results.

Variances and indexes

You can use two types of measurements to quantify the results: variances and indexes. A *variance* measures the difference between two amounts, and an *index* measures an efficiency ratio. To determine the variances and the indexes, compare numbers with the EV: in this case, $4,320. To measure the schedule performance, compare the EV against the PV. To measure cost performance, compare the EV against the AC.

Four equations will give you this information:

- ✦ Schedule variance: SV = EV – PV
- ✦ Cost variance: CV = EV – AC
- ✦ Schedule performance index: SPI = EV / PV
- ✦ Cost performance index: CPI = EV / AC

Here are the glossary definitions of those terms.

Schedule variance (SV). A measure of schedule performance expressed as the difference between the earned value and the planned value.

Cost variance (CV). The amount of budget deficit or surplus at a given point in time, expressed as the difference between earned value and actual cost.

Schedule performance index (SPI). A measure of schedule efficiency expressed as the ratio of earned value to planned value.

Cost performance index (CPI). A measure of cost efficiency of budgeted resources expressed as the ratio of earned value to actual cost.

The preceding four simple measurements give you a lot of objective information about project performance. A negative schedule variance says that you accomplished less work than planned. You might not be behind on the critical path, but the accomplishment rate is less than expected. A positive schedule variance says that you accomplished more than planned. Again, you have to compare progress with your critical path to determine whether you're ahead or behind schedule.

The negative cost variance says that you spent more than was budgeted for the work accomplished. Conversely, a positive cost variance says that you spent less than was budgeted for the work.

In a nutshell, when you look at a cost or schedule performance index, you're looking to see how efficient you are. An SPI or CPI of less than 1.00 indicates underperformance; in other words, you are either behind in accomplishing work or over budget. Conversely, an SPI or CPI greater than 1.00 indicates that you're performing well — accomplishing more work than planned or spending less to do it.

The CPI is considered the single most reliable indicator of the health of the project.

Look at the variances and indexes for the garden project. The frame is completed, so you earned everything you planned. Therefore, there will not be a schedule variance, and the schedule performance index will be 1.0:

EV – PV = SV
2,400 – 2,400 = 0

EV / PV = SPI
2,400 / 2,400 = 1.0

However, note these more-telling numbers for the cost information:

EV – AC = CV
2,400 – 2,500 = –100

EV / AC = CPI
2,400 / 2,500 = .96

The preceding equations indicate that you spent $100 more than planned and were 96% cost efficient. This means that for every dollar you spent, you earned 96 cents.

For index measurements, you should carry out to two decimal places.

You can try the same calculations for the planks before looking at the answers in the sidebar "Plank EV calculations."

The questions on the exam might ask you to calculate information for a specific work package or for the project as a whole. For the project as a whole, you sum the value of the work for PV, EV, and AC and then do your calculations, using the cumulative values.

Earned value doesn't tell you what happened; it only points out that things aren't going according to plan.

A common way to graph earned value information is to chart the EV and AC numbers against the performance measurement baseline (PMB), as shown in Figure 1-6.

Plank EV calculations

- SV: 1,920 – 2,400 = –480
- SPI: 1,920 / 2,400 = .80
- CV: 1,920 – 2,300 = –380
- CPI: 1,920 / 2,300 = .83

The work is $480 less than planned and 80% efficient on the schedule. The work cost $380 more than the value, which means that the cost efficiency is 83%. Another way of looking at this is that for every dollar spent on the project, $0.83 is being earned. Not a good situation.

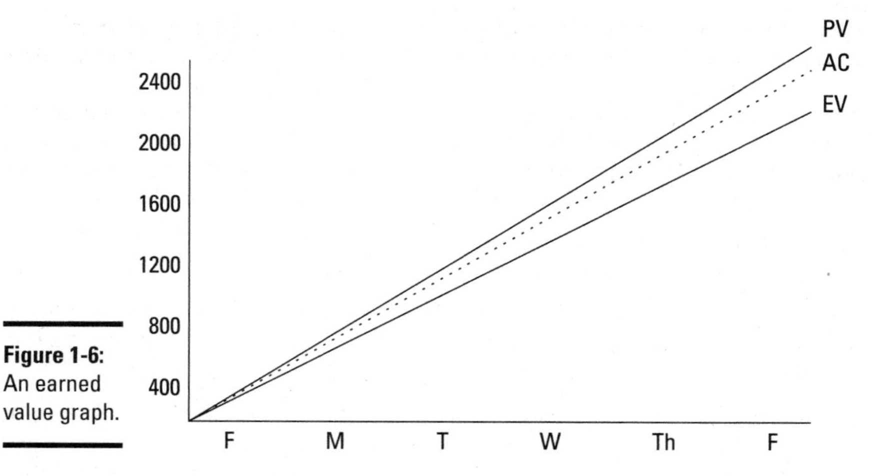

Figure 1-6: An earned value graph.

A negative schedule variance or an SPI less than 1.0 does not necessarily mean that you're behind schedule. You have to check your critical path to determine your true schedule situation.

When looking at variances, any negative variance indicates that your performance isn't going how you want. You're either accomplishing less or spending more than you planned.

And when looking at indexes, any index less than 1.00 indicates that your performance isn't going how you want. A CPI of .90 indicates that for every dollar you spend, you're getting only 90 cents of value.

Forecasting

One of the benefits of EV is that it gives you a quantifiable way to forecast final budget results. Keep in mind, though, that a forecast using EV won't be as accurate as a new, bottom-up forecast. However, it does take a lot less time.

A forecast adds the actual cost of work thus far, and develops an estimate to complete (ETC) the additional work. The new total of the AC + bottom-up ETC is the estimate at completion (EAC).

Estimate to complete. The expected cost to finish all the remaining project work.

Estimate at completion. The expected total cost of completing all work expressed as the sum of the actual cost to date and the estimate to complete.

If you don't have time to complete a new, bottom-up ETC for the remaining work, you can use any of the following formulas. Each formula represents a different set of assumptions, so make sure you understand the scenario and assumptions regarding future work before developing your EAC.

EAC = BAC – EV + AC

This equation is used if the current cost variance is not expected to continue. It assumes that any existing variance is a one-time event. Most people don't consider this a valid way of calculating the EAC.

EAC = ((BAC – EV) / CPI) + AC

This equation has a shortcut: BAC/CPI. This is used if the current cost variance is expected to continue at the same rate. Some people consider this the best case scenario EAC.

EAC = ((BAC – EV) / (CPI × SPI)) + AC

This equation is used if the schedule and cost are significant to project success, and their performance is expected to continue at the same rate. Some people consider this the most likely scenario; others, the worst case.

You can work through each of these equations, given the cumulative data for the garden project. To make it a little easier, just use the deck information and don't worry about the plants right now.

1. **Figure the cumulative PV, EV, and AC.**
   - PV = 4,800
   - EV = 4,320
   - AC = 4,800
2. **Figure out the CPI and SPI.**

   SPI = 4,320 / 4,800 = .90

   CPI = 4,320 / 4,800 = .90

3. **Work the equations.**

EAC = BAC – EV + AC
12,100 – 4,320 + 4,800 = 12,580

EAC = ((BAC – EV) / CPI) + AC
((12,100 – 4,320) / .90) + 4,800 = 13,444

EAC = ((BAC – EV) / (CPI × SPI)) + AC
((12,100 – 4,320) / (.90 × .90)) + 4,800 = 14,405

Because the project is both over budget and behind schedule, you would expect to see the EAC higher than the BAC when you take into consideration the budget performance, and even more so when you take into consideration the schedule performance.

At this point, the project is 50% complete. There is time to look for ways to catch up on the schedule, but you probably won't be able to make up the costs: What is spent is spent. To compensate, you'll probably need to either reduce the number of plants you get or get less-expensive plants. However, because the earned value numbers provide an early warning, you have time to make proactive decisions rather than reaching the end of the project and running out of money when you no longer have the opportunity to develop corrective or preventive actions.

Variance at completion

You can use a formula called a variance at completion (VAC) to see the difference between the original BAC and the current EAC. This tells you the amount of additional funding you need to complete the project.

Variance at Completion. A projection of the amount of budget deficit or surplus, expressed as the difference between the budget at completion and the estimate at completion.

BAC – EAC = VAC

Using the various EACs calculated earlier in this example, you can see the VACs.

EAC = 12,580
VAC = 12,100 – 12,580 = –480

EAC = 13,444
VAC = 12,100 – 13,444 = –1,344

EAC = 14,450
VAC = 12,100 – 14,405 = –2,305

To-complete performance index

You might encounter one more equation on the PMP exam. The *to-complete performance index* (TCPI) indicates how efficiently you have to perform for the rest of the project to meet your original BAC or your new EAC. It takes the remaining work and divides it by the remaining funds.

To-complete performance index (TCPI). A measure of the cost performance that is required to be achieved with the remaining resources in order to meet a specified management goal, expressed as the ratio of the cost to finish the outstanding work to the remaining budget.

Here are the formulas for TCPI:

TCPI = (BAC – EV) / (BAC – AC)

TCPI = (BAC – EV) / (EAC – AC)

For the garden project, you would calculate the following with the BAC in the denominator:

(12,100 – 4,320) / (12,100 – 4,800) = 1.07

This means to achieve the BAC, for the remainder of the project, you need to get $1.07 worth of value for every dollar you spend. This is a great equation to see whether your expectations are realistic. Given that you are halfway done and also that you are thus far getting 90 cents for every dollar, it isn't likely that you will improve by 17 cents on the dollar from now on. However, future work is different from past work, so it's possible. The point is that this index lets you know how efficient you need to be to meet a budget objective.

If you have a different EAC that you're working toward, use the EAC as the denominator. Here is the equation using the EAC of $13,444 in the denominator. In this example, I chose the EAC = BAC / CPI to indicate that I expect future work to continue at the same efficiency as past work.

(12,100 – 4,320) / (13,444 – 4,800) = .90

This example demonstrates that if future work continues at the same cost efficiency, and I am working toward an EAC that reflects that assumption, then I need to continue to perform at a .90 cost performance efficiency.

Earned value rules roundup

Here is everything about earned value you need to memorize for the exam.

- **PV:** Planned value; what you plan to spend to accomplish the work: in other words, the budget
- **EV:** Earned value; the value of what you got
- **AC:** Actual cost; what you spent for what you got
- **BAC:** Budget at completion; the total PV or the project
- **ETC:** Estimate to complete; the expected remaining cost of the project or WBS work element
- **EAC:** Estimate at completion; the expected total cost of the project or WBS element when the scope is completed
- **VAC:** Variance at completion; the difference between the BAC and the EAC
- **TCPI:** To-complete performance index; the efficiency ratio you have to achieve to meet a budget target (BAC or EAC)

Variances and indexes. Variances are good for specific information; indexes are good for showing relative performance information.

- **For variance and indexes:** Always start with EV.
- **When looking for information on schedule:** Use PV.
- **When looking for information on cost:** Use AC.

For a variance, subtract:

- SV = EV – PV
- CV = EV – AC

  Remember: Negative is bad; positive is good.

For an index, divide:

- SPI = EV / PV
- CPI = EV / AC

  Remember: Less than 1.0 is bad; greater than 1.0 is good.

Three steps to EAC. The three easy steps to calculate an estimate at completion are

Step 1: Start with the work remaining: (BAC – EV).

Step 2: Divide by a factor:

- 1.0 = (BAC – EV)
- CPI = (BAC – EV) / CPI
- CPI × SPI = (BAC – EV) / (CPI × SPI)

Step 3: Add the AC:

- 1.0 = (BAC – EV) + AC
- CPI = ((BAC – EV) / CPI) + AC
- CPI × SPI = ((BAC – EV) / (CPI – SPI)) + AC

To-complete performance index. The work remaining divided by the budget remaining:

- Work remaining: BAC – EV
- Budget remaining: BAC – AC or EAC = AC

  (BAC – EV) / (BAC – AC)

More cost control techniques

I discuss performance reviews in the Control Schedule process in Book VII, Chapter 3. Regardless of whether your project uses formal earned value management methods, comparing the baseline costs to the actual incurred costs is still important.

In a performance review, focus your attention on the outliers: specifically, those work packages with index factors that are outside the variance thresholds. For instance, if you have a threshold of a 10% cost variance, you would want to focus the review on those work packages that are close to or less than .90.

For variances that are increasing, or outside the variance threshold, you will need to identify the cause of the variance so you can determine the appropriate preventive or corrective action.

You would also want to look at trends in the numbers. For example, is the EAC getting farther away from the BAC? Are the schedule or cost performance indexes getting farther away from 1.0 or closer? This information lets you know whether you need to employ corrective or preventive actions to manage the schedule and budget.

FOR THE EXAM

The monitoring and controlling knowledge and skills that you should expect to see tested for controlling costs and using earned value include:

- Project performance metrics focusing on costs
- Variance and trend analysis techniques
- Performance measurement techniques, specifically earned value
- Cost analysis techniques, including forecasting

Reserve analysis is a technique used to compare the remaining reserve with the current project status. You can analyze both contingency reserve and management reserve. Review contingency reserve to assess reserves used to mitigate risks. If a risk event has passed without the risk occurring and there were contingency funds set aside for that risk, they can be released. If more risks have occurred than planned, you may find that the remaining reserves are insufficient.

Control Cost: Outputs

The outcome of this process is the actual work performance information, such as the cumulative cost and schedule variances and the cumulative cost and schedule performance indexes. You will also have forecasts and the associated data to explain the assumptions you made for those forecasts.

As needed, you will make change requests and update various project management plan components, project documents, and organizational process assets. The following list shows some of the more common elements you may need to update:

- **Cost management plan:** If there are significant cost variances, you may need to revisit estimating techniques as well as levels of accuracy needed for estimating and reporting.
- **Cost baseline:** If changes have occurred or risk events have materialized, the baseline may be updated (but only after going through the formal change control process).
- **Cost estimates:** Cost estimates may be updated to reflect the most current information.
- **Basis of estimates:** As cost estimates are adjusted, the underlying basis of the estimates are also updated.
- **Causes of variances:** Make sure to also catalog the corrective actions taken to address the variances.
- **Lessons learned:** Record information that can be used later in the project and by other projects.

Figure 1-7 shows an example of an EV status report that shows the common earned value measurements, the root cause of variances, and the impact on key objectives.

EARNED VALUE STATUS REPORT

Project Title: ______________________ **Date Prepared:** __________

Budget at Completion (BAC): ______________ **Overall Status:** __________

	Current Reporting Period	Current Period Cumulative	Past Period Cumulative
Planned value (PV)	*Value of the work planned to be accomplished*		
Earned value (EV)	*Value of the work actually accomplished*		
Actual cost (AC)	*Cost for the work accomplished*		
Schedule variance (SV)	*EV-PV*		
Cost variance (CV)	*EV-AC*		
Schedule performance index (SPI)	*EV/PV*		
Cost performance index (CPI)	*EV/AC*		
Root Cause of Schedule Variance:			
Describe the cause of any schedule variances.			
Impact on Deliverables, Milestones, or Critical Path:			
Describe the impact on deliverables, milestones, and the critical path and any intended actions to address the variances.			
Root Cause of Cost Variance:			
Describe the cause of any cost variances.			
Impact on Budget, Contingency Funds, or Reserve:			
Describe the impact on the project budget, contingency funds and reserves, and any intended actions to address the variances.			
Percent planned		*PV/BAC*	
Percent earned		*EV/BAC*	
Percent spent		*AC/BAC*	
Estimates at Completion (EAC):			
EAC w/CPI [BAC/CPI]			
EAC w/ CPIxSPI [AC+((BAC-EV)/(CPIxSPI))]			
Selected EAC, Justification and explanation			
There are many valid methods of deriving estimates at completion. Two of them are listed above. Whichever method you choose, document the method and justify the approach.			
To complete performance index (TCPI)		*(BAC-EV)/(BAC-AC)**	

*Another common equation for TCPI is (BAC-EV)/(EAC-AC).

Page 1 of 1

Figure 1-7: An earned value status report form.

Work performance information for the Control Cost process can be easily abused to hide cost variances. For example, if a project team lead takes delivery of a purchased item but the invoice has not yet been paid, the project could show the earned value of that purchase but not the incurred cost. If you take the credit for the EV without estimating the AC in your status report, you are not showing the true cost status. To avoid this type of behavior, you need to have clear reporting expectations in your cost management plan.

The following honesty standards from the Code of Ethics and Professional Conduct relate to work performance measurements in schedule as well as cost:

- We are truthful in our communications and in our conduct.
- We provide accurate information in a timely manner.
- We do not engage in or condone behavior that is designed to deceive others, including but not limited to, making misleading or false statements, stating half-truths, providing information out of context, or withholding information that, if known, would render our statements as misleading or incomplete.

Key Terms

The new terms in this chapter focus on earned value management. There are a lot of new terms here, and they have precise technical meanings, so make sure you have a solid understanding of all the terms before you take the exam.

- Cost baseline
- Performance measurement baseline
- Cost management plan
- Earned value management (EVM)
- Planned value (PV)
- Earned value (EV)
- Actual cost (AC)
- Budget at completion (BAC)
- Schedule variance (SV)
- Cost variance (CV)

✦ Schedule performance index (SPI)
✦ Cost performance index (CPI)
✦ Estimate to complete (ETC)
✦ Estimate at completion (EAC)
✦ Variance at completion (VAC)
✦ To-complete performance index (TCPI)

Chapter Summary

The information in this chapter may show up on test questions as earned value calculations or as definitions. In addition, you may see some of the earned value equations discussed in this chapter on the exam in different knowledge areas. For example, you may see a test question that asks you about schedule variances, or the risk impacts of a performance index less than .90, or even when reviewing contractor status reports. Therefore, as you go over the information in this chapter, keep in mind how it could be used in other contexts.

✦ The Control Cost process compares the cost baseline and funding requirements against the work performance data. Using variance analysis and earned value techniques, you can determine the status of the budget and see whether corrective or preventive actions are required.

✦ Earned value management integrates scope, schedule, and budget performance to provide an objective overview of the project's performance. It uses planned value (PV), earned value (EV), and actual cost (AC) along with the budget at completion (BAC) to develop quantitative measures for variance and efficiency.

✦ You should know the following equations for the PMP exam:
  - $SV = EV - PV$
  - $CV = EV - AC$
  - $SPI = EV / PV$
  - $CPI = EV / AC$
  - $EAC = BAC / CPI$
  - $TCPI = (BAC - EV) / (BAC - AC)$

er Summary

- In general, a negative variance and an index less than 1.0 indicate performance is less than expected. A positive variance and an index greater than 1.0 indicate that performance is favorable to plan.
- Forecasts add the AC to an estimate to complete (ETC) to determine an estimate at completion (EAC). The assumptions about the ETC can give you varying EACs.
- The VAC tells you the difference between your BAC and your EAC.
- A TCPI tells you how efficient you have to perform to achieve the original budget.

Prep Test

Multiple Choice

1 **Which of the following is not a common cause of cost overruns?**

A ❍ Inaccurate estimating
B ❍ Unplanned, in-scope work
C ❍ Contractor underrun
D ❍ A risk event occurring

2 **The measure of work performed expressed in terms of the budget authorized for is known as**

A ❍ Budget at completion
B ❍ Earned value
C ❍ Planned value
D ❍ Actual cost

3 **The equation to determine the amount of work you planned to accomplish versus the amount of work you actually accomplished is**

A ❍ EV – PV
B ❍ EV – AC
C ❍ PV – EV
D ❍ AC – EV

4 **To demonstrate how efficiently you are performing to budget, which equation should you use?**

A ❍ EV / PV
B ❍ PV / EV
C ❍ EV / AC
D ❍ AC / EV

5 **If you want to develop a forecast that shows the impact of your cost and schedule performance, which EAC should you use?**

A ❍ EAC = BAC – EV + AC
B ❍ EAC = ((BAC – EV) / CPI) + AC
C ❍ EAC = BAC ÷ CPI
D ❍ EAC = ((BAC – EV) / (CPI × SPI)) + AC

6 **The measurement that indicates how well you have to perform to meet a budget target is the**

A ❍ Cost performance index
B ❍ To-complete performance index
C ❍ Schedule performance index
D ❍ Estimate at completion

Scenario 1

You have a project to build a brick enclosure with four walls that are 10 feet high. The planned value for each wall is $10,000, and you plan to build one wall per week. At the end of the second week, you have completed the first wall and have 6 feet of the second wall built. You have spent $18,000 so far.

1 **What is your earned value?**

A ❍ $20,000
B ❍ $16,000
C ❍ $18,000
D ❍ $24,000

2 **What is your cost variance?**

A ❍ –2,000
B ❍ –4,000
C ❍ 4,000
D ❍ 2,000

3 **What is your SPI?**

A ❍ .90
B ❍ 1.11
C ❍ .80
D ❍ 1.25

4 **Assuming that your cost performance remains the same for the rest of the project, what is your EAC?**

A ❍ 42,000
B ❍ 44,000
C ❍ 50,000
D ❍ 44,444

5 **What is the TCPI to meet the original BAC?**

A ❍ 1.05

B ❍ 1.06

C ❍ 1.09

D ❍ 91

Answers

Multiple Choice

1 **C.** Contractor underrun. A contractor underrun would be more of a cause of a project underrun, not overrun. *Check out "Control Costs."*

2 **B.** Earned value. The measure of the work performed is the earned value. *See "Earned value management."*

3 **A.** EV – PV. The schedule variance is the difference between the planned value and the earned value. *Look at "Variances and indexes."*

4 **C.** EV ÷ AC. You would use the cost performance index. *Review "Variances and indexes."*

5 **D.** EAC = ((BAC – EV) ÷ (CPI × SPI)) + AC. Use the equation that includes the SPI and CPI in the denominator. *Go over "Forecasting."*

6 **B.** To-complete performance index. The TCPI tells you how efficiently you need to perform to hit a budget target. *I discuss this in "To-complete performance index."*

Scenario 1

1 **B.** $16,000. You earned $10,000 for the first wall and 60% × $10,000 ($6,000) for the second wall. *Go over "Monitoring with EVM."*

2 **A.** –2,000. You earned $16,000 and paid $18,000 to earn it. *Check out "Variances and indexes."*

3 **C.** .80. Your SPI is 16,000/20,000. *See "Variances and indexes."*

4 **D.** 44,444. The EAC is BAC ÷ CPI, 40,000/.90. *Look over the information in "Forecasting."*

5 **C.** 1.09. The TCPI divides the work remaining by the funds remaining (BAC - EV) / (BAC - AC), (40,000 - 16,000) / (40,000 - 18,000). *Go over "To-complete performance index."*

Chapter 2: Controlling Quality

Exam Objective

- **Control quality and ensure that project deliverables align with the quality standards established in the project quality plan by using appropriate tools and techniques (such as testing, inspection, and control charts) to adhere to customer requirements.**

Just like the other quality processes, the Control Quality process focuses on product quality as well as project quality. Because much of the quality improvement and quality control work you do on projects comes from the factory floor, many tools and techniques are adopted to meet project needs.

As I discuss in the chapter on controlling project scope (Book VII, Chapter 2), a very close relationship exists between quality control and scope validation. Control Quality is concerned with comparing deliverables against the quality plan and quality metrics to ensure that the deliverables are correct and meet the requirements. After this is done, the verified deliverables go through the Validate Scope process for customer acceptance.

Another aspect of this process is that here, the project manager checks that approved change requests were implemented as approved. This is one of the aspects of *project* scope that's analyzed and controlled.

Note that some of the tools and techniques are discussed in Book IV, Chapter 2, and Book VI, Chapter 1, where I go over planning project quality and assuring project quality, respectively. When planning for quality, the techniques from those chapters are used to plan measurements, tolerances, and procedures. In this process, you apply those measurements, tolerances, and procedures. The results from applying the measurements are inputs to the Perform Quality Assurance process.

Quick Assessment

1. Deliverables come from the Direct and Manage Project Work process into the Control Quality process. From there, they go to the ______ ______ process for customer acceptance.

2. A key point to remember in all quality processes is "______ over inspection."

3. (True/False). Approved change requests are validated as having been implemented correctly as part of the Control Quality process.

4. ______ are a good way to identify where in the process problems could occur.

5. Where would you find the roles and responsibilities associated with the Control Quality process?

6. To determine whether a measurement meets a requirement, you should use ______ sampling.

7. If you want to rank defects by the number of times they occur, you should use a(n) ______ ______.

8. Which technique uses upper and lower specification limits?

9. If you are looking at a scatter diagram and notice that while one variable increases another decreases, what type of correlation do you have?

10. The results of quality control measurements go to the ______ ______ ______ process.

Answers

1. Validate Scope. Deliverables come from the Direct and Manage Project Work process into the Control Quality process. From there, they go to the Validate Scope process for customer acceptance. *I discuss this in "Quality Control Basics."*

2. Prevention. Preventing defects is more cost effective than finding them during inspection. *Look over the information in "Quality Control Basics."*

3. True. One of the outputs of the Control Quality process is validated changes. *Look over "Validating change requests."*

4. Flow charts. Flow charts show the steps in a process, which enables you to see where possible problems in the process could occur. *See the information under "Flow charts."*

5. Quality management plan. The quality management plan describes how you will perform quality assurance and quality control on the project. It includes information on roles and responsibilities for all quality activities. *For more information, check out "Control Quality: Inputs."*

6. Attribute. Attribute sampling indicates whether a result has been met; variable sampling indicates the degree to which a result has been met. *Look over the information in "Run charts and control charts."*

7. Pareto chart. A Pareto chart is a histogram that ranks the defects by the number of times they occur, such as defect X shows up more than defect Y, which shows up more than defect Z. *You can read more about Pareto charts in "Histograms and Pareto charts."*

8. Control chart. A control chart uses upper and lower control limits as well as upper and lower specification limits. *Look over the information in "Run charts and control charts."*

9. Negative. A negative correlation means that an increase in one variable causes a decrease in a different variable. A positive correlation means that an increase in one variable causes an increase in a different variable. *You can read about positive and negative correlations in "Scatter diagrams."*

10. Perform Quality Assurance. In the Perform Quality Assurance process, the quality control results are reviewed to determine whether the quality processes are functioning appropriately. *Read about this in "Control Quality: Outputs."*

Quality Control Basics

I discuss the flow of deliverables in Book VII, Chapter 2. Deliverables go through four processes:

1. Deliverables are created in the Direct and Manage Project Work process.
2. They are verified as correct in the Control Quality process.
3. Verified deliverables are ready for inspection and acceptance in the Validate Scope process.
4. Accepted deliverables are ready for the Close Project or Phase process.

In this chapter, I focus on Step 2, verifying that the deliverables are correct.

Control Quality. Monitoring and recording results of executing the quality activities to assess performance and recommend necessary changes.

Notice that the preceding definition notes *results,* not *deliverables.* Keep in mind that a good portion of quality control is associated with results, but another aspect assesses whether the project is performing well in addition to whether the processes are working correctly. I discuss some of this when talking about the Perform Quality Assurance process in Book VI, Chapter 1.

Because this is a quality process, you always have to remember that prevention is preferred over inspection! Preventing a problem or defect in the design process is better than finding it after the deliverable is complete and having to repair it!

Control Quality: Inputs

The first item you reference is the quality management plan (see Book IV, Chapter 2, for more information on the quality management plan), which is part of the project management plan. The quality management plan provides direction for the Control Quality process. For example, it can have the following information:

- Information for control charts includes the upper and lower control limits and the upper and lower specification limits.
- The number of items to sample if you use statistical sampling, the criteria you are sampling for, and the measurements for attribute and/or variable sampling. Statistical sampling is described in Book IV, Chapter 2.
- Flow charts of an existing process that you're looking to improve.

Your quality management plan will also define the roles and responsibilities for quality control and identify the organizational process assets, such as any policies and procedures that need to be followed.

Quality metrics are the specific measurements that need to be met for the results to meet the quality requirements. For my running example, the childcare center project, you could have the following metrics for schedule performance:

- 90% of all activities must start within 3 days of their scheduled start.
- 100% of all activities on the critical path must finish on or before their scheduled finish date.
- No activity on a path with float shall use more than 50% of the float.

A quality checklist helps you make sure that all the proper steps are being followed to comply with policies, regulations, or processes. You can use a *punch list* (a fancy construction term for a list of unfinished matters that require attention) for the construction part of the childcare project to ensure all the construction requirements are met and that the center is ready to open.

The information in the quality plan, metrics, and checklists is used with the work performance data and the deliverables. The work performance data come from the Direct and Manage Project Work process. The work performance data are usually used to determine whether the *project* performance is acceptable. The deliverables are used to determine whether the *product* performance is acceptable.

Validating change requests

I mention in the introduction of this chapter that the Control Quality process is where change requests are validated. In Book VII, Chapter 1, I talk about the Perform Integrated Change Control process, showing a flow chart of the change request, the change log, analysis, decision, document updates, communication, and implementation. Verification that the change was implemented correctly takes place in this process. The approved change requests are an input to Control Quality. The implementation of those change requests is reviewed; if the change requests are implemented as directed, they are *validated.* This process, shown in Figure 2-1, closes the loop on the change request process.

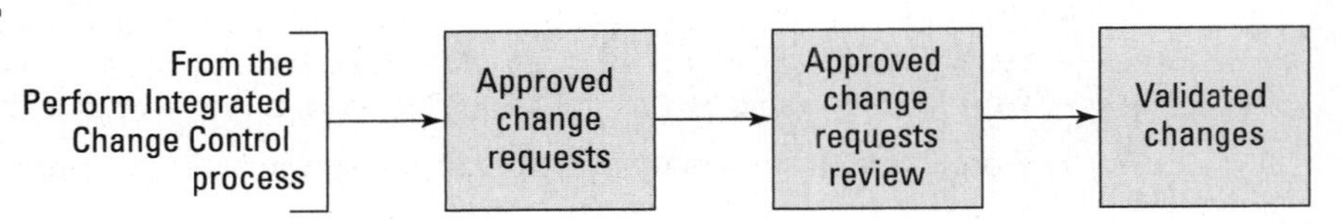

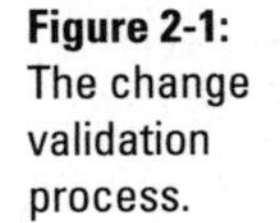

Figure 2-1: The change validation process.

Following the change request through the Perform Integrated Change Control process and then validating that it was implemented correctly in the Control Quality process may not seem like such a big deal, but when you're implementing a scope change — particularly a big scope change — you need to spend sufficient time making sure you understand the requirements, deliverables, resources, and risks associated with that change. Additionally, the schedule and budget documents need to reflect the change. When validating the change in the Control Quality process, you make sure that the work breakdown structure (WBS), schedule, budget, resource requirements, and all other documentation are updated and consistently reflect the approved change.

Example of validating change requests

To bring life to this subject, I show you an example. When I discuss controlling scope (Book VII, Chapter 2), I talk about events that cause scope change. One of those was the customer seeing the product and wanting changes. Using a scenario from my running example of the childcare center, assume that the parents come to the center after it's framed but before any of the electric, plumbing, and HVAC work is done. Some of the parents think it would be a good idea to increase the size of the playroom and decrease the size of the eating area. The contractor is on site and says that could be done and that he can give an estimate for cost and schedule implications by the end of the week.

Carry this scenario further and assume that the change control process was used, the schedule impact was only a week, and the budget impact was $12,000. The change control board (read about the CCB in Book VII, Chapter 1) decides to accept this change. The decision is communicated to the parents, and the change is incorporated. As part of the quality control process, you want to look at the plans to see that they were changed as specified by the parents. You should check the schedule to make sure the new work doesn't have a schedule impact of greater than one week, and check the budget to ensure that the $12,000 is recorded — but no more than that. You should also do a walk-through after the change is implemented to make sure the area was reconfigured correctly.

Control Quality: Tools and Techniques

Many of the tools and techniques in this process are easiest to understand when you're applying them in a fixed, predictable, repetitive environment. The tools in the sections that follow originated in the world of manufacturing.

To make the information in this section a little easier to absorb, I use a fictional case study, departing from the childcare center for a process improvement project for an IT help desk.

Seven basic quality tools

The following tools are known as the seven basic quality tools:

- Flow charts
- Cause-and-effect diagrams
- Checksheets
- Histograms
- Pareto charts
- Control charts
- Scatter diagrams

Every quarter, the support departments at Cynergy2, Inc., send a survey to their customers (Cynergy2 employees) to see whether the department is meeting the needs of its stakeholders. The support departments include human resources, information technology, legal, maintenance, food services, and security. For the past several quarters, the satisfaction with the IT department has been on the decline. Now the Chief Operating Officer wants something done about that. A relatively new hire, Karen, is assigned to this process improvement project. Karen has a background in process improvement and experience in statistics, quantitative analysis, and quality improvement.

Flow charts

After initial review of the satisfaction surveys, Karen determines that the greatest source of dissatisfaction centers around calls to the help desk, so she decides to start her analysis there. The first thing she does is develop a flow chart of the process that the caller goes through when calling the help desk.

Flow charts are a good way to identify where in the process problems could occur.

Using the flow chart in Figure 2-2, Karen identifies two areas of concern:

✦ There are no assigned specialists for Internet connectivity issues. If the hardware or software specialists are busy, no one addresses the Internet calls. Not all hardware and software professionals have network expertise in connecting to the Internet.

✦ If the call is not answered in three minutes, callers are asked to leave a message for a callback. Customers do not want a callback; they want their problems solved immediately.

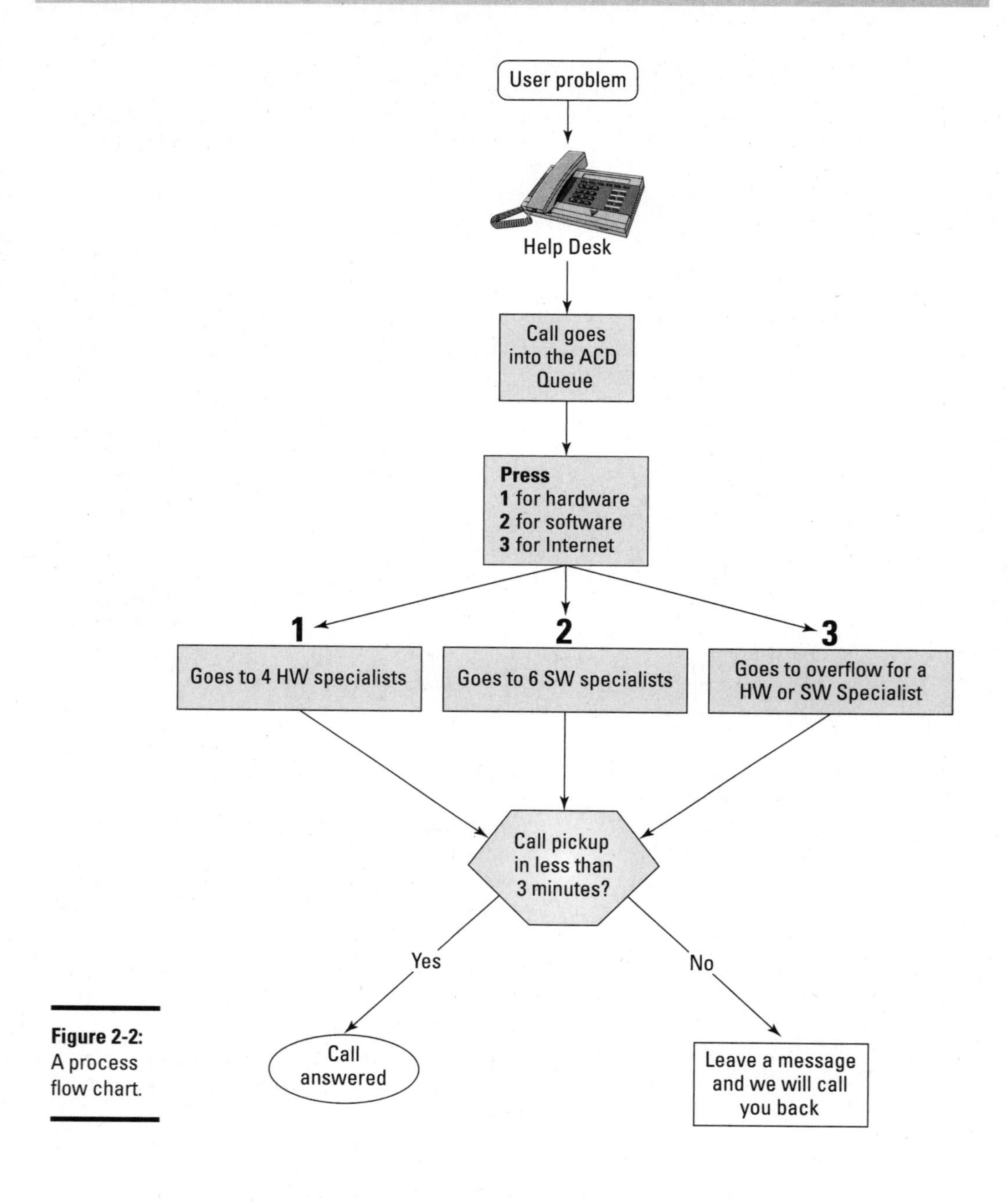

Figure 2-2: A process flow chart.

Cause-and-effect diagrams

The next step Karen decides to take is to create a cause-and-effect diagram to look at the factors that can lead to the low satisfaction rating for the help desk.

A *cause-and-effect diagram,* which illustrates how one or more factors can lead to a problem or defect, can be very useful when you're performing a root-cause analysis of a problem or defect. By working backward from the defect, you ask *How did that happen?* or *Why did that happen?* These questions lead to the inputs to the process or the product that could be potential causes of defects. You can break each branch of the diagram into limbs and continue to decompose them until you have sufficient detail to identify the source of the problem. Figure 2-3 has a classic cause-and-effect diagram that lists six possible causes of a problem: time, equipment, personnel, energy, and so on.

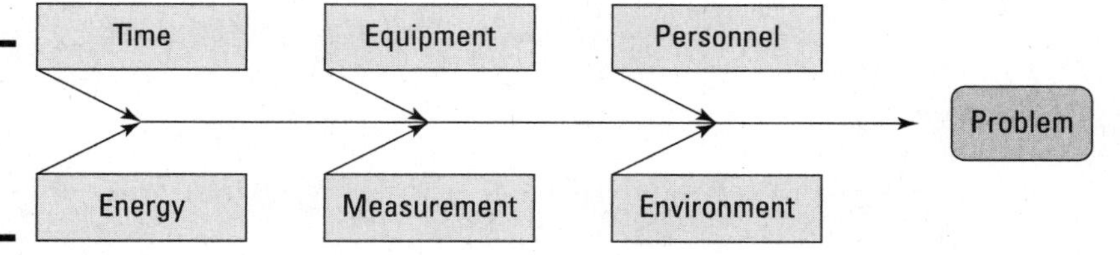

Figure 2-3: A cause-and-effect diagram.

A cause-and-effect diagram is also known as a *fishbone diagram* or an *Ishikawa diagram.* Expect to see any of these terms on the exam.

Analyzing the cause-and-effect diagram, you can analyze how each of those variables could have an impact on the help desk.

- **Time:** The time of day can affect the number of people staffing the help desk and the number of people at work.
- **Energy:** There have been instances of the Automated Call Distribution (ACD) system spontaneously rebooting. No one has figured out what causes this to happen.
- **Equipment:** The ACD hardware and software itself could be causing some of the problems. The headsets that the employees are using are outdated, and sometimes cause static.

- **Measurements:** The measurements for the ACD metrics are measuring the call start from the time a person picks up the phone, not from the time the call goes into the ACD queue.
- **Personnel:** There is a high turnover for employees on the help desk. The average tenure is six months. Even though staff members might have the technical skills, they're not familiar with some of the legacy software or the policies and procedures at Cynergy2, Inc.
- **Environment:** The help desk staff doesn't have cubicles, and they sit near the break room, where people tend to congregate and chat. There is a lot of background noise.

Any of these factors could be broken down further. For example, the personnel branch could be broken into orientation and training on legacy systems, policies and procedures, and the basics of network troubleshooting.

Checksheets

Checksheets can be used to count the number of times that an event occurs or to list the steps to perform a process correctly. In my example, Karen uses checksheets to mark the number of times that the ACD system spontaneously reboots and also the number of times employees indicate that their headsets have static. This information will be transferred to the histograms and Pareto charts that I discuss next.

Histograms and Pareto charts

The next thing Karen did was use the information from the IT department survey to rank the reasons for dissatisfaction. She started out by creating a histogram that uses bars to demonstrate the number of times each cause of dissatisfaction was checked. Then she ranked these in order, using a *Pareto chart,* which is a specific type of histogram ordered by frequency of occurrence that shows how many results each identified cause generates. Figure 2-4 shows Karen's histogram, and Figure 2-5 shows her Pareto chart. Notice that the Pareto chart has a line that tracks the cumulative percentage of defects. The left side vertical axis shows the number of defects. The right side vertical axis shows the cumulative percent of defects.

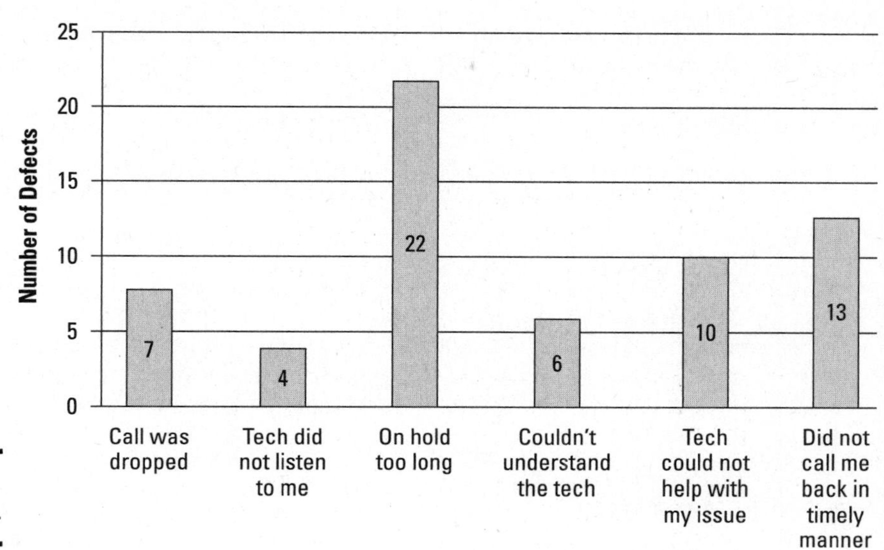

Figure 2-4: A histogram.

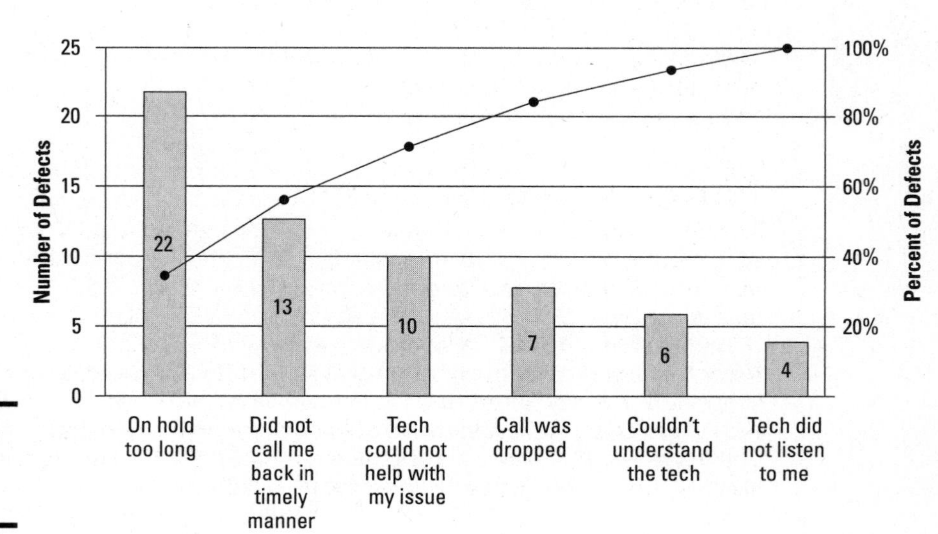

Figure 2-5: A Pareto chart.

A Pareto chart is sometimes referenced in conjunction with the "80/20 rule," which states that 80% of the problems come from 20% of the causes.

Based on the histogram, it was clear that Karen needed to address the issue of people being on hold too long, and then look at improving the time for calling people back. If she could improve those two issues, more than one-half of the complaints would be addressed.

Run charts and control charts

The department metric for answering calls is that a person, not a machine, answers 95% of all calls within three minutes. Karen decided to use a run chart (as shown in Figure 2-6), which charts the history and pattern of variation, to see whether certain times of day had longer average hold times than others.

The ACD system can put out reports for any day that shows the volume of calls and the average hold time. So that Karen didn't need to look at the data for the last year, she used the principles of statistical sampling to select 20 random days in the past year.

The concept of sampling is that you don't have to test every single item to infer quality. You can test a sample.

The fluctuation in the sample data shows common-cause variation. In other words, you would expect the average hold time to vary because of the variables in the process (people, time of day, amount of training). If Karen noted any irregularities, she would look for a special cause, such as someone being out sick, a software upgrade installation, a holiday, or some other unusual event. Figure 2-6 shows Karen's sampling data in a run chart.

When Karen analyzed the data from the run chart, she found that the average hold time was just longer than 2.5 minutes (152 seconds). The longest average hold time was 7 minutes. The range of hold times is from 1 second to 10:43 (10 minutes, 43 seconds). There was a definite spike in the average hold time when people first arrived at work. Hold time steadily decreased until it spiked when people returned from lunch, and then it steadily declined throughout the afternoon until employees went home.

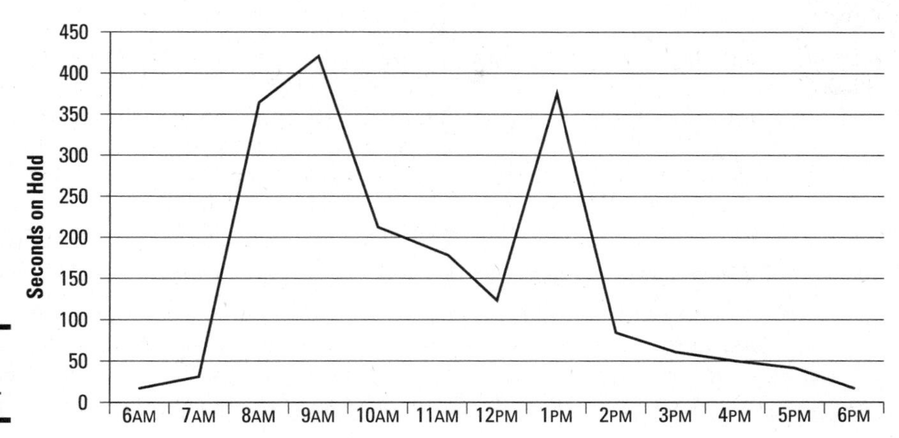

Figure 2-6: A run chart.

Karen decided to put the run chart data on a control chart (see Figure 2-7). A *control chart* is a graphic display of process data over time and against established control limits, and that has a centerline that assists in detecting a trend of plotted values toward either control limit. It's like a run chart, but it shows control limits, and it can show specification limits as well.

I define control limits and specification limits in Book IV, Chapter 2, but here are the definitions again.

Control limit. The area composed of three standard deviations (SD) on either side of the centerline, or mean, of a normal distribution of data plotted on a control chart that reflects the expected variation in the data.

Specification limit. The area, on either side of the centerline, or mean, of data plotted on a control chart that meets the customer's requirements for a product or service. This area may be greater than or less than the area defined by the control limits.

For Karen, showing the control limits didn't make sense because the process is clearly out of control. Instead, she decided to show the upper specification limit and the average hold time. Figure 2-7, plotting the run chart with the average hold times against the upper specification limit (that is, the metric), illustrates the average hold time is significantly greater than the metric.

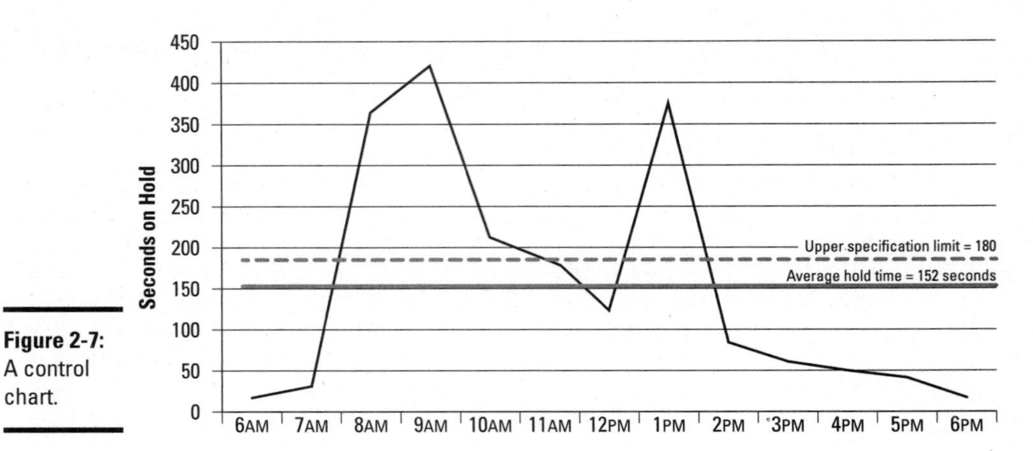

Figure 2-7: A control chart.

From 8 a.m. to 10:59 a.m., the average hold time is greater than the upper specification; from 1 p.m. to 1:59 p.m., hold times are greater than the upper specification, too.

When you're testing, you might have some situations where you're determining whether a result meets the requirement. This is *attribute sampling*. Other times, you might be determining the degree to which a result meets a requirement. That is *variable sampling*.

Using the concepts of attribute and variable sampling, Karen can select any period and determine whether the average hold time meets the upper specification limit. She can also use attribute sampling to randomly select a number of calls throughout the day to see whether each call is within the specification limit. Simply put, the metric is met or not met. Karen can also perform variable sampling to determine the degree to which a result conforms. In other words, by looking at the individual hold time measurements for a call, she can determine the degree to which it is compliant with the metric. Because the metric has an upper specification limit of 180 seconds, a call that is answered at 210 seconds is 117% of the limit, or 17% over the limit.

You might hear about the Rule of Seven when talking about control charts. The Rule of Seven states that seven data points trending in one direction (up or down) or seven data points on one side of the mean indicate that the process isn't random. This means that you should check the measurement to determine whether something is influencing the process. This would be a special cause variation because it's highly unlikely that in a random process, you would find this type of behavior.

Scatter diagrams

Before devising an action plan, Karen wanted to see whether any particular variables had an impact on either the hold time or the customer satisfaction. She used a scatter diagram (see Figure 2-8) because that shows the relationship between two variables. The first thing she measured was the relationship between the number of help desk staff and the percent of time the help desk was within the upper specification limit. As expected, there was a *positive correlation,* which means that as one variable increases, the other increases. A perfect 1:1 correlation gives you a straight diagonal line.

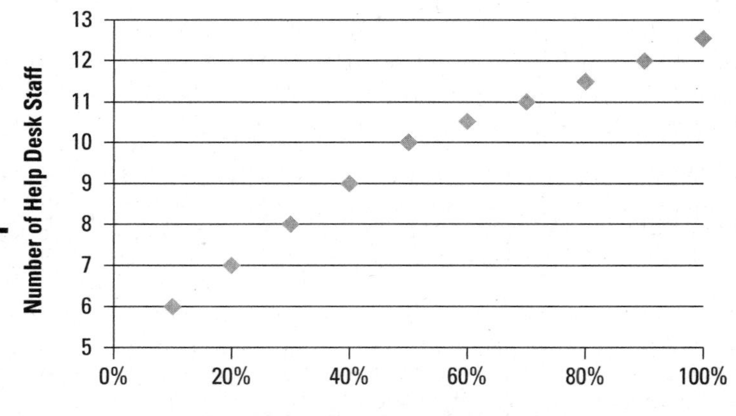

Figure 2-8: Scatter diagram with a positive correlation.

The next thing Karen measured is the relationship between the hold time and the customer satisfaction rating. This result showed a negative correlation (see Figure 2-9), where an increase in the hold time leads to a decrease in the satisfaction.

Karen was curious whether there was any relationship between the day of the week and the hold time. As it turns out, there was a curvilinear correlation, which means the ends of the measurements are relatively even and there is an increase or decrease in the mid measurements. Figure 2-10 shows that hold time was less Monday and Friday than Tuesday through Thursday.

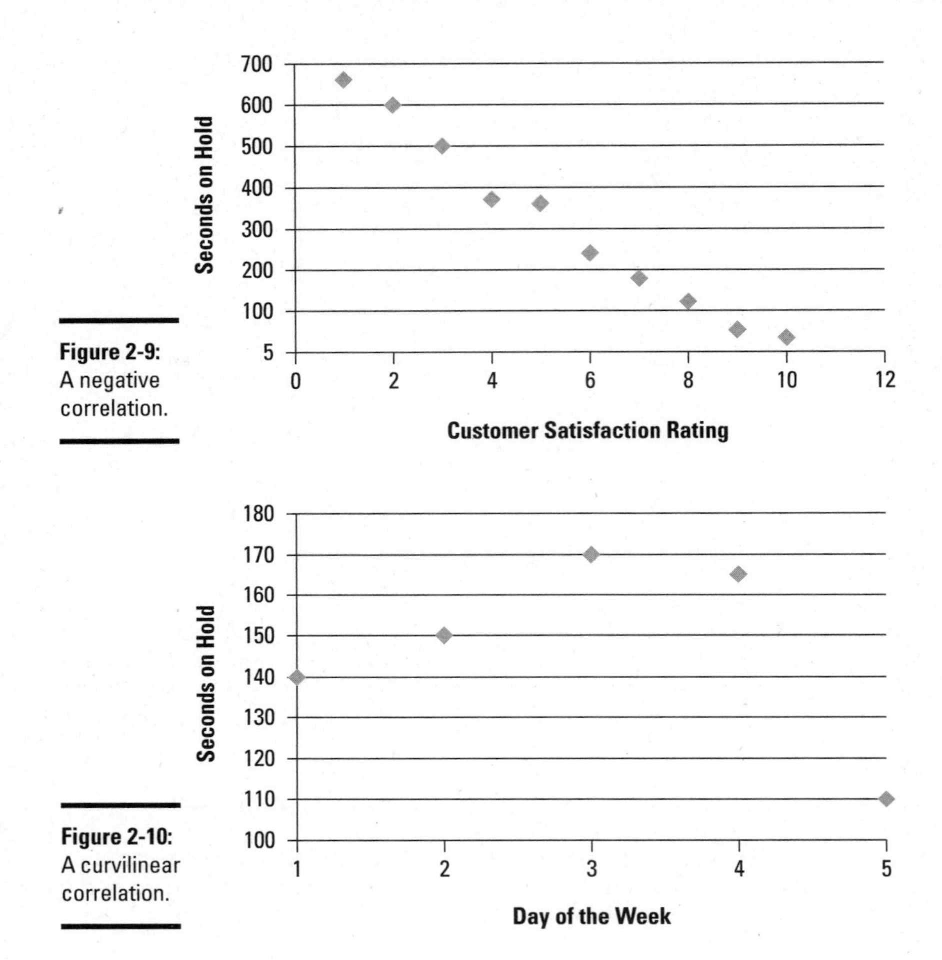

Figure 2-9: A negative correlation.

Figure 2-10: A curvilinear correlation.

Finally, she wanted to see whether the weather and temperature had any bearing on hold time. She thought that maybe more people skipped work when it was nice outside. The results (see Figure 2-11) were random, however, indicating no correlation.

Based on Karen's research and analysis, she can make some recommendations for changes to the process, including some corrective actions, to bring the results in line with expectations.

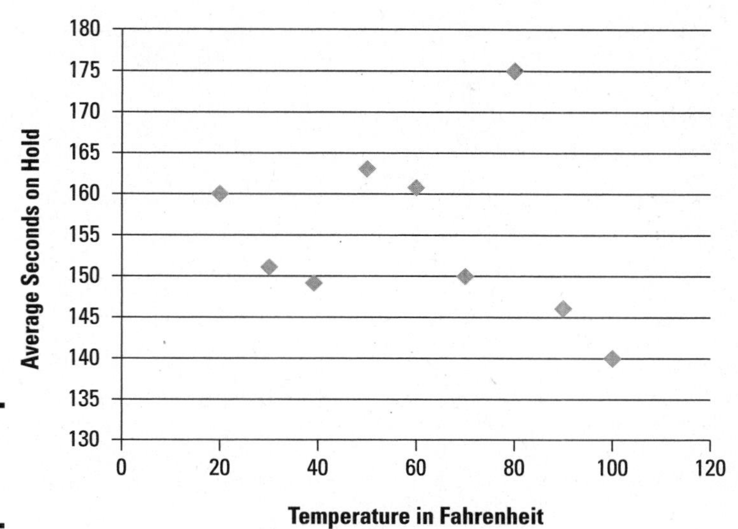

Figure 2-11: No correlation.

The final technique is inspection. I discuss inspection at length in the Validate Scope process (see Book VII, Chapter 2). Inspection can be used to determine whether the results comply with the requirements, much like in the Validate Scope process. It can also be used to validate defect repairs and other approved changes.

You need to be familiar with these quality definitions for the exam.

Control chart. A graphic display of process data over time and against established control limits, and that has a centerline that assists in detecting a trend of plotted values toward either control limit.

Flow chart. The depiction in a diagram format of the inputs, process actions, and outputs of one or more processes within a system.

Pareto chart. A histogram, ordered by frequency of occurrence, that shows how many results were generated by each identified cause.

Inspection. Examining or measuring to verify whether an activity, component, product, result, or service conforms to specified requirements.

The following definitions are not from the *PMBOK Guide,* but you should know them for the exam.

Attribute sampling. A statistical sampling method that indicates whether the result conforms to the target measurement

Variable sampling. A statistical sampling method that indicates the degree to which the result conforms as rated on a continuous scale

Tolerance. Indicates that the result is acceptable if it falls within a specified range

Cause-and-effect diagram. Diagrams that define the inputs to a process or product to identify potential causes of defects

Histogram. A bar chart showing a distribution of variables

Run chart. Shows trends in the variation of a process over time — often used in conjunction with control charts

Scatter diagram. Shows the relationship between two variables

The knowledge and skills you will be tested on from this chapter include

- Project control limits, such as variances, tolerances, and thresholds for project performance
- Project performance metrics
- Variance and trend analysis techniques
- Problem-solving techniques: in particular, the tools you can use to determine root cause analysis

Control Quality: Outputs

The results of the Control Quality process are what you would expect:

- The quality measurements are recorded as indicated in the Plan Quality Management process. The measurements go to the Perform Quality Assurance process.
- Deliverables and results are verified, or a change request is submitted to bring them into compliance.
- Changes are validated as appropriate.
- Work performance information is generated, such as the number and cause of defects.
- Documentation is updated:
  - The project management plan. The quality management plan and the process improvement plan

- Project documents. Metrics and quality standards
- Organizational process assets. Lessons learned and quality checklists

The following responsibility standards from the Code of Ethics and Professional Conduct are demonstrated in the "Ethics and quality control" sidebar and are applicable to all aspects of the project.

- ✦ Report unethical or illegal conduct to appropriate management and, if necessary, to those affected by the conduct.
- ✦ Bring violations of the code of Ethics and Professional Conduct to the attention of the appropriate body for resolution.
- ✦ File ethics complaints only when they are substantiated by facts.
- ✦ Pursue disciplinary action against an individual who retaliates against a person raising ethics concerns.

Ethics and quality control

Reporting the facts about quality control measurements is critical to delivering a product that meets stakeholder needs. It is also a matter of ethics. The following fictional example demonstrates the relationship between ethics and quality.

You are reviewing a control chart for part failures from a vendor who is manufacturing a component for you. You notice several instances over the past three months where the number of defects is greater than the upper control limit. You visit the plant and discover that the vendor is using parts that are not the quality agreed upon in the firm fixed price contract. You review the contract and it clearly states that the vendor will use "premium parts." The parts in the component are lower grade "standard parts."

You report the situation to your program manager and to the vendor's project manager, Victor. Victor says the "premium parts" are not necessary and the product will work just as well with the "standard parts." You state that your organization agreed to a higher price contract because of the "premium parts." You inform Victor that you are going to write up this situation, and you expect Victor to rework all the components that already have "standard parts." In addition, there should not be any delivery delays. You advise Victor that if the situation is not resolved immediately, you will be compelled to file an ethics violation with the appropriate bodies.

Several hours later, you receive a call from Bob, a team member from Victor's project team. Bob informs you that he was aware of the situation involving using lesser-quality parts and that when he raised the concern with Victor, Victor told Bob that if Bob didn't like what was happening, he could find another job. You thank Bob for calling and add the information Bob gave you to the report.

Key Terms

You may be familiar with these terms from the Plan Quality process (Book IV, Chapter 2) or the Perform Quality Assurance process (Book VI, Chapter 1). As you review the terms in the Control Quality process, think about how they are used to control project and product quality.

- Flow charts
- Cause-and-effect diagrams
- Fishbone diagrams
- Ishikawa diagrams
- Checksheets
- Histograms
- Pareto charts
- Run charts
- Scatter diagrams
- Control charts
- Upper control limit
- Lower control limit
- Upper specification limit
- Lower specification limit
- Common cause
- Random cause
- Special cause
- Attribute sampling
- Variable sampling
- Rule of Seven
- Positive correlation
- Negative correlation
- Curvilinear correlation
- Inspection
- Tolerance

Chapter Summary

You need to be familiar with the many techniques of the Control Quality process for the exam. The measurements that result from this process become inputs to the Perform Quality Assurance process.

- Quality control is all about making sure that project and product results are consistent with the quality management plan. You can apply many different techniques to measure and ensure the quality requirements are met for both the project and the product.
- The quality plan, quality metrics, and quality checklists are used with the work performance measurements and deliverables to determine whether the work is done correctly.
- Control Quality also validates that approved changes are implemented correctly.
- The Seven Basic Quality Tools are used to measure conformance to quality requirements. These tools include
  - *Flow charts:* Find places in a process where errors could occur.
  - *Cause-and-effect diagrams:* Find the variables that cause defects.
  - *Checksheets:* Count the number of times an event occurs, or provide steps to follow when performing work.
  - *Histograms:* Count the number of defects by their cause.
  - *Pareto charts:* Rank order defects by their cause.
  - *Control charts:* Provide oversight to a process over time to determine whether it is in control; uses upper and lower control limits and the process mean. Can be used with run charts.
  - *Scatter diagrams:* Show the relationship between two variables.
- You can use statistical sampling techniques rather than test every deliverable. While sampling, you can perform attribute and variable sampling.
- Inspection is used to examine or measure a deliverable for compliance.
- The output will be verified deliverables or a change request. The project management plan, project documents, and organizational process assets will be updated as appropriate.

Prep Test

1 **What input do you use to make sure all the proper steps are being followed to comply with a process or a policy?**

A ❍ Work performance measurement
B ❍ Quality metrics
C ❍ Organizational process assets
D ❍ Quality checklist

2 **Which tool is used to identify and decompose the factors that can lead to a defect or a problem?**

A ❍ Fishbone diagram
B ❍ Run chart
C ❍ Statistical sampling
D ❍ Pareto chart

3 **As a result of looking at reasons why your organization's projects come in late, you identify seven main causes that explain 95% of late deliveries. You created a bar chart that ranks them in order of occurrence. What tool did you use to do this?**

A ❍ Histogram
B ❍ Checksheet
C ❍ Pareto chart
D ❍ Scatter diagram

4 **Normal variation in a process is called**

A ❍ Special cause
B ❍ Common cause
C ❍ Variable cause
D ❍ Attributable cause

5 **You look at last week's timecards for your project team. You have a control chart to plot how long team members spend on your project. Last week, all numbers were significantly down from team members in Wisconsin because the plant was closed for 2 days for a massive snowstorm. This is an example of**

A ❍ Bad luck
B ❍ Variable attribute
C ❍ Special cause
D ❍ Common cause

6 **Which tool has upper and lower specification limits?**

A ❍ Histogram
B ❍ Control chart
C ❍ Checksheet
D ❍ Scatter diagram

7 **How is the upper control limit set on a control chart?**

A ❍ Wherever the customer wants it
B ❍ 2 SD above the mean
C ❍ 1 SD above the mean
D ❍ 3 SD above the mean

8 **The specification limits relate to the requirements of the**

A ❍ Process
B ❍ Project
C ❍ Sponsor
D ❍ Customer

9 **If you have seven data points below the mean, you should be concerned that the process is not random. This is known as**

A ❍ Statistical sampling
B ❍ Normal variance
C ❍ The Rule of Seven
D ❍ Special cause

10 **You create a chart that shows a strong correlation between adding staff and increased customer satisfaction. This is an example of**

A ❍ Positive correlation
B ❍ Random correlation
C ❍ Negative correlation
D ❍ Curvilinear correlation

11 **You asked your team members to turn in their status reports every Thursday. You get 40% of them first thing in the morning, about 20% throughout the day, and the other 40% at the close of business. What kind of correlation is this?**

A ❍ Positive correlation
B ❍ Random correlation
C ❍ Negative correlation
D ❍ Curvilinear correlation

Answers

1 **D.** Quality checklist. A quality checklist tells you the steps you need to follow to comply with a process or policy. *Go over "Control Quality: Inputs."*

2 **A.** Fishbone diagram. A fishbone diagram — also known as an Ishikawa diagram or a cause-and-effect diagram — shows the factors that can lead to problems or defects. *Review "Cause-and-effect diagrams."*

3 **C.** Pareto chart. A rank-ordered bar chart that shows the causes of defects is a Pareto diagram. If you did not put the bars in order, it would be a histogram. *Check out "Histograms and Pareto charts."*

4 **B.** Common cause. Normal variation in a process is a *common cause.* An unusual event that causes a variation in a process is a *special cause. See "Run charts and control charts."*

5 **C.** Special cause. The snowstorm caused a variation in the results; this was a special cause. *Look at "Run charts and control charts."*

6 **B.** Control chart. A control chart has upper and lower control limits and upper and lower specification limits. *Read "Run charts and control charts."*

7 **D.** 3 SD above the mean. The control limits are 3 standard deviations from the mean. *Go over "Run charts and control charts."*

8 **D.** Customer. The specification limits are the voice of the customer. The control limits are the voice of the process. *Review the information in "Run charts and control charts."*

9 **C.** The Rule of Seven. Seven points in a row or seven data points on either side of the mean indicate a process is not random. This is called the Rule of Seven. *Check out "Run charts and control charts."*

10 **A.** Positive correlation. Positive correlation means that as one variable increases, the other variable increases. *See "Scatter diagrams."*

11 **D.** Curvilinear correlation. A curvilinear correlation starts and ends around the same level, and the points in between are either higher or lower than the end points. *Read "Scatter diagrams."*

Chapter 3: Controlling Communications and Stakeholders

Exam Objectives

- **Communicate project status and continue to ensure the project is aligned with business needs.**
- **Minimize the impact of issues with the project schedule, cost, and resources by using the issue register to manage issues and assign corrective actions.**

Controlling Communications and Controlling Stakeholder Engagement are similar. In fact, you will notice that the only difference in the inputs, tools and techniques, and outputs is that Control Communications includes project communications as an input.

This similarity between the two processes is not surprising given that communication is the main vehicle you use when working with stakeholders. The main distinction between the two processes is that Controlling Communications is concerned with ensuring that the communications management plan is effective, and Controlling Stakeholder Engagement is concerned with ensuring that the stakeholder management plan is effective.

The information in these two processes can seem pretty generic, so to make the information relevant, think about situations on current and past projects that you can relate to.

Quick Assessment

1. The process of monitoring and controlling communications through the entire project life cycle to ensure the information needs of the project stakeholders are met is ______ ______.

2. Ignoring cultural differences and having preconceptions about the audience are examples of ______ ______.

3. (True/False). Lessons learned are considered project communications.

4. ______ is a communication blocker that assumes certain groups of people think or act in a similar way.

5. Hearing only the information you want to hear is a communication blocker referred to as ______ ______.

6. The process of monitoring overall project stakeholder relationships and adjusting strategies and plans for re-engaging stakeholders is ______ ______ ______.

7. A stakeholder who is actively against your project is ______.

8. Where would a dispute between stakeholders be recorded?

9. To hold productive meetings, would you have weekly meetings, publish the issue log, or manage conflict?

10. Which two project documents are likely to be updated as part of the Control Communications process?

Answers

1 Control Communications. Control Communications ensures that the communications management plan is effective. *To see the definition, go to the "Control Communications" section.*

2 Communication blockers. There are many ways to inhibit good communication — you can see a list in the *"Communication blockers" section.*

3 True. Lessons learned are one of the many communications you will record, index, and distribute on a project. *Read more in the "Control Communications: Outputs" section.*

4 Stereotyping. Stereotyping can occur when you assume people with specific skills sets, ethnicity, age, or other generalization think or act the same. *Read more about it in the "Communication blockers" section.*

5 Selective listening. Focusing on what you want to hear (say, the project schedule is currently doing well) instead of not listening to other information (say, there is a trend toward overrunning the budget) is an example of selective listening. *See the "Communication blockers" section.*

6 Control Stakeholder Engagement. Ensuring that stakeholders are participating effectively on your project is part of controlling their engagement. *See the "Control Stakeholder Engagement" section.*

7 Resistant. Stakeholders who are aware of your project but don't support it are resistant. *You can read about them in the "Control Stakeholder Engagement: Inputs" section.*

8 Issue log. An issue log is used to document and monitor elements under discussion or in dispute between project stakeholders. *For more information on this topic, read the "Control Stakeholder Engagement: Inputs" section.*

9 Manage conflict. If conflict occurs in your meeting, you need to effectively manage it so that it stays professional and productive. *Go over the information in the "Holding productive meetings" section.*

10 Stakeholder register and issue log. There may be additional documents you update, but you should expect to update at least these two. *See information in the "Control Stakeholder Engagement: Outputs" section.*

Control Communications

Control Communications ensures that the communications management plan is effective. The communications management plan may evolve and be updated throughout the project as new stakeholders enter the project, new information needs are identified, and communications requirements change.

Control Communications. Monitoring and controlling communications throughout the entire project life cycle to ensure that the information needs of the project stakeholders are met.

Control Communications: Inputs

As with all main controlling processes in a knowledge area, you start with the relevant project management plan elements, the actual results, work performance data, and organizational process assets (OPAs).

The elements of the project management plan that you will use are the communications management plan and the stakeholder management plan. Compare the information in those plans with the communications that were actually delivered as well as the associated work performance data, such as

- ✦ When information was distributed
- ✦ Whom information was delivered to
- ✦ Additional information requests
- ✦ Feedback on the information, timeliness, or medium

Project communications includes status reports, performance reports, forecasts, presentations, updated project documents and project management plan elements, lessons learned, correspondence, minutes, and so forth.

You may use the issue log to identify any issues that need to be communicated. For example, the sponsor or PMO may want to be notified about any issues that have high impacts or would negatively affect key stakeholders.

Control Communications: Tools and Techniques

When comparing the results of the communications process, you may engage experts in meetings to help determine whether the process is working effectively — and if not, how to improve it. Sometimes it's a matter of changing how information is presented. You can use information management systems to improve the usability and readability of information by putting data in charts, tables, and graphic formats (such as a dashboard or story board).

Communication blockers

If effective communication is an issue, you can check whether any of the following common communication blockers are the culprit. As you can well intuit, *communication blockers* are things people do that inhibit good communication. The following list highlights common communication blockers along with an example or a brief explanation.

- **Using the wrong communication media:** You wouldn't send a corrective action notification via e-mail. You would have that kind of communication in person, one-on-one.
- **Making erroneous assumptions about your audience:** For example, sometimes we make the mistake of assuming that people already know what we know. If you leave out what you consider introductory information and only address more specific issues, your audience might not understand your message. Having a lack of common understanding leads to ineffective communication.
- **A receiver in an area with a lot of background activity:** The background activity can reduce the recipient's ability to hear your message or focus on your message because she is distracted.
- **Withholding information:** Sometimes team members withhold performance issues or challenges until it's too late to do anything about them. Another example is if your sponsor knows that a reorganization is going to impact your project but withholds that information, blocking the flow of communication.
- **Ignoring cultural differences:** Different organizations have different cultures with regards to work hours, quality of work, accountability, and so on. If you assume that a contractor has the same culture as your organization, you will have issues.
- **Stereotyping:** Assuming that all technical people think in a certain way or that all senior management will act in a certain manner reduces your ability to really hear what someone from one of those groups is saying.
- **Having preconceptions about the audience:** Similar to stereotyping, if you're at a meeting and you have preconceptions about how your audience will behave, you may miss cues about what your audience is thinking, or you might not deliver the information the audience is interested in.
- **Displaying emotions and reactive behavior:** Part of being professional is not letting your emotions get in the way of your communication. Communicating with a person acting emotionally is difficult.
- **Employing selective listening:** Selective listening means that someone is hearing only the parts of the message he wants to hear. For example, say you're presenting a status report to your sponsor. You state that for

the most part, the project is on track, but there are a few areas of concern with regards to the schedule. However, the sponsor hears only the part about how things are on track and ignores or avoids the information about the schedule concerns.

- **Engaging in power games:** Making decisions and taking actions based on political gain, or trying to dominate a situation based on your power, can inhibit open and honest communication.
- **Management by memo:** There are times when an e-mail or a memo is appropriate; however, you can't manage a project via memo, and you can't deliver critical information via e-mail. You have to have face-to-face interaction.
- **Sending mixed messages:** An example of a mixed message is when a team member states she understands what you want, but her facial expression seems confused, or she's disorganized and asks the same questions again.

Control Communications: Outputs

The outputs from this process are the standard outputs:

- **Work performance information:** Information about the effectiveness of the communications process, such as the timeliness of reports, the effectiveness of presentations, and so forth.
- **Change requests:** Corrective or preventive action needed to bring performance into alignment with the plan, or to meet changing stakeholder information requirements.
- **Project management plan updates:** The communications management plan is the most likely document you will update, although the stakeholder management plan may also require updates as well.
- **Project documents updates:** Performance reports, forecasts, and issue logs are the most likely documents that will need updating.
- **Organizational process assets updates:** All project documentation, including lessons learned, outcomes of issue resolution, and corrective actions.

Control Stakeholder Engagement

When you're first initiating and planning your project, you should spend time identifying your stakeholders and determining how to best leverage them for the good of your project. When you first identify stakeholders for your project, you may have created a Power/Support grid (see Book II,

Chapter 3, for a sample) to analyze stakeholder involvement in your project. During planning, you may have created a stakeholder engagement assessment matrix to show a stakeholder's initial support for your project and the desired level of support for your project. See upcoming Table 3-1 for an example of a stakeholder engagement assessment matrix.

The power/support grid and stakeholder assessment matrix are key components that help you develop your stakeholder management plan. In this process, you will revisit the stakeholder management plan to determine whether it's having the intended effect or you need to revisit the plan and find more effective ways to engage the project stakeholders.

Control Stakeholder Engagement. Monitoring overall project stakeholder relationships and adjusting strategies and plans for reengaging stakeholders.

Control Stakeholder Engagement: Inputs

The project management plan contains the stakeholder management plan and the communications management plan that provide information on how to engage and communicate with stakeholders. The power/support grid and stakeholder assessment matrix are key components of the stakeholder management plan that help develop the stakeholder management plan. In this process, you will revisit the stakeholder management plan and compare it with work performance data to determine whether it's having the intended effect or you need to find more effective ways to engage the project stakeholders.

Table 3-1, which I also show in Book V, Chapter 3, demonstrates the process, building on my running example of a childcare center.

Table 3-1 Stakeholder Engagement Matrix

Stakeholder	*Unaware*	*Resistant*	*Neutral*	*Supportive*	*Leading*
Manny	B			A	
Jocelyn		B	A		
Jamie				B	A
Kim	B		A		

Assume that your issue log has an entry that indicates that Manny (the community affairs liaison in HR) was interested in having an auditorium space at Cynergy, Inc., to communicate with large groups of people from the community. In the beginning of the childcare center project, it looked like both projects were viable. However, Morgan Cuthbert (the sponsor) has just told Manny that because of lower than projected sales, she is forced to choose between the auditorium and the childcare center, and she has chosen to put the auditorium on hold. At this point, you're concerned that Manny will no longer be such a strong supporter of your project. In fact, he may even become a resistor.

You look over the minutes from the last three meetings and notice that even though Manny was invited, he did not show up. Further research reveals that he was supposed to have attended a grand opening for Baby Gap as a way of showing community outreach and talking about the childcare center at Cynergy, Inc. You have found out that he cancelled at the last minute. This type of work performance data and project documentation help you to build a clearer picture of Manny's current engagement level in the project. He has gone from unaware, to supportive, to at the very best neutral, but possibly even resistant.

To control Manny's engagement level, you will want to meet with him — and possibly other stakeholders — to determine his state of support and see how you can get him actively engaged in the project again.

Control Stakeholder Engagement: Tools and Techniques

Another example that demonstrates how stakeholder engagement can be controlled involves the city inspector. In the following scenario, you will see how a stakeholder's engagement (the city inspector) has a potential to affect the project and also how the project team uses information management systems, expert judgment, and meetings.

Inspector issue and impact

On November 8, the following issue was entered in the issue log:

> Rick Johnson is new building inspector; he was hired by the city on October 10. He is scheduled to do his inspection on the childcare center on December 1. At a local builder's association meeting, the general contractor for the childcare center heard that Rick has not approved buildings that didn't have their documentation complete and indexed per the instructions Rick sent 10 days prior to his visit. This has caused a delay in the approval for several buildings in the city.

Fast-forward two days to November 10. You have not received the documentation request from Rick, and the contractors do not work the week of Thanksgiving.

You meet with the general contractor, several of the subcontractors, and the facilities manager to determine the impact and then brainstorm solutions. The group determines the following impacts:

- **Scope impact:** There may be additional unplanned work to provide all the documentation in a specific presentation style.
- **Schedule impact:** If the inspector doesn't sign off on the childcare build-out on December 1, it will cause a day-for-day slip in the schedule. The childcare center may open late, especially with the winter holidays reducing the number of work hours in the month.
- **Cost impact:** If contractors are willing to work overtime in December to get the paperwork and documentation indexed correctly, it will lead to a schedule overrun.

The group decides to consult with J.J. Shoals, a contractor who successfully passed the city inspection, in order to minimize the risk of not passing the inspection. They set up a meeting with the J.J. three days later and develop a work plan to gather, organize, and present the information in the format that worked for J.J. previously.

Holding productive meetings

Meetings are a common method of sharing communication and engaging stakeholders in projects. Project managers spend considerable time leading meetings. Some are informal meetings involving a few team members, some are project team meetings, and some are formal presentations to management and other key stakeholders. Some of the key guidelines to effective meetings are

- Have meetings only when necessary.
- Make the purpose of each meeting clear.
- Prepare, distribute, and follow an agenda.
- Make sure the right people are at the meeting and also that only people who need to be present are invited.
- Encourage participation.
- Manage conflict if and when it occurs.
- Issue minutes.
- Follow up on action items.

When distributing information, you can use hard copy or electronic information. You can push out the information, you can have people pull it as needed, or you can deliver it interactively. I discuss push and pull communication methods in Book IV, Chapter 4.

Control Stakeholder Engagement: Outputs

The outputs from this process are similar to the outputs from the Control Communications process:

- **Work performance information:** Information about the effectiveness of the stakeholder engagement process, such as the level of support and participation in the project.
- **Change requests:** Corrective or preventive action needed to bring engagement into alignment with the plan, or to meet changing stakeholder engagement levels.
- **Project management plan updates:** The stakeholder management plan is the most likely document you will update, although the communications management plan and the human resource management plans may also require updates as well.
- **Project documents updates.** The stakeholder register and issue logs are the most likely documents that will need updating.
- **Organizational process assets updates:** All project documentation, including lessons learned, outcomes of issue resolution, and corrective actions.

Key Terms

There are no new key terms in this chapter.

Chapter Summary

In this chapter, I talk about controlling communications and stakeholder engagement.

- To be successful, you need to follow effective communication techniques and avoid communication blockers.
- Evaluate the effectiveness of the communications management plan.
- Have meetings only when necessary, and follow the guidelines for effective meetings.
- Assess the level of participation and engagement of project stakeholders and take corrective or preventive actions to optimize engagement levels.

Prep Test

Multiple Choice

1 Which input is an example of a communication?

A ❍ A pending issue
B ❍ A performance report
C ❍ The communications management plan
D ❍ The stakeholder register

2 Work performance data for Control Communications includes

A ❍ The number of tasks started
B ❍ The number of change requests
C ❍ When information was distributed
D ❍ The level of stakeholder engagement

3 When a project includes stakeholders from multiple organizations, you have a higher risk of

A ❍ Using the wrong communicating media
B ❍ Withholding information
C ❍ Ignoring cultural differences
D ❍ Engaging in power games

4 A functional manager isn't providing the resource support she promised. You are noting that she indicated support for the project, but it appears that she's somewhat resistant. You need to take actions to get her to support your project. What process are you involved in?

A ❍ Manage Communications
B ❍ Control Communications
C ❍ Manage Stakeholder Engagement
D ❍ Control Stakeholder Engagement

5 **Because the portfolio review committee has to review dozens of reports each meeting, the committee has asked for a simpler way to review information rather than a table. You develop a stop light chart for them. This is part of which process?**

A ❍ Manage Communications
B ❍ Control Communications
C ❍ Manage Stakeholder Engagement
D ❍ Control Stakeholder Engagement

6 **A grid that shows current versus desired stakeholder engagement is part of which input to the Control Stakeholder Engagement process?**

A ❍ Communications management plan
B ❍ Organizational process assets
C ❍ Stakeholder management plan
D ❍ Stakeholder register

7 **To hold effective meetings, you should**

A ❍ Manage conflict.
B ❍ Lead by example.
C ❍ Release the agenda two hours prior to the meeting.
D ❍ Discourage participation so you get through the agenda.

Scenario 1

You give a presentation for upper management that highlights your project's achievements from the previous quarter. At the end, you hear the Director of Finance state that he didn't see the value in the presentation because he wasn't very familiar with the project.

1 **What type of communication blocker occurred?**

A ❍ A receiver with a lot of background activity
B ❍ Withholding information
C ❍ Stereotyping
D ❍ Making erroneous assumptions about the audience

2 **What guideline for productive meeting management was not followed?**

A ❍ Make sure only the people who need to be there are invited.
B ❍ Encourage participation.
C ❍ Make the purpose of each meeting clear.
D ❍ Issue minutes.

Scenario 2

After completing the requirements gathering and concept development phase of your project, you're moving into the design phase. In the prior phase, you used in-house expertise, but now you'll be using contracted architects and engineers. You heard that the architect often delivers late and makes changes without fully documenting them.

1 **This is an example of where you need to**

A ❍ Control stakeholder engagement.
B ❍ Control communications.
C ❍ Manage the budget.
D ❍ Manage integration.

Answers

Multiple Choice

1. **B.** A performance report. Performance reports, minutes, status reports, and presentations are all examples of project communications. *Go over "Control Communications: Inputs."*

2. **C.** When information was distributed. You can also track whom information was delivered to and also feedback about the communication. *Review "Control Communications: Inputs."*

3. **C.** Ignoring cultural differences. Organizations have different internal cultures. The more organizations you have on a project, the greater likelihood that cultural differences will be overlooked. *Check out "Control Communications: Inputs."*

4. **D.** Control Stakeholder Engagement. Checking stakeholders' level of engagement and taking action to encourage them to have the desired level of engagement is part of controlling their engagement. *Check out "Control Stakeholder Engagement."*

5. **B.** Control Communications. Making sure communications meet the needs of the stakeholders is part of controlling communications. *Look over "Control Communications."*

6. **C.** Stakeholder management plan. A stakeholder engagement assessment matrix can be part of the stakeholder management plan. *See the information in "Control Stakeholder Engagement: Inputs."*

7. **A.** Manage conflict. Keeping conflict productive is important. If conflict becomes negative or nonproductive, you need to step in and manage it. *You can find this in "Holding productive meetings."*

Scenario 1

1. **D.** Making erroneous assumptions about the audience. You assumed that the Director of Finance was informed and interested in the presentation. *Go over the information in "Communication blockers."*

2. **A.** Make sure only the people who need to be there are invited. The Director of Finance did not need to be there and did not find value in the presentation. *Look at "Holding productive meetings."*

Scenario 2

1. **A.** Control stakeholder engagement. You will need to closely monitor the architect and continue to adjust your strategy to ensure he does not disrupt the project. *Review the information in "Control Stakeholder Engagement."*

Chapter 4: Managing Your Risks and Procurements

Exam Objectives

- **Actively employ risk management techniques as documented in the risk management plan to minimize the impact of risk on the project.**
- **Conduct risk reassessment on a regular basis and implement response strategies as indicated in the risk register.**
- **Administer contracts and measure contractor performance.**
- **Identify and quantify variances and determine appropriate preventive and corrective actions.**

Monitoring and controlling risks is a complex process — and, when done well, ensures that you're practicing good project management principles. By practicing risk management, your project will be a lot smoother and have a greater probability of meeting its objectives.

In Book V, Chapter 1, I spend quite a bit of time talking about planning for risks. This juncture is where you use all that knowledge gained in identifying, prioritizing, quantifying, and developing responses to risk. In Control Risks, you will spend time assessing the effectiveness of the risk management process overall as well as determining whether it is being used: in other words, a *risk audit.*

Managing contracts includes monitoring the contractors' performance as well as making sure that the terms and conditions of the contract are followed. Contract administration includes managing payments, changes, performance reviews, and the day-to-day interaction with the contractor. All these activities need to be conducted while integrating the contractor work with in-house work or with the work of other contractors. The more contractors you have, the more complex it becomes.

Quick Assessment

1. ______ ______ identifies new risks, analyzes existing risks, and closes outdated risks.

2. To identify where performance could go over a performance threshold in the future, you should employ a(n) ______ ______.

3. Comparing accomplishments against a schedule of technical achievements is called ______ ______ ______.

4. A contested change where the buyer and seller cannot agree on compensation is a(n) ______, a(n) _____, or a(n) ______.

5. (True/False). Contract administration may be handled by a department that is entirely separate from the project.

6. Which input provides information on schedule variances, forecasts, and funds expended?

7. To review the risk management process and the individual risk responses, you should conduct a(n) ______ ______.

8. If you want to indicate that failure to deliver on time constitutes a breach of contract, which clause should you include in a contract?

9. What are two types of alternative dispute resolution?

10. An event that is the result of elements of nature, or "an act of God," is referred to in contractual language as ______ ______.

Answers

1 Risk reassessment. Risk reassessment occurs after the initial in-depth identification, analysis, and response to risks. It occurs throughout the project. *Read up on "Risk reassessment."*

2 Variance and trend analysis. A trend analysis will indicate whether there is a likelihood of breaching a performance threshold if current performance trends continue. *Go over the information in "Variance and trend analysis."*

3 Technical performance measurement. Technical performance measurement compares planned technical achievements with actual technical achievements. *You can read more about this in "Technical performance measurement."*

4 Claim, dispute, appeal. *Claims, disputes,* and *appeals* are all terms that are used to describe a situation where the buyer and seller cannot agree on compensation. *You can read about this in "Claims and disputes."*

5 True. Contract administration is often handled by a legal department, contracts department, or procurement department, not the project. *For more information, see "Contract administration."*

6 Work performance reports. Work performance reports contain information on the status of the project, including technical achievements, schedule status, and budget information. *Check out Table 4-1, which talks about risk-monitoring inputs.*

7 Risk audit. A risk audit assesses individual risk responses for effectiveness, and it reviews the entire risk management process to determine whether it's being followed and whether it's appropriate for the project. *Read up on this in "Risk audit."*

8 Time is of the Essence. When a Time is of the Essence clause is in a contract, it means that on-time delivery is so important that failure to deliver on time is considered a breach of contract. *Read more about this in "Control Procurements."*

9 Mediation and arbitration. Both mediation and arbitration are less formal and less costly than litigation. *See "Claims and disputes" for more information.*

10 *Force majeure. Force majeure* events allow a delay in performance due to circumstances beyond one's control. I define *force majeure* in the section on *"Force majeure and liquidated damages."*

Control Risks: Inputs

To effectively monitor and manage risks, you need to have a 24/7, 360-degree view on what's happening with your project. In Control Risks, you continue the cycle of identifying, analyzing, and responding to risks.

Control Risks. Implementing risk response plans, tracking identified risks, monitoring residual risks, identifying new risks, and evaluating the risk process effectiveness throughout the project.

You will be monitoring risks and identifying new risks throughout the entire life of the project. While executing the plan, you will have additional information: namely, performance information. Every time you get a status report from the team members, and every time you prepare a performance report for your sponsor, you should be looking at the work performance measurements and work performance information to determine whether new risks are on the horizon that you should put through the risk planning cycle.

You should be familiar with the content in the inputs by now, but because they are so critical to effectively identifying and responding to risks, Table 4-1 lists them, with the input on the left, and the content from the input on the right.

Table 4-1 Risk Monitoring Inputs

Input	*Content*
Project Management Plan	Risk management plan, including: Approach for allocating reserves Reporting formats Timing and frequency for risk reassessment Risk audit approach
Risk register	Risk ID Risk statement Probability Impact by objective Risk score Response Revised probability, impact, and score Risk owner Actions Status Risk triggers Watch list

Input	*Content*
Work Performance Data	Status of deliverables Percent of work actually completed Technical achievements Actual start and finish dates of schedule activities Remaining work to be done on in-progress work Costs committed Costs incurred Status of the implementation of change requests Corrective actions taken Preventive actions taken Status of defect repairs
Work performance reports	Percent complete of work in progress Schedule variance Schedule performance index Cost variance Cost performance index Work completed in the current period Work planned for completion but not complete, along with the reasons why Funds expended during the current period Any variance in the funds expended, along with the reasons why Status of existing risks and issues Any new risks or issues Forecast for future schedule performance Forecast for future cost performance Resource utilization variances Summary of changes requested and changes implemented Any quality findings New and resolved assumptions
Other	Assumption Log Issue log

You can see that there is quite a bit of information you need to gather and synthesize to effectively manage your risks.

Control Risks: Tools and Techniques

To effectively manage risks on your project, you should reassess existing risks on a regular basis as well as identify new risks. You should also analyze project performance, forecasts, trends, and reserve utilization. A risk audit will help ensure that the risk management process is working effectively. These techniques are discussed in more detail in the following sections.

Risk reassessment

Much of the work in Monitor and Control Risks takes place in reassessing the risks that you already identified and documented in the risk register. For a refresher on all the information in the risk register, review Book V, Chapter 1. You should take some time at every team meeting to identify new risks and discuss active risks. At the points in time documented in the risk management plan, you should do a really thorough review of the entire register. This is often done at the close of one phase and the start of another. Common actions in risk reassessment include

- Identifying new risks, analyzing the probability and impact, and developing a risk response plan
- Identifying any risk triggers that have occurred to tell you whether you need to implement a response plan or a contingency plan
- Determining whether any risk events have become active, indicating that you need to implement the response strategy
- Determining whether any events occurred that you didn't plan for — and need a workaround for
- Assessing whether the probability or impact for any risks has changed
- Assessing whether the risk response strategy is still appropriate, or whether you need to take a different approach
- Determining whether residual risks have grown and whether you need to develop more robust responses
- Identifying any secondary risks that have emerged and putting them through the risk planning cycle
- Determining whether events have evolved to the point where you should take preventive or corrective actions for any new or existing risks
- Reviewing your watch list to see whether any risk events should be escalated up to the active risk list
- Reassessing the risk tolerance levels of the sponsor, performing organization, and other stakeholders to determine if they have shifted
- Identifying any risk events that have passed so that you can close them

Keeping the risk register up to date can take some time, but you can see that if you ask these questions, perform the assessments, and continue to identify new events, your project will perform much better than if you just did risk management at the beginning of the project or once every few months.

Analysis

Comparing the planned work against the actual work and also the planned costs against the actual costs generates good performance information. To really understand what's happening on your project, though, you need to compare information across documents. A quality issue in one deliverable could result in a cost or schedule risk down the line. This type of risk analysis helps you stay on top of your project.

Variance and trend analysis

After you begin generating performance reports, reviewing the reports and monitoring and controlling risks will go hand in hand. Whenever you see a variance outside the threshold, you should investigate the cause of the variance and determine whether it poses a risk to the project. If it does, you will move immediately to identifying that as a risk and developing a response to it.

A trend analysis is a method you can use to determine whether project performance is at risk. If your CPI is trending from .95 to .93 to .91, you know to take action soon, or you will be outside the threshold established in the project management plan (covered Book V, Chapter 3).

Technical performance measurement

Technical performance measurement is another way to determine whether your progress is on track. You might have a plan in place promising certain functionality by a point in time, but you haven't achieved that functionality. Or you might have planned to have a specific number of bugs or defects fixed by a certain date, but that didn't happen. This should be considered a risk.

Reviewing the risk log is a good idea, but go over the Assumption Log (see Book III, Chapter 1) as well. You should be looking for new assumptions, if the existing assumptions are valid, whether they changed, or finding any can be closed out. And while you're at it, do the same thing for the issue log.

Reserve analysis

When developing risk responses, you set aside time and money for contingency reserve to reduce the risk of time and cost overruns. As you progress through the project, you will allocate some of the schedule reserve as needed, and you will need to use some of the budget reserve either for contingency funds for identified risks or for unforeseen expenditures. At the same time, as you progress through the project, the amount of uncertainty — and, therefore, risk — is reduced.

Reserve analysis looks at the amount of risk on the project and the amount of schedule and budget reserve to determine whether the reserve is sufficient for the remaining risk. You can expect to spend a certain percentage in each phase of the life cycle, or you might allocate it by milestone. If appropriate, you might be able to release some project reserve from the project, or you might need to ask for more, depending on how the project is going.

Risk audit

A risk audit looks at the risk management process overall as well as the responses to individual risks. The audit can be relatively informal and conducted during a team meeting, or it might be formal and conducted by an outside risk management expert. The purpose of a risk audit is to evaluate the effectiveness of the risk management process. Some of the items that a risk audit addresses are

- Was the risk management planning sufficient?
- Did the team do a good job in identifying risks?
- Were the probability and impact (PxI) tables appropriate for the project?
- Were the correct quantitative analysis techniques used?
- How effective were the risk responses?
- Are the risks being monitored and managed appropriately?

A risk audit also considers the effectiveness of risk responses by answering questions, such as

- Was the selected strategy effective?
- Did the risk event occur as expected?
- Did the response affect the risk event as expected?
- Were other options available that would have been more effective?
- What actions can be taken to increase the effectiveness of the response?

The risk audit can be used for lessons learned. You can document areas for improvement as well as areas that worked well that you can share with other project teams. The Risk Audit form shown in Figure 4-1 is a generic example of what you can expect to see during a risk audit.

RISK AUDIT

Project Title: ______________________ Date Prepared: ______________________

Project Audit: ______________________ Audit Date: ______________________

Risk Event Audit:

Event	Cause	Response	Comment
List the event from the risk register.	*Identify the root cause of the event.*	*Describe the response implemented.*	*Discuss if there was any way to have foreseen the event and respond to it more effectively.*

Risk Response Audit:

Event	Response	Successful	Actions to Improve
List the event from the risk register.	*List the risk response.*	*Indicate if the response was successful.*	*Identify any opportunities for improvement in risk response.*

Risk Management Process Audit:

Process	Followed	Tools and Techniques Used
Plan Risk Management	*Indicate if the various processes were followed as indicated in the risk management plan.*	*Identify tools and techniques used in the various risk management processes and whether they were successful.*
Identify Risks		
Perform Qualitative Risk Analysis		
Perform Quantitative Risk Analysis		
Plan Risk Responses		
Monitor and Control Risks		

Description of Good Practices to Share:

Describe any practices that should be shared for use on other projects. Include any recommendations to update and improve risk forms, templates, policies, procedures, or processes to ensure these practices are repeatable.

Description of Areas for Improvement:

Describe any practices that need improvement, the improvement plan, and any follow-up dates or information for corrective action.

Figure 4-1: A Risk Audit form.

Control Risks: Outputs

You will update the risk register based on the risk reassessment. You add new risks as well as their analysis and response strategy. Existing risks will be updated as needed, and some risks will be closed out. The register should also indicate which responses were enacted and how effective they were.

The risk management plan, and any of the other subsidiary management plans and baselines from the project management plan, might require updating depending upon the results of this process. Assumption Logs (Book III, Chapter 1) and other appropriate project documents should be updated to reflect the outcome of this process as well. Organizational process assets are updated with information from risk audits, such as lessons learned. If your organization has a risk database, you should make sure that's kept up to date as part of your risk management activities.

Many times, risk management entails corrective and preventive actions. These need to go through the change management process in the form of a change request.

Monitor and Control Project Risk is the primary process that will be used to test knowledge and skills on risk identification and analysis techniques and risk response techniques.

Control Procurements

Much like how the majority of your time managing the project is reflected in the Direct and Manage Project Work process, the majority of your time managing contracts is reflected in the Control Procurements process.

Control Procurements. Managing procurement relationships, monitoring contract performance, and making changes and corrections to contracts as needed.

During this process, the seller must meet the procurement requirements, and the buyer must perform according to the terms of the contract. This includes appropriate and timely payments and also contract change management. Thus, you can see that both the buyer and the seller will work with the procurement agreement to ensure that both parties are fulfilling their contractual commitments.

This process requires significant integration across the project. Here are some examples of integration. There are, of course, others, depending upon the nature of the project:

- **Scope:** You need to verify and control the contractor scope. You should recall that verifying scope is the process of formally accepting the result. As a buyer, you want to make sure the contractor is delivering all the scope and only the scope that was promised. You also need to ensure that no one in your organization is making "constructive" changes to the contract.
- **Constructive change:** When a contractor performs work beyond the contract requirements, without a formal order under the changes clause, either due to an informal order from, or through the fault of, the buyer.
- **Schedule:** The contractors' deliverables need to be coordinated with other deliverables. Many contracts have milestone payments based on deliveries, and some have incentives based on timely or early delivery. In addition, some contracts have a clause that indicates that late delivery is considered a material breach.

  Time is of the Essence is a contract clause that indicates that on-time delivery is mandatory, and therefore, contractually binding. Failure to act or deliver within the stated time frame constitutes a breach of contract.
- **Cost:** You need to ensure that the contractor is paid only for work that's verified and accepted. If interim payments are scheduled, make sure that you're approving payments consistent with the results. In other words, if the contractor is scheduled to be 50% complete, yet only 25% of the work is done, make sure that you're paying 25% of the contract and not 50%.
- **Quality:** You use the same quality control techniques on contractor results as you do for in-house work. This ensures that the deliverables meet the requirements and specifications.
- **Communication:** The contractor needs to submit status reports that you will reference when developing your project performance reports. Many times, contracts will specify the format and timing of the reports.
- **Risk:** Information in the contractors risk log should be integrated with the project risk log. Additionally, there may be risks associated with contracting that you should manage throughout the project.

Obviously, the more contractors you have on a project, the more work this entails. For complex procurements, or for projects with multiple vendors, you might have a procurement administrator or a contracting officer's representative to provide oversight to the contractor and manage much of this work. This is particularly true when the organization has a centralized contracting department.

Control Procurements: Inputs

The procurement management plan (part of the project management plan) provides guidance on who will manage various aspects of the procurement as well as how to go about it. This includes information on how to use the payment systems, contract change control system, and performance reviews.

You use the baselines in the project management plan and compare them against the work performance reports and work performance data provided by the contractor. You should also compare the performance reports against the actual agreements and the procurement documents.

Change requests can include a change to the statement of work (SOW) for the contract, or to the contract itself.

Control Procurements: Tools and Techniques

The fundamental aspects of controlling procurements are analyzing performance, managing disputes, and administering the contract. I discuss each separately.

Analyzing performance

To analyze the contractor's performance, review his performance reports. This can be as simple as looking at a contractor status report. Or, for complex procurements, this review includes all-day performance reviews, on-site inspections, and contract audits. The contractor status report can include the same type of information you gather from your in-house team members.

To discuss performance reviews, on-site inspections, and audits, consider this scenario. Assume that you just took over managing an aerospace project. The design, development, and manufacturing for a jet engine are outsourced to Speed of Sound (SOS) Jets. You are reviewing the performance reports, including the following summary graphic shown in Figure 4-2.

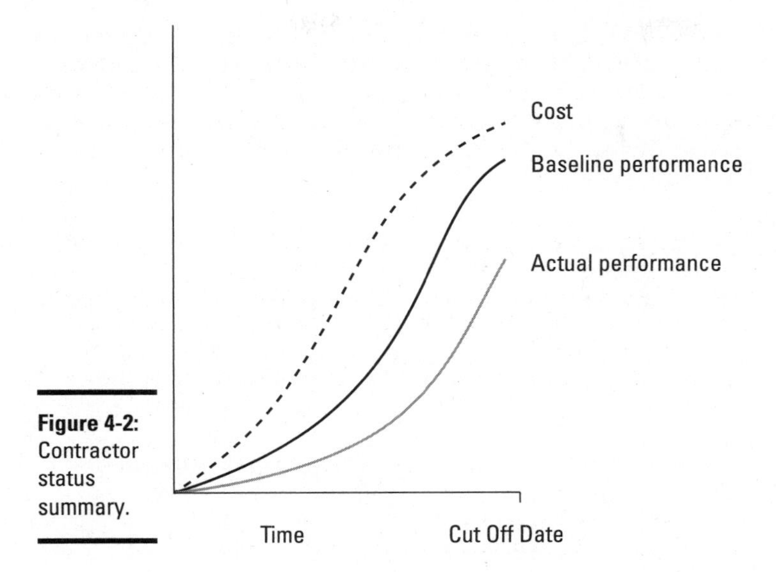

Figure 4-2: Contractor status summary.

The contractor status graph in the figure shows you that the actual results are less than (behind) your baseline, and that your costs are greater than your baseline. In other words, the contractor is behind and over budget.

Procurement performance review

Based on the contractor status report, you decide that you need to go to the contractor's location and have a meeting. You convene with your contracting officer, the SOS representative assigned to this contract, your technical lead, and your quality assurance team lead. You ask the SOS contractor to have his project manager, technical lead, contract administrator, and any key suppliers he deems appropriate present for the meeting. You also tell SOS that you want all technical drawings and documentation available and that you would like a tour of the facilities where the work is being done.

At the meeting, you begin by introducing yourself and asking the SOS project manager, Kevin, to bring you up to date on the past 18 months of work. Kevin states that SOS is 90% done with design and 65% done with development, but hasn't started manufacturing. He states that SOS had problems with the thrust on the first prototype and had to go back and redesign some parts. The redesign, retooling, and machining put SOS behind schedule and over budget. The second prototype, which just entered the testing phase, is meeting the requirements and specifications so far.

Your technical expert is reviewing the drawings and concurs with the project manager's explanation. You ask Kevin to discuss ways to get the schedule back on track and look for ways to minimize the overrun while the technical lead and QA team member tour the facility and look at the new prototype.

Inspection and audit

In addition to touring the facility and checking out the new prototype, the quality assurance team member and technical lead validate the progress as reported and also verify that the work done so far is acceptable. They are also looking at the processes for material check-in, usage, and reporting to make sure that your company is charged only for material used on your project.

Your contracting officer and the SOS contract administrator are going through the contract and reviewing the terms to make sure that everyone has a clear understanding of the implications of the cost and schedule overruns. SOS believes there have been some constructive changes to the original design. The two contracts people are discussing this issue. If they can't come to a resolution about the situation, it might turn into a claim that will need to be settled per the contractual language.

Claims and disputes

As I mention, the contract team members are reviewing the contract and discussing claims, disputes, and constructive changes. (I define constructive changes earlier in the section "Control Procurements.") Take a look at the claims and dispute resolution options.

The information in this section should not be construed as legal advice. For specific legal consultation, you should consult with the appropriate council.

Claim. A request, demand, or assertion of rights by a seller against a buyer, or vice versa, for consideration, compensation, or payment under the terms of a legally binding contract, such as for a disputed change.

Alternate Dispute Resolution (ADR). A means to settle claims or disputes without litigation. The two primary means of ADR are Arbitration and Mediation.

Mediation. A method of ADR used to settle claims and disputes informally. An independent party aids in settling the claim or dispute between the parties.

Arbitration. A method of ADR used to settle claims and disputes without litigation. An impartial third party, usually a professional arbitrator, hears the testimony and reviews evidence from both sides. Both parties agree that arbitration will be binding, meaning that the arbitrator's award is final.

A claim can also be called a *dispute* or an *appeal.* A claim can occur when the parties can't agree whether there has been a change, or the appropriate compensation for a change. Here's a snippet of a conversation between the buyer's QA lead and the seller's technical lead:

QA: I would like to see the results of the XYZ performance integration test.

TL: We didn't do the performance integration test; it wasn't in the contract.

QA: You need to do that test. Otherwise, how can you prove that the engine integrates with the XYZ?

This could be a situation where the QA lead is introducing a change. On the other hand, the performance integration test may be in-scope work, depending on how the contract is written. Assuming that the performance integration test is not in scope, but the contractor performs the test based on the QA person saying the contractor needs to perform the test, there could be a dispute on the charges associated with running the test.

The contract will have a section describing how disputes and claims should be handled. The preferred method of handling disputes is to first try and negotiate a settlement. If the two parties can't come to an agreement, they will have to use some form of ADR.

The first ADR method to try is mediation, which is less formal and less costly than arbitration. Mediators are professionals who work with both parties to try and come to a negotiated settlement. If mediation isn't successful, the parties can use arbitration. Arbitration is more formal than mediation — because there is a licensed arbitrator — but is less formal and less costly than litigation. Arbitration includes testimony and evidence from both sides and is legally binding.

Force majeure and liquidated damages

Two additional contractual terms that you should be familiar with for the exam are *force majeure* and liquidated damages.

Force majeure is usually associated with natural disasters or "acts of God." It allows the seller a delay for delivery.

Force Majeure. An event that is the result of elements of nature; sometimes also referred to as "acts of God." A *force majeure* event allows a party to delay its contractual obligations because of circumstances beyond its control, such as unusually bad weather, natural disasters, political uprisings, strikes, and so on.

Liquidated Damages. A contract provision that establishes a predetermined award if a party fails to perform as promised. Liquidated damages can only be compensatory damages — to make the injured party whole again. If they are disproportionately large, they are unenforceable.

Liquidated damages are damages that are reimbursed on a set value. For example, say that SOS had a penalty of $1,000 per day for late delivery. If a supplier delivered material to SOS eight days late and caused SOS to be late and have an $8,000 penalty, SOS could go after the supplier for the $8,000 — but no more. An amount higher than $8,000 would be considered punitive damages. Punitive damages are damages that are meant to punish the offender for egregious behavior. They are not normally awarded in contract law.

Contract administration

The contract administration function is about using the internal systems to maintain contract compliance. For example, all changes to the scope of work, the schedule, or contractual terms must follow the contractually stipulated terms and conditions. If specific forms need to be filled out, or if only specific people can sign an amendment, then those procedures need to be followed.

The payment system is used to match up a contract number, the SOW, invoices, and accounts payable categories. All invoices need to be matched to an SOW on an active contract. In some instances, the project manager may need to sign off before an invoice is paid.

A records management system keeps all correspondence associated with a contract in order. The system includes procedures, software, and processes needed to maintain the contract information throughout the life of the contract.

The monitoring and controlling knowledge and skills that apply to managing your own project also apply to managing a contractor. Expect to see test questions regarding administering procurements that deal with the following knowledge and skills:

- ✦ Project performance metrics (cost, duration, effort)
- ✦ Controlling performance against the project management plan
- ✦ Variance and trend analysis techniques

- Change management techniques
- Integrated change control techniques
- Cost analysis techniques
- Problem-solving techniques, including root cause analysis
- Risk identification and analysis techniques
- Risk response techniques
- Performance measurement and tracking techniques, including CPM, PERT, and EVM
- Reporting procedures

Control Procurements: Outputs

Work performance information includes cost, schedule, and technical performance information from the vendor. This information will be integrated with the in-house performance information to create work performance reports in the Monitor and Control Project Work process. In addition, performance information about the vendor should be collected. This includes information about potential issues that could result in claims or disputes.

The organizational process assets and the procurement documentation are kept up to date via the records management system. Examples of documentation include

- Schedules
- Payment records
- Change requests
- Performance reports
- Audit results
- Letters, memos, and meeting minutes
- Technical documentation
- Formal acceptance of deliverables

Throughout the contract performance period, change requests will likely be needed. These need to follow the change process outlined in the contract and go through the project Integrated Change Control process. The buyer is concerned only with those changes that affect the contractual terms. If the seller is making changes that are transparent to the buyer and don't affect any contractual obligations, those changes are not documented in the buyer's change control system.

Monitoring and Controlling summary

Books VII and VIII describe the processes in the Monitoring and Controlling process group. The information in these two books makes up 25% of the exam: in other words, 50 questions. To do well on those 50 questions, you need to know the tools, techniques, and outputs associated with the processes as well as have proficiency in the skills and knowledge associated with analyzing performance against the project management plan and taking appropriate action. Many of the questions will integrate the Code of Ethics and Professional Conduct. Expect to see questions that require knowledge and skills associated with the following:

✓ Project control limits variance, thresholds, tolerance	Book VII, Chapter 1 Book VIII, Chapter 2
✓ Project performance metrics	Book VII, Chapter 1 Book VII, Chapter 3 Book VIII, Chapter 1 Book VIII, Chapter 2
✓ Controlling performance against the project management plan	Book VII, Chapter 1 Book VII, Chapter 2
✓ Variance and trend analysis techniques	Book VII, Chapter 1 Book VII, Chapter 2 Book VII, Chapter 3 Book VIII, Chapter 1 Book VIII, Chapter 2
✓ Change management techniques	Book VII, Chapter 1
✓ Integrated change control techniques	Book VII, Chapter 1
✓ Cost analysis techniques	Book VIII, Chapter 1
✓ Problem solving techniques, including root cause analysis	Book VIII, Chapter 2
✓ Risk identification, analysis techniques, and risk response techniques	Book VIII, Chapter 4
✓ Performance measurement and tracking techniques, including CPM, PERT, and EVM	Book VII, Chapter 3 Book VIII, Chapter 1
✓ Reporting procedures	Book VII, Chapter 1

As in all control processes, the project team updates project management plan components and project documents to maintain accurate and current records.

There are numerous ways that contracts and contractual relationships can be abused. The Code of Ethics and Professional Conduct addresses opportunities for misconduct in the standards on responsibility and honesty. Be prepared for procurement administration questions to address both ethical as well as technical issues on the exam. Specific standards that are likely to be included in procurement questions include the following:

- We protect proprietary or confidential information that has been entrusted to us.
- We respect the property rights of others.
- We make commitments and promises, implied or explicit, in good faith.
- We do not engage in dishonest behavior with the intention of personal gain or at the expense of another.

Key Terms

Terms having to do with procurements are mostly legal in nature. It seems like a different language sometimes. However, it's important to understand how these terms apply to contracts and procurements in a project. This chapter is one of the few chapters with key terms not defined in the *PMBOK Guide*.

- Constructive changes
- Time is of the Essence
- Claims
- Negotiation
- Alternate Dispute Resolution (ADR)
- Mediation
- Arbitration
- *Force majeure*
- Liquidated damages

...r Summary

Control Risk is a process you will engage in throughout the project. This chapter described the activities necessary to continuously manage risk on your project. I also discussed the day-to-day management and administration of contracts.

- Controlling risks uses information from work in progress, work performance reports, and risk reassessment to identify new risks, check the status of existing risks, and close out old risks.
- All new risks identified need to go through the entire risk analysis and response cycle.
- Risk reassessment looks at the status of risks to see whether the analysis has changed, any risk triggers have occurred, the responses are effective, and residual risk is still acceptable.
- You should review work performance reports to look for variance or trends that indicate a need for corrective or preventive action.
- Comparing the amount of reserve remaining against the amount of risk remaining is a way to determine whether you have sufficient reserve.
- A risk audit reviews the effectiveness of the risk management processes and risk responses.
- Controlling procurements is concerned with monitoring seller performance and following the terms and conditions in the contract.
- Keeping all the vendor(s) work aligned and integrated with in-house project work is important.
- You can use work performance reports, performance reviews, inspections, and audits to assess the seller progress.
- Contract changes need to go through the contract change control system. Constructive changes can lead to disputes or claims. If the change, the timing of the change, or the payment for the change is not agreed to, you need to use negotiation, mediation, or arbitration to come to a resolution.

Prep Test

Multiple Choice

1 Which technique would you employ to do all of the following?

* **Assess whether the risk response strategy is still appropriate. You may need to take a different approach.**

* **Determine whether the residual risks have grown. If so, you may need to develop more robust responses.**

* **Identify any secondary risks that have emerged and put them through the risk planning cycle.**

A ❍ Technical performance measurement
B ❍ Risk reanalysis
C ❍ Risk reassessment
D ❍ Reserve analysis

2 If you want late deliveries to indicate a breach of contract, you should

A ❍ Include a *force majeure* clause in the contract.
B ❍ Include a Time is of the Essence clause in the contract.
C ❍ Make sure that liquidated damages are included in the contract.
D ❍ Perform an audit and inspection on the seller's premises.

3 Visiting the seller's location to see whether processes and procedures are being followed and also to assess the quality of the work is

A ❍ Inspection and audit
B ❍ Performance reporting
C ❍ Procurement performance review
D ❍ Contract administration

4 Which is the least preferred method of settling claims?

A ❍ Litigation
B ❍ Mediation
C ❍ Negotiation
D ❍ Arbitration

5 **Damages that are compensatory in nature and paid at a previously agreed upon rate are**

A ❍ Punitive damages

B ❍ Constructive damages

C ❍ Liquidated damages

D ❍ Real damages

Scenario 1

When looking at performance reports, you notice that over the past four weeks, a work package has continued to get further and further behind. The work package isn't on the critical path, but if things continue this way, it is likely to become the new critical path and cause the project to be late.

1 **This assessment is an example of**

A ❍ Risk reassessment

B ❍ Trend analysis

C ❍ Reserve analysis

D ❍ Performance measurement

Scenario 2

Based on your experience in software development, you expected to have 100 defects after the first build. You estimated that you could have 40 cleared by the first week, 65 by the second week, 90 by the third week, and all 100 cleared by the fourth week. At the end of the second week, you see that you have cleared 67 defects.

1 **This is an example of**

A ❍ Risk reassessment

B ❍ Trend analysis

C ❍ Reserve analysis

D ❍ Technical performance measurement

Scenario 3

In a performance review, you state that your project is 60% done. You've applied $75,000 of the $100,000 allocated for cost reserves and 8 of the 12 weeks of schedule reserves.

1 **Which risk monitoring technique would you use, and which status would it indicate?**

- **A** ❍ Reserve analysis shows that you are on schedule and over budget.
- **B** ❍ Reserve analysis shows that you are at risk of going over budget and beyond your scheduled due date.
- **C** ❍ Trend analysis shows that your CPI and SPI will be greater than 1.0 at the end of the project.
- **D** ❍ Trend analysis shows that your CPI and SPI will be less than 1.0 at the end of the project.

Scenario 4

A number of risk events have occurred on the project lately. You put together a team to discover why. The team finds that the risk analysis process wasn't being followed correctly. Many of the risks that occurred were on the watch list, but they should have had a higher probability and impact score. You are concerned about more misuse of the risk management process.

1 **To help you determine whether people are using the processes correctly, you conduct**

- **A** ❍ A risk audit
- **B** ❍ A risk reassessment
- **C** ❍ A trend analysis
- **D** ❍ A status meeting

Scenario 5

Your supplier notifies you that his delivery will be a week late because a tornado destroyed part of his warehouse, including some of the materials that were about to be shipped to you.

1 **You can't hold the supplier at fault because your contract has what kind of clause?**

- **A** ❍ Liquidated damages
- **B** ❍ *Force majeure*
- **C** ❍ Constructive change
- **D** ❍ ADR

Answers

Multiple Choice

1. **C.** Risk reassessment. Risk reassessment accomplishes all these actions. *Look into "Risk reassessment."*
2. **B.** Include Time is of the Essence in the contract. If a Time is of the Essence clause is in a contract, late delivery is considered a breach of contract. *Look over "Control Procurements."*
3. **A.** Inspection and audit. Walking around the seller site is an example of inspection and audit. *Check out "Analyzing performance."*
4. **A.** Litigation. Litigation is the least preferred method of settling claims because it takes the most time and is the most costly. Negotiation, mediation, and arbitration are all better options, if possible. *Go to "Claims and disputes."*
5. **C.** Liquidated damages. Liquidated damages reimburse damages at an agreed-upon stipulated rate. *See information in "Force majeure and liquidated damages."*

Scenario 1

1. **B.** Trend analysis. Trend analysis looks at past performance for trends that put the project performance at risk. *See "Variance and trend analysis."*

Scenario 2

1. **D.** Technical performance measurement. Technical performance measurement can measure the number of defects fixed. *Go over "Variance and trend analysis."*

Scenario 3

1. **B.** Reserve analysis shows that you're at risk of going over budget and beyond your scheduled due date. The reserve analysis shows that a greater percent of budget and schedule reserve has been used than the percent of scope that has been accomplished. *Check out "Reserve analysis."*

Scenario 4

1 **A.** A risk audit. A risk audit can tell you whether risk processes are being followed correctly. *Look at the information in "Risk audit."*

Scenario 5

1 **B.** *Force majeure. Force majeure* gives an obligated party an excuse not to perform if circumstances arise beyond its control. *Review "Force majeure and liquidated damages."*

Book IX

Closing Your Project and the Code of Ethics and Professional Conduct

LESSONS LEARNED

Project Title: ____________ Date Prepared: ____________

Project Performance Analysis	What Worked Well	What Can Be Improved
Requirements definition and management	*List any practices or incidents that were effective in defining and managing requirements.*	*List any practices or incidents that can be improved in defining and managing requirements.*
Scope definition and management	*List any practices or incidents that were effective in defining and managing scope.*	*List any practices or incidents that can be improved in defining and managing scope.*
Schedule development and control	*List any practices or incidents that were effective in developing and controlling the schedule.*	*List any practices or incidents that can be improved in developing and controlling the schedule.*
Cost estimating and control	*List any practices or incidents that were effective in developing estimates and controlling costs.*	*List any practices or incidents that can be improved in developing estimates and controlling costs.*
Quality planning and control	*List any practices or incidents that were effective in planning, assuring, and controlling quality. Specific defects are addressed elsewhere.*	*List any practices or incidents that can be improved in planning, assuring, and controlling quality. Specific defects are addressed elsewhere.*
Human resource availability, team development, and performance	*List any practices or incidents that were effective in working with team members and developing and managing the team.*	*List any practices or incidents that can be improved in working with team members and developing and managing the team.*
Communication management	*List any practices or incidents that were effective in planning and distributing information.*	*List any practices or incidents that can be improved in planning and distributing information.*
Stakeholder management	*List any practices or incidents that were effective in managing stakeholder expectations.*	*List any practices or incidents that can be improved in managing stakeholder expectations.*
Reporting	*List any practices or incidents that were effective in reporting project performance.*	*List any practices or incidents that can be improved in reporting project performance.*
Risk management	*List any practices or incidents that were effective in the risk management process. Specific risks are addressed elsewhere.*	*List any practices or incidents that can be improved in the risk management process. Specific risks are addressed elsewhere.*
Procurement planning and management	*List any practices or incidents that were effective in planning, conducting, and administering contracts.*	*List any practices or incidents that can be improved in planning, conducting, and administering contracts.*
Process improvement information	*List any processes that were developed that should be continued.*	*List any processes that should be changed or discontinued.*
Product-specific information	*List any practices or incidents that were effective in delivering the specific product, service, or result.*	*List any practices or incidents that can be improved in delivering the specific product, service, or result.*
Other	*List any other practices or incidents that were effective, such as change control, configuration management, etc.*	*List any other practices or incidents that can be improved, such as change control, configuration management, etc.*

Page 1 of 2

For more, read the article on closing knowledge and skills at `www.dummies.com/extras/pmpcertificationaio`.

Contents at a Glance

Chapter 1: Closing Your Contracts and Your Project

Exam Objectives

- **Confirm that the project scope and deliverables are complete by attaining final acceptance by the project sponsor and customer.**
- **Facilitate project closure by transferring ownership and management of project deliverables.**
- **Formally close the project and all contracts by obtaining legal, financial, and administrative closure, thus eliminating further liability.**
- **Write the final project report that communicates final project performance, including any variances and project issues. Distribute to appropriate stakeholders.**
- **Conduct a thorough project review to collect and document lessons learned and contribute them to the organization's knowledge base.**
- **Collect, organize, and archive project and contract documents and records to comply with regulatory requirements, retain for future projects, and be available for audit purposes.**
- **Gain customer and stakeholder feedback to determine satisfaction level, enhance relationships, and provide constructive project evaluation.**

There are a lot of exam objectives for the Closing process group even though it only has two processes: Close Project or Phase and Close Procurements. In this chapter, you see that the actions needed to conduct an effective close-out are similar regardless of whether you are closing a procurement, a phase, or a project.

Closure does not occur only at the end of the project. You can conduct closure activities at any time in the project. Keep in mind that one of the processes is Close Project or Phase. You will be closing out some phases of the project early in the project life cycle. In addition, you will perform close-out activities on procurements as they are completed instead of waiting until the end of the project to close out procurements.

Quick Assessment

1 (True/False). Contracts are closed only at the close of the project.

2 Terminating a contract early because of a change in marketplace conditions is known as _____ _____ _____.

3 Mediation is a type of _____ _____ _____.

4 What technique would you use to determine what worked well on a procurement and what can be improved?

5 Identifying best practices that can be passed on and understanding the source of poor performance is documented in a(n) _____ _____ report.

6 Which document should you measure project completion against?

7 (True/False). Close-out activities begin after the product has undergone final acceptance.

8 A contract that is terminated because one of the parties is about to default is said to be terminated for _____.

9 Two very important stakeholders you should approach for information about your project are your _____ and your _____.

10 (True/False). If a project is terminated early or put on hold, you should conduct project closure activities.

Answers

1. False. Contracts can be closed out at any point in the project. *See "Closing Your Procurements."*

2. Termination for convenience. Terminating a contract for convenience does not imply fault for either party; it indicates that there is no longer a need for the project or that circumstances have changed. *Look at the information in "Terminating for convenience."*

3. Alternative Dispute Resolution. Mediation and arbitration are both types of Alternative Dispute Resolution (ADR). *Check out "Dispute resolution."*

4. Procurement audit. A procurement audit is used to determine what worked well on a procurement and what can be improved so future procurements are managed better. *Read the information in "Procurement audits."*

5. Lessons learned. A lessons learned report documents information you want to pass on for future projects, both good and bad. *Go over "Learning from projects."*

6. Project management plan. You measure project completion against the project management plan, which contains the scope statement, baselines, and other relevant project information. *Go over the information in "Close Project or Phase: Inputs."*

7. False. Close-out activities should be conducted throughout the project. You should close each phase in the project life cycle as well as collect lessons learned throughout the project. *See the section "Close Project or Phase: Inputs."*

8. Cause. If either party defaults or is about to default, the other party can terminate the contract for cause. *See "Termination for cause."*

9. Sponsor, customer. You should always determine your customer's level of satisfaction with the product and the project. After all, your customer is the reason why the project exists. Your sponsor can give you a strategic perspective of how well you met your project objectives. *See "Whom to talk to."*

10. True. If a project is terminated early, you should document the scope that was completed, the scope that is in progress, and any lessons learned from the project. *Look at "Close Project or Phase: Tools and Techniques."*

Knowledge and Skills for the Closing Processes

Closing processes don't just happen at the end of a project. They happen whenever you close a procurement or a phase. Keep the following list of cross-cutting skills in mind as you read through the information in this chapter.

- Information management tools, techniques, and methods
- Targeting communications to intended audiences

Questions in the Closing process group account for 8% of the exam. You should expect 16 questions on the two processes in this process group.

Closing Your Procurements

Close Procurements is one of the two closing processes. This process supports the Close Project or Phase process but doesn't necessarily happen at the same time. However, to close the project, *all* procurements must be closed. The exception to this is if you have open claims or appeals. Open claims are handled by the legal department.

Because contracts are legal documents, the project manager does not usually have the authority to close them out. Generally, the project manager will inform a contract administrator that the contract project work has been completed. It is then up to the contract administrator to formally close out the contract.

Close Procurements. Completing each procurement.

To close out a procurement, you use the procurement management plan for the details and guidelines associated with contract closure. All procurement documents need to be indexed for lessons learned and future reference. Procurement documents include performance reports, invoices, and contractual change documentation. Your organization may use information from contractor performance reports and documentation to evaluate contractors for future work.

Terminating a contract

Contracts can be terminated for a variety of reasons, such as termination by mutual agreement, termination for cause, and termination for convenience.

Terminating a contract by mutual agreement is self-explanatory. If both parties agree that the contract should be cancelled, they need to follow the requirements in the termination clause of the contract. Termination for cause and termination for convenience have different contractual obligations associated with them, so look at both of those methods of termination a little closer.

Termination for cause

Termination for cause occurs when either party has breached or is about to breach the contract. This is also known as *defaulting* on the contract.

Here are two examples of seller default:

✦ The seller can't deliver the quality of work promised, and there is no evidence that the seller will be able to.

✦ The clause Time is of the Essence is in the contract, and it's abundantly clear that the seller can't meet the delivery date. (Read more about Time is of the Essence in Book VIII, Chapter 3.)

The following are examples of buyer default:

✦ The buyer is in significant arrears for payment, and it's obvious that the buyer can't catch up on back payments and make future payments.

✦ The buyer is obligated to provide some element or component of the deliverable for the seller to be able to complete the contract. If the buyer doesn't deliver the element, the buyer is defaulting on its part of the contract.

Terminating for convenience

Many contracts have a clause that allows the buyer to terminate the contract at its convenience. Examples of reasons to terminate for convenience include the following:

✦ Another project takes higher priority, and the company decides to cancel or delay the current project.

✦ The market changes, and there is no longer a need for the project.

✦ Because of a reorganization, new leadership has other priorities.

✦ Financial landscape has shifted. A company's quarterly earnings were worse than expected, and the organization has decided to cut costs based on projected earnings.

A contract terminated for convenience doesn't reflect poorly on either party. It just means there is no longer a need for the contracted goods.

Compensation

Depending on the reason for termination (cause or convenience), there is a difference in the compensation due to the seller. If a contract is terminated for cause, the buyer need only reimburse the seller for the accepted work. However, if the contract is terminated for convenience, the buyer must reimburse the seller for accepted work and any preparations for work and any partially completed work. Here's a scenario from my running childcare center example.

You get a call from the sponsor, Morgan Cuthbert, to come to her office right away. When you get there, Morgan informs you that she has great news. The cafeteria vendor has informed her that it can reorganize the kitchen area and make room for a separate food storage and food prep area for the child-care center. The cafeteria is adjacent to the childcare center, so by building a simple doorway, you will have plenty of kitchen space. This is great news because you can use the planned kitchen space for other activities for the childcare center.

Although this is good news, you realize that the kitchen contractor, Kit's Kitchens, has already drawn up plans for the kitchen, laid in the rough plumbing, and preordered some cabinets. You understand that you have to terminate Kit's contract and pay for any work in progress. Upon returning to your desk, you call the kitchen contractor and set up a meeting.

At the meeting, you explain the situation to Kit and assure her that you have every intention of paying for completed work, work in progress, and any preparation for future work.

The following week you meet with Kit again. She tallied expenses for work in progress for the electrician, plumber, and carpenter. You think the expenses are fair and agree to them. There is a $500 cancellation fee for the cabinets. You talk with the general contractor to see whether the cabinets can be used anywhere else in the childcare center so you don't have to count the $500 as a total loss. It turns out that you can use the cabinets for art supplies and sleeping mats. Therefore, you decide to keep the cabinet order as is.

At the end of the meeting, you agree to provide all the documentation to the contract administrator and get the invoices through the system. You assure Kit that you will move ahead with contract closure and get her payment as soon as possible.

In this scenario, the contract termination was in no way a reflection of the work that Kit provided. The contract will go through the termination process, the buyer will compensate the seller fairly, and the contract will be closed.

The roles and responsibilities associated with early contract termination should be clearly documented in the contract.

Close Procurements: Tools and Techniques

When closing contracts, you need to make sure all claims are resolved. You should also review the entire procurement process so you can learn from the current procurement to improve future procurements. I talk about both techniques in the following sections.

Dispute resolution

In the event of a disagreement that the contracted parties can't resolve via negotiation, they need to follow the dispute resolution clause in the contract. Most contracts require the parties to enter into some type of mediation or arbitration. Some contracts require the issue be resolved by using one of these forms of ADR, and others require that ADR be tried before the least appealing alternative of litigation. (Read more about ADR, mediation, and arbitration in Book VIII, Chapter 4.)

When the issue or claim can't be resolved while the project is active, the claim may remain open even though the project has been closed.

Procurement audits

A *procurement* audit is a formal review of the procurement process on a single procurement, or for the procurement process used on the project as a whole. The purpose is to review each process in the procurement to identify those areas that worked well as well as those areas that can be improved in the future.

The audit begins by looking at the procurement planning process:

- Was the make-or-buy analysis complete?
- Was the contract type appropriate?
- How effective was the procurement management plan?
- Did the statement of work (SOW) accurately reflect the work that needed to be done without saying how it should be done?
- Were the procurement bid documents complete?
- Were the source selection criteria appropriate?

The procurement audit should also review the following information for conducting procurements:

- ✦ Were a sufficient number of qualified sellers identified?
- ✦ Did the bidder conference go smoothly and answer all bidder questions? (See Book VI, Chapter 3.)
- ✦ Did the procurement negotiations end up with a win-win situation?
- ✦ Was the contract developed and signed in a timely manner?
- ✦ Was the contract complete without requiring numerous changes and revisions?
- ✦ Was the contract sufficiently clear so as not to result in numerous disputes and misunderstandings?

While administering the contract, the procurement audit will assess the following:

- ✦ How well contract changes were handled
- ✦ Performance reports and performance reviews
- ✦ How well inspections at the seller location went
- ✦ The effectiveness of the payment system
- ✦ The completeness and organization of the project records
- ✦ How well disputes and issues were handled

When auditing vendors, you want to record areas that worked well and areas that should be improved the next time. This information can be used the next time a similar procurement is needed.

A sample procurement audit form is shown in Figure 1-1. The form is generic, but it shows the type of information that you would gather for a procurement audit.

PROCUREMENT AUDIT

Project Title: ______________________ DatePrepared: ______________________

Project Auditor: ______________________ Audit Date: ______________________

Vendor Performance Audit

What Worked Well:	
Scope	*Describe aspects of product scope that were handled well.*
Quality	*Describe aspects of product quality that were handled well.*
Schedule	*Describe aspects of the project schedule that were handled well.*
Cost	*Describe aspects of the project cost that were handled well.*
Other	*Describe any other aspects of the procurement that were handled well.*
What Can Be Improved:	
Scope	*Describe aspects of the product scope that could be improved.*
Quality	*Describe aspects of the product quality that could be improved.*
Schedule	*Describe aspects of the project schedule that could be improved.*
Cost	*Describe aspects of the project cost that could be improved.*
Other	*Describe any other aspects of the procurement that could be improved.*

Procurement Management Process Audit

Process	Followed	Tools and Techniques Used
Plan Procurements	*yes or no*	*Describe any tools or techniques that were effective for the process.*
Conduct Procurements	*yes or no*	*Describe any tools or techniques that were effective for the process.*
Administer Procurements	*yes or no*	*Describe any tools or techniques that were effective for the process.*
Close Procurements	*yes or no*	*Describe any tools or techniques that were effective for the process.*

Description of Good Practices to Share:

Describe any good practices that can be shared with other projects or that should be incorporated into organization policies, procedures or processes. Include information on lessons learned.

Description of Areas for Improvement:

Describe any areas that should be improved with the procurement process. Include information that should be incorporated into policies, procedures or processes. Include information on lessons learned.

Figure 1-1: A Procurement Audit form.

Close Procurements: Outputs

A key part of closing a contract is reviewing the SOW and ensuring that all elements are complete and accepted. You should go through the deliverables list to make sure that all the deliverables meet the contractual requirements, all procedures and contract clauses were followed, and also that all the technical and other contract documentation is available.

It's a good practice to formally accept deliverables throughout the life of the contract, especially for large contracts. Closing the contract should merely formalize all the accepted work that has been delivered. After you accept all the work, you notify the contract administrator that the terms of the contract have been met. The contract administrator can then take the necessary steps to formally close out the contract.

Because a contract is a legal document, it's important to collect and archive all procurement documentation and correspondence. The following is a partial list of information that you need to collect, index, and archive:

- Schedules
- Invoices and payment history
- Performance reports
- Technical documentation
- Contract change requests
- Corrective action reports
- Contract disputes and their resolutions
- Inspections
- Audits
- Performance evaluations

The contract documentation is a part of the overall project documentation that you need to archive prior to project closure. The following sections take a look at that final process.

Procurements need to be closed out from the legal, financial, and administrative perspectives. Legally, you need to make sure the statement of work is complete and also that all deliverables have been formally accepted. Administratively, you want to make sure that all the terms and conditions of the contract have been followed and also that the procurement documentation has been appropriately archived. Financially, you need to make sure all the payments have been made, including award fees, incentive fees, and fixed fees as appropriate.

Close Project or Phase

The Close Project or Phase process marks the culmination of a phase in the project life cycle or the completion of the entire project.

DEFINITION

Close Project or Phase. Finalizing all activities across all Project Management process groups to formally complete the project or phase.

Close Project or Phase: Inputs

To formally close a phase in the project life cycle or the entire project, you need to compare the accepted deliverables to the information in the project management plan. Remember: "Accepted deliverables" are an output from the Validate Scope process (see Book VII, Chapter 2).

Accepted deliverables

At the end of a *phase,* you should get formal approval and acceptance for any completed deliverables. At the end of the *project,* you have all accepted deliverables, the approvals for each deliverable, and the final approval and acceptance for the final product.

The project management plan

The project management plan documents the project life cycle and has instructions on how to close out a project phase. Each phase has specific deliverables that need to be complete and accepted before it can be considered closed. Oftentimes, additional criteria need to be met before considering a phase closed. Some examples are identified in the following section.

Organizational process assets

Your organizational process assets (OPAs) describe phase and project closure guidelines. Examples of phase closure criteria include

- **Performance reviews:** At the end of the phase, the project sponsor and/or customer along with the project management team discuss the performance metrics for the phase and the project overall. They look at the risk events that occurred during the current phase, the status of issues, and any corrective actions that need to be taken.
- **Project management plan updates:** The end of a phase is a good time to make sure that all the elements of the project management plan are accurate and up to date. Some project managers wait for a phase gate to update the plans with the latest version.

- **Project document updates:** If you have an iterative life cycle, you can collect information for the next iteration during the Close Project or Phase process. You can also go through the assumption and risk logs and close out any out-of-date items, and update the remaining items. Some project managers collect new requirements, changes, assumptions, and risks when they formally initiate the new phase.
- **Lessons learned:** It's a good practice to collect lessons learned as you go through the project. At the end of each phase, formalizing the lessons learned for the phase and integrating those lessons into the next phase helps ensure that you don't repeat the same mistakes. I discuss lessons learned in greater detail shortly.

Close Project or Phase: Tools and Techniques

You'll use your team expertise and customer feedback to measure deliverables against elements in the project management plan to determine whether the project is complete. The project scope statement documents product scope, product acceptance criteria, and project deliverables. You should review the project scope statement; requirements documentation; baselines for scope, schedule and cost; and any other relevant information in the project management plan to make sure that you successfully met all the project and product completion requirements.

Analytical techniques are used to record final project performance measurements for technical, schedule, and budget performance. The causes of any variances should be identified and recorded in a lessons learned document.

Conduct a lessons learned meeting at least at the end of every phase because you often have different resources in different phases. Make sure to get stakeholder input from those people who leave the project before it's complete.

In the event that the project terminates before completion, you will conduct the formal closure process with the existing information. You want to document the progress that was made, the work that remains unfinished, and the reason for project termination. Oftentimes, a project is restarted months or even years later, so having good records of the project's status when it was closed is helpful.

Close Project or Phase: Outputs

The results of the Close Project or Phase process include a project review with lessons learned and a final report that you will distribute to appropriate stakeholders. You also need to formally transition project resources (team members) and the final product and then organize the project archives.

A project review accomplishes two outcomes: the lessons learned document and the final project report. You will use interviewing and feedback techniques similar to those you used when you were first identifying requirements and defining scope (see Book III, Chapter 1) to collect and compile feedback. First I discuss gathering information for lessons learned and then move into discussing the final report.

Learning from projects

To make sure it will benefit future projects, conducting a meaningful lessons learned exercise takes time and effort. Notice I said *meaningful*. Lessons learned is different from documenting all the reasons why a project wasn't successful. It takes discipline to identify the root cause of good as well as not-so-good results. In addition, you need to document them in a way that they can be used and useful for future projects.

Here are some quick examples of not-so-great documentation and then some better documentation. Although each scenario might be relevant to your project, the not-so-great examples aren't productive information to pass along. Consider my alternatives.

> *Not so great*
>
> Don't expect Jim to work on weekends because he has kids in soccer practice.
>
> *Better*
>
> Document in the Team Operating Agreement people's availability to work overtime so they can fit it into their schedule if needed.
>
> *Not so great*
>
> Make sure you ask Jennifer from Marketing whether she has anything to add before you baseline your budget.
>
> *Better*
>
> Do a full stakeholder analysis to identify all stakeholders who will have requirements for the project.

Whom to talk to

Here are some ways you can conduct a lessons learned exercise. You could all stakeholders to come together and share what worked and what they would do differently next time. Another approach is to interview people one-on-one or in small groups to get more specific and perhaps sensitive information. You should include suppliers and vendors in your lessons learned. You can take the information from a contract close-out report and a procurement audit, or you can interview the contractor about his experience working on the project. The point is that you want a broad spectrum of input for the lessons learned document.

Don't wait until the end of the project to collect your lessons learned information. At the minimum, you should gather this info at the end of each phase — especially for long projects! By the end of a long project, some team members will have moved on, and most team members will have forgotten events that occurred in the beginning phases.

For those topics that you think can help improve the performance of projects in the future, you should share the results with management, the Project Management Office (PMO), and other project managers. The same is true for sharing events that went poorly on your project so others don't find themselves in the same situation.

Two very important stakeholders you should approach for information about your project are your sponsor and your customer. In addition to identifying areas for improvement and those areas that worked well, conduct a satisfaction survey. This can be informal, such as asking how you can do a better job of satisfying them in the future, or you can send an electronic survey. Ask open-ended questions when asking them how the project went from their perspective. This will help maintain and improve your working relationship.

An important part of closing a phase and the project is to measure stakeholder satisfaction. The obvious stakeholder you want to check with is the customer. However, don't forget other stakeholders, such as your team members and the sponsor. If something you're doing isn't working for team members, you want to know about the issue so you can address it.

What to talk about

When collecting information about the project, have specific and general questions designed to get people talking. You might want to gather information about specific areas of the project, such as

- Effectiveness of requirements gathering
- How well scope was controlled
- The quality of the schedule
- How well communication worked
- Effectiveness of risk management

The lessons learned form in Figure 1-2 is a starting place for some of the relevant areas you can inquire about when collecting lessons learned.

LESSONS LEARNED

Project Title: ______________________ Date Prepared: ______________________

Project Performance Analysis

	What Worked Well	What Can Be Improved
Requirements definition and management	*List any practices or incidents that were effective in defining and managing requirements.*	*List any practices or incidents that can be improved in defining and managing requirements.*
Scope definition and management	*List any practices or incidents that were effective in defining and managing scope.*	*List any practices or incidents that can be improved in defining and managing scope.*
Schedule development and control	*List any practices or incidents that were effective in developing and controlling the schedule.*	*List any practices or incidents that can be improved in developing and controlling the schedule.*
Cost estimating and control	*List any practices or incidents that were effective in developing estimates and controlling costs.*	*List any practices or incidents that can be improved in developing estimates and controlling costs.*
Quality planning and control	*List any practices or incidents that were effective in planning, assuring, and controlling quality. Specific defects are addressed elsewhere.*	*List any practices or incidents that can be improved in planning, assuring. and controlling quality. Specific defects are addressed elsewhere.*
Human resource availability, team development, and performance	*List any practices or incidents that were effective in working with team members and developing and managing the team.*	*List any practices or incidents that can be improved in working with team members and developing and managing the team.*
Communication management	*List any practices or incidents that were effective in planning and distributing information.*	*List any practices or incidents that can be improved in planning and distributing information.*
Stakeholder management	*List any practices or incidents that were effective in managing stakeholder expectations.*	*List any practices or incidents that can be improved in managing stakeholder expectations.*
Reporting	*List any practices or incidents that were effective in reporting project performance.*	*List any practices or incidents that can be improved in reporting project performance.*
Risk management	*List any practices or incidents that were effective in the risk management process. Specific risks are addressed elsewhere.*	*List any practices or incidents that can be improved in the risk management process. Specific risks are addressed elsewhere.*
Procurement planning and management	*List any practices or incidents that were effective in planning, conducting, and administering contracts.*	*List any practices or incidents that can be improved in planning, conducting, and administering contracts.*
Process improvement information	*List any processes that were developed that should be continued.*	*List any processes that should be changed or discontinued.*
Product-specific information	*List any practices or incidents that were effective in delivering the specific product, service, or result.*	*List any practices or incidents that can be improved in delivering the specific product, service, or result.*
Other	*List any other practices or incidents that were effective, such as change control, configuration management, etc.*	*List any other practices or incidents that can be improved, such as change control, configuration management, etc.*

Page 1 of 2

Figure 1-2: The Lessons Learned form.

LESSONS LEARNED

Risks and Issues

ID	Risk or Issue Description	Response	Comments
Identifier.	*Identify specific risks that occurred that should be considered to improve organizational learning.*	*Describe the response and its effectiveness.*	*Indicate what should be done to improve future project performance.*

Quality Defects

ID	Defect Description	Resolution	Comments
Identifier.	*Identify quality defects that should be considered to improve organizational effectiveness.*	*Describe how the defects were resolved.*	*Indicate what should be done to improve future project performance.*

Vendor Management

Vendor	Issue	Resolution	Comments
List the vendor.	*Describe any issues, claims, or disputes that occurred.*	*Describe the resolution.*	

Other

Areas of Exceptional Performance	Areas for Improvement
Identify areas of exceptional performance that can be passed on to other teams.	*Identify areas that can be improved on for future projects.*

Page 2 of 2

Your lessons learned become part of the organization's knowledge base, which means that they will be OPAs for the next project.

The final report and archiving information

Your final project reports should include information on the project objectives and how you met them, and also explain any variances from the success criteria. A key component in the final report is a final financial accounting and analysis. You should compare the final total expenditures with the original budget and identify the causes of variances. For complex multiyear projects, you'll want to show the information based on the organization's fiscal year and compare that with the original funding requirements. Additional accounting information that may be required includes

- A comparison of the financial metrics, such as NPV, FV, and so forth, that were used to justify the project in the first place. (See Book II, Chapter 1.)
- Final earned value (EV) numbers and metrics if EVM is being used. (See Book VIII, Chapter 1, for EVM metrics.)
- A description of the work packages that had significant variances and a root cause analysis on the variance.
- Significant variances.
- Validation or explanation of assumptions about cost estimates, including the "cost of money." (See Book II, Chapter 1.)

The final report will be sent to all key stakeholders identified in the communication management plan.

Hopefully, you collected and organized your project documentation throughout the project. That ongoing effort makes it a lot easier when you have to archive information at the end. How you archive information depends on the nature of the project. For some projects, you may want to have a box of files or set of notebooks organized alphabetically, chronologically, or by topic. In other situations, all your archives will be electronic and posted to an intranet. Some of the information you archive may be sensitive and can be stored only in a secure facility.

Personally, if I manage a one-year project, I take about four weeks to complete the transition, conduct a lessons learned session, write the final report, and organize and archive the project records. You should archive at least

- The charter, project management plan, and project documents — especially all signed documents with approvals
- Baselines, performance reports, variance analysis, and final results
- Written communications, presentations, and reports

- Stakeholder satisfaction surveys and lessons learned
- Assumption, risk, and issue logs
- Procurement documentation and records
- Technical documentation

Archiving information is usually the last activity on a project. Frequently, the project manager is the only person still active at this point. The archived information is helpful for future projects. In many cases, regulations require that you maintain records and documentation for a specified amount of time: for example, warranty information, changes that involve regulations, and project information that could be audited for taxes or legal compliance or used in contractual legal disputes and lawsuits.

Transitioning the product and resources

Having a few loose ends at the end of the project is not uncommon. Usually, new projects require your attention, so you need to make sure you take any open items and assign them to someone for follow-up and closure. When transitioning a product or service to either a customer or to operations, you need to train the recipients on how to work the new product and how to support and maintain it. If there isn't formal documentation and training for this purpose, make sure you spend sufficient time transferring your knowledge to whoever will be maintaining the product or service.

After the lessons learned and the project documentation is collected and organized, you can begin to release your resources. For team members, write up a performance assessment. This can be formal or informal. You should identify the behaviors and actions that contributed to the project's success as well as any areas for improvement. If your organization doesn't have policies about this type of action, use your discretion on how you approach this. Most people want to improve, but you need to be sensitive and not hand out unsolicited advice!

An important part of releasing resources is having a celebration or some kind of event to acknowledge what the team has accomplished and thank the members for their contributions and participation. For large projects, this can be a nice event or dinner with awards, certificates, and speeches by senior management. Or, you could go as casual as having a potluck. Whatever the case, make sure you take the time to thank people and leave them with a feeling of closure.

Closing processes summary

The information in this chapter will account for 16 questions on the PMP exam. To do well on those 16 questions, you will need to have proficiency in the skills and knowledge associated with closing contracts, closing phases and the project, conducting a project review with lessons learned, archiving information, and transitioning the final product to the customer or operations. The following list identifies the knowledge and skills you will need as well as the section in this chapter that discusses the relevant information.

- Contract closure requirements — "Closing Your Procurements"
- Basic project accounting principles — "The final report and archiving information"
- Close-out procedures — "Close Project or Phase"
- Feedback techniques — "Learning from projects"
- Project review techniques — "The project review"
- Archiving techniques and statutes — "The final report and archiving information"
- Compliance with relevant statutes — "The final report and archiving information" and organizational policies
- Transition planning techniques — "Transitioning the product and resources"

If your project was at a work site, make sure that all the equipment is in better shape than when you found it, the supplies are stocked appropriately, and the area is neat and clean.

Key Terms

There aren't too many new terms in this chapter. By the time you reach the Closing processes, you already have come across most of the relevant terms.

- Termination for cause
- Termination for convenience
- Procurement audit

er Summary

This chapter discusses the two processes that have to do with closing activities: Close Project or Phase and Close Procurements. Both processes entail collecting, organizing, and archiving information as well as documenting areas that went well and areas that didn't go so well.

- You will close out each project procurement when the contract is complete. Contracts can be considered complete when the statement of work (SOW) is complete and all contractual obligations have been fulfilled.
- Sometimes, procurements are closed before they are complete. In some situations, both parties agree to terminate the contract early. In other situations, contracts are terminated early for cause, or for convenience. The amount of compensation is different, depending on whether the contract is terminated for cause or convenience.
- Before the contract can be closed, all open invoices need to be paid, and all disputes need to be resolved via negotiation, mediation, arbitration — or, in the worst case scenario, litigation.
- When contractual obligations have been met, you notify the contract administrator, who formally closes the contract.
- A procurement audit assesses the effectiveness of the procurement processes and the specific vendor or contractor for future reference.
- All procurement documentation and records need to be indexed and archived. This information becomes part of the overall project close-out.
- You should close out each phase of the project. The phase deliverables should be formally accepted and signed off. In addition, you should update all documentation and conduct a lessons learned exercise from the phase. If the project is closed before completion, you should document the reasons why.
- Doing a good lessons learned exercise entails a 360-degree interview and discussion with stakeholders. You should ask general and specific questions. The lessons learned will become part of the project close-out documentation. It should also record areas that can be used for other projects to increase their probability for success and reduce the probability of failure.
- After the project is complete, you release team members and other project resources, such as locations, equipment, and material.
- Make sure that the product or result is properly transitioned to the customer or the operational division that will maintain it.

Prep Test

Multiple Choice

1 Which is not a reason for early contract termination?

A ❍ For convenience
B ❍ For cause
C ❍ *Force majeure*
D ❍ Mutual agreement

2 Under which conditions will you have to reimburse a vendor for expenses incurred for preparing to do work for you?

A ❍ If you don't deliver a key component needed to start the work
B ❍ If there is a Time is of the Essence clause
C ❍ If the vendor can't meet the deliverable requirements
D ❍ If you change your mind about doing the project

3 If you want to review the procurement processes to determine the extent they were followed and how well they worked, you should conduct a(n)

A ❍ Inspection
B ❍ Walk-through
C ❍ Procurement validation
D ❍ Procurement audit

4 When is the best time to formally accept contract deliverables?

A ❍ At the end of a phase
B ❍ At the end of the project
C ❍ During quality control
D ❍ At the beginning of a phase

5 Completion of the project is measured against the

A ❍ Project scope statement
B ❍ Requirements documentation
C ❍ Project management plan
D ❍ Scope baseline

6 **Which information is not relevant for a lessons learned document?**

- **A** ❍ Which team members received bonuses
- **B** ❍ Methods to improve requirements gathering
- **C** ❍ An effective technique for team building
- **D** ❍ A risk response that worked well

7 **Writing a performance assessment for the lead engineer is part of which closing activity?**

- **A** ❍ Archiving documentation
- **B** ❍ Conducting lessons learned
- **C** ❍ Accepting all deliverables
- **D** ❍ Releasing project resources

8 **The final activity on the project is**

- **A** ❍ Sending out a survey to assess stakeholder satisfaction
- **B** ❍ Archiving project information
- **C** ❍ Closing out a contract
- **D** ❍ Transitioning the product or service to operations or the customer

Scenario 1

The electrician on your project hasn't showed up for work the past two days. You drove by his place of business, and it was abandoned.

1 **This is an example of termination for**

- **A** ❍ Convenience
- **B** ❍ Default
- **C** ❍ Completion
- **D** ❍ Untimely delivery

Scenario 2

You're ready to close out a contract for the design and development of a secure network in your new location. The contractor sends you an invoice that includes $35,000 worth of work you don't think you should be billed for. You're fine with the majority of the bill, but you think that the $35,000 is the contractor's responsibility. After discussing this with the contractor, you're not able to come to a negotiated settlement, so you have to find a more formal way of resolving the issue.

1 Of the following, which is the least preferable way to resolve this dispute?

A ❍ Litigation
B ❍ Mediation
C ❍ Arbitration
D ❍ Binding arbitration

2 Which of the following is the most informal way to resolve the dispute?

A ❍ Litigation
B ❍ Mediation
C ❍ Arbitration
D ❍ Binding arbitration

Answers

Multiple Choice

1 **C.** *Force majeure. Force majeure* allows the obligated party to delay or not perform contractual duties. It isn't a reason for early contract termination. *See "Terminating a contract." For more information on* force majeure, *you can look over Book VIII, Chapter 4.*

2 **D.** If you change your mind about doing the project. If you change your mind about doing a project, you're terminating for convenience. You must pay the seller for accepted goods and preparation expenses for any work not yet delivered. *Look at "Compensation."*

3 **D.** Procurement audit. A procurement audit reviews the processes and the performance on a procurement or on the procurement process as a whole. *Go to "Procurement audits."*

4 **A.** At the end of a phase. You should accept deliverables as they are complete, but at the very least, at the end of each phase. *See the information in "Close Procurements: Outputs."*

5 **C.** Project management plan. Project completion is measured against the project management plan. *Review "The project management plan."*

6 **A.** Which team members received bonuses. Information on team member performance, bonuses, or feedback is not part of the lessons learned document. *Go over "Learning from projects."*

7 **D.** Releasing project resources. Part of releasing project resources is providing feedback to team members. *Check out "Transitioning the product and resources."*

8 **B.** Archiving project information. Archiving project information is usually the last activity performed on a project. *See "The final report and archiving information."*

Scenario 1

1 **B.** Default. The electrician is out of business. He has breached his contract by not finishing the work. *Check out "Termination for cause."*

Scenario 2

1 **A.** Litigation. Litigation is costly and time consuming. As such, it is the least desirable method to resolve conflict. *Review "Dispute resolution."*

2 **B.** Mediation. Mediation can be as informal as having a third party review the situation and make a decision. *Go over the information in "Dispute resolution."*

Chapter 2: The PMI Code of Ethics and Professional Conduct

PMI has developed and published a Code of Ethics and Professional Conduct ("the Code") that describes the expectations of project management practitioners. The Code articulates the ideals that we (as project managers) should aspire to, and those behaviors that are considered mandatory. The purpose of the Code of Ethics and Professional Conduct is to instill confidence in the project management profession and to help an individual become a better practitioner.

Because there aren't any questions that are solely based on the Code, I have been sprinkling the standards throughout the text of all the minibooks. In this chapter, I present the standards in one place to give you further understanding of how they might be integrated into exam questions.

There are no exam objectives associated with the information in this chapter. Rather, you will see questions that incorporate situations that would require you to apply standards from the Code along with the technical information from the process groups and knowledge areas.

The Code focuses on four areas: responsibility, respect, fairness, and honesty. In this chapter, I look at each of these four elements and how they apply to projects and the PMP exam.

Quick Assessment

1 The four values in the Code of Ethics and Professional Conduct are responsibility, ______, fairness, and ______.

2 The two types of standards in the Code of Ethics are ______ and ______.

3 (True/False). You are not bound by the Code of Ethics until after you earn your PMP credential.

4 ______ is our duty to show a high regard for ourselves, others, and the resources entrusted to us. Resources entrusted to us may include people, money, reputation, the safety of others, and natural or environmental resources.

5 A person's legal or moral responsibility to promote the best interest of an organization or other person with whom she is affiliated is known as ______ ______ ______.

6 You applied for a job as a project manager with Ajax Contractors, Inc., but you didn't get the job. A month later, you heard that Ajax hired the nephew of the CEO, who is less qualified than you are. Which standard does this violate?

7 Making decisions based on the best interests of society, public safety, and the environment is part of which standard?

8 Ethics complaints fall under which standard?

9 Which section of the Code addresses assessing our own impartiality and objectivity?

10 Developing project status reports that are consistent with the Code requires that we provide accurate information in a timely manner. Which standard articulates the need to provide accurate information in a timely manner?

Answers

1. Respect, honesty. The four values in the Code of Ethics and Professional Conduct are responsibility, respect, fairness, and honesty. *Look over "About the Code."*

2. Aspirational, mandatory. Aspirational standards are those we should strive to meet. Mandatory standards are those we have to meet. *See information in "About the Code."*

3. False. You are bound by the Code of Ethics as soon as you apply for your PMP credential, if you are a member of PMI, or if you volunteer for PMI. *This information is in "About the Code."*

4. Respect. Respect is defined by the Code as our duty to show a high regard for ourselves, others, and the resources entrusted to us. Resources entrusted to us may include people, money, reputation, the safety of others, and natural or environmental resources. *Check out the section on "Respect."*

5. Duty of loyalty. Duty of loyalty is defined as a person's legal or moral responsibility to promote the best interest of an organization or other person with whom she is affiliated. *Duty of loyalty is defined in the section on "Fairness mandatory standards."*

6. Fairness. The Fairness standard doesn't allow the organization to discriminate against others based on nepotism. *Review "Fairness mandatory standards."*

7. Responsibility. We have a responsibility to make decisions and take actions based on the best interests of our stakeholders, including the public, the environment, and society as a whole. *You will see this standard in the section "Responsibility aspirational standards."*

8. Responsibility. The responsibility standard includes information on reporting violations of the Code and ethics complaints. *Check out "Responsibility mandatory standards."*

9. Fairness. Part of being fair is making sure we can be objective and that we don't have a conflict of interest in any given situation. *See "Fairness aspirational standards."*

10. Honesty. The honesty aspirational standard states that we provide accurate information in a timely manner. *You will find this statement in the section on "Honesty aspirational standards."*

About the Code

The Code describes the ideals for project management and the appropriate behaviors in our roles as project managers. It can also be used as a reference to guide our behavior when we are faced with difficult situations. The Code applies to the following groups of people:

- All PMI members
- Anyone who holds a PMI certification (including the PMP)
- Anyone applying for a certification
- Anyone who volunteers with PMI

The Code was developed when PMI asked practitioners from around the globe to identify those values that were most important in decision making and guiding their project management actions. Based on the feedback from the global community, the four values that the Code is based on were identified as

- Responsibility
- Respect
- Fairness
- Honesty

There are two aspects to each value: aspirational standards and mandatory standards. And the standards are not mutually exclusive. An act or omission can be both aspirational and mandatory.

- **Aspirational standards:** Those standards that describe the conduct we should strive to uphold as project management practitioners.
- **Mandatory standards:** Those standards that are firm requirements. They may limit or prohibit behavior.

Practitioners whose conduct is not in accordance with the mandatory standards are subject to disciplinary procedures before the PMI Ethics Review Committee.

You can find the Code at the PMI website. A copy is also integrated into the PMP Exam Handbook, also found on the PMI website. You can go to PMI online at `www.pmi.org` and type **Code of Ethics and Professional Conduct** into the Search box.

The Code is not copyrighted. Throughout this chapter, I quote the description of the value and the aspirational and mandatory standards verbatim.

Responsibility

The responsibility standards are about taking ownership for our actions, decisions, and the consequences that result from them. Here is the definition of responsibility from the Code.

Responsibility is our duty to take ownership for the decisions we make or fail to make, the actions we take or fail to take, and the consequences that result.

Responsibility aspirational standards

The following are the six aspirational standards under responsibility. Remember that aspirational standards are standards we strive to uphold. The following is from the Code of Ethics and Professional Conduct:

1. We make decisions and take actions based on the best interests of society, public safety, and the environment.
2. We accept only those assignments that are consistent with our background, experience, skills, and qualifications.
3. We fulfill the commitments that we undertake — we do what we say we will do.
4. When we make errors or omissions, we take ownership and make corrections promptly. When we discover errors or omissions caused by others, we communicate them to the appropriate body as soon they are discovered. We accept accountability for any issues resulting from our errors or omissions and any resulting consequences.
5. We protect proprietary or confidential information that has been entrusted to us.
6. We uphold this Code and hold each other accountable to it.

Discussion

As you look at the standards here, see whether you can think of the type of questions you would see on the exam. For example, you might see questions that ask what you should do if what is in the best interest of the project schedule is to move forward without another round of testing even though the safety director has recommended it. In this situation, you are looking at the good of the project schedule and probably some stakeholder satisfaction issues and weighing them against the need for public safety.

Regardless of what you would do in real life, for these questions, you want to stick with the Code and select the answer that indicates that if safety issues were at stake, you would run the extra round of testing.

Another area you need to watch in this section is not taking on projects that you're not qualified to manage. If there is a project with a type of technology, or regulations that you're not familiar with, you're probably not qualified to manage that project. At the very least, you're obligated to disclose your concerns over your lack of experience.

The standard about not disclosing proprietary and confidential information is a pretty black-and-white issue. You shouldn't have any problem with those questions. A more difficult question is what to do if you see someone else not behaving in concert with the Code. It can be very hard to "make waves" if you see someone behaving inconsistently with this Code. However, if that person is a PMP and not in alignment with the values, you are required to hold him accountable to the Code.

Responsibility mandatory standards

The two types of mandatory standards for responsibility are regulations and legal requirements, and ethics complaints.

Regulations and legal requirements

There are two mandatory standards for regulations and legal requirements. Remember: *Mandatory requirements are not negotiable!* The following is from the Code of Ethics and Professional Conduct:

1. We inform ourselves and uphold the policies, rules, regulations, and laws that govern our work, professional, and volunteer activities.
2. We report unethical or illegal conduct to appropriate management and, if necessary, to those affected by the conduct.

Ethics complaints

The ethics complaint standards have to do with violating the Code and reporting violations by others. The following is from the Code of Ethics and Professional Conduct:

3. We bring violations of this Code to the attention of the appropriate body for resolution.
4. We only file ethics complaints when they are substantiated by facts.
5. We pursue disciplinary action against an individual who retaliates against a person raising ethics concerns.

Discussion

For regulations and legal requirements, make sure that you understand the policies, regulations, and rules associated with the work you're doing. In addition, if you see someone behaving unethically or illegally, you are required to report her.

The section on ethics complaints will govern your relationship with PMI after you apply to take the exam. If you see a violation of this Code, you must report it to the Ethics Review Committee. However, make sure that you can substantiate the facts of the case. Bringing an ethics violation to the committee is a serious undertaking. People can have their memberships and their certifications revoked if their behavior is egregious enough. In the event of an investigation, you have the responsibility to cooperate with PMI in obtaining the facts about the case.

Respect

Respect is our duty to show a high regard for ourselves, others, and the resources entrusted to us. Resources entrusted to us may include people, money, reputation, the safety of others, and natural or environmental resources.

An environment of respect engenders trust, confidence, and performance excellence by fostering mutual cooperation — an environment where diverse perspectives and views are encouraged and valued.

Respect aspirational standards

The respect aspirational standards are about appreciating diversity in culture, opinion, and points of view. They also address the professionalism with which we conduct ourselves. The following is from the Code of Ethics and Professional Conduct:

1. We inform ourselves about the norms and customs of others and avoid engaging in behaviors they might consider disrespectful.
2. We listen to others' points of view, seeking to understand them.
3. We approach directly those persons with whom we have a conflict or disagreement.
4. We conduct ourselves in a professional manner, even when it is not reciprocated.

Discussion

When the exam asks questions about culture, many times we think about different cultures as representing people from different countries — but that isn't the only scenario in which we experience diverse cultures. Here are some other examples:

- ✦ Differences in ages or generations can mean different means of communication and different work ethics.
- ✦ If you change jobs and go to a different company, or even just a new department, the work rules and norms may be different.
- ✦ Different geographical areas, even if they are in the same country, have different work styles.

You might see the term *ethnocentrism* on the exam. This term means the tendency to see the world from one's own ethnic perspective and not understand that there are alternative world views. The majority of the questions having to do with different cultures can be correctly answered by embracing diversity and having an open mind and tolerance for different points of view.

You might see questions on the exam that provide a scenario wherein a team member complains about your management style. The proper response is to approach that person directly and seek to understand what is causing the conflict. However, sometimes, we shy away from direct contact, or we are inclined to complain about the team member to others. For this section of the exam, you have to aspire to be more communicative and direct than you are accustomed to.

Regarding professionalism, I know that when someone is treating me disrespectfully or unprofessionally, I have a hard time responding professionally. For me, this is something I need to keep aspiring to! This includes gossip! Not only do you have an ethical obligation to not participate in gossip, but you should also actively discourage others from this behavior.

Respect mandatory standards

The following mandatory respect standards have to do with power, influence, and behavior. The following is from the Code of Ethics and Professional Conduct:

1. We negotiate in good faith.
2. We do not exercise the power of our expertise or position to influence the decisions or actions of others in order to benefit personally at their expense.

3. We do not act in an abusive manner toward others.
4. We respect the property rights of others.

Discussion

You might see some questions about contracts and procurements that talk about negotiating in good faith. Some of these questions might even state that the person with whom you're negotiating has adopted a win-lose attitude to the negotiation. Regardless, you're required to negotiate in good faith and mutual cooperation.

Contracts aren't the only place where you need to negotiate on your project. Sometimes you need to negotiate the competing constraints, or negotiate with functional managers for resources. In these situations, you have to assume that the person you are negotiating with is doing his best, and approach the situation from a win-win perspective.

Other standards in this area require that you influence with integrity, and not with power or to the detriment of others. I think it's pretty obvious treating others unfairly, disrespectfully, or abusively is not okay. Nor is it okay to disrespect the personal, intellectual, or real property of others. By the way, this includes copyrighted material. It is against the Code to copy and use others' work without their express permission.

Many of the questions about respect will be situational. You will have to assume you are in the position of the project manager and select the appropriate response.

Fairness

Fairness is our duty to make decisions and act impartially and objectively. Our conduct must be free from competing self-interest, prejudice, and favoritism.

Fairness aspirational standards

The aspirational fairness standards are concerned with making sure that all relevant parties have equal opportunities. This will be especially prevalent in procurement questions. The aspirational standards also address impartiality and transparency in decision making. The following is from the Code of Ethics and Professional Conduct.

1. We demonstrate transparency in our decision-making process.
2. We constantly reexamine our impartiality and objectivity, taking corrective action as appropriate.
3. We provide equal access to information to those who are authorized to have that information.
4. We make opportunities equally available to qualified candidates.

Discussion

One way to demonstrate transparency in decision making is to develop a decision-making process and establish decision-making criteria. In the procurement chapters (see Book V, Chapter 2, and Book VI, Chapter 3), you can see this as developing and applying source selection criteria. This can apply to other types of decisions as well.

The other standards in this section can be easily applied to procurements and hiring or promoting team members.

Fairness mandatory standards

The mandatory fairness standards address objectivity, conflicts of interest, favoritism, and discrimination. The following is from the Code of Ethics and Professional Conduct:

1. We proactively and fully disclose any real or potential conflicts of interest to the appropriate stakeholders.
2. When we realize that we have a real or potential conflict of interest, we refrain from engaging in the decision-making process or otherwise attempting to influence outcomes, unless or until
   - We have made full disclosure to the affected stakeholders.
   - We have an approved mitigation plan.
   - We have obtained the consent of the stakeholders to proceed.
3. We do not hire or fire, reward or punish, or award or deny contracts based on personal considerations, including but not limited to, favoritism, nepotism, or bribery.
4. We do not discriminate against others based on, but not limited to, gender, race, age, religion, disability, nationality, or sexual orientation.
5. We apply the rules of the organization (employer, Project Management Institute, or other group) without favoritism or prejudice.

Discussion

The Code has two key definitions in the first mandatory standard.

Conflict of Interest. A situation that arises when a practitioner of project management is faced with making a decision or doing some act that will benefit the practitioner or another person or organization to which the practitioner owes a duty of loyalty, and at the same time will harm another person or organization to which the practitioner owes a similar duty of loyalty. The only way practitioners can resolve conflicting duties is to disclose the conflict to those affected and allow them to make the decision about how the practitioner should proceed.

Duty of Loyalty. A person's responsibility, legal or moral, to promote the best interest of an organization or other person with whom she is affiliated.

The rules about conflicts of interest apply to actual and perceived conflicts. Here's an example: Say that you're an officer in a PMI chapter, you happen to provide training, and the board is looking at offering a training course. You should excuse yourself from the discussion because you could be perceived as having a conflict of interest even if you didn't promote yourself at the expense of others.

For conflict of interest situations, be as conservative as possible by disclosing information even if you think it not relevant to the situation. Better to over-disclose than be accused of conflict of interest.

The remaining standards are about not showing favoritism and not discriminating in any way, shape, or form. Exam questions that address these standards are fairly easy to spot — and as long as you choose the answer that shows the high moral ground, you will do fine on these questions.

Honesty

The Code defines honesty as our duty to understand the truth and act in a truthful manner both in our communications and in our conduct.

Honesty aspirational standards

The aspirational honest standards are about keeping our word and fully disclosing all relevant information. The following is from the Code of Ethics and Professional Conduct:

1. We earnestly seek to understand the truth.
2. We are truthful in our communications and in our conduct.
3. We provide accurate information in a timely manner.
4. We make commitments and promises, implied or explicit, in good faith.
5. We strive to create an environment in which others feel safe to tell the truth.

Discussion

Think about your performance reports or your status reports. You want to put the best information forward. You want to talk about the good things that have happened on the project. After all, not many people want to discuss risks and challenges, especially if you think you can correct them before someone finds out, or if you have a plan to make things right again. However, this behavior goes against the honesty standards. In addition, if a team member gives you information you believe might not be wholly true, you have a duty to find out the truth. You also need to make sure to not penalize team members for coming to you with risks or challenges. You need to create an environment where people can tell you the truth without fear of abusive responses. These standards are probably some of the same rules you had growing up: Tell the truth, be on time, and keep your promises.

Honesty mandatory standards

The mandatory honesty standards take the aspirational standards one step further by stating that we must not engage in deceptive or dishonest behavior. The following is from the Code of Ethics and Professional Conduct:

1. We do not engage in or condone behavior that is designed to deceive others, including but not limited to, making misleading or false statements, stating half-truths, providing information out of context or withholding information that, if known, would render our statements as misleading or incomplete.
2. We do not engage in dishonest behavior with the intention of personal gain or at the expense of another.

Discussion

These mandatory standards carry over from the aspirational standards. In addition to telling the truth, you can't commit the sin of omission or misleading someone, or not speaking up if someone misinterprets what you told her. It can be difficult to confess that your projects are in trouble, especially if you expect a punitive response. However, you have a duty and an obligation to disclose the whole truth.

This concept applies to estimating and planning as well. If you're given an unrealistic deadline from your sponsor, you have an obligation to inform her that the deadline is unrealistic — and tell her why it is unrealistic. If your team members are giving you optimistic estimates and you know about it, you have an obligation to discuss the situation with them and get more realistic estimates.

Some of these standards might be easier than others to apply, but they all represent the high moral ground. Keep that in mind when you come across these questions on the exam.

Key Terms

Although you may not see the majority of these terms on the exam, you may see ethnocentrism, conflict of interest, and duty of loyalty on the exam. However, you need to be familiar with all the terminology in the context of behaving ethically and in accordance with the Code.

- Code of Ethics and Professional Conduct
- Responsibility
- Respect
- Fairness
- Honesty
- Aspirational standards
- Mandatory standards
- Ethnocentrism
- Conflict of interest
- Duty of loyalty

Chapter Summary

The Code of Ethics and Professional Conduct will not be overtly tested, but the concepts in the Code will be included in the questions. Therefore, you need to be familiar with the expectations of how we, as project managers, behave.

Chapter Summary

- ✦ The Code of Ethics and Professional Conduct describes the ideals for project management and the appropriate behaviors in your role as project manager. The Code applies to the following groups of people:
  - All PMI members
  - Anyone who holds a PMI certification (including the PMP)
  - Anyone applying for a certification
  - Anyone who volunteers with PMI
- ✦ The four values on which the standards are based are responsibility, respect, fairness, and honesty. Each has aspirational standards and mandatory standards. Aspirational standards describe the conduct you should strive to uphold as a project management practitioner. Mandatory standards are firm requirements. They may limit or prohibit behavior.
- ✦ Responsibility is your duty to take ownership for the decisions you make or fail to make, the actions you take or fail to take, and the consequences that result.
- ✦ Respect is your duty to show a high regard for yourself, others, and the resources entrusted to you, including people, money, reputation, the safety of others, and natural or environmental resources.
- ✦ Fairness is your duty to make decisions and act impartially and objectively. Your conduct must be free from competing self-interest, prejudice, and favoritism.
- ✦ Honesty is your duty to understand the truth and act in a truthful manner both in your communications and in your conduct.

Prep Test

1 **Your organization is bidding on a contract to do an extensive home remodeling job for a well-known celebrity. You will be the project manager on the job. Part of the job entails custom glass mosaic work. Your organization is planning on using Gabe to do the mosaic work. Gabe is a good worker and has worked with tile for five years. His customers are always happy with the work he does. You are concerned, though, that he may not be qualified to do the mosaic work because of the intricate design and detailed cuts needed. What is the best approach to this situation?**

A ❍ Ask Gabe whether he thinks he can do high-quality work on the job.

B ❍ Tell your company that there isn't anyone qualified to do the work. If your company chooses to put Gabe in as a resource, the company should indicate that his experience is with tile.

C ❍ Call the customer and discuss your concerns.

D ❍ Do nothing. As long as you are qualified to do your job, that is all you have to worry about.

2 **Your boss called you into the office and told you that the company was going to be downsizing shortly. You are being promoted to a supervisory role, but several of your colleagues will be let go. Later that day, Sandra approaches you in tears, saying that she heard there were going to be layoffs, and she was scared she was going to be let go. She asks you whether you know anything. How should you respond?**

A ❍ Tell her not to worry: You are sure she will have a job after the reorganization.

B ❍ Help her brush up her resume and tell her about a job placement service you know about.

C ❍ Tell her information like that is all rumor or gossip until proven otherwise.

D ❍ Tell your boss that Sandra is crying and spreading rumors around the office.

3 **Your PMP exam is scheduled for two weeks from now. You're trying to balance work, family, and studying. When you get into work, you have a voice mail from PMI, which is investigating an ethics complaint about your co-worker Matt. It appears that he has been inappropriately disclosing confidential information about the CAPM exam. The person on the Ethics Committee has asked you to call her back. What should you do?**

A ❍ Call her back. You are required to cooperate in ethics investigations.

B ❍ Avoid her calls. You are not a PMP yet, and hopefully, you can take your test without getting in the middle of an investigation.

C ❍ Tell Matt he better clean up his act because he is under investigation.

D ❍ Call the Ethics Committee person back and tell her you don't know Matt.

4 **You're managing a project to develop and deploy a project management methodology for your organization. You were blind-copied on an e-mail in which three team members were discussing ways to undermine your work and get a proprietary methodology implemented instead. The e-mails were derogatory and belittling to you, and you are hurt and annoyed that these team members are working toward their own agenda. How should you handle this?**

- **A** ❍ Inform their manager that they are behaving unprofessionally and that you want them pulled from the team.
- **B** ❍ Send their e-mail to other team members as an example of the type of behavior you are not going to tolerate.
- **C** ❍ Report them to PMI for an ethics violation.
- **D** ❍ Call a meeting and ask them their reasons for wanting a proprietary methodology.

5 **As a consultant, you've worked with a number of different companies. You just got off an assignment where people worked at home, answered e-mails on weekends, and seemed to sleep with their e-mail open. You just started a new assignment. You sent out an e-mail Friday around 4:30 p.m., asking the team to let you know about meeting Monday at 10 a.m. It's now Sunday, and you haven't heard a peep. What standard should you apply to keep the relationship with the client in good standing?**

- **A** ❍ Listen to others and seek to understand them.
- **B** ❍ Inform yourself about the norms and customs of others and avoid engaging in behaviors they might consider disrespectful.
- **C** ❍ Conduct yourself in a professional manner, even when it's not reciprocated.
- **D** ❍ Make decisions and take actions based on the best interests of the company.

6 **Your responsibility assignment matrix (RAM) shows that you're supposed to have Kyle as a resource for the entire month of April. It's April 12, and so far, Kyle has been around for only 30 hours. He claims that a lot of problems are happening in his department right now, and he's trying to take care of everything at once. You realize you need to meet with his manager. How should you approach this?**

- **A** ❍ Talk to his manager to see whether you can work out a situation where you can have Kyle but still make sure that the functional manager's department isn't left short-handed.
- **B** ❍ Escalate the issue to the project sponsor.
- **C** ❍ Approach Kyle's boss and tell him that he isn't living up to his word.
- **D** ❍ Tell Kyle that he needs to give you 40 hours per week. He can deal with the issues in his department after the work on your project is done.

7 **You have various options how to test a specific component. Your team operating agreement says that for decisions, you will ask all team members to state their opinions in less than three minutes, and then you will call a vote. The largest voting block will carry the decision. Which value does this demonstrate?**

A ❍ Providing equal access to information

B ❍ Examining your impartiality

C ❍ Demonstrating transparency in the decision-making process

D ❍ Disclosure of perceived conflicts of interest

8 **You're an independent contractor, and you've been asked to be a team member for a company you worked with before on a large project for the local parks and recreation agency. However, you're not comfortable taking the assignment because you know someone on the selection committee. What values should you look to when making your decision?**

A ❍ You're okay because the selection committee can't discriminate in its selection process.

B ❍ You're okay if you disclose your relationship with all affected stakeholders and have their consent to proceed.

C ❍ You can't take the assignment. Your friendship with someone on the selection committee is a conflict of interest.

D ❍ You should decline because it puts your friend in a situation of having a conflict of interest.

9 **A new employee just gave you an estimate that seems aggressive. What should you do first?**

A ❍ Seek to understand how he came up with the estimate.

B ❍ Let him know that you're not interested in aggressive estimates but in realistic estimates.

C ❍ Let his boss know that she should review his estimates before they are forwarded to you.

D ❍ Go with the estimate he gave you but hold him to it.

10 **Carrie just came to your office and let you know that she can't make the deadline she promised you. There are some problems with the component she is working on, and she needs more time. You problem-solve with her to help come up with various solutions while letting her know you appreciate her advance warning and honesty. Which value are you demonstrating?**

A ❍ Providing accurate information in a timely manner

B ❍ Creating an environment where others feel safe to tell the truth

C ❍ Seeking to understand the truth

D ❍ Not engaging in dishonest behavior

11 **Last month, you missed a milestone by two weeks. When you reported this to the steering committee, you were severely chastised in front of 15 executives and 6 of your peers. You have to report to the same committee tomorrow. You just found out that one of the deliverables is having a problem passing the validation review, which could cause a schedule slip of up to four days. How should you address this?**

A ❍ Report the progress on your overall project to date and report on the existing risks, including the potential schedule slip.

B ❍ Report the progress to date. The schedule hasn't slipped yet, so you don't need to address this tomorrow.

C ❍ Tell the team it needs to do whatever it takes to get back on schedule because you don't want a replay of last week.

D ❍ Make sure the team lead for the deliverable is in the meeting to experience what happens when she misses a deadline.

Answers

1 **B.** The Responsibility standard states that you accept only those assignments that are consistent with your background, experience, skills, and qualifications. *See "Responsibility aspirational standards."*

2 **C.** The Responsibility standard states that you protect proprietary or confidential information that has been entrusted to you. *Look over "Responsibility aspirational standards."*

3 **A.** The Responsibility standard requires that you cooperate in ethics investigations. *See "Responsibility mandatory standards."*

4 **D.** This scenario demonstrates approaching those persons with whom you have a conflict with directly and conducting yourself in a professional manner. *See "Respect aspirational standards."*

5 **B.** Your new assignment clearly has different norms about work hours. You should inform yourself about the company culture and practices. *Read "Respect aspirational standards."*

6 **A.** You should negotiate in good faith so the functional area is taken care of and your project needs are met. *Go to "Respect mandatory standards."*

7 **C.** This demonstrates transparency in decision making. *Go over "Fairness aspirational standards."*

8 **B.** You should disclose your relationship. If everyone agrees to a solution that allows the parks and recreation agency to make a fair and impartial selection, you can still be part of the team. *You can read about this in "Fairness mandatory standards."*

9 **A.** First, you should understand the estimating method that the employee used. Maybe he knows a way to get the work done faster than you've seen in the past. *Check out "Honesty aspirational standards."*

10 **B.** By problem-solving and generating options, you're providing a safe environment where she can be honest about what's going on. *Go to "Honesty aspirational standards."*

11 **A.** You need to report current status and the risk of missing a deadline. To not report this is misleading the steering committee and withholding relevant information. *Look at "Honesty mandatory standards."*

Appendix A: What's on the Website

In This Appendix

- System requirements
- Accessing the prep exam on the website
- What you'll find on the website
- Troubleshooting

System Requirements

Make sure that your computer meets the minimum system requirements shown in the following list. If your computer doesn't match up to most of these requirements, you may have problems using the software and files on the website. For the latest and greatest information, please refer to the ReadMe file located on the website.

- A PC running Microsoft Windows 98, Windows 2000, Windows NT4 (with SP4 or later), Windows Me, Windows XP, Windows Vista, Windows 7, or Windows 8
- A Macintosh running Apple OS X or later
- A PC running a version of Linux with kernel 2.4 or greater
- An Internet connection

If you need more information on the basics, check out these Wiley books: *PCs For Dummies,* by Dan Gookin; *Macs For Dummies*, by Edward C. Baig; *Windows Vista For Dummies, Windows 7 For Dummies,* and *Windows 8 For Dummies,* all by Andy Rathbone.

Accessing the Prep Exam on the Website

Fire up your Internet browser and enter **http://www.dummies.com/extras/pmpcertificationaio** in the Address field. Click the link for the prep exam, and then follow these steps to access the free downloadable prep exam file.

1. **Click the Register or Login Now link to register or login.**

   If you have never accessed the prep exam on the book's web page before, you will need to set up an account by registering. In the future if you want to download the exam again for some reason, you will only have to login.

2. **After you have registered, you will be taken to the PMP Certification All-in-One For Dummies, Second Edition web page. Click the Downloads tab and download the prep exam file to your computer.**

   Make sure you can remember where you've saved the file.

3. **Unzip the downloaded file on your Windows computer.**

   Note that the interface will not function properly unless you first unzip the file.

4. **Click start.exe to open the interface.**

5. **Read through the license agreement, and then click the Accept button to browse the contents.**

6. **If you experience trouble with the `start.exe` file or interface, please refer to the product `ReadMe.txt` file.**

What You'll Find on the Website

The prep exam on the website is designed to simulate the actual PMP exam: each question has multiple choice answers. The online prep exam is not adaptive, though, and it is not timed, so you might want to time yourself to gauge your speed.

With each question, you find out whether you answered the question correctly by clicking on the Explanation button. If you answered incorrectly, you are told the correct answer with a brief explanation of why it's correct.

The prep exam contains the prep test questions from the end of each chapter in the book. If you perform well on the prep exam, you're probably ready to tackle the real thing.

Troubleshooting

I tried my best to compile programs that work on most computers with the minimum system requirements. Alas, your computer may differ, and some programs may not work properly for some reason.

The two likeliest problems are that you don't have enough memory (RAM) for the programs you want to use, or you have other programs running that are affecting installation or running of a program. If you get an error message such as `Not enough memory` or `Setup cannot continue`, try one or more of the following suggestions and then try using the software again:

- **Turn off any antivirus software running on your computer.** Installation programs sometimes mimic virus activity and may make your computer incorrectly believe that it's being infected by a virus.
- **Close all running programs.** The more programs you have running, the less memory is available to other programs. Installation programs typically update files and programs, so if you keep other programs running, installation may not work properly.
- **Have your local computer store add more RAM to your computer.** This is, admittedly, a drastic and somewhat expensive step. However, adding more memory can really help the speed of your computer and allow more programs to run at the same time.

Customer Care

If you have trouble with the Prep Test, please call the Wiley Product Technical Support phone number at (800) 762-2974. Outside the United States, call 1(317) 572-3994. You can also contact Wiley Product Technical Support at `http://support.wiley.com`. John Wiley & Sons will provide technical support only for installation and other general quality control items. For technical support on the applications themselves, consult the program's vendor or author.

To place additional orders or to request information about other Wiley products, please call (877) 762-2974.

Appendix B: Practice Test

1 **Assume that your project evaluates risk impacts as Low, Moderate, and High as follows: Low 0.1 - 0.2, Moderate 0.3 - 0.4, High 0.5 - 0.9. These ratings**

A ❍ Are wrong. They must be linear.
B ❍ Cannot sum to 1.0 because 1.0 would reflect a case of certainty.
C ❍ Must be the same for every project in your department's portfolio.
D ❍ Demonstrate a degree of risk aversion.

2 **Which stakeholder looks at the financial return from a group of projects and programs?**

A ❍ The project manager
B ❍ The PMO manager
C ❍ The portfolio manager
D ❍ The program manager

3 **You performed a quantitative risk analysis on your project. The output of this analysis**

A ❍ Shows the probability of achieving your project's schedule and cost objectives.
B ❍ Shows the probability of achieving your project risk objectives.
C ❍ Lists risks that require responses in the near term.
D ❍ Identifies trends in qualitative risk analysis results.

4 **Tone and inflection is what component of communication?**

A ❍ Verbal
B ❍ Nonverbal
C ❍ Para language
D ❍ Linguistics

5 **You work at a multinational organization. Your latest project includes people in four time zones, people who work from their homes, and technical experts from around the globe. This is an example of**

A ❍ A virtual team
B ❍ Cultural diversity
C ❍ A reduced travel budget
D ❍ Geographical dispersion

6 **The process most concerned with maintaining the integrity of project baselines is**

A ❍ Control Costs
B ❍ Monitor and Control Project Work
C ❍ Perform Integrated Change Control
D ❍ Control Scope

7 **Verified deliverables are an input to which process?**

A ❍ Close Project or Phase
B ❍ Close Procurements
C ❍ Validate Scope
D ❍ Control Scope

8 **Which stakeholder provides the funding for the project?**

A ❍ Senior management
B ❍ The finance department
C ❍ The portfolio steering committee
D ❍ The sponsor

9 **Before closing the project, project scope is measured against**

A ❍ The project management plan
B ❍ The work breakdown structure (WBS)
C ❍ The earned value (EV)
D ❍ The cost plus incentive fee

10 **A vendor who failed to attend the bidder conference because of illness asks for a repeat. To minimize the burden on the contracting organization, the vendor offers the use of its conference room to serve breakfast and lunch. What should you do?**

A ❍ Escalate this matter to your sponsor for guidance.
B ❍ You can repeat the conference, but only in the same facilities and under the same conditions as everyone else.
C ❍ If the vendor provides evidence of the claimed illness, go ahead.
D ❍ You cannot present a private bidder conference for one client.

11 **In a communication model, the sender is responsible for the following:**

A ❍ Understanding the information correctly
B ❍ Making sure the information is received in its entirety
C ❍ Decoding the message contents
D ❍ Making the content clear and complete

12 Developing the project management plan entails

A ❍ Documenting the actions necessary to define, prepare, integrate, and coordinate all subsidiary plans

B ❍ Carrying out the project by performing the activities included therein

C ❍ Coordinating changes across the entire project

D ❍ Integrating and coordinating all project documents and stakeholder expectations

13 You're meeting with your team to focus efforts on accomplishing the project objectives and working as a team. This is an example of

A ❍ Negotiation skills

B ❍ Leadership

C ❍ Influencing

D ❍ Listening

14 To be successful, you need to manage stakeholder engagement. The skills you will need to do this successfully include all the following except

A ❍ Negotiating

B ❍ Presenting

C ❍ Public speaking

D ❍ Controlling change

15 One of your resources has been transferred to a more critical project in the organization. You're looking to see the best way to spread her work among the remaining team members until you can find a replacement. What tool should you use to accomplish this?

A ❍ Variance analysis

B ❍ Resource analysis

C ❍ Schedule compression

D ❍ Resource optimization

16 Validate Scope is the process of

A ❍ Obtaining formal acceptance of the project scope by the project management team

B ❍ Obtaining all appropriate sign-offs from the project team

C ❍ Formalizing acceptance of the completed project deliverables

D ❍ Documenting the scope for the project stakeholders

17 **A procurement audit is a structured review of the procurement process starting from the**

A ❍ Plan Procurement Management process
B ❍ Close Procurements process
C ❍ Litigation pre-trial discovery process
D ❍ Mediation and arbitration result

18 **Some of your colleagues started up a project management training business. It appears from their flyers that they are members of PMI, but you know that's false. What should you do about it?**

A ❍ Steer clear; they are misrepresenting themselves.
B ❍ Send them a registered letter asking who they are.
C ❍ Report them to the Better Business Bureau.
D ❍ Inform PMI.

19 **The project charter is an input to which of the following processes?**

A ❍ Collect Requirements
B ❍ Create WBS
C ❍ Validate Scope
D ❍ Control Scope

20 **Projects are typically authorized for one or more of the following reasons except**

A ❍ Market demand
B ❍ Employee request
C ❍ Legal requirements
D ❍ Technological advance

21 **The scope statement identifies the**

A ❍ Project manager
B ❍ Business case for the project
C ❍ Assumptions and exclusions
D ❍ Team responsible for project delivery

22 **What is the difference between decomposition in activity definition and in scope definition?**

A ❍ The final outputs are deliverables in activity definition.
B ❍ The final outputs are activities in activity definition.
C ❍ There is no difference.
D ❍ The output is a network diagram in activity definition.

23 **Which process is the most dependent upon the nature of the deliverables being created and the work being performed?**

A ❍ Create WBS
B ❍ Define Scope
C ❍ Direct and Manage Project Work
D ❍ Monitor and Control Project Work

24 **Which of the following is true about quality management?**

A ❍ The product quality management processes are the same, regardless of the project.
B ❍ The project quality management processes are the same, regardless of the product.
C ❍ Quality management is concerned with the product. Integrated change control is concerned with the project.
D ❍ Customer satisfaction and quality are essentially the same.

25 **You're conducting a performance review from the last several reporting periods. You notice that the TCPI has gone from 1.04 to 1.05 to 1.07. What's going on in your project?**

A ❍ Your cost performance is improving.
B ❍ Your schedule performance is improving.
C ❍ Your forecast is improving.
D ❍ Your cost performance is deteriorating.

26 **You're trying to figure out how an error was introduced into a product. You look at all the inputs that could have led to the defect. The appropriate technique to chart this type of analysis is the**

A ❍ Pareto chart
B ❍ Run diagram
C ❍ Scatter diagram
D ❍ Ishikawa diagram

27 **As the project manager, you're involved in administrative activities, such as finalizing open claims, updating records, making sure all payments are finalized, and archiving the information for future use. These activities occur**

A ❍ At the end of the project
B ❍ When a contract is complete
C ❍ During the monitoring and controlling process
D ❍ During the executing process

28 **Your organization is looking at teaming up with another organization to respond to a very lucrative long-term RFP. However, you have grave misgivings about the other organization. The committee in charge of assessing the teaming arrangement must have a unanimous decision to move forward. Everyone else on the Executive Committee is for it. You really don't want to rock the boat, but you feel compelled to vote against the decision. What's the best way to approach the committee with this information?**

A ❍ Arrange for a third party to enter the negotiations and muddy the water.

B ❍ Send an anonymous letter to the Executive Committee.

C ❍ Send an anonymous letter to your proposed partner.

D ❍ Prepare your facts and make your case to the Executive Committee.

29 **Project objectives should include all the following except**

A ❍ Date by which the project should be completed

B ❍ Budget

C ❍ Quality parameters

D ❍ Risk assessment

30 **To shift the risk to the seller, which type of contract should you use?**

A ❍ Time and materials

B ❍ Firm fixed price

C ❍ Cost plus fixed fee

D ❍ Fixed price incentive

31 **The primary advantage of the bottom-up estimate is the increased accuracy in the estimates. What is a consideration that the project team must keep in mind?**

A ❍ The relationship of the data to other variables

B ❍ The additional cost associated with this level of detail

C ❍ The size of the project

D ❍ The level of experience of the estimator

32 **The management style used by a project manager who makes decisions without considering input by other team members is**

A ❍ *Laissez-faire*

B ❍ Judgmental

C ❍ Autocratic

D ❍ Bureaucratic

33 **You're negotiating an FPIF contract with a vendor. The target cost is $400,000. The target profit is 10%. The incentive split is 70/30. These are all part of the contract payment terms and incentive structure. If actual costs are $475,000, what is the actual profit?**

A ❍ $40,000
B ❍ $17,500
C ❍ $492,500
D ❍ $475,000

34 **A strike has caused delays on your project, but your company's policy is to honor labor contract commitments even during strikes, so you didn't hire non-union replacement workers. You had some contingency time, and you anticipate the new labor agreement will change the project costs. What technique can you use to determine whether your plan will require corrective action?**

A ❍ What-if scenario analysis
B ❍ Re-baselining the schedule
C ❍ Analogous estimating
D ❍ Resource optimization

35 **The purpose of a change control system is to**

A ❍ Ensure that project team members work the same plan.
B ❍ Make sure that changes to the statement of work (SOW) are approved.
C ❍ Assess the impact of changes on cost or schedule before deciding to implement them.
D ❍ All the above.

36 **Close Project or Phase inputs include all the following except**

A ❍ Project management plan
B ❍ Accepted deliverables
C ❍ Variance analysis
D ❍ Organizational process assets

37 **You're bidding on a contract with a government agency. At the bidder conference, you discover that a good friend from college is the government's contract officer. What is the appropriate plan of action?**

A ❍ Because you probably see eye to eye on most issues, this relationship could be a significant advantage to the government.
B ❍ Establish a policy of dealing only with your friend's subordinates.
C ❍ Avoid any decisions or actions that could be interpreted as a conflict of interest.
D ❍ Disclose your past relationship, given that it is a potential conflict of interest.

38 **The role that initiates projects that are part of a program is**

A ❍ The PMO Director
B ❍ The program manager
C ❍ The sponsor
D ❍ The Portfolio Committee

39 **The items at the lowest level of the WBS are referred to as**

A ❍ Control accounts
B ❍ Tasks
C ❍ Work packages
D ❍ Activities

40 **Which of the following is not a component of the human resource management plan?**

A ❍ Project organization charts
B ❍ Resource requirements
C ❍ Roles and responsibilities
D ❍ Staffing management plan

41 **Which is the highest level of performance for a project team?**

A ❍ Forming
B ❍ Storming
C ❍ Norming
D ❍ Performing

42 **A type of power that you might have as a project manager because you are very good friends with the owner of the company is**

A ❍ Referent
B ❍ Formal
C ❍ Expert
D ❍ Forcing

43 **You're negotiating the payment terms, incentives, penalties, and fees for an FPIF contract. The target cost is $500,000. The target profit is 10%. The incentive split is 70/30. If actual costs are $475,000, what is the actual profit?**

A ❍ $60,000
B ❍ $57,500
C ❍ $50,000
D ❍ $532,500

44 **Which is not part of the Control Scope process?**

A ❍ Making sure that scope creep doesn't occur on the project
B ❍ Managing project and product scope changes
C ❍ Analyzing variance between the baseline and the deliverables
D ❍ Obtaining customer validation for the final deliverable

45 **Your SPI for a control account is 1.07. What should you report about this at your performance review?**

A ❍ Give the root cause for the negative variance and your planned corrective action.
B ❍ Nothing; it is within the tolerance level.
C ❍ Give the root cause for the positive variance and the projected finish date.
D ❍ Nothing; you have sufficient float.

46 **Many projects are broken into phases to make them easier to manage. Which of the following phases is most likely to be associated with the initiating process group?**

A ❍ Planning
B ❍ Testing
C ❍ Development
D ❍ Concept

47 **The project is closed, and all documents have been finalized. These documents become a part of the**

A ❍ Accepted deliverables
B ❍ Organizational process assets
C ❍ Scope statement
D ❍ Risk register updates

48 **You're a contract project manager, midway through an assignment. Another project comes along at a 50% higher hourly rate. Can you take it?**

A ❍ As a contract project manager, you can leave immediately.
B ❍ You can begin to phase out of the old project and have team members pick up more of the project, while phasing into the new project.
C ❍ This is a conflict of interest, which you must disclose. You might be able to take the project if all stakeholders agree to the plan.
D ❍ You can give two weeks' notice and take the assignment.

49 **Your organization is developing a new product for launch in October of this year. The investment is $5,450,000. You expect to recapture $3,000,000 by October of the following year and the remaining $2,450,000 by April of the next year. This forecast is known as**

A ❍ Benefit-cost ratio
B ❍ Future value
C ❍ Net present value
D ❍ Payback period

50 **You measure completion of product scope against**

A ❍ The scope statement
B ❍ The product requirements
C ❍ The project management plan
D ❍ The scope management plan

51 **The skill and capacity required to complete project activities is**

A ❍ Authority
B ❍ Competency
C ❍ Role
D ❍ Responsibility

52 **Your new lab has state-of-the-art everything. The problem is that much of the high-end equipment has periodic problems, which shuts down operations. Which statement reflects your situation?**

A ❍ You have high-quality equipment, but low grade.
B ❍ The grade is low, but the precision is high.
C ❍ You have very accurate equipment, but the quality is low.
D ❍ You have high-grade equipment, but low quality.

53 **All the following are results from developing a project team except**

A ❍ Improving individualism
B ❍ Improving team member skills
C ❍ Improving trust
D ❍ Improving team member knowledge

54 **Your EV is $650,000, and your AC is $639,000. Your BAC is $1,200,000. What is your EAC?**

A ❍ $1,220,657
B ❍ $1,120,657
C ❍ $1,176,471
D ❍ $1,211,000

55 **Your cost analyst brings you the latest bad news on the budget performance. He shows you a bar chart that ranks all the reasons for cost variance, including labor, usage variance, overtime, and so on. What type of chart is he showing you?**

A ❍ Pareto chart
B ❍ Cause-and-effect diagram
C ❍ Flow chart
D ❍ Run chart

56 **What is a risk reassessment used for?**

A ❍ To validate the accuracy of the data
B ❍ To determine whether assumptions are valid
C ❍ To identify new risks and update the probability and impact
D ❍ To correct errors in the original risk assessment

57 **The Close Project process**

A ❍ Occurs only once in each project
B ❍ Ensures the project is successful
C ❍ May occur after each project phase
D ❍ Is not always required

58 **You have a major deliverable due on Thursday, and your progress report is due Friday. The team ran into some snags on the deliverable but identified the issue and plans to work on it over the weekend. The team is confident the issue can be resolved by Saturday afternoon, so that by Monday, everything will be back on track. What should you report in your progress report?**

A ❍ Take a vacation day Friday, and submit your report Monday after the issue is resolved.
B ❍ Report that everything is on track. By the time the sponsor reads the report, that will be the case.
C ❍ Give the sponsor a detailed analysis of the cause and effect of the issue and the task breakdown you are using to resolve it. Make sure to acknowledge the diligent team members who will be working over the weekend in your progress report.
D ❍ Advise the sponsor of the status of the deliverable and the corrective action you have planned.

59 **The project manager must identify ________, determine their requirements, and then manage and influence those requirements to ensure a successful project.**

A ❍ Team members
B ❍ Subject matter experts
C ❍ Sponsors
D ❍ Stakeholders

60 **Where should you document the project life cycle?**

A ❍ The scope statement

B ❍ The requirements documentation

C ❍ The project management plan

D ❍ Scope management plan

61 **The right to make and approve decisions is**

A ❍ Authority

B ❍ Competency

C ❍ Role

D ❍ Responsibility

62 **To produce your product, you're working with chemicals that must be kept between 46 and 48 degrees at all times. Therefore, you have a number of devices that constantly measure and adjust the temperature in the enclosure where the chemicals are stored. You are most concerned that these devices have a high degree of**

A ❍ Relevance

B ❍ Precision

C ❍ Accuracy

D ❍ Control

63 **To effectively manage your project team, you need to engage in**

A ❍ Conflict management

B ❍ Norming behavior

C ❍ Negotiating

D ❍ Setting project standards

64 **You're managing a project and determine the only way to resolve a vendor problem is to have it resolved by a neutral third party. To accomplish this, you should use**

A ❍ Claims resolution guidelines

B ❍ Litigation

C ❍ Alternative dispute resolution (ADR)

D ❍ A team operating agreement

65 **As a result of comparing planned project performance against the performance measurements, you submit a change request. Which of the following is not considered a change request?**

A ❍ A modification of the in-scope and out-of-scope work in the scope statement

B ❍ A new and updated cost estimate

C ❍ A new requirement for a key task

D ❍ An update to the Assumption Log

66 **As the project manager, you need to ensure that all project work is complete prior to closing the project. Which document would be the most appropriate to review?**

A ❍ Scope management plan
B ❍ Project management plan
C ❍ Cost performance index
D ❍ Integrated schedule

67 **You're the project manager of a team of workers that is doing a job at a client site. You walk into the area where your team is working and notice that people have their feet up on the desks, the trash cans are overflowing, and fast-food bags are strewn about. You call your team together and tell them that this type of behavior is completely inappropriate and you expect them to clean up the work space and keep it neat. This exemplifies which ethics standard?**

A ❍ Being truthful in our conduct
B ❍ Conducting ourselves in a professional manner, even when it is not reciprocated
C ❍ Respecting the property rights of others
D ❍ Reporting unethical conduct

68 **Information from the stakeholder register is used in which process?**

A ❍ Develop Project Charter
B ❍ Plan Communications Management
C ❍ Control Communications
D ❍ Perform Quality Assurance

69 **Which document defines the cost variance thresholds for the project?**

A ❍ The change management plan
B ❍ The resource management plan
C ❍ The cost management plan
D ❍ The cost baseline

70 **Which process is concerned with documenting uncertain events that can influence your project objectives?**

A ❍ Control Risks
B ❍ Plan Risk Management
C ❍ Plan Risk Responses
D ❍ Identify Risks

71 **The QC results show that a process is consistently out of control. You ask the QA lead to give you a chart that shows you the upper control limit and lower control limit and where the problems occurred. You are asking for a**

A ❍ Control chart
B ❍ Run chart
C ❍ Pareto chart
D ❍ Fishbone diagram

72 **You and your sponsor are in disagreement over the best way to handle a discrepancy in the latest procurement audit. You decide that because this isn't a really big deal and the sponsor outranks you, you should emphasize the areas of the audit that you agree on and downplay the differences. This is an example of**

A ❍ Avoiding
B ❍ Collaborating
C ❍ Compromising
D ❍ Smoothing

73 **Often, project managers do not have position power, so they need to rely on**

A ❍ Negotiation skills
B ❍ Leadership
C ❍ Influencing
D ❍ Listening

74 **Your EV is $825,000, and your AC is $865,000. Your BAC is $1,200,000. What is your EAC?**

A ❍ $1,263,158
B ❍ $1,140,592
C ❍ $1,200,000
D ❍ $1,240,000

75 **At the close of the development phase of your project, you review the risk register to determine whether the risk responses were effective and accomplished the intended result. This is called a**

A ❍ Risk analysis
B ❍ Risk audit
C ❍ Performance measurement
D ❍ Risk reassessment

76 **During the Close Project or Phase process, there is an outstanding dispute with a supplier. You are considering arbitration as an option to resolve it. Arbitration is an example of**

A ❍ Litigation

B ❍ Alternative dispute resolution (ADR)

C ❍ A unilateral negotiation

D ❍ Trial without a jury

77 **You've been offered a job as a program manager at a new firm. You've managed projects before but never something as large and complex as the program you would be managing. Your friend who is employed by the organization talked you up, and you think that person might have overstated your qualifications. This new job would mean a 20% increase in pay and an opportunity to really improve your skills in your profession. When you go to interview, what should your approach be?**

A ❍ Find out from your friend what criteria is being used to select the candidate.

B ❍ Do your research on the company and highlight your areas of strength as well as your lack of experience with a program this large.

C ❍ Apply for the PgMP so you can honestly state you are working on becoming a certified program manager.

D ❍ Tell your boss you are out looking so he has time to replace you.

78 **The purpose of stakeholder analysis is all the following except**

A ❍ Identify alternative stakeholders.

B ❍ Identify the influence and interest of the various stakeholders.

C ❍ Document stakeholder expectations.

D ❍ Identify the potential impact or support of each stakeholder.

79 **Which of the following is not considered when calculating cost of quality?**

A ❍ Training

B ❍ Rework

C ❍ Appraisal

D ❍ Quality function deployment

80 **Your procurement documents clearly state that all bidders must have at least five references for similar work. You want to make sure the selected vendor has sufficient experience and satisfied customers. Asking for five references is an example of**

A ❍ Screening criteria

B ❍ Weighting criteria

C ❍ Scoring criteria

D ❍ Ranking criteria

81 **Direct and Manage Project Work comprises**

A ❍ Integrating and coordinating all project plans to create a consistent, coherent document

B ❍ Performing the work defined in the project management plan to achieve the project's objectives

C ❍ Coordinating changes across the entire project

D ❍ The activities needed to identify, define, combine, unify, and coordinate the various processes and project management activities

82 **A contractor, at your desk, is very annoyed that even though a change was authorized, he's not getting paid what he thinks is a fair price. You think it is a fair price, though. The contractor's next action should be to**

A ❍ File a claim

B ❍ Charge you extra next time a change comes through

C ❍ Make it up in overtime

D ❍ Not work with you again

83 **Reviewing, approving, or denying preventive and corrective actions is part of which process?**

A ❍ Direct and Manage Project Work

B ❍ Monitor and Control Project Work

C ❍ Perform Integrated Change Control

D ❍ Control Scope

84 **Your firm laid off everybody and shut down. You decided to use the forced "vacation" to get your PMP certification before applying for a new job. You received your eligibility letter from PMI and scheduled the exam for two weeks hence. You have no doubts that you'll pass, but you aren't taking any chances and will study every day. In the meantime, you start applying for jobs. Do you put PMP on your resume?**

A ❍ Sure. You will be certified by the time an interview would be scheduled.

B ❍ You can state that you will be taking the exam and expect to receive your certification on the scheduled date.

C ❍ Yes, if you put PMP (Pending) after your name.

D ❍ You can say you are a certified project manager as long as you do not use any registered PMI terms, such as PMP or PMI.

85 **Which of the following is an output of the Estimate Activity Resources process?**

A ❍ Activity cost estimates

B ❍ Resource breakdown structure

C ❍ Requested changes

D ❍ Resource calendars

86 **The output of the Determine Budget process is**

A ❍ Project funding requirements
B ❍ Cost baseline
C ❍ Project schedule updates
D ❍ All the above

87 **To mitigate any misunderstandings on the project team, you document your authority level with regards to decision making, prioritization, conflict resolution, and escalation. This is likely to be recorded in which document?**

A ❍ The project management plan
B ❍ The project charter
C ❍ The team operating agreement
D ❍ The project scope statement

88 **You generally have very high standards for work performance, tie rewards to these standards, and make sure that the rewards are what your team appreciates. The motivation theory you espouse is**

A ❍ Theory X
B ❍ Contingency Theory
C ❍ Expectancy Theory
D ❍ Goal-setting Theory

89 **Evaluating overall project performance on a regular basis to provide confidence that the project will satisfy the relevant quality standards is referred to as**

A ❍ Plan Quality
B ❍ Perform Quality Assurance
C ❍ Control Quality
D ❍ Perform Quality Management

90 **There are outstanding issues, claims, and disputes with one supplier for your project. A common method for addressing these is through**

A ❍ Scope verification
B ❍ Procurement audits
C ❍ Negotiated settlements
D ❍ Lessons learned

91 **Project objectives, project approval requirements, and high-level milestones are all components of which document?**

A ❍ The charter
B ❍ The strategic plan
C ❍ The scope statement
D ❍ The WBS

92 **You're documenting the methods you'll use to integrate staff onto the team and how you will release staff. You're also noting training needs and safety requirements for the team. Which document compiles this information?**

A ❍ Staffing management plan

B ❍ Responsibility assignment matrix

C ❍ Resource requirements

D ❍ Resource calendars

93 **Crashing can**

A ❍ Reduce project duration and cost

B ❍ Reduce schedule duration by increasing the assignment of resources on critical path activities

C ❍ Compress the schedule by overlapping activities that would normally be done in sequence

D ❍ Resequence activities to maximize float

94 **You're managing a project with specific performance criteria. You want a contract that encourages the seller to meet or exceed these performance criteria. What type of contract should you select?**

A ❍ Cost plus incentive fee

B ❍ Cost plus fixed fee

C ❍ Firm fixed price

D ❍ Time and material

95 **Your organization has had problems controlling changes in the past, so on your new project, you implement a Change Control board. People aren't familiar with this type of process and are resisting your proposal. You reassure them by telling them**

A ❍ Members can make changes as needed, but those who are not members cannot.

B ❍ The Change Control board need deal only with those changes that might jeopardize the project.

C ❍ The role of the board is to make sure that only changes beneficial to the project are authorized.

D ❍ The configuration management system automates almost everything anyway, so the job of the board is very straightforward.

96 **You accept a position in a new organization as project manager of a project that's not been meeting its performance measures. You meet with the team members and realize that they are deeply concerned about their job security and bonuses because the previous manager threatened to withhold their bonuses if work didn't improve. You recognize that according to Maslow's Hierarchy of Needs model, this team is dealing with**

A ❍ Esteem needs
B ❍ Physiological needs
C ❍ Safety and security needs
D ❍ Social needs

97 **Which of the following tools cannot be used to determine the root cause of a problem?**

A ❍ Fishbone diagram
B ❍ Ishikawa diagram
C ❍ Checklist
D ❍ Flow chart

98 **The client for your project to develop a new decking finish has discovered that the finishing component runs if it isn't allowed to set for 48 hours. You need to develop a different finishing component. This means changes to the development and testing work, delaying your delivery date by six weeks, and adding a significant amount to the project cost to cover the rework. You create a change request, and it's approved. What else must you do?**

A ❍ Write up the incident for preventive action.
B ❍ Develop new quality assurance standards.
C ❍ Notify the Change Control board.
D ❍ Update the project baselines.

99 **As a project manager, the conflict management approach that you would tend not to use because it does not lead to an ongoing positive result is**

A ❍ Problem solving
B ❍ Compromise
C ❍ Collaboration
D ❍ Avoidance

100 **A project conflict has arisen on how to integrate new software midstream during your IT project. You wish to gather the team and incorporate multiple viewpoints to quickly resolve this conflict. Which conflict resolution mode would you apply?**

A ❍ Withdrawing

B ❍ Smoothing

C ❍ Forcing

D ❍ Collaborating

Sample Test Answers

1 **D.** This is an uneven distribution that is skewed, so more risks will land in the high-risk rating, showing that the organization has a low risk tolerance. *See Book V, Chapter 1.*

2 **C.** The portfolio manager is interested in financial performance for all the projects and programs in a portfolio. *See Book I, Chapter 2.*

3 **A.** Quantitative risk analysis can show you the probability of meeting cost and schedule objectives. *See Book V, Chapter 1.*

4 **C.** Tone and inflection are referred to as *para language* communication. *See Book IV, Chapter 4.*

5 **A.** A geographically diverse team is a virtual team. *See Book VI, Chapter 2.*

6 **C.** Perform Integrated Change Control ensures that only approved changes are integrated into the project baselines. *See Book VII, Chapter 1.*

7 **C.** Verified deliverables come from Control Quality and go into Validate Scope for customer acceptance. *See Book VII, Chapter 2.*

8 **D.** If there isn't a defined customer who is paying for it, the sponsor provides funding for the project. *See Book II, Chapter 3.*

9 **A.** Product scope completion is measured against requirements. Project scope completion is measured against the project management plan. *See Book IX, Chapter 1.*

10 **D.** This is a Fairness standard. The offer of the vendor to provide breakfast, lunch, and a room would have the appearance of favoritism and could impede the impartiality of the selection. The bidder conference is a technique to provide equal access to information. If a bidder is unable to attend, the buyer cannot make special arrangements. Look at *PMI Code of Ethics and Professional Conduct 4.2. See Book IX, Chapter 2.*

11 **D.** The sender's responsibility is to make sure the information is clear and complete and also to confirm that the receiver understood the message correctly. The other answers are the responsibility of the receiver. *See Book IV, Chapter 4.*

12 **A.** Defining, preparing, integrating, and coordinating all subsidiary plans is a key part of developing a project management plan. *See Book III, Chapter 1.*

13 **B.** Getting people to work together toward a common end is leadership. *See Book VI, Chapter 2.*

14 **D.** Controlling change is important to a successful project. However, negotiating, presenting, and public speaking are important in managing stakeholder engagement. *See Book VI, Chapter 3.*

15 **D.** Use resource optimization to make sure no resources are over-worked and that the work is spread out as evenly as possible among the remaining resources. *See Book VII, Chapter 3.*

16 **C.** Verify Scope is about the customer or sponsor formally accepting the project deliverables. *See Book VII, Chapter 2.*

17 **A.** A procurement audit starts with the very first procurement process, Plan Procurement Management. *See Book V, Chapter 2.*

18 **D.** This is a Responsibility mandatory standard, meaning that you are required to bring violations of the Code to the attention of the appropriate body for resolution: in this case, PMI. Review the *PMI Code of Ethics and Professional Conduct 2.3. See Book IX, Chapter 2.*

19 **A.** The project charter and the stakeholder register are inputs to the Collect Requirements process. *See Book III, Chapter 1.*

20 **B.** A project would not be started for an employee request unless there were other compelling reasons, such as a business need or any of the other listed options. *See Book I, Chapter 2.*

21 **C.** Assumptions and exclusions are documented in the project scope statement. *See Book III, Chapter 2.*

22 **B.** Outputs from scope definition are work packages. In activity definition, the outputs are activities. *See Book III, Chapter 3.*

23 **C.** The majority of the product work is accomplished in the Direct and Manage Project Work process. The Direct and Manage Project Work process is wholly dependent upon the nature of the product, service, or result. *See Book VI, Chapter 1.*

24 **B.** The processes used to manage the project quality are the same, regardless of the product. Managing the product quality depends upon the product, service, or result. *See Book IV, Chapter 2.*

25 **D.** A TCPI higher than 1.0 indicates that you have more scope left than you do budget. Therefore, this situation is deteriorating. *See Book VIII, Chapter 1.*

26 **D.** An Ishikawa diagram looks for the root cause of defects. *See Book VIII, Chapter 2.*

27 **B.** Finalizing open claims, updating records, and finalizing payments are all part of the Close Procurements process. You can close out a contract at any point in the project life cycle. *See Book IX, Chapter 1.*

28 **D.** You have a responsibility to take actions and be truthful in your communication about what you believe are the best interests of the organization. This is a Responsibility aspirational standard and an Honesty aspirational standard. Review the *PMI Code of Ethics and Professional Conduct 2.2 and 5.2. See Book IX, Chapter 2.*

29 **D.** A risk assessment is not a project objective. *See Book II, Chapter 2.*

30 **B.** A firm fixed price contract shifts the risk to the seller to deliver all the scope at a set price. *See Book V, Chapter 2.*

31 **B.** The additional accuracy takes time, and therefore costs more, to develop. *See Book III, Chapter 3, and Book IV, Chapter 1.*

32 **C.** The autocratic style is top-down, where the leader makes the decisions. *See Book VI, Chapter 2.*

33 **B.** The incentive fee is $40,000. The difference between target and actual is –$75,000. –$75,000 × 30% = –$22,500. Therefore, $40,000 – $22,500 = $17,500. *See Book VI, Chapter 3, and Book V, Chapter 2.*

34 **A.** A what-if scenario analysis is a modeling technique that allows you to see the effect of various scenarios on your schedule. *See Book VII, Chapter 3.*

35 **D.** The change control system ensures all team members are working to the same plan, that all changes to any aspect of the project are approved, and that there is an analysis of the impact of a change before it is approved. *See Book VII, Chapter 1.*

36 **C.** A variance analysis is not an input to closing the project or a phase. *See Book IX, Chapter 1.*

37 **D.** This is a Fairness mandatory standard; therefore, you must disclose real or potential conflicts of interest to the appropriate stakeholders. *See Book IX, Chapter 2.*

38 **B.** The program manager is responsible for initiating projects within the program. *See Book I, Chapter 2.*

39 **C.** A work package is the lowest level of the WBS. *See Book III, Chapter 2.*

40 **B.** Resource requirements are not part of the human resources plan. *See Book IV, Chapter 3.*

41 **D.** Teams are at their most efficient in the performing phase. *See Book VI, Chapter 2.*

42 **A.** Referent power is based on your charisma and personality, or on whom you know. *See Book VI, Chapter 2.*

43 **B.** The target profit is $50,000. There is a positive variance of $25,000. 30% of $25,000 is $7,500. Therefore, the profit is $57,500. *See Book V, Chapter 2.*

44 **D.** Obtaining customer validation is part of the Validate Scope process. *See Book VII, Chapter 2.*

45 **C.** This is a positive variance. You should report this as well as the cause. *See Book VII, Chapter 3, and Book VIII, Chapter 1.*

46 **D.** Concept is most closely associated with developing a charter and identifying stakeholders as well as other initiating activities. *See Book I, Chapter 3.*

47 **B.** Project documents become organizational process assets that can be used by future projects. *See Book IX, Chapter 1.*

48 **C.** This is a Fairness mandatory standard. Therefore, you must refrain from engaging in the decision-making process or otherwise attempting to influence outcomes, unless or until: You make a full disclosure to the affected stakeholders; you have an approved mitigation plan; and you have obtained the consent of the stakeholders to proceed. *Review the PMI Code of Ethics and Professional Conduct 4.3. See Book IX, Chapter 2.*

49 **D.** The forecast of when you recapture your investment and start making a profit is the payback period. *See Book II, Chapter 1.*

50 **B.** The product scope completion is measured against product requirements. *See Book III, Chapter 2.*

51 **B.** Competency describes the skill or skill level of an individual. *See Book IV, Chapter 3.*

52 **D.** "State-of-the-art" indicates high grade. However, the problems indicate low quality. *See Book IV, Chapter 2.*

53 **A.** Team development does not improve individualism. *See Book VI, Chapter 2.*

54 **C.** First you have to determine your CPI by dividing EV by AC. This gives you a CPI of 1.02. The EAC equation of BAC / CPI gives you this answer. *See Book VIII, Chapter 1.*

55 **A.** A chart that ranks the problems by frequency is a Pareto chart. *See Book VIII, Chapter 2.*

56 **C.** Risk reassessment looks for new risks and updates the information on existing risks. *See Book VIII, Chapter 4.*

57 **C.** You perform closure activities at least at the end of each phase and each project. *See Book IX, Chapter 1.*

58 **D.** C is a good option, but the sponsor probably doesn't want to know all the technical details — only that you have the situation under control. This is an Honesty aspirational standard, which indicates that you need to provide accurate information in a timely manner. *Review the PMI Code of Ethics and Professional Conduct. See Book IX, Chapter 2.*

59 **D.** You should identify stakeholders and their requirements. *See Book II, Chapter 3.*

60 **C.** The project life cycle is documented in the project management plan. *See Book III, Chapter 1.*

61 **A.** Authority is the right to make decisions. *See Book IV, Chapter 3.*

62 **C.** Because you have a very tight temperature tolerance, your measurements need to be accurate. *See Book IV, Chapter 2.*

63 **A.** Managing conflict is a key ingredient in effective team management. *See Book VI, Chapter 2.*

64 **C.** Mediation and arbitration are types of alternative dispute resolution (ADR). *See Book VIII, Chapter 4.*

65 **D.** The Assumption Log is a dynamic document that should be continuously updated. All the other answer choice items represent a change that needs to be submitted to the CCB. *See Book VII, Chapter 1.*

66 **B.** The project management plan is used to ensure that the project is complete. *See Book IX, Chapter 1.*

67 **C.** This is a Respect mandatory standard that states we respect the property rights of others. *Review the PMI Code of Ethics and Professional Conduct 3.3. See Book IX, Chapter 2.*

68 **B.** You will plan your communications based on stakeholder requirements. *See Book II, Chapter 3.*

69 **C.** The cost management plan contains the cost variance thresholds. *See Book IV, Chapter 1.*

70 **D.** Identifying risks is about looking for what can affect an objective and then documenting that event. *See Book V, Chapter 1.*

71 **A.** A control chart has upper and lower control limits, and also charts whether a process is in control. *See Book VIII, Chapter 2.*

72 **D.** Smoothing is used when you need to maintain a relationship or have little relative power. *See Book VI, Chapter 2.*

73 **C.** If you don't have position power, you need to rely on your ability to influence others. *See Book VI, Chapter 2.*

74 **A.** Your CPI is .95. The EAC is BAC / CPI. EAC = 1,200,000 / .95 = 1,263,158. *See Book VIII, Chapter 1.*

75 **B.** A risk audit looks to see whether the risk management processes and the risk responses are appropriate for the project. *See Book VIII, Chapter 4.*

76 **B.** Arbitration is a form of ADR. *See Book IX, Chapter 1.*

77 **B.** You have a responsibility to identify both your strengths and weaknesses. Just because you haven't managed something this big doesn't mean that you can't. However, the employer has a right to know. This is a Responsibility aspirational standard. *Review the PMI Code of Ethics and Professional Conduct 2.2. See Book IX, Chapter 2.*

78 **A.** The purpose is not to identify alternative stakeholders, but rather to identify the influences, interests, expectations, and effects of the stakeholders. *See Book II, Chapter 3.*

79 **D.** Quality function deployment is not considered a cost of quality. It is a technique used in planning quality. *See Book IV, Chapter 2.*

80 **A.** The five references are screening criteria. *See Book V, Chapter 2.*

81 **B.** Performing the work defined in the project management plan to achieve the project's objectives is the *PMBOK Guide* glossary definition of Direct and Manage Project Execution. *See Book VI, Chapter 1.*

82 **A.** The contractor can file a claim if he feels the situation is unfair. *See Book VIII, Chapter 4.*

83 **C.** Perform Integrated Change Control looks at all change requests and approves or denies them. *See Book VII, Chapter 1.*

84 **B.** Claiming to PMP certification is against the Honesty mandatory standard that states you do not engage in dishonest behavior with the intention of personal gain or at the expense of another. *Review the PMI Code of Ethics and Professional Conduct. See Book IX, Chapter 2.*

85 **B.** A resource breakdown structure is an output of the Estimate Activity Resources process. *See Book III, Chapter 3.*

86 **D.** Funding requirements, the cost baseline, and updates to project documents, including the project schedule, are all outputs from the Determine Budget process. *See Book IV, Chapter 1.*

87 **B.** The project charter has a section to document the PM authority. *See Book II, Chapter 2.*

88 **C.** Expectancy Theory is about motivating people based on their expectations. *See Book VI, Chapter 2.*

89 **B.** Quality assurance makes sure the project can satisfy the quality standards. *See Book VI, Chapter 1.*

90 **C.** As you close out contracts, you will want to make sure that all open claims are negotiated and settled. *See Book IX, Chapter 1.*

91 **A.** The charter documents the project objectives, project approval requirements, and high-level milestones. *See Book II, Chapter 2.*

92 **A.** Information on bringing on staff and releasing staff, as well as training requirements, is part of the staffing management plan. *See Book IV, Chapter 3.*

93 **B.** Crashing reduces time on the critical path by adding resources or extending work periods. *See Book III, Chapter 3.*

94 **A.** An incentive fee encourages contractors to meet specified performance criteria. *See Book V, Chapter 2.*

95 **C.** A change control board (CCB) ensures that beneficial changes are approved and implemented, and also that only approved changes are implemented. *See Book VII, Chapter 1.*

96 **C.** The team members can't work effectively if they're worried about being fired or having their bonuses negatively affected. They are worried about work survival and security needs. *See Book VI, Chapter 2.*

97 **C.** A checklist does not identify a root cause. *See Book VIII, Chapter 2.*

98 **D.** After the change is approved, you need to update your baseline. *See Book VII, Chapter 1.*

99 **D.** Avoidance does not usually lead to a long-term positive outcome. *See Book VI, Chapter 2.*

100 **D.** Collaboration uses the team's input and is an effective way to gather multiple points of view. *See Book VI, Chapter 2.*

Appendix C: Lab Work

This appendix has a number of exercises that will help you remember key terms and vocabulary you need for the PMP exam. The first lab has definitions of knowledge areas and process groups, which will help set the framework for all the processes in project management. The remaining exercises focus on a specific knowledge area. This is a different approach than how the information is presented in the chapters of this book, which organize information by process group. Here, you are asked to recall information by knowledge area. This will keep your brain nimble when recalling processes, inputs, tools, techniques, outputs, and vocabulary. You can find the answers to each lab in the back half of this appendix.

Good luck!

Knowledge Area and Process Groups

Fill in the blank with the name of the correct knowledge area or process group.

1. Project ______ Management includes the processes necessary to purchase or acquire the products, services, or results needed from outside the project team.
2. ______ ______ are those processes performed to finalize all activities across all Process Groups to formally close a project or phase.
3. Project ______ Management includes the processes involved in planning, estimating, budgeting, financing, funding, managing, and controlling costs so that the project can be completed within the approved budget.
4. ______ are those processes performed to establish the scope of the project, refine the objectives, and define the course of action required to attain the objectives that the project was undertaken to achieve.
5. Project ______ Management includes the processes of conducting risk management planning, identification, analysis, response planning, and controlling risk on a project.

6. Project ______ Management includes the processes and activities of the performing organization that determine quality policies, objectives, and responsibilities so that the project will satisfy the needs for which it was undertaken.
7. ______ ______ ______ ______ are those processes required to track, review, and regulate the progress and performance of the project; identify any areas in which changes to the plan are required; and initiate the corresponding changes.
8. Project ______ Management includes the processes required to ensure that the project includes all the work required, and only the work required, to complete the project successfully.
9. Project ______ ______ Management includes the processes that organize, manage, and lead the project team.
10. ______ ______ are those processes performed to complete the work defined in the project management plan to satisfy the project specifications.
11. Project ______ Management includes the processes and activities needed to identify, define, combine, unify, and coordinate the various processes and project management activities within the Project Management process groups.
12. Project ______ Management includes the processes required to manage the timely completion of a project.
13. Project ______ Management includes the processes required to identify all people or organizations impacted by the project, analyzing stakeholder expectations and impact on the project, and developing appropriate management strategies for effectively engaging stakeholders in project decisions and execution.
14. ______ ______ are those processes performed to define a new project or a new phase of an existing project by obtaining authorization to start the project or phase.
15. Project ______ Management includes the processes that are required to ensure timely and appropriate planning, collection, creation, distribution, storage, retrieval, management, control, monitoring, and ultimate disposition of project information.

PMP Foundation

The following list of terms comes from Chapters 1–3 of the *PMBOK Guide*. These terms are discussed in Book I of this book. There's also a table with selected definitions from the *PMBOK Guide* glossary. Match the term with the appropriate definitions. *Hint:* Not all terms will be used.

Functional organization	Project management office
Project phase	Project management
Matrix organization	Enterprise environmental factors (EEFs)
Project	Progressive elaboration
Progressive elaboration	Organizational process assets (OPAs)
Project life cycle	Program
Portfolio	Projectized organization

Term	Definition
	A collection of logically related project activities that culminates in the completion of one or more deliverables.
	Conditions, not under the immediate control of the team, that influence or direct the project, program, or portfolio.
	A temporary endeavor undertaken to create a unique product, service, or result.
	The application of knowledge, skills, tools, and techniques to project activities to meet the project requirements.
	The series of phases that a project passes through from its initiation to its closure.
	Any organizational structure in which the project manager shares responsibility with the functional managers for assigning priorities and for directing the work of persons assigned to the project.
	Plans, processes, policies, procedures, and knowledge basis that are specific to and used by the performing organization.
	The iterative process of increasing the level of detail in a project management plan as greater amounts of information and more accurate estimates become available.

Project Integration Management

Here is a list of terms and processes from Project Integration Management. The following table contains selected definitions from the *PMBOK Guide* glossary. Match each term with the appropriate definition.

Develop Project Charter	Project management plan
Close Project or Phase	Project charter
Defect repair	Monitor and Control Project Work
Corrective action	Perform Integrated Change Control
Preventive action	Direct and Manage Project Execution
Change request	Develop Project Management Plan

Term	*Definition*
	An intentional activity to modify a nonconforming product or product component.
	Tracking, reviewing, and reporting the progress to meet the performance objectives defined in the project management plan.
	A document issued by the project initiator or sponsor that formally authorizes the existence of a project and also provides the project manager with the authority to apply organizational resources to project activities.
	The document that describes how the project will be executed, monitored, and controlled.
	A formal proposal to modify any document, deliverable, or baseline.
	Leading and performing the work defined in the project management plan and implementing approved changes to achieve the project's objectives.
	An intentional activity that ensures the future performance of the project work is aligned with the project management plan.
	Finalizing all activities across all project management process groups to formally complete the project or phase.
	Developing a document that formally authorizes the existence of a project and provides the project manager with the authority to apply organizational resources to project activities.
	Defining, preparing, and coordinating all subsidiary plans and integrating them into a comprehensive project management plan.
	An intentional activity that realigns the performance of the project work with the project management plan.
	Reviewing all change requests; approving changes and managing changes to deliverables, organizational process assets, project documents, and project management plan; and communicating their disposition.

Project Scope Management

In the right column, enter the name of the Project Scope Management process most associated with the tool, technique, or output identified in the left column.

Tool, technique, or output	Project Scope Management process
Rolling wave planning	
Product analysis	
Requirements traceability matrix	
Accepted deliverables	
Assumption	
Decomposition	
Work performance measurements	
WBS dictionary	
Constraint	
Group creativity techniques	
Variance analysis	
Work package	
Project scope statement	
Scope change	
Scope baseline	
Inspection	
Prototypes	
Control account	
Scope management plan	

Project Time Management

The left column holds glossary terms from the Project Time Management knowledge area. The right column has *PMBOK Guide* glossary definitions for the terms. Match the term to the *PMBOK Guide* glossary definition by entering the definition number next to the term.

Term	Definition
___ Milestone	1. A schedule compression technique in which activities or phases normally done in sequence are performed in parallel for at least a portion of their duration.
___ Network diagram	2. The amount of time whereby a successor activity can be advanced with respect to a predecessor activity.
___ Effort	3. A technique used to shorten the schedule duration for the least incremental cost by adding resources.
___ Duration	4. The total amount of time that a schedule activity may be delayed or extended from its early start date without delaying the project finish date or violating a schedule constraint.
___ Analogous estimating	5. A technique for estimating the duration or cost of an activity or a project using historical data from a similar activity or project.
___ Lead	6. A significant point or event in the project, program, or portfolio.
___ Lag	7. The logical relationship in which a successor activity cannot finish until a predecessor activity has finished.
___ Backward pass	8. A critical path technique for calculating the late start and late finish dates by working backward through the schedule model from the project end date.
___ Early finish date	9. The amount of time whereby the successor activity is required to be delayed with respect to a predecessor activity.
___ Total float	10. The total number of work periods (not including holidays or other nonworking periods) required to complete a schedule activity or work breakdown structure component. Usually expressed as workdays or workweeks. Sometimes incorrectly equated with elapsed time.
___ Crashing	11. The number of labor units required to complete a schedule activity or work breakdown structure component, often expressed in hours, days, or weeks.
___ Fast-tracking	12. A graphical representation of the logical relationships among the project schedule activities.
___ Finish-to-finish	13. In the critical path method, the earliest possible point in time when the uncompleted portions of a schedule activity can finish based on the schedule network logic, the data date, and any schedule constraints.

Project Cost Management

The following is a list of earned value (EV) terms and processes from Project Cost Management. Use the following table of selected definitions from the *PMBOK Guide* glossary to match the term with the appropriate definition. *Hint:* Not all terms are used.

Budget

Schedule variance

Cost performance index

Planned value (PV)

Cost variance

Earned value (EV)

Estimate at completion

Cost performance baseline

Actual cost (AC)

Performance measurement baseline

Estimate to complete

Budget at completion

Schedule performance index

Term	Definition
	A measure of schedule efficiency expressed as the ratio of earned value to planned value.
	The expected total cost of completing the work expressed as the sum of the actual cost to date and the estimate to complete.
	The authorized budget assigned to scheduled work.
	The expected cost to finish all the remaining project work.
	A measure of the cost efficiency of budgeted resources expressed as the ratio of earned value to actual cost.
	The amount of budget deficit or surplus at a given point in time, expressed as the difference between the earned value and the actual cost.
	The sum of all the budgets established for the work to be performed.
	The measure of work performed expressed in terms of the budget authorized for that work.
	A measure of schedule performance expressed as the difference between the earned value and the planned value.

Earned Value

For the following, add the equation that matches the earned value (EV) acronym.

SV:

SPI:

CV:

CPI:

ETC:

EAC:

In the following scenario, use the PV, EV, AC, and BAC values for a project to complete the calculations for SV, CV, SPI, CPI, ETC, and EAC. Round to two decimal places for index calculations.

PV = 125,000
EV = 117,000
AC = 133,000
BAC = 225,000

SV:

SPI:

CV:

CPI:

ETC:

EAC:

Project Quality Management

Match the term or process from Project Quality Management next to the appropriate definition in the following table of selected definitions. *Hint:* Note that not all the terms are defined in the *PMBOK Guide* glossary; some are defined throughout this book.

Control chart	Grade
Variable sampling	Scatter diagram
Accuracy	Flowcharting
Customer satisfaction	Pareto chart
Precision	Quality
Cause-and-effect diagram	Specification limits
Attribute sampling	Tolerance

Term	*Definition*
	An assessment of correctness.
	The depiction in a diagram format of the inputs, process actions, and outputs of one or more processes within a system.
	The degree to which a set of inherent characteristics fulfills requirements.
	A category or rank used to distinguish items that have the same functional use but do not share the same requirements for quality.
	A measure of exactness.
	A histogram, ordered by frequency of occurrence, that shows how many results were generated by each identified cause.
	A graphic display of process data over time and against established control limits, and that has a centerline that assists in detecting a trend of plotted values toward either control limit.
	The quantified description of acceptable variation for a quality requirement.
	A decomposition technique that helps trace an undesirable effect back to its root cause.
	The area, on either side of the centerline, or mean, of data plotted on a control chart that meets the customer's requirements for a product or service. This area may be greater than or less than the area defined by the control limits.
	A correlation chart that uses a regression line to explain or to predict how the change in an independent variable will change a dependent variable.

Fill in the blanks with the appropriate quality management tools or technique.

1. If you want to eliminate defects, and you want to start with the element that causes the most defects, you should use a(n) ______ ______.
2. If you're trying to identify where quality problems could occur, you should use ______.
3. Providing training and documenting processes are examples of ______ ______.
4. To measure your project practices against those of comparable projects or organizations in order to identify best practices and generate ideas for improvement, you should use ______.
5. A(n) ______ ______ is used to determine whether a process is stable or has predictable performance.

Project Human Resource Management

In the right column of the following table, enter the name of the Project Human Resource Management process most associated with the tool, technique, or output in the left column.

Tool, technique, or output	*Project Human Resource Management process*
Recognition and rewards	
Organizational charts	
Pre-assignment	
Team-building activities	
Organizational theory	
Conflict management	
Ground rules	
Issue log	
Virtual teams	
Training	
Responsibility assignment matrix (RAM)	

Project Communications Management

In the left column, enter the name of the process, term, or output that matches the definition in the right column.

Process, term, or output	Definition
	Creating, collecting, distributing, storing, retrieving, and the ultimate disposition of project information in accordance with the communications management plan.
	A component of the project, program, or portfolio management plan that describes how, when, and by whom information about the project will be administered and disseminated.
	Developing an appropriate approach and plan for project communications based on stakeholder's information needs and requirements as well as available organizational assets.
	Thoughts or ideas are translated into language by the sender.
	Used for very large volumes of information, or for very large audiences, and requires the recipients to access the communication content at their own discretion.
	Performance reports, deliverable status, schedule progress, and costs incurred.
	Monitoring and controlling communications throughout the entire project life cycle to ensure the information needs of the project stakeholders are met.

Project Risk Management

In the following table, match the term next to the appropriate *PMBOK Guide* glossary definition. *Hint:* Not all terms are used.

Fallback plan	Reserve	Risk register
Risk transference	Trigger	Risk tolerance
Risk mitigation	Threat	Delphi technique
Risk avoidance	Risk register	Risk acceptance
Risk	Opportunity	Probability and impact matrix

Term	Definition
	A provision in the project management plan to mitigate cost and/or schedule risk. Often used with a modifier (for example, management reserve, contingency reserve) to provide further detail on what types of risk are meant to be mitigated.
	A risk response strategy whereby the project team works to eliminate the threat or protect the project from its impact.
	An uncertain event or condition that, if it occurs, has a positive or negative effect on one or more project objectives.
	A risk response strategy whereby the project team acts to reduce the probability of occurrence or impact of a risk.
	The degree, amount, or volume of risk that an organization or individual will withstand.
	The document in which the results of risk analysis and risk response planning are recorded.
	A risk response strategy whereby the project team shifts the impact of a threat to a third party, together with ownership of the response.
	A grid for mapping the probability of each risk occurrence and its impact on project objectives if that risk occurs.
	A risk response strategy whereby the project team decides to acknowledge the risk and not take any action unless the risk occurs.
	An event or situation that indicates that a risk is about to occur.

Project Procurement Management

Fill in the blank(s) with the name of the correct process or term. Not all definitions are in the *PMBOK Guide* glossary.

1. ______ ______ is the process of managing procurement relationships, monitoring contract performance, and making changes and corrections as appropriate.
2. The profit component of compensation to the seller is a(n) ______.
3. ______ ______ ______is the process of documenting project procurement decisions, specifying the approach, and identifying potential sellers.
4. ______ ______ is the process of obtaining seller responses, selecting a seller, and awarding a contract.

5. A type of contract involving payment to the seller for the seller's actual costs, plus a fee typically representing the seller's profit. ______ ______ contracts often include incentive clauses where if the seller meets or exceeds selected project objectives, such as schedule targets or total cost, then the seller receives from the buyer an incentive or bonus payment.

6. ______ ______ is the process of completing each project procurement.

7. A(n) ______ is a mutually binding agreement that obligates the seller to provide the specified product or service or result and obligates the buyer to pay for it.

8. A(n) ______ ______ ______ is an agreement that sets the fee that will be paid for a defined scope of work regardless of the cost or effort to deliver it.

Project Stakeholder Management

In the following table, match the term next to the appropriate *PMBOK Guide* glossary definition.

Identify Stakeholders

Plan Stakeholder Management

Manage Stakeholder Engagement

Control Stakeholder Engagement

Stakeholder register

Stakeholder management plan

Stakeholder engagement assessment matrix

Power/interest grid

Stakeholder analysis

Issue

Term	Definition
	A classification model used for stakeholder analysis.
	A component of the project management plan that identifies the management strategies required to effectively engage stakeholders.
	Monitoring overall stakeholder relationships and adjusting strategies and plans for engaging stakeholders.
	Systematically gathering and analyzing quantitative and qualitative information to determine whose interests should be taken into account throughout the project.

(continued)

Term	Definition
	Identifying the people, groups, or organizations that could impact or be impacted by a decision, an activity, or an outcome of the project; and analyzing and documenting relevant information regarding their interests, involvement, interdependencies, influence, and potential impact on project success.
	A tool used to indicate the current and desired level of stakeholder engagement.
	Communication and working with stakeholders to meet their needs/expectations, address issues as they occur, and foster appropriate stakeholder engagement in project activities throughout the project life cycle.
	A document including the identification, assessment, and classification of project stakeholders.
	Developing appropriate management strategies to effectively engage stakeholders throughout the project life cycle, based on the analysis of their needs, interests, and potential impact on project success.
	A point or matter in question or in dispute, or a point or matter that is not settled and is under discussion or over which there are opposing views or disagreements.

Appendix C Answers

Knowledge Areas and Process Groups

1. Project Procurement Management includes the processes to purchase or acquire the products, services, or results needed from outside the project team.
2. Closing Processes are those processes performed to finalize all activities across all Process Groups to formally close a project or phase.
3. Project Cost Management includes the processes involved in planning, estimating, budgeting, financing, funding, managing, and controlling costs so that the project can be completed within the approved budget.
4. Planning processes are those processes performed to establish the scope of the project, refine the objectives, and define the course of

action required to attain the objectives that the project was undertaken to achieve.

5. Project Risk Management includes the processes of conducting risk management planning, identification, analysis, response planning, and controlling risk on a project.

6. Project Quality Management includes the processes and activities of the performing organization that determine quality policies, objectives, and responsibilities so that the project will satisfy the needs for which it was undertaken.

7. Monitoring and Controlling processes are those processes required to track, review, and regulate the progress and performance of the project; identify any areas in which changes to the plan are required; and initiate the corresponding changes.

8. Project Scope Management includes the processes required to ensure that the project includes all the work required, and only the work required, to complete the project successfully.

9. Project Human Resource Management includes the processes that organize, manage, and lead the project team.

10. Executing processes are those processes performed to complete the work defined in the project management plan to satisfy the project specifications.

11. Project Integration Management includes the processes and activities needed to identify, define, combine, unify, and coordinate the various processes and project management activities within the Project Management process groups.

12. Project Time Management includes the processes required to manage the timely completion of a project.

13. Project Stakeholder Management includes the processes required to identify all people or organizations impacted by the project, analyzing stakeholder expectations and impact on the project, and developing appropriate management strategies for effectively engaging stakeholders in project decisions and execution.

14. Initiating processes are those processes performed to define a new project or a new phase of an existing project by obtaining authorization to start the project or phase.

15. Project Communications Management includes the processes that are required to ensure timely and appropriate planning, collection, creation, distribution, storage, retrieval, management, control, monitoring, and ultimate disposition of project information.

PMP Foundation

Term	Definition
Project phase	A collection of logically related project activities that culminates in the completion of one or more deliverables.
Enterprise environmental factors (EEFs)	Conditions, not under the immediate control of the team, that influence, or direct the project, program, or portfolio.
Project	A temporary endeavor undertaken to create a unique product, service, or result.
Project management	The application of knowledge, skills, tools, and techniques to project activities to meet the project requirements.
Project life cycle	The series of phases that a project passes through from its initiation to its closure.
Matrix organization	Any organizational structure in which the project manager shares responsibility with the functional managers for assigning priorities and for directing the work of persons assigned to the project.
Organizational process assets (OPAs)	Plans, processes, policies, procedures, and knowledge basis that are specific to and used by the performing organization.
Progressive elaboration	The iterative process of increasing the level of detail in a project management plan as greater amounts of information and more accurate estimates become available.

Project Integration Management

Term	Definition
Defect repair	An intentional activity to modify a nonconforming product or product component.
Monitor and Control Project Work	Tracking, reviewing, and reporting the progress to meet the performance objectives defined in the project management plan.
Project charter	A document issued by the project initiator or sponsor that formally authorizes the existence of a project, and provides the project manager with the authority to apply organizational resources to project activities.
Project management plan	The document that describes how the project will be executed, monitored, and controlled.

Term	Definition
Change request	A formal proposal to modify any document, deliverable, or baseline.
Direct and Manage Project Execution	Leading and performing the work defined in the project management plan and implementing approved changes to achieve the project's objectives.
Preventive action	An intentional activity that ensures the future performance of the project work is aligned with the project management plan.
Close Project or Phase	Finalizing all activities across all project management process groups to formally complete the project or phase.
Develop Project Charter	Developing a document that formally authorizes the existence of a project and provides the project manager with the authority to apply organizational resources to project activities.
Develop Project Management Plan	Defining, preparing, and coordinating all subsidiary plans and integrating them into a comprehensive project management plan.
Corrective action	An intentional activity that realigns the performance of the project work with the project management plan.
Perform Integrated Change Control	Reviewing all change requests; approving changes, and managing changes to deliverables, organizational process assets, project documents, and project management plan; and communicating their disposition.

Project Scope Management

Tool, technique, or output	Project Scope Management process
Rolling wave planning	Create WBS
Product analysis	Define Scope
Requirements traceability matrix	Collect Requirements
Accepted deliverables	Validate Scope
Assumption	Define Scope
Decomposition	Create WBS

(continued)

Tool, technique, or output	*Project Scope Management process*
Work performance measurements	Control Scope
WBS dictionary	Create WBS
Constraint	Define Scope
Group creativity techniques	Collect Requirements
Variance analysis	Control Scope
Work package	Create WBS
Project scope statement	Define Scope
Scope change	Control Scope
Scope baseline	Create WBS
Inspection	Validate Scope
Prototypes	Collect Requirements
Control account	Create WBS
Scope management plan	Plan Scope Management

Project Time Management

Term	*Definition*
6 Milestone	1. A schedule compression technique in which activities or phases normally done in sequence are performed in parallel for at least a portion of their duration.
12 Network diagram	2. The amount of time whereby a successor activity can be advanced with respect to a predecessor activity.
11 Effort	3. A technique used to shorten the schedule duration for the least incremental cost by adding resources.
10 Duration	4. The total amount of time that a schedule activity may be delayed or extended from its early start date without delaying the project finish date or violating a schedule constraint.
5 Analogous estimating	5. A technique for estimating the duration or cost of an activity or a project using historical data from a similar activity or project.

Term	Definition
2 Lead	6. A significant point or event in the project, program, or portfolio.
9 Lag	7. The logical relationship in which a successor activity cannot finish until a predecessor activity has finished.
8 Backward pass	8. A critical path technique for calculating the late start and late finish dates by working backward through the schedule model from the project end date.
13 Early finish date	9. The amount of time whereby the successor activity is required to be delayed with respect to a predecessor activity.
4 Total float	10. The total number of work periods (not including holidays or other nonworking periods) required to complete a schedule activity or work breakdown structure component. Usually expressed as workdays or workweeks. Sometimes incorrectly equated with elapsed time.
3 Crashing	11. The number of labor units required to complete a schedule activity or work breakdown structure component, often expressed in hours, days, or weeks.
1 Fast-tracking	12. A graphical representation of the logical relationships among the project schedule activities.
7 Finish-to-finish	13. In the critical path method, the earliest possible point in time when the uncompleted portions of a schedule activity can finish based on the schedule network logic, the data date, and any schedule constraints.

Project Cost Management

Term	Definition
Schedule performance index	A measure of schedule efficiency expressed as the ratio of earned value to planned value.
Estimate at completion	The expected total cost of completing the work expressed as the sum of the actual cost to date and the estimate to complete.
Planned value (PV)	The authorized budget assigned to scheduled work.
Estimate to complete	The expected cost to finish all the remaining project work.
Cost performance index	A measure of the cost efficiency of budgeted resources expressed as the ratio of earned value to actual cost.

(continued)

Term	*Definition*
Cost variance	The amount of budget deficit or surplus at a given point in time, expressed as the difference between the earned value and the actual cost.
Budget at completion	The sum of all the budgets established for the work to be performed.
Earned value (EV)	The measure of work performed expressed in terms of the budget authorized for that work.
Schedule variance	A measure of schedule performance expressed as the difference between the earned value and the planned value.

Earned Value

SV:	EV – PV
SPI:	EV / PV
CV:	EV – AC
CPI:	EV / AC
ETC:	BAC – EV (may be divided by CPI or CPI × SPI)
EAC:	AC + ((BAC – EV) / CPI) *Note:* Divisor may be CPI × SPI or other variants

PV = 125,000
EV = 117,000
AC = 133,000
BAC = 225,000

SV:	–8,000
SPI:	.94
CV:	–16,000
CPI:	.88
ETC:	108,000
EAC:	255,682

Project Quality Management

Term	*Definition*
Accuracy	An assessment of correctness.
Flowcharting	The depiction in a diagram format of the inputs, process actions, and outputs of one or more processes within a system.
Quality	The degree to which a set of inherent characteristics fulfills requirements.
Grade	A category or rank used to distinguish items that have the same functional use but do not share the same requirements for quality.
Precision	A measure of exactness.
Pareto chart	A histogram, ordered by frequency of occurrence, that shows how many results were generated by each identified cause.
Control chart	A graphic display of process data over time and against established control limits, and that has a centerline that assists in detecting a trend of plotted values toward either control limit.
Tolerance	The quantified description of acceptable variation for a quality requirement.
Cause-and-effect diagram	A decomposition technique that helps trace an undesirable effect back to its root cause.
Specification limits	The area, on either side of the centerline, or mean, of data plotted on a control chart that meets the customer's requirements for a product or service. This area may be greater than or less than the area defined by the control limits.
Scatter diagram	A correlation chart that uses a regression line to explain or to predict how the change in an independent variable will change a dependent variable.

1. If you want to eliminate defects, and you want to start with the element that causes the most defects, you should use a Pareto chart.
2. If you are trying to identify where quality problems could occur, you should use flowcharting.
3. Providing training and documenting processes are examples of preventive costs.
4. To measure your project practices against those of comparable projects or organizations in order to identify best practices and generate ideas for improvement, you should use benchmarking.
5. A control chart is used to determine whether a process is stable or has predictable performance.

Project Human Resource Management

Tool, technique, or output	Project Human Resource Management process
Recognition and rewards	Develop Project Team
Organizational charts	Plan Human Resource Management
Pre-assignment	Acquire Project Team
Team-building activities	Develop Project Team
Organizational theory	Plan Human Resource Management
Conflict management	Manage Project Team
Ground rules	Develop Project Team
Issue log	Manage Project Team
Virtual teams	Acquire Project Team
Training	Develop Project Team
Responsibility assignment matrix (RAM)	Plan Human Resource Management

Project Communications Management

Process, term, or output	Definition
Manage Communications	Creating, collecting, distributing, storing, retrieving, and the ultimate disposition of project information in accordance with the communications management plan.
Communications management plan	A component of the project, program, or portfolio management plan that describes how, when, and by whom information about the project will be administered and disseminated.
Plan Communications Management	Developing an appropriate approach and plan for project communications based on stakeholder's information needs and requirements, and available organizational assets.
Encode	Thoughts or ideas are translated into language by the sender.
Pull communication	Used for very large volumes of information, or for very large audiences, and requires the recipients to access the communication content at their own discretion.
Project communications	Performance reports, deliverable status, schedule progress, and costs incurred.
Control Communications	Monitoring and controlling communications throughout the entire project life cycle to ensure the information needs of the project stakeholders are met.

Project Risk Management

Term	*Definition*
Reserve	A provision in the project management plan to mitigate cost and/or schedule risk. Often used with a modifier (for example, management reserve, contingency reserve) to provide further detail on what types of risk are meant to be mitigated.
Risk avoidance	A risk response strategy whereby the project team works to eliminate the threat or protect the project from its impact.
Risk	An uncertain event or condition that, if it occurs, has a positive or negative effect on one or more project objectives.
Risk mitigation	A risk response strategy whereby the project team acts to reduce the probability of occurrence or impact of a risk.
Risk tolerance	The degree, amount, or volume of risk that an organization or individual will withstand.
Risk register	The document in which the results of risk analysis and risk response planning are recorded.
Risk transference	A risk response strategy whereby the project team shifts the impact of a threat to a third party, together with ownership of the response.
Probability and Impact Matrix	A grid for mapping the probability of each risk occurrence and its impact on project objectives if that risk occurs.
Risk acceptance	A risk response strategy whereby the project team decides to acknowledge the risk and not take any action unless the risk occurs.
Trigger condition	An event or situation that indicates that a risk is about to occur.

Project Procurement Management

1. Control Procurements is the process of managing procurement relationships, monitoring contract performance, and making changes and corrections as appropriate.
2. The profit component of compensation to the seller is a fee.
3. Plan Procurement Management is the process of documenting project procurement decisions, specifying the approach, and identifying potential sellers.
4. Conduct Procurements is the process of obtaining seller responses, selecting a seller, and awarding a contract.

5. A type of contract involving payment to the seller for the seller's actual costs, plus a fee typically representing seller's profit. Cost-reimbursable contracts often include incentive clauses where if the seller meets or exceeds selected project objectives, such as schedule targets or total cost, then the seller receives from the buyer an incentive or bonus payment.
6. Close Procurements is the process of completing each project procurement.
7. A contract is a mutually binding agreement that obligates the seller to provide the specified product or service or result and obligates the buyer to pay for it.
8. A fixed-price contract is an agreement that sets the fee that will be paid for a defined scope of work regardless of the cost or effort to deliver it.

Project Stakeholder Management

Term	*Definition*
Power/interest grid	A classification model used for stakeholder analysis.
Stakeholder management plan	A component of the project management plan that identifies the management strategies required to effectively engage stakeholders.
Control Stakeholder Engagement	Monitoring overall stakeholder relationships and adjusting strategies and plans for engaging stakeholders.
Stakeholder analysis	Systematically gathering and analyzing quantitative and qualitative information to determine whose interests should be taken into account throughout the project.
Identify Stakeholders	Identifying the people, groups, or organizations that could impact or be impacted by a decision, an activity, or an outcome of the project; and analyzing and documenting relevant information regarding their interests, involvement, interdependencies, influence, and potential impact on project success.
Stakeholder engagement assessment matrix	A tool used to indicate the current and desired level of stakeholder engagement.
Manage Stakeholder Engagement	Communication and working with stakeholders to meet their needs/expectations, address issues as they occur, and foster appropriate stakeholder engagement in project activities throughout the project life cycle.

Term	Definition
Stakeholder register	A document including the identification, assessment, and classification of project stakeholders.
Plan Stakeholder Management	Developing appropriate management strategies to effectively engage stakeholders throughout the project life cycle, based on the analysis of their needs, interests, and potential impact on project success.
Issue	A point or matter in question or in dispute, or a point or matter that is not settled and is under discussion or over which there are opposing views or disagreements.

Appendix D: Exam Objective Cross Walk

The PMP exam tests information in each of five domains: initiating, planning, executing, monitoring and controlling, and closing. To optimize your chances of doing well on the exam, remember the following information about how the exam is designed and how the exam objectives are tested.

- Each domain has associated tasks that assess a project manager's competence in that domain.
- Each domain has knowledge and skills that are required to competently perform the tasks in that domain.
- In addition to the knowledge and skills associated with each domain, cross-cutting knowledge and skills are used in multiple domains and tasks.
- The information from the PMI Code of Ethics and Professional Conduct (the Code) is integrated into exam questions.

Information in this appendix summarizes

- Domain tasks and where you can find them (domain tasks are listed as objectives in the front of each chapter)
- Domain-specific knowledge and skills
- Cross-cutting knowledge and skills, as well as the minibooks that have processes where the cross-cutting knowledge and skills are applied
- Code of Ethics and Professional Conduct standards, as well as where you can find an example of how each standard could be integrated into an exam question

Domain Tasks

The domain tasks assess your competence in each domain. The domain and the percent of exam questions from that domain are listed in the following tables.

Table D-1	Initiating, 13%
Task 1	
Book II, Chapter 1	Meet with the sponsor, customer, and other subject matter experts and review available information to evaluate the feasibility of new products or services, keeping in mind given assumptions and constraints.
Task 2	
Book II, Chapter 2	Given business and compliance requirements, define the high-level scope needed to meet customer expectations.
Task 3	
Book II, Chapter 3	Analyze stakeholders to identify expectations and gain support for the project.
Task 4	
Book II, Chapter 2	Use historical data, information on the environment, and expert judgment to identify and document high-level risks, assumptions, and constraints. Use the information to propose an approach to carry out the project.
Task 5	
Book II, Chapter 2	Analyze stakeholder requirements to document the scope, milestones, and deliverables and complete a project charter.
Task 6	
Book II, Chapter 2	Gain commitment for the project and formalize project management authority by obtaining approval for the project charter.

Table D-2	Planning, 24%
Task 1	
Book III, Chapter 2	Using the project charter, lessons learned, and requirements-gathering techniques, such as interviews, brainstorming, focus groups, and so on, assess the project requirements, assumptions, and constraints to determine project deliverables.
Task 2	
Book III, Chapter 2	Deconstruct the project into a WBS in order to manage the project scope.

Task 3	
Book IV, Chapter 1	Using cost-estimating techniques, develop a budget plan based on the project scope in order to manage project cost.
Task 4	
Book III, Chapter 3	Using the scope and resource plan, create a project schedule to manage the timely completion of the project.
Task 5	
Book IV, Chapter 3	Develop roles and responsibilities and an organizational structure as part of the human resource management plan to help manage project staff.
Task 6	
Book IV, Chapter 4	Use stakeholder requirements and the project organizational structure to create a communications plan that will help manage the flow of project information.
Task 7	
Book V, Chapter 1	Review the project scope and schedule to determine what, if any, scope or resources will need to be procured.
Task 8	
Book IV, Chapter 2	Review the project scope to determine the quality requirements and standards needed to meet stakeholder expectations.
Task 9	
Book III, Chapter 1	Define and document how changes will be addressed to track and manage changes throughout the project.
Task 10	
Book V, Chapter 1	Create a risk management plan that provides guidance for identifying, analyzing, prioritizing, and developing response strategies to manage uncertainty throughout the project.
Task 11	
Book III, Chapter 1	Present the project management plan to attain approval before executing the project.
Task 12	
Book III, Chapter 1	Hold a kick-off meeting to start the project and communicate key project information.

Table D-3	Executing, 30%
Task 1	
Book VI, Chapter 2	Acquire and manage project resources, both internal and external, to execute the project. Follow the procurement management plan for acquiring external resources.
Task 2	
Book VI, Chapter 1	Execute project activities defined in the project management plan to create project deliverables on time and within budget.
Task 3	
Book VI, Chapter 1	Follow the quality management plan, using appropriate tools and techniques to assure work and scope meet the quality requirements and standards.
Task 4	
Book VI, Chapter 1	Follow the change management plan with regards to processes and procedures and implement approved changes.
Task 5	
Book VIII, Chapter 4	Actively employ risk management techniques as documented in the risk management plan to minimize the impact of risk on the project.
Task 6	
Book VI, Chapter 2	Employ leadership, training, motivating, mentoring, and other interpersonal skills to maximize team performance.
Book VI, Chapter 3	Implement the procurement of project resources in accordance with the procurement plan.
Book VI, Chapter 3	Ensure a common understanding by setting expectations in accordance with the project plan to align the stakeholder and team members.

Table D-4	Monitoring and Controlling, 25%
Task 1	
Book VII, Chapter 1 Book VII, Chapter 2 Book VII, Chapter 3 Book VIII, Chapter 3	Measure project performance, identify and quantify variances, and determine appropriate preventive and corrective actions. Communicate status to stakeholders per the communication management plan.

Task 2	
Book VII, Chapter 1 Book VII, Chapter 2 Book VII, Chapter 3	Ensure baseline integrity by updating the project management plan in response to approved changes and communicating those approved changes to the team.
Task 3	
Book VIII, Chapter 2	Control quality and ensure that project deliverables are aligned with the quality standards established in the project quality plan by using appropriate tools and techniques (such as testing, inspection, and control charts) to adhere to customer requirements.
Task 4	
Book VIII, Chapter 3	Conduct risk reassessment on a regular basis and implement response strategies as indicated in the risk register.
Task 5	
Book VI, Chapter 3	Minimize the impact of issues with the project schedule cost and resources by using the issue register to manage issues and assign corrective actions.
Task 6	
Book VIII, Chapter 3	Communicate project status and continue to ensure the project is aligned with business needs.
Book VIII, Chapter 4	Administer contracts and measure contractor performance, identify and quantify variances, and determine appropriate preventive and corrective actions.

Table D-5	**Closing, 8%**
Task 1	
Book IX, Chapter 1	Confirm that the project scope and deliverables are complete by attaining final acceptance by the project sponsor and customer.
Task 2	
Book IX, Chapter 1	Facilitate project closure by transferring ownership and management of project deliverables.

(continued)

Table D-5 (continued)

Task 3	
Book IX, Chapter 1	Formally close the project and all contracts by obtaining legal, financial, and administrative closure, thus eliminating further liability.
Task 4	
Book IX, Chapter 1	Write the final project report that communicates final project performance, including any variances and project issues. Distribute to appropriate stakeholders.
Task 5	
Book IX, Chapter 1	Conduct a thorough project review to collect and document lessons learned and contribute them to the organization's knowledge base.
Task 6	
Book IX, Chapter 1	Collect, organize, and archive project and contract documents and records to comply with regulatory requirements, retain for future projects, and be available for audit purposes.

Domain-Specific Knowledge and Skills

The following knowledge and skills are listed by domain. In the final chapter of each process group in the book, I identify the knowledge and skills listed in that process group and where you can find examples.

Initiating Knowledge and Skills

Initiating knowledge and skills are used to initiate the project and phases in the project life cycle.

- Cost-benefit analysis
- Business case development
- Project selection criteria (for example, cost, feasibility, impact)
- Stakeholder-identification techniques
- Risk-identification techniques
- Elements of a project charter

Planning Knowledge and Skills

Planning knowledge and skills are used to elaborate the project objectives that were identified in the initiating processes.

- Requirements-gathering techniques
- Work breakdown structure (WBS) tools and techniques
- Time-, budget-, and cost-estimation techniques
- Scope-management techniques
- Resource-planning process
- Workflow-diagramming techniques
- Types and uses of organization charts
- Elements, purpose, and techniques of project planning
- Elements, purpose, and techniques of communications planning
- Elements, purpose, and techniques of procurement planning
- Elements, purpose, and techniques of quality management planning
- Elements, purpose, and techniques of change management planning
- Elements, purpose, and techniques of risk management planning

Executing Knowledge and Skills

Executing knowledge and skills are used to manage the project work and the team members.

- Project-monitoring tools and techniques
- Elements of a statement of work
- Interaction of work breakdown structure elements within the project schedule
- Project-budgeting tools and techniques
- Quality-standard tools
- Continuous-improvement processes

Monitor and Control Knowledge and Skills

Monitoring and controlling skills are used make sure the project is proceeding as planned and to take appropriate actions to correct product and project progress as needed.

- Performance measurement and tracking techniques (for example, EV, CPM, PERT)
- Project control limits (for example, thresholds, tolerance)
- Project performance metrics (for example, efforts, costs, milestones)
- Cost-analysis techniques
- Variance and trend analysis techniques
- Project plan management techniques
- Change management techniques
- Integrated change control processes
- Risk identification and analysis techniques
- Risk-response techniques (for example, transference, mitigation, insurance, acceptance)
- Problem-solving techniques (including root cause analysis)
- Reporting procedures

Closing Knowledge and Skills

Closing knowledge and skills are used to close out the project, a phase in the project life cycle, and procurement contracts.

- Contract closure requirements
- Basic project accounting principles
- Close-out procedures
- Feedback techniques
- Project-review techniques
- Archiving techniques and statutes
- Compliance (statute/organization)
- Transition planning techniques

Cross-Cutting Skills and Knowledge

Cross-cutting knowledge and skills cut across all process groups. You will need the skills throughout your project. However, you may need them with more frequency or intensity during some process groups than others. Therefore, at the beginning of each process group, I inserted a sidebar that identifies the cross-cutting skills you are most likely to use in that process group. The following table identifies the minibook or minibooks with the processes where each specific cross-cutting skill would most likely be used.

Table D-6 Cross-cutting Skills and Knowledge

	Minibook							
	II	III	IV	V	VI	VII	VIII	IX
Active listening	X	X	X	X	X			
Brainstorming techniques		X	X	X				
Conflict resolution techniques		X	X		X			
Cultural sensitivity and diversity		X	X	X	X			
Data-gathering techniques	X	X	X	X	X	X	X	X
Decision-making techniques		X	X	X	X			
Facilitation	X	X	X	X	X			
Information management tools, techniques, and methods		X	X	X	X	X	X	X
Leadership tools and techniques		X	X	X	X			
Negotiating		X	X	X	X			
Oral and written communication techniques, channels, and applications	X	X	X	X	X	X	X	X
Presentation tools and techniques					X	X	X	
Prioritization/time management					X			
Problem-solving tools and techniques		X	X	X	X	X	X	
Project management software		X	X	X		X	X	
Relationship management		X	X	X	X	X	X	
Stakeholder impact analysis	X	X	X	X	X	X	X	
Targeting communications to intended audiences (for example, team, stakeholders, customers)		X	X	X	X	X	X	
Team motivation methods					X			

Code of Ethics and Professional Conduct

The Code of Ethics and Professional Conduct (the Code) guides our behavior as project managers. It establishes standards that are mandatory and standards that we should aspire to (aspirational standards). The standards cover responsibility, respect, fairness, and honesty. The following table shows the standard in the left column; the right column shows where in the book you can find a discussion on the standard. I emphasized some of the standards in multiple locations because they are particularly relevant in the executing and monitoring and controlling processes. Any standard can show up in a question from any process group. I also point them out in specific chapters just to give you an idea of how a standard can be applied in an exam question.

Table D-7 Code of Ethics and Professional Conduct

Responsibility Aspirational Standards	*Find Here*
We make decisions and take actions based on the best interests of society, public safety, and the environment.	Book VI, Chapter 2
We accept only those assignments that are consistent with our background, experience, skills, and qualifications.	Book VII, Chapter 1
We fulfill the commitments that we undertake — we do what we say we will do.	Book VII, Chapter 1
When we make errors or omissions, we take ownership and make corrections promptly. When we discover errors or omissions caused by others, we communicate them to the appropriate body as soon they are discovered. We accept accountability for any issues resulting from our errors or omissions and any resulting consequences.	Book VII, Chapter 1
We protect proprietary or confidential information that has been entrusted to us.	Book VIII, Chapter 4
We uphold this Code and hold each other accountable to it.	Book VII, Chapter 1
Responsibility Mandatory Standards	
We inform ourselves and uphold the policies, rules, regulations, and laws that govern our work, professional, and volunteer activities.	Book I, Chapter 2
We report unethical or illegal conduct to appropriate management and, if necessary, to those affected by the conduct.	Book VIII, Chapter 2
We bring violations of this Code to the attention of the appropriate body for resolution.	Book VIII, Chapter 2

Responsibility Mandatory Standards	
We file ethics complaints only when they are substantiated by facts.	Book VIII, Chapter 2
We pursue disciplinary action against an individual who retaliates against a person raising ethics concerns.	Book VIII, Chapter 2
Respect Aspirational Standards	
We inform ourselves about the norms and customs of others and avoid engaging in behaviors they might consider disrespectful.	Book VI, Chapter 2
We listen to others' points of view, seeking to understand them.	Book VI, Chapter 2
We approach directly those persons with whom we have a conflict or disagreement.	Book VI, Chapter 2
We conduct ourselves in a professional manner, even when it is not reciprocated.	Book VI, Chapter 2
Respect Mandatory Standards	
We negotiate in good faith.	Book VI, Chapter 3
We do not exercise the power of our expertise or position to influence the decisions or actions of others in order to benefit personally at their expense.	Book VI, Chapter 2
We do not act in an abusive manner toward others.	Book VI, Chapter 2
We respect the property rights of others.	Book VI, Chapter 3 Book VIII, Chapter 4
Fairness Aspirational Standards	
We demonstrate transparency in our decision-making process.	Book VI, Chapter 2
We constantly reexamine our impartiality and objectivity, taking corrective action as appropriate.	Book VI, Chapter 3
We provide equal access to information to those who are authorized to have that information.	Book VI, Chapter 3
We make opportunities equally available to qualified candidates.	Book VI, Chapter 3
Fairness Mandatory Standards	
We proactively and fully disclose any real or potential conflicts of interest to the appropriate stakeholders.	Book VI, Chapter 3

(continued)

Table D-7 (continued)

Fairness Mandatory Standards	
When we realize that we have a real or potential conflict of interest, we refrain from engaging in the decision-making process or otherwise attempting to influence outcomes, unless or until * We have made full disclosure to the affected stakeholders. * We have an approved mitigation plan. * We have obtained the consent of the stakeholders to proceed.	Book VI, Chapter 3
We do not hire or fire, reward or punish, or award or deny contracts based on personal considerations, including but not limited to, favoritism, nepotism, or bribery.	Book VI, Chapter 2
We do not discriminate against others based on, but not limited to, gender, race, age, religion, disability, nationality, or sexual orientation.	Book VI, Chapter 2
We apply the rules of the organization (employer, Project Management Institute, or other group) without favoritism or prejudice.	Book VII, Chapter 1
Honesty Aspirational Standards	
We earnestly seek to understand the truth.	Book VI, Chapter 3 Book VIII, Chapter 3
We are truthful in our communications and in our conduct.	Book VI, Chapter 3 Book VII, Chapter 3 Book VIII, Chapter 3
We provide accurate information in a timely manner.	Book VI, Chapter 3 Book VII, Chapter 3 Book VIII, Chapter 3
We make commitments and promises, implied or explicit, in good faith.	Book VIII, Chapter 4
We strive to create an environment in which others feel safe to tell the truth.	Book VI, Chapter 2
Honesty Mandatory Standards	
We do not engage in or condone behavior that is designed to deceive others, including but not limited to, making misleading or false statements, stating half-truths, providing information out of context or withholding information that, if known, would render our statements as misleading or incomplete.	Book VII, Chapter 3 Book VIII, Chapter 3
We do not engage in dishonest behavior with the intention of personal gain or at the expense of another.	Book VIII, Chapter 4

Appendix E: Glossary

1. Inclusions and Exclusions

This glossary includes terms that are:

- Unique or nearly unique to project management (e.g., project scope statement, work package, work breakdown structure, critical path method).
- Not unique to project management, but used differently or with a narrower meaning in project management than in general everyday usage (e.g., early start date).

This glossary generally does not include:

- Application area-specific terms.
- Terms used in project management which do not differ in any material way from everyday use (e.g., calendar day, delay).
- Compound terms whose meaning is clear from the combined meanings of the component parts.
- Variants when the meaning of the variant is clear from the base term.

As a result of the above inclusions and exclusions, this glossary includes:

- A preponderance of terms related to Project Scope Management, Project Time Management, and Project Risk Management, since many of the terms used in these Knowledge Areas are unique or nearly unique to project management.
- Many terms from Project Quality Management, since these terms are used more narrowly than in their everyday usage.
- Relatively few terms related to Project Human Resource Management, Project Communications Management, and Project Stakeholder Management, since most of the terms used in these Knowledge Areas do not differ significantly from everyday usage.
- Relatively few terms related to Project Cost Management, Project Integration Management, and Project Procurement Management, since many of the terms used in these Knowledge Areas have narrow meanings that are unique to a particular application area.

2. Common Acronyms

AC	actual cost
ACWP	actual cost of work performed
BAC	budget at completion
CCB	change control board
COQ	cost of quality
CPAF	cost plus award fee
CPFF	cost plus fixed fee
CPI	cost performance index
CPIF	cost plus incentive fee
CPM	critical path methodology
CV	cost variance
EAC	estimate at completion
EF	early finish date
EMV	expected monetary value
ES	early start date
ETC	estimate to complete
EV	earned value
EVM	earned value management
FF	finish-to-finish
FFP	firm fixed price contract
FMEA	failure mode and effect analysis
FP-EPA	fixed price with economic price adjustment
FPIF	fixed price incentive fee
FS	finish to start
IFB	invitation for bid
LF	late finish date
LOE	level of effort
LS	late start date
OBS	organizational breakdown structure
PDM	precedence diagramming method
PMBOK	Project Management Body of Knowledge
PV	planned value
QFD	quality function deployment
RACI	responsible, accountable, consult, and inform

RAM	responsibility assignment matrix
RBS	risk breakdown structure
RFI	request for information
RFP	request for proposal
RFQ	request for quotation
SF	start-to-finish
SOW	statement of work
SPI	schedule performance index
SS	start-to-start
SV	schedule variance
SWOT	strengths, weaknesses, opportunities, and threats
T&M	time and material contract
WBS	work breakdown structure

3. Definitions

Many of the words defined here have broader, and in some cases different, dictionary definitions.

The definitions use the following conventions:

- In some cases, a single glossary term consists of multiple words (e.g., risk urgency assessment).
- When synonyms are included, no definition is given and the reader is directed to the preferred term (i.e., see preferred term).
- Related terms that are not synonyms are cross-referenced at the end of the definition (i.e., see also related term).

Acceptance Criteria. A set of conditions that is required to be met before deliverables are accepted.

Accepted Deliverables. Products, results, or capabilities produced by a project and validated by the project customer or sponsors as meeting their specified acceptance criteria.

Accuracy. Within the quality management system, *accuracy* is an assessment of correctness.

Acquire Project Team. The process of confirming human resource availability and obtaining the team necessary to complete project activities.

Acquisition. Obtaining human and material resources necessary to perform project activities. Acquisition implies a cost of resources, and is not necessarily financial.

Activity. A distinct, scheduled portion of work performed during the course of a project.

Activity Attributes. Multiple attributes associated with each schedule activity that can be included within the activity list. Activity attributes include activity codes, predecessor activities, successor activities, logical relationships, leads and lags, resource requirements, imposed dates, constraints, and assumptions.

Activity Code. One or more numerical or text values that identify characteristics of the work or in some way categorize the schedule activity that allows filtering and ordering of activities within reports.

Activity Cost Estimates. The projected cost of the schedule activity that includes the cost for all resources required to perform and complete the activity, including all cost types and cost components.

Activity Duration. The time in calendar units between the start and finish of a schedule activity. See also *duration.*

Activity Duration Estimate. A quantitative assessment of the likely amount or outcome for the duration of an activity.

Activity Identifier. A short, unique numeric or text identification assigned to each schedule activity to differentiate that project activity from other activities. Typically unique within any one project schedule network diagram.

Activity List. A documented tabulation of schedule activities that shows the activity description, activity identifier, and a sufficiently detailed scope of work description so project team members understand what work is to be performed.

Activity Network Diagrams. See *project schedule network diagram.*

Activity-on-Node (AON). See *precedence diagramming method (PDM).*

Activity Resource Requirements. The types and quantities of resources required for each activity in a work package.

Actual Cost (AC). The realized cost incurred for the work performed on an activity during a specific time period.

Actual Duration. The time in calendar units between the actual start date of the schedule activity and either the data date of the project schedule if the schedule activity is in progress or the actual finish date if the schedule activity is complete.

Adaptive Life Cycle. A project life cycle, also known as change-driven or agile methods, that is intended to facilitate change and require a high degree of ongoing stakeholder involvement. Adaptive life cycles are also iterative and incremental, but differ in that iterations are very rapid (usually 2–4 weeks in length) and are fixed in time and resources.

Additional Quality Planning Tools. A set of tools used to define the quality requirements and to plan effective quality management activities. They include, but are not limited to: brainstorming, force field analysis, nominal group techniques and quality management and control tools.

Adjusting Leads and Lags. A technique used to find ways to bring project activities that are behind into alignment with plan during project execution.

Advertising. The process of calling public attention to a project or effort.

Affinity Diagram. A group creativity technique that allows large numbers of ideas to be classified into groups for review and analysis.

Agreements. Any document or communication that defines the initial intentions of a project. This can take the form of a contract, memorandum of understanding (MOU), letters of agreement, verbal agreements, email, etc.

Alternative Analysis. A technique used to evaluate identified options in order to select which options or approaches to use to execute and perform the work of the project.

Alternatives Generation. A technique used to develop as many potential options as possible in order to identify different approaches to execute and perform the work of the project.

Analogous Estimating. A technique for estimating the duration or cost of an activity or a project using historical data from a similar activity or project.

Analytical Techniques. Various techniques used to evaluate, analyze, or forecast potential outcomes based on possible variations of project or environmental variables and their relationships with other variables.

Application Area. A category of projects that have common components significant in such projects, but are not needed or present in all projects. Application areas are usually defined in terms of either the product (i.e., by similar technologies or production methods) or the type of customer (i.e., internal versus external, government versus commercial) or industry sector (i.e., utilities, automotive, aerospace, information technologies, etc.). Application areas can overlap.

Applying Leads and Lags. A technique that is used to adjust the amount of time between predecessor and successor activities.

Apportioned Effort. An activity where effort is allotted proportionately across certain discrete efforts and not divisible into discrete efforts. [Note: Apportioned effort is one of three earned value management (EVM) types of activities used to measure work performance.]

Approved Change Request. A change request that has been processed through the integrated change control process and approved.

Approved Change Requests Review. A review of the change requests to verify that these were implemented as approved.

Assumption. A factor in the planning process that is considered to be true, real, or certain, without proof or demonstration.

Assumptions Analysis. A technique that explores the accuracy of assumptions and identifies risks to the project from inaccuracy, inconsistency, or incompleteness of assumptions.

Attribute Sampling. Method of measuring quality that consists of noting the presence (or absence) of some characteristic (attribute) in each of the units under consideration. After each unit is inspected, the decision is made to accept a lot, reject it, or inspect another unit.

Authority. The right to apply project resources, expend funds, make decisions, or give approvals.

Backlog. A listing of product requirements and deliverables to be completed, written as stories, and prioritized by the business to manage and organize the project's work.

Backward Pass. A critical path method technique for calculating the late start and late finish dates by working backward through the schedule model from the project end date.

Bar Chart. A graphic display of schedule-related information. In the typical bar chart, schedule activities or work breakdown structure components are listed down the left side of the chart, dates are shown across the top, and activity durations are shown as date-placed horizontal bars. See also *Gantt chart.*

Baseline. The approved version of a work product that can be changed only through formal change control procedures and is used as a basis for comparison.

Basis of Estimates. Supporting documentation outlining the details used in establishing project estimates such as assumptions, constraints, level of detail, ranges, and confidence levels.

Benchmarking. Benchmarking is the comparison of actual or planned practices, such as processes and operations, to those of comparable organizations to identify best practices, generate ideas for improvement, and provide a basis for measuring performance.

Bidder Conference. The meetings with prospective sellers prior to the preparation of a bid or proposal to ensure all prospective vendors have a clear and common understanding of the procurement. Also known as contractor conferences, vendor conferences, or pre-bid conferences.

Bottom-Up Estimating. A method of estimating project duration or cost by aggregating the estimates of the lower-level components of the work breakdown structure (WBS).

Brainstorming. A general data gathering and creativity technique that can be used to identify risks, ideas, or solutions to issues by using a group of team members or subject matter experts.

Budget. The approved estimate for the project or any work breakdown structure component or any schedule activity.

Budget at Completion (BAC). The sum of all budgets established for the work to be performed.

Buffer. See *reserve.*

Business Case. A documented economic feasibility study used to establish validity of the benefits of a selected component lacking sufficient definition and that is used as a basis for the authorization of further project management activities.

Business Value. A concept that is unique to each organization and includes tangible and intangible elements. Through the effective use of project, program, and portfolio management disciplines, organizations will possess the ability to employ reliable, established processes to meet enterprise objectives and obtain greater business value from their investments.

Buyer. The acquirer of products, services, or results for an organization.

Cause and Effect Diagram. A decomposition technique that helps trace an undesirable effect back to its root cause.

Central Tendency. A property of the central limit theorem predicting that the data observations in a distribution will tend to group around a central location. The three typical measures of central tendency are the mean, median, and mode.

Change Control. A process whereby modifications to documents, deliverables, or baselines associated with the project are identified, documented, approved, or rejected.

Change Control Board (CCB). A formally chartered group responsible for reviewing, evaluating, approving, delaying, or rejecting changes to the project, and for recording and communicating such decisions.

Change Control System. A set of procedures that describes how modifications to the project deliverables and documentation are managed and controlled.

Change Control Tools. Manual or automated tools to assist with change and/or configuration management. At a minimum, the tools should support the activities of the CCB.

Change Log. A comprehensive list of changes made during the project. This typically includes dates of the change and impacts in terms of time, cost, and risk.

Change Request. A formal proposal to modify any document, deliverable, or baseline.

Charter. See *project charter.*

Checklist Analysis. A technique for systematically reviewing materials using a list for accuracy and completeness.

Checksheets. A tally sheet that can be used as a checklist when gathering data.

Claim. A request, demand, or assertion of rights by a seller against a buyer, or vice versa, for consideration, compensation, or payment under the terms of a legally binding contract, such as for a disputed change.

Claims Administration. The process of processing, adjudicating, and communicating contract claims.

Close Procurements. The process of completing each project procurement.

Close Project or Phase. The process of finalizing all activities across all of the Project Management Process Groups to formally complete a project or phase.

Closed Procurements. Project contracts or other procurement agreements that have been formally acknowledged by the proper authorizing agent as being finalized and signed off.

Closing Process Group. Those processes performed to finalize all activities across all Process Groups to formally close a project or phase.

Code of Accounts. A numbering system used to uniquely identify each component of the work breakdown structure (WBS).

Collect Requirements. The process of determining, documenting, and managing stakeholder needs and requirements to meet project objectives.

Colocation. An organizational placement strategy where the project team members are physically located close to one another in order to improve communication, working relationships, and productivity.

Communication Constraints. Restrictions on the content, timing, audience, or individual who will deliver a communication usually stemming from specific legislation or regulation, technology, or organizational policies.

Communication Methods. A systematic procedure, technique, or process used to transfer information among project stakeholders.

Communication Models. A description, analogy or schematic used to represent how the communication process will be performed for the project.

Communication Requirements Analysis. An analytical technique to determine the information needs of the project stakeholders through interviews, workshops, study of lessons learned from previous projects, etc.

Communication Technology. Specific tools, systems, computer programs, etc., used to transfer information among project stakeholders.

Communications Management Plan. A component of the project, program, or portfolio management plan that describes how, when, and by whom information about the project will be administered and disseminated.

Compliance. A general concept of conforming to a rule, standard, law, or requirement such that the assessment of compliance results in a binomial result stated as "compliant" or "noncompliant."

Conduct Procurements. The process of obtaining seller responses, selecting a seller, and awarding a contract.

Configuration Management System. A subsystem of the overall project management system. It is a collection of formal documented procedures used to apply technical and administrative direction and surveillance to: identify and document the functional and physical characteristics of a product, result, service, or component; control any changes to such characteristics; record and report each change and its implementation status; and support the audit of the products, results, or components to verify conformance to requirements. It includes the documentation, tracking systems, and defined approval levels necessary for authorizing and controlling changes.

Conflict Management. Handling, controlling, and guiding a conflictual situation to achieve a resolution.

Conformance. Within the quality management system, conformance is a general concept of delivering results that fall within the limits that define acceptable variation for a quality requirement.

Conformance Work. In the cost of quality framework, conformance work is done to compensate for imperfections that prevent organizations from completing planned activities correctly as essential first-time work. Conformance work consists of actions that are related to prevention and inspection.

Constraint. A limiting factor that affects the execution of a project, program, portfolio, or process.

Context Diagrams. A visual depiction of the product scope showing a business system (process, equipment, computer system, etc.), and how people and other systems (actors) interact with it.

Contingency. An event or occurrence that could affect the execution of the project that may be accounted for with a reserve.

Contingency Allowance. See *reserve*.

Contingency Reserve. Budget within the cost baseline or performance measurement baseline that is allocated for identified risks that are accepted and for which contingent or mitigating responses are developed.

Contingent Response Strategies. Responses provided which may be used in the event that a specific trigger occurs.

Contract. A contract is a mutually binding agreement that obligates the seller to provide the specified product or service or result and obligates the buyer to pay for it.

Contract Change Control System. The system used to collect, track, adjudicate, and communicate changes to a contract.

Control. Comparing actual performance with planned performance, analyzing variances, assessing trends to effect process improvements, evaluating possible alternatives, and recommending appropriate corrective action as needed.

Control Account. A management control point where scope, budget, actual cost, and schedule are integrated and compared to earned value for performance measurement.

Control Chart. A graphic display of process data over time and against established control limits, which has a centerline that assists in detecting a trend of plotted values toward either control limit.

Control Communications. The process of monitoring and controlling communications throughout the entire project life cycle to ensure the information needs of the project stakeholders are met.

Control Costs. The process of monitoring the status of the project to update the project costs and managing changes to the cost baseline.

Control Limits. The area composed of three standard deviations on either side of the centerline or mean of a normal distribution of data plotted on a control chart, which reflects the expected variation in the data. See also *specification limits.*

Control Procurements. The process of managing procurement relationships, monitoring contract performance, and making changes and corrections as appropriate.

Control Quality. The process of monitoring and recording results of executing the quality activities to assess performance and recommend necessary changes.

Control Risks. The process of implementing risk response plans, tracking identified risks, monitoring residual risks, identifying new risks, and evaluating risk process effectiveness throughout the project.

Control Schedule. The process of monitoring the status of project activities to update project progress and manage changes to the schedule baseline to achieve the plan.

Control Scope. The process of monitoring the status of the project and product scope and managing changes to the scope baseline.

Control Stakeholder Engagement. The process of monitoring overall project stakeholder relationships and adjusting strategies and plans for engaging stakeholders.

Corrective Action. An intentional activity that realigns the performance of the project work with the project management plan.

Cost Aggregation. Summing the lower-level cost estimates associated with the various work packages for a given level within the project's WBS or for a given cost control account.

Cost Baseline. The approved version of the time-phased project budget, excluding any management reserves, which can be changed only through formal change control procedures and is used as a basis for comparison to actual results.

Cost Management Plan. A component of a project or program management plan that describes how costs will be planned, structured, and controlled.

Cost of Quality. A method of determining the costs incurred to ensure quality. Prevention and appraisal costs (cost of conformance) include costs for quality planning, quality control (QC), and quality assurance to ensure compliance to requirements (i.e., training, QC systems, etc.). Failure costs (cost of nonconformance) include costs to rework products, components, or processes that are non-compliant, costs of warranty work and waste, and loss of reputation.

Cost Performance Index (CPI). A measure of the cost efficiency of budgeted resources expressed as the ratio of earned value to actual cost.

Cost Plus Award Fee Contracts (CPAF). A category of contract that involves payments to the seller for all legitimate actual costs incurred for completed work, plus an award fee representing seller profit.

Cost Plus Fixed Fee Contract (CPFF). A type of cost-reimbursable contract where the buyer reimburses the seller for the seller's allowable costs (allowable costs are defined by the contract) plus a fixed amount of profit (fee).

Cost Plus Incentive Fee Contract (CPIF). A type of cost-reimbursable contract where the buyer reimburses the seller for the seller's allowable costs (allowable costs are defined by the contract), and the seller earns its profit if it meets defined performance criteria.

Cost Variance (CV). The amount of budget deficit or surplus at a given point in time, expressed as the difference between the earned value and the actual cost.

Cost-Benefit Analysis. A financial analysis tool used to determine the benefits provided by a project against its costs.

Cost-Reimbursable Contract. A type of contract involving payment to the seller for the seller's actual costs, plus a fee typically representing seller's profit. Cost-reimbursable contracts often include incentive clauses where, if the seller meets or exceeds selected project objectives, such as schedule targets or total cost, then the seller receives from the buyer an incentive or bonus payment.

Crashing. A technique used to shorten the schedule duration for the least incremental cost by adding resources.

Create WBS. The process of subdividing project deliverables and project work into smaller, more manageable components.

Criteria. Standards, rules, or tests on which a judgment or decision can be based or by which a product, service, result, or process can be evaluated.

Critical Chain Method. A schedule method that allows the project team to place buffers on any project schedule path to account for limited resources and project uncertainties.

Critical Path. The sequence of activities that represents the longest path through a project, which determines the shortest possible duration.

Critical Path Activity. Any activity on the critical path in a project schedule.

Critical Path Method. A method used to estimate the minimum project duration and determine the amount of scheduling flexibility on the logical network paths within the schedule model.

Customer. Customer is the person(s) or organization(s) that will pay for the project's product, service, or result. Customers can be internal or external to the performing organization.

Customer Satisfaction. Within the quality management system, a state of fulfillment in which the needs of a customer are met or exceeded for the customer's expected experiences as assessed by the customer at the moment of evaluation.

Data Date. A point in time when the status of the project is recorded.

Data Gathering and Representation Techniques. Techniques used to collect, organize, and present data and information.

Decision Tree Analysis. A diagramming and calculation technique for evaluating the implications of a chain of multiple options in the presence of uncertainty.

Decomposition. A technique used for dividing and subdividing the project scope and project deliverables into smaller, more manageable parts.

Defect. An imperfection or deficiency in a project component where that component does not meet its requirements or specifications and needs to be either repaired or replaced.

Defect Repair. An intentional activity to modify a nonconforming product or product component.

Define Activities. The process of identifying and documenting the specific actions to be performed to produce the project deliverables.

Define Scope. The process of developing a detailed description of the project and product.

Deliverable. Any unique and verifiable product, result, or capability to perform a service that is required to be produced to complete a process, phase, or project.

Delphi Technique. An information gathering technique used as a way to reach a consensus of experts on a subject. Experts on the subject participate in this technique anonymously. A facilitator uses a questionnaire to solicit ideas about the important project points related to the subject. The responses are summarized and are then recirculated to the experts for further comment. Consensus may be reached in a few rounds of this process. The Delphi technique helps reduce bias in the data and keeps any one person from having undue influence on the outcome.

Dependency. See *logical relationship.*

Dependency Determination. A technique used to identify the type of dependency that is used to create the logical relationships between predecessor and successor activities.

Design of Experiments. A statistical method for identifying which factors may influence specific variables of a product or process under development or in production.

Determine Budget. The process of aggregating the estimated costs of individual activities or work packages to establish an authorized cost baseline.

Develop Project Charter. The process of developing a document that formally authorizes the existence of a project and provides the project manager with the authority to apply organizational resources to project activities.

Develop Project Management Plan. The process of defining, preparing, and coordinating all subsidiary plans and integrating them into a comprehensive project management plan.

Develop Project Team. The process of improving competencies, team member interaction, and overall team environment to enhance project performance.

Develop Schedule. The process of analyzing activity sequences, durations, resource requirements, and schedule constraints to create the project schedule model.

Diagramming Techniques. Approaches to presenting information with logical linkages that aid in understanding.

Dictatorship. A group decision-making technique in which one individual makes the decision for the group.

Direct and Manage Project Work. The process of leading and performing the work defined in the project management plan and implementing approved changes to achieve the project's objectives.

Discrete Effort. An activity that can be planned and measured and that yields a specific output. [Note: Discrete effort is one of three earned value management (EVM) types of activities used to measure work performance.]

Discretionary Dependency. A relationship that is established based on knowledge of best practices within a particular application area or an aspect of the project where a specific sequence is desired.

Document Analysis. An elicitation technique that analyzes existing documentation and identifies information relevant to the requirements.

Documentation Reviews. The process of gathering a corpus of information and reviewing it to determine accuracy and completeness.

Duration (DU or DUR). The total number of work periods (not including holidays or other nonworking periods) required to complete a schedule activity or work breakdown structure component. Usually expressed as workdays or workweeks. Sometimes incorrectly equated with elapsed time. Contrast with *effort.*

Early Finish Date (EF). In the critical path method, the earliest possible point in time when the uncompleted portions of a schedule activity can finish based on the schedule network logic, the data date, and any schedule constraints.

Early Start Date (ES). In the critical path method, the earliest possible point in time when the uncompleted portions of a schedule activity can start based on the schedule network logic, the data date, and any schedule constraints.

Earned Value (EV). The measure of work performed expressed in terms of the budget authorized for that work.

Earned Value Management. A methodology that combines scope, schedule, and resource measurements to assess project performance and progress.

Effort. The number of labor units required to complete a schedule activity or work breakdown structure component, often expressed in hours, days, or weeks.

Emotional Intelligence. The capability to identify, assess, and manage the personal emotions of oneself and other people, as well as the collective emotions of groups of people.

Enterprise Environmental Factors. Conditions, not under the immediate control of the team, that influence, constrain, or direct the project, program, or portfolio.

Estimate. A quantitative assessment of the likely amount or outcome. Usually applied to project costs, resources, effort, and durations and is usually preceded by a modifier (i.e., preliminary, conceptual, feasibility, order-of-magnitude, definitive). It should always include some indication of accuracy (e.g., $\pm x$ percent). See also *budget* and *cost.*

Estimate Activity Durations. The process of estimating the number of work periods needed to complete individual activities with estimated resources.

Estimate Activity Resources. The process of estimating the type and quantities of material, human resources, equipment, or supplies required to perform each activity.

Estimate at Completion (EAC). The expected total cost of completing all work expressed as the sum of the actual cost to date and the estimate to complete.

Estimate Costs. The process of developing an approximation of the monetary resources needed to complete project activities.

Estimate to Complete (ETC). The expected cost to finish all the remaining project work.

Execute. Directing, managing, performing, and accomplishing the project work; providing the deliverables; and providing work performance information.

Executing Process Group. Those processes performed to complete the work defined in the project management plan to satisfy the project specifications.

Expected Monetary Value (EMV) Analysis. A statistical technique that calculates the average outcome when the future includes scenarios that may or may not happen. A common use of this technique is within decision tree analysis.

Expert Judgment. Judgment provided based upon expertise in an application area, knowledge area, discipline, industry, etc., as appropriate for the activity being performed. Such expertise may be provided by any group or person with specialized education, knowledge, skill, experience, or training.

External Dependency. A relationship between project activities and non-project activities.

Facilitated Workshops. An elicitation technique using focused sessions that bring key cross-functional stakeholders together to define product requirements.

Failure Mode and Effect Analysis (FMEA). An analytical procedure in which each potential failure mode in every component of a product is analyzed to determine its effect on the reliability of that component and, by itself or in combination with other possible failure modes, on the reliability of the product or system and on the required function of the component; or the examination of a product (at the system and/or lower levels) for all ways that a failure may occur. For each potential failure, an estimate is made of its effect on the total system and of its impact. In addition, a review is undertaken of the action planned to minimize the probability of failure and to minimize its effects.

Fallback Plan. Fallback plans include an alternative set of actions and tasks available in the event that the primary plan needs to be abandoned because of issues, risks, or other causes.

Fast Tracking. A schedule compression technique in which activities or phases normally done in sequence are performed in parallel for at least a portion of their duration.

Fee. Represents profit as a component of compensation to a seller.

Finish Date. A point in time associated with a schedule activity's completion. Usually qualified by one of the following: actual, planned, estimated, scheduled, early, late, baseline, target, or current.

Finish-to-Finish (FF). A logical relationship in which a successor activity cannot finish until a predecessor activity has finished.

Finish-to-Start (FS). A logical relationship in which a successor activity cannot start until a predecessor activity has finished.

Firm-Fixed-Price Contract (FFP). A type of fixed price contract where the buyer pays the seller a set amount (as defined by the contract), regardless of the seller's costs.

Fishbone diagram. See *Cause and Effect Diagram*.

Fixed Formula Method. An earned value method for assigning a specified percentage of budget value for a work package to the start milestone of the work package with the remaining budget value percentage assigned when the work package is complete.

Fixed Price Incentive Fee Contract (FPIF). A type of contract where the buyer pays the seller a set amount (as defined by the contract), and the seller can earn an additional amount if the seller meets defined performance criteria.

Fixed Price with Economic Price Adjustment Contracts (FP-EPA). A fixed-price contract, but with a special provision allowing for predefined final adjustments to the contract price due to changed conditions, such as inflation changes, or cost increases (or decreases) for specific commodities.

Fixed-Price Contracts. An agreement that sets the fee that will be paid for a defined scope of work regardless of the cost or effort to deliver it.

Float. Also called slack. See *total float* and *free float*.

Flowchart. The depiction in a diagram format of the inputs, process actions, and outputs of one or more processes within a system.

Focus Groups. An elicitation technique that brings together prequalified stakeholders and subject matter experts to learn about their expectations and attitudes about a proposed product, service, or result.

Forecast. An estimate or prediction of conditions and events in the project's future based on information and knowledge available at the time of the forecast. The information is based on the project's past performance and expected future performance, and includes information that could impact the project in the future, such as estimate at completion and estimate to complete.

Forward Pass. A critical path method technique for calculating the early start and early finish dates by working forward through the schedule model from the project start date or a given point in time.

Free Float. The amount of time that a schedule activity can be delayed without delaying the early start date of any successor or violating a schedule constraint.

Functional Manager. Someone with management authority over an organizational unit within a functional organization. The manager of any group that actually makes a product or performs a service. Sometimes called a line manager.

Functional Organization. A hierarchical organization where each employee has one clear superior, and staff are grouped by areas of specialization and managed by a person with expertise in that area.

Funding Limit Reconciliation. The process of comparing the planned expenditure of project funds against any limits on the commitment of funds for the project to identify any variances between the funding limits and the planned expenditures.

Gantt Chart. A bar chart of schedule information where activities are listed on the vertical axis, dates are shown on the horizontal axis, and activity durations are shown as horizontal bars placed according to start and finish dates.

Grade. A category or rank used to distinguish items that have the same functional use (e.g., "hammer") but do not share the same requirements for quality (e.g., different hammers may need to withstand different amounts of force).

Ground Rules. Expectations regarding acceptable behavior by project team members.

Group Creativity Techniques. Techniques that are used to generate ideas within a group of stakeholders.

Group Decision-Making Techniques. Techniques to assess multiple alternatives that will be used to generate, classify, and prioritize product requirements.

Guideline. An official recommendation or advice that indicates policies, standards, or procedures for how something should be accomplished.

Hammock Activity. See *summary activity.*

Hard Logic. See *mandatory dependency*.

Histogram. A special form of bar chart used to describe the central tendency, dispersion, and shape of a statistical distribution.

Historical Information. Documents and data on prior projects including project files, records, correspondence, closed contracts, and closed projects.

Human Resource Management Plan. A component of the project management plan that describes how the roles and responsibilities, reporting relationships, and staff management will be addressed and structured.

Idea/Mind Mapping. Technique used to consolidate ideas created through individual brainstorming sessions into a single map to reflect commonality and differences in understanding and to generate new ideas.

Identify Risks. The process of determining which risks may affect the project and documenting their characteristics.

Identify Stakeholders. The process of identifying the people, groups, or organizations that could impact or be impacted by a decision, activity, or outcome of the project; and analyzing and documenting relevant information regarding their interests, involvement, interdependencies, influence, and potential impact on project success.

Imposed Date. A fixed date imposed on a schedule activity or schedule milestone, usually in the form of a "start no earlier than" and "finish no later than" date.

Incentive Fee. A set of financial incentives related to cost, schedule, or technical performance of the seller.

Incremental Life Cycle. A project life cycle where the project scope is generally determined early in the project life cycle, but time and cost estimates are routinely modified as the project team's understanding of the product increases. Iterations develop the product through a series of repeated cycles, while increments successively add to the functionality of the product.

Independent Estimates. A process of using a third party to obtain and analyze information to support prediction of cost, schedule, or other items.

Influence Diagram. A graphical representation of situations showing causal influences, time ordering of events, and other relationships among variables and outcomes.

Information Gathering Techniques. Repeatable processes used to assemble and organize data across a spectrum of sources.

Information Management Systems. Facilities, processes, and procedures used to collect, store, and distribute information between producers and consumers of information in physical or electronic format.

Initiating Process Group. Those processes performed to define a new project or a new phase of an existing project by obtaining authorization to start the project or phase.

Input. Any item, whether internal or external to the project that is required by a process before that process proceeds. May be an output from a predecessor process.

Inspection. Examining or measuring to verify whether an activity, component, product, result, or service conforms to specified requirements.

Inspections and Audits. A process to observe performance of contracted work or a promised product against agreed-upon requirements.

Interpersonal Skills. Ability to establish and maintain relationships with other people.

Interrelationship Digraphs. A quality management planning tool, the interrelationship digraphs provide a process for creative problem-solving in moderately complex scenarios that possess intertwined logical relationships.

Interviews. A formal or informal approach to elicit information from stakeholders by talking to them directly.

Invitation for Bid (IFB). Generally, this term is equivalent to request for proposal. However, in some application areas, it may have a narrower or more specific meaning.

Issue. A point or matter in question or in dispute, or a point or matter that is not settled and is under discussion or over which there are opposing views or disagreements.

Issue Log. A project document used to document and monitor elements under discussion or in dispute between project stakeholders.

Iterative Life Cycle. A project life cycle where the project scope is generally determined early in the project life cycle, but time and cost estimates are routinely modified as the project team's understanding of the product increases. Iterations develop the product through a series of repeated cycles, while increments successively add to the functionality of the product.

Lag. The amount of time whereby a successor activity is required to be delayed with respect to a predecessor activity.

Late Finish Date (LF). In the critical path method, the latest possible point in time when the uncompleted portions of a schedule activity can finish based on the schedule network logic, the project completion date, and any schedule constraints.

Late Start Date (LS). In the critical path method, the latest possible point in time when the uncompleted portions of a schedule activity can start based on the schedule network logic, the project completion date, and any schedule constraints.

Lead. The amount of time whereby a successor activity can be advanced with respect to a predecessor activity.

Lessons Learned. The knowledge gained during a project which shows how project events were addressed or should be addressed in the future with the purpose of improving future performance.

Lessons Learned Knowledge Base. A store of historical information and lessons learned about both the outcomes of previous project selection decisions and previous project performance.

Level of Effort (LOE). An activity that does not produce definitive end products and is measured by the passage of time. [Note: Level of effort is one of three earned valued management (EVM) types of activities used to measure work performance.]

Leveling. See *resource leveling.*

Life Cycle. See *project life cycle.*

Log. A document used to record and describe or denote selected items identified during execution of a process or activity. Usually used with a modifier, such as issue, quality control, action, or defect.

Logical Relationship. A dependency between two activities, or between an activity and a milestone.

Majority. Support from more than 50 percent of the members of the group.

Make-or-Buy Analysis. The process of gathering and organizing data about product requirements and analyzing them against available alternatives including the purchase or internal manufacture of the product.

Make-or-Buy Decisions. Decisions made regarding the external purchase or internal manufacture of a product.

Manage Communications. The process of creating, collecting, distributing, storing, retrieving, and the ultimate disposition of project information in accordance with the communications management plan.

Manage Project Team. The process of tracking team member performance, providing feedback, resolving issues, and managing team changes to optimize project performance.

Manage Stakeholder Engagement. The process of communicating and working with stakeholders to meet their needs/expectations, address issues as they occur, and foster appropriate stakeholder engagement in project activities throughout the project life cycle.

Management Reserve. An amount of the project budget withheld for management control purposes. These are budgets reserved for unforeseen work that is within scope of the project. The management reserve is not included in the performance measurement baseline (PMB).

Management Skills. The ability to plan, organize, direct, and control individuals or groups of people to achieve specific goals.

Mandatory Dependency. A relationship that is contractually required or inherent in the nature of the work.

Market Research. The process of gathering information at conferences, online reviews, and a variety of sources to identify market capabilities.

Master Schedule. A summary-level project schedule that identifies the major deliverables and work breakdown structure components and key schedule milestones. See also *milestone schedule.*

Material. The aggregate of things used by an organization in any undertaking, such as equipment, apparatus, tools, machinery, gear, material, and supplies.

Matrix Diagrams. A quality management and control tool used to perform data analysis within the organizational structure created in the matrix. The matrix diagram seeks to show the strength of relationships between factors, causes, and objectives that exist between the rows and columns that form the matrix.

Matrix Organization. Any organizational structure in which the project manager shares responsibility with the functional managers for assigning priorities and for directing the work of persons assigned to the project.

Methodology. A system of practices, techniques, procedures, and rules used by those who work in a discipline.

Milestone. A significant point or event in a project, program, or portfolio.

Milestone List. A list identifying all project milestones and normally indicates whether the milestone is mandatory or optional.

Milestone Schedule. A summary-level schedule that identifies the major schedule milestones. See also *master schedule*.

Monitor. Collect project performance data with respect to a plan, produce performance measures, and report and disseminate performance information.

Monitor and Control Project Work. The process of tracking, reviewing, and reporting the progress to meet the performance objectives defined in the project management plan.

Monitoring and Controlling Process Group. Those processes required to track, review, and regulate the progress and performance of the project; identify any areas in which changes to the plan are required; and initiate the corresponding changes.

Monte Carlo Analysis. A technique that computes or iterates the project cost or project schedule many times using input values selected at random from probability distributions of possible costs or durations, to calculate a distribution of possible total project cost or completion dates.

Monte Carlo Simulation. A process which generates hundreds or thousands of probable performance outcomes based on probability distributions for cost and schedule on individual tasks. The outcomes are then used to generate a probability distribution for the project as a whole.

Most Likely Duration. An estimate of the most probable activity duration that takes into account all of the known variables that could affect performance.

Multi-Criteria Decision Analysis. This technique utilizes a decision matrix to provide a systematic analytical approach for establishing criteria, such as risk levels, uncertainty, and valuation, to evaluate and rank many ideas.

Near-Critical Activity. A schedule activity that has low total float. The concept of near-critical is equally applicable to a schedule activity or schedule network path. The limit below which total float is considered near critical is subject to expert judgment and varies from project to project.

Negotiated Settlements. The process of reaching final equitable settlement of all outstanding issues, claims, and disputes through negotiation.

Negotiation. The process and activities to resolving disputes through consultations between involved parties.

Network. See *project schedule network diagram*.

Network Analysis. See *schedule network analysis*.

Network Logic. The collection of schedule activity dependencies that makes up a project schedule network diagram.

Network Path. Any continuous series of schedule activities connected with logical relationships in a project schedule network diagram.

Networking. Establishing connections and relationships with other people from the same or other organizations.

Node. One of the defining points of a schedule network; a junction point joined to some or all of the other dependency lines.

Nominal Group Technique. A technique that enhances brainstorming with a voting process used to rank the most useful ideas for further brainstorming or for prioritization.

Nonconformance Work. In the cost of quality framework, nonconformance work is done to deal with the consequences of errors and failures in doing activities correctly on the first attempt. In efficient quality management systems, the amount of nonconformance work will approach zero.

Objective. Something toward which work is to be directed, a strategic position to be attained, a purpose to be achieved, a result to be obtained, a product to be produced, or a service to be performed.

Observations. A technique that provides a direct way of viewing individuals in their environment performing their jobs or tasks and carrying out processes.

Opportunity. A risk that would have a positive effect on one or more project objectives.

Optimistic Duration. An estimate of the shortest activity duration that takes into account all of the known variables that could affect performance.

Organizational Breakdown Structure (OBS). A hierarchical representation of the project organization that illustrates the relationship between project activities and the organizational units that will perform those activities.

Organizational Process Assets. Plans, processes, policies, procedures, and knowledge bases that are specific to and used by the performing organization.

Organizational Project Management Maturity. The level of an organization's ability to deliver the desired strategic outcomes in a predictable, controllable, and reliable manner.

Output. A product, result, or service generated by a process. May be an input to a successor process.

Parametric Estimating. An estimating technique in which an algorithm is used to calculate cost or duration based on historical data and project parameters.

Pareto Diagram. A histogram, ordered by frequency of occurrence, that shows how many results were generated by each identified cause.

Path Convergence. A relationship in which a schedule activity has more than one predecessor.

Path Divergence. A relationship in which a schedule activity has more than one successor.

Payment Systems. The system used to provide and track supplier's invoices and payments for services and products.

Percent Complete. An estimate expressed as a percent of the amount of work that has been completed on an activity or a work breakdown structure component.

Perform Integrated Change Control. The process of reviewing all change requests; approving changes and managing changes to deliverables, organizational process assets, project documents, and the project management plan; and communicating their disposition.

Perform Qualitative Risk Analysis. The process of prioritizing risks for further analysis or action by assessing and combining their probability of occurrence and impact.

Perform Quality Assurance. The process of auditing the quality requirements and the results from quality control measurements to ensure that appropriate quality standards and operational definitions are used.

Perform Quantitative Risk Analysis. The process of numerically analyzing the effect of identified risks on overall project objectives.

Performance Measurement Baseline. An approved, integrated scope-schedule-cost plan for the project work against which project execution is compared to measure and manage performance. The PMB includes contingency reserve, but excludes management reserve.

Performance Reporting. See *work performance reports.*

Performance Reports. See *work performance reports.*

Performance Reviews. A technique that is used to measure, compare, and analyze actual performance of work in progress on the project against the baseline.

Performing Organization. An enterprise whose personnel are most directly involved in doing the work of the project or program.

Pessimistic Duration. Estimate of the longest activity duration that takes into account all of the known variables that could affect performance.

Phase. See *project phase.*

Phase Gate. A review at the end of a phase in which a decision is made to continue to the next phase, to continue with modification, or to end a project or program.

Plan Communications Management. The process of developing an appropriate approach and plan for project communications based on stakeholder's information needs and requirements and available organizational assets.

Plan Cost Management. The process that establishes the policies, procedures, and documentation for planning, managing, expending, and controlling project costs.

Plan Human Resource Management. The process of identifying and documenting project roles, responsibilities, required skills, reporting relationships, and creating a staffing management plan.

Plan Procurement Management. The process of documenting project procurement decisions, specifying the approach, and identifying potential sellers.

Plan Quality Management. The process of identifying quality requirements and/or standards for the project and its deliverables, and documenting how the project will demonstrate compliance with quality requirements.

Plan Risk Management. The process of defining how to conduct risk management activities for a project.

Plan Risk Responses. The process of developing options and actions to enhance opportunities and to reduce threats to project objectives.

Plan Schedule Management. The process of establishing the policies, procedures, and documentation for planning, developing, managing, executing, and controlling the project schedule.

Plan Scope Management. The process of creating a scope management plan that documents how the project scope will be defined, validated, and controlled.

Plan Stakeholder Management. The process of developing appropriate management strategies to effectively engage stakeholders throughout the project life cycle, based on the analysis of their needs, interests, and potential impact on project success.

Planned Value (PV). The authorized budget assigned to scheduled work.

Planning Package. A work breakdown structure component below the control account with known work content but without detailed schedule activities. See also *control account.*

Planning Process Group. Those processes required to establish the scope of the project, refine the objectives, and define the course of action required to attain the objectives that the project was undertaken to achieve.

Plurality. Decisions made by the largest block in a group, even if a majority is not achieved.

Policy. A structured pattern of actions adopted by an organization such that the organization's policy can be explained as a set of basic principles that govern the organization's conduct.

Portfolio. Projects, programs, subportfolios, and operations managed as a group to achieve strategic objectives.

Portfolio Management. The centralized management of one or more portfolios to achieve strategic objectives.

Practice. A specific type of professional or management activity that contributes to the execution of a process and that may employ one or more techniques and tools.

Precedence Diagramming Method (PDM). A technique used for constructing a schedule model in which activities are represented by nodes and are graphically linked by one or more logical relationships to show the sequence in which the activities are to be performed.

Precedence Relationship. The term used in the precedence diagramming method for a logical relationship. In current usage, however, precedence relationship, logical relationship, and dependency are widely used interchangeably, regardless of the diagramming method used. See also *logical relationship.*

Precision. Within the quality management system, *precision* is a measure of exactness.

Predecessor Activity. An activity that logically comes before a dependent activity in a schedule.

Predictive Life Cycle. A form of project life cycle in which the project scope, and the time and cost required to deliver that scope, are determined as early in the life cycle as possible.

Preferential Logic. See *discretionary dependency.*

Preferred Logic. See *discretionary dependency.*

Preventive Action. An intentional activity that ensures the future performance of the project work is aligned with the project management plan.

Prioritization Matrices. A quality management planning tool used to identify key issues and evaluate suitable alternatives to define a set of implementation priorities.

Probability and Impact Matrix. A grid for mapping the probability of each risk occurrence and its impact on project objectives if that risk occurs.

Procedure. An established method of accomplishing a consistent performance or result, a procedure typically can be described as the sequence of steps that will be used to execute a process.

Process. A systematic series of activities directed towards causing an end result such that one or more inputs will be acted upon to create one or more outputs.

Process Analysis. A process analysis follows the steps outlined in the process improvement plan to identify needed improvements.

Process Decision Program Charts (PDPC). The PDPC is used to understand a goal in relation to the steps for getting to the goal.

Process Improvement Plan. A subsidiary plan of the project management plan. It details the steps for analyzing processes to identify activities that enhance their value.

Procurement Audits. The review of contracts and contracting processes for completeness, accuracy, and effectiveness.

Procurement Documents. The documents utilized in bid and proposal activities, which include the buyer's Invitation for Bid, Invitation for Negotiations, Request for Information, Request for Quotation, Request for Proposal, and seller's responses.

Procurement Management Plan. A component of the project or program management plan that describes how a project team will acquire goods and services from outside the performing organization.

Procurement Performance Reviews. A structured review of the seller's progress to deliver project scope and quality, within cost and on schedule, as compared to the contract.

Procurement Statement of Work. Describes the procurement item in sufficient detail to allow prospective sellers to determine if they are capable of providing the products, services, or results.

Product. An artifact that is produced, is quantifiable, and can be either an end item in itself or a component item. Additional words for products are material and goods. Contrast with *result.* See also *deliverable.*

Product Analysis. For projects that have a product as a deliverable, it is a tool to define scope that generally means asking questions about a product and forming answers to describe the use, characteristics, and other the relevant aspects of what is going to be manufactured.

Product Life Cycle. The series of phases that represent the evolution of a product, from concept through delivery, growth, maturity, and to retirement.

Product Scope. The features and functions that characterize a product, service, or result.

Product Scope Description. The documented narrative description of the product scope.

Program. A group of related projects, subprograms, and program activities managed in a coordinated way to obtain benefits not available from managing them individually.

Program Evaluation and Review Technique (PERT). A technique for estimating that applies a weighted average of optimistic, pessimistic, and most likely estimates when there is uncertainty with the individual activity estimates.

Program Management. The application of knowledge, skills, tools, and techniques to a program to meet the program requirements and to obtain benefits and control not available by managing projects individually.

Progressive Elaboration. The iterative process of increasing the level of detail in a project management plan as greater amounts of information and more accurate estimates become available.

Project. A temporary endeavor undertaken to create a unique product, service, or result.

Project-Based Organizations (PBOs). A variety of organizational forms that involve the creation of temporary systems for the performance of projects. PBOs conduct the majority of their activities as projects and/or provide project over functional approaches.

Project Calendar. A calendar that identifies working days and shifts that are available for scheduled activities.

Project Charter. A document issued by the project initiator or sponsor that formally authorizes the existence of a project and provides the project manager with the authority to apply organizational resources to project activities.

Project Communications Management. Project Communications Management includes the processes that are required to ensure timely and appropriate planning, collection, creation, distribution, storage, retrieval, management, control, monitoring, and the ultimate disposition of project information.

Project Cost Management. Project Cost Management includes the processes involved in planning, estimating, budgeting, financing, funding, managing, and controlling costs so that the project can be completed within the approved budget.

Project Funding Requirements. Forecast project costs to be paid that are derived from the cost baseline for total or periodic requirements, including projected expenditures plus anticipated liabilities.

Project Governance. The alignment of project objectives with the strategy of the larger organization by the project sponsor and project team. A project's governance is defined by and is required to fit within the larger context of the program or organization sponsoring it, but is separate from organizational governance.

Project Human Resource Management. Project Human Resource Management includes the processes that organize, manage, and lead the project team.

Project Initiation. Launching a process that can result in the authorization of a new project.

Project Integration Management. Project Integration Management includes the processes and activities needed to identify, define, combine, unify, and coordinate the various processes and project management activities within the Project Management Process Groups.

Project Life Cycle. The series of phases that a project passes through from its initiation to its closure.

Project Management. The application of knowledge, skills, tools, and techniques to project activities to meet the project requirements.

Project Management Body of Knowledge. An inclusive term that describes the sum of knowledge within the profession of project management. As with other professions, such as law, medicine, and accounting, the body of knowledge rests with the practitioners and academics that apply and advance it. The complete project management body of knowledge includes proven traditional practices that are widely applied and innovative practices that are emerging in the profession. The body of knowledge includes both published and unpublished materials. This body of knowledge is constantly evolving. PMI's *PMBOK® Guide* identifies a subset of the project management body of knowledge that is generally recognized as good practice.

Project Management Information System. An information system consisting of the tools and techniques used to gather, integrate, and disseminate the outputs of project management processes. It is used to support all aspects of the project from initiating through closing, and can include both manual and automated systems.

Project Management Knowledge Area. An identified area of project management defined by its knowledge requirements and described in terms of its component processes, practices, inputs, outputs, tools, and techniques.

Project Management Office (PMO). An organizational structure that standardizes the project-related governance processes and facilitates the sharing of resources, methodologies, tools, and techniques.

Project Management Plan. The document that describes how the project will be executed monitored, and controlled.

Project Management Process Group. A logical grouping of project management inputs, tools and techniques, and outputs. The Project Management Process Groups include initiating processes, planning processes, executing processes, monitoring and controlling processes, and closing processes. Project Management Process Groups are not project phases.

Project Management Staff. The members of the project team who perform project management activities such as schedule, communications, risk management, etc.

Project Management System. The aggregation of the processes, tools, techniques, methodologies, resources, and procedures to manage a project.

Project Management Team. The members of the project team who are directly involved in project management activities. On some smaller projects, the project management team may include virtually all of the project team members.

Project Manager (PM). The person assigned by the performing organization to lead the team that is responsible for achieving the project objectives.

Project Organization Chart. A document that graphically depicts the project team members and their interrelationships for a specific project.

Project Phase. A collection of logically related project activities that culminates in the completion of one or more deliverables.

Project Procurement Management. Project Procurement Management includes the processes necessary to purchase or acquire products, services, or results needed from outside the project team.

Project Quality Management. Project Quality Management includes the processes and activities of the performing organization that determine quality policies, objectives, and responsibilities so that the project will satisfy the needs for which it was undertaken.

Project Risk Management. Project Risk Management includes the processes of conducting risk management planning, identification, analysis, response planning, and controlling risk on a project.

Project Schedule. An output of a schedule model that presents linked activities with planned dates, durations, milestones, and resources.

Project Schedule Network Diagram. A graphical representation of the logical relationships among the project schedule activities.

Project Scope. The work performed to deliver a product, service, or result with the specified features and functions.

Project Scope Management. Project Scope Management includes the processes required to ensure that the project includes all the work required, and only the work required, to complete the project successfully.

Project Scope Statement. The description of the project scope, major deliverables, assumptions, and constraints.

Project Stakeholder Management. Project Stakeholder Management includes the processes required to identify all people or organizations impacted by the project, analyzing stakeholder expectations and impact on the project, and developing appropriate management strategies for effectively engaging stakeholders in project decisions and execution.

Project Statement of Work. See *statement of work.*

Project Team. A set of individuals who support the project manager in performing the work of the project to achieve its objectives.

Project Team Directory. A documented list of project team members, their project roles, and communication information.

Project Time Management. Project Time Management includes the processes required to manage the timely completion of the project.

Projectized Organization. Any organizational structure in which the project manager has full authority to assign priorities, apply resources, and direct the work of persons assigned to the project.

Proposal Evaluation Techniques. The process of reviewing proposals provided by suppliers to support contract award decisions.

Prototypes. A method of obtaining early feedback on requirements by providing a working model of the expected product before actually building it.

Quality. The degree to which a set of inherent characteristics fulfills requirements.

Quality Audits. A quality audit is a structured, independent process to determine if project activities comply with organizational and project policies, processes, and procedures.

Quality Checklists. A structured tool used to verify that a set of required steps has been performed.

Quality Control Measurements. The documented results of control quality activities.

Quality Function Deployment (QFD). A facilitated workshop technique that helps to determine critical characteristics for new product development.

Quality Management and Control Tools. They are a type of quality planning tools used to link and sequence the activities identified.

Quality Management Plan. A component of the project or program management plan that describes how an organization's quality policies will be implemented.

Quality Management System. The organizational framework whose structure provides the policies, processes, procedures, and resources required to implement the quality management plan. The typical project quality management plan should be compatible to the organization's quality management system.

Quality Metrics. A description of a project or product attribute and how to measure it.

Quality Policy. A policy specific to the Project Quality Management Knowledge Area, it establishes the basic principles that should govern the organization's actions as it implements its system for quality management.

Quality Requirement. A condition or capability that will be used to assess conformance by validating the acceptability of an attribute for the quality of a result.

Quantitative Risk Analysis and Modeling Techniques. Commonly used techniques for both event-oriented and project-oriented analysis approaches.

Questionnaires and Surveys. Written sets of questions designed to quickly accumulate information from a large number of respondents.

RACI. A common type of responsibility assignment matrix that uses responsible, accountable, consult, and inform statuses to define the involvement of stakeholders in project activities.

Records Management System. A specific set of processes, related control functions, and tools that are consolidated and combined to record and retain information about the project.

Regression Analysis. An analytic technique where a series of input variables are examined in relation to their corresponding output results in order to develop a mathematical or statistical relationship.

Regulation. Requirements imposed by a governmental body. These requirements can establish product, process, or service characteristics, including applicable administrative provisions that have government-mandated compliance.

Reporting Systems. Facilities, processes, and procedures used to generate or consolidate reports from one or more information management systems and facilitate report distribution to the project stakeholders.

Request for Information (RFI). A type of procurement document whereby the buyer requests a potential seller to provide various pieces of information related to a product or service or seller capability.

Request for Proposal (RFP). A type of procurement document used to request proposals from prospective sellers of products or services. In some application areas, it may have a narrower or more specific meaning.

Request for Quotation (RFQ). A type of procurement document used to request price quotations from prospective sellers of common or standard products or services. Sometimes used in place of request for proposal and, in some application areas, it may have a narrower or more specific meaning.

Requested Change. A formally documented change request that is submitted for approval to the integrated change control process.

Requirement. A condition or capability that is required to be present in a product, service, or result to satisfy a contract or other formally imposed specification.

Requirements Documentation. A description of how individual requirements meet the business need for the project.

Requirements Management Plan. A component of the project or program management plan that describes how requirements will be analyzed, documented, and managed.

Requirements Traceability Matrix. A grid that links product requirements from their origin to the deliverables that satisfy them.

Reserve. A provision in the project management plan to mitigate cost and/or schedule risk. Often used with a modifier (e.g., management reserve, contingency reserve) to provide further detail on what types of risk are meant to be mitigated.

Reserve Analysis. An analytical technique to determine the essential features and relationships of components in the project management plan to establish a reserve for the schedule duration, budget, estimated cost, or funds for a project.

Residual Risk. A risk that remains after risk responses have been implemented.

Resource. Skilled human resources (specific disciplines either individually or in crews or teams), equipment, services, supplies, commodities, material, budgets, or funds.

Resource Breakdown Structure. A hierarchical representation of resources by category and type.

Resource Calendar. A calendar that identifies the working days and shifts on which each specific resource is available.

Resource Histogram. A bar chart showing the amount of time that a resource is scheduled to work over a series of time periods. Resource availability may be depicted as a line for comparison purposes. Contrasting bars may show actual amounts of resources used as the project progresses.

Resource Leveling. A technique in which start and finish dates are adjusted based on resource constraints with the goal of balancing demand for resources with the available supply.

Resource Optimization Techniques. A technique that is used to adjust the start and finish dates of activities that adjust planned resource use to be equal to or less than resource availability.

Resource Smoothing. A technique which adjusts the activities of a schedule model such that the requirement for resources on the project do not exceed certain predefined resource limits.

Responsibility. An assignment that can be delegated within a project management plan such that the assigned resource incurs a duty to perform the requirements of the assignment.

Responsibility Assignment Matrix (RAM). A grid that shows the project resources assigned to each work package.

Result. An output from performing project management processes and activities. Results include outcomes (e.g., integrated systems, revised process, restructured organization, tests, trained personnel, etc.) and documents (e.g., policies, plans, studies, procedures, specifications, reports, etc.). Contrast with *product.* See also *deliverable.*

Rework. Action taken to bring a defective or nonconforming component into compliance with requirements or specifications.

Risk. An uncertain event or condition that, if it occurs, has a positive or negative effect on one or more project objectives.

Risk Acceptance. A risk response strategy whereby the project team decides to acknowledge the risk and not take any action unless the risk occurs.

Risk Appetite. The degree of uncertainty an entity is willing to take on, in anticipation of a reward.

Risk Audits. Examination and documentation of the effectiveness of risk responses in dealing with identified risks and their root causes, as well as the effectiveness of the risk management process.

Risk Avoidance. A risk response strategy whereby the project team acts to eliminate the threat or protect the project from its impact.

Risk Breakdown Structure (RBS). A hierarchical representation of risks according to their risk categories.

Risk Categorization. Organization by sources of risk (e.g., using the RBS), the area of the project affected (e.g., using the WBS), or other useful category (e.g., project phase) to determine the areas of the project most exposed to the effects of uncertainty.

Risk Category. A group of potential causes of risk.

Risk Data Quality Assessment. Technique to evaluate the degree to which the data about risks is useful for risk management.

Risk Management Plan. A component of the project, program, or portfolio management plan that describes how risk management activities will be structured and performed.

Risk Mitigation. A risk response strategy whereby the project team acts to reduce the probability of occurrence or impact of a risk.

Risk Reassessment. Risk reassessment is the identification of new risks, reassessment of current risks, and the closing of risks that are outdated.

Risk Register. A document in which the results of risk analysis and risk response planning are recorded.

Risk Threshold. Measure of the level of uncertainty or the level of impact at which a stakeholder may have a specific interest. Below that risk threshold, the organization will accept the risk. Above that risk threshold, the organization will not tolerate the risk.

Risk Tolerance. The degree, amount, or volume of risk that an organization or individual will withstand.

Risk Transference. A risk response strategy whereby the project team shifts the impact of a threat to a third party, together with ownership of the response.

Risk Urgency Assessment. Review and determination of the timing of actions that may need to occur sooner than other risk items.

Role. A defined function to be performed by a project team member, such as testing, filing, inspecting, or coding.

Rolling Wave Planning. An iterative planning technique in which the work to be accomplished in the near term is planned in detail, while the work in the future is planned at a higher level.

Root Cause Analysis. An analytical technique used to determine the basic underlying reason that causes a variance or a defect or a risk. A root cause may underlie more than one variance or defect or risk.

Scatter Diagram. A correlation chart that uses a regression line to explain or to predict how the change in an independent variable will change a dependent variable.

Schedule. See *project schedule* and see also *schedule model.*

Schedule Baseline. The approved version of a schedule model that can be changed only through formal change control procedures and is used as a basis for comparison to actual results.

Schedule Compression. Techniques used to shorten the schedule duration without reducing the project scope.

Schedule Data. The collection of information for describing and controlling the schedule.

Schedule Forecasts. Estimates or predictions of conditions and events in the project's future based on information and knowledge available at the time the schedule is calculated.

Schedule Management Plan. A component of the project management plan that establishes the criteria and the activities for developing, monitoring, and controlling the schedule.

Schedule Model. A representation of the plan for executing the project's activities including durations, dependencies, and other planning information, used to produce a project schedule along with other scheduling artifacts.

Schedule Network Analysis. The technique of identifying early and late start dates, as well as early and late finish dates, for the uncompleted portions of project schedule activities. See also *backward pass, critical path method, critical chain method,* and *resource leveling.*

Schedule Network Templates. A set of activities and relationships that have been established that can be used repeatedly for a particular application area or an aspect of the project where a prescribed sequence is desired.

Schedule Performance Index (SPI). A measure of schedule efficiency expressed as the ratio of earned value to planned value.

Schedule Variance (SV). A measure of schedule performance expressed as the difference between the earned value and the planned value.

Scheduling Tool. A tool that provides schedule component names, definitions, structural relationships, and formats that support the application of a scheduling method.

Scope. The sum of the products, services, and results to be provided as a project. See also *project scope* and *product scope.*

Scope Baseline. The approved version of a scope statement, work breakdown structure (WBS), and its associated WBS dictionary, that can be changed only through formal change control procedures and is used as a basis for comparison.

Scope Change. Any change to the project scope. A scope change almost always requires an adjustment to the project cost or schedule.

Scope Creep. The uncontrolled expansion to product or project scope without adjustments to time, cost, and resources.

Scope Management Plan. A component of the project or program management plan that describes how the scope will be defined, developed, monitored, controlled, and verified.

Secondary Risk. A risk that arises as a direct result of implementing a risk response.

Selected Sellers. The sellers which have been selected to provide a contracted set of services or products.

Seller. A provider or supplier of products, services, or results to an organization.

Seller Proposals. Formal responses from sellers to a request for proposal or other procurement document specifying the price, commercial terms of sale, and technical specifications or capabilities the seller will do for the requesting organization that, if accepted, would bind the seller to perform the resulting agreement.

Sensitivity Analysis. A quantitative risk analysis and modeling technique used to help determine which risks have the most potential impact on the project. It examines the extent to which the uncertainty of each project element affects the objective being examined when all other uncertain elements are held at their baseline values. The typical display of results is in the form of a tornado diagram.

Sequence Activities. The process of identifying and documenting relationships among the project activities.

Seven Basic Quality Tools. A standard toolkit used by quality management professionals who are responsible for planning, monitoring, and controlling the issues related to quality in an organization.

Simulation. A simulation uses a project model that translates the uncertainties specified at a detailed level into their potential impact on objectives that are expressed at the level of the total project. Project simulations use computer models and estimates of risk, usually expressed as a probability distribution of possible costs or durations at a detailed work level, and are typically performed using Monte Carlo analysis.

Soft Logic. See *discretionary dependency.*

Source Selection Criteria. A set of attributes desired by the buyer which a seller is required to meet or exceed to be selected for a contract.

Specification. A document that specifies, in a complete, precise, verifiable manner, the requirements, design, behavior, or other characteristics of a system, component, product, result, or service and the procedures for determining whether these provisions have been satisfied. Examples are: requirement specification, design specification, product specification, and test specification.

Specification Limits. The area, on either side of the centerline, or mean, of data plotted on a control chart that meets the customer's requirements for a product or service. This area may be greater than or less than the area defined by the control limits. See also *control limits.*

Sponsor. A person or group who provides resources and support for the project, program, or portfolio and is accountable for enabling success.

Sponsoring Organization. The entity responsible for providing the project's sponsor and a conduit for project funding or other project resources.

Staffing Management Plan. A component of the human resource plan that describes when and how project team members will be acquired and how long they will be needed.

Stakeholder. An individual, group, or organization who may affect, be affected by, or perceive itself to be affected by a decision, activity, or outcome of a project.

Stakeholder Analysis. A technique of systematically gathering and analyzing quantitative and qualitative information to determine whose interests should be taken into account throughout the project.

Stakeholder Management Plan. The stakeholder management plan is a subsidiary plan of the project management plan that defines the processes, procedures, tools, and techniques to effectively engage stakeholders in project decisions and execution based on the analysis of their needs, interests, and potential impact.

Stakeholder Register. A project document including the identification, assessment, and classification of project stakeholders.

Standard. A document that provides, for common and repeated use, rules, guidelines, or characteristics for activities or their results, aimed at the achievement of the optimum degree of order in a given context.

Start Date. A point in time associated with a schedule activity's start, usually qualified by one of the following: actual, planned, estimated, scheduled, early, late, target, baseline, or current.

Start-to-Finish (SF). A logical relationship in which a successor activity cannot finish until a predecessor activity has started.

Start-to-Start (SS). A logical relationship in which a successor activity cannot start until a predecessor activity has started.

Statement of Work (SOW). A narrative description of products, services, or results to be delivered by the project.

Statistical Sampling. Choosing part of a population of interest for inspection.

Subnetwork. A subdivision (fragment) of a project schedule network diagram, usually representing a subproject or a work package. Often used to illustrate or study some potential or proposed schedule condition, such as changes in preferential schedule logic or project scope.

Subproject. A smaller portion of the overall project created when a project is subdivided into more manageable components or pieces.

Successor Activity. A dependent activity that logically comes after another activity in a schedule.

Summary Activity. A group of related schedule activities aggregated and displayed as a single activity.

SWOT Analysis. Analysis of strengths, weaknesses, opportunities, and threats of an organization, project, or option.

Tailor. The act of carefully selecting process and related inputs and outputs contained within the *PMBOK® Guide* to determine a subset of specific processes that will be included within a project's overall management approach.

Technique. A defined systematic procedure employed by a human resource to perform an activity to produce a product or result or deliver a service, and that may employ one or more tools.

Templates. A partially complete document in a predefined format that provides a defined structure for collecting, organizing, and presenting information and data.

Threat. A risk that would have a negative effect on one or more project objectives.

Three-Point Estimate. A technique used to estimate cost or duration by applying an average of optimistic, pessimistic, and most likely estimates when there is uncertainty with the individual activity estimates.

Threshold. A cost, time, quality, technical, or resource value used as a parameter, and which may be included in product specifications. Crossing the threshold should trigger some action, such as generating an exception report.

Time and Material Contract (T&M). A type of contract that is a hybrid contractual arrangement containing aspects of both cost-reimbursable and fixed-price contracts. Time and material contracts resemble cost-reimbursable type arrangements in that they have no definitive end, because the full value of the arrangement is not defined at the time of the award. Thus, time and material contracts can grow in contract value as if they were cost-reimbursable-type arrangements. Conversely, time and material arrangements can also resemble fixed-price arrangements. For example, the unit rates are preset by the buyer and seller, when both parties agree on the rates for the category of senior engineers.

Time-Scaled Schedule Network Diagram. Any project schedule network diagram drawn in such a way that the positioning and length of the schedule activity represents its duration. Essentially, it is a bar chart that includes schedule network logic.

To-Complete Performance Index (TCPI). A measure of the cost performance that is required to be achieved with the remaining resources in order to meet a specified management goal, expressed as the ratio of the cost to finish the outstanding work to the remaining budget.

Tolerance. The quantified description of acceptable variation for a quality requirement.

Tornado Diagram. A special type of bar chart used in sensitivity analysis for comparing the relative importance of the variables.

Tool. Something tangible, such as a template or software program, used in performing an activity to produce a product or result.

Total Float. The amount of time that a schedule activity can be delayed or extended from its early start date without delaying the project finish date or violating a schedule constraint.

Tree Diagram. A systematic diagram of a decomposition hierarchy used to visualize as parent-to-child relationships a systematic set of rules.

Trend Analysis. An analytical technique that uses mathematical models to forecast future outcomes based on historical results. It is a method of determining the variance from a baseline of a budget, cost, schedule, or scope parameter by using prior progress reporting periods' data and projecting how much that parameter's variance from baseline might be at some future point in the project if no changes are made in executing the project.

Trigger Condition. An event or situation that indicates that a risk is about to occur.

Unanimity. Agreement by everyone in the group on a single course of action.

Validate Scope. The process of formalizing acceptance of the completed project deliverables.

Validated Deliverables. Deliverables that are result of executing quality control process to determine correctness.

Validation. The assurance that a product, service, or system meets the needs of the customer and other identified stakeholders. It often involves acceptance and suitability with external customers. Contrast with *verification*.

Value Engineering. An approach used to optimize project life cycle costs, save time, increase profits, improve quality, expand market share, solve problems, and/or use resources more effectively.

Variance. A quantifiable deviation, departure, or divergence away from a known baseline or expected value.

Variance Analysis. A technique for determining the cause and degree of difference between the baseline and actual performance.

Variance At Completion (VAC). A projection of the amount of budget deficit or surplus, expressed as the difference between the budget at completion and the estimate at completion.

Variation. An actual condition that is different from the expected condition that is contained in the baseline plan.

Velocity. A measure of a team's productivity rate at which the deliverables are produced, validated, and accepted within a predefined interval. Velocity is a capacity planning approach frequently used to forecast future project work.

Verification. The evaluation of whether or not a product, service, or system complies with a regulation, requirement, specification, or imposed condition. It is often an internal process. Contrast with *validation*.

Voice of the Customer. A planning technique used to provide products, services, and results that truly reflect customer requirements by translating those customer requirements into the appropriate technical requirements for each phase of project product development.

WBS Dictionary. A document that provides detailed deliverable, activity, and scheduling information about each component in the work breakdown structure.

Weighted Milestone Method. An earned value method that divides a work package into measurable segments, each ending with an observable milestone, and then assigns a weighted value to the achievement of each milestone.

What-If Scenario Analysis. The process of evaluating scenarios in order to predict their effect on project objectives.

Work Authorization. A permission and direction, typically written, to begin work on a specific schedule activity or work package or control account. It is a method for sanctioning project work to ensure that the work is done by the identified organization, at the right time, and in the proper sequence.

Work Authorization System. A subsystem of the overall project management system. It is a collection of formal documented procedures that defines how project work will be authorized (committed) to ensure that the work is done by the identified organization, at the right time, and in the proper sequence. It includes the steps, documents, tracking system, and defined approval levels needed to issue work authorizations.

Work Breakdown Structure (WBS). A hierarchical decomposition of the total scope of work to be carried out by the project team to accomplish the project objectives and create the required deliverables.

Work Breakdown Structure Component. An entry in the work breakdown structure that can be at any level.

Work Package. The work defined at the lowest level of the work breakdown structure for which cost and duration can be estimated and managed.

Work Performance Data. The raw observations and measurements identified during activities being performed to carry out the project work.

Work Performance Information. The performance data collected from various controlling processes, analyzed in context and integrated based on relationships across areas.

Work Performance Reports. The physical or electronic representation of work performance information compiled in project documents, intended to generate decisions, actions, or awareness

Workaround. A response to a threat that has occurred, for which a prior response had not been planned or was not effective.

Index

Symbols and Numerics

A

B

C

D

E

F

G

H

I

J

K

L

M

N

O

P

Q

R

S

T

U

V

W

About the Author

Cynthia Snyder is a well-known project management speaker, consultant, and trainer. She was the project manager for the team that updated PMI's *Project Management Body of Knowledge—Fourth Edition*. She's also the author of many books, including *A Project Manager's Book of Forms* and *A User's Manual to the PMBOK Guide* (Wiley) as well as *PMP Certification All-in-One For Dummies* and *Project 2013 For Dummies*. Her books have been translated into several languages.

Cynthia provides consulting and training services for government and private industry. Her consulting focuses on project management maturity, PMO startups, and positioning project management as a core competency for organizations.

Author's Acknowledgments

Publishing a book is not a solo endeavor. It takes many people to get information from the author's head into the reader's hands. If you are reading this, it is because the following people at John Wiley & Sons, Inc. have been instrumental in getting you this information.

Thank you to Connie Santisteban for stepping into the Dummies role and supporting me in completing the work.

Mark Enochs is an extraordinary editor and has made working on this update as easy as it could possibly be. Thank you for being a pleasure to work with, Mark.

Teresa Artman provided great feedback, with an amazing eagle-eye, and made sure all the updates stayed in sync! I am grateful to Teresa for her guidance and help.

Joseph Kestel provided excellent feedback on the content. I am grateful to have had his expert guidance.

Saving the best for last, thank you to my wonderful husband, Dexter Dionisio for ongoing and loving support.

Publisher's Acknowledgments

Acquisitions Editor: Connie Santisteban

Senior Project Editor: Mark Enochs

Senior Copy Editor: Teresa Artman

Special Help: Rebecca Senninger

Technical Editor: Joseph Kestel

Editorial Assistant: Amanda Graham

Sr. Editorial Assistant: Cherie Case

Project Coordinator: Katie Crocker

Project Manager: Laura Moss-Hollister

Assistant Producers: Sean Patrick, Marilyn Hummel

Cover Image: © iStockphoto.com / ngkaki